ELÉ

EARLY
CHILDHOOD
INCLUSION

Focus on Change

EARLY

CHILDHOOD

INCLUSION

Focus on Change

edited by

Michael J. Guralnick, Ph.D.
University of Washington, Seattle

·P A U L·H·
BROOKES
PUBLISHING C⁰

Baltimore • London • Toronto • Sydney

Paul H. Brookes Publishing Co.
Post Office Box 10624
Baltimore, Maryland 21285-0624

www.brookespublishing.com

Typeset by PRO-IMAGE Corporation, York, Pennsylvania.
Manufactured in the United States of America by
Hamilton Printing Company, Rensselaer, New York.

The vignettes in this book are based on the authors' experiences. Some of the
vignettes represent actual people and actual circumstances. Names and other
identifying details have been changed to protect individuals' identities. Some
of the vignettes are composite accounts that do not represent the lives or
experiences of specific individuals, and no implications should be inferred.

Library of Congress Cataloging-in-Publication Data

Early childhood inclusion: focus on change/edited by Michael J. Guralnick
      p.   cm.
    Includes bibliographical references and index.
    ISBN 1-55766-491-9
    1. Inclusive education—United States.   2. Early childhood education—
United States.   3. Handicapped children—Education (Early childhood)—
United States.   I. Guralnick, Michael J.

LC1201 .E29 2001
372.21'0973—dc21

00-46744

British Library Cataloguing in Publication data are available from the British
Library.

Contents

About the Editor

Michael J. Guralnick, Ph.D., is Director of the Center on Human Development and Disability (CHDD) and Professor of Psychology and Pediatrics at the University of Washington, Seattle. Comprising both a University Affiliated Program and a Mental Retardation and Developmental Disabilities Research Center, the CHDD is one of the largest interdisciplinary research and training centers in the United States, addressing issues directly related to developmental disabilities. More than 600 faculty and staff members and doctoral and postdoctoral students operate within the four CHDD buildings on the campus of the University of Washington and in community sites to conduct basic and applied research, to provide clinical services to individuals and their families, to provide interdisciplinary clinical and research training, and to provide technical assistance and outreach training to practitioners and community agencies.

Dr. Guralnick has directed research and development projects in the fields of early childhood intervention, inclusion, peer relationships, and pediatric education. He has published more than 100 articles and book chapters and 7 edited volumes. Dr. Guralnick's publications have appeared in a diverse group of well-respected journals, including *Child Development, Pediatrics, American Journal on Mental Retardation, Journal of Early Intervention, Developmental Psychology, Journal of Developmental and Behavioral Pediatrics, Journal of Applied Developmental Psychology,* and *Development and Psychopathology.* He currently directs a major research project supported by the National Institute of Child Health and Human Development designed to determine the effectiveness of a comprehensive early intervention program in promoting the peer-related social competence of young children with developmental delays.

Dr. Guralnick received the 1994 Research Award from the American Association on Mental Retardation and the 1997 Distinguished Research Award from The Arc of the United States. He is past President of both the American Association of University Affiliated Programs and the Council for Exceptional Children's Division for Early Childhood and is former Chair of the Mental Retardation and Developmental Disabilities Research Center Directors. He is currently Chair of the International Society on Early Intervention and is President-Elect of the Academy on Mental Retardation.

Contributors

Harriet Able-Boone, Ph.D.
Associate Professor
School of Education
University of North Carolina at Chapel
  Hill
Campus Box #3500
Chapel Hill, NC 27599

Shirin D. Antia, Ph.D.
Professor
College of Education
Department of Special Education,
  Rehabilitation, and School
  Psychology
University of Arizona
Tucson, AZ 85721

Don Bailey, Ph.D.
Director
Frank Porter Graham Child
  Development Center
Professor of Medical Allied Health
  Research
Professor of Education
University of North Carolina at Chapel
  Hill
Campus Box #8180
Chapel Hill, NC 27599

Marie E. Brand, M.S.
Faculty, School of Education
State University of New York at
  New Paltz
75 South Manheim Boulevard
Room 205
New Paltz, NY 12561

Mary Beth Bruder, Ph.D.
Professor and Director
Division of Child and Family Studies
University of Connecticut Health Center
263 Farmington Avenue
Farmington, CT 06030

Virginia Buysse, Ph.D.
Assistant Director
Frank Porter Graham Child
  Development Center
University of North Carolina at Chapel
  Hill
Campus Box #8180
Chapel Hill, NC 27599

Carol J. Caperton, M.S.
Project Manager
American Speech-Language-Hearing
  Association
10801 Rockville Pike
Rockville, MD 20852

Allen C. Crocker, M.D.
Associate Professor of Pediatrics and
  Maternal and Child Health
Harvard University
Program Director
Institute for Community Inclusion
Children's Hospital
300 Longwood Avenue
Boston, MA 02115

Karen E. Diamond, Ph.D.
Professor
Department of Child Development and
  Family Studies
Purdue University
1267 CDFS Building
West Lafayette, IN 47907

Carl J. Dunst, Ph.D.
Research Scientist
Orelena Hawks Puckett Institute
18A Regent Park Boulevard
Asheville, NC 28806
Research Director
Family, Infant, and Preschool Program
Western Carolina Center
Morganton, NC 28655

Elizabeth J. Erwin, Ed.D.
Associate Professor and Coordinator
Program in Special Education
School of Education
Department of Educational and
    Community Programs
Queens College of the City University of
    New York
Flushing, NY 11367

Susan Forrest, M.Ed.
Georgia State University
University Plaza
Atlanta, GA 30303

Alan Gartner, Ph.D.
Professor
Co-Director
National Center on Educational
    Restructuring and Inclusion
The Graduate Center
The City University of New York
365 Fifth Avenue
New York, NY 10016

Michael J. Guralnick, Ph.D.
Director
Center on Human Development and
    Disability
Professor of Psychology and Pediatrics
University of Washington
Seattle, WA 98195

Marci J. Hanson, Ph.D.
Professor
Department of Special Education
San Francisco State University
1600 Holloway Avenue
San Francisco, CA 94132

Fiona K. Innes, Ph.D.
Research Analyst
American Institutes for Research
Pelavin Research Center and Education
    Statistics Services Institute
1000 Thomas Jefferson, NW
Suite 400
Washington, D.C. 20007

Frank W. Kohler, Ph.D.
Assistant Professor of Special
    Education
University of Northern Iowa
155 Schindler Education Center
Cedar Falls, IA 50613

Linda M. Levine, Ed.D.
Adjunct Assistant Professor
Department of Special Education,
    Rehabilitation, and School
    Psychology
University of Arizona
Tucson, AZ 85721

Dorothy Kerzner Lipsky, Ph.D.
Director
National Center on Educational
    Restructuring and Inclusion
The Graduate Center
The City University of New York
365 Fifth Avenue
New York, NY 10016

Gail G. McGee, Ph.D.
Associate Professor of Psychiatry and
    Behavioral Sciences
Emory University School of
    Medicine
718 Gatewood Road
Atlanta, GA 30322

R.A. McWilliam, Ph.D.
Research Scientist
Frank Porter Graham Child
    Development Center
University of North Carolina at
    Chapel Hill
Campus Box #8180
Chapel Hill, NC 27599

Rebecca S. Morrison, Ph.D.
Visiting Assistant Professor
The Ohio State University
356 Arps Hall
1945 North High Street
Columbus, OH 43210

Marion O'Brien, Ph.D.
Director
Sunnyside Infant-Toddler Program
Professor
Department of Human Development
    and Family Life
The University of Kansas
Lawrence, KS 66045

Samuel L. Odom, Ph.D.
Otting Professor of Special
    Education
Indiana University
201 North Rose
Bloomington, IN 47405

Diane Paul-Brown, Ph.D.
Director
Clinical Issues in Speech-Language
    Pathology
American Speech-Language-Hearing
    Association
10801 Rockville Pike
Rockville, MD 20852

Stephanie M. Porter, M.S.N., R.N.
Director of Clinical Services
Institute for Community Inclusion
Children's Hospital
300 Longwood Avenue
Boston, MA 02115

Mary Jane K. Rapport, Ph.D., P.T.
Assistant Professor
Departments of Pediatrics and
    Rehabilitation Medicine
University of Colorado Health
    Sciences Center
Denver, CO 80262

Mary Ann Romski, Ph.D.
Professor of Communication,
    Psychology, and Educational
    Pyschology and Special
    Education
Department of Communication
Georgia State University
University Plaza
Atlanta, GA 30303

Diane M. Sainato, Ph.D.
Associate Professor of Special Education
The Ohio State University
356 Arps Hall
1945 North High Street
Columbus, OH 43210

Barbara Schwartz, Ph.D.
Director
Department of Teaching and Learning
Quality Improvement Center for
    Disabilities
New York University School of
    Education
726 Broadway
5th Floor
New York, NY 10003

Rose A. Sevcik, Ph.D.
Associate Professor
Department of Psychology
Georgia State University
University Plaza
Atlanta, GA 30303

Barbara J. Smith, Ph.D.
Associate Research Professor
School of Education
University of Colorado–Denver
1380 Lawrence Street
Suite 650
Denver, CO 80204

Leslie C. Soodak, Ph.D.
Associate Professor of Education
Pace University
861 Bedford
Pleasantville, NY 10570

Zolinda Stoneman, Ph.D.
Director
Institute on Development and
    Disability: A University Affiliated
    Program
Professor of Child and Family
    Development
The University of Georgia
850 College Station Road
Athens, GA 30602

Matthew J. Stowe, J.D.
Research Associate
Beach Center on Families and
    Disability
The University of Kansas
3126 Haworth Hall
Lawrence, KS 66045

Phillip S. Strain, Ph.D.
Professor of Educational Psychology
University of Colorado–Denver
1380 Lawrence Street
Suite 650
Denver, CO 80217

Ann Turnbull, Ed.D.
Co-Director
Beach Center on Families and
    Disability
Professor
Department of Special Education
The University of Kansas
3111 Haworth Hall
Lawrence, KS 66045

**H. Rutherford Turnbull III, LL.B./J.D.,
    LL.M.**
Co-Director
Beach Center on Families and
    Disability
The University of Kansas
3111 Haworth Hall
Lawrence, KS 66045

Patricia W. Wesley, M.Ed.
Director
Partnerships for Inclusion
Frank Porter Graham Child
    Development Center
University of North Carolina at Chapel
    Hill
Sheryl-Mar Suite 100
521 South Greensboro Street
Carrboro, NC 27510

Pamela J. Winton, Ph.D.
Research Fellow
Frank Porter Graham Child
    Development Center
University of North Carolina at Chapel
    Hill
Campus Box #8185
Chapel Hill, NC 27599

Mark Wolery, Ph.D.
Professor of Special Education
Peabody College
Vanderbilt University
Nashville, TN 37203

Craig Zercher, M.A.
Doctoral Candidate
Department of Special Education
San Francisco State University
1600 Holloway Avenue
San Francisco, CA 94132

Preface

This is a book about change—at least hoped for change. The focus is on early childhood inclusion, a field characterized by a philosophy and practice that encourages full participation of children with disabilities and their families in everyday activities with their typically developing peers. On the surface, the press for inclusion of young children with disabilities seems benign; upon closer inspection, however, success requires substantial changes in the way our society thinks, feels, and acts. In time, inclusion will likely achieve profound changes in the lives of children with disabilities and their families.

Unquestionably, the foundation for change toward meaningful inclusion is in place at so many levels and in so many ways. Even a cursory review of the field will reveal that much has been accomplished since the early 1980s. Yet, despite progress well deserved and often hard won, the pace of change has slowed perceptibly in recent years; fragmentation is apparent; and, perhaps most disturbing, no direction, coherent plans, or national leadership can be found.

The intent of *Early Childhood Inclusion: Focus on Change* is not to whine about or lay blame for this state of affairs. The field simply may have underestimated the difficulties in achieving the goals of early childhood inclusion and perhaps failed to recognize the complexity of the issues that need to be addressed and the depths of the philosophical and ideological divisions among those affected by this movement. To the contrary, the purpose of this book is to increase awareness of the need for change and, it is hoped, to serve as a catalyst for progress.

To accomplish this, a large number of distinguished professionals, whose careers have been central to the progress that has been achieved, agreed to consider these issues in *Early Childhood Inclusion: Focus on Change*. In so doing, factors influencing the various goals of inclusion have been identified, barriers to change examined, and, of most value, directions for change proposed. As will be seen, it has become rapidly apparent that meaningful progress can only be achieved through a national-in-scope effort encompassing the interrelated domains of systems change, program development, and research. One such plan, including mechanisms for carrying out the plan, is presented in the final chapter of this book. Consequently, the reader will be provided not only with rationales indicating what changes are necessary but also with a framework to guide an agenda for change.

I am most indebted to many of this book's chapter authors for countless discussions over the years. Indeed, what has been especially gratifying is the high level of enthusiasm expressed by all of these authors to contribute their ideas and expertise to address the challenging task of focusing on change in the field of early childhood inclusion. I know I speak for many of the contributors when I say that this task has been a therapeutic experience, channeling frustrations with the pace and nature of change in early childhood inclusion into a more productive and optimistic view of the future of this field.

Numerous others have also made *Early Childhood Inclusion: Focus on Change* possible. Once again, Carolyn Hamby has provided expert editorial assistance. There is considerable doubt that this book would have been completed without her management and editorial expertise; certainly it would have been greatly flawed without her participation. Finally, the staff of Paul H. Brookes Publishing Co. continue to provide substantial and highly professional support in their efforts to bring to our profession the highest quality publications.

EARLY
CHILDHOOD
INCLUSION

Focus on Change

I

Introduction and Overview

1

MICHAEL J. GURALNICK

A Framework for Change in Early Childhood Inclusion

The year 1975 will always be remembered by the disability community for the passage of the Education for All Handicapped Children Act (PL 94-142). In that landmark and wonderfully crafted piece of legislation, the right of children with disabilities to obtain a free and appropriate public education was firmly and unequivocally established. Modified and extended by subsequent amendments and reauthorizations (e.g., the Education of the Handicapped Act Amendments of 1986 [PL 99-457], the Individuals with Disabilities Education Act [IDEA] of 1990 [PL 101-476], the IDEA Amendments of 1991 [PL 102-119] and 1997 [PL 105-17]) and supported by related legislation (Rehabilitation Act of 1973 [PL 93-112], Americans with Disabilities Act of 1990 [PL 101-336]), programs of services and supports have evolved such that infants, toddlers, and preschool children who are developmentally at risk and their families have become part of a meaningful early intervention system (Guralnick, 1997b, 1998). At the beginning of the 21st century, although eligibility requirements and the details of the practices and the forms taken by the service system vary from place to place, young children and their families in communities all across the United States have access to early intervention programs.

Unquestionably, one of the most far-reaching and perhaps radical components of this legislation is related to the prospect of providing services and supports to young children with disabilities together with typically developing children in what is now referred to as inclusive environments. As practiced, inclusion takes many forms and varies substantially in terms of the degree to which children with and without disabilities are actually included with one another. (Details of these variations are discussed shortly.) Nevertheless, the defining feature of inclusion for young children is the existence of *planned participation* between children with and without disabilities in the context of children's educational/developmental programs. Inclusion replaces terms such as *mainstreaming* and *integration,* which provided useful frameworks during early periods as the nature and meaning of participation between children with and without disabilities evolved. Of note, many professionals, families, and advocates do not limit inclusion to mean

3

involvement only in educational/developmental programs but extend the concept to the participation of children with disabilities and their families in typical activities found in their neighborhoods and communities. This broader conceptualization of inclusion is adopted throughout this book.

In many respects, the press for inclusion was a reaction against the stigma and isolation that almost inevitably accompanied one's "disability status": a circumstance reinforced by the separation of children with disabilities characteristic of educational settings before the passage of PL 94-142. Against the background of the emergence of principles of *normalization* (Wolfensberger, 1972) and the civil rights movement, questions intensified as to the ethics and legitimacy of a practice that discouraged a sense of community belonging in families and children with disabilities. At the same time, increasing recognition of the lost developmental and social opportunities that likely resulted from limiting experiences almost exclusively to children with similar special needs began to emerge, as did an appreciation by the professional community that developmental differences are primarily variations of common developmental processes that require accommodations rather than an entirely separate set of approaches and practices.

Combined with concerns regarding the low expectations that seemed to continue to accompany children who were grouped in terms of developmental status, the energies of advocates coalesced to encourage efforts that promoted interactions between children with and without disabilities in every manner and at every level. Over time, the values and principles regarding a sense of belonging, developmental continuity, respect for and celebration of individual differences, expansion of social and educational opportunities, and raised expectations for children with disabilities were joined with legal concepts related to procedural and substantive due process, to equal protection requirements, and to constitutional principles of minimum intrusion (Turnbull, Ellis, Boggs, Brooks, & Biklen, 1981). Together they established a powerful set of arguments that resulted in the language in PL 94-142 (as well as subsequent amendments and reauthorizations applied to young children) intended to promote inclusive practices.

It is important to recognize that the inclusive aspects of PL 94-142 were based primarily on ideological, theoretical, and legal grounds. At the time, little empirical evidence could be found to suggest that children with disabilities would, for example, achieve a greater sense of belonging from participation in an inclusive environment, that meaningful friendships would develop between children with and without disabilities, that social or other aspects of development of children with disabilities would be enhanced as a consequence of opportunities to interact with typically developing children, or that contact among children with diverse characteristics would engender a respect for individual differences. From a developmental perspective, there was hope that children would challenge and learn from one another, and various forms of social learning theory and imitation were appealed to that suggested the potential benefits of inclusive environments. Again, however, virtually no empirical basis existed, and the early published works using paradigms such as imitation (e.g., Guralnick, 1976) were at best crude attempts to understand a most complex process.

Moreover, particularly for young children, the field had only meager experience with programs that included children with and without disabilities. The diverse forms that inclusive programs might take, whether these programs could feasibly encompass all children with disabilities, or how individual family choice was to be weighed had simply not been examined in any systematic manner. The question of how to deliver traditional special education and related services in these new environments loomed as a major concern.

Perhaps it was this lack of experience with inclusive programs and the absence of a firm empirical basis for most of the stated and implied expectations for inclusion that led to the carefully worded statement about preschool inclusion found in PL 94-142:

> To the maximum extent appropriate, [children with disabilities]. . .are educated with children who are not [disabled], and that special classes, separate schooling, or other removal of [children with disabilities] from the regular educational environment occurs only when the nature or severity of the [disability] is such that education in regular classes with the use of supplementary aids and services cannot be achieved satisfactorily. (§ 612[5][b])

This statement directs educational agencies to seek out ways to educate children with disabilities together with typically developing children. The language also indicates a presumption for placement of children in general education environments but does identify conditions under which other placements could occur (i.e., "only when the nature or severity of the [disability] is such that services cannot be achieved satisfactorily"). Translating this cautious language into practice, however, was and is a complex issue. Defining what constitutes satisfactory progress and the required level of supplementary aids and services could and would serve as points of contention. Similarly, the qualification "to the maximum extent appropriate" added another element of ambiguity. Corresponding language and requirements applied to infants and toddlers in subsequent legislation (PL 102-119, PL 105-17) specifying that services and supports be provided in natural environments created similar difficulties for this group of young children and their families.

Finally, to complicate matters further, regulations for PL 94-142 mandated that each educational system have available an array of environments that vary in restrictiveness and that, to the extent appropriate, children were to be placed in the *least restrictive* of those environments. It was in this context of determining the least restrictive environment that the various forms of inclusion would be realized and justified. Moreover, the concept of least restrictiveness served as the basis for the tensions that emerged when inclusion was put into practice. Questions included the following: Is it appropriate to emphasize educational or social benefits? To what extent should classroom structure be altered in the interests of inclusion? What limits should be placed on resources to provide supplementary aids and services? Answers to these and other vexing questions would contribute to program design and placement decisions within the least restrictive framework. The challenge, it seems, was to apply this principle of least restrictiveness over time, to determine which questions were appropriate, to evaluate practices carefully, and, ultimately, to develop the meaning of least restrictiveness within contemporary beliefs and practices (Biklen, 1982).

Evaluating all of this in historical context, it is reasonable to consider the legislative intent regarding inclusion as both a means to remedy past failures and inequities and to serve as a catalyst for change. Despite all of the uncertainties and tensions, the message could be construed as, "Move ahead; press this issue; develop rationales for making decisions; and experiment wisely, vigorously, and creatively, but remain committed to this new paradigm." Indeed, the field of early intervention took this message seriously.

A CALL FOR CHANGE

The stage was set for what was intended to be a remarkable and inexorable shift in the expectations for and experiences of individuals with disabilities. However, it soon became apparent that the conceptual and practical implications of legislation that fostered inclusion were both extraordinary and demanding even (or especially) when applied to young children. In essence, it required *change* in virtually every facet of the evolving system of early intervention services and supports, as the early intervention system maintained strong historical ties to the larger educational system that operated primarily within a segregated model. For preschool-age children in particular, the very foundations of the systems themselves were challenged, encouraging educational agencies to rethink their traditional administrative structures with attendant changes in how resources were to be allocated and how and by whom decisions were to be made. Although a long-term perspective was needed, similar changes in the training of personnel at all levels, as well as changes in early childhood program staffing patterns, were implied by the press for inclusion. These changes were relevant not only to general early childhood educators and to early childhood special educators but also to members of all disciplines who were now asked to alter their practices to accommodate new inclusive approaches. At minimum, co-teaching and consultant models were needed to meet both the spirit and the letter of inclusion.

Efforts to promote education reform, redesign policies, restructure personnel preparation programs, and alter existing professional practices were forced to confront attitude and belief systems that were grounded in years of training and experience and supported by well-developed professional infrastructures. For educational staff in particular, adapting instructional materials and curricula—including incorporating the use of assistive technology—constituted not just a technical challenge but also a conceptual one, as special educational practices and beliefs about how children learn and develop now had to accommodate to general early childhood educators' practices and beliefs. Differences in approaches became most apparent when children with highly specialized needs were to be included, such as those with autism or complex special health care needs. Could a developmental approach that was common to general early childhood education practice work? How could the highly intensive and specialized techniques often needed for these children fit within the general early childhood program? These concerns were expressed by all involved, including parents, administrators, teachers, and related personnel.

At a more personal level, change was called for in the ways in which children with and without disabilities interacted socially with one another. Many children with disabilities were socially isolated, and inclusive programs were seen as a means of altering that state of affairs. Questions that plagued both parents and professionals centered on whether meaningful relationships, not just perfunctory acceptance, would form between children with and without disabilities. Would an understanding of and respect for individual differences emerge through experience with one another? How could staff incorporate activities in inclusive programs to support these social interaction processes? Could the foundation for a broader inclusive community that extended to families and neighborhoods be established? To be sure, early childhood programs were becoming more diverse, particularly with regard to their multicultural composition, yet children with a heterogeneous array of disabilities constituted an even more complex challenge for change.

Finally, change was occurring in other aspects of the early intervention system, and it had important implications for change in inclusive practices. In particular, emerging concepts of family centeredness, family empowerment, and family choice were forever altering the nature of parent–professional relationships. As parents increasingly exercised their new decision-making roles about all matters of their child's program, including type of placement, parents' perceptions of and commitment to inclusive practices added a new and once again highly complex dimension to the entire process. Issues regarding how *their* child would gain access to the needed special education and related services and how the program would work to minimize rejection of *their* child by peers rapidly moved discussions of inclusive practices from a theoretical to a very practical level.

PATTERNS OF CHANGE

Despite these and other numerous and diverse challenges to change, there remained an optimism in the field that the principles and practices of inclusion at the early childhood level would ultimately be agreed on and realized. No one, of course, thought it would be easy, yet neither did the anticipated changes seem unreasonable nor unreachable over the course of time. Indeed, in 1978, the essence of this optimism was captured in an anthology that described new models and approaches designed to "integrate" or "mainstream" young children in early childhood environments (Guralnick, 1978). A high level of activity followed in virtually every aspect of the early childhood system, and more and more children were being served in inclusive environments (e.g., Wolery, Holcombe-Ligon, et al., 1993). Personnel preparation programs were modified, new inclusive models were developed and evaluated, many administrative barriers were removed,

and a productive dialogue was established between relevant constituencies at all levels. Together, these efforts culminated in the ability of education professionals to create inclusive programs that seemed to work.

The accomplishments of the 1980s were truly impressive (see Guralnick, 1990a). Nevertheless, as discussed in the following sections of this chapter, what failed to emerge was a comprehensive, national, and well-coordinated effort to clarify, define, and foster inclusive practices. No goals were set, momentum was difficult to sustain, and the process seemed fractionated despite islands of excellence in various communities. Conceptualization of the issues and corresponding expectations for outcomes never fully developed. Consequently, continuing research and program development were not carried out within a systematic framework. A lack of focus became a critical concern.

Four goal domains, which are consistent with the rationale and expectations for inclusive programs discussed previously, provide a perspective on the status of inclusive programs and the issues that were still unresolved in the 1990s: 1) access, 2) feasibility, 3) developmental and social outcomes, and 4) social integration. In this chapter, each of these four goal domains provides a basis for specifying explicit goals and corresponding expectations for inclusion. Each goal then is evaluated in terms of existing research and practice patterns to determine the extent to which individual goals have been realized. With this framework and information, it is hoped that the field will be in a better position to establish an agenda for change.

Access

Universal access to inclusive programs for infants, toddlers, and preschoolers constitutes an obvious and essential goal (see Table 1.1). The reasonable expectation is

Table 1.1.   Goal and outcome criteria for the goal domain of access

Goal	Outcome criteria
Universal access to inclusive programs	1. Availability of inclusive programs in local community
	2. Maximum participation with typically developing children in typical activities

that all communities will have developed and refined inclusive models that become meaningful placement options for young children with disabilities. Indeed, substantial progress toward universal access was achieved in the 1980s. One report indicated that nearly three quarters of U.S. programs that serve preschool-age children enroll at least one child with a disability (Wolery, Holcombe-Ligon, et al., 1993). Although more conservative percentages are likely to be more accurate when considering the high number of nonrespondents in survey studies (see Buysse, Wesley, Bryant, & Gardner, 1999), individual states also have reported considerable progress over time for both preschool-age children (Dinnebeil, Mc-Inerney, Fox, & Juchartz-Pendry, 1998) and infants and toddlers (Bruder, Staff, & McMurrer-Kaminer, 1997). The figures for preschool-age children are impressive when it is realized that public schools rarely provide programs for typically developing young children. As a consequence, programs that involve typically developing children either needed to be established or needed arrangements made with private preschool or child care programs or with public programs such as Head Start. Even more complex arrangements were needed to establish inclusive child care options for agencies that are responsible for infants and toddlers with disabilities.

Other evidence, however, suggests that we are far from achieving the goal of universal access to inclusive programs, irrespective of the forms that these inclusive programs may take. As might be expected from the complex arrangements with community preschools or

child care programs needed to gain access to typically developing children, this state of affairs has created numerous policy barriers regarding contractual arrangements for services, financial responsibilities, personnel standards, transportation, and many others (see Smith & Rose, 1993). Most of these issues still await resolution in many communities. Moreover, reports indicate that inclusive experiences are still not available to a substantial proportion of families (Cavallaro, Ballard-Rosa, & Lynch, 1998; Kochanek & Buka, 1999; McWilliam et al., 1995). In the study by Cavallaro and colleagues (1998), for example, findings indicated that more than one quarter of local education agencies (LEAs) in California did not provide an inclusive option to families in their community. Co-location of separate programs for children with and without disabilities was the predominant service model, but even here it was not clear whether many of these programs arranged opportunities for social interaction between the two groups (social inclusion). Even when community inclusion programs are available, inclusive placements do not necessarily follow (Kochanek & Buka, 1999). In addition, surveys of inclusive options suggest fewer opportunities in high-quality accredited programs, even with a most liberal interpretation of survey results (McDonnell, Brownell, & Wolery, 1997). Indeed, the lack of quality inclusive options clearly limits access as many parents choose specialized programs because of these concerns (see Bailey, McWilliam, Buysse, & Wesley, 1998). Also of concern is that many newly created inclusive programs seemingly disintegrate after funding or leadership is no longer provided (Peck, Furman, & Helmstetter, 1993). The absence of an infrastructure and a general commitment to and advocacy for inclusive programs to help resolve differences of approach, opinion, or values of the constituencies involved is most evident in the descriptions of these programs. Furthermore, inclusive options are more readily available to children with mild disabilities than to children with more significant problems (Buysse, Bailey, Smith, & Simeonsson, 1994). This occurs despite evidence that even children with severe disabilities can be accommodated within some type of inclusive environment (Hanline, 1990).

Data on inclusive child care options for infants and toddlers, most of whom have significant disabilities, are very limited. Despite progress in many communities, parents of infants and toddlers with disabilities report having difficulties locating community-based child care. In fact, infants with established disabilities as well as those at risk enter child care later and spend fewer hours in child care than do typically developing children (Booth & Kelly, 1998). In addition, nearly half of mothers of children with special needs who do not wish to remain home after the birth of their child were not planning to return to work because of difficulties with finding quality child care (Booth & Kelly, 1999). From a different perspective, analyses of services for infants and toddlers in early intervention programs specifically selected to be "exemplary in values and concepts," including community inclusion, revealed that only approximately one third of the services were provided in inclusive environments (Kochanek & Buka, 1998). Similarly, only a small fraction of infants and toddlers with disabilities in California receive services in inclusive environments (other than their homes) (Cavallaro et al., 1998). The importance of inclusive experiences

in child care should not be underestimated, even if they occur only on a part-time basis. Not only does child care constitute the primary inclusive option for infants and toddlers, it also provides most families with their first experience with families in their communities in a formal and structured environment.

Even policy makers have become impatient with the pace of inclusive practices, strengthening the individualized education program (IEP) in the reauthorization of the IDEA amendments of 1997 in an effort to maximize the involvement of children with disabilities in general program activities. Requirements for the IEP emphasize the importance of focusing on the services, adjustments, and accommodations needed to ensure a child's participation in general programs. Moreover, required now are explanations on the IEP as to the extent to which a child with a disability will *not* participate in general activities. These requirements clearly encourage participants who are developing the IEP to consider carefully how to maximize inclusive experiences. Additional provisions of this reauthorization encourage inclusive practices by requiring a more central role for the general educator in developing the IEP and mandating participation of parents in determining their child's placement in a particular program.

These concerns about access to inclusive programs are complicated further when the type of inclusive program is considered (see the next section). The fact is that the level of *planned participation* between children with and without disabilities varies substantially across program types, even though all program types are considered and consider themselves to be inclusive. Indeed, the term *inclusion* is generally used in its broadest sense to refer to children with disabilities whose programs include participation with children without disabilities, despite that the level of participation may be minimal (see Cavallaro et al., 1998). However, the absence of options or failure to select an option that can readily accommodate children with disabilities and provide for far more extensive involvement in inclusive activities also can be said to restrict access. This important but often overlooked issue effectively restricts access and is discussed in the following sections.

Types of Inclusive Programs   Although no official or even generally accepted typology exists for the range of available early childhood inclusion program types, the program options that exist for preschool-age children tend to parallel the special educational continuum of least restrictive environments (Taylor, 1988). Specifically, the following four general categories seem representative of current placement options. The first consists of *full inclusion*. In this option, children with disabilities are to be full participants in the general program environment. All activities are intended to be well adapted to children's needs, and IEPs are designed to be accommodated within the general early childhood curriculum. Depending on the number of children with special needs in the classroom or the severity of the children's disabilities, early childhood special educators and other specialists provide services on an intermittent or continuing basis.

The program and all of the children in it remain the responsibility of the general early childhood educator, although both special educational and related services can be provided by specialized staff. Ideal and most consistent with an inclusive framework is that both special education and related services are well integrated into the ongoing curriculum and general program activities are implemented by all staff. This is usually accomplished through some combination of consultation (Buysse & Wesley, 1993), team process (Bruder, 1996), and integrated strategies for providing specialized services (McWilliam, 1996b).

The second type of program, the *cluster model,* shares many characteristics with the full inclusion model. However, it is distinguished by the fact that a small group of children with disabilities is essentially grafted onto an existing program that serves typically developing children, bringing with it its own staff. Moreover, this cluster of children with special needs frequently is assigned a separate physical location within the larger program, usually an alcove or some other physically designated area.

In this model, the general early childhood teacher is responsible for all children, and children with disabilities are expected to participate in most, but not all, of the usual program activities. Some activities that are unique to children with disabilities are planned within this model. Conceptually, the cluster model can operate in a manner similar to the full inclusion model, although the clustering itself, the constant presence of a special education teacher (often an early childhood special educator), and the expectation of greater involvement of the special education teacher with the children with disabilities immediately establish some level of separation. This model can be efficient, but a tendency toward separate activities beyond those that may have been planned originally can result in substantial functional separation. Staff in this model, as in the full inclusion model, must constantly work together to maximize consultant and team approaches and to develop ways to integrate related services.

The third model, most appropriately labeled *reverse inclusion,* differs dramatically from the previous two models in that its foundation is a specialized program to which a relatively small group (usually 25%–40% of the total) of typically developing children is added. Generally staffed by early childhood special educators, this model often remains true to its "special needs" tradition, although accommodations for the typically developing children can create a program pattern that exhibits many similarities to general early childhood programs. In fact, variations across programs in terms of structure, curriculum, educational philosophy, and so forth of this reverse inclusion model can be substantial. Every effort is made to develop activities that include all children, and this model is also very efficient and can easily integrate the services provided by specialists.

The fourth and final model, *social inclusion,* provides the least contact between children with and without disabilities. Although housed in the same general location, programs for typically developing children and children with disabilities are maintained in separate spaces with separate staffs. Accordingly, curricula, educational philosophies, and other program features are likely to differ substantially between the two types of programs. Planned contact between the two groups generally occurs during free play and other recreational activities and is intended to provide opportunities for social interaction. Virtually all services are provided in the context of the specialized program.

These four types of inclusive program options can be operated by public or private agencies and located in community centers, private facilities, or public schools. Dual enrollment (enrollment in specialized and inclusive programs at different times of the day or days of the week) is also an option, especially when child care is needed (see Odom et al., 1999). However, dual enrollment creates very different educational/developmental opportunities. In most instances, the specialized program is conventional, with all services being provided in that context, whereas the inclusive option is a child care or similar program. Socialization with typically developing children in

general child care is, of course, important, but without a knowledgeable and well-trained child care or nursery staff, the likelihood of achieving a productive socialization experience is reduced. Frequently, the complementary inclusive program is not involved or seemingly committed to the child's larger educational/developmental program. Unfortunately, effective communication across dual programs is extremely difficult to accomplish (Donegan, Ostrosky, & Fowler, 1996).

The Priority of Full Inclusion Programs   Many in the field might argue that the availability of this array of inclusive options for young children with disabilities may well be appropriate and can best meet children's individual needs while balancing multiple goals. After all, this seems to be what was intended by PL 94-142 and is consistent with the notion of ensuring the availability of alternative programs that vary in terms of restrictiveness (i.e., degree of contact with typically developing children and participation in typical program activities). Of course, the specialized option (no planned participation with typically developing children) remains as well. Yet, as Taylor (1988) pointed out most thoughtfully, whereas this principle of least restrictive alternatives once served the disability field well, it may now be inconsistent with contemporary thinking and stand as a barrier to children's full participation in typical educational and community activities. Although Taylor's (1988) paper should be consulted for the detailed development of this position, he pointed out how the principle of least restrictive environments in today's framework can actually legitimize restrictive environments. As Taylor discussed, by striving to ensure the existence of alternative placements, the least restrictive principle fails to recognize that service intensity and type of program constitute independent issues except in extreme instances; it implies a "readiness" model; it is not compatible with a true parent–professional partnership; as practiced it may actually infringe on children's rights; it may require children to experience increasing numbers of transitions should they move toward more inclusive options; and it diverts attention to issues related to environment rather than to supports and services.

This position could be interpreted to suggest that the only appropriate inclusive placement is a fully inclusive one. However, as persuasive as this argument is, options other than full inclusion may well be appropriate for children even at the early childhood level. We just do not know. The concern, and it is as much programmatic as philosophical, is that no general, agreed-on *justification or rationale* for placing children in *any* program option has been established. Simply put, the field has not yet adequately addressed issues with regard to *why* these various options exist and what unique benefits they may confer. Should such a framework be developed, we will then be in a better position to address questions such as the following: Under what conditions should children be limited only to social inclusion? What child needs or program characteristics would lead to considerations of placing a child in a reverse inclusion program? Is it acceptable for decisions to be based primarily on the availability of slots or ease and efficiency with which specialized services can be provided? Are there valid concerns that the intensive specialized services for children with disabilities cannot be accommodated without disrupting the entire general early childhood program? How are decisions affected by assessments of program quality? Is it likely that children's social and educational development will be compromised as a consequence of participation in full inclusion programs? Will children with disabilities be isolated or even rejected by their peers

in fully inclusive environments? Is peer rejection minimized in reverse inclusion programs? Failure to consider these and other questions that are specific to existing options allows participants to make placement decisions that are unexamined in light of both value judgments and available knowledge.

Should such a rationale be developed, it may well reveal that the choice of inclusive program type for many children with disabilities unnecessarily limits involvement with typically developing children and participation in typical activities. For example, why is it that in California only approximately one third of the children with disabilities in reporting LEAs participate in fully inclusive programs and only one half of the children with mild disabilities are fully included (Cavallaro et al., 1998)? Could more children benefit from participation in full inclusion programs? Indeed, the new language of the IDEA Amendments of 1997 with respect to IEP development and placement decisions is asking for a more thoughtful level of decision making. As noted previously, required for the IEP are new statements that focus participants on what needs to be done to maximize general classroom involvement and that explain *why* children are *not* participating in all activities. This constitutes an important direction and serves to encourage the development of rationale bases for placement decisions. For completeness, development of such a rationale should encompass a justification for placement in a specialized program as well. In fact, even in exemplary programs, child placement in an inclusive or specialized environment is unrelated to child, maternal, or service provider characteristics (Kochanek & Buka, 1999).

A related concern with respect to the absence of a well-established rationale for decisions is that virtually no motivation for change is generated. Rather than accepting what is available as a result of an ambiguous set of circumstances, being armed with a rationale allows the important issues to shift within this framework to the conditions necessary to maximize inclusion. Answers to all of the previous questions are, of course, tied to certain conditions (e.g., adequate resources and methods to promote inclusion). Accordingly, entering into a dialogue about these conditions may well constitute one of the most important strategies for altering the current pattern of inclusive options. Important information, at least at a general or group level, that relates to questions that are relevant to a rationale for deciding on specific placements is already available, including specialized placements. This information is summarized later in this chapter and in the remainder of this book. Consequently, discrepancies between what exists and what needs to be created can be identified. Goals and future directions for research and program development can follow.

Should communities undergo such a review and analysis, this process may, over time, yield results that produce important changes at a systems and general program level. Such a process is to be encouraged now, despite that more knowledge needs to be acquired. Discomfort at the level of uncertainty that exists with respect to an emerging framework to help inform decisions about inclusive options will vary from community to community, but, as will be seen, useful information that is relevant to many of the important questions is, in fact, available. Professionals who participate in research should be available not only to bring their knowledge to the attention of all those involved but also to do so in a convenient and interpretable manner. Moreover, the specific issues that could benefit from the attention of researchers would become apparent as this process of developing a rationale continues. Of note, the absence of infor-

mation is especially glaring for infants and toddlers, and we have only a limited understanding of the meaning of "natural environments" for these young children.

Finally, the ultimate challenge is to apply such a framework (rationale) to an individual child and family, especially when some level of uncertainty is inevitable. Of course, a child's individual needs remain of paramount importance, and the links between a rationale and information about program options in relation to the needs of a given child and family may create tension in many circumstances. These decisions will also remain personal ones, and certain factors that govern those decisions may never be identified. Nevertheless, decisions on a child-by-child basis can become increasingly informed when presented within a well-designed rationale that frames the issues and communicates what is known. It is under these circumstances and through this process that a more thoughtful understanding of the meaning of the priority of full inclusion can be achieved.

Summary   Available evidence suggests a mixed picture with regard to children's access to inclusive programs. Considerable progress, especially for preschool-age children, has been achieved, and, although a more recent phenomenon, efforts to ensure access for infants and toddlers are moving forward. Yet, universal access to inclusive programs of any type for young children with disabilities is far from a reality. A substantial proportion of families are still not offered an inclusive option. Even when offered to families, the poor quality of many programs effectively limits access. Of considerable concern is the absence of a systems-level infrastructure designed to maintain existing programs and to foster the systematic expansion of inclusive options. Moreover, there seems to be no well-developed framework justifying either the development of various inclusive options or a rationale for matching children with program types. No corresponding rationale for placement in specialized environments exists either. As a consequence, decisions about placement options, especially when considering options other than full inclusion, are likely to be uneven at best. The reauthorization of IDEA seeks to maximize the participation of children with disabilities in fully inclusive environments, but fully inclusive programs do not seem to be emphasized in community environments. For needed change to occur, a dynamic new framework is required that utilizes our existing and emerging knowledge base to identify what must be accomplished to ensure that children find their way to the most appropriate program.

Feasibility

The concept of feasibility is important and represents a recognition of and respect for the integrity of general early childhood or early intervention programs (see Table 1.2). Inclusive practices, when properly carried out, ultimately require change and accommodation at the program level to ensure an appropriate experience for children with disabilities. However, it is not the intent of inclusive practices to alter in a significant way the fundamental assumptions and structure of a particular program's model, thereby altering the experience for typically developing children. If that disruptive outcome were to occur, it is hard to imagine continued support for inclusive programs. Indeed, court cases have established that teachers in inclusive programs cannot be required to devote an unusually large proportion of their time to children with disabilities, nor are programs required to alter their nature radically (*Daniel R.R. v. State Board of Education,* 1989; see Lipsky & Gartner, 1997, pp. 86, 305). Feasibility, then, refers to the ability of a particular program to retain its core philosophical and programmatic ap-

proach while successfully meeting the individual needs of all children in the program (Guralnick, 1982). In a meaningful sense, then, feasibility reflects critical dimensions of program quality.

Feasibility is a particularly challenging goal for general early childhood programs that are now faced with accommodating children with a wide range of disabilities (usually in the full inclusion model). Yet, significant challenges exist for other types of inclusive programs as well. Reverse inclusion programs, for example, often dominated by an early childhood special education approach, may need to incorporate more of a developmental model to meet the needs of typically developing children—a circumstance that may challenge the basic features of a model designed originally for children with special needs. The commitment of any program to experiment with variations of their model and the availability of resources to support those adjustments are critical for ensuring that programs are feasible. In many respects, then, feasibility presents both a program integrity issue and a resource issue.

Program Integrity   The goal of universal access to inclusive programs can easily be quantified, even for various program types (see the previous "Access" section). In contrast, the goal domain of feasibility has not been fully developed and therefore does not readily lend itself to such straightforward objective measures. Nevertheless, a number of measurement approaches can be suggested. For example, with regard to program integrity, teaching and administrative staff could conduct self-evaluations about the accommodations required and their impact on the program. Judgments then could be made about the compatibility of the altered program with the program's model and approach. Alternatively, observations of the ecology of the program by personnel not identified with the program could provide converging informa-

Table 1.2.   Goal and outcome criteria for the goal domain of feasibility

Goal	Outcome criteria
Accommodate to and meet individualized needs of children with and without disabilities without disrupting the integrity of a program's model	1. Self-evaluations by program staff regarding program integrity 2. Independent observations to evaluate the appropriateness of curriculum adjustments, flow of activities, classroom atmosphere, distribution of teacher–child interactions, and so forth 3. Instructional time, child engagement, and progress toward IFSP or IEP objectives are in accord with expectations 4. Specialist expertise available to meet individualized child needs delivered in a manner consistent with program model 5. Children with disabilities not stigmatized by teachers or program practices

tion regarding the application of the general or overall curriculum, the flow of activities, classroom atmosphere, the distribution of teacher–child interactions (e.g., time devoted to children with and without disabilities), and other dimensions. These observations then would be compared with expectations based on the program's philosophical and programmatic approach.

The limited and extremely preliminary data on this issue do suggest that the general integrity of early childhood programs can be feasibly maintained when children with disabilities are included. Survey research with general early childhood educators as respondents indicates that the range of activities is not restricted as a consequence of the presence of children with disabilities and that educators perceive that their general activities can be relatively easily adapted to accommodate children with disabilities (Wolery, Schroeder, et al., 1994). Similar results (i.e., minor accommodations) were obtained in a more recent study of practitioners (general educators, special educators, related services personnel, paraprofessionals) involved in early childhood inclusive programs (Stoiber, Gettinger, & Goetz, 1998). Accommodations were perceived to be more major for children with certain disorders (e.g., autism, behavior disorders), however. In addition, observations of interaction patterns of children and teachers in inclusive environments suggest an ecology that can accommodate all children (Kontos, Moore, & Giorgetti, 1998). Feasibility using engagement as the measure (i.e., time spent by children in appropriate interactions with teachers, peers, or curricular activities) is also suggested. Analyses by McCormick, Noonan, and Heck (1998) indicated high levels of engagement in similar activities for children with and without disabilities in community-based programs using what seemed to be the cluster model. Nevertheless, no well-defined system exists to examine this goal domain, including expectations related to the flow of program activities, the frequency and consistency of teacher–child relationships, and other important features that can index the integrity of the program's philosophical and programmatic approach. This is an important task for future work.

In fact, given the often contentious debate regarding the application of a general early childhood model articulated within the framework of developmentally appropriate practices (DAP; Bredekamp, 1987; Bredekamp & Copple, 1997) to children with disabilities, legitimate concern about the feasibility of inclusive programs can be raised (e.g., Carta, Schwartz, Atwater, & McConnell, 1991). The degree of program structure, the importance of assessment and evaluation, the nature and extent of the interactions that occur between adults and children, and the relative emphasis on socioemotional as opposed to other developmental goals are among the issues that can affect feasibility. Numerous efforts toward reconciling the perspective of the primarily early childhood special education tradition with that of the general early childhood tradition have been attempted (Bredekamp, 1993; Guralnick, 1993; Wolery, 1997), and many common themes can now be comfortably identified.

Of note, research comparing inclusive and specialized programs with respect to developmental appropriateness for preschool-age children has yielded similar outcomes (approximately 50% of inclusive and specialized programs met minimum criteria for developmental appropriateness; La Paro, Sexton, & Snyder, 1998). Comparisons between specialized and inclusive programs for toddlers also have produced similar results (Bruder & Staff, 1998). Although issues of overall program quality can be raised by these and other studies (Buysse et al., 1999), it nevertheless seems that generally agreed-on quality practices are commonly shared across widely differing programs. Yet, judging by the extraordinary effort that has been required to achieve some common ground at a conceptual level regarding DAP, it seems that much remains to be accomplished at a day-to-day level, particularly when considering the many full inclusion programs that are administered by the general early childhood community. Moreover, issues regarding the availability of special educational and related resources and their effective integration into a program's model are likely areas of concern for feasibility. These topics, which directly address the program's ability to meet the individualized needs of children with disabilities, are examined in the following sections.

Special Educational Resources

Feasible programs provide the context for educational/developmental activities that are closely linked to individualized needs of children with disabilities. At a minimum, the objectives specified in the IEP for preschool-age children and those in the individualized family service plan (IFSP) for infants and toddlers must be carried out in a thoughtful way. To accomplish this, *specific* curriculum adaptations often are required, and sophisticated instructional technologies must be incorporated into the daily activities of the overall program. The feasibility of this task has been amply demonstrated given adequate training and resources (e.g., Wolery & Fleming, 1993). Although evaluation approaches for feasibility with respect to meeting the child's needs have not been firmly established, measures of instructional time, child engagement, and the rate of child progress toward achieving objectives have been suggested (McWilliam, Trivette, & Dunst, 1985; Wolery & Fleming, 1993).

It is this aspect of feasibility that places demands on resources, particularly personnel. Experts in instructional technology and disability issues in general must be available to provide advice, training, and even direct child services on occasion (see Guralnick, 1999a). Without access to this expertise, the possibilities of carrying out an appropriate individualized program are remote for many children with disabilities. For the cluster, reverse inclusion, and social inclusion models, experts are usually readily available. However, for full inclusion programs, available evidence suggests that a large number of programs neither work with nor are supported by special education professionals (McDonnell et al., 1997; Wolery, Martin, et al., 1994). In fact, a survey by Cavallaro and colleagues (1998) showed that the majority of inclusive programs did not provide any services to children with disabilities in the inclusive environment. Given the overall absence of training of general educators in the disability field (e.g., Wolery,

Brookfield, et al., 1993), significant concerns can be raised about the ability of a substantial proportion of full inclusion programs to provide appropriate individualized activities for children with disabilities. This is a major threat to the feasibility of these programs.

Related Services Resources   Feasible inclusive programs not only require special educational expertise but also require related services that utilize the skills of specialists, such as occupational therapists or speech-language pathologists. The question of feasibility relates to both the availability of these specialized services and how they are provided. With respect to availability, extant data suggest that specialists are in short supply in full inclusion programs (McDonnell et al., 1997; Wolery, Venn, et al., 1994). As a consequence, considerable concern exists with respect to developing and implementing an individualized program that incorporates the perspectives of relevant disciplines in full inclusion environments. This seems to be especially problematic for community-based preschool and child care programs.

With regard to the form through which these specialized services are provided, many early childhood models hold that an approach that *integrates* at many levels the knowledge and skills provided by various specialists (including special educators) is most effective and consistent with the way children learn about the world. The more conventional "pull-out" types of services are discouraged by most general early childhood models as being both disruptive and inconsistent with the program's overall conceptual model. The clear preference in these programs is for "integrated therapy" in which specialists weave their services into the ongoing activities and routines of the program itself (see McWilliam, 1996b). Close consultation between education and specialist personnel, even if services are provided by the specialist in the program

environment (usually in the context of general activities), is part of this highly demanding collaborative approach.

In reality, numerous variations of integrated therapy models can be identified and are found in practice (McWilliam, 1995). These variations allow programs to incorporate more easily related services into their activities to meet children's individual needs and, of importance, do not depend on the type of inclusion (or segregated) model. Accordingly, feasibility can potentially be achieved within this framework.

Despite that research has not demonstrated the superiority of one approach over another (i.e., integrated or pull-out) on children's development (McWilliam, 1996a), integrated therapy approaches are far more prevalent and accepted at the beginning of the 21st century than at any other time. In fact, more and more professionals profess a need for integrative approaches. At the same time, substantial differences exist among disciplines as to the value and practice of integrated therapies (McWilliam & Bailey, 1994), and nonintegrated models remain a major force in practice (McWilliam, 1995). Reasons for this include the fact that integrated therapy requires specialists to alter historically grounded and well-established practices. Collaborative approaches are perhaps even more time-consuming than individual practice, as specialists must become familiar with a child's total program, adapt standard practice models, and enter into negotiations with staff to achieve consensus. Indeed, the limited time and opportunities available for collaboration is a recurring theme as voiced by specialists and teachers alike (Buysse, Wesley, & Keyes, 1998; McWilliam, 1995; Stoiber et al., 1998). Larger systems issues of financial considerations and billing practices are also relevant.

There is little doubt that conceptual issues and how these issues are translated into day-to-day practices that are associated with integrated therapy approaches will require resolution to achieve feasible programs. Perhaps more fundamental is the limited supply of well-trained specialists in general, not only in full inclusion programs. In fact, the training issue is a serious one, as personnel shortages have been well documented and changes in preservice training for professional groups that is compatible with inclusive practices are not nearly keeping pace with the expected demand (Winton, 1993; Yoder, Coleman, & Gallagher, 1990). Of considerable importance, parents have consistently identified staff training and the availability of special services as concerns with respect to placing their children in inclusive programs (Bailey & Winton, 1987; Blacher & Turnbull, 1982; Guralnick, 1994). It is ironic that, to some extent, the practice of integrated therapy may exacerbate parents' concerns regarding the availability of specialized services, as the visibility of therapists and particularly therapist–child interactions (and therefore perceived intensity of services) may be reduced. Moreover, many parents seem to be interested primarily in obtaining nonintegrated related services from specialists because they believe that it provides more obvious evidence of service provision that is individualized and even most effective (McWilliam et al., 1995). As a consequence, parental choice may challenge the feasibility of inclusive models (particularly full inclusion models) by encouraging or even insisting on practices that are not compatible with the early childhood program's philosophy. In fact, parent satisfaction is an important element for all dimensions of feasibility and requires the development of a thoughtful process of parent–professional relationships around issues related to inclusion. This process would complement parental decision making already established as part of placement and program planning procedures.

Stigma   Finally, programs should be considered feasible only if they minimize the possibility that the child with a disability will be stigmatized as a result of experiences in the inclusive environment (see Goffman, 1963). This is a difficult construct to measure, but care must be taken by staff to ensure that efforts to meet an individual child's needs do not occur in a manner that unduly separates the child with a disability from his or her peers and that intervention programs are provided in a respectful manner. Virtually no direct information is available on this issue (Stoneman, 1993). However, results from preliminary studies indicate that in comparison with typically developing children, teachers tend to be less involved with children with disabilities during free play in inclusive programs (Kontos et al., 1998), the possible frustration experienced by teachers as a result of compliance concerns and the extra assistance required by children with disabilities (Quay, 1991), and data in related fields regarding how readily and subtly prejudicial categories about people with disabilities are formed suggest potential concern. Self-assessments and assessments provided by observers as to the manner and style with which services are provided to children with disabilities, how questions that arise about a child's disability are responded to, and self-exploration of staff attitudes toward people with disabilities may serve as useful strategies for evaluating whether the inclusive experience is contributing to the stigmatization of the child with disabilities. Moreover, this dimension of feasibility may well have important implications for the goal of social integration, which is discussed in the section "Social Integration."

Summary   The goal of feasibility for inclusive programs represents a framework for ensuring the integrity of programs and the quality of the inclusive experience for children with and without disabilities. Despite its importance, it is perhaps the least well-developed and articulated goal, as limited programmatic work or research has been carried out. Issues of importance include maintaining the integrity of the program's model, particularly as indexed by the nature of adult–child interactions, engagement, and the ability to adapt appropriately the program's curriculum; ensuring that individualized special educational interventions occur as planned; providing specialized therapies in a manner that is consistent with the program's model; and minimizing the possibility of stigmatizing children with disabilities in the way services are delivered and how the program is organized to adapt to children's diverse skills, behaviors, and abilities. Agreeing on and developing criteria and corresponding measures of feasibility constitute important future tasks for the field and provide a more specific framework for establishing program quality. Evidence does suggest that program integrity can be maintained. Studies of practitioner perceptions and direct observations support this position. Program quality, as assessed by indicators of DAP, also seems to be unaffected by including children with disabilities. Most research, however, has focused on full inclusion programs or the cluster model. Nevertheless, concerns with regard to the availability of special educational and related services to help meet children's individualized needs (in full inclusion programs in particular), as well as differences of opinion on models of service delivery, constitute substantial threats to the feasibility of inclusive programs.

Developmental and Social Outcomes

The third goal of inclusive programs relates to the developmental (e.g., language, cognition, motor) and social outcomes of children with and without disabilities. The appropriate goal here actually should be modest (i.e., children will do at least as well developmentally

and socially in inclusive programs as they do in specialized ones). Particularly for children with disabilities, a rationale certainly can be developed to suggest that these children may derive unique benefits from participation in inclusive environments that can enhance development in general. Arguments related to higher expectations that are likely to be found in inclusive environments and the more demanding nature of those environments have been put forward (see Guralnick, 1990a, 1990b). Nevertheless, it is reasonable to expect inclusive programs to provide an environment that can accommodate children with disabilities, meet their individualized needs in a nonstigmatizing manner, and not have a negative impact on typically developing children in the program. As a consequence, developmental and social outcomes should be unaffected by participation in specialized or inclusive programs (see Table 1.3).

Even if programs are considered to be feasible, it is still important to evaluate the developmental and social outcomes of all children. Theoretically, feasible programs should be more likely to yield appropriate developmental and social outcomes, but hardly any information is available on this important linkage. As noted, formal criteria for identifying feasible programs remain to be established. Even when this is accomplished, however, there may well be circumstances that are not evaluated by the feasibility measures agreed on and that can be problematic with respect to confidence that the developmental and social outcome goals are achieved. For example, the larger number of children generally found in inclusive as compared to specialized programs may provide distractions to children with disabilities that adversely influence a variety of developmental domains. Similarly, the social environment provided by typically developing peers may be of concern for children with disabilities, as relationships between children with and without

Table 1.3.   Goal and outcome criteria for the goal domain of developmental and social outcomes

Goal	Outcome criteria
Children will do at least as well developmentally and socially in inclusive programs as they do in specialized programs	1. Norm- or criterion-referenced measures of cognitive, language, motor, or other aspects of development 2. Diverse aspects of peer-related social interactions and social competence 3. Establishing friendships

disabilities may become strained. Over time, this may substantially restrict the development of a competent pattern of peer-related social interactions for children with disabilities. Accordingly, direct outcome, in addition to feasibility, measures are needed.

Developmental Domains   In essence, the issue to be examined is whether, under optimal though realistic conditions, children's developmental and social outcomes are affected by participation in inclusive programs. This can best be addressed by comparing feasible inclusive programs with well-established specialized ones. In the absence of established criteria for feasibility, the closest approximation to these conditions is comparisons involving inclusive model demonstration or research-oriented programs, either community based or university operated. Specialized programs involved in the comparisons should also be well-established community programs or, occasionally, research-oriented models. This type of comparative analysis was carried out by Buysse and Bailey (1993), who evaluated and summarized outcomes of 22 studies that met children's chronological age, study design (i.e., emphasized a comparative between- or within-groups research design), and outcome measure criteria. Although as a group these studies exhibited many methodological problems as revealed by an analysis of threats to internal and external validity, consistent patterns did nevertheless emerge. Specifically, irrespective of the developmental domains assessed, no differences were found to result from children's participation in inclusive or specialized

programs. This conclusion applies to typically developing children as well (e.g., Odom, DeKlyen, & Jenkins, 1984). Studies of the cognitive aspects of children's play continue to support the finding that inclusive environments do not create circumstances that limit development (Guralnick, Connor, Hammond, Gottman, & Kinnish, 1996a; McCabe, Jenkins, Mills, Dale, & Cole, 1999). Of note, few studies included children with severe disabilities. Nonetheless, a later comparative study that focused on toddlers with severe and moderate disabilities in inclusive and specialized environments also did not detect differences in the developmental progress of children (Bruder & Staff, 1998). Of importance, in this particular investigation and other studies, programmatic characteristics differed between the environments (e.g., often more intensive special educational or therapeutic services were provided in the specialized environments, and teacher–child ratios were higher in those environments). In most instances, however, the quality of the inclusive environments, the level and array of available specialized services, and perhaps developmental advantages associated with inclusive programs seemed sufficient to ensure developmental outcomes that were equivalent to specialized environments.

This analysis by Buysse and Bailey (1993) accepted all inclusive program types, relatively few of which could be classified as full inclusion. However, a study that used a quasi-experimental design did compare two different inclusive program types: full inclusion and reverse inclusion with a specialized program on developmental outcomes for heterogeneous groups of children with mild and moderate disabilities (Mills, Cole, Jenkins, & Dale, 1998). Overall differences on developmental outcomes using conventional analyses were not found to be statistically significant among the three groups, thereby supporting the general pattern found in previous work. Focusing on the full inclusion and specialized programs, analyses of changes over time within the two groups and comparisons between children classified as high or low functioning between groups failed to detect any differences. Accordingly, in these analyses, specialized programs do not provide detectable developmental benefits in comparison to full inclusion programs for heterogeneous groups of children with mild and moderate disabilities. There was some suggestion that a reverse inclusion program, in comparison to both the specialized and full inclusion program types, may offer some developmental advantages for children who are higher functioning but disadvantages for children considered to be lower functioning (Cole, Mills, Dale, & Jenkins, 1991; Mills et al., 1998). These differences are small, however, and in the absence of an understanding of the mechanisms (e.g., type of curriculum, teacher–child interactions [see Guralnick, 1981b, 1982]) which mediate these effects (i.e., process-outcome studies), no clear pattern regarding the relationship among program type, child characteristics, and developmental outcome is evident. For children with severe disabilities, another recent quasi-experimental study comparing full inclusion and specialized programs indicated that the full inclusion program may provide more developmental advantages for these children (Hundert, Mahoney, Mundy, & Vernon, 1998). Taken together, the evidence suggests that children who are in feasible inclusive programs do at least as well as children who are in specialized programs. This conclusion must remain tentative, however, as few well-designed studies have been carried out.

Social Development   The comparative analysis by Buysse and Bailey (1993) that focused on children's peer-related social development suggested a somewhat different pattern. Specifically, as they reviewed, a number of studies reported increased levels of social interactions for children with disabilities when participating in inclusive as compared with specialized environments. Of note, the peer interactions of typically developing children do not seem to be affected by their involvement with children with disabilities. Later studies confirmed these patterns for the level of peer-related social interactions (Guralnick, Connor, et al., 1996a; Guralnick, Connor, Hammond, Gottman, & Kinnish, 1996b). However, no changes have been observed in the extent to which children establish friendships as a consequence of participation in inclusive or specialized environments (Guralnick, Gottman, & Hammond, 1996). Analyses further suggest that when advantages for inclusive environments are found, increases in the peer-related social interactions can most likely be attributed to the social demands placed on children with disabilities by their typically developing peers (Guralnick, Connor, et al., 1996a; see also McGee, Paradis, & Feldman, 1993). This finding regarding the specific role of typically developing children suggests the importance of the programmatic factor related to the proportion of children with and without disabilities in the inclusive environment. Specifically, this finding may explain why increases in social interactions by children with disabilities are less apparent when they are in an environment that contains a relatively small proportion of typically developing children (i.e., reverse inclusion program; see Guralnick & Groom, 1988b).

Moreover, and of considerable importance, this increase occurs primarily in the form of higher levels (primarily frequency) of social interactions with peers rather than in the form of more developmentally advanced levels of social competence. Consequently, it may well be that inclusive programs, particularly the full and cluster models, provide a stimulating, interactive environment that encourages a high level of social interactions. To achieve social outcomes in the form of more sophisticated skills related to socially competent interactions, however, simple placement in inclusive programs is not adequate. More comprehensive interventions that are directed specifically toward fostering children's peer-related social competence may well be required (Guralnick, 1999b; Guralnick & Neville, 1997).

Summary It seems that well-designed inclusive programs produce no adverse developmental or social effects for children in general in comparison with specialized programs and may even provide a modest advantage in terms of the frequency of peer interactions for children with disabilities. In contrast, there is no evidence for or reason to expect similar outcomes for programs in which the integrity of the program's model is disrupted by including children with disabilities, for programs without resources that are sufficient to meet children's individual needs, or for programs that stigmatize children with disabilities (i.e., programs that are not feasible). Consequently, communities that make efforts to increase the number of feasible inclusive programs will not be disappointed when developmental and social outcomes of participating children are evaluated.

More definitive research to address this issue and perhaps to clarify the relationship to specific criteria for feasibility or to programmatic factors that mediate

child outcomes is certainly warranted (see Buysse & Bailey, 1993; Guralnick, 1981b). These factors may be especially informative if consistent evidence suggests that different types of inclusive programs provide advantages for children with certain developmental, behavioral, or physical characteristics. When this information becomes available, programs that are most likely to ensure optimal outcomes for children irrespective of the type or severity of their disability can be designed. This information, therefore, will have considerable practical and clinical utility and allow professionals and parents to make well-informed decisions about placement and programs on a child-by-child basis.

Of note, practical and ethical concerns that restrict the placement of children in inclusive and specialized programs to ensure equivalence of factors that can influence developmental and social outcomes will limit the quality of the experimental designs that address these questions. Accordingly, in the absence of prospective, randomized, controlled comparisons, quasi-experimental designs may well constitute the basis for evaluating developmental and social outcomes. Given these constraints, using a variety of child characteristics (e.g., type and severity of disability) to match children in feasible inclusive programs to children in existing specialized programs may be the best option (e.g., Brown, Horn, Heiser, & Odom, 1996). Although matching will never be perfect and other often unknown confounds are inevitable, continued reports of no detrimental effects on developmental and social outcomes, at minimum, of inclusive practices will further increase confidence that this important goal can be achieved. Other evaluation approaches that closely monitor *expected outcomes* for children will also add to this knowledge base.

Social Integration

The goal of inclusive programs that is most directly and firmly rooted in the ideology of inclusion relates to the nature of the social relationships that occur between children with and without disabilities. The hope is that by participating in common activities that are supported by program priorities that exemplify an inclusive philosophy and value system, meaningful social relationships will result (Guralnick, 1978, 1990a, 1999c). This expectation for *social integration* is a demanding one, as it tests typically developing children's ability and willingness to understand and then, it is hoped, move beyond differences in the developmental, behavioral, and even certain physical characteristics of their peers. Challenges to the social skills of children with disabilities are equally demanding, and many parents of children with disabilities express concerns that their child's behavior will contribute to his or her social rejection in inclusive environments (Guralnick, Connor, & Hammond, 1995).

The goal of *social integration* and the goal related to social outcomes discussed in the previous section are associated in complex ways. In one sense, the increased frequency of social interactions that often is found in full inclusion environments implies at least some level of social involvement with typically developing children. This is important because a meaningful level of social integration likely is necessary for children to gain the potential developmental benefits related to cognitive, communicative, general prosocial, and other skills that have been associated with productive peer relations (Bates, 1975; Garvey, 1986; Hartup, 1983; Howes, 1988; Rubin & Lollis, 1988). However, as discussed in the next section, a high level of *social separation,* especially when considering forms of peer interactions involving extended social ex-

changes, can exist even under these circumstances.

In fact, previous (Guralnick 1981a) and recent reviews (Guralnick, 1999c) of the literature on social integration continue to reveal the existence of substantial separation between children with and without disabilities in inclusive environments. Despite the heterogeneity of participant samples in these studies, the diversity of the approaches selected to evaluate social integration (e.g., direct observations, peer sociometrics), or the way social integration is indexed (e.g., actual social exchanges, friendships, prosocial behavior), separate subgroups based on children's developmental status tend to form (e.g., Cavallaro & Porter, 1980; Guralnick, 1980; Minnett, Clark, & Wilson, 1994; Nabors, 1997; Strain, 1984). Of importance, the context for observational studies has almost always been free play. It is precisely in this situation, when children are less constrained by adult structure, that accurate assessments of the quality of social behaviors with peers and preference patterns can be obtained. Moreover, these conclusions were based on analyses of social integration from the perspective of the typically developing children. That is, the question addressed was whether in inclusive environments typically developing children interacted with children with disabilities or children without disabilities in the environment based simply on the number of children available in each group or whether children's developmental status influenced social interaction patterns (i.e., subgroup preferences).

Nature of Social Integration   Of course, social interactions between children can take many forms, and the extent to which children are socially integrated may differ accordingly. Variations in play quality, complexity, and intimacy all affect the social demands placed on play partners. As might be expected, analyses of the different forms of social interaction have revealed a complex and differentiated perspective of social integration and have provided insight into the nature of the relationships that occur between children with and without disabilities in inclusive environments (Guralnick, 1999c). The series of studies conducted by Guralnick and his colleagues focusing on children with mild cognitive delays (Guralnick et al., 1998; Guralnick, Connor, et al., 1996a; Guralnick, Gottman, et al., 1996; Guralnick & Groom, 1987, 1988a; Guralnick & Paul-Brown, 1984, 1986, 1989) provides details of these variations in social integration. Specifically, social integration was analyzed within three constructs: 1) connectedness, 2) interpersonal relationships, and 3) accommodations. Results from this series of studies are summarized next (see Table 1.4).

Connectedness refers to the quantitative analysis of peer-related social interactions evaluated in relation to the availability of children who represent groups that differ in developmental status. In a real sense, these preference patterns constitute an "equity" criterion and can be applied separately to different characteristics of social interactions. Specifically, when more passive measures of connectedness are evaluated, such as parallel play or onlooker behavior, separation occurs only to a minor extent. Consequently, all children move about the inclusive program freely and engage in activities and toy play without regard to developmental status. Therefore, many opportunities exist for observational learning. For more interactive measures of connectedness, however, such as extended group play, substantial social separation is apparent. Typically developing children clearly prefer other typically developing children to children with developmental delays; they interact with children with delays approximately half as often as expected, based on availability (see Guralnick, Gottman,

et al., 1996; Guralnick & Groom, 1987). For the most demanding and intimate form of connectedness, friendships, the preference by typically developing children for other typically developing children is even stronger (Guralnick, Gottman, et al., 1996).

The quality of the interpersonal relationships that occur between children with and without mild developmental delays provides an additional perspective on social integration. When these assessments are carried out, the pattern of preferences is similar to the assessment of connectedness. In particular, social exchanges, when they do occur, are not overly negative. However, detailed analyses of utterance-by-utterance evaluations of social-communicative exchanges strongly suggest the language of separation. For example, inclusionary statements by typically developing children, such as "let's" or "we," or justifications for requests occur less frequently when interacting with children who have delays in comparison with interactions with other typically developing children (Guralnick & Paul-Brown, 1984, 1989). A disproportionately high level of disagreements and an unusually high level of tension displayed during conflicts further suggest that strained interpersonal relationships exist between children with delays and children without delays (Guralnick & Paul-Brown, 1989; Guralnick et al., 1998).

Despite these circumstances, additional analyses revealed that typically developing children made important accommodations to the cognitive and linguistic levels of the children with delays. Typically developing children worked hard to clarify communications, frequently using a directive mode when relating to ensure understanding, using multiple modalities when interacting, and making adjustments in syntactic aspects of speech in accordance with their playmates' cognitive and linguistic levels (Guralnick & Paul-Brown, 1984,

Table 1.4. Goal and outcome criteria for the goal domain of social integration

Goal	Outcome criteria
Meaningful social relationships between children with and without disabilities will be evident in inclusive environments	1. Connectedness of social interactions, including measures of passive and extended play as well as friendships 2. Quality of interpersonal relationships 3. Appropriateness of accommodations made by typically developing children in social situations

1989). This pattern suggests a sensitivity to individual differences of play partners and a willingness and ability of typically developing children to make appropriate accommodations.

Of note, when social separation occurs, related research with groups of younger typically developing children matched developmentally to children with delays has indicated that typically developing children who are the same chronological age as children with delays are not simply responding to playmates' developmental levels but rather to characteristics associated with the child's developmental status (see Guralnick, 1999c). That is, separation goes beyond what might occur based on children's differences in developmental level. Of importance, close inspection of this pattern of social separation suggests that these social relationships may best be characterized by the tendency of typically developing children not to reject children with disabilities but rather to ignore or exclude them, in part, simply through preferences for other typically developing children.

As indicated previously, although not studied in as much detail as for children with mild developmental delays, separation in virtually all forms of social interaction seems to be characteristic of inclusive environments for children with a wide range of types and severities of disability (Guralnick, 1981a, 1999c). Social separation can be detected even for children with communication disorders (Gertner, Rice, & Hadley, 1994; Guralnick, Connor, et al., 1996b). Generally, however, the greater the severity of a child's disability,

the greater the social separation found in these free play environments. It is ironic that the social inclusion model yields what seems to be the least amount of social integration, as demonstrated in perhaps the earliest study of this issue (Devoney, Guralnick, & Rubin, 1974). Meaningful exchanges between children with and without disabilities occurred in that investigation only with proper teacher structuring, a finding replicated repeatedly over the years. Limited familiarity and the awkwardness of the "designated" social play situation in the social inclusion model add to the already existing factors discussed in the next section that contribute to this high level of social separation.

Finally, it should be noted that when social separation is defined from the perspective of the children with delays, a very different pattern is obtained. Instead of separation, evidence suggests that children with disabilities either exhibit no preference or prefer typically developing children. This important finding suggests that complete social integration is indeed achieved from the perspective of children with disabilities (see Guralnick, 1981a, 1999c, for details).

The Forces that Affect Social Separation The forces that tend to produce social separation seem powerful, being resistant to explicit efforts to promote integration. Despite many strategies that are carried out in inclusive programs—such as specific teaching about disability or diversity issues, intensive efforts to encourage social interactions, and activities designed to promote inclusion in general—social separation seems to be maintained even across the school year (Diamond, LeFurgy, & Blass, 1993; Guralnick, 1980; Ispa, 1981; Jenkins, Odom, & Speltz, 1989). That is not to say that programs that exhibit state-of-the-art inclusive practices, experimenting with new techniques to develop positive relationships among all children, will not yield benefits. Such efforts need to be pursued vigorously. Studies on changes in children's attitudes resulting from specific interventions suggest potential, although their impact on actual peer relationships, including friendships, remains to be demonstrated (Favazza & Odom, 1997). Clearly, then, the absence of social integration from the perspective of typically developing children constitutes a significant concern for one of the core goals of inclusive programs.

A diverse set of factors is likely to be responsible for this absence of desired social integration. As described elsewhere (Guralnick, 1999c), perhaps of most significance is the set of expectations about children with disabilities held by typically developing children as transmitted by family members throughout the child's early years (see Stoneman, 1993). In many instances, these prior expectations are communicated via expressed or, more commonly, through implied parental attitudes toward disability and diversity. The degree to which parents encourage or arrange specific experiences with children with disabilities is important. To the extent that these expectations of typically developing children as they enter inclusive environments are not accepting of children with disabilities, as is generally the case (see Favazza & Odom, 1997), social integration patterns are certain to be affected. These patterns, it is hoped, can be modified by the inclusive preschool experience, but, as noted previously, this is difficult to accomplish. In addition, extensive experiences with children with disabilities are not likely to occur in the homes or communities of typically developing children, even when

both participate in an inclusive preschool program. Evidence suggests that young children with disabilities have less well-developed community-based peer social networks (Guralnick, 1997a; Lewis, Feiring, & Brooks-Gunn, 1987; Stoneman, Brody, Davis, & Crapps, 1988) and have difficulties with establishing linkages between social relationships that are formed with peers in the preschool or child care environment and those in their neighborhoods (Guralnick, 1997a). Even parents of children with disabilities have difficulty with establishing relationships with parents of typically developing children when both participate in the same inclusive program (Bailey & Winton, 1989; Stoneman, 1993).

Moreover, research has clearly documented that children with developmental delays (and many other groups of children with disabilities as well) exhibit peer interaction problems that go beyond delays expected on the basis of their developmental level (Guralnick, 1999b; Guralnick & Neville, 1997). Because selection of play partners depends substantially on children's common interests, abilities, backgrounds, and styles of relating (e.g., Rubin, Lynch, Coplan, Rose-Krasnor, & Booth, 1994), these unusual peer interaction problems place children with disabilities at an added disadvantage. As discussed previously, participation in inclusive programs raises only the level of social interactions, not the level of social competence. Consequently, interventions that succeed in promoting competence with peers (a social outcome) will likely enhance social integration as well.

Summary   Critical aspects of the goal of social integration have not been achieved. To be sure, positive signs exist, particularly in relation to integration for more passive forms of social interactions, accommodations by typically developing children, and integration from the perspective of children with delays. However, high expectations for the development of meaningful and productive social relationships between children with and without disabilities have been tempered by an understanding of the dynamics of connectedness and interpersonal relationships, the unusual difficulties in peer competence manifested by children with disabilities, and concerns about the attitudes that many typically developing children hold with regard to children with disabilities by the time they enter inclusive early childhood environments. As a consequence, efforts to alter larger societal perceptions of individuals with disabilities, to design strategies that are intended to foster specific dimensions of social integration in inclusive environments, and to develop interventions that enhance children's social competence constitute major areas that demand change to achieve higher levels of social integration.

Finally—and, in some ways, alternatively—the state of knowledge regarding social integration may also serve as a catalyst for articulating a more specific set of expectations for social integration. Is it reasonable to expect children with disabilities to form close friendships with typically developing children? If so, how would we expect the nature of this relationship to differ from the relationship between two typically developing children? How would these social interaction patterns be expected to vary in accordance with children's chronological age or the type or severity of a child's disability? These and related questions are extraordinarily difficult to address, as they force us to confront deeply held ideologies and value systems. No goal domain is more sensitive to values or engenders a greater personal reaction than that involving social relationships. Nevertheless, the time may be right for a thorough review and discussion of goals and expectations as well as the programmatic implications that relate to the most fundamental goal of inclusion, social integration.

FACTORS THAT INFLUENCE INCLUSION GOALS

Through thoughtful and persistent efforts, much has been accomplished with respect to meeting the expectations for and achieving the four goals of inclusion. As indicated in numerous chapters throughout this book, important changes have occurred in virtually every area related to improving inclusive practices. Fundamental reform in the education system is occurring, policies at all levels are being modified or developed to accommodate the unique issues created by inclusive programs, legal decisions are serving as catalysts for change, and attitudes and beliefs of families of typically developing children as well as of the children themselves are being challenged by inclusive practices. The attitudes and beliefs of parents of children with disabilities are being similarly challenged as they are faced with making decisions that best meet the needs of their child and family yet require their child to engage in demanding but often uncertain patterns of interacting created by inclusive practices. Training at preservice and in-service levels for general early childhood educators, for early childhood special educators, and for professionals from virtually all relevant specialties is gradually being altered to accommodate to the goals and practices of inclusion. Correspondingly, the entire ecology of infant and toddler programs, child care, and preschool programs, including Head Start, has shifted in an effort to accommodate the highly individualized needs of children with disabilities. Efforts are also under way to include children in the broad array of community activities. Innovations in collaborative educational models, strategies for delivering assistive technologies, approaches to promote social competence, the design of instructional technologies adapted to children with diverse abilities and skills, strategies for easing transitions, and finding ways to ensure that multicultural issues are addressed constitute important service delivery patterns that have improved inclusive practices substantially. Progress also has been achieved toward including special groups of children with disabilities in inclusive environments, such as those with autism, hearing impairments, or complex health care needs. Children from these groups create unique challenges for inclusive programs at many levels. Accordingly, spurred by a vision of an inclusive community, supported by legislation and legal decisions, and encouraged by the ability of the field to develop effective inclusive programs, professionals, parents, administrators, and advocates have, through these many influential factors, permanently altered the life patterns of many young children with disabilities and their families.

These accomplishments notwithstanding, analyses of the status of the four goal domains for inclusive practices presented in this chapter suggest either that progress has slowed considerably in recent years or that conditions for furthering progress are not in evidence. It now seems that numerous conceptual and practical problems must be resolved for the pace of change to increase. In particular, the goal of universal access to inclusive programs is far from being realized and is further compounded by the existence of different types of inclusive programs that may unnecessarily restrict the participation of children with disabilities with typically developing children. Clarifying the purposes, conceptual bases, advantages, and disadvantages of these various types of inclusive programs and providing a rationale for placement of *individual children* in each program type undoubtedly will uncover the diversity of assumptions and meanings of inclusion held by various constituencies, yet this is a necessary step for appropriate change to result. Similarly, the absence of generally agreed-on

criteria for establishing feasible programs is of concern and limits understanding of quality environments and associations of program ecology with developmental and social outcomes. Concerns about staff training and availability of needed resources are long-standing problems, and many families continue to choose less inclusive and even noninclusive environments because of these issues. However, evidence suggests that participation of children with disabilities in feasible inclusive programs does not adversely affect their developmental or social progress. In fact, there may be some advantage to children with disabilities in terms of an increased level of social interactions. Typically developing children's progress also seems unaffected, yet this information is based on a relatively small number of studies that were carried out primarily in research or demonstration programs. As a consequence of this and other factors, there does not seem to be widespread public or professional understanding that inclusive programs, especially full inclusion programs, can produce outcomes similar to those in specialized programs for the vast majority of young children with disabilities. Correspondingly, there seems to be only limited leadership in attempting to clarify this knowledge base or to resolve conceptual or empirical issues. Even with a recognition of the possibilities for and the value of inclusive programs, the failure to generate strategies that press for systematic, national-in-scope programs focused on local communities to develop feasible inclusive programs that will result in positive outcomes for all involved is a significant barrier to future progress. Finally, although perhaps unrealistic in retrospect, the high expectations for social integration, particularly in the form of more extended forms of social play activities and the development of friendships, have not been met from the perspective of typically developing children. Given the complexity of this issue and the powerful forces that seem to be operating across so many dimensions to produce social separation, a comprehensive and long-term plan to reconceptualize the nature, meaning, and expectations for social integration is likely to be required in the context of a focus on change.

ORGANIZATION OF THIS BOOK

Given this background, the primary purpose of this volume is to describe factors that influence the goals of inclusion, to articulate the barriers that prevent these goals from being realized, and, most important, to establish an agenda for change. As suggested in the final chapter, an agenda that is national in scope may well be essential for significant progress to be achieved.

Figure 1.1 depicts what seem to be the most salient factors that can influence the four goal domains (access, feasibility, developmental and social outcomes, social integration) of inclusion discussed in this chapter. As expected, some factors can influence all four inclusion goals, whereas the influence of others is likely to be limited to only one particular goal. Similarly, these factors are interrelated in complex ways, and their interactions are discussed in the context of specific issues.

Each of these influential factors corresponds to a chapter in the book. Specifically, education reform (Chapter 2, Lipsky & Gartner) at the highest levels will be required to ensure universal access to inclusive programs and will affect feasibility as well. The continuing effort to alter policies (Chapter 3, Smith & Rapport) such as those related to transportation, financing, standards, certification, and others will have an important impact on inclusive programs. Similarly, legal issues (Chapter 4, Stowe & H.R. Turnbull) that are relevant to inclusive practices have historically played an important role in clarifying and often fos-

tering inclusion and will continue to do so in the future.

Parents have been the primary catalysts for change in the disability field, and inclusion is no exception. The attitudes and beliefs of parents of typically developing children (Chapter 5, Stoneman) and of parents of children with disabilities (Chapter 6, Erwin, Soodak, Winton, & A. Turnbull) can substantially influence most of the goals of inclusion. The attitudes and beliefs of typically developing children themselves (Chapter 7, Diamond & Innes), although closely aligned with the values of their parents, may nevertheless be subject to change through participation in inclusive programs and thereby influence some of the goals of inclusion, particularly social integration.

Training (Chapter 8, Buysse, Wesley, & Boone) of all relevant personnel clearly is a central issue, and successful inclusion in any form cannot be achieved without a comprehensive and well-articulated program of preservice and in-service training. Program ecology—particularly adult–child interactions, engagement in activities, and the classroom structure of the various programs—will be influenced by the training of staff as well as other factors. In turn, program ecology affects so many of the goals of inclusion. Accordingly, program ecology will have a substantial impact on the goals of inclusion. These issues are examined separately for infants and toddlers (Chapter 9, Bruder) and for children in child care (Chapter 10, O'Brien), preschool (Chapter 11, Odom & Bailey), and Head Start (Chapter 12, Schwartz & Brand). A separate chapter considers the ecology of inclusion of children in community activities (Chapter 14, Dunst).

There exist as well important service delivery issues that must be addressed. Considerations of multicultural influences (Chapter 18, Hanson & Zercher), collaborative models, especially for chil-

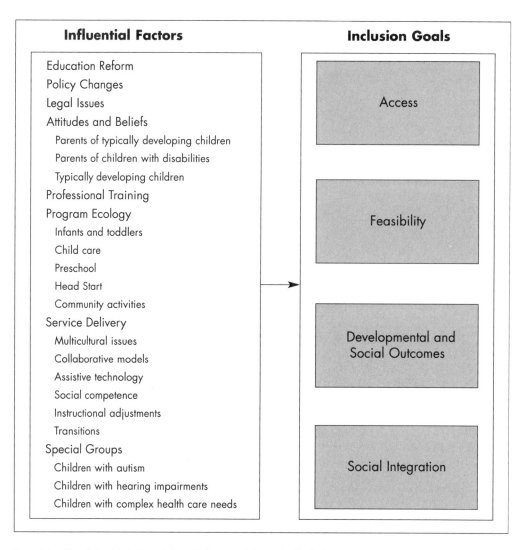

Influential Factors

Education Reform
Policy Changes
Legal Issues
Attitudes and Beliefs
   Parents of typically developing children
   Parents of children with disabilities
   Typically developing children
Professional Training
Program Ecology
   Infants and toddlers
   Child care
   Preschool
   Head Start
   Community activities
Service Delivery
   Multicultural issues
   Collaborative models
   Assistive technology
   Social competence
   Instructional adjustments
   Transitions
Special Groups
   Children with autism
   Children with hearing impairments
   Children with complex health care needs

Inclusion Goals

Access

Feasibility

Developmental and
Social Outcomes

Social Integration

Figure 1.1.   The relationship between influential factors and the goals of inclusion.

dren with communication disorders (Chapter 19, Paul-Brown & Caperton), assistive technology (Chapter 20, Romski, Sevcik, & Forrest), social competence (Chapter 21, Guralnick), instructional adjustments (Chapter 22, McWilliam, Wolery, & Odom), and transitions (Chapter 13, Sainato & Morrison) will be required to ensure the success of inclusive programs. Finally, certain groups of children pose unique and difficult challenges for inclusion and are therefore discussed separately. Groups considered are children with autism (Chapter 15, Strain, McGee, & Kohler), children with hearing impairments (Chapter 16, Antia & Levine), and children with complex health care needs (Chapter 17, Crocker & Porter).

In the final chapter of the book, these four goal areas are revisited, and an agenda for change is proposed (Chapter 23, Guralnick). In particular, the various factors that influence the goals of inclusion are integrated in an effort to encourage the creation of a coherent program of systems change, program development, and research in the field of early childhood inclusion.

REFERENCES

Americans with Disabilities Act of 1990, PL 101-336, 42 U.S.C.§§§ 12101 *et seq.*

Bailey, D.B., Jr., McWilliam, R.A., Buysse, V., & Wesley, P.W. (1998). Inclusion in the context of competing values in early childhood education. *Early Childhood Research Quarterly, 13,* 27–47.

Bailey, D.B., Jr., & Winton, P.J. (1987). Stability and change in parents' expectations about mainstreaming. *Topics in Early Childhood Special Education, 7,* 73–88.

Bailey, D.B., Jr., & Winton, P.J. (1989). Friendship and acquaintance among families in a mainstreamed day care center. *Education and Training in Mental Retardation, 24,* 107–113.

Bates, E. (1975). Peer relations and the acquisition of language. In M. Lewis & L.A. Rosenblum (Eds.), *The origins of behavior: Vol. 4. Friendship and peer relations* (pp. 259–292). New York: John Wiley & Sons.

Biklen, D. (1982). The least restrictive environment: Its application to education. In G. Melton (Ed.), *Child and youth services* (pp. 121–144). Binghamton, NY: The Haworth Press.

Blacher, J., & Turnbull, A.P. (1982). Teacher and parent perspectives on selected social aspects of preschool mainstreaming. *The Exceptional Child, 29,* 191–199.

Booth, C.L., & Kelly, J.F. (1998). Child-care characteristics of infants with and without special needs: Comparisons and concerns. *Early Childhood Research Quarterly, 13,* 603–622.

Booth, C.L., & Kelly, J.F. (1999). Child-care and employment in relation to infants' disabilities and risk factors. *American Journal on Mental Retardation, 104,* 117–130.

Bredekamp, S. (Ed.). (1987). *Developmentally appropriate practice in early childhood programs serving children from birth through age 8.* Washington, DC: National Association for the Education of Young Children.

Bredekamp, S. (1993). The relationship between early childhood education and early childhood special education: Healthy marriage or family feud? *Topics in Early Childhood Special Education, 13,* 248–273.

Bredekamp, S., & Copple, C. (1997). *Developmentally appropriate practice in early childhood programs* (Rev. ed.). Washington, DC: National Association for the Education of Young Children.

Brown, W.H., Horn, E.M., Heiser, J.G., & Odom, S.L. (1996). Innovative Practices Project BLEND: An inclusive model of early intervention services. *Journal of Early Intervention, 20,* 364–375.

Bruder, M.B. (1996). Interdisciplinary collaboration in service delivery. In R.A. McWilliam (Ed.), *Rethinking pull-out services in early intervention: A professional resource* (pp. 27–48). Baltimore: Paul H. Brookes Publishing Co.

Bruder, M.B., & Staff, I. (1998). A comparison of the effects of type of classroom and service characteristics on toddlers with disabilities. *Topics in Early Childhood Special Education, 18,* 26–37.

Bruder, M.B., Staff, I., & McMurrer-Kaminer, E. (1997). Toddlers receiving early intervention in childcare centers: A description of a service delivery system. *Topics in Early Childhood Special Education, 17,* 185–208.

Buysse, V., & Bailey, D.B., Jr. (1993). Behavioral and developmental outcomes in young children with disabilities in integrated and segregated settings: A review of comparative studies. *The Journal of Special Education, 26,* 434–461.

Buysse, V., Bailey, D.B., Jr., Smith, T.M., & Simeonsson, R.J. (1994). The relationship between child characteristics and placement in specialized versus inclusive early childhood programs. *Topics in Early Childhood Special Education, 14,* 419–435.

Buysse, V., & Wesley, P.W. (1993). The identity crisis in early childhood special education: A call for professional role clarification. *Topics in Early Childhood Special Education, 13*(4), 418–429.

Buysse, V., Wesley, P.W., Bryant, D., & Gardner, D. (1999). Quality of early childhood programs in inclusive and noninclusive settings. *Exceptional Children, 65,* 301–314.

Buysse, V., Wesley, P.W., & Keyes, L. (1998). Implementing early childhood inclusion: Barriers and support factors. *Early Childhood Research Quarterly, 13,* 169–184.

Carta, J.J., Schwartz, I.S., Atwater, J.B., & McConnell, S.R. (1991). Developmentally appropriate practice: Appraising its usefulness for young children with disabilities. *Topics in Early Childhood Special Education, 11*(1), 1–20.

Cavallaro, C.C., Ballard-Rosa, M., & Lynch, E.W. (1998). A preliminary study of inclusive special education services for infants, toddlers, and preschool-age children in California. *Topics in Early Childhood Special Education, 18,* 169–182.

Cavallaro, S.A., & Porter, R.H. (1980). Peer preferences of at-risk and normally developing children in preschool mainstream classrooms. *American Journal of Mental Deficiency, 84,* 357–366.

Cole, K.N., Mills, P.E., Dale, P.S., & Jenkins, J.R. (1991). Effects of preschool integration for children with disabilities. *Exceptional Children, 58,* 36–45.

Daniel R.R. v. State Board of Education, 874 F.2d 1036, 1047 (5th Cir. 1989).

Devoney, C., Guralnick, M.J., & Rubin, H. (1974). Integrating handicapped and nonhandicapped preschool children: Effects on social play. *Childhood Education, 50,* 360–364.

Diamond, K., LeFurgy, W., & Blass, S. (1993). Attitudes of preschool children toward their peers with disabilities: A year-long investigation in integrated classrooms. *The Journal of Genetic Psychology, 154,* 215–221.

Dinnebeil, L.A., McInerney, W., Fox, C., & Juchartz-Pendry, K. (1998). An analysis of the perceptions and characteristics of childcare personnel regarding inclusion of young children with special needs in community-based programs. *Topics in Early Childhood Special Education, 18,* 118–128.

Donegan, M.M., Ostrosky, M.M., & Fowler, S.A. (1996). Children enrolled in multiple programs: Characteristics, supports, and barriers to teacher communication. *Journal of Early Intervention, 20,* 95–106.

Education for All Handicapped Children Act of 1975, PL 94-142, 20 U.S.C. §§ 1400 *et seq.*

Education of the Handicapped Act Amendments of 1986, PL 99-457, 20 U.S.C. §§1400 *et seq.*

Favazza, P.C., & Odom, S.L. (1997). Promoting positive attitudes of kindergarten-age children toward people with disabilities. *Exceptional Children, 63,* 405–418.

Garvey, C. (1986). Peer relations and the growth of communication. In E.C. Mueller & C.R. Cooper (Eds.), *Process and outcome in peer relationships* (pp. 329–345). San Diego: Academic Press.

Gertner, B.L., Rice, M.L., & Hadley, P.A. (1994). Influence of communicative competence on peer preferences in a preschool classroom. *Journal of Speech and Hearing Research, 37,* 913–923.

Goffman, E. (1963). *Stigma.* Upper Saddle River, NJ: Prentice Hall.

Guralnick, M.J. (1976). The value of integrating handicapped and nonhandicapped preschool children. *American Journal of Orthopsychiatry, 46,* 236–245.

Guralnick, M.J. (Ed.). (1978). *Early intervention and the integration of handicapped and nonhandicapped children.* Baltimore: University Park Press.

Guralnick, M.J. (1980). Social interactions among preschool children. *Exceptional Children, 46,* 248–253.

Guralnick, M.J. (1981a). The efficacy of integrating handicapped children in early education settings: Research implications. *Topics in Early Childhood Special Education, 1*(1), 57–71.

Guralnick, M.J. (1981b). Programmatic factors affecting child–child social interactions in mainstreamed preschool programs. *Exceptional Education Quarterly, 1*(4), 71–91.

Guralnick, M.J. (1982). Mainstreaming young handicapped children: A public policy and ecological systems analysis. In B. Spodek (Ed.), *Handbook of research on early childhood education* (pp. 456–500). New York: The Free Press.

Guralnick, M.J. (1990a). Major accomplishments and future directions in early childhood mainstreaming. *Topics in Early Childhood Special Education, 10*(2), 1–17.

Guralnick, M.J. (1990b). Peer interactions and the development of handicapped children's social and communicative competence. In H. Foot, M. Morgan, & R. Shute (Eds.), *Children helping children* (pp. 275–305). Sussex, England: John Wiley & Sons.

Guralnick, M.J. (1993). Developmentally appropriate practice in the assessment and intervention of children's peer relations. *Topics in Early Childhood Special Education, 13*(3), 344–371.

Guralnick, M.J. (1994). Mothers' perceptions of the benefits and drawbacks of early childhood mainstreaming. *Journal of Early Intervention, 18,* 168–183.

Guralnick, M.J. (1997a). The peer social networks of young boys with developmental delays. *American Journal on Mental Retardation, 101,* 595–612.

Guralnick, M.J. (1997b). Second generation research in the field of early intervention. In M.J. Guralnick (Ed.), *The effectiveness of early intervention* (pp. 3–20). Baltimore: Paul H. Brookes Publishing Co.

Guralnick, M.J. (1998). Effectiveness of early intervention for vulnerable children: A developmental perspective. *American Journal on Mental Retardation, 102,* 319–345.

Guralnick, M.J. (1999a). Early childhood intervention: Evolution of a system. In M. Wehmeyer & J.R. Patton (Eds.), *Mental retardation in the 21st century* (pp. 37–58). Austin, TX: PRO-ED.

Guralnick, M.J. (1999b). Family and child influences on the peer-related social competence of young children with developmental delays. *Mental Retardation and Developmental Disabilities Research Reviews, 5,* 21–29.

Guralnick, M.J. (1999c). The nature and meaning of social integration for young children with mild developmental delays in inclusive settings. *Journal of Early Intervention. 22,* 70–86.

Guralnick, M.J., Connor, R., & Hammond, M. (1995). Parent perspectives of peer relations and friendships in integrated and specialized programs. *American Journal on Mental Retardation, 99,* 457–476.

Guralnick, M.J., Connor, R., Hammond, M., Gottman, J.M., & Kinnish, K. (1996a). Immediate effects of mainstreamed settings on the social interactions and social integration of preschool children. *American Journal on Mental Retardation, 100,* 359–377.

Guralnick, M.J., Connor, R., Hammond, M., Gottman, J.M., & Kinnish, K. (1996b). The peer relations of preschool children with communication disorders. *Child Development, 67,* 471–489.

Guralnick, M.J., Gottman, J.M., & Hammond, M.A. (1996). Effects of social setting on the friendship formation of young children differing in developmental status. *Journal of Applied Developmental Psychology, 17,* 625–651.

Guralnick, M.J., & Groom, J.M. (1987). The peer relations of mildly delayed and nonhandicapped preschool children in mainstreamed playgroups. *Child Development, 58,* 1556–1572.

Guralnick, M.J., & Groom, J.M. (1988a). Friendships of preschool children in mainstreamed playgroups. *Developmental Psychology, 24,* 595–604.

Guralnick, M.J., & Groom, J.M. (1988b). Peer interactions in mainstreamed and specialized classrooms: A comparative analysis. *Exceptional Children, 54,* 415–425.

Guralnick, M.J., & Neville, B. (1997). Designing early intervention programs to promote children's social competence. In M.J. Guralnick (Ed.), *The effectiveness of early intervention* (pp. 579–610). Baltimore: Paul H. Brookes Publishing Co.

Guralnick, M.J., & Paul-Brown, D. (1984). Communicative adjustments during behavior-request episodes among children at different developmental levels. *Child Development, 55,* 911–919.

Guralnick, M.J., & Paul-Brown, D. (1986). Communicative interactions of mildly delayed and normally developing preschool children: Effects of listener's developmental level. *Journal of Speech and Hearing Research, 29,* 2–10.

Guralnick, M.J., & Paul-Brown, D. (1989). Peer-related communicative competence of preschool children: Developmental and adaptive characteristics. *Journal of Speech and Hearing Research, 32,* 930–943.

Guralnick, M.J., Paul-Brown, D., Groom, J.M., Booth, C.L., Hammond, M.A., Tupper, D.B., & Gelenter, A. (1998). Conflict resolution patterns of preschool children with and without developmental delays in heterogeneous playgroups. *Early Education and Development, 9,* 49–77.

Hanline, M.F. (1990). A consulting model for providing integration opportunities for preschool children with disablities. *Journal of Early Intervention, 14,* 360–366.

Hartup, W.W. (1983). Peer relations. In E.M. Hetherington (Ed.), P.H. Mussen (Series Ed.), *Handbook of child psychology: Vol. 4. Socialization, personality, and social development* (pp. 103–196). New York: John Wiley & Sons.

Howes, C. (1988). Peer interaction of young children. *Monographs of the Society for Research in Child Development, 53*(1, Serial No. 217).

Hundert, J., Mahoney, B., Mundy, F., & Vernon, M.L. (1998). A descriptive analysis of developmental and social gains of children with severe disabilities in segragated and inclusive preschools in Southern Ontario. *Early Childhood Research Quarterly, 13,* 49–65.

Individuals with Disabilities Education Act Amendments of 1991, PL 102-119, 20 U.S.C. §§ 1400 *et seq.*

Individuals with Disabilities Education Act Amendments of 1997, PL 105-17, 20 U.S.C. §§ 1400 *et seq.*

Individuals with Disabilities Education Act (IDEA) of 1990, PL 101-476, 20 U.S.C. §§ 1400 *et seq.*

Ispa, J. (1981). Social interactions among teachers, handicapped children, and nonhandicapped children in a preschool. *Journal of Applied Developmental Psychology, 1,* 231–250.

Jenkins, J.R., Odom, S.L., & Speltz, M.L. (1989). Effects of social integration on preschool children with handicaps. *Exceptional Children, 55,* 420–428.

Kochanek, T.T., & Buka, S.L. (1998). Patterns of service utilization: Child, maternal, and service provider factors. *Journal of Early Intervention, 21,* 217–231.

Kochanek, T.T., & Buka, S.L. (1999). Influential factors in inclusive versus non-inclusive placements for preschool children with disabilities. *Early Education and Development, 10,* 191–208.

Kontos, S., Moore, D., & Giorgetti, K. (1998). The ecology of inclusion. *Topics in Early Childhood Special Education, 18,* 38–48.

La Paro, K.M., Sexton, D., & Snyder, P. (1998). Program quality characteristics in segregated and inclusive childhood settings. *Early Childhood Research Quarterly, 13,* 151–167.

Lewis, M., Feiring, C., & Brooks-Gunn, J. (1987). The social networks of children with and without handicaps: A developmental perspective. In S. Landesman & P. Vietze (Eds.), *Living environments and mental retardation* (pp. 377–400). Washington, DC: American Association on Mental Retardation.

Lipsky, D.K., & Gartner, A. (1997). *Inclusion and school reform: Transforming America's classrooms.* Baltimore: Paul H. Brookes Publishing Co.

McCabe, J.R., Jenkins, J.R., Mills, P.E., Dale, P.S., & Cole, K.N. (1999). Effects of group composition, materials, and developmental level on play in preschool children with disabilities. *Journal of Early Intervention, 22,* 164–178.

McCormick, L., Noonan, M.J., & Heck, R. (1998). Variables affecting engagement in inclusive preschool classrooms. *Journal of Early Intervention, 21,* 160–176.

McDonnell, A.P., Brownell, K., & Wolery, M. (1997). Teaching experience and specialist support: A survey of preschool teachers employed in programs accredited by NAEYC. *Topics in Early Childhood Special Education, 17,* 263–285.

McGee, G.G., Paradis, T., & Feldman, R.S. (1993). Free effects of integration on levels of autistic behavior. *Topics in Early Childhood Special Education, 13*(1), 57–67.

McWilliam, R.A. (1995). Integration of therapy and consultative special education: A continuum in early intervention. *Infants and Young Children, 7,* 29–38.

McWilliam, R.A. (1996a). A program of research on integrated versus isolated treatment in early intervention. In R.A. McWilliam (Ed.), *Rethinking pull-out services in early intervention: A professional resource* (pp. 71–102). Baltimore: Paul H. Brookes Publishing Co.

McWilliam, R.A. (Ed.). (1996b). *Rethinking pull-out services in early intervention: A professional resource.* Baltimore: Paul H. Brookes Publishing Co.

McWilliam, R.A., & Bailey, D.B., Jr. (1994). Predictors of service-delivery models in center-based early intervention. *Exceptional Children, 61,* 56–71.

McWilliam, R.A., Lang, L., Vandiviere, P., Angell, R., Collins, L., & Underdown, G. (1995). Satisfaction and struggles: Family perceptions of early intervention services. *Journal of Early Intervention, 19,* 43–60.

McWilliam, R.A., Trivette, C.M., & Dunst, C.J. (1985). Behavior engagement as a measure of the efficacy of early intervention. *Analysis and Intervention in Developmental Disabilities, 5,* 59–71.

Mills, P.E., Cole, K.N., Jenkins, J.R., & Dale, P.S. (1998). Effects of differing levels of inclusion on preschoolers with disabilities. *Exceptional Children, 65,* 79–90.

Minnett, A., Clark, K., & Wilson, G. (1994). Play behavior and communication between deaf and hard of hearing children and their hearing peers in an integrated preschool. *American Annals of the Deaf, 139,* 420–429.

Nabors, L. (1997). Playmate preferences of children who are typically developing for their classmates with special needs. *Mental Retardation, 35,* 107–113.

Odom, S.L., DeKlyen, M., & Jenkins, J.R. (1984). Integrating handicapped and nonhandicapped preschoolers: Developmental impact on non-handicapped children. *Exceptional Children, 51,* 41–48.

Odom, S.L., Horn, E.M., Marquart, J., Hanson, M.J., Wolfberg, P., Beckman, P., Lieber,

J., Shouming, L., Schwartz, I., Janko, S., & Sandall, S. (1999). On the forms of inclusion: Organizational context and individualized service models. *Journal of Early Intervention, 22,* 185–199.

Peck, C.A., Furman, G.C., & Helmstetter, E. (1993). Integrated early childhood programs: Research on the implementation of change in organizational contexts. In C.A. Peck, S.L. Odom, & D.D. Bricker (Eds.), *Integrating young children with disabilities into community programs: Ecological perspectives on research and implementation* (pp. 187–205). Baltimore: Paul H. Brookes Publishing Co.

Quay, L.C. (1991). Caregivers' interactions with nonhandicapped and mainstreamed handicapped children in caregiving and instructional activities. *Early Education and Development, 2,* 261–269.

Rehabilitation Act of 1973, PL 93-112, 29 U.S.C. §§ 701 *et seq.*

Rubin, K.H., & Lollis, S.P. (1988). Origins and consequences of social withdrawal. In J. Belsky & T. Nezworski (Eds.), *Clinical implications of attachment* (pp. 219–252). Mahwah, NJ: Lawrence Erlbaum Associates.

Rubin, K.H., Lynch, D., Coplan, R., Rose-Krasnor, L., & Booth, C.L. (1994). "Birds of a feather. . .": Behavioral concordances and preferential personal attractions in children. *Child Development, 65,* 1778–1785.

Smith, B.J., & Rose, D.F. (1993). *Administrator's policy handbook for preschool mainstreaming.* Cambridge, MA: Brookline Books.

Stoiber, K.C., Gettinger, M., & Goetz, D. (1998). Exploring factors influencing parents' and early childhood practitioners' beliefs about inclusion. *Early Childhood Research Quarterly, 13,* 107–124.

Stoneman, Z. (1993). The effects of attitude on preschool integration. In C.A. Peck, S.L. Odom, & D.D. Bricker (Eds.), *Integrating young children with disabilities into community programs: Ecological perspectives on research and implementation* (pp. 223–248). Baltimore: Paul H. Brookes Publishing Co.

Stoneman, Z., Brody, G.H., Davis, C.H., & Crapps, J.M. (1988). Childcare responsibilities, peer relations, and sibling conflict: Older siblings of mentally retarded children. *American Journal on Mental Retardation, 93,* 174–183.

Strain, P.S. (1984). Social behavior patterns of nonhandicapped and nonhandicapped-developmentally disabled friend pairs in mainstream preschools. *Analysis and Intervention in Developmental Disabilities, 4,* 15–28.

Taylor, S.J. (1988). Caught in the continuum: A critical analysis of the principle of the least restrictive environment. *Journal of The Association for Persons with Severe Handicaps, 13,* 41–53.

Turnbull, H.R., III, Ellis, J.W., Boggs, E.M., Brooks, P.O., & Biklen, D.P. (1981). *The least restrictive alternative: Principles and practices.* Task Force on Least Restriction Legislative and Social Issues Committee. Washington, DC: American Association on Mental Deficiency.

Winton, P.J. (1993). Providing family support in integrated settings: Research and recommendations. In C.A. Peck, S.L. Odom, & D.D. Bricker (Eds.), *Integrating young children with disabilities into community programs: Ecological perspectives on research and implementation* (pp. 65–80). Baltimore: Paul H. Brookes Publishing Co.

Wolery, M. (1997). Encounters with general early education: Lessons being learned. *Journal of Behavioral Education, 7,* 91–98.

Wolery, M., Brookfield, J., Huffman, K., Schroeder, C., Martin, C.G., Venn, M.L., & Holcombe, A. (1993). Preparation in preschool mainstreaming as reported by general early education faculty. *Journal of Early Intervention, 17,* 298–308.

Wolery, M., & Fleming, L.A. (1993). Implementing individualized curricula in integrated settings. In C.A. Peck, S.L. Odom, & D.D. Bricker (Eds.), *Integrating young children with disabilities into community programs: Ecological perspectives on research and implementation* (pp. 109–132). Baltimore: Paul H. Brookes Publishing Co.

Wolery, M., Holcombe-Ligon, A., Brookfield, J., Huffman, K., Schroeder, C., Martin, C.G., Venn, M.L., Werts, M.G., & Fleming, L.A. (1993). The extent and nature of preschool mainstreaming: A survey of general early educators. *The Journal of Special Education, 27,* 222–234.

Wolery, M., Martin, C.G., Schroeder, C., Huffman, K., Venn, M.L., Holcombe, A., Brookfield, J., & Fleming, L.A. (1994). Employment of educators in preschool mainstreaming: A survey of general early educators. *Journal of Early Intervention, 18,* 64–77.

Wolery, M., Schroeder, C., Martin, C.G., Venn, M.L., Holcombe, A., Brookfield, J., Huffman, K., & Fleming, L.A. (1994). Classroom activities and areas: Regularity of use and perceptions of adaptability by general early educators. *Early Education and Development, 5,* 181–194.

Wolery, M., Venn, M.L., Holcombe, A., Brookfield, J., Martin, C.G., Huffman, K., Schroeder, C., & Fleming, L.A. (1994). Employment of related service personnel in preschool programs: A survey of general early educators. *Exceptional Children, 61,* 25–39.

Wolfensberger, W. (1972). *The principle of normalization in human services.* Toronto, Canada: National Institute on Mental Retardation.

Yoder, D.E., Coleman, P.P., & Gallagher, J.J. (1990). *Personnel needs: Allied health personnel meeting the demands of Part H, PL 99-457.* Unpublished manuscript. Chapel Hill: University of North Carolina, Carolina Institute for Child and Family Policy.

II

Overarching Influences

2

DOROTHY KERZNER LIPSKY

ALAN GARTNER

Education Reform and Early Childhood Inclusion

Broad issues of education reform interrelate with early childhood inclusion in a reciprocal relationship. Issues of education reform provide a context for early childhood inclusion; in turn, the implementation of early childhood inclusion programs influences the schools at all educational levels. Thus, for example, as increasing numbers of children with disabilities enter the public schools having participated in early childhood inclusion programs, their parents are more likely to advocate integrated rather than specialized programs. To the extent that the implementation of inclusive education practices in public schools is limited, the pressure to expand early childhood inclusion programs is reduced. To the extent that the absence of preschool programs in general limits opportunities for children with disabilities to be included, action in response to the increasing calls for universal preschool education will provide the environments for inclusion to take place. This chapter describes some of the broad school reforms and their potential for effect on early childhood inclusion.

FROM PARALLEL SYSTEMS TO THE PRESUMPTION OF INCLUSION

Special education has been successful in meeting access goals (i.e., the "child find" requirements) of the Education for All Handicapped Children Act of 1975 (PL 94-142). Over the course of the 1980s and into the 1990s, however, there was growing concern about the outcomes of students with disabilities. Numerous studies, including the Congressionally mandated National Longitudinal Transition Study (NLTS), found limited outcomes across a wide range of measures, including student learning, dropout rates, graduation rates, postsecondary education and training, employment, and residential independence (The Transition Experiences of Youth with Disabilities, 1993).

Despite strong progress made by many youth with disabilities in the four outcomes areas [employment, wages, postschool education, and residential independence], the NLTS found substantial gaps between youth with disabilities and their peers in general education. A particularly important difference relates to the lower level of educational attainment of many youth with disabilities, which does not bode well for their long-term economic future. (Blackorby & Wagner, 1996, p. 410; for a discussion of these limited outcomes, see Chapter 2 of Lipsky & Gartner, 1997)

At the same time, there was also increasing concern about the growth of special education programs and their continuing separation from general education. This was occurring despite PL 94-142's requirement that each state establish procedures to ensure that

> To the maximum extent appropriate, [children with disabilities], including children in public or private institutions or other care facilities, are educated with children who are not [disabled], and that special classes, separate schooling, or other removal of [children with disabilities] from the regular educational environment occurs only when the nature or severity of the [disability] is such that education in regular classes with the use of supplementary aids and services cannot be achieved satisfactorily. (§612[5][B])

In the early 1980s, in response to growing concern about the effectiveness of separate special education programs, Madeleine Will, then assistant secretary of the U.S. Department of Education, called for general and special educators to share responsibility for students with learning problems. Will's efforts, labeled the Regular Education Initiative (REI), were limited to students with mild disabilities. Nonetheless, the REI created a furor. Many special educators responded defensively, both denigrating the need for change and arguing that general education would be neither willing nor able to serve students with disabilities. As the first major challenge to the separate special education system from within the federal government, the REI served to "break the ice" and thus provided an opening for substantive change. Nearly two decades earlier, Dunn (1968) questioned whether separate special education was justifiable for children with mild mental retardation. Indeed, he presaged much of the current debate, challenging general education's failure to serve a broader range of children.

In response, a number of researchers and practitioners challenged the fundamental design of two separate systems. These included Stainback and Stainback (1984), who called for the "merger" of general and special education; Biklen (1985), who called for "integrating" special and general education; and Gartner and Lipsky (1987), who called for going "beyond special education" to a unitary and "refashioned mainstream." Nisbet summarized these reform efforts and appropriately emphasized the restructuring required:

> These initiatives departed from the earlier reform attempts of mainstreaming and integration in their appreciation of the need for broader structural reform. Rather than adding a new service, creating a new specialist, or identifying a new category of disability, these initiatives challenged underlying assumptions about students' learning and the established relationship between general and special education. They became the precursors to a movement that suggests that, rather than ever separating students on the basis of disability, all students should be included from the beginning of their school careers, by right, in the opportunities and responsibilities of public schooling. Inclusion requires the restructuring of both the assumptions and the organization of public education in this country. (1995, p. 152)

In the Individuals with Disabilities Education Act (IDEA) Amendments of 1997 (PL 105-17), Congress addressed the issues of limited student outcomes and continuing segregation of students with disabilities from the education of their typically developing peers. Without requiring inclusion, it nonetheless connected the two issues.

Inclusion is not defined in the federal legislation; indeed, the word does not appear in the law, nor does *mainstreaming* or *integration*. In a summary of pedagogical and research foundations of inclusive schooling practices, McGregor and Vogelsberg noted that critics of inclusive schooling practices portray advocates as "zealots," who in proposing "general education placement of students with disabilities [deny] them the individualized, special education supports that they need" (1999, p. 9). On the contrary, McGregor and Vogelsberg emphasized the definition of inclusion that speaks to the provision of needed supports within general education environments:

> Inclusion is the provision of services to students with disabilities, including those with severe impairments, in the neighborhood school, in age-appropriate classes, with the necessary support services and supplementary aids (for the child and the teacher) both to assure the child's success—academic, behavioral, and social—and to prepare the child to participate as a full and contributing member of the society. (Lipsky & Gartner, 1996, p. 763, cited in McGregor & Vogelsberg, 1999, p. 9)

THE DEVELOPMENT OF INCLUSIVE EDUCATION

Central to the development of inclusive education is a reconceptualization of disability, special education, and the common school. Instead of focusing on the impairments of the individual, a shift is required in the understanding of the extent to which the disability results from a mismatch between the individual's needs and the services to be provided by the school (or other human services agency). If the response is to educate a student with disabilities in a separate and segregated environment, then the resulting labeling and stigmatization themselves have harmful consequences. If the school (or education system as a whole) fails to respond to the needs of the individual student, then it is a failing school (or system). An inclusive school system, then, is a place where diversity, not homogenization, is valued.

> Differences hold great opportunities for learning. Differences offer a free, abundant, and renewable resource. I would like to see our compulsion for eliminating differences replaced by an equally compelling focus on making use of these differences to improve schools. What is important about people—and about schools—is what is dif-

ferent, not what is the same. (Barth, 1990, pp. 514–515)

Kunc pointed out the benefits for "typical" students:

> As a collective commitment to educate *all* [emphasis in original] children takes hold and "typical" students realize that "those kinds" do belong in their school and classes, typical students will benefit by learning that their own membership in the class and in the society is something that has to do with human rights rather than academic or physical ability. In this way, it is conceivable that the students of inclusive schools will be liberated from the tyranny of earning the right to belong. It is ironic that the students who were believed to have the least worth and value may be the only ones who can guide us off the path of social destruction. (1992, p. 39)

It is not diversity in the abstract but rather a recognition that in a diverse population there are a multitude of strengths and capacities. Sacks cited the views of Temple Grandin, a biologist who has autism:

> She thinks there has been too much emphasis on the negative aspects of autism and insufficient attention, or respect, paid to the positive ones. She believes that, if some parts of the brain are faulty or defective, others are highly developed. . . . [M]oved by her own perception of what she possesses so abundantly and lacks so conspicuously, Temple inclines to a modular view of the brain, the sense that it has a multiplicity of separate, autonomous powers or "intelligences"— much as the psychologist Howard Gardner proposes in his book *Frames of Mind.* (1995, p. 290)

It is not only a matter of neurological development. In her pungent phrase, Minow (1990) talked of the "dilemma of difference," as expressed in social arrangements and problem framing. This can be seen in considering the options available for providing services to a student who is deaf. Using the case of Amy Rowley (*Board of Education v. Rowley,* 1982), Minow pointed out that the Henrik Hudson (New York) school system assumed that the problem was Amy's: "Because she was different from other students, the solution must focus on her" (1990, p. 82). Instead of a conceptualization of teaching and learning as a one-to-one relationship between teacher and student, Minow asserted that one can conceptualize the classroom as a learning community and Amy as a collaborative worker with her classmates. This shifts the focus from Amy, making the "problem" not hers but one that involves all of the students.

> After all, if Amy cannot communicate with her classmates, they cannot communicate with her, and all lose the benefits of exchange. Moreover, conducting the class in both spoken and sign language would engage all the students in the difficult and instructive experience of communicating across traditional lines of difference. All the students could learn to struggle with problems of translation and learn to empathize by experiencing first hand discomfort with an unfamiliar mode of instruction. It would be educational for all of them to discover that all languages are arrangements of signs and to use group action to improve the situation of an individual. (1990, p. 84)

Viewing the social nature of the "problem"—and its solution—provides a different stance toward the "dilemma of difference." It no longer makes the trait of hearing impairment (or any other disability) signify or isolate the individual. Rather, it requires societal institutions, schools, and early childhood programs alike to reframe their understanding of difference and to restructure their responses to it.

Reauthorization of IDEA

In the findings section of the reauthorized IDEA, the Congress provided a conceptual framework for considering the education of students with disabilities. It stated, in part, that the education of students with disabilities can be made more effective by

> Having high expectations for students and ensuring their success in the general curriculum

> [Ensuring] that special education can become a service for children rather than a place to which they are sent

> Providing incentives for whole school approaches

These expressions of belief and intent are actualized in the law's provisions designed to ensure that students with disabilities have access to the general curriculum and receive regular assessment (and public reporting) of their progress, the presumption that they will be educated with peers without disabilities (with supports and services, as needed), and that the school will take responsibility for students' goals-directed learning.

The U.S. Department of Education's "IDEA '97: Final Regulations, Major Issues" stated,

> Prior to 1997, the federal law did not specifically address general curriculum involvement of students with disabilities. The 1997 reauthorization shifted the focus of IDEA to one of improving teaching and learning, with a specific focus on the individualized education program (IEP) as the primary tool for enhancing the student's involvement and progress in the general curriculum. (1999)

Furthermore, the 1997 reauthorization of IDEA and its regulations require that the IEP for each student with a disability include not only a statement of the child's present levels of educational performance but also

> How the child's disability affects the child's involvement and progress in the general curriculum

> A statement of measurable annual goals related to meeting the child's needs that result from the child's disability to enable the child to be involved and progress in the general curriculum

> A statement of the special education and related services and supplemental aids and services necessary to enable the child to progress in the general education curriculum

> A statement of the program modifications or supports for school personnel that will be provided for the child to advance appropriately toward attaining the annual goals, to be involved and progress in the general curriculum, and partici-

pate in extracurricular and other nonacademic activities and be educated with nondisabled peers. (1999)

A new provision in the law requires the involvement of general education personnel in the development of the child's IEP in order to ensure that someone who is familiar with the general education curriculum is represented. In addition, it provides an opportunity for the general education teacher(s) to propose incorporation in the student's IEP of the supplementary aids and services needed by the child *and* the teacher for the child to be involved and to progress in the general education curriculum.

Not only is involvement in the general education curriculum required for children with disabilities, but that involvement is to be standards based. Specifically, the 1997 IDEA amendments require that children with disabilities be included in general state and district assessment programs, with appropriate adaptations and modifications, as necessary. Alternative assessments are to be provided for children who cannot participate in the general assessment activities. This is estimated by the federal government to be fewer than 2% of the school-age population, or approximately 5%–20% of children with disabilities. The results of these assessments are to be made public and provided to the parents of children with disabilities with the same frequency and in the same detail as reported on the assessment of students without disabilities.

Although the participation of children with disabilities in the general curriculum is required regardless of the type of environment in which the student receives services, the law expresses the anticipation that students with disabilities will be educated with their peers without disabilities:

IDEA presumes that the first placement option considered for each disabled student by the stu-

dent's placement team, which must include the parent, is the school the child would attend if not disabled, with appropriate supplementary aids and services to facilitate such placement. Thus, before a disabled child can be placed outside the regular education environment, the full range of supplementary aids and services that if provided would facilitate the student's progress in the regular classroom must be considered. (IDEA '97, 1999)

Any decision for a child with disabilities not to participate with children without disabilities in academic, extracurricular, or nonacademic activities must be educationally justified on the student's IEP. In no case may a decision for a child with disabilities not to participate in the general education program be based on the child's category of disability, the current availability of service options, space availability, attitudes of school personnel, or availability of needed staff or their lack of training.

Of importance, the requirements regarding the placement of school-age children with disabilities have their parallel at the early childhood level. These requirements clearly apply to preschool-age children but also the birth-to-3 group. For this younger group,

IDEA 1997 focused on the provision of early intervention services in natural environments, ensuring that early intervention [EI] services be provided in natural environments and that EI services be provided in some other environments only if EI services for a child cannot be achieved in a natural environment. The regulations contain a provision requiring that IFSPs [individualized family service plans] include a statement of the natural environments in which the services are to be provided for the child and a justification of the extent, if any, to which the services will not be provided in the natural environment. (Grzywacz, 1999, p. 8; see also Chapter 4)

For students ages 3–5 years, under Part B of IDEA the schools operate these programs. Thus, education reform efforts, including inclusive education, can have direct influence at the same time as they "trickle down" to the natural environment issues that focus on children from birth to 3 years old, served under Part C of the law.

AGENDA FOR CHANGE: EXEMPLARY PRACTICES

Growing evidence as to limited outcomes for students in special education programs, reported most prominently in the NLTS, mirrored similar concerns about education in general. Beginning with the publication in 1983 of *A Nation at Risk*, a flood of books, reports, and studies questioned the efficacy of American public education, both overall and in comparison with other countries. Indeed, the poor state of general education was one of the reasons cited by opponents of the REI; they claimed that general education would be neither willing nor able to serve children with disabilities (see Lloyd, Singh, & Repp 1991, especially chapters by Hocutt, Martin, & McKinney; Kauffmann; Gottlieb, Alter, & Gottleib; and Fuchs & Fuchs). This view continues as of the beginning of the 21st century (see, e.g., Crockett & Kauffman, 1999).

Villa and Thousand (1995) summarized 10 rationales for inclusive education:

1. Changing assumptions about the future society and its characteristics and needs
2. The limited efficacy of separate special education programs
3. The substantive requirements of federal law
4. The procedural issues in the federal law
5. The growing number of students who are eligible for special education services
6. The disjointedness of dual systems
7. The financial costs of dual systems
8. The harmful effects of separation on children
9. Positive evidence from an increasing number of inclusive education programs
10. Support for inclusive education from a growing number and range of organizations, both general and special education

Nevertheless, reforms in general and special education have occurred largely separate from one another. Generally, the large-scale reform efforts of general education have ignored special education. The developments of inclusive education programs, however, have provided a seedbed for addressing common needs in both general and special education. This includes the incorporation in inclusive education of

1. Formulations of broad conceptual designs from education in general (e.g., Edmonds' correlates of school effectiveness [Lezotte, 1989] and Gardner's multiple intelligences [Goldman & Gardner, 1989])
2. Features of comprehensive education reform (e.g., Slavin's [1997] Success for All and Roots and Wings programs and Levin's [1997] "accelerated schools" model)
3. The adoption of proven instructional strategies (e.g., cooperative learning and peer learning programs [Lipsky & Gartner, 1997, see especially Chapter 12])

The core conceptualization of inclusive education is that children with disabilities are more like than different from children without disabilities and will be best served in a unitary system in which children and staff receive needed support services and supplementary aids. This is not an improved or "fixed" special education system, alongside the general education mainstream; rather, it is a restructured, singular, and seamless system.

Looking at the issue from the perspective of overall school change, in the introduction to a synthesis of recommended practices about inclusive schooling, McGregor and Vogelsberg wrote,

The presence of students with disabilities in general education classrooms stimulates educators to consider the match [among] classroom climate, curriculum, teaching practices, and the needs of students with identified learning differences. . . . [A]lthough students labeled as exceptional do not represent the only source of diversity in the general education classroom, their presence provides a catalyst for teachers to consider the diverse learning needs of all of their students in the design of instructional activities. (1999, p. 5)

In a survey of more than 1,000 school districts implementing inclusive education programs (National Study of Inclusive Education, 1995), the National Center on Educational Restructuring and Inclusion (NCERI) identified seven factors that are necessary for inclusion to be effective:

1. Visionary leadership, which could come from a variety of sources (e.g., superintendents, principals, teachers and other school professionals, parents, university personnel)

2. Collaboration (between general and special educators, evaluation and classroom personnel, related services providers and classroom instructors)

3. Refocused use of assessment (viz., less addressed to sorting of students and more addressed to identifying their instructional needs)—This has been strengthened by IDEA 1997's requirement that students with disabilities be included in a district's general program of student learning outcomes.

4. Supports for staff (especially time for systematic professional development and flexible planning time) and stu-

dents (i.e., supplementary aids and support services)

5. Appropriate funding levels and formulas—This has been reinforced by the IDEA 1997 requirement that states adopt "placement neutral" funding formulas.

6. Effective parental involvement— This has been strengthened by the IDEA 1997 requirement that parents participate in all placement decisions.

7. Curricula adaptations and effective instructional practices—The most common of these reported were cooperative learning, multilevel instruction, activity-based learning, mastery learning, use of instructional technology, peer support, and tutoring programs.

These seven factors are similar to factors that characterize inclusive schools, reported by the "Working Forum on Inclusive Schools," sponsored by 10 national education organizations (Creating Schools for All Our Students, 1995).

Of note, McGregor and Vogelsberg (1999) summarized the research concerning education structures and practices that support inclusive schooling. They identified responsive instructional practices, strategies to accommodate specific barriers to learning, ways of creating caring and supportive learning communities, and organizational structures that support responsive schooling practices.

Responsive instructional practices include integrated approaches to curricular content; instruction that is delivered in a manner that capitalizes on different ways of learning; teaching for thinking, problem solving, and understanding; and assessment integrally connected to learning and teaching.

Strategies to accommodate specific barriers to learning include explicit instruction in "how to learn," curricular modifications and adaptations, and planning for the full range of learners at the design point (i.e., "universal design") of instruction, rather than retrofitting (i.e., remediation or modification) later, and an appreciation of differences that is fostered throughout the curriculum.

Creating caring and supportive learning communities includes using cooperative structures that promote the value of learning together and helping others; classroom practices that teach self-control, problem solving, and community values; and linking instruction to real experiences that expand the concepts of classroom, curriculum, and community.

Organizational structures that support inclusive schooling practices include alternative approaches to a highly segmented school day and heterogeneous school grouping practices, cross-grade grouping, time for teaming and reflection that foster collaborative approaches to instruction, role-release activities that enable adults to work in a mutually supportive and collaborative manner, and building-based strategies and resource allocation.

CONCLUSION

How a society treats its youngest children, including those with disabilities, is critical both for its future and as a measure of the society's values. A number of issues and themes emerged in the 1990s that give particular relevance to inclusive early childhood programs for all children. These include a growing recognition that 1) the early years provide a significant opportunity for influencing the long-term development of an individual, 2) the expansion of child care programs as part of "welfare reform" efforts offers an opportunity both for program expansion and for integration, 3) among professionals, parents, advocates, and policy

makers, it is the responsibility of the society to provide needed early intervention programs for children with disabilities, and 4) quality early intervention programs for children with disabilities require the existence of early childhood programs for all children.

The growing recognition that early childhood programs are important for children with significant disabilities produces a conundrum, however, as it relates to the expansion of inclusive education programs. This is the issue that Taylor raised more than a decade ago in his challenge to the least restrictive environment (LRE) principle: "The LRE principle confuses segregation and integration on the one hand with intensity of services on the other" (1998, p. 48). Only as there is the reality—and its recognition—that needed early childhood services, regardless of the level of intensity, can be provided effectively in inclusive environments will parents choose such environments.

At the same time, school districts must recognize both the benefits of early childhood inclusion and the IDEA 1997 requirement that providing services in the general education environment must be considered as the first alternative for all children with disabilities. In many school districts, the absence of such services has relegated children to segregated special classrooms. To counter this, those involved in the school systems' evaluation and placement of children must come to recognize the benefits of effective inclusive education programs, while the federal government and state education agencies must exercise with greater diligence their supervision and oversight responsibilities. The beginning of the 21st century is an opportune time for the expansion of inclusive education opportunities in early childhood programs with the juxtaposition of the overall expansion of early childhood programs, the strictures of the federal law, the presence of models of excellent inclusive early childhood programs, the potential downward pressure from the public schools as they implement inclusive education, and growing parental recognition that their children can receive needed *and* quality services in an inclusive environment.

REFERENCES

Barth, R. (1990). A personal vision of a good school. *Phi Delta Kappan, 71,* 512–521.

Biklen, D. (Ed.). (1985). *The complete school: Integrating special and general education.* New York: Teachers College Press.

Blackorby, J., & Wagner, M. (1996). Longitudinal postschool outcomes of youth with disabilities: Findings from the National Longitudinal Transition Study. *Exceptional Children, 62*(5), 399–413.

Board of Education v. Rowley, 102 S. Ct. 3034 (1982).

Creating schools for all our students: What twelve schools have to say. (1995). Reston, VA: Council for Exceptional Children.

Crockett, J.B., & Kauffman, J.M. (1999). *The least restrictive environment: Its origins and interpretations in special education.* Mahwah, NJ: Lawrence Erlbaum Associates.

Dunn, L.M. (1968). Special education for the mildly retarded: Is much of it justifiable? *Exceptional Children, 35,* 5–22.

Education for All Handicapped Children Act of 1975, PL 94-142, 20 U.S.C. §§ 1400 *et seq.*

Gartner, A., & Lipsky, D.K. (1987). Beyond special education: Toward a quality system for all students. *Harvard Educational Review, 57*(4), 367–395.

Goldman, J., & Gardner, H. (1989). Multiple paths to educational effectiveness. In D.K. Lipsky & A. Gartner (Eds.), *Beyond separate education: Quality education for all* (pp. 121–139). Baltimore: Paul H. Brookes Publishing Co.

Grzywacz, P. (1999, February 26). Early children: The year in review. *The Special Educator, 14*(14), 8–10.

IDEA '97: Final regulations, major issues. (1999, March 12). *Federal Register.*

Individuals with Disabilities Education Act (IDEA) Amendments of 1997, PL 105-17, 20 U.S.C. §§ 1400 *et seq.*

Kunc, N. (1992). The need to belong: Rediscovering Maslow's hierarchy of needs. In R. Villa, J.S. Thousand, W. Stainback, & S. Stainback (Eds.),

Restructuring for caring and effective education: An administrative guide to creating heterogeneous schools (pp. 25–39). Baltimore: Paul H. Brookes Publishing Co.

Levin, H.M. (1997). Doing what comes naturally: Full inclusion in accelerated schools. In D.K. Lipsky & A. Gartner (Eds.), *Inclusion and school reform: Transforming America's classrooms* (pp. 389–400). Baltimore: Paul H. Brookes Publishing Co.

Lezotte, L.W. (1989). School improvement based on the effective schools research. In D.K. Lipsky & A. Gartner (Eds.), *Beyond special education: Quality education for all* (pp. 25–37). Baltimore: Paul H. Brookes Publishing Co.

Lipsky, D.K., & Gartner, A. (1997). *Inclusion and school reform: Transforming America's classrooms.* Baltimore: Paul H. Brookes Publishing Co.

Lloyd, J.W., Singh, N.N., & Repp, A.C. (Eds.). (1991). *The regular education initiative: Alternative perspectives on concepts, issues, and models.* Sycamore, IL: Sycamore Publishing Co.

McGregor, G., & Vogelsberg, R.T. (1998). *Inclusive schooling practices: Pedagogical and research foundations: A synthesis of the literature that informs best practices about inclusive schooling.* Allegheny University of the Health Sciences, Consortium on Inclusive Schooling Practices (Available from Paul H. Brookes Publishing Co., Baltimore).

Minow, M. (1990). *Making all the difference: Inclusion, exclusion, and American law.* Ithaca, NY: Cornell University Press.

A nation at risk. (1983). Washington, DC: National Commission on Excellence in Education.

National study of inclusive education. (1995). New York: City University of New York, Graduate Center, National Center on Educational Restructuring and Inclusion.

Nisbet, J. (1995). Educational reform: Summary and recommendations. In *The national reform agenda and people with mental retardation: Putting people first* (pp. 151–165). Washington, DC: President's Committee on Mental Retardation.

Sacks, O. (1995). *An anthropologist on Mars.* New York: Alfred A. Knopf.

Slavin, R.E. (1997). Including inclusion in school reform: Success for All and Roots and Wings. In D.K. Lipsky & A. Gartner (Eds.), *Inclusion and school reform: Transforming America's classrooms* (pp. 375–387). Baltimore: Paul H. Brookes Publishing Co.

Stainback, W., & Stainback, S. (1984). A rationale for the merger of regular and special education. *Exceptional Children, 51,* 102–112.

Taylor, S.J. (1988). Caught in the continuum: A critical analysis of the principle of the least restrictive environment. *Journal of The Association for Persons with Severe Handicaps, 13*(1), 41–53.

The transition experiences of youth with disabilities: A summary of findings from the National Longitudinal Transition Study of Special Education Students. (1993). Palo Alto, CA: SRI International.

Villa, R.A., & Thousand, J.S. (1995). The rationales for creating inclusive schools. In R.A. Villa & J.S. Thousand (Eds.), *Creating an inclusive school.* Alexandria, VA: Association for Supervision and Curriculum Development.

3

BARBARA J. SMITH

MARY JANE K. RAPPORT

Public Policy in Early Childhood Inclusion

Necessary But Not Sufficient

Even though IDEA [Individuals with Disabilities Education Act] does not mandate regular class placement for every disabled student, IDEA assumes that the first placement option considered for each student by the student's placement team, which must include the parent, is the school the child would attend if not disabled, with appropriate supplementary aids and services to facilitate such placement. Thus, before a disabled child can be placed outside the regular educational environment, the full range of supplementary aids and services that, if provided, would facilitate the student's placement in the regular classroom setting must be considered. (34 C.F.R. Appendix A, p. 12471)

This chapter describes several issues related to public policy that affect inclusive practices for young children. These issues include the evolutionary nature of policy and, in particular, early childhood inclusion policy, the status of inclusion policy, the importance of evaluating policy, and whether policy is sufficient to create and sustain high-quality inclusion practices.

THE CHANGING NATURE OF POLICY

According to Seekins and Fawcett (1986), public policies commit the government to certain goals, determine whose interests and values will prevail, and regulate and distribute resources. In the United States, public policies exist as laws, regulations, executive orders, guidelines, and so forth that have been promulgated at the federal, state, or local level. Gallagher (1996) described public policy as a *social hypothesis* that certain procedures will enhance the welfare of the target group of citizens for which it was designed. In addition, he and his colleagues (Gallagher, Harbin, Eckland, & Clifford, 1994) defined *public policy* as the rules

The authors acknowledge the contributions of several colleagues whose work assisted either directly or indirectly in the preparation of material for this chapter: Michael J. Guralnick, Deborah Rose, Phillip S. Strain, and Sharon Walsh.

This manuscript was prepared in part with support from the U.S. Department of Education, Office of Special Education Programs, Grant No. H324R980047-99, to the University of Colorado–Denver. However, the opinions expressed are not necessarily those of the U.S. Department of Education, Office of Special Education Programs, or the University of Colorado–Denver.

and standards by which scarce public resources are allocated to meet social needs. According to these definitions, *inclusion public policy* refers to the rules and standards that govern the allocation of resources to promote the goals, values, and social hypothesis that including children with disabilities in educational and other programs and services with their peers without disabilities enhances their welfare. Moreover, public policy has been described as evolutionary—changing with the times and circumstances (LaVor, 1976b). Indeed, if public policy is a social hypothesis, then it follows that as society's values and knowledge change, so, too, will public policy.

Inclusion policy has, in fact, evolved in many ways. First, the perception that children should be provided an inclusionary environment has changed over time. The question of which children with disabilities are "better" or "worse" candidates for inclusion has been debated in policy arenas for years (see Chapter 15). Our values and knowledge bases have evolved to recognize that the quality of the programs is the critical factor. As values and knowledge change over time, rather than make determinations about *which children* should be included, perhaps policies will determine how to support *high-quality environments and services.*

Second, early inclusion efforts sometimes amounted to trivial physical integration during short periods of unplanned activities such as lunch or playtime. The field now ascribes to more planned social and educational participation in all activities (Division for Early Childhood [DEC], 1996). Therefore, policies need to promote these more meaningful inclusion options (see Chapter 1). As an example, at one point typical practice involved assigning only to the child with a disability in an inclusive environment an aide or service provider who follows the child from activity to activity. The current trend is to attempt to

provide the support of these personnel to the general education teacher or integrate the services into the activities of the classroom as a whole so that the child is treated more like the other children in the environment.

Simply put, inclusion policy evolves as the thinking and database about inclusion in society evolve. The terminology related to children with disabilities being with their peers without disabilities has changed over time in the consumer and professional literature as well as in policy (Odom et al., 1999). Terms such as *mainstreaming, least restrictive environment, continuum of alternative placements, integration, inclusion,* and *involvement and progress in the general curriculum* represent different points in time and different valued outcomes since the 1970s. The provisions related to inclusion in the original Individuals with Disabilities Education Act (IDEA), which was passed in 1975 as the Education for all Handicapped Children Act (PL 94-142), referred only to least restrictive environments and to a continuum of placement options. More recent, the IDEA Amendments of 1997 (PL 105-17) contain many provisions for ensuring access to the "general curriculum" for 3- to 21-year-olds and to "natural environments" for birth to 3-year-olds. These concepts and policies reflect a more proactive and purposeful policy with a clear preference for children with disabilities to be educated and receive services with their age-mates without disabilities in typical early childhood environments. These examples of policies and how they have an impact on services to children point out the importance of parents' and professionals' being involved in the details of policy development. This involvement can help guide the policy toward recommended practice, as well as current values and knowledge. A brief history of the evolution of policy development in the area of inclusion follows.

INCLUSION POLICY: THE PAST

Before the early 1970s, the primary inclusion policy initiatives focused on accessibility to goods and services. For instance, federal legislation for developing captioned films for individuals with hearing impairments was passed in 1965 (Captioned Films for the Deaf Act, PL 89-258), and an act to eliminate architectural barriers for people with physical disabilities was passed in 1968 (Elimination of Architectural Barriers to Physically Handicapped Act, PL 90-480) (LaVor, 1976a). Another early policy concept related to inclusion practices was the doctrine of least restrictive alternative. Johnson described how this doctrine had been applied by the mid-1970s by the courts and was used in federal legislation to guard against arbitrary and capricious placement and treatment decisions for individuals with disabilities:

> In essence, this doctrine provides that, when government pursues a legitimate goal that may involve the restricting of fundamental liberty, it must do so using the least restrictive alternative available. Applied to education, courts have ruled in principle that special education systems or practices are inappropriate if they remove children from their expanded peer group without benefit of constitutional safeguards. Placement in special environments for educational purposes can, without appropriate safeguards, become a restriction of fundamental liberties.
>
> It is required, then, that substantive efforts be made by educators to maintain handicapped children with their peers in a regular education setting and that the state (as represented by individual school districts) bear the burden of proof when making placements or when applying treatments which involve partial or complete removal of handicapped children from their normal peers.
>
> This doctrine represents for handicapped children the right to be educated in the regular class, however defined, unless clear evidence is available that partial or complete removal is necessary. Factors idiosyncratic to school districts (such as organizational arrangements, technological differences in delivery systems, agency jurisdictional problems, and/or lack of adequate local, state, or federal financial support) may not be considered as reasons for abrogation of the right of an individual child to the least restrictive alternative necessary to meet his/her unique educational needs. (1976, p. 60)

The least restrictive alternative doctrine was supported in early court decisions in the 1960s and 1970s regarding the right to treatment for people with disabilities, including *Pennsylvania ARC (PARC) v. The Commonwealth of Pennsylvania* (1972) and *Mills v. The Board of Education of the District of Columbia* (1972). These two cases put forth the notion that individuals with disabilities have the right to be served in the least restrictive environment and that right may not be compromised without due process. These early court cases helped drive the development of future laws and regulations pertaining to the education rights of children with disabilities. The concept of educating children with disabilities in the general classroom environment was evident in some state laws by the early 1970s. Although not using the term *least restrictive alternative,* the following excerpt from a Tennessee law of that era includes many of the concepts and terms used today in IDEA and other inclusion policies:

> To the maximum extent practicable, handicapped children shall be educated along with children who do not have handicaps and shall attend regular classes. Impediments to learning and to the normal functioning of handicapped children in the regular school environment shall be overcome by the provision of special aids and services rather than by separate schooling for the handicapped. (Abeson & Ballard, 1976, p. 88)

In 1973, Section 504 of the Rehabilitation Act (PL 93-112) was passed by Congress to prohibit the discrimination of individuals with disabilities in public services—an important policy step toward community inclusion. Section 504 also contained an important, albeit incremental, inclusion concept requiring that children with disabilities be educated in the school closest to their home.

In 1974, the Education of the Handicapped Act Amendments (PL 93-380) were passed. Many of the provisions of these amendments were precursors to the more broadly sweeping Education for All Handicapped Children Act of 1975 (PL 94-142), described next. PL 93-380 contained a provision that, although not mandating that states serve all children with disabilities, such services, when provided, should be in the least restrictive environment (LRE).

PL 94-142 established a right to a free appropriate public education (FAPE) for all children with disabilities. As noted previously, this law, which later became IDEA, required states that accepted federal funds under this law to educate all children with disabilities and to do so in the LRE. PL 94-142 adopted the concept of providing necessary supports and services for the child to be educated in the LRE. However, many subsequent congressional revisions to the IDEA, as well as administrative clarifications and regulations by the U.S. Department of Education, have been needed over the years to define LRE further. These subsequent policies have attempted to address the incremental progress that state and local education agencies were making toward the goal of educating children with disabilities with children who do not have disabilities and to reflect the changing knowledge base and social values. For instance, in the preschool arena, many education agencies (following early IDEA regulations) originally interpreted the LRE provision to mean 1) if there were no school-funded general early childhood opportunities available, they did not need to educate preschoolers with disabilities in inclusive environments, and 2) locating a segregated preschool class in a general elementary school met the LRE requirements. More recent policies have been needed to advance the thinking beyond these convenient solutions to more complex ones, such as collaborative arrangements in the community with child care or Head Start as the early education environment for children with disabilities and in which special education and related services could be provided.

The Head Start Act of 1964 (PL 88-452) has been another important early childhood inclusion policy. Passed by Congress as part of the War on Poverty, the Head Start Act was geared to children living in poverty but was amended by the mid-1970s to 1) require that 10% of the population served by Head Start be children with disabilities and 2) create resource access projects to provide training and materials to Head Start programs related to teaching children with disabilities. Thus, early on, Head Start became a major inclusion option for children in the 3- to 5-year age range. Head Start policy has also evolved over time. At one point, the eligibility criteria that Head Start and IDEA used to determine a child's disability were different (Smith & Rose, 1993). Therefore, school districts, having the responsibility for providing a FAPE to all children with disabilities under IDEA, found it difficult to place those children in Head Start because Head Start used different definitions to determine which children had eligible disabilities. On the basis of reports of this problem, in the early 1990s, the Head Start Act was amended to bring the Head Start eligibility definitions more in line with those of IDEA to facilitate collaboration with public schools.

In 1990, the Americans with Disabilities Act (ADA; PL 101-336) became law and expanded the civil rights and antidiscrimination protections of Section 504 of the Rehabilitation Act. The ADA intends to ensure people with disabilities equality of opportunity, full participation, independent living, and economic self-sufficiency. The ADA addresses employment, public accommodations and services, telecommunications, and miscellaneous provisions tied to the legal procedures and processes guaranteed under the law. Many of the education-specific provisions of the ADA are already addressed when a school is in compliance with Section 504 and IDEA. For very young children, the ADA opened the doors to community programs such as child care, recreational programs, and other similar opportunities available to children of their age. This was a significant change for many private child care centers that, before the ADA, were under no federal legal mandate to include young children with disabilities in their programs. Since 1990, these programs and facilities have been required to provide equal opportunity and to avoid discrimination in application and enrollment criteria and processes. Child care programs must make reasonable accommodations (i.e., they do not have to alter their fundamental purpose or program to accommodate a child with a disability). However, if a child with a disability can participate with reasonable accommodations, then he or she may not be denied access solely because of his or her disability.

Concurrent with policy changes at the federal level, many states have amended their policies and procedures. Some state laws, regulations, and guidelines are attempting to provide the policy and funding bases for more meaningful inclusion (Smith & Rose, 1993). Many states' policies are also providing resources for training and technical assistance to improve the knowledge and skills for professionals to work collaboratively and to meet the individual needs of all children in inclusive environments.

Finally, national policy evolved most recently in the 1997 amendments to IDEA (PL 105-17). The 1997 amendments represent a major milestone. They are the first major revision of IDEA since the enactment of PL 94-142 in 1975.

Although the main purpose of IDEA remains the assurance of a FAPE for children with disabilities, the 1997 amendments and the attendant regulations published in March 1999 make clear the preference for inclusion. The amendments and accompanying regulations have taken the concept of LRE much further toward meaningful inclusion. Many of the new provisions are described in the following sections. For the purposes of this chapter, however, it is important to note that IDEA 1997 attempts to address many of the previous challenges to inclusion. For example, IDEA 1997 includes prohibitions on state education funding formulas that have the effect of segregation by funding classrooms rather than services that can be delivered anywhere (see 34 C.F.R. § 300.130], and the individualized education program (IEP) provisions now require consideration about involvement in the general education curriculum and the participation of general educators in the IEP process (34 C.F.R. § 300.340–350). IDEA 1997 policies are described in detail next to explain current inclusion policy, because they represent the latest national policy that affects inclusion for young children with disabilities.

INCLUSION POLICY: THE PRESENT

At the federal level, the main policy governing inclusion in early intervention and early education is IDEA 1997, yet the term *inclusion* is not used in the legislation. Instead, IDEA 1997 uses terms such as *LRE, participation in the general curriculum,* and *natural environments.* First is a review of the relevant provisions of Part C of IDEA, the Early Intervention Program for Infants and Toddlers with Disabilities, which governs services to children from birth to 3 years. Then, Part B of IDEA, Assistance to States for the Education of Children with Disabilities, is described for children from 3 to 21 years.

Table 3.1. Part C of IDEA, Early Intervention Program for Infants and Toddlers with Disabilities—Inclusion Provisions (34 C.F.R. Part 303)

Section 303.12 EARLY INTERVENTION SERVICES

(a) Natural environments
To the maximum extent appropriate to the needs of the child, early intervention services must be provided in natural environments, including the home and community settings in which children without disabilities participate.

Section 303.18 NATURAL ENVIRONMENTS

As used in this part, natural environments means settings that are natural or normal for the child's age peers who have no disabilities.

Section 303.167 INDIVIDUALIZED FAMILY SERVICE PLANS (IFSPs)

Each application must include—

(c) Policies and procedures to ensure that—

(1) To the maximum extent appropriate, early intervention services are provided in natural environments; and

(2) The provision of early intervention services for any infant or toddler occurs in a setting other than a natural environment only if early intervention cannot be achieved satisfactorily for the infant or toddler in a natural environment.

Section 303.344 CONTENT OF AN IFSP

(d) Early intervention services

(1) (ii) The natural environments, as described in Sec. 303.12(b), Sec. 303.18, in which early intervention services will be provided, and a justification of the extent, if any, to which the services will not be provided in a natural environment.

Part C: The Early Intervention Program for Infants and Toddlers with Disabilities

In IDEA 1997, Part H, the Infant and Toddler Program, was changed to Part C. Regulations for Part C, the Early Intervention Program for Infants and Toddlers with Disabilities, were issued by the U.S. Department of Education in April 1998 and were reopened for comment in 1999. These regulations incorporated statutory changes from IDEA 1997 as well as changes to provide consistency between Part C and Part B of IDEA. Final regulations for IDEA 1997 were issued in March 1999, and the Part C section contained several technical changes that were not included in the previous regulatory changes.

The Part C regulations emphasize the provision of early intervention services in "natural environments." The concept of natural environments, as an extension of the LRE requirement under Part B, was first included in the then Part H regulations after the 1991 Amendments of IDEA. Table 3.1 contains the Part C regulations pertaining to natural environments including the relevant section related to the individualized family service plan (IFSP).

The federal statutory and regulatory language emphasizes the importance of providing services in natural environments. Part C of IDEA contains the legal presumption for providing early intervention services for infants or toddlers in natural environments. Early intervention services are defined in the IDEA 1997 statute as "developmental services that to the maximum extent appropriate are provided in natural environments, including home and community settings in which children without disabilities participate" (§ 1432). Natural environments are further defined in regulations as "settings that are natural or normal for the child's age peers who have no disabilities" (34 C.F.R. § 303.18).

Federal law includes both the legal requirements for early intervention and the foundation for implementation of services in natural environments, but the specifics as to how such requirements should be addressed are left up to each state. As such, IDEA requires that states develop policies and procedures to ensure that, to the maximum extent appropriate, early intervention services are provided in natural environments and occur elsewhere only if early intervention cannot be achieved satisfactorily in a natural environment. In an effort to facilitate implementation around providing services in natural environments, Part C also requires that each IFSP identify the natural environment in which services are to be provided and justify the extent, if any, to which the services will not be provided in the natural environment. Thus, the legal interpretation indicates that all early intervention services should occur in environments that are natural for the child's age-peers without disabilities, unless there is justification of the need for early intervention supports and services to be delivered in some other environment. This exception should occur only when the IFSP team, including the child's parent(s), determines that goals and objectives related to the child's development cannot be achieved satisfactorily through intervention in environments that are natural for other children of the same age.

Part B: Assistance to States for the Education of Children with Disabilities

Part B of IDEA applies to the education for children with disabilities who are 3 to 21 years old. The requirements for 3- through 5-year-olds are, therefore, contained in Part B of IDEA, not Part C.

In Part C of IDEA, the Infants and Toddlers Program, the concept of "natural environment" is used to refer to inclusive environments for children from birth to 3 years (see Table 3.1). In Table 3.2, the provisions in the regulations governing Part B that pertain to serving 3- to 21-year-olds in inclusive environments are described. Congress used different terminology for preferred environments in Part C for infants and toddlers than in

Part B for children 3 to 21 years old. The term *natural environments* used in Part C refers to environments that are natural or normal for the child's age-peers without disabilities. The terms used in Part B are more educational-environment based (i.e., *LRE, general curriculum,* etc.). This is an artifact of the preschool provisions being "housed" in Part B—the part of the law that primarily describes services for school-age children.

Part B attempts to recognize the importance of changing procedures for 3- through 5-year-olds from the school-age population, as applicable. This is evident in the section of the law governing the IEP. Under this section, when it refers to requiring a statement in the IEP of "how a child's disability affects the child's involvement and progress in the general curriculum," it makes a distinction for preschool-age children: "For preschool children, as appropriate, how the disability affects the child's participation in appropriate activities" (34 C.F.R. § 300-347). The regulations did not respond to field requests to the U.S. Department of Education to describe what "appropriate activities" might refer to. It was the recommendation of the DEC of the Council for Exceptional Children that *appropriate activities* be defined as "activities, materials, and environments that are chronologically age relevant and developmentally and individually appropriate" (DEC, 1998). In another example of age-related adaptations related to the LRE provisions, in Appendix 1 of the regulations ("Analysis of Comments"), the following guidance is given for preschool placement options: "The full continuum of alternative placements at 34 C.F.R. § 300.551, including integrated placement options, such as community-based settings with typically developing age-peers, must be available to preschool children with disabilities" (p. 12639).

Included in Table 3.2 are many of the provisions related to the IEP, because

Table 3.2.   Part B of IDEA, Assistance to States for the Education of Children with Disabilities—Inclusion Provisions (34 C.F.R. Part 300)

Section 300.28 SUPPLEMENTARY AIDS AND SERVICES

As used in this part, the term *supplementary aids and services* means aids, services, and other supports that are provided in regular education classes or other education-related settings to enable children with disabilities to be educated with nondisabled children to the maximum extent appropriate in accordance with section 300.550–300.556.

Section 300.130 LEAST RESTRICTIVE ENVIRONMENT

(a) General. The state must have on file with the Secretary procedures that ensure that the requirements of sections 300.550–300.556 are met including the provisions in section 300.551 requiring a continuum of alternative placements to meet the unique needs of each child with a disability. (b) Additional requirements, (1) If the State uses a funding mechanism by which the State distributes State funds on the basis of the type of setting where a child is served, the funding mechanism may not result in placements that violate the requirements of paragraph (a) of this section. (2) If the State does not have policies and procedures to ensure compliance with paragraph (b) (1) of this section, the State must provide the Secretary an assurance that the State will revise the funding mechanism as soon as feasible to ensure that such mechanism does not result in placements that violate that paragraph.

Section 300.235 PERMISSIVE USE OF FUNDS

(a)(1) Funds provided to a LEA under Part B of the act may be used for the following activities: (1) For the costs of special education and related services and supplementary aids and services provided in a regular class or other education-related setting to a child with a disability in accordance with the IEP of the child, even if one or more nondisabled children benefit from such services. (2). . .to develop and implement a fully integrated and coordinated service system. . . .

Section 300.340 DEFINITIONS RELATED TO IEPs

Individualized education program or IEP means a written statement for each child with a disability that is developed, reviewed, and revised in accordance with section 300.341–300.350.

Section 300.342 WHEN IEPs MUST BE IN EFFECT

(b)(2) The child's IEP is accessible to each regular education teacher, special education teacher, related service provider, and other service provider who is responsible for its implementation; and (3) Each teacher and provider described in paragraph (b)(2) of this section is informed of—(i) His or her specific responsibilities related to implementing the child's IEP; and (ii) The specific accommodations, modifications, and supports that must be provided for the child in accordance with the IEP.

Section 300.344 IEP TEAM

(a) The public agency shall ensure that the IEP team for each child with a disability includes—(1) The parents of the child; (2) At least one regular education teacher of such child (if the child is or may be participating in the regular education environment); (3) a representative of the local educational agency who—. . .is knowledgeable about the general curriculum. . . . [the other provisions related to team membership do not relate to LRE]

Section 300.346 DEVELOPMENT, REVIEW AND REVISION OF IEP

(d) Requirements with respect to regular education teachers. The regular education teacher of a child with a disability, as a member of the IEP Team, must, to the extent appropriate, participate in the development, review and revision of the IEP, including assisting in the determination of—(1) appropriate positive behavioral interventions and strategies for the child and (2) supplementary aids and services, program modifications, or supports for school personnel that will be provided for the child. . . .

Section 300.347 CONTENT OF IEP

(a) General. The IEP for each child with a disability must include—
(1) A statement of the child's present levels of educational performance, including—(i) how the child's disability affects the child's involvement and progress in the general curriculum [i.e., the same curriculum as for nondisabled children]; or (ii) for preschool children, as appropriate, how the disability affects the child's participation in appropriate activities;
(2) A statement of measurable annual goals, including benchmarks or short-term objectives, related to—(i) Meeting the child's needs that result from the child's disability to enable the child to be involved in and progress in the general curriculum; or for preschool children, as appropriate to participate in appropriate activities and (ii) Meeting each of the child's other educational needs that result from the child's disability;
(3) A statement of the special education and related services and supplementary aids and services to be provided to the child, or on behalf of the child, and a statement of the program modifications or supports

(continued)

Table 3.2.   (*continued*)

for the school personnel that will be provided for the child—(i) To advance appropriately toward attaining the annual goals; (ii) To be involved and progress in the general curriculum in accordance with paragraph (a) (1) of this section and to participate in extracurricular and other nonacademic activities; and (iii) To be educated and participate with other children with disabilities and nondisabled children in the activities described in this section.

(4) An explanation of the extent, if any, to which the child will not participate with nondisabled children in the regular class and in the activities described in paragraph (a) (3) of this section.

(5) (i) A statement of any individual modifications in the administration of State or district-wide assessments of student achievement that are needed in order for the child to participate in the assessment; and (ii) If the IEP Team determines that the child will not participate in a particular State or district-wide assessment of student achievement (or part of an assessment), a statement of—(A) Why that assessment is not appropriate for the child; and (B) How the child will be assessed.

Section 300.550–556 LEAST RESTRICTIVE ENVIRONMENT (LRE)

(b) Each public agency shall ensure—(1) that to the maximum extent appropriate, children with disabilities, including children in public or private institutions or other care facilities, are educated with children who are not disabled; and (2) special classes, separate schooling or other removal of children with disabilities from the regular educational environment occurs only if the nature or severity of the disability is such that education in regular classes with the use of supplementary aids and services cannot be achieved satisfactorily.

Section 300.551 CONTINUUM OF ALTERNATIVE PLACEMENTS

(a) Each public agency shall ensure that a continuum of alternative placements is available to meet the needs of children with disabilities for special education and related services. (b) The continuum required in paragraph (a) of this section must—(1) Include the alternative placements listed in the definition of special education under section 300.26 (instruction in regular classes, special classes, special schools, home instruction, and instruction in hospitals and institutions); and (2) Make provision for supplementary services (such as resources room or itinerant instruction) to be provided in conjunction with regular class placement.

Section 300.552 PLACEMENTS

In determining the educational placement of a child with a disability, including a preschool child with a disability, each public agency shall ensure that—(a) The placement decision—(1) Is made by a group of persons, including the parents, and other persons knowledgeable about the child, the meaning of the evaluation data, and the placement options; and (2) Is made in conformity with the LRE provisions of this subpart, including section 300.550–300.554; (b) The child's placement—(1) Is determined at least annually; (2) Is based on the child's IEP; and (3) Is as close as possible to the child's home; (c) Unless the IEP of a child with a disability requires some other arrangement, the child is educated in the school that he or she would attend if nondisabled; (d) In selecting the LRE, consideration is given to any potential harmful effect on the child or on the quality of services that he or she needs; and (e) A child with a disability is not removed from education in age-appropriate regular classrooms solely because of needed modifications in the general curriculum.

Section 300.553 NONACADEMIC SETTINGS

In providing or arranging for the provision of nonacademic and extracurricular services and activities, including meals, recess periods, and the services and activities set forth in section 300.306, each public agency shall ensure that each child with a disability participates with nondisabled children in those services and activities to the maximum extent appropriate to the needs of that child.

Section 300.554 CHILDREN IN PUBLIC OR PRIVATE INSTITUTIONS

Except as provided in section 300.600(d), each SEA must ensure that section 300.550 is effectively implemented, including, if necessary, making arrangements with public and private institutions (such as a memorandum of agreement or special implementation procedures).

Section 300.555 TECHNICAL ASSISTANCE AND TRAINING ACTIVITIES

Each SEA shall carry out activities to ensure that teachers and administrators in all public agencies—(a) Are fully informed about their responsibilities for implementing section 300.550; and (b) Are provided with technical assistance and training necessary to assist them in this effort.

Section 300.556 MONITORING ACTIVITIES

(a) The SEA shall carry out activities to ensure that section 300.550 is implemented by each public agency.

(b) If there is evidence that a public agency makes placements that are inconsistent with section 300.550, the SEA shall—(1) Review the public agency's justification for its actions; and (2) Assist in planning and implementing any necessary corrective action.

the IDEA priority to include children in typical environments and in the general curriculum is woven throughout the IEP requirements. The IEP is primary to enhancing the child's involvement in the "regular" education environment. The IEP describes the services to be provided to the child and the environment in which they will be provided. The priority for inclusion is reflected in the provisions related to 1) the *content* of the IEP (i.e., statements regarding access to the general curriculum and appropriate activities and justification for nonparticipation in regular class and activities [34 C.F.R. § 300.347]) and 2) requirements of the IEP *team* (i.e., the requisite involvement of a regular education teacher [34 C.F.R. § 300.344] and access to and knowledge of the IEP by all teachers and related services providers of the child [34 C.F.R. § 300.342]). These are new requirements and emphases.

Other inclusion-related provisions include the definition of *supplementary aids and services* (34 C.F.R. § 300.28). The term is defined in such a manner as to make it clear that these non–special education and related services are to be provided if necessary to successfully include a child with a disability in a regular education environment and/or general curriculum. Therefore, services such as teacher training and other supports beyond special education and related services must be provided in the regular education environment if they enhance the successful inclusion of a child with a disability. The amendments also include 1) prohibitions on state education funding formulas that have the result of creating segregation (e.g., formulas that pay for classes rather than services [34 C.F.R. § 300.130]) and 2) a clear preference for education in the regular classroom to the extent that 34 C.F.R. § 300. 235 clarifies that IDEA funds are to be used for special education, related services, and supplementary aids and services in the regular

class even if children without disabilities in that environment benefit from them. In other words, this addresses the problem, noted previously, that personnel who were funded to provide specialized services were not allowed also to work with peers without disabilities.

EVALUATING INCLUSION POLICY: WHAT DO WE KNOW?

There are few instances in the literature of either policy analyses or impact studies specific to early childhood inclusion policy. In 1988, the National Association of State Directors of Special Education (NASDSE; 1988) and the Great Lakes Area Regional Resource Center (GLARRC; 1988) conducted surveys on early childhood inclusion policies. The two studies reported similar problems: 1) ambiguities related to fiscal policies that allow inclusive options for young children (i.e., use of public special education funds), 2) a lack of policy related to agency responsibility for ensuring program quality in natural (non–school based) environments, 3) ambiguities related to policies that ensure that personnel who are providing special education services in natural environments meet public school standards, and 4) other concerns about meeting state and federal special education mandates in non–school environments that offer inclusive and natural opportunities.

A limited evaluation of the early childhood provisions of IDEA is reported annually by the U.S. Department of Education (DoE), Office of Special Education Programs, in its *Annual Report to Congress on the Implementation of IDEA*. There have been 20 such reports to date; the most recent reports data from the 1996–1997 school year (DoE, 1998). According to that report, it is unclear how many infants and toddlers are served in natural environments other than the home, and it is unclear how many of those are served in the home as a preferred option of the parents. The report states that 53% of infants and toddlers with disabilities were served in their home, 28% in early intervention classrooms, and 10% in outpatient facilities. For preschool-age children, 51.6% were served in general classes (programs designed primarily for children without disabilities), 31% in separate classes, 10% in resource rooms, and 3% in their homes. Although not a policy study per se, researchers in North Carolina reported that 34% of the early childhood programs that they studied included children with disabilities (Buysse, Wesley, Bryant, & Gardner, 1999). The researchers noted that this is fewer than that reported in national studies. Finally, as McLean and Dunst (1999) pointed out, most early childhood inclusion policy or systems studies have focused on classrooms to the exclusion of family child care and other community inclusion opportunities.

In 1990 and again in 1993, the Research Institute on Preschool Mainstreaming (funded by the U.S. Department of Education, Office of Special Education Programs [OSEP]) conducted national policy surveys, the results of which are discussed next. Following are summaries of the data from the two studies as well as additional information collected for purposes of updating those data for this chapter.

Issues in Inclusion Policies for Preschool-Age Children

If policy is a social hypothesis that certain procedures will enhance the welfare of a population, then it follows that it is important to evaluate whether the policy is having the intended effect. A comparison of the data from the two national surveys collected by the Research Institute on Preschool Mainstreaming in 1990 (Smith & Rose, 1993) and again in 1993 provides information related to policies and their effects over time. The information represents a sample from various groups that were directly involved in programs for young children with disabilities (e.g., state and local education administrators, child care and Head Start directors, parents). An examination of the questions and results from the two surveys is contained in Table 3.3.

Overall, the results indicate a slight increase (+4%) in the amount of preschool mainstreaming/integration that was taking place in 1993 compared with 1990, but fewer people noted a lack of local policy related to preschool mainstreaming/integration. It is difficult to be specific about where the growth in integration might have occurred. These results suggest that more preschool integration was occurring in 1993 along with the existence of more local policies related to integration.

Nearly all barriers to inclusion reportedly declined between 1990 and 1993. However, there was an increase (+4%) between 1990 and 1993 in the percentage of respondents who indicated that there were values or attitudes that served as barriers. Comments from several respondents in the 1993 survey described these values or attitudes:

- "Regular early childhood educators and administrators often lack both the knowledge and training to serve children with disabilities objectively."

- "Such values are evidenced at many levels: parents of children with disabilities, parents of children without disabilities, teachers, administrators. It is the 'fear factor.' It is also a difference in belief regarding the scope and purpose of special education services."

- "A few persons at state and local levels believe that segregated settings are best for preschool children. Therefore, we sometimes see only one setting offered as placement for preschool children."

- "Some programs strongly believe in special education preschool programs."
- "People are still unsure of children with disabilities being with their 'normal' child."
- "Concern re: the special-needs child requiring too much of the teacher's time, with not enough attention being given to typical students."

It is important to note that these 1993 comments are nearly identical to the comments about values and attitudes that were reported in 1990 (Smith & Rose, 1993).

The remaining seven items related to policy barriers all declined in the years between the first and second surveys. The greatest change (–14%) was in the respondents' view of whether there were conflicting eligibility policies between

public schools and other providers of service. Many of the policy conflicts noted in 1990 were related to the difference between Head Start eligibility and that of IDEA described previously. The criteria were brought more in line in later amendments to Head Start. Also, in 1990, the ADA was passed, which made it more difficult for child care programs to have discriminatory eligibility requirements. The second largest change was in the reduction of perceived policy barriers related to fiscal or contracting procedures (–12%). The two greatest continuing challenges to preschool mainstreaming/integration were values/attitudes toward inclusion and policy barriers related to personnel training and experience.

The 1990 survey was a larger sample with a broader representation (Smith, Salisbury, & Rose, 1992) than in the 1993 survey. It elicited responses from 278 people (a response rate of 47%) with return

Table 3.3.   Barriers to inclusion: Comparison of 1990 and 1993 Research Institute on Preschool Mainstreaming Survey data

Question/issue	1990 results (Yes response)	1993 results (Yes response)	Net change
Is preschool mainstreaming/integration taking place?	88%	92%	+4%
Is there a lack of local policy related to preschool mainstreaming/integration?	58%	46%	–12%
Are there barriers to preschool integration related to program quality and/or program supervision and accountability policies?	33%	28%	–5%
Are there barriers to preschool integration related to fiscal or contracting policies (e.g., procedures for funding inclusive settings)?	47%	35%	–12%
Are there barriers to preschool integration related to transportation policies?	27%	23%	–4%
Are there barriers to preschool integration related to policies governing the use of private agencies/institutions?	33%	30%	–3%
Are there conflicting eligibility policies between public schools and providers of integrated services?	28%	14%	–14%
Are there practices or policy barriers to preschool integration related to personnel training and experience?	59%	49%	–10%
Are there barriers to preschool integration related to curricula or methods?	27%	25%	–2%
Are there values or attitudes that serve as barriers to preschool integration?	58%	62%	+4%

Funded by the U.S. Department of Education, Office of Special Education Programs (OSEP).

rates varying from a high of 71% from state education agency (SEA) preschool (§ 619) coordinators to a low of 20% from federal and regional Office of Special Education Programs and Head Start representatives. The 1993 survey had responses from 124 people (a response rate of 43%) with return rates varying from a high of 67% from SEA preschool (§ 619) coordinators to a low of 15% from parents. Noting the differences in samples, the discrepancies between response groups in the 1993 survey yield several interesting points. First, although only 23% of the total responses indicated that there were policy barriers related to transportation, 100% of the parents and 47% of the local special education directors believed that this was an area in which there were policy barriers. Second, only 14% of all respondents found there to be disincentives to preschool inclusion related to conflicts in eligibility policies between public schools and private providers. However, there seemed to be a large discrepancy among the respondents. Although only 41% of the local special education directors and 40% of the Head Start Resource Access Projects reported these conflicts to be a barrier, 100% of the Interagency Coordinating Council, 91% of the state directors of special education, and 89% of the preschool (§ 619) coordinators considered it a barrier.

It is important, also, that in the 1990 study, when asked for copies of policies that presented the perceived barrier, respondents later reported that they found that the policy did not, in fact, exist! Rather, the barrier was a misinterpretation of a policy (Smith & Rose, 1993).

Several new questions were included in the 1993 survey. Table 3.4 summarizes those data. Two of the questions asked respondents whether knowledge of the long-term impact of inclusion on 1) children with disabilities and 2) those

who are typically developing would facilitate the expansion of inclusive programs. Eighty-eight percent (for children with disabilities) and 86% (for typically developing children) of the respondents answered that it would make a difference. All of the parent respondents answered affirmatively to this question as well. Not surprising, 65% of respondents said that the possibilities of communitywide integration would improve if children with disabilities could manage their own behavior, and 79% said that there would be more integrated opportunities if service providers knew how to promote the development of friendships between children with disabilities and their typically developing peers.

Finally, respondents were asked to identify which groups exert the most influence on school districts' policies and procedures related to preschool inclusion. Almost half (41%) said that principals and other administrators exert the most influence. This group was the choice of 100% of the parents and 64% of Head Start directors. Although none of the parents thought that they exerted the most influence, 37% of the other respondents named parents as the group with the most influence.

Data Collection in 1999

To supplement the 1990 and 1993 data, the authors conducted a short survey and one focus group in 1999 asking SEA preschool (Section 619 of IDEA) coordinators the current status of challenges to inclusive preschool programs in their state. Despite the low response rate to the survey ($N = 9$ [18%]), one important trend was noticeable. There continue to be large differences in the extent to which states offer inclusive programs and experiences for young children. For example, one state reported that there are only "a few places around the state that have some type of inclusion program at the preschool level," while another

Table 3.4.   1993 Research Institute on Preschool Mainstreaming Survey data

Additional questions/issues asked in 1993	1993 responses
Would it be helpful to know the long-term impact of preschool integration on children with disabilities?	Yes (88%)
Would it be helpful to know the impact of preschool integration on typically developing children?	Yes (86%)
Would options for integration improve if children with disabilities could manage their own behavior?	Yes (65%)
Would there be more integrated opportunities if providers knew how to promote the development of friendships?	Yes (79%)
Which group exerts the most control on school district policies and procedures related to preschool integration?	
Principals and other administrators	41%
Parents	37%
Teachers/direct service personnel	20%
Others	12%
The public	7%

Funded by the U.S. Department of Education, Office of Special Education Programs (OSEP).

reported that "all our preschool services are inclusive." One state described a barrier that has prohibited the implementation of inclusive preschool programs and is representative of a scenario that is known to exist in other states. Specifically, most of the preschool programs for children with disabilities are located within elementary school buildings or on elementary school campuses. The state legislature does not provide preschool programs for typically developing 3- to 5-year-olds, and these funding policies have been interpreted as limiting the preschool programs to children with disabilities and stifling inclusion opportunities with same-age peers.

The states that responded to the 1999 survey and the six that participated in the focus group continue to identify some of the same challenges and barriers that were first identified and discussed in 1990. Among the states was variability as to which areas continue to present challenges. Several states indicated that funding policies (e.g., funding for programs for "typically developing children") continue to be a barrier. Other states reported challenges in program standards that ensure compliance with the requirement to provide education programs and related services in the LRE or in natural environments (i.e., accountability in community environments). In addition, there continue to be challenges related to transportation and coordination between programs.

Issues in Inclusion Policies for Infants and Toddlers

Even fewer reported policy studies are related to inclusion for infants and toddlers. Gallagher and colleagues (1994) described three general stages in policy evolution: policy development, policy approval, and policy application. With the more recent emphasis on the provision of early intervention services in natural environments, many states have had to shift from the policy application stage back to the policy development and policy approval stages to incorporate changes that are necessary for an alternative model of service delivery.

In an effort to generate similar information to that collected from SEA preschool (§ 619) coordinators on challenges or barriers to inclusive preschool services, a similar survey was sent to Part C coordinators. Although the response rate of 12% ($N = 6$) makes it difficult to generalize the information, conversations with experts around the United States informally validated the survey responses. Many of the barriers to preschool inclusion are also barriers for states in their efforts to provide young children and their families with inclusive early intervention services under Part C. This is particularly troublesome because it is known that children who begin their early childhood careers in segregated environments often continue to be placed in those types of environments (Miller, Strain, McKinley, Heckathorn, & Miller, 1995). Several Part C coordinators were quick to point out that personnel training is a major barrier to the delivery of appropriate and quality inclusive early intervention services. Both lack of funding and lack of collaboration across programs impede the ability of states to overcome the personnel issue. Access to child care programs that are high quality as a "natural environment" is a dilemma for many families and programs (Buysse et al., 1999; Cost, Quality, and Child Outcomes Study Team, 1995; Janko, Schwartz, Sandall, Anderson, & Cottam, 1997).

Like the challenges facing preschool inclusion, well-entrenched attitudes and beliefs that favor segregated service delivery models are also a substantial barrier to the implementation of early intervention services in natural environments. Changes in state funding models, state policy around service delivery, and the need to provide early intervention in alternative environments have threatened the existence of many programs that are designed to provide early intervention in specialized environments. In many states, parents and professionals struggle with changing existing systems from center-based early intervention programs to itinerant special services in natural environments such as the home or child care environment. This decentralization of service delivery poses a number

of similar challenges described previously in the section "Issues in Inclusion Policies for Preschool-Age Children" and leads to parental and professional concerns and fears.

As service delivery models change, so do the requirements around billing and third-party reimbursement. In several states, the use of third-party insurance benefits is one of the biggest challenges to overcome in the provision of early intervention services in natural environments. This challenge is particularly significant in states that have a requirement around mandatory utilization of the family's third-party benefits. One such challenge or dilemma stems from the discrepancy between health insurance rules that require physician supervision of services to be reimbursed and the desire to provide services to children and families in environments outside health care facilities, where there are no physicians. This stipulation often works in opposition to the IDEA federal requirements of providing early intervention services in natural environments.

Part B of IDEA requires agencies other than education to comply with the legal responsibilities outlined in the law, but Part C does not have the same requirement. Such a requirement under Part C might be the impetus necessary to make changes such as allowing infants and toddlers who are eligible for Medicaid to gain access to services in natural environments using Medicaid resources. Similar regulatory and policy changes may be necessary for private insurers who have stringent limitations on providers, environments, and types and amounts of therapy services. Any contemplated policy change is complicated by the fact that rules governing the implementation of Medicaid and other third-party resources vary from state to state. The barriers identified in one state cannot be assumed to exist in another state. Therefore, the mechanism for overcoming such barriers may vary considerably across states as well as between counties or other local governing entities.

AGENDA FOR CHANGE: IS PUBLIC POLICY SUFFICIENT FOR CREATING CHANGE?

This chapter has discussed the purpose of public policy and its evolutionary character; examined how policies related to inclusion have changed over time; reviewed the major federal policy (IDEA 1997) as it relates to early intervention and educational inclusion; and reviewed information on the prevalence of inclusive programming in early childhood, whether the policy challenges to the inclusion of young children have changed over time, and what the existing challenges are. This discussion has noted the following:

- There is a dearth of policy research efforts looking particularly at inclusion policies and their implementation and effectiveness in meeting desired goals for young children.

- The policy research that is available points to slow progress in the effectiveness of current policies to advance inclusion for young children. Although IDEA has required educating children in the LRE for more than 20 years, only approximately 51% of preschool-age children with disabilities are being educated in inclusive environments. One study reported a smaller percentage of programs that are inclusive than earlier reported (34% versus more than 50%). There were still the same perceived policy challenges in the mid- to late 1990s that there were in 1990. There seems to be the same perception that fiscal and contracting policies limit con-

tracting with or creating normalized environments, personnel preparation does not facilitate individually and developmentally appropriate environments for all children, schools' transportation policies limit access to more natural environments, and ambiguity of program accountability between lead agencies and typical environments remains.

- There were *greater* challenges to inclusion in people's attitudes and beliefs in 1993 than there were in 1990.

- The perceived policy barriers did not in fact exist in the 1990 study—only the *belief* that they did.

- Factors other than policy are reported to be important in advancing inclusion. These factors include knowledge of effects of inclusion, knowledge and skills of personnel to promote friendships, and children's abilities to manage their own behavior.

- The quality of the majority of natural environments is mediocre at best.

Clearly, these data present a picture of little progress in early childhood inclusion related to policy development. However, several cautions are worth noting. First, it is unclear whether what is reported in studies as policy barriers are really perceptions and beliefs about what policies say rather than the effect of actual policy. Second, there is little research on the effects of public policy on early childhood inclusion. Third, the studies have not been evaluations of early childhood inclusion policies (i.e., they have studied either an individual's perceptions of policy or policies that did not have as their sole intent to promote early childhood inclusion). The intent of a policy is critical in the appropriate evaluation of it. Thus, in the first instance, in the Smith and Rose (1993) study, many of the challenges reported by the survey respondents were in fact a misinterpretation of IDEA requirements. In the second instance, IDEA had as its overarching goal access to a FAPE for all children with disabilities, not how to create high-quality inclusive practices. A better evaluation of the impact that public policy can have on promoting early childhood inclusion is a rigorous, multimethod study of a policy specifically designed to promote early childhood inclusion versus an educational rights policy such as IDEA. Such a study should include policy analysis and qualitative, descriptive, and comparative methods (Knapp, 1995). Buysse and colleagues (1999) suggested developing and evaluating policies that 1) affect personnel skills associated with child outcomes, 2) promote child care licensing requirements that reflect both developmental and chronological age as the basis for grouping and class size, 3) promote individually as well as developmentally appropriate practice, and 4) improve overall program quality.

Most studies have focused on federal policy or the implementation of federal policy at the state and local levels. However, state and local policy may go beyond federal requirements. The effects of state policy are evident in inclusion policy research efforts (Harvey, Voorhees, & Landon, 1997; McLeskey & Henry, 1999). Also, as noted previously, most studies have focused on classroom inclusion versus other community inclusion opportunities (McLean & Dunst, 1999). However, from the available information, there seem to be some important links among successful inclusion and policy, administrative procedures, and systems change efforts. These links include leadership philosophy, beliefs, and behavior (Harvey et al., 1997; Peck, Hayden, Wandschneider, Peterson, & Richarz, 1989; Smith & Rose, 1993); policies targeted at remediation of specific inclusion barriers such as eligibility criteria and funding formulas (Harvey et al., 1997; Smith & Rose, 1993); policies and proce-

dures that require and support collaborative systems and planning among agencies (Fink & Fowler, 1997; Harvey et al., 1997; Rous, Hemmeter, & Schuster, 1999; Smith & Rose, 1993), and policies and procedures that promote training and technical assistance (Buysse et al., 1999; Smith & Rose, 1993).

It seems that public policy alone may not be sufficient for promoting inclusive practices. However, given that policy establishes goals and determines the use of public resources, it is probably necessary. Indeed, policy could be viewed as the floor of possibilities upon which a structure can be built by actions that change attitudes and beliefs, that promote better understanding among stakeholders, including parents, schools, child care providers, health providers, and payers, and that increase resources—both fiscal and human. Policies can facilitate improvements in the non–policy-related factors such as personnel skills. For instance, according to McDonnell, Brownell, and Wolery (1997), fewer than half of the teachers in National Association for the Education of Young Children–accredited early childhood community programs that enroll children with disabilities have the benefit of the services of an early childhood special educator. Also, participation as a member of the IEP team was significantly less for teachers in community programs than for teachers in public schools. The emphasis in IDEA 1997 on ensuring necessary special services in typical environments as well as mandating the participation of the general educator on the IEP team may address these threats to quality inclusion. Policy research and validation efforts are needed to document whether IDEA 1997 does have this effect.

With the limited information available, one can conclude that some policy problems have not improved or have improved very little. However, people report that there are other important influences that could promote the practice of inclusion: broader knowledge by all stakeholders about the benefits of inclusion for both children with disabilities and typically developing peers, the ability of children with disabilities to manage their behavior, and recognition that school administrators and parents are the most important stakeholders for improving inclusion policies and opportunities.

There have been many recommendations for action that go beyond the realm of policy (Harvey et al., 1997; Rose & Smith, 1993; Smith & Rose, 1993; Washington & Andrews, 1998). Training and technical assistance initiatives assist in decreasing and eliminating the barriers associated with personnel preparation and quality programs (see Chapter 8). Both of these efforts may be a link to moving forward in positive directions as better prepared personnel will be able to provide quality programs and services to meet the needs of all young children in the community. Training and technical assistance have been shown to result in systems change (Rous et al., 1999). Personnel who are trained to work with typically developing children can learn new skills associated with adapting to the needs of children with disabilities in their environments. Personnel who are trained to work with children with disabilities can learn to provide their expertise in the natural environment and to support the teacher. Both groups can learn to work as a team rather than independently (Harvey et al., 1997; Rosenkoetter, 1998; Smith, Miller, & Bredekamp, 1998). Personnel who are trained to collect data systematically and reflect on inclusive practices in a university–school research partnership had positive effects on inclusive practices, collaboration, and beliefs (Gettinger, Stoiber, & Lange, 1999).

Taking a look at high-quality inclusive programs as a resource is another place to begin (Harvey et al., 1997; Smith & Rose, 1993). The examples that these programs can share provide the opportunity to begin to break down some of the barriers and challenges. Peer-to-peer consultation (e.g., administrator to administrator, teacher to teacher, parent to parent) allows individuals from successful inclusive environments to give relevant support and advice to their peers who are attempting the transition to inclusive practices. The respondents to the surveys discussed in this chapter said that stakeholders need information on the impact of inclusion. Other strategies reported in the literature include person-to-person dialogue to share information, fears, and experiences. These exchanges can allay fears, build trust, and build awareness of successful inclusion efforts. Clearly, there are individuals who do not believe that inclusion is important for young children, who do not know how to accomplish inclusion, or who are afraid of change. These individuals could benefit from strategies that emerge from these exchanges (Janko et al., 1997; Peck et al., 1989; Rose & Smith, 1993; Rose & Smith, 1994; Strong & Sandoval, 1999).

A better understanding among stakeholders about why and how to provide inclusive opportunities can be accomplished through collaborative planning at the community level (Smith & Rose, 1993; Strain, Smith, & McWilliam, 1996; Washington & Andrews, 1998). Indeed, IDEA 1997 contains language that encourages the use of Part B funds (up to 5%) by local school districts to "develop and implement a coordinated services system" (34 C.F.R. § 300.244). Such coordinated service system activities may include coordination around transition of a child from Part C services to Part B services, interagency financial arrangements, and interagency personnel development. These efforts can bring together Head Start, child care, parents, schools, and others as appropriate to build a vision and system of early childhood services and supports for all children. These collaborative efforts can result in better understanding of the various programs, of the needs of families of young children, and of how to meet the diverse needs of all children in the community. These efforts can result in a better and more efficient use of limited resources by promoting sharing and reallocation of space, funds, transportation, personnel training opportunities, and so forth. Finally, these efforts can result in communication and respect across programs and between programs and families.

CONCLUSION

Policy that promotes inclusion is necessary. As defined at the beginning of this chapter, public policy is related to the knowledge base and values of a society. As of 2000, policies have not been sufficient to result in a significant increase in inclusion. However, given the data on attitudes and beliefs, they may reflect current values. Perhaps through the other strategies noted in this chapter and elsewhere in this book, society's values, attitudes, and beliefs toward inclusion will improve. Then, perhaps, public policies can be sufficiently directed toward inclusion. Policy can lay a foundation and policy can foster systems change, but training, information, peer support, experience, collaborative planning, and other skill- and trust-building strategies can foster the personal change needed for supportive attitudes and values necessary for effective inclusion practices.

REFERENCES

Abeson, A., & Ballard, J. (1976). State and federal policy for exceptional children. In F.J. Weintraub, A. Abeson, J. Ballard, & M.L. LaVor (Eds.), *Public policy and the education of exceptional children* (pp. 83–95). Reston, VA: Council for Exceptional Children.

Americans with Disabilities Act (ADA) of 1990, PL 101-336, 42 U.S.C §§12101 *et seq.*

Buysse, V., Wesley, P., Bryant, D., & Gardner, D. (1999). Quality of early childhood programs in inclusive and non-inclusive settings. *Exceptional Children, 65*(3), 301–314.

Captioned Films for the Deaf Act of 1965, PL 89-258.

Cost, Quality, and Child Outcomes Study Team. (1995). *Cost, quality and child outcomes in child care centers: Public report.* Denver: University of Colorado at Denver, Economics Department.

Division for Early Childhood of the Council for Exceptional Children. (1996). *Position on inclusion.* Denver, CO: Author.

Division for Early Childhood of the Council for Exceptional Children. (1998). *Letter to Tom Irvin, Office of Special Education Programs, U.S. Department of Education.* Denver, CO: Author.

Education for All Handicapped Children Act of 1975, PL 94-142, 20 U.S.C. §§1400 *et seq.*

Education of the Handicapped Act Amendments of 1974, PL 93-380, 88 Stat. 576.

Elimination of Architectural Barriers to Physically Handicapped Act of 1968, PL 90-480.

Fink, D., & Fowler, S. (1997). Inclusion, one step at a time: A case study of communication and decision making across program boundaries. *TECSE, 17*(3), 337–362.

Gallagher, J.J. (1996). Unpublished manuscript. Chapel Hill: The University of North Carolina, Frank Porter Graham Child Development Center.

Gallagher, J.J., Harbin, G.L., Eckland, J., & Clifford, R. (1994). State diversity and policy implementation: Infants and toddlers. In L.J. Johnson, R.J. Gallagher, M.J. Montagne, J.B. Jordan, J.J. Gallagher, P.L. Hutinger, & M.B. Karnes (Eds.), *Meeting early intervention challenges: Issues from birth to three* (2nd ed., pp. 235–250). Baltimore: Paul H. Brookes Publishing Co.

Gettinger, M., Stoiber, K., & Lange, J. (1999). Collaborative investigation of inclusive early education practices: A blueprint for teacher–researcher partnership. *Journal of Early Intervention, 65*(3), 257–265.

Great Lakes Area Regional Resource Center (GLARRC). (1988). *Issues assessment summary.* Planners Conference on Integration and the Least Restrictive Environment for Young Children, Chicago, IL.

Harvey, J., Voorhees, M., & Landon, T. (1997). The role of the state department of education in promoting integrated placement options for preschoolers: Views from the field. *Topics in Early Childhood Special Education, 17*(3), 387–409.

Head Start Act of 1964 (PL 88-452).

Individuals with Disabilities Education Act (IDEA) of 1990, PL 101-476, 20 U.S.C. §§ 1400 *et seq.*

Individuals with Disabilities Education Act Amendments of 1997, PL 105-17, 20 U.S.C. §§ 1400 *et seq.*

Janko, S., Schwartz, I.S., Sandall, S., Anderson, K., & Cottam, C. (1997). Beyond microsystems: Unanticipated lessons about the meaning of inclusion. *Topics in Early Childhood Special Education, 17,* 286–306.

Johnson, R.A. (1976). Renewal of school placement systems for the handicapped. In F.J. Weintraub, A. Abeson, J. Ballard, & M.L. LaVor (Eds.), *Public policy and the education of exceptional children* (pp. 47–61). Reston, VA: Council for Exceptional Children.

Knapp, M.S. (1995). How shall we study comprehensive, collaborative services for children and families? *Educational Researcher, 24,* 5–16.

LaVor, M.L. (1976a). Federal legislation for handicapped persons. In F.J. Weintraub, A. Abeson, J. Ballard, & M.L. LaVor (Eds.), *Public policy and the education of exceptional children* (pp. 96–111). Reston, VA: Council for Exceptional Children.

LaVor, M.L. (1976b). Time and circumstances. In F.J. Weintraub, A. Abeson, J. Ballard, & M.L. LaVor (Eds.), *Public policy and the education of exceptional children* (pp. 293–303). Reston, VA: Council for Exceptional Children.

McDonnell, A., Brownell, K., & Wolery, M. (1997). Teaching experience and specialist support: A survey of preschool teachers employed in programs accredited by NAEYC. *TECSE, 17*(3), 263–285.

McLean, M., & Dunst, C. (1999). On the forms of inclusion: The need for more information. *Journal of Early Intervention, 22*(3), 200–202.

McLeskey, J., & Henry, D. (1999). Inclusion: What progress is being made across states? *TEACHING Exceptional Children, 31,* 56–62.

Miller, L., Strain, P., McKinley, J., Heckathorn, K., & Miller, S. (1995). The effectiveness of integrated and segregated preschools in terms of school-aged placements. *Case in Point, IX,* 16–25.

Mills v. The Board of Education of the District of Columbia (1972).

National Association of State Directors of Special Education (NASDSE). (1988, October 26). Preschool survey results. *Special Net.*

Odom, S.L., Horn, E., Marquart, J., Hanson, M.J., Wolfberg, P., Beckman, P., Lieber, J., Li, S., Schwartz, I., Janko, S., & Sandall, S. (1999). On the forms of inclusion: Organizational context and individualized service models. *Journal of Early Intervention, 22*(3), 185–199.

Peck, C.A., Hayden, L., Wandschneider, M., Peterson, K., & Richarz, S. (1989). Development of integrated preschools: A qualitative inquiry into sources of resistance among parents, administrators, and teachers. *Journal of Early Intervention, 13,* 353–364.

Pennsylvania ARC (PARC) v. The Commonwealth of Pennsylvania (1972).

Rehabilitation Act of 1973, PL 93-112, 29 U.S.C. §§ 701 *et seq.*

Rose, D.F., & Smith, B.J. (1993). Preschool mainstreaming attitude barriers and strategies for addressing them. *Young Children, 48,* 59–62.

Rose, D.F., & Smith, B.J. (1994). Providing public education services to preschoolers with disabilities in community-based programs: Who's responsible for what? *Young Children, 49,* 64–68.

Rosenkoetter, S. (1998). Together we can. . .suggestions from the pioneers of classroom blending of multiple early childhood programs. *Young Exceptional Children, 1,* 7–16.

Rous, B., Hemmeter, M.L., & Schuster, J. (1999). Evaluating the impact of the STEPS model on development of community-wide transition systems. *Journal of Early Intervention, 22*(1), 38–50.

Seekins, T., & Fawcett, S. (1986). Public policy making and research information. *The Behavior Analyst, 9,* 35–45.

Smith, B., Miller, P., & Bredekamp, S. (1998). Sharing responsibility: DEC-, NAEYC-, and Vygotsky-based practices for quality inclusion. *Young Exceptional Children, 2,* 11–20.

Smith, B., & Rose, D. (1993). *Administrator's policy handbook for preschool mainstreaming.* Cambridge, MA: Brookline Books.

Smith, B.J., Salisbury, C.L., & Rose, D.F. (1992). Policy options for preschool mainstreaming. *Case in Point, VII,* 17–30.

Strain, P., Smith, B., & McWilliam, R. (1996). The widespread adoption of service delivery recommendations: A systems change perspective. In S. Odom & M. McLean (Eds.), *Early intervention/early childhood special education: Recommended practices.* Austin, TX: PRO-ED.

Strong, K., & Sandoval, J. (1999). Mainstreaming children with a neuromuscular disease: A map of concerns. *Exceptional Children, 65*(3), 353–366.

U.S. Department of Education. (1998). *Twentieth annual report to Congress on the implementation of the Individuals with Disabilities Education Act.* Washington, DC: U.S. Government Printing Office.

Washington, V., & Andrews, J.D. (1998). *Children of 2010.* Washington, DC: National Association for the Education of Young Children.

4

MATTHEW J. STOWE

H. RUTHERFORD TURNBULL III

Legal Considerations of Inclusion for Infants and Toddlers and for Preschool-Age Children

This chapter analyzes the inclusion requirements of the Individuals with Disabilities Act (IDEA) and its amendments as they apply to infants and toddlers (under Part C) and to preschool-age children (under Part B). It begins by describing the general federal policy in favor of integration/inclusion and against segregation. Then, in recognition that the essential inclusion requirements were originally set out in Part B (the so-called "least restrictive environment" [LRE] requirements) and that they therefore constitute the basis for interpreting the Part C requirements (the so-called "natural environment" [NE] requirements), the chapter authors de-scribe the LRE requirements under Part B and the leading court decisions interpreting them. After laying this foundation for further analysis of the inclusion requirements, the authors then examine the requirements as they apply to preschool-age children. Finally, the chapter authors reconcile the various differences within Part C and between it and Part B.

Anyone who analyzes the NE requirements under Part C immediately confronts a difficulty, namely, the relatively sparse body of law interpreting Part C itself. Aside from Part C's own language and the implementing regulations (which essentially parrot Part C's language), there is very little from the U.S. Department of Education (DOE) or from case law to aid the analysis.

For that reason, the chapter authors attempt to understand Part C's NE requirements in light of the language of Part C and its regulations and in light of the meaning ascribed to LRE under Part B. They then develop an analogy between Part B, on the one hand, and Part C, on the other. The authors lay the Part B and Part C purposes and language side by side to show how the DoE's and the courts' interpretation of Part B informs— or should inform—the interpretation of Part C.

This portion of the chapter does not rely on analogy alone; it references the DOE's annual reports to Congress concerning IDEA implementation. In referencing these reports, the chapter authors argue that the DOE, by reporting what is happening in Part C with respect to NE, implicitly approves the inclusion practices under Part C.

Because the very principles that favor inclusion and oppose segregation are so much a core concept of federal disability policy, the chapter authors examine the values, desired outcomes, and purposes of the Part B and Part C LRE/NE provisions. At this point, the authors also explain the various interests of the affected stakeholders—the child, the family, and the provider system/state. They argue that there is a necessary and proper tradeoff of these interests, and the tradeoff process should be guided by criteria that relate principally to the benefit that will accrue to the infant/toddler.

The chapter concludes with the recognition that there are ways to reconcile the sometimes competing interests of the various stakeholders. The message is that Part C's NE mandate is not as powerful as Part B's LRE mandate but that there is sufficient flexibility within the individualized family service plan (IFSP) process to ensure that inclusion/NE is achieved along with child and family development and the satisfaction of state interests.

METHODS OF ANALYSIS AND USE OF PRESUMPTIONS

This chapter uses what lawyers know as an *interest analysis* and a *textual analysis*. Interest analysis identifies the interested parties (stakeholders), the nature of their interests, and the congruence or difference among those interests. With respect to inclusion of infants/toddlers and preschool-age children, the five interested parties are children with disabilities, their families, and their service providers; children without disabilities; and the state as an administrative and fiscal unit receiving federal funds and expending its own.

Textual analysis closely parses the language of the law (IDEA and its regulations) and of the cases that interpret the law to determine what the rule of law is, the rationale for that rule, and the principles and values that underlie the law. By explicating the text to determine these factors, it becomes possible to interpret the inclusion provisions in Part B and Part C.

Finally, it is helpful to connect the LRE/NE provisions to a very traditional legal technique for shaping behavior. That technique is called *presumptions*. The most familiar of legal presumptions is that a person is presumed to be innocent of a crime until he or she is convicted of it. A comparable presumption in disability law is that a student (including an infant/toddler) will be included in general school environments, to the maximum extent appropriate for (beneficial to) the student. Both presumptions shape the behavior of those affected by them. In the case of the presumption of innocence, it puts the state to the task of proving guilt beyond a reasonable doubt (a very high standard of proof). In the case of the presumption of inclusion, it puts the providers to the task of justifying any removal from the typical environments (general education classrooms for school-age children, or the NEs for infants/toddlers). By requiring the providers to justify removal from the NEs, the presumption causes the decision makers (IFSP team) to begin with the NE and to move incrementally away from it; the presumption shapes their behavior and the results of their behavior.

The discussion that follows uses the interest analysis, a textual analysis, and the presumption of integration to explicate Part B (early childhood education) and Part C (infant/toddler) inclusion provisions. The authors begin by describing the general federal policy in favor of integration/inclusion and against segregation.

GENERAL FEDERAL POLICY

It is long-settled federal policy that individuals with disabilities should not be isolated from the communities in which they live, work, and attend school. The legislative basis for this policy was first articulated in 1973 with the enactment of the antidiscrimination provisions of the Rehabilitation Act (PL 93-112), commonly known as Section 504 (§ 794). Shortly thereafter, Congress restated the policy by enacting the Education for All Handicapped Children Act of 1975 (PL 94-142). With the enactment of the Americans with Disabilities Act (ADA) in 1990 (PL 101-336), Congress made its most recent statement in favor of inclusion and against segregation.

These three statutes attack segregation in two ways: by prohibiting discrimination and by providing entitlements. Antidiscrimination statutes aim to prevent prejudicial action in the public and private sectors, whereas entitlement statutes aim to provide a special benefit that an individual can receive if he or she meets certain standards of eligibility.

Two of the statutes (Section 504 and ADA) are civil rights laws that prohibit discrimination, on the basis of disability, against an *otherwise qualified* person with a disability; the person is "otherwise qualified" if he or she can, with reasonable accommodations, participate in a federally assisted program. Section 504 requires state and local education agencies to provide nonacademic services in as inclusive an environment as possible and to educate a student with disabilities with students without disabilities unless they can demonstrate that even after providing supplemental aids and services, that child cannot be educated in an inclusive environment (Title 34, C.F.R. § 104.34). Similarly, ADA requires state and local governments to provide services in integrated environments (§ 12101); as interpreted by the Supreme Court in 1999, ADA is an antisegregation, prointegration statute, with limitations (*Olmstead v. L.C.,* 1999).

The third statute, the federal special education law, now termed the Individuals with Disabilities Education Act (IDEA), is a federal entitlement statute that provides federal funds to states on the condition that they engage in certain types of behavior. Included among those behaviors is the very straightforward one of not segregating students merely because they have disabilities. It applies to infants and toddlers (§§ 1443–1445), to early education (preschool) (§ 1419), and to students ages 6 through 21 (§§ 1411 *et seq.*).

DEDICATION TO THE PRINCIPLES OF INTEGRATION/INCLUSION

Although the primary purpose of IDEA is to ensure that all students with disabilities are provided a free appropriate public education (FAPE), inclusion is specifically emphasized as an integral part of FAPE. In Part A, the general provisions section of IDEA, the Congress finds that "disability. . .in no way diminishes the right of individuals to participate in or contribute to society" (§ 1400[c][1]). This "right to participate" is one of the two cornerstones on which rests the IDEA policy in support of inclusion. The second cornerstone, also mentioned in the general provisions part, was formed by more than 20 years of research and experience. It is the evidence that children with disabilities can be effectively educated within the general curriculum to the maximum extent appropriate by providing services in the general classroom whenever necessary (§ 1400[c][5]). Studies have demonstrated that academic performance or developmental progress among integrated children is comparable to that of children in segregated placements (Buysse & Bailey, 1993; Gartner & Lipsky, 1987; see also Chapter 1). IDEA is results-oriented legislation that recognizes that integration aligns ethical and practical considerations into one unarguable answer to the questions of how best to structure special education for children with disabilities: as a service to be provided rather than a place to be sent (§ 1400[c][5][C]).

THE LEGAL RIGHTS AND PROTECTIONS QUESTION

To support inclusion, IDEA creates procedural and substantive requirements to which the states must adhere. The question is to what extent and in what situations does IDEA require that children with disabilities be included in educational environments with their peers without disabilities. This question is particularly important with regard to children who are not yet of school age (younger than 6 years) and who therefore do not have a "general classroom" to attend. This chapter collects and analyzes the legal requirements related to inclusion of children with disabilities ages birth to 5 years, but first it is necessary to understand the LRE mandate of IDEA as it applies to school-age children.

PART B: THE REQUIREMENTS THAT SUPPORT INTEGRATION/INCLUSION

To clarify the inclusion requirements of IDEA as it applies to school-age children with disabilities, this section begins with an examination of the statute, regulations, and case law interpreting the LRE

mandate of Part B. The chapter authors then make distinctions in how these requirements apply to preschool children.

General Commitment to Integration

Part B, covering students ages 3–21, establishes the core requirements of the statute. These include the requirement that all children with disabilities be provided a FAPE in the LRE based on an individualized and nondiscriminatory evaluation (§§ 1400 *et seq.*). The requirements also mandate that due process procedures be established, that parents and children be included in the decision-making process, and that transition (into adulthood) be a carefully performed process for achieving specified outcomes (§§ 1400 *et seq.*). Together, these requirements emphasize three core concepts in the education of individuals with disabilities: 1) inclusion—involvement of each child with a disability in the general curriculum to the maximum extent possible while addressing the unique needs of the child; 2) empowerment—involvement of the parents and the child, as well as general and special education personnel, in making individualized decisions to support each child's education; and 3) productivity—preparation of the child for employment and other postschool activities in integrated environments (Title 34, C.F.R. § 300, Appendix A).

The first and third of these core concepts demonstrate the extent to which Part B is dedicated to inclusion, both in the classroom and in society. This goal is further reflected in the specific requirements of transition planning and transition services in Part B. For instance, when a child reaches age 14, each child's individualized education program (IEP) is required to include a statement of the transition service needs of the child (Title 34 C.F.R. § 300.374[b][1][i]).

LRE in Part B: The Statute and Regulations

Section 1412(a)(5) provides that to be eligible for Part B funds, a state must demonstrate that it has in effect policies and procedures to ensure that

> To the maximum extent appropriate, children with disabilities. . .are educated with children who are not disabled, and that special classes, separate schooling, or other removal of children with disabilities from the regular educational environment occurs only when the nature or severity of the disability of a child is such that education in regular classes with the use of supplementary aids and services cannot be achieved satisfactorily. (§ 1412[a][5][A])

This is the LRE provision of Part B. It requires inclusion, either full or partial, in all three school environments: the general class, extracurricular activities, and other nonacademic activities (§ 1414[d][1][A][iii]). Full inclusion is preferred over partial inclusion, and partial inclusion is preferred over segregated service delivery. The calculus for determining the appropriate placement for a child includes a presumption that, whenever possible, children with disabilities will be included in all activities with children without disabilities, including lunch, recess, gym, and other nonacademic activities at the school (Title 34, C.F.R. §§ 300.553, 300.306). The statute recognizes that even children who because of their disability cannot be educated in a general classroom often still can benefit from interaction with their peers without disabilities. As the regulations state, provision of nonacademic services in as inclusive an environment as possible is especially important for children whose educational needs necessitate their being with other children with disabilities for most of the day (Title 34, C.F.R. § 104.34).

In addition, a continuum of alternative placements must be made available to support the LRE presumption. This continuum must include, at least, the alternative placements listed under regulation Section 300.26 (general classes, special classes, special schools, home instruction, and instruction in residential environments). The local education agency (LEA) or state education agency (SEA) must also supply any supplementary aids and services (e.g., resource room and itinerant instruction) that will allow for a greater amount of inclusion for a child with disabilities (§ 1412[a][5]).

Special classes, separate schooling, or other removal of students with disabilities from the general education environment may be justified only when the child's education cannot be achieved satisfactorily in the general classroom even with supplementary aids and services (§ 1412[a][5][A]). This requirement has two prongs: First, the LEA, in considering whether supplementary aids and services can prevent removal, must make good faith efforts to allow the child to benefit from the general classroom, and second, the LEA must make those aids and services available when they are necessary for the child to benefit from educational programs or to allow for a more inclusive placement.

Furthermore, the child's IEP must include an explanation of the extent, if any, to which the child will not participate in activities across all three domains with children without disabilities (§ 1414[d][1][A][iii]). There must be a justification for not educating the child with disabilities in the general classroom, and that justification must also explain the extent of noninclusive activities (§ 1414[d][1][A][iv]).

The regulations do allow consideration to be given to the distance of the proposed placement from the child's home in determining whether a placement is in the LRE (Title 34, C.F.R.

§ 300.552[a][3]). The regulations create a preference for education of the child with disabilities in the school that the child would have attended if he or she did not have a disability (Title 34, C.F.R. § 300.552[c]). Before 1999, when new regulations were promulgated, the notes to the regulations stated, "The parent's right to challenge the placement . . .extends. . .to placement in a distant school. . . . An equally appropriate education may exist closer to home" (Title 34, C.F.R. § 300.522, 1992, note 1). The note indicated that the home-school preference extended to placements in which all other factors are equal but was silent on how much weight this factor was to be given compared with other LRE factors. The notes were removed from the final regulations released in 1999 (Title 34, C.F.R. §§ 300.550–300.552, March 1999). Some courts have seemed to give considerable weight to the home-school preference in ruling whether a placement is in the LRE (*Fuhrmann v. East Hanover Board of Education*, 1993).

In promulgating the 1999 regulations, the DOE made several significant changes. First, it changed the introductory paragraph to emphasize that the regulations applied to all children with disabilities who are entitled to a FAPE (Title 34, C.F.R. §§ 300.550–300.552, March 1999). Second, it changed Subsection (a)(1) to emphasize that placement decisions are a function of the IEP team and should reflect the input of the parents and other "persons knowledgeable" (Title 34, C.F.R. § 300.552[a][1]). Third, the regulations allow the team to consider "any potential harmful effect on the child or on the quality of services that he or she needs" when selecting the LRE (Title 34, C.F.R. § 300.552[d]). Last, they forbid removal of children with disabilities from "age-appropriate regular classrooms solely because of needed modifications in the general curriculum" (Title 34, C.F.R.

§ 300.552[e]). The overall effect of these changes is to strengthen Part B's LRE presumption.

LRE in Case Law: The Holland Decision

No significant cases have interpreted the 1997 statute and the 1999 regulations. There are, however, earlier cases that have become touchstones in interpreting the statute, especially Section 1412(a)(5), the basic LRE provision. Because Part B (early childhood, ages 3–5) and Part C (birth–3) are understandable in light of the leading cases, the chapter authors examine them here. One of the leading cases is *Board of Education v. Holland* (1994). There the question was the meaning of the requirement that children with disabilities be "mainstreamed" (the term popularly used at the time for inclusion) to the maximum extent appropriate. The court identified four factors as relevant in determining whether a placement is appropriate: 1) benefits available in a general classroom compared with those available in a special education classroom, 2) the nonacademic benefits of interaction with children without disabilities, 3) the effect of the presence of the child with disabilities on others, and 4) the costs of supplementary aids and services necessary for inclusion.

As for the first factor, the court found that the presumption favoring inclusion was not overcome by evidence that a special education placement may be academically superior to placement in a general classroom: "The Act's presumption in favor of mainstreaming requires that a handicapped child be educated in a regular classroom if the child can receive a satisfactory education there, even if it is not the best academic setting for that child" (*Board of Education v. Holland*, 1994, p. 1403). Comparably greater academic benefit, after the threshold level is reached, does not trump the LRE requirement.

The second factor involves benefits that the child would receive through interaction with peers without disabilities. Modeling behavior, reducing stigma, and developing social skills are a few of the benefits that can fall under this part of the test. Academic benefits are often tied into these nonacademic factors. For example, improved self-esteem and increased motivation as a result of inclusion will often result in better academic progress. Accordingly, this second factor reflects the "fundamental purpose of the IDEA's mainstreaming requirement" (*Board of Education v. Holland,* 1994, p. 1403).

The third factor addresses the possible negative effects of including the child with disabilities in the general classroom, including effects on other children and the teacher. The court noted that "if other children are disadvantaged by the presence of the handicapped child, mainstreaming is not appropriate" (*Board of Education v. Holland,* 1994, p. 1403; Title 34, C.F.R. § 300.552). In making this determination, the school district or LEA "must consider all reasonable means to minimize the demands on the teacher" (*Board of Education v. Holland,* 1994, p. 1403; Title 34, C.F.R. § 300.552). Supplemental aids and services, such as the employment of a teacher's aide, can sometimes accommodate a child's need for additional attention.

The fourth and final inquiry is cost. The court said that "if the cost of educating a handicapped child in a regular classroom is so great that it would significantly impact upon the education of other children in the district, then education in a regular classroom is not appropriate" (*Board of Education v. Holland,* 1994, p. 1404; *Greer v. Rome City School District,* 1991). In making this determination, the cost comparison is between a special education environment and a general classroom environment with aids and related services. Later in this chapter,

it becomes clear that these four factors are appropriate for Part C decision making and interpretation.

LRE and Other Court Decisions

The federal appellate courts have applied various interpretations of the LRE mandate ("A free appropriate education," 1994). Only the Seventh, Ninth, and Third Circuit Courts of Appeals have actually followed the Holland test. The others have generally employed an older approach, established in the Roncker case ("A free appropriate education," 1994).

In *Roncker v. Walter* (1983), the court created a test that incorporated the policy mandates of individualization, appropriateness, and LRE. The proper inquiry, said the Sixth Circuit Court of Appeals, is into whether the needed services, available in the proposed more restrictive environment, could be feasibly provided in an environment that permitted a greater degree of integration. This is the "feasibility-portability" test. When deciding whether a noninclusive environment is superior to an inclusive one, the school district must first determine whether the services or advantages of the more restrictive placement can be feasibly provided in (made portable to or imported to) the inclusive environment.

It is useful to compare Roncker and Holland with respect to cost. Roncker said cost can be validly considered because excessive spending on a single child may deprive other children of services (except in cases in which the LEA has failed to provide a proper continuum of services). By contrast, Holland said cost can make a placement inappropriate only when it is "so great that it would significantly impact upon the education of other children in the district" (*Board of Education v. Holland,* 1994, pp. 1398, 1404). The difference between Roncker and Holland may be significant, though it is difficult to determine whether courts favor one or the other test. Under Roncker, the LEA may defend against a more inclusive placement by asserting that making that placement available (meeting the feasibility and portability tests) may "deprive" other students of services to which they are entitled. The effect must be great: deprivation. If the LEA asserts that the child's placement will cause deprivation to other children, then that child's team must show otherwise. Under Roncker, deprivation seems to be the bottom line. Under Holland, however, the bottom line is "significant (adverse) impact" on other children's education; that impact need not rise to the level of "deprivation." Accordingly, it seems that the LEA has a better, more flexible, cost defense under Holland. That result weakens the LRE presumption. Regardless of which standard or test is used, the courts have a lot of leeway in deciding whether a state or local educational agency has fulfilled the LRE mandate of Part B. Compare the language used in Daniel R.R. ("Given the tolerance [of a wide range of educational abilities] embodied in the EHA [now the IDEA], we cannot predicate access to regular education on the child's ability to perform on par with nonhandicapped children" [*Daniel R.R. v. State Board of Education,* 1989]) with the holding in Devries (i.e., that the disparity in cognitive ability with nonhandicapped children is too difficult to bridge [*Devries v. Fairfax County School,* 1989]). Devries determined that a 17-year-old with an IQ score of 74—who actively participated in activities with his peers without disabilities, was accepted by his peers, and successfully held and was promoted in a job—had "no appropriate peer group, academically, socially, or vocationally" (*Devries v. Fairfax County School,* 1989). It is difficult to reconcile these two cases and others like them. The former case seems more LRE-positive; the latter seems to rest on antiquated stereotypes and under-

lying prejudice, not on the evidence that the student was able to perform effectively in inclusive academic and employment settings. If anything, the latter case should be decided differently under the 1997 amendments to IDEA and the 1999 implementing regulations.

It is useful to note a new trend that apparently would not apply the LRE mandate to private placement decisions of parents. In *Cleveland Heights v. Boss* (1998), the Sixth Circuit Court held, on the basis of the Supreme Court decision in *Florence City School District Four v. Carter* (1993), that the failure of the private school placement to satisfy the LRE mandate does not bar reimbursement for private school placement costs when the school district has failed to supply an appropriate education. Parental placement decisions under this rule are seemingly not bound by the LRE mandate.

LRE AND PRESCHOOL PLACEMENT

Having set out Part B's LRE provisions and indicated the variety of their meaning for children ages 6–21 (as interpreted by the federal courts of appeals), it is now appropriate to describe Part B's LRE provisions for children ages 3–5.

Part B Application to Preschool-Age Children

One difference between the two age groups is that by the strict language of the statute, the state is not held to the FAPE requirement for preschool-age children if the FAPE rule would be "inconsistent with state law or practice" (§ 1412[a][1][B][i]). If a state decides not to extend FAPE, then the LRE mandate is not required for preschool placements, because the LRE mandate applies only to "all preschool children with disabilities who are entitled to receive FAPE" (Title 34, C.F.R. §§ 300.550–300.552, March 1999). Although this concern is minimized by the fact that every state currently extends FAPE to ages 3–5, there are other differences in Part B's application to preschool children.

A second difference is that a LEA is usually not required to provide a preschool program for children without disabilities (even in states that extend FAPE to children ages 3–5) and therefore is not required to initiate such programs just to satisfy the LRE mandate (Title 34, C.F.R. §§ 300.550–300.552, March 1999).

Notwithstanding the absence of a general education requirement for infants and toddlers and preschool-age children, the LRE principle is still powerful. For example, in *P.J. v. State of Connecticut Board of Education* (1992), the court said, "In each case the public agency must ensure that each child's placement is in the LRE." The court then relied on a list of examples given in the note to the regulations and listed alternative methods through which a LEA could meet the LRE requirement. These include the following:

1. Providing opportunities for the participation (even part time) of preschool-age children with disabilities in other preschool programs operated by public agencies (such as Head Start)
2. Placing children with disabilities in private school programs for preschool-age children without disabilities or private preschool programs that integrate children with and without disabilities
3. Locating classes for preschool-age children with disabilities in general elementary schools (Title 34, C.F.R. § 300.552, 1992, note 1)

The courts have interpreted these alternatives to require the school district to meet the LRE requirement in the placement of preschool-age children with disabilities (*P.J. v. State of Connecticut Board of Education,* 1992), and some have even implied that the LEA might have to offer placements beyond those that currently exist if required to meet the needs of the child (*Board of Education of Lagrange School District v. Illinois State Board of Education,* 1998). Although this note has been removed from the regulations, the reasons for doing so do not seem to reflect disagreement with the courts' interpretation of the statute's requirements (Title 34, C.F.R. §§ 300.550-300.552, March 1999), nor do any of the changes give any reason to believe that similar interpretation will not be used; courts will merely rely more on the statement of the LRE requirement in regulation Section 300.552 and the legislative history behind the words "including a preschool child with a disability" (Title 34, C.F.R. § 300.552).

In a preschool placement situation in which there is no duty to provide preschool environments for children without disabilities, some courts interpret the duty created by Part B to be need based, with the contents of the preschool-age child's IEP describing the extent to which the LRE is mandated for the child. That was the approach in *T.R. v. Kingwood Township Board of Education* (1998) in which a half-day placement in an inclusive environment, plus an afternoon resource center placement, constituted the LRE because the child did not need an afternoon program. The afternoon program was added to accommodate the parents, who believed their child did need a full-day program.

The lack of duty to provide preschool environments for children without disabilities may also undermine the "associational rights" argument for inclusion (see *Hulme v. Dellmuth,* 1991). It is difficult to argue that children with disabilities have a right to associate with their peers without disabilities in a preschool environment when children without disabilities have no right whatsoever to preschool programs. IDEA grants rights and services that level the playing field between individuals with and without disabilities in an educational environment. It does nothing more, because access to early education, much less the LRE in early education, is not a right for preschool-age children under IDEA.

Analysis of Part B as Applicable to Preschool-Age Children

The consequences of these provisions and court decisions are that the LEA must engage in a decision-making process that can result in an LRE placement as follows:

1. *FAPE or placement for preschool-age children with disabilities:* The first inquiry in any case involving preschool-age children (ages 3–5) with disabilities is whether the school district is required to extend them the benefits of the LRE requirement of Part B. This inquiry has two parts: a) does the state extend FAPE under Part B to preschool-age children (which all states currently do), and b) does the state provide preschool services to children without disabilities? If either part of this test is met, then the state must educate preschool-age children with disabilities in an inclusive environment to the maximum extent possible.

2. *Appropriate placement:* If the LRE mandate does apply, then the school district must provide an appropriate placement. An appropriate placement for a preschool-age child in a district that does not provide preschool for children without disabilities may be limited by the extent to which the child is found to need preschool services. Full-day preschool placement is not required in all situations. If the school district does not currently offer an appropriate program, it must use one of the available

alternative methods for meeting its duty to provide an appropriate environment.

3. *Presumptive placement:* If there is an appropriate placement to which preschool-age children without disabilities are normally sent, then that environment is the presumptive environment for preschool-age children with disabilities. This presumption can be overcome only when the placement is inappropriate for the child, even with supplementary aids and services. Only then does the next LRE become the presumptive environment (and so on down the continuum of placements). Where each environment rests on the continuum of placements is determined by a number of factors, including how far the placement is from the child's home, the amount of interaction with children without disabilities that the placement allows, the extent to which the child is involved in the general curriculum, and the benefits that the placement provides the child. Furthermore, inclusion is measured across the three fields of academics, extracurricular activities, and other nonacademic activities.

PART C: INFANTS AND TODDLERS

Having described Part B as it applies to school-age and preschool-age children, it is now appropriate to describe Part C, for, as noted in this chapter's introduction, Part C is interpreted in part in light of Part B. That "in part" qualifier is important, for the purposes of Part B and Part C differ.

Purpose of Early Childhood Intervention

Part C has four explicit purposes: child development, cost containment/placement avoidance, family capacity building, and institutional prevention. These factor into the inclusion analysis under Part C.

Part C of IDEA, covering children ages birth to 3, was first added to the legislation in 1986 (Education of the Handicapped Amendments of 1986, PL 99-457). Congress recognized that there was "an urgent and substantial need to enhance the development of infants and toddlers with disabilities and to minimize their potential for developmental delay" (§ 1431[a][1]). Congress was undoubtedly swayed by the evidence indicating that greater educational benefits resulted for children with disabilities who received early intervention services than for those who did not; with greater benefits come reduced special education costs. Furthermore, Congress recognized that the capacity of infants and toddlers to succeed in any educational program depends on that child's family (U.S. DOE, 1998). Part C therefore takes a family-systems approach by including the goal of enhancing families' capacity to meet the special needs of their infants and toddlers with disabilities. In Part C, families not only take an active role in the formation of the service plan for their child but are themselves entitled to services to enhance their ability to meet the developmental needs of their infant or toddler (§ 1436[a][2]).

Part C's purposes also encompass inclusion principles. One of the findings in Part C is that there is "an urgent and substantial need to minimize the likelihood of institutionalization of individuals with disabilities and maximize the potential for their independently living in society" (§ 1431[a][3]). This dedication to inclusion is operationalized by NE, and the commitment to independence for individuals with disabilities is achieved through inclusion.

As noted, these four purposes factor into the inclusion analysis under Part C. Child development can ensure that the child avoids special education placement.

Cost reduction is achieved with inclusion, for, on the whole, a single system of services is less expensive to operate than a dual system; family capacity building enables the infant or toddler to stay with the family, in the environment that is most typical for children without disabilities; and prevention of institutionalization is a strategy for inclusion.

Transition from Part C to Part B

When an infant or toddler with disabilities reaches age 3, he or she generally becomes ineligible for services under Part C and becomes eligible for services under Part B. IDEA recognizes, however, that this shift in services can be problematic for both the child with disabilities and his or her family and should, instead, be "seamless" (§ 1412[a][9]). Section 1412(a)(9) therefore requires that "by the third birthday of such child, an individualized education program (IEP) . . .or. . .an individualized family service plan (IFSP) has been developed and is being implemented for the child" (§ 1412[a][9]). The LEA must participate in transition planning conferences (§ 1412[a][9]).

Although Part C generally is inapplicable for any child who is receiving a FAPE under Part B (§ 1419[h]), the IFSP may serve as the IEP for the child when appropriate. Whether at this stage an IEP or IFSP will be used to plan for service delivery is decided by both the parents and the LEA (§ 1414[d][2][B]). Both the agency and the parents must agree to use an IFSP to substitute for an IEP, and the IFSP must still "contain the material described in sec. 1436" and be developed "in accordance with this (1414) section" (§ 1414[d][2][B]).

One difficulty in the substitution of the IFSP for an IEP is that Section 1436 contains references to NEs and Section 1414 refers to participation with children without disabilities (§§ 1414 [a][1][A][II–III], 1436[d][5]). Although the courts have not yet addressed the question of which section prevails when they are in conflict with each other, the statute allows flexibility in service delivery when parents and the LEA agree that an IFSP would better serve the needs of the child. It is therefore logical to assume that the type of plan will dictate the type of requirements. Otherwise, there would be little reason to allow the election of an IFSP plan.

Statutory Requirements of Part C

Part C includes two provisions that directly deal with the issue of inclusive environments. The first requires states to adopt "policies and procedures to ensure that. . .to the maximum extent appropriate, early intervention services are provided in NEs, and occur in a setting other than an NE only when early intervention cannot be achieved satisfactorily for the infant or toddler in an NE" (§ 1435[a][16]). The second requires that included in the infant or toddler's IFSP is a statement concerning the NEs in which early intervention services shall be provided, including a justification of the extent, if any, to which the services will not be provided in an NE (§ 1436[d]).

The only definition of NEs in the statute itself is nested within the definition of early intervention services that states that NEs include the home and community environments in which children without disabilities participate (§ 1432[4][G]). As with services under Part B, "to the maximum extent" must mean, at the least, that when given a choice between providing services in an NE or a non-NE, the NE, all other factors being equal, is the proper placement. "To the maximum extent" also suggests that even if one service (e.g., medical) can be performed only in a non-NE, that fact alone does not remove or lessen the obligation to provide any other needed services in an NE. "To the maximum extent" implies that there are degrees of inclu-

sion, the most inclusive of which is preferred to all less inclusive locations for service delivery. "To the maximum extent" therefore suggests that each service must be evaluated independently for its appropriateness in an NE (Title 34, C.F.R. §§ 303.322[c][3][iii], 303.344 [d][1]). This requirement is especially important because Part C does not include any requirement that a continuum of alternative placements be made available.

As with Part B, any placement of an infant or toddler with disabilities must first be shown to be "appropriate." Where the provision of the service would not be appropriate in an NE, it does not have to be delivered in one (§ 1436[d][5]). IDEA states that "the provision of early intervention services for any infant or toddler should occur in an environment other than a natural environment only when early intervention cannot be achieved satisfactorily for the infant or toddler in a natural environment" (§ 1435[a][16]). Although this is similar to the Part B requirements for removal from the general classroom and general curriculum, there are several differences, the importance of which is not clarified by examination of the statute on its face.

What does early intervention mean in this context? Any delivery of services at all? Services that produce some benefit (like Part B)? Or services that promote maximum developmental progress? And how do we decide when it has been satisfactorily achieved? What is satisfactory? Does "achieved" imply reaching a goal? Does "satisfactorily for the infant" mean that family needs and parental desires should not be considered in determining whether services can be delivered in an NE?

Questions also revolve around the definition of *natural environment*. Are there more and less "natural" environments? How should a choice be made between placements when there is more than one NE in which services could be delivered? Who has the final authority to make such a choice if the IFSP team cannot come to a consensus? The LEA? What if the parents will not accept the decision? The statute alone does not give us the answers to these questions.

It may seem that such intensive scrutiny of the statute's language is unwarranted. Courts, families, and state agencies could simply give the statute the common sense interpretation that any reasonable person might infer. Unfortunately, some of this hair splitting cannot be dealt with so easily, especially by a parent who is questioning the placement choice for his or her infant or toddler.

Where can a parent, provider, or administrative officer look for answers to the complicated questions that arise when applying LRE to the complexities of individual circumstances? A few answers are forthcoming from the courts. It could be argued that Part B and Part C have analogous inclusion provisions and that an intense analysis of Part C is therefore unnecessary. Although it is to a certain extent true that Part B and Part C have similar mandates, to say that the inclusion and benefit questions are the same in each part ignores the real and potential differences in litigating each type of case. Differences in statutory language/mandates, in age groups covered, in age-related needs of each group, and in the purposes of Part C could and probably will produce answers to these questions that lead to very different results for infants and toddlers with disabilities and their families than those reached under Part B.

Part C and the Courts

Very few cases have directly dealt with Part C provisions. None of them has discussed NEs, inclusion, or LRE, but although there may not be any case law for direct precedent on NE issues, one case does demonstrate how courts may deal with Part C provisions and placement issues.

In *Still v. DeBuono* (1996), the placement of the toddler E.M. initially was disputed. The school system (and E.M.'s IFSP team) called for social work in parent–child groups, special instruction in group and individual environments, and speech therapy to be provided for 5 hours per week at the Child Development Center. E.M.'s parents wanted applied behavior analysis treatment in the home and sought it privately. The district subsequently modified E.M.'s IFSP to discontinue services at the Child Development Center and to provide for individual speech-language therapy at Lenox Hill Hospital. The parents again refused and brought suit against the school district to compensate them for the private in-home applied behavior analysis treatments. Initially, the issues included whether the school district had provided an appropriate placement and appropriate services for E.M. The school district eventually admitted that it had failed to provide an adequate IFSP and based its opposition to the parents' claim mainly on the fact that the applied behavior analysis in-home services were provided in part by unlicensed student aids (although under the direction of a licensed provider).

One important feature of the court's analysis deals with its omission of LRE. If this had been a Part B case, an LRE issue would have surfaced alongside a discussion of the appropriateness or inappropriateness of each placement. That the LRE issue is not even mentioned in this case may suggest a practical difference between Part B and Part C unevidenced in the statute: that courts, families, and school districts are not or have not been placing the same kind of importance on the NE requirement of Part C that they have historically placed on the LRE mandate of Part B.

The second important feature is the reliance on case law construing analogous provisions of Part B to guide its approach to Part H (now Part C). The court cites two Supreme Court cases, *Burlington School Comm. v. Department of Education* (1985) and *Florence City School District Four v. Carter* (1993), to the effect that the provisions of Part B in those cases are strikingly similar in both their basic structure and purpose to those of Part H (now Part C). This suggests that a court will consider precedent in interpreting the provisions of other parts of IDEA if they are sufficiently analogous to the provisions in Part C. This approach accesses a much greater volume of judicial authority from which to predict future judicial treatment of Part C issues, limited only by the extent to which those precedents are not transferable because of Part C structure and purpose.

Agency Regulations and Regulatory History

Having determined that Part C and judicial interpretation provide little guidance concerning the NEs provisions, it is now appropriate to consider whether the regulations and their history fill the void. To a degree, they do, but probably not sufficiently.

The regulations of April 1999 have a few provisions that are relevant to NEs. *Natural environments* are defined as "settings that are natural or normal for the child's age peers who have no disabilities" (Title 34, C.F.R. § 303.18). This definition requires NEs to be evaluated by comparison with environments that are typical for children without disabilities. It requires that this comparison be based on an equivalent number of years since birth (preventing a nonnatural placement from being justified by evaluations that say things such as "operating at a 1-year-old level").

Even more significant than what the regulations say concerning NEs is what the Office of Special Education Programs (OSEP) has declined to say and its expla-

nation for doing so. When it submitted the proposed Part C regulations in 1997 (Comments to Proposed Rules for the Early Intervention Program for Infants and Toddlers with Disabilities, 1997), OSEP invited comments. One commentator suggested that proposed Section 303.322 (the regulation on evaluation and assessment) incorporate the new requirement relating to NEs (U.S. DOE, 1993, 58 Federal Register 40958, 40986). The Secretary declined to adopt the suggestion, saying, "Like all other aspects of services to a particular child, the setting for service delivery must be determined through the IFSP process." The Secretary was clarifying the difference between the evaluation process and the IFSP process (U.S. DOE, 1993, 58 Federal Register 40958, 40986). It is not in the evaluation stage that the environment for intervention services should be determined. That is a purpose of the IFSP (U.S. DOE, 1993, 58 Federal Register 40958, 40986).

Another commentator asked the DOE to clarify the flexibility afforded to service providers in determining which environments are "natural" for children with disabilities and to provide a detailed list of examples or other means to clarify when a child should be served in an NE (U.S. DOE, 1993, 58 Federal Register 40982). Another commentator requested that the DOE provide flexibility to states in determining which environments are NEs (U.S. DOE, 1993, 58 Federal Register 40982). Some commentators expressed concern that the families' needs and wishes not be ignored in determining the location of service delivery (U.S. DOE, 1993, 58 Federal Register 4098). Yet another requested that the DOE provide parents with the option of choosing the environment in which their children receive services (U.S. DOE, 1993, 58 Federal Register 40982). Answering the questions together, the Secretary declined to adopt any of the recommendations, saying,

No further guidance is appropriate at this time. Decisions on the early intervention services to be provided to a child and his or her family, including decisions on the location of service delivery, are made in the development of the IFSP. . . . The Secretary contemplates that the range of available options will be reviewed at the IFSP meeting. . .in which the parents of the child are full participants. (U.S. DOE, 1993, 58 Federal Register 40983)

By refusing to address these questions and referencing the IFSP process, the Secretary reinforces the agency's commitment to several policies of early intervention services. One is that neither the family nor the state is intended to make placement decisions on its own. The IFSP process incorporates the judgments of both the family and the representatives of the local education authority. Together with other members of the IFSP team, they must come to a decision concerning the appropriate environment for delivery of services. The Secretary seems confident that these questions, especially about when NEs should be used and about family needs and wishes, are sufficiently answered in the statute to allow the IFSP team to address these questions on an individualized basis for each child. It is the policy for individualized education that the Secretary is trying to protect by silence. Instead of providing flexibility to the states or families in determining the proper environment for service delivery, the Secretary advocates flexibility to the IFSP team as a whole and refuses to fence in or place restrictions on its decision-making ability.

The consequence of the Secretary's approach is to place the definition of NEs and the criteria for deciding which of several possible placements meets the NE standard in the hands of a team. By deferring to process, the Secretary denigrates substance. Unlike Part B, which is replete with substantive standards, OSEP's approach to Part C seems almost entirely process based, with results that predictably may be less favorable to the NE than would be obtained for the same child at an older age under Part B.

Agency Reports and Professional Standards

The 1997 report to Congress from the DOE on IDEA provides additional information on what Congress intended to achieve through early intervention. The report cites a review of the professional literature on early intervention by Bailey and Wolery (1992) which suggests seven specific goals of early intervention. (U.S. DOE, 1998, pp. i-xxxiv, I-1 to IV-16, A-1 to A-265; IV-5 [1998]). These goals are to

(1) support families in achieving the goals they have for themselves and their children, (2) promote children's active engagement, independence, and mastery of the environment, (3) promote progress in key developmental domains, (4) build and support children's social competence, (5) promote the generalized use of skills in a variety of relevant settings, (6) provide and prepare children for normalized life experiences, and (7) prevent the emergence of future problems or disabilities. (U.S. DOE, 1998, pp. i-xxxiv, I-1 to IV-16, A-1 to A-265; IV-5 [1998])

These goals are more specific and detailed than the purposes outlined in Part C. The purposes outlined in Part C are the aims of the statute as a whole, but these goals are criteria for judging when early intervention is successful.

The significance of OSEP's approval —and, perhaps, adoption—of the Bailey-Wolery criteria becomes clear if one examines the natural environment provisions. Part C authorizes early intervention services to be delivered in nonnatural environments only when early intervention cannot be successfully achieved in a natural environment (§ 1435[a][16][B]) The Bailey-Wolery goals help define what the DOE considers to be successful early intervention. Which of these goals applies to any individual service would be determined by the IFSP. It is obviously not intended that all of these goals be addressed by each service provided, but that the IFSP provide for services to address all of these goals.

Analogy of Part C to Part B

The chapter authors have argued that Part B and Part C should be read together to determine what Part C means by NEs because the core provisions of IDEA are in Part B, because Part C lacks specificity, and because the courts may interpret Part C on the basis of how they interpret Part B. It is therefore timely to read Part B and Part C side by side and determine the analogous provisions of each.

Threshold Question for Analogy The Still court (*Still v. DeBuono,* 1996) is the only one to address the question of whether interpretations of Part B can generally be applied to early intervention provisions and requirements. In Still, the court found that the Part B section in question was strikingly similar to the analogous early intervention section in both its basic structure and its purpose, despite also observing that the provisions were distinct in notable respects. The Still case suggests that in many instances Part B and Part C provisions will correlate sufficiently to rely on rulings from Part B to support arguments in Part C (*Still v. DeBuono,* 1996, p. 888). The test is whether the provisions in Part C are strikingly similar in purpose and structure so that the principles involved in Part B fit well within the context of Part C. If so, the analogy should hold considerable weight.

The LRE and NE requirements are sufficiently analogous to apply a case law analogy from Part B to Part C, in most instances. Both mandate the inclusion of the child, to the maximum extent appropriate, in a typical environment. Both define a typical environment as one that is typical for a child without disabilities of the same age (*Still v. DeBuono,* 1996). The difference between the two provisions lies mainly in which environ-

ments are "typical" for the age groups that each part serves. Part C includes the home in the typical environment because, for an infant or a toddler without disabilities, the home is a usual or typical environment for that child's activities and education (§ 1432[1]). Part B, in contrast, serves children who are presumptively at an age at which school or preschool is the usual or typical environment for them to learn and receive services (§ 1412[a][1]).

Comparison of Part B and Part C Language The "removal" language of Part B presumes that the child begins in a typical environment and requires the LEA to justify any attempt to take the child out of that placement. Leaving this language out of Part C is not suggestive of a lack of a presumption in favor of an NE in Part C, because it would be pointless to talk of removal when an infant or toddler is not usually placed in any educational environment until services under IDEA begin. Thus, the "removal" language merely reflects a difference created by the age of children to whom services are being provided. Part C still mandates that an infant's or a toddler's IFSP include a "justification of the extent, if any, to which the services will not be provided in a natural environment" (§ 1436[d][5]).

"Only when the nature and severity of the disabilities is such that education in regular classes. . .cannot be achieved satisfactorily" in the Part B LRE requirement defines when an inclusive environment is not the "appropriate" environment for a child with disabilities (§ 1412[a][5][A]). The only acceptable justification under the statute for the IEP team's placing a child in a noninclusive environment is that the nature and severity of the disability makes the more inclusive placement inappropriate (Title 34, C.F.R. §§ 300.553–300.306). Note that other family and individual strengths and needs may—and in some areas must— still be considered in other parts of IEP development; they just may not be used to justify a failure to integrate.

In Part C, the inclusion language is less specific. Section 1435(a)(16)(B) states that "the provision of early intervention services. . .occurs in a setting other than a natural environment only when early intervention cannot be satisfactorily achieved for the infant or toddler in a natural environment" (§ 1435[a][16][B]). It does not put any restriction on the weighing of the infant's or toddler's needs and strengths that are unrelated to disability. In other words, it could be argued under Part C that if a child's strengths are better used in a segregated environment than they can be in an inclusive environment, then early intervention cannot be "satisfactorily achieved" in the inclusive environment, which can therefore be claimed to be inappropriate.

As the previous example demonstrates, the determination of what is "satisfactorily achieved" is left up to the discretion of the IFSP team to a greater extent than it is under Part B. If an IFSP team determines that a program that is not inclusive is sufficiently more beneficial to the infant or toddler's development, then the team could attempt to justify that placement as within the language of Part C merely by arguing that some benefits (though arguably unrelated to the child's disability) cannot be satisfactorily achieved in the inclusive environment. The weakness in this argument lies in the analogy to Part B. If the courts determine that "satisfactorily achieved" has equivalent meanings in Part B and Part C, then the considerations that lead to a determination of whether early intervention can be satisfactorily achieved would also have to be equivalent.

Another difference between Part C and Part B is that Part C does not parallel Part B in applying the inclusion mandate to the three domains of academics,

extracurricular, and other activities (§ 1414[d][1][A][iii]). Nevertheless, it provides for the same broad inclusion mandate in somewhat simpler terms. Part B's LRE requirement says that children with disabilities must be educated to the maximum extent appropriate for children without disabilities, therefore requiring a regulation that clarifies that the presumption in favor of inclusion applies to all school activities. Part C simply requires that services be provided in NEs to the maximum extent appropriate (§ 1435[a][16]).

Under Part B, then, the child has a claim to take part in any general education activities at his or her school. By contrast, Part C services are provided only on the basis of need: Only the services and activities that have some connection with the infant's or toddler's IFSP plan and that meet his or her developmental needs must be provided. Of course, if the IFSP team decides that an infant's or toddler's appropriate placement includes full or partial placement in an inclusive group environment, then the inclusive presumption (as in Part B, three domains) arguably covers any and all activities provided by that environment for children without disabilities. These activities, such as lunch or an outing, are usually part and parcel of a program and not divisible from the educational portion of the placement.

Applying the Holland Case to Part C   By analogy, the Holland case can be used (through the methods outlined in Still) to interpret the NE requirements in Part C. To form the analogy, one must ask how each of the four factors of the Holland test could be applied to early intervention under Part C and its requirement for service delivery in both group and home environments. For analogy to Part C, it is useful to think of the Holland case as if the court had substituted "natural environments" for "general classroom."

The first factor was the academic benefit of the general classroom compared with the special education classroom (*Board of Education v. Holland,* 1994). For infants and toddlers, the line between academic and nonacademic benefit is elusive at best. The simplest way to draw the line is between benefits that flow directly from services and those that are inherently conferred by the very nature of the environment. Therefore, for academic benefit to be "successfully achieved," the services provided must be able to confer some benefit in the chosen environment. Maximum benefit is not necessary under Part B and should not be necessary under Part C. Benefits are inherently conferred by the very nature of the environment (inclusive setting in Part B, NE in Part C). The maximum academic benefit potential of an environment under Part B is secondary in importance to the maximum inclusion policy (*Board of Education v. Holland,* 1994, pp. 1398, 1402).

The court in Holland made these statements "in light of the recognition of the nonacademic value of such integration" (*Board of Education v. Holland,* 1994, pp. 1398, 1402). For Holland to apply, a court might require that similar nonacademic value be demonstrated in a Part C program. The difficulty of this showing would depend on factors such as the age of the child and the nature or extent of his or her disability and is also affected by the type of NE at issue.

NEs, unlike inclusive school environments, include the home (§ 1432[4][G]). Because a home often is not integrated, the application of Holland to other cases questioning Part C mandates will not always be possible from the perspective of such nonacademic values as modeling peers without disabilities. Other nonacademic values might be conferred by a home environment, such as learning to function in the infant's or toddler's primary environment. In any case, some

nonacademic values may need to be demonstrated. When group environments are used, this difficulty almost vanishes, considering that most services delivered in group environments for infants and toddlers attempt to benefit the infant or toddler in what could be classified as nonacademic ways.

Holland's second factor (nonacademic benefit) would easily be adapted to group environment use, but as the factor was stated by the court, it would have limited use in situations in which the NE is the home. By rephrasing the question in more general terms, it becomes easier to see how a court might apply this part of the test in such situations. An integrated environment provides benefits by allowing the children with disabilities to interact with children without disabilities. That is its nature. To apply this to the home environment, a similar question should be asked. Specifically, what nonacademic benefits does the home environment provide that are absent in other non-NEs? Family capacity building, stigma reduction, and environmental familiarity are only a few of the nonacademic benefits of service delivery in a home environment that might be argued.

As with the other factors of the Holland test, the "effect on others" factor's application to Part C delivery of services differs greatly between group environments and the home environment. For group environments, this factor is largely unchanged; the age of the children or that the group environment is called an NE instead of the LRE makes no difference in this kind of analysis. For a home environment, this inquiry may not apply at all. If there are no other "students," then there is no reason to weigh any potential harm. The only other people generally present in the home environment are family members. By analogy, disadvantages to the family caused by service delivery in the home could be factored in under this step of the Holland test, but because the family is not entitled to FAPE and is presumably not even in pursuit of an education within the home, this factor is generally inapplicable.

The final factor is cost (*Board of Education v. Holland,* 1994). For group environments under the NE requirement of Part C, this factor is just as applicable (maybe more so, given the cost containment purpose of Part C) and can be applied relatively unchanged. The same can be said for delivery in a home environment. A home environment may have different cost considerations than a group or inclusive classroom environment, but the threshold question remains the same.

Generally speaking, an analogy between Holland and the Part C NE requirement is easily accomplished when the environments at issue are group environments. When the placement and delivery of services are in the home, the Holland test seems less analogous. The main purpose of inclusion, as noted in the Holland case, is to provide benefits to children with disabilities through interaction with their peers without disabilities. For placement in a home environment, this purpose seems inapposite. The home is a completely noninclusive environment. The need to prevent stigma and to harvest the benefits of greater family involvement, in an atmosphere that might well make an infant or toddler more receptive to services, must be the basis on which any analogy between LRE and home placement rests.

Findings and Analysis: General Framework Formed

The framework for the applying of the LRE mandate to children with disabilities ages 3–5 can be much more easily compared with the placement of school-age children than can the NE mandate of Part C. It is therefore useful to analyze the legal requirements and assess the values and outcomes involved in applying the NE mandate in the two situations in which it arises: for children with disabilities ages birth–3 and for children with disabilities ages 3–5 whose parents agree, along with the agency, to have their child served under an IFSP instead of an IEP.

Appropriate: The Threshold "Benefit" or "Successful Achievement" Question   Before any environment can be considered for delivery of services, it must be appropriate in that delivery of the services in that environment will benefit the infant or toddler. This is true for both natural and nonnatural environments (*Board of Education v. Holland,* 1994). Although there is no mandate for benefit to be maximized, consideration of the level of benefit that a service provides in a particular environment, given the purposes and findings of Part C, should be evaluated (§ 1431). In determining whether the level and scope of benefits received are sufficient to reach the "successful achievement" threshold, the Bailey-Wolery goals of early intervention should be examined.

The Still test would probably allow some reliance on Part B case law, as the statutes are similar in both purpose and structure with consideration to the question of the benefit. In *Board of Education v. Rowley* (1982), the Supreme Court held that any program must yield some benefit but not maximized benefit. How much benefit is required? The method and environment determined by the school district generally are given deference as long as there is some benefit and the environment does not conflict with the LRE mandate.

Presumptive Placement   The "successfully achieved" question is only one of the factors that is used to determine the proper environment for service delivery to an infant or toddler with disabilities. The IFSP team must also factor in the presumption for natural environments, what natural environments are available, and the needs of the infant or toddler.

Natural Environments versus Other Environments   An NE is the environment that would be natural or typical for a child without disabilities of the same age in the same location (Title 34, C.F.R. § 303.18). When two or more environments produce a similar level of benefit to the child, an NE must be chosen for delivery over a non-NE (§ 1435[a][16]). If the Holland test can be applied to Part C, then there is a rebuttable presumption for placement in an NE and the reasons justifying the rebuttal must be explained in the IFSP before nonnatural placement may occur (*Board of Education v. Holland,* 1994). In making the determination, the four factors of Holland may be considered: 1) educational benefits, 2) nonacademic benefits, 3) effect on others, and 4) costs. Educational benefits under Part B correlate with skill development under Part C, and nonacademic benefits under Part B correspond with social and family capacity development under Part C. Effect on others in the home environment might include other siblings and family members. The cost analysis should include an examination of the costs to the parents as well as the costs to the school district.

Home versus Inclusive Group Environment   When there are several NEs that would be "appropriate" for delivery of services, the home environment is the first to be considered for delivery of services. It is the primary NE for an infant or toddler (102nd Congress, 1991). However, there is nothing to indicate that the preference for the home rises to the level of a rebuttable presumption. Given the emphasis on prevention of future developmental delay and future costs associated with special education, this preference for the home is only one factor to be considered in the IFSP meeting when determining which of several

optional and appropriate NEs is the most appropriate for delivery of any particular service (U.S. DOE, 1993, 58 Federal Register 40958, 40974). Arguably more important are the seven goals of early intervention and whether the needs of the child suggest that significant additional benefit would result from service delivery in a group environment.

Maximum Extent   The state's mandate to maximize service provision within natural environments includes two components. First, each service provided must be examined individually for its potential for being delivered in an NE. Second, the more natural or inclusive environments should be given preference over less natural or inclusive environments.

Mix and Match Services   Even if some services cannot be effectively delivered in an NE, other intervention services must still be delivered in NEs to the extent appropriate, given the previously mentioned factors (102nd Congress, 1991). Although infants and toddlers sometimes require extensive medical intervention, in which case the appropriate environment for most services probably will be a hospital or a rehabilitation environment, any intervention services that can appropriately be delivered in an NE, given the extent of the child's medical condition, must be delivered in that environment (102nd Congress, 1991). Accordingly, school districts and IFSP teams will often have to mix and match service environments—hospital, rehabilitation center, home, and so forth—to meet the "maximum extent" mandate for delivery of effective individualized services.

Partial versus Full Inclusion   Mixing and matching of services is also an issue when the choice is between home and group environments. Each service should be determined individually, with weight also being given to the IFSP plan as a whole. Where some group interaction would produce a desired benefit, the child should be served in a group environment in part, even if all other services are best provided in the home, as noted in a 1994 OSEP letter to Zimenoff. Furthermore, the level of participation within any particular group environment should be considered when measuring the level of inclusion. By analogy to Part B, group environments that approach total inclusion should have preference over those that provide partial inclusion, and those that provide partial inclusion should be preferred to noninclusive environments (*Board of Education v. Holland,* 1994). An example of a partially inclusive environment for Part C service delivery is a child care program that serves children with disabilities for some activities separately from children without disabilities but also includes activities in which the two groups are integrated.

IFSP: The Forum Where the Decisions Are Made   Which environments are "natural," when a child should be served in an NE, and which NE will best serve the child all are determinations that the IFSP team must make (U.S. DOE, 1998, 64 Federal Register 18290)? Neither the state nor the parents may unilaterally determine the location for delivery of services (U.S. DOE, 1998, 64 Federal Register 18290). Family needs and wants must be considered in delivery of services to both them and their infant or toddler as well as the goals of early intervention (U.S. DOE, 1998). The statute and regulations are designed to provide flexibility and individualized programming for the infant or toddler with disabilities and flexibility to the IFSP team in making the determination of the proper location for service delivery (U.S. DOE, 1998, 64 Federal Register 18290). Some, none, or all of the factors in the Holland case might be applicable to such decision making. If the IFSP team determines a nonnatural location for service delivery to be appropriate, then it must justify that placement in the IFSP plan (§§ 1436[d][5]).

Value Basis, Outcomes, and Purposes

The chapter authors have parsed the language of Part B and Part C and that of their respective regulations, have examined the case law and its potential transference from Part B to Part C, and have analyzed Part B and Part C to determine their analogy to each other. What else remains to be done? Simply, one must analyze Part B and Part C with respect to their values, proposed outcomes, and purposes. That analysis may shed light on the meaning of NEs. The "interest analysis" technique is applied here.

For the Child   Although Part C is a family-focused statute, the child is still intended to be the primary beneficiary of services. This intended benefit takes priority even over the NE mandate. Likewise, the NE requirement takes priority over the wants and needs of the family.

Minimize Developmental Delay and Institutionalization, Maximize Independence   The primary purpose of early intervention for an infant or a toddler with disabilities is, simply put, benefit (§ 1431[a][1]). Benefit covers a broad spectrum of specific goals and general purposes of early intervention. The purposes of the IDEA generally are to prepare and enable individuals with disabilities to lead "productive and independent adult lives" (§ 1400[c][5][E][ii]). Part C expands on these provisions with specific policies to develop the capacity of infants and toddlers, minimize their potential for developmental delay, and minimize the likelihood that they will be institutionalized (§ 1431[a][3]).

Finally, there are the seven goals inherent in early intervention itself (outlined in Bailey & Wolery's 1992 review of the professional literature), which include providing and preparing children for normalized life experiences, promoting progress in key developmental domains, and preventing the emergence of future problems or disabilities (U.S. DOE, 1998, pp. i-xxxiv, I-1 to IV-16, A-1 to A-265; IV-5). These goals can be condensed and restated: 1) meeting infants' or toddlers' immediate needs and promoting progress and independence in their immediate environments, 2) reducing the effects of and forestalling further development of disabilities, thereby reducing the need for special education services, and 3) promoting independence and productivity.

Appropriate over Inclusion, Benefit over Inclusion   Part B deals with a school-age child who will need additional or supplementary services to achieve eventual independence as an adult (§§ 1401[29], [30]). The early intervention program envisions an infant or toddler in his or her earliest stages of development to whom services can be granted to reduce his or her developmental delay and need for special education services when he or she reaches school age (§ 1431; 102nd Congress, 1991). The early intervention program is a preemptive strike against developmental delay. Although it shares the ultimate goal of promoting eventual independence and productivity when the children with disabilities become adults, it is even more ambitious: It proposes that the needs of children with disabilities, upon reaching the age in which Part B services begin, may be reduced (§ 1431[a][2]).

The goals of the Part C NE mandate also differ from the goals of the Part B LRE mandate. Part B's requirement is focused on inclusion of the child with disabilities in environments with children without disabilities (§ 1412[a][5][A]), yet one of the NEs under Part C is the home, generally speaking a noninclusive environment (§ 1432[4][G]). Indeed, for most infants and toddlers without disabilities, the main environment for human development is the home, and the home is often the best place for building the

capacity of families, a goal that Part B does not attempt to encompass. The benefits of family capacity building and normalization of the child's environment are given at least equal footing with the benefits of interaction with children without disabilities under Part C. This suggests a change in the reasoning behind the inclusion mandate in Part C from that of Part B. In Part B, inclusion is considered a right in and of itself, a right of association (§§ 1400[c][1]; *Hulme v. Dellmuth,* 1991). In Part C, inclusion is qualified to be, at best, a right of normalization (having services provided in the environment where children without disabilities are typically or generally placed).

Child over Family Possibility   In the proposed rules for early intervention services in 1992, the DOE noted that

> The statute adds a requirement that early intervention services, to the maximum extent appropriate, be provided in natural environments. . . . This requirement will be implemented. . .with the clarification that services must be provided in natural environments to the maximum extent appropriate to the needs of the child. (DOE, 1991, 57 Federal Register 18986, 19002; Title 34, C.F.R. § 303.12[b])

This rule was indeed adopted, and later the statute itself was amended to say, "achieved satisfactorily for the infant or toddler" (§ 1435[a][16][B]). It seems that Congress intends that the IFSP team should inquire into whether an NE is appropriate for service delivery. This inquiry may be read as limited to the needs of the child and excluding the needs and wants of the family and school district. It is difficult to comprehend why the Congress made this one exception to the consideration of family needs in early intervention service delivery; it seems conspicuously out of place in a program that mandates family-directed evaluation and services (Title 34, C.F.R. §§ 303.12[b], 1435[a][3]). It is this very conspicuousness, though, that makes the intention of the Congress seem so clear. In the end, it is the needs of the infant or toddler with disabilities that must govern any determination of the location of service delivery in an NE (Title 34, C.F.R. § 303.12[b]).

For the Family Part C, unlike Part B, recognizes that children live with families and that children with disabilities can be assisted most effectively and efficiently by increasing the ability of their families to meet their needs. Therefore, Part C includes provisions that address family capacity, collaboration with professionals, and family needs and wants.

Family Capacity and Collaboration Mandate Part C is committed to developing the parent–professional partnership (U.S. DOE, 1998). In developing the IFSP, professionals must collaborate with families (§ 1436[a][3]). OSEP recognizes the importance of families and their role in the development of an infant or toddler with a disability and has been taking steps to promote an increase in the participation of families served through IDEA (U.S. DOE, 1998). OSEP has proposed that the following four steps be used to strengthen the working relationship among families, professionals, and administrators: 1) increase involvement of families in decision making, 2) improve information available to families, 3) link families to other resources and supports in the community, and 4) reduce the adversarial nature of dispute resolution by encouraging mediation (U.S. DOE, 1998).

During the transition of an infant or a toddler into a Part B program, good collaboration is particularly important (U.S. DOE, 1998). During this transition, the relationship between parents and professionals may change. For most families, the location for delivery of services will change from the home to a school environment. The goals and objectives of Part B services also become more child cen-

tered and less family oriented (U.S. DOE, 1998). This may also be the first time the child is included in environments with children without disabilities. The regulations stress the importance of parent participation during these transition periods (Title 34, C.F.R. § 303.148).

Family-Directed Services Argument Against Child over Family In 1986, Part H (now Part C) required that a family-centered approach be used in serving eligible children from birth to age 3 (U.S. DOE, 1998). This approach recognizes that professionals now understand that beyond issues related directly to the child are family issues that must be addressed if the child is to be effectively served by the early intervention program. To understand better the impact of a disability on the child, at the time and in the future, one must understand the environment in which the child lives and develops (U.S. DOE, 1998). This focus is evidenced in Part C by the importance given to families at the IFSP meeting. Part C requires that families have a significant part in the development of the IFSP, that the IFSP team consider the entire family when deciding on services, and that the IFSP team decide on services that increase the capacity of families to meet the special needs of their infants and toddlers with disabilities (§ 1436[a]).

The emphasis on assisting families to meet the needs of their children with disabilities is also evidenced in Part C by the strength of the parental consent requirement. In Part C, if a parent does not consent with respect to a service described in the IFSP, then that service (but not other services in the plan) cannot be provided. Other proffered services, consented to by the parents, must still be provided (§ 1436[e]). Unlike Part B, which provides that parental consent can be overruled in a due process hearing, Part C provides that parents have the absolute right to accept or refuse any service in the IFSP (§ 1436[e]).

The home is the primary NE for infants and toddlers with disabilities (102nd Congress, 1991). This emphasis on providing services in the home environment reflects the importance of families in providing and receiving services under the IFSP. As with inclusion in a group environment, the home environment provides to the child and the family benefits that are more difficult to achieve in other environments. Family security and feelings of control over the services being provided to the infant or toddler are fostered by providing services in the home environment. The child may well be more receptive to services in the home environment. The danger of stigma can be reduced by increasing the functional capacity of the child and the child's family in a supportive home environment. At home, stigma or feelings of difference will not erode the child's feelings of self-worth, and a solid family support structure can be built.

Cost and the Family's Needs and Wants Part B of IDEA prevents LEAs or SEAs from requiring the parents to pay or use private insurance, if it would result in any financial expense for the family, to pay any services related to providing a child with disabilities an education (§ 1401[8]). Part C's mandate is not as strong. It provides that early intervention services be provided at no cost except where federal or state law provides for a system of payments by families, including a schedule of sliding fees (§ 1432[4][B]). Under Part C, states have the option of shifting some of the cost for services to parents. This cost shift cannot be decided by a school district but must come from a mandate of the state legislature (§ 1432[4][B]). In addition, the regulations provide that no fees may be charged to parents for 1) implementing the child-find requirements, 2) evaluation and assessment, 3) service coordination, 4) administrative and coordinative activities relating to development, review, and evaluation of IFSPs, and 5) ad-

ministrative and coordinative activities relating to implementation of procedural safeguards (Title 34, C.F.R. § 303.521[b]).

Nevertheless, cost shifting for the expense of delivery of services is allowable, although the regulations also provide that in states that require a FAPE to be provided to children from birth, any service that the state requires to be provided must be provided at no cost to the parent (Title 34, C.F.R. § 303.521[c]). These provisions place the power to decide who pays how much for services entirely in the hands of each state legislature, with one significant exception: Services will not be denied or withheld solely because the family cannot afford the service (Title 34, C.F.R. § 303.520 [b][3][ii]). To financially burden the family is deemed discretionary for the states, but refusal of service for indigence is not.

Under Holland, cost is a factor in determining the location for delivery of Part B services. In Holland, the cost was examined solely from the point of view of the school district. Because Part B services must be provided at no cost to the parents, there is no need to consider cost with relation to its effect on the family.

In Part C, by contrast, cost to the family could be a significant factor in parental support for IFSP decisions on location for delivery of services. Home and group environments will create different cost concerns for families, as will natural and nonnatural environments. These cost concerns could directly affect whether a service location will meet the goals and purposes of the early education program. If a location for service delivery would be financially difficult for a family, then the financial burden on the family's capacity to meet the needs of their child with a disability must be addressed. Otherwise, the overall purpose for which the early intervention program was created may be impeded.

Several problems arise if cost to the family is not considered in determining the appropriate location for service delivery. First, families that would be heavily burdened by the cost for a particular service may refuse a much-needed service altogether. Second, parents may be forced to accept, in lieu of no services at all, services that place a financial burden on the family. Third, parents who have difficulty meeting the burden of some services at the optimum location for delivery may dishonestly report observations about their child's development and disability to receive services in a manner that the family can afford. This undermines the IFSP process and contravenes the cooperative and coordinated approach to individualized family assessment and service delivery. So, although the IFSP NE requirement uses the words "for the infant or toddler," it must be remembered that the ability of the infant or toddler to benefit from services often depends on the financial needs and concerns of the family. The IFSP team, if it is to fulfill the purpose of early intervention, must consider the indirect effects of the location of service delivery as related to the financial concerns of the parents and family.

For the System   The system itself is also a stakeholder in the provision of IDEA, as are the taxpayers whose money supports the system. For the system, services must be effective and efficient to justify the amount and use of funds. Therefore, Part C addresses the capacity of the service system, provides measures for accountability, and allows states to put some of the cost burden directly on families.

Infrastructure and Policies   Part C seeks not only to build family capacity but also to increase the capacity of states and LEAs to locate, evaluate, and deliver services to infants and toddlers with disabilities (§ 1435). Part C requires states to designate a lead agency, form an interagency

coordinating council to advise the lead agency, and ensure that early intervention funds are being properly used (§§ 1435[a][10], 1437[a], 1441[a]). These policies and infrastructure requirements are designed to allow flexibility to the states in developing their version of the early intervention program while retaining some minimum standards to ensure that each program meets the goals of early intervention. The state's interest in individualizing its program to maximize the effectiveness of state resources and programs is therefore not compromised by the federal government's interest in tracking the use of federal funds and effectiveness of the provisions of IDEA.

Identification, Public Awareness, and Underrepresented Groups   Each state must also find and identify all of the infants and toddlers who are now or will be within the state and need early intervention services (§ 1435[a][5]). This requirement focuses on three goals: 1) identify infants and toddlers currently needing services in the state and procedures for identifying future infants and toddlers who might be in need of early intervention services, 2) increase public awareness so that parents of infants and toddlers will know that early intervention services are available if their child needs them, and 3) give special attention to the infants and toddlers born to underrepresented groups so that they will not be overlooked (Title 34, C.F.R. §§ 303.164, 303.165, 303.20, 303.321).

Quality of Services and Quality of Outcomes   The state also has great motivation to increase the quality of services and outcomes that result from early intervention services. The quality of early intervention services may have a direct effect on the quantity of disability-related services that are needed as the child grows. Moreover, the state may desire to continue to receive federal funds to help it serve its citizens with disabilities and their families. IDEA is not an unsupervised program; the state must justify its expenditures and show some positive results in order to continue to enjoy federal aid (§ 1437[b]). Although it may be unlikely that a state would be refused funding altogether, it is possible that the federal oversight and correction standards procedures would become significantly more stringent if a state does not demonstrate a minimal level of quality of outcome.

Cost   One of the most serious differences between Part B and Part C provisions concerns the cost of services (U.S. DOE, 1999, 64 Federal Register 12406, 12536). Part B is a no-cost-to-parents law, but this rule does not apply to Part C services (U.S. DOE, 1999, 64 Federal Register 12406, 12536).

Under Part C, parents may be required to pay fees for services (§ 1432 [4][B]). Indeed, the DOE amended a proposed regulation (§ 303.520[d]) that would have prohibited states from requiring the use of private insurance for services that qualify (U.S. DOE, 1999, 64 Federal Register 12406, 12536). Part B already contains such a provision (Title 34, C.F.R. § 300.142). This decision reflects a federal concern regarding whether states, with the current level of federal assistance, can meet the costs that would be required under such a policy (U.S. DOE, 1999, 64 Federal Register 12406, 12536). Although early intervention may promise reduced expenditures for special education in the future, states still have a strong interest in the present cost of services. Without adequate funding, none of the IDEA programs (Parts A–D as initiated by states) can be successful. States also do not want to impose tax increases to meet IDEA costs. Some states have even argued that they would have to withdraw from the early intervention program altogether if they were forced to shoulder the entire burden of funding its

services (U.S. DOE, 1999, 64 Federal Register 12406, 12536).

AGENDA FOR CHANGE: RECONCILING OUTCOMES, PERSPECTIVES, AND PLACEMENT PRESUMPTIONS

This chapter has thus far traced the general federal policy in favor of inclusion, described the LRE provisions of Part B and their interpretation by the courts, and applied both Part B and Part C to the NE provisions. In all of this, there are differences and, indeed, discrepancies that can be justified by the values, desired outcomes, and purposes of Part B and Part C (compared and contrasted with each other) and by the interests of the stakeholders. Here the chapter authors reconcile the sometimes competing interests of the stakeholders, and the chapter concludes by arguing that Part C's NE mandate, although not supporting inclusion as powerful as Part B's, is strong enough to accommodate the various interests and to provide a foundation for the child to profit from Part B's LRE requirements.

Outcomes that Are Compatible and Mutually Supportive across Child, Family, and System

Part C of the IDEA does not directly attempt to reconcile the needs, capacities, and perspectives of the infant or toddler, the family, and the system. Instead, it tries to provide a forum in which all competing interests can be made congruent. This forum is, of course, the IFSP meeting (§ 1436). Given that benefiting children with disabilities is the ultimate purpose of early intervention (a family systems focus recognizes that helping the family and helping the child are intimately interrelated), the outcome goals for the child with disabilities, the family, and the system must be considered in the choice of the location for service delivery.

Presumption of Placement: Group Environments

There are basically two general categories in which services may be provided: group environments and home environments. Each has its own value and individual effect on outcomes for the child, the family, and the system. Group environments particularly support traditional concepts of inclusion.

Values   Group environments have a host of values. Interaction and association with others is one. Support and encouragement from others outside the family can significantly affect the child's attitude toward learning and interaction with others—two factors that are so important in making progress in the achievement of early intervention and Part B goals (U.S. DOE, 1998). Group environment can also reduce stigma and improve the self-esteem of the child. Developmental factors also warrant a group environment. Modeling peer-age children's positive behavior, building adaptive skills, and forming good social skills are facilitated by service delivery in a group environment. Finally, fiscal benefits accrue from some group environments. Hiring special individuals to provide time-consuming services within the home environment can be especially costly when compared with a child care program that already includes individuals who are qualified to perform the service.

The Maximization of Inclusion   When a group environment is the only place for appropriate delivery of services, the question becomes, "To what extent can these services be provided in an environment that integrates infants and toddlers with and without disabilities?" The answer should be easy: Often, most of the benefits favoring a group environment over the home environment also suggest that inclusion is necessary for the child to benefit from the group environment. Modeling, for instance, is better achieved when the child is exposed to children without disabilities so that the behaviors that they are, in fact, modeling reflect the functional norm in the child's culture and are not colored by the manifestations of another's disabilities. Stigma also can be significantly reduced by inclusion.

Even with services that are commonly provided for Part B children in noninclusive environments, such as those designed to facilitate the education and adaptation of children with visual impairments, an infant's or toddler's needs often differ significantly from those with the same disability in later age groups and do not indicate that a noninclusive program will provide the same level of benefit. An infant or a toddler who is blind, for example, may need intensive instruction, which a special school or group environment specifically for blind children could provide but which also could be provided in the home. Perhaps the intensity of the services could not reach a level that some programs specifically designed for blind children do, but it would build the family capacity to provide support and would begin the infant or toddler's education in the place where it will first and foremost be used.

Outcome Relevance   Parents sacrifice some control with group environments, but that alone does not exclude them from those environments (U.S. DOE, 1998). Steps can be taken to include them even in this portion of service delivery (U.S. DOE, 1998). Many programs use this parental resource to reduce costs while building the capacity of the primary caregivers of the infant or toddler with disabilities (U.S. DOE, 1998).

Group environments are in many ways the easiest for school districts to use because they have been doing it for years. It allows them to combine and coordinate service delivery in the system as a whole. It also allows them to control costs by gathering resources at a single location.

Presumption of Placement: Home Environment

Unlike group environments, home environments are noninclusive in that they do not provide for interaction with individuals without disabilities. Nevertheless, they have their own values to recommend them.

Values   The primary placement for infants and toddlers under Part C is the home (102nd Congress, 1991). That is so because the home environment is the usual one for infants and toddlers without disabilities. The home environment also is a place where delivery of services can easily incorporate the family and where the infant or toddler will feel most secure and comfortable and, therefore, most receptive to the services. Home delivery creates little of the stigma that often accompanies public placements (although inclusion reduces this danger). The home environment gives the child a chance to begin in the environment where he or she will receive the maximum amount of support and encouragement from the people who matter the most to the child: his or her parents. Cost also sometimes can be addressed best in the home environment, especially where the child needs very intensive care and interaction with caregivers. Such a need could often overpower the resources available at an inclusive group environment and undermine the capacity building goal in a noninclusive group environment. Furthermore, the cost in these environments for a full-time aide might be prohibitive, whereas in the home, family members can provide many of the ongoing services.

Maximization of Benefit   Placement in the home will usually reflect that the need and right of the infant or toddler for interaction in a group environ-ment with children without disabilities is only a secondary concern of the IFSP team. The home environment in many cases provides the best opportunity for capacity building and prevention of some forms of developmental delay. From a Part B perspective, this placement is the result of a decision that turns the LRE mandate on its ear. Generally, the IFSP team will have determined that the benefits received from service delivery in the home environment outweigh considerations that would suggest placement in an inclusive group environment. Simply put, they will find that in this case and with this child, developmental benefit is more important than inclusion. Because the child is an infant or a toddler, many of the benefits that an inclusive group environment can provide, a home environment can provide better.

Outcome Relevance   The home environment can be problematic for the providers who balk at trying to coordinate service delivery for 100 students at 100 different locations. The cost of some services will probably be more for both the family and the locations, especially during the initial program setup for home delivery of services. This cost hopefully will be reduced as the infant or toddler and family build their respective capacities, as will the structural difficulties for the state and local agencies through establishment and evolution of the individualized system for service delivery.

Presumption of Placement: Alternative Placements

Although Part C seems to indicate that environments are either classified as group or home or natural or unnatural, the reality is a lot less clear. Many environments are difficult to categorize and must be carefully examined in the IFSP process.

Hypothetical Situations   There are many placements that Part C does not consider, including service delivery at a neighbor's, friend's, or relative's house. Neither the IDEA nor its regulations mention this type of placement explicitly (§§ 1400 *et seq.*; Title 34, C.F.R. §§ 303 *et seq.*). In its Twentieth Annual Report to Congress, the DOE listed eight different environments in which data are collected (U.S. DOE, 1999): 1) early intervention classroom, 2) family child care, 3) general nursery school/child care, 4) residential facility, 5) home, 6) hospital (inpatient), 7) outpatient service facility, and 8) other. This chapter has generally discussed environments in terms of home or group environments, NEs or non-NEs, and inclusive or noninclusive environments, because these are divisions incorporated into the law. These eight environments demonstrate that there are many environment choices within these divisions. The example of a friend's, neighbor's, or relative's house comes under the label "other" environments, but that gives no more guidelines on how to treat such an environment for service delivery.

Need for Flexibility   The equity of situations such as the hypothetical requires a flexible approach to the requirements of the NE. The purposes of the NE mandate as outlined by the Congress, DOE, and others should be the focus for this decision. For instance, a "most-like" approach would compare a newly proposed environment with others that are clearly NEs to determine whether the proposed environment qualifies under the definition of NE. For example, the hypothetical suggests an environment that most resembles a home environment, but with some differences. The neighbor's home, in the absence of the parents, could weaken the generally strong family capacity-building argument in favor of home environments but could also add an opportunity for fostering one source for community support of that family's capacity. Those values should

be determined along with any limitations of a newly considered environment. Whether stigma might attach or whether infants and toddlers without disabilities are commonly introduced to similar environments also should be considered.

The important thing is not to view the NE mandate as closing doors on any opportunities for the infant or toddler and his or her family. The Secretary refused to elaborate further on which environments could be considered "natural" and said that such decisions are to be in the hands of the IFSP team to allow it flexibility in forming an IFSP (U.S. DOE, 1993, 58 Federal Register 40958, 40974). There could be no clearer an answer. The IFSP meeting is intended to contemplate the whole range of available options as related to meeting the individualized needs of the child and the family (U.S. DOE, 1993, 58 Federal Register 40958, 40974).

The range of options available to the IFSP team is not limited by state accreditation and licensing requirements (*Still v. DeBuono,* 1996). The Still case held that where there were no licensed or accredited individuals available to perform a needed service, sufficiently qualified individuals may do so even if not accredited or licensed to do so. The state may not refuse to provide services merely because there are no licensed individuals available to perform the service. The state may only refuse to provide or pay when there is no one who is qualified to perform the services (*Still v. DeBuono,* 1996).

Another side of that coin is, unfortunately, that child care facilities will often refuse to serve as a location for early intervention services even if that means they will not be a "state accredited" child care facility. Nevertheless, some of these facilities are violating a mandate to provide services to infants and toddlers with disabilities, a mandate located not within IDEA but in Section 504 requirements or in ADA (§ 794). The threshold question in these cases is whether the child care facility is receiving federal funds (§ 794). If so, they are subject to liability for discrimination under 504 (§ 794). Federal funds are in part available to almost every child care facility in some capacity, and the vast majority of them use these funds. Many child care facilities actually receive funds from IDEA's Part B program itself (§ 1419). If the facility receives no federal funds, then the ADA still applies.

CONCLUSION

It is beyond argument that Part C has enlarged the net of inclusion and the opportunities for infants and toddlers and their families to participate in the regular ebb and flow of their own communities. There remain, however, several other considerations.

From the perspective of early intervention service delivery, there are service delivery considerations. A host of issues arise as the child makes the transition from Part C to Part B programs, especially with regard to preserving the family-focused Part C services and the role of families in the early development of their infants and toddlers with disabilities. What specific assurances are there—not just in IDEA but in practice—that infants and toddlers and their families will make the transition smoothly into the Part B program? What assurances do families have that school districts will use or incorporate the IFSP, in whole or in part, within the child's IEP? What assurances are there that the child's developmental, behavioral, and physical needs are evaluated and responded to as adequately in the preschool period as they have been during the infant-toddler years?

The list of "what assurances" goes on and on. The point, very simply, is that Part C promises a family-focused and child-focused program, whereas Part B programs promise a child-focused pro-

gram, with the family as a secondary beneficiary. More to the point, there are different legal assurances—and different programmatic perspectives—on "natural environments" and "least restrictive environments."

These different legal and programmatic considerations have ramifications for the child, family, and education system. The needs of infants and toddlers differ from the needs of young preschool-age children, and their families' needs differ as well. Needs vary and change across time and circumstance, and they are responded to (if at all) by different programs in different ways. The special role of families in the early development of infants and toddlers is a foundation of Part C. It is not nearly so foundational within Part B. The question that needs to be asked, therefore, is what are the consequences to the child and family if an infant or toddler is moved into a less or even a more inclusive program upon making the transition to child-focused Part B services?

The NE mandate within Part C is not as strong as the presumption in favor of inclusion/least restriction in Part B. The trade-off is that Part C seems to be more favorable than Part B when it comes to such matters as individualization of services, family-directed service provision, and flexibility in decision-making processes. It seems beyond cavil that the tools are there—within Part C—to accomplish the goals for infants and toddlers as well as preschool-age children. What is particularly notable is the great amount of discretion that Part C allows, especially with respect to the place of service delivery, that is to say, the operational definition of "natural environment." This wide range of discretion may explain why (as other authors have pointed out) there is such inconsistency in placement decisions and such an absence of access to inclusive placements for infants and toddlers, but there may be other factors that explain why inconsistency seems the norm.

One of those factors may well be that state agencies (sometimes, the education agency, sometimes the health-welfare agency) and state/local agencies use the flexibility that Part C gives them to design programs that do, indeed, meet the needs of the infants/toddlers and families by responding to the diversity of their needs and of the communities in which their needs are to be met. However, in some situations, the agencies and professionals involved may not want or be able to meet the needs of the child and family.

Even if there is inclusion-favorable policy, professional capacity, and willingness, there remains the cardinal rule: individualize for the infant/toddler and family. Policy decisions, made at state and local levels, and professional judgments, made at the point-of-service level, may need to be variable and inconsistent to meet this cardinal rule. Discretion, coupled with diversity in state, local, and community factors and with the variety of child and family needs, seems to be quite defensible, and with it, the results—inconsistency—may also be defensible.

Another explanation looks at the families. One must acknowledge that families themselves are not of a single mind about placements in NEs. Given a choice between the family home as a place of service delivery and center-based service delivery (and given that each is or can be made appropriate for the infant/toddler and family), some families may prefer the former over the latter, or vice versa.

Any preference in turn may reflect several factors about families and the service system. It may suggest that families are not exercising their rights to claim placement in inclusive center-based programs; and, more basically, it may reflect their lack of knowledge of their rights (rather than a reluctance or inability to exercise them).

Knowledge is power, and rights are powerful; but first there must be knowledge. The absence of it—an informed constituency of parents/families—may be attributed to a variety of sources, including, without limitation, professionals and parent-advocacy/service organizations. These may not be reaching the families in ways that are meaningful to families, especially those that are from ethnically, culturally, and linguistically diverse backgrounds.

Moreover, the lack of knowledge may be attributed to the "snowed under/overwhelmed" factor: The birth of a child with a disability is usually unexpected and, even for families that know their child will be born with a disability or for families that have experience with disability, accompanied by many new challenges for the family. Family priorities may not include learning about and acting on Part C (or even Part B) rights.

Finally, there may be conflict involving the state's policy, the practice of local agencies, the judgment of professionals, the needs of the infant/toddler, and the priorities of families. It may be that some families are capable—within a multiconstituency conflict arena—of enforcing their rights to service in NEs, but it may be more likely that they are not. After all, families that are well experienced in the ways of IDEA (Part B or Part C) and disability and that have the financial, emotional, and professional resources to enforce their rights invariably find that there is a high cost to enforcement, one that they may be willing to pay but one that they may just as soon forego. For all of the rights (and information-acquiring) provisions of IDEA, there still remains this fact, one that Congress has not seen fit to address sufficiently: In the relationship among policy, agencies, and professionals on the one hand and families on the other, the balance of power lies with the former—so, too, does (and should) the balance of duty. Until the service system adopts a more proinclusive posture, it will be uphill, all the way, for families that want the natural and least restrictive, most typical, environment.

REFERENCES

23 IDELR 440, OSEP letter to Zimenoff. (1994, July).

A free appropriate education in the least restrictive environment: Promises made, promises broken by the Individuals with Disabilities Education Act. (1994, Fall). *Dayton Law Review, 20,* 243.

Americans with Disabilities Act (ADA) of 1990, PL 101-336, 42 U.S.C. §§ 12101 *et seq.*

Board of Education of Lagrange School District v. Illinois State Board of Education, 1998 U.S. Dist. LEXIS 17916, 17925 (N.D. Ill. Dist. Ct. 1998).

Board of Education v. Holland, 4 F.3d 1398 (9th Cir. 1994).

Board of Education v. Rowley, 458 US 176 (1982).

Burlington School Comm. v. Department of Education, 471 U.S. 359 (1985).

Buysse, V., & Bailey, D. (1993). Behavioral and developmental outcomes in young children with disabilities in integrated and segregated settings: A review of comparative studies. *Journal of Special Education, 26,* 434–461.

Cleveland Heights-University Heights City School District v. Boss, 144 F.3d 391 (6th Cir. 1998).

Comments to Proposed Rules for the Early Intervention Program for Infants and Toddlers with Disabilities, 62 Fed. Reg. no. 204, October 22, 1997.

Daniel R.R. v. State Board of Education, 874 F.2d 1036, 1047 (5th Cir. 1989).

Devries v. Fairfax County School, 882 F.2d 876, 879 (4th Cir. 1989).

Early Intervention Program for Infants and Toddlers with Disabilities, part three Rule, 57 Fed. Reg. 18986, 19002, (1991).

Early Intervention Program for Infants and Toddlers with Disabilities, part three Rule, 58 Fed. Reg. 40958, 40974, (1993).

Early Intervention Program for Infants and Toddlers with Disabilities, part three Rule, 58 Fed. Reg. 40958, 40986, (1993).

Early Intervention Program for Infants and Toddlers with Disabilities, part three Rule, 58 Fed. Reg. 40982, (1993).

Early Intervention Program for Infants and Toddlers with Disabilities, part three Rule, 58 Fed. Reg. 40983, (1993).

Early Intervention Program for Infants and Toddlers with Disabilities, part three Rule, 64 Fed. Reg. 18290, (1998).

Early Intervention Program for Infants and Toddlers with Disabilities, part two Rule. 64 FR 12406, 12536. (1999).

Education for All Handicapped Children Act of 1975, PL 94-142, 20 U.S.C. §§ 1400 *et seq.*

Education of the Handicapped Amendments of 1986, PL 99-457, 20 U.S.C. §§ 1400 *et seq.*, 97 Stat. 1357.

Florence City School District Four v. Carter, 510 U.S. 7, 15 (1993).

Fuhrmann v. East Hanover Board of Education, 993 F2d 1031 (3rd Cir. 1993).

Gartner, A., & Lipsky, D.K. (1987). Beyond special education: Toward a quality system for all students. *Harvard Educational Review, 57,* 367, 375.

Greer v. Rome City School District, 950 F.2d 688 (11th Cir. 1991).

Hulme v. Dellmuth, 439 A.2d 582 (E.D. Pa. 1991).

Individuals with Disabilities Education Act (IDEA) of 1990, PL 101-476, 20 U.S.C. §§ 1400 *et seq.*

Individuals with Disabilities Education Act Amendments of 1991, PL 102-119, 20 U.S.C. §§ 1400 *et seq.*

Olmstead v. L.C., 119 S. Ct. 2176 (1999).

P.J. v. State of Connecticut Board of Education, 788 F.Supp. 673, 680 (Conn. Dist. Ct. 1992).

Rehabilitation Act of 1973, PL 93-112, 29 U.S.C. §§ 701 *et seq.*

Roncker v. Walter, 700 F.2d 1058, 1063 (6th Cir. 1983).

Still v. DeBuono, 101 F.3d 888 (NY Dist. Ct., 1996).

T.R. v. Kingwood Township Board of Education, 32 F.Supp. 2d 720, 731 (N.J. Dist Ct. 1998).

U.S. Department of Education. (1998). *Nineteenth annual report to Congress on the implementation of the Individuals with Disabilities Education Act.* Washington, DC: Author.

U.S. Department of Education. (1999). *Twentieth annual report to Congress on the implementation of the Individuals with Disabilities Education Act.* Washington, DC: Author.

5

ZOLINDA STONEMAN

Attitudes and Beliefs of Parents of Typically Developing Children

Effects on Early Childhood Inclusion

To reject a stereotype that we learned from our parents is a little like rejecting them. (Triandis, 1971, p. 104)

Parents of typically developing young children can affect the success of preschool inclusion programs. This influence is exerted through their direct influence on preschool programs as well as through their socialization of their children. These parents can directly affect the inclusion of children with disabilities through their choice of a preschool program for their child and through the influence that they exert on the program once their child is enrolled. The actions that they take can often be traced back to their attitudes toward inclusion and toward children with disabilities. In addition to these actions, parents indirectly influence inclusionary preschool programs through their socialization of their own children, who then become the typically developing peers in inclusionary programs. These indirect socialization influences include teaching their children about different aspects of disability,

controlling their children's access to experiences, transmitting emotional responses related to people with disabilities, and socializing their children's behavior. The goals that parents have for socializing their children and the parenting behaviors in which they engage to achieve this desired socialization can be linked to their attitudes and beliefs.

THEORETICAL MODELS OF ATTITUDE

Before discussing in greater depth the paths of influence through which the attitudes of parents of typically developing children influence preschool inclusion, it is important to consider what is meant by the construct *attitude*. More than 20 years ago, Fishbein and Ajzen (1975) commented that theorists did not agree on a definition of what constitutes an attitude. That is still the case at the beginning of the 21st century. Social psychologists have generated a rich and prolific body of research literature focusing on attitudes. A literature search can yield literally thousands of research papers on this topic. However, this work often has been disappointing because researchers have experienced difficulty in documenting a consistent, robust link between people's reported attitudes and their actual behavior. The link between attitudes and behavior has eluded researchers because of ambiguity in defining what constitutes an attitude, as well as difficulty in operationalizing the complex, multifaceted relationship that exists between an attitude and a resulting behavior performed in a specific environmental context. In this chapter, the conceptual scheme described by Triandis (1971) is used to organize information concerning attitudes. Although Triandis was not the first to develop this scheme, his book *Attitude and Attitude Change* provides a clear presentation of the framework. Triandis suggested that an attitude has three interrelated components: *cognition, affect,* and *behavioral intent.*

The cognitive component of an attitude is the knowledge or information that the person holding an attitude has about the referent. It is a "network of thoughts about categories of people" (Triandis, Adamopoulos, & Brinberg, 1984, p. 22). If a parent believes that including young children with disabilities in a typical child care center harms the other children in the program by diverting teacher attention, then the parent forms an attitude toward preschool inclusion on the basis of that cognition. Families provide young children with the knowledge and information about different disabilities that they need to form attitudes. Most of this information is conveyed by parents. As children grow and develop, they may increasingly notice differences among children. They then turn to their parents for an explanation of what those differences mean.

Affect, the second component of an attitude, refers to the emotional reaction elicited by the referent (Triandis, 1971).

A mother who is eating with her young child in a restaurant may be seated at a table next to a child who has cerebral palsy and is drooling and spewing food on herself because the child is motorically unable to eat neatly. The mother may feel repulsion toward this child and may express this emotion facially or verbally. Another parent and child may be present when a person has a tonic-clonic seizure (formerly called a grand mal seizure), and the parent may experience and express fear. These emotional reactions experienced by parents can be transmitted to children. The children may learn to feel disgust about the inability of a child with a physical disability to eat neatly and may learn to fear people who have seizures. However, when parents' emotional reactions are positive, they can instill in children a favorable emotional response toward those with disabilities.

The third component of an attitude, behavioral intent, is a predisposition to act in a certain manner, including a desire to seek or avoid contact with the referent of an attitude (Triandis, 1971). The mother in the restaurant described previously may turn away from the child with cerebral palsy, or she and her family may leave the restaurant. The parent who fears the person who is having a seizure may move away quickly or may freeze in place and stare at the person. Parents may not directly teach their children how to behave in the presence of a person with a disability. Frequently, children learn appropriate behavior patterns vicariously from watching and modeling the behavior of their parents and other significant adults.

As stated previously, there is not always a direct relationship among an individual's knowledge, emotional reactions, behavioral dispositions, and actual behavior. Triandis (1971; Triandis et al., 1984) described one aspect of the problem. When attitudes are measured, information is usually obtained about a class of people (e.g., children with disabilities). The judgment that guides behavior, however, is in response to one attitude object with multiple attributes. Stoneman (1993) gave the example of a young child with Down syndrome, who also is blond, is fair-skinned, is in pigtails, frequently wears a Muppets shirt, and has a missing front tooth and a charming smile. A parent's attitude toward including this child in child care will, in part, reflect an amalgamation of attitudes held toward each of the girl's characteristics.

Conversely, a single characteristic that is particularly salient to the observer may predominate. Consider, for example, how attitudes about including this little girl in a child care classroom may change when the observer learns that the girl's mother is addicted to crack cocaine or that the girl frequently bites other children hard enough to draw blood. Either of these characteristics, both unrelated to Down syndrome, may influence a parent of a typically developing child not to want her child to have this little girl as a classmate or as a friend. Söder (1990) criticized disability attitude research because it has examined responses to people on the basis of only one characteristic, their disability. "This single characteristic is supposed to be so relevant that respondents can base their judgments on this information alone" (p. 229). This is rarely the case.

Fishbein and Ajzen (1975) stressed the importance of understanding the social context when trying to understand attitude–behavior convergence. They posited that the social environment can enhance or attenuate the attitude–behavioral relationship as individuals are influenced by their beliefs about what important "social others" expect them to do in given situations. Thus, social norms may cause a parent to behave in a manner that is inconsistent with his or her attitudes but is in accordance with per-

ceived social norms and expectations. How people react to people with disabilities reflects situational/contextual influences (Söder, 1990).

THE CONSTRUCT OF PARENT ATTITUDES TOWARD DISABILITY

There has been an ongoing debate about whether there is a generalized attitude that extends across people with different disabling conditions. Measurement instruments generally assume the existence of such a generalized set of attitudes (Gething, 1991). There seems to be empirical support for this generalized attitude, but there are also numerous studies documenting differing attitudes depending on the specific disability being studied. Jones (1974) found that there exists toward people with disabilities a general attitude, which cuts across different disabilities, but also found evidence for more specific attitudes toward individuals with different disabling conditions. He suggested that attitudes toward people with different disabilities are hierarchical in nature; some disabilities are associated with more negative public attitudes than others (Jones, 1974). Gething (1991) created multiple parallel forms of the Interaction with Disabled Persons Scale, focusing on the comfort of the respondent with people with specific disabilities. Findings from this study support the existence of a general attitude toward people with disabilities but also document differences between different conditions at the extremes of the attitude dimension.

The theory of reasoned action (Ajzen & Fishbein, 1980; Fishbein & Ajzen, 1975) predicts that attitudes toward specific practices (e.g., preschool inclusion) would predict corresponding actions accurately, whereas more general attitudes (e.g., attitudes toward disability) would be less likely to relate to behavior. Gottlieb and Siperstein (1976) stressed the importance of specifying the attitude referent in disability studies. General attitudes toward children with disabilities might be important in understanding parents' attitudes toward inclusion, but attitudes toward children with a specific disability might be more powerful in predicting parents' reactions toward individual children with disabilities attending inclusive preschool programs. Leonard and Crawford (1989) posited the existence of two levels of attitudes, societal and personal. According to this conceptualization, parents can have positive attitudes toward children with disabilities at a societal level, desiring full, inclusive lives for those children, while, at a personal level, being very concerned about their own child's being in an inclusive preschool.

Wide differences exist in the attitudes of parents of children without disabilities toward including preschool children with different disabilities (Green & Stoneman, 1989). Children with physical and sensory disabilities cause the least concern; children with mental retardation, emotional disturbance, and behavior problems make parents the most uncomfortable. Level of disability has also been demonstrated to be relevant to attitudes (Gottlieb & Siperstein, 1976; Jones, 1974; Stoneman, 1997); reactions to individuals who have more severe mental retardation, for example, are more negative than attitudes toward those who have mild mental retardation. In the Green and Stoneman study, the more severe the child's mental retardation, the more concerned parents of children without disabilities were about including that child.

In conceptualizing parental attitudes, it is important to differentiate among general attitudes toward disability, attitudes held toward young children with disabilities, and attitudes held toward preschool inclusion. As Söder noted, "We don't want disabilities, we don't envy those who are disabled. . .this does not mean that we devalue persons with disabilities" (1990, p. 235). Attitudes are more positive when the referent is a person with a disability rather than a disability label (Whiteman & Lukoff, 1965). In addition, each of these attitude constructs is further elucidated when a specific type and severity of disability is included in the referent information. A parent's attitude about including a child with a hearing loss in a preschool program might be very different from that same parent's attitude about including a child who has a severe emotional disorder. Perhaps the answer to the question, "Is *parent attitudes toward disability* a meaningful construct?" is, "Yes, it is one of numerous meaningful attitude constructs that are useful in understanding how the attitudes of parents of typically developing children may have an impact on preschool inclusion."

HOW PARENT ATTITUDES ARE FORMED

Virtually all theorists agree that attitudes are learned (Allport, 1954; Fishbein & Ajzen, 1975; Triandis, 1971). Frequently, attitudes are formed on the basis of minimum information or experience with the attitude referent. The following sections briefly discuss influences that shape parent attitudes toward preschool inclusion and toward young children with disabilities: family of origin, personal experience, culture and religion, spouse and significant others, and education (see Figure 5.1).

Family of Origin

Social frames are the lenses through which the social world is filtered and meaning is constructed (Klein, 1995). Childhood recollections are thought to act as social frames, influencing the way people view the social world as adults. Many parents formed their attitudes about people with disabilities when they

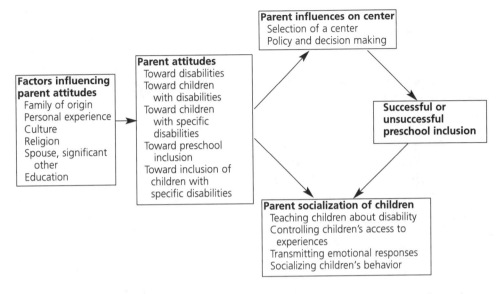

Figure 5.1.   Paths of influence through which the attitudes of parents of typically developing children can influence the success of preschool inclusion.

were young, living with their families of origin. Often, everything that people know and believe about an attitude object is what parents and others told them when they were children (Triandis et al., 1984). This may be particularly true for attitudes about people with disabilities. Until recently, segregated schools and living environments kept people with disabilities largely from public view. Thus, it is likely that parents had only minimal contact with people with disabilities during their childhood. They learned from their families how to think about people with disabilities. When they become adults, parents pass on those attitudes to their own children.

Personal Experience

In addition to what they learned from their families when they were young, parents base their attitudes on their own personal experiences with people with disabilities. There is a general belief that direct experience with classes of people reduces the negative attitudes and stereotypes held toward that group of people. Gottlieb, Corman, and Curci (1984)

termed this the *contact hypothesis*. Barsch (1964) suggested that serving children with disabilities in segregated educational environments would unknowingly serve to maximize negative attitudes among the general population. Not all scholars agree that contact, by itself, results in positive attitude change. Yuker (1983) argued that researchers should not "waste time" studying the effects of general, undefined "contact" with individuals with disabilities but, instead, should focus efforts on defining the precise nature and duration of contact and the nature of the interpersonal relationships involved. He concluded that "contact with a disabled person is most apt to change a nondisabled individual's attitudes when the two persons are of equal status, when they are working toward common goals, when the contact is intimate rather than casual, and when the contact is pleasant or rewarding to both parties" (Yuker, 1983, pp. 101–102). Leonard and Crawford (1989) suggested that some forms of personal contact may emphasize similarities, leading to greater acceptance. Conversely, when people without disabilities have higher status than the person with a disability, which is the norm in many interactions, positive attitude change is not expected (Yuker, 1983).

The contact hypothesis predicts that parents' attitudes toward preschool inclusion are related to their previous experiences with people with disabilities. There is some evidence in the literature that direct personal experience with children with specific disabilities "softens the perception of seriousness" of that disability and may bring about a higher level of acceptance (Barsch, 1964). Parents of children in inclusive environments have been found to hold more favorable attitudes about inclusion than parents of children in segregated environments (Diamond & LeFurgy, 1994; Green & Stoneman; 1989; Miller et al., 1992). This may indicate that the experience of having children in inclusive preschool programs influences parent attitudes in a positive manner. Conversely, of course, it may indicate that parents with more positive attitudes about inclusion are more likely to place their children in inclusive environments.

Among parents whose children were in inclusive programs, Green and Stoneman (1989) found that parents who perceived their child's experience as successful were more supportive of inclusion than were parents who evaluated their child's experience less positively. In addition, parents who had positive life experiences with people with disabilities were more supportive of preschool inclusion than were parents whose experiences were more negative (Green & Stoneman, 1989). Green and Stoneman concluded that the most important variable that affects parent attitudes about inclusion seemed to be the quality, rather than quantity, of experience with people with disabilities and with inclusionary preschool environments.

Ajzen, Timko, and White (1982) argued that lack of direct experience with an attitude object will increase the likelihood that attitudes are pliable and can change over time. Attitudes that are based on personal experience, once formed, are more resistant to change. Stoneman (1993) cautioned that poor-quality inclusion programs may actually do harm, making parents of typically developing children less accepting of future inclusionary efforts. If in the rapid proliferation of preschool inclusion programs these programs are implemented without trained staff or adequate resources, then the resulting low-quality services may shut the door for future development of effective, high-quality programs.

Culture and Religion

Disability is a socially determined construct that is defined differently in various cultures and societies (Barnett, 1986; Brooks & Baumeister, 1977; Farber & Rowitz, 1986; Mink, 1997). Mink, for example, concluded that in cultures that are not highly technological, conditions such as mental retardation are less salient and less likely to be diagnosed and labeled, whereas groups who place high value on cognitive competence, such as the Euro-American middle-class culture and middle-class Chinese immigrants, are more likely to identify a child who learns slowly as having mental retardation and, thus, having a disability. Recent evidence confirms the existence of cross-cultural differences in beliefs about and attributions of disability and about effective strategies for overcoming a disability (Danseco, 1997; Furnham & Akande, 1997; Selway & Ashman, 1998). Parental norms, beliefs, and values are derived from and reflect the parents' culture; these norms and values then define differing goals for the cultural socialization of children (McCollum & McBride,

1997). In addition, models of educational inclusion vary across cultures; any discussion of inclusionary practices must be considered in cultural context (Bowd, 1992).

Religion also influences parental attitudes toward people with disabilities. Religious teachings can support both positive and negative attitudes. Different religious groups have quite different teachings about disability, including disability as a punishment for sins of the parents, God as a healer of disability, people with disabilities as being favored by God or as being demon or evil spirit possessed, and people with disabilities as objects of pity and charity (Danseco, 1997; Rose, 1997; Selway & Ashman, 1998; Stratford, 1994). Thus, both cultural and religious forces shape parents' attitudes toward people with disabilities.

Spouse and Significant Others

Parent attitudes toward inclusion are influenced contemporaneously by the attitudes and beliefs of their marital partners and significant other adults in their lives. Green and Stoneman (1989) found that the attitudes of mothers of typically developing children were related to the positiveness of the mothers' past experiences with people with disabilities, as well as to other personal factors. The primary predictors of fathers' attitudes toward inclusion were the attitudes of their wives. Green and Stoneman (1989) suggested that this pattern may reflect a family system in which mothers set the tone for family attitudes toward inclusion, whereas fathers, who tend to be less involved in the day-to-day aspects of child care, adopt the views held by their wives. It is plausible that other adults also influence parent attitudes, such as a relative or neighbor whose child has had a positive (or negative) experience in an inclusive environment.

Education

There is some evidence to suggest that sometimes better-educated parents of typically developing children have more positive attitudes about preschool inclusion than do less well-educated parents (Green & Stoneman, 1989; Guralnick, 1994; Stoiber, Gettinger, & Goetz, 1998). These relationships tend to be modest in size. This is consistent with the often-replicated finding in the attitude literature that people with increased education are less likely to have negative stereotypes and prejudices (Allport, 1954).

RESEARCH ON PARENT ATTITUDES TOWARD PRESCHOOL INCLUSION

Across multiple studies, the general attitudes of parents (mothers have been more frequently studied than fathers) of typically developing children toward preschool inclusion have been found to be very positive. Findings concerning the positivity of parent attitudes are consistent across different types of inclusive environments, including Head Start and First Chance Programs (Blacher & Turnbull, 1982; Miller et al., 1992; Stoiber et al., 1998), public school kindergartens (Stoiber et al., 1998; Turnbull, Winton, Blacher, & Salkind, 1983), university-based model programs (Bailey & Winton, 1987; Stoiber et al., 1998), community child care (Green & Stoneman, 1989; Guralnick, 1994; Miller et al., 1992; Peck, Hayden, Wandschneider, Peterson, & Richarz, 1989; Stoiber et al., 1998), and public school preschools (Miller et al., 1992). Parents of typically developing children who do not attend inclusive programs also tend to hold positive attitudes (Diamond & LeFurgy, 1994; Green & Stoneman, 1989; Miller et al., 1992; Reichart et al., 1989). The most consistently reported benefit of inclusion, as viewed by parents, is the anticipation that children will learn to be sensitive to and accepting of differences (Bailey & Winton, 1987; Diamond & LeFurgy, 1994; Green & Stoneman, 1989; Guralnick, 1994; Peck, Carlson, & Helmstetter, 1992; Reichart et al., 1989; Turnbull et al., 1983).

The upbeat nature of these findings, however, is qualified by strong concerns on the part of parents that preschool/child care teachers and paraprofessional classroom staff lack adequate training to implement quality inclusionary practices (Bailey & Winton, 1987; Green & Stoneman, 1989; Guralnick, 1994; Turnbull et al., 1983). Thus, although parents of typically developing children believe that including children with disabilities is a positive, enriching practice, they are skeptical that preschool staff members have the skills needed to implement inclusion in a way that enhances the quality of the educational experience for all children. These concerns parallel the concerns of child care providers, who report that teachers lack the specialized training needed for inclusionary environments, particularly for working with children with more substantial disabilities (Buysse, Wesley, Keyes, & Bailey, 1996; Stoiber et al., 1998). It is regrettable that during the 1990s, as inclusionary programs multiplied, parent concerns about inadequate personnel preparation continued to compromise their enthusiasm about preschool inclusion.

In addition to inadequate training of personnel, other drawbacks to inclusion perceived by parents included possible social rejection or teasing of children with disabilities (Bailey & Winton, 1987; Guralnick, 1994; Turnbull et al., 1983), inadequate staff–child ratios (Peck et al., 1989), concerns about children with disabilities receiving adequate therapeutic services and individualized instruction (Green & Stoneman, 1989; Guralnick, 1994; Peck et al., 1989; Turnbull et al.,

1983), and lack of teacher attention for children without disabilities (Green & Stoneman, 1989; Guralnick, 1994). These concerns are less pervasive than parent concerns about trained personnel, but they deserve attention nonetheless.

One of the most cogent statements about preschool inclusion was made by Bailey, McWilliam, Buysse, and Wesley (1998), who suggested that if all community child care programs were of high quality, were family centered, and addressed the unique learning needs of each child, then most barriers to inclusion would be eliminated. This holds true for parent attitudes toward inclusion. Parents of typically developing children think that inclusion is a good idea but only in high-quality preschool programs with well-trained staff and adequate resources.

IMPACT OF PARENT ATTITUDES ON TEACHERS AND ADMINISTRATORS

Teachers and administrators can be influenced by parents who are in the process of selecting a preschool program for their child, as well as by the parents of children who attend their center. These influences can affect the decisions that teachers and administrators make about including children with disabilities in their classrooms and in their centers.

Parent Attitudes Influence the Selection of a Center

One mechanism through which the attitudes of parents of typically developing children can influence inclusive programs is through the selection of a preschool program. As mentioned previously, parents of children in inclusive environments hold more favorable attitudes about inclusion than do parents of children in segregated environments (Diamond & LeFurgy, 1994; Green & Stoneman; 1989; Miller et al., 1992). One possible explanation for this finding is that parents who have more positive attitudes about inclusion are more likely to place their children in inclusive environments. Obviously, many factors enter into parents' selection of a preschool program for their children. One might expect the final decision to be a result of an interaction between parent attitudes toward inclusion and their attitudes toward other aspects of the preschool program.

A parent who is opposed to inclusion may select a certain preschool for her child because of its excellent program quality and proximity to her home, despite that children with disabilities attend the program. Another parent may want her child to go to school with a diverse group of children but may avoid an inclusive program because the teachers have questionable training and the building is not well maintained. For a parent who has very strong negative attitudes about inclusion, the presence of children with disabilities in a program might be the deciding factor in the selection of a center, but such parents are a small minority.

The possibility that parents might not select a center because it includes children with disabilities is probably of particular concern for proprietary child care centers, especially those located in communities where numerous child care options exist. When for-profit centers face strong competition from other preschool providers, administrators may be especially sensitive to issues that draw parents to their center or keep them away. Child care administrators may be reluctant to accept children with disabilities if they believe that some parents may withdraw their children or never enroll their children because of the presence of children with disabilities. In areas where child care shortages exist, which is frequently the case, concerns about losing parents to other centers would be less salient. In these communities, market

forces would ensure that all center slots were full, even if some parents chose other programs because a particular center served children with disabilities.

Parent selection factors are less of an issue in federally funded programs such as Head Start and some prekindergarten programs in which inclusion of children with disabilities is mandated. If parents want the service and are eligible, they have no choice but to have their child attend programs with classmates who have disabilities. With the advent of the Americans with Disabilities Act (ADA) of 1990 (PL 101-336), the importance of parent attitudes in influencing whether a center includes children with disabilities has been lessened. ADA includes a strong federal requirement that preschool programs not violate the civil rights of children with disabilities by denying them access to services that are available to their peers without disabilities. Most center personnel remain uninformed about the relevance of the ADA to child care environments (Eiserman, Shisler, & Healey, 1995). In one study, approximately one third of child care providers indicated that they had declined service to a child with a disability in the past 3 years (Eiserman et al., 1995). Over time, as enforcement of ADA provisions increases, centers will no longer be able to discriminate against children with disabilities by denying them admission to the program. Thus, regardless of whether parents of typically developing children do or do not support inclusion, centers will accept children with disabilities because it is the law.

Parents' Attitudes Influence Center Policy and Decision Making

Parental influence over center programs does not end with the selection of a center. Parents of children enrolled in preschool programs exert considerable influence over administrators and teachers, affecting center policies and decision making. Preschool programs operate in a "sociopolitical context" (Marchant, 1995; Peck et al., 1989). Peck and colleagues (1989) presented a model of reciprocal control that posits that all constituents of preschool programs have influence over and are influenced by the behavior of others in the system. Making changes in the preschool program, such as including children with disabilities, can disrupt the equilibrium of this system and may result in negative consequences or, at the minimum, in the need to renegotiate relationships and procedures.

Parents of children currently attending a center can make demands on the center administrators. Parents may demand that the administrator release from the program children whom they believe to be disruptive. They may advocate for a reduction of class size or hiring of additional staff to accommodate the needs of participating children with disabilities, or they may request the placement of children with disabilities in specific classrooms or groupings. The theory of reasoned action (Ajzen & Fishbein, 1980; Fishbein & Ajzen, 1975) suggests that whether attitude-based behaviors occur is, in part, a function of perceived social pressure. In the preschool context, whether parents with negative inclusion attitudes exert pressure may be due, in part, to the views of other parents. When parents share similar views, they can increase their influence by banding together with other similarly minded parents to try to bring about change. Groups of parents working together can have a dramatic effect on center policies and practices. If the parents are motivated by concerns over the inclusion of children with disabilities in the program or concerns about how those children are being supported in the center, then the parents can wield substantial influence over administrators and other center personnel.

PARENTS AS SOURCES OF INFLUENCE OVER THEIR CHILDREN

The previous sections discussed direct influences that parents' attitudes toward inclusion can exert on preschool programs. Next is consideration of how parents indirectly influence preschools by socializing their children toward certain developmental and social goals.

Teaching Children about Disability

Young children learn about people with disabilities from information that they receive from significant adults in their environment. Children learn to identify which people have disabilities, to understand the nature and causes of disability, to make attributions about behavior, and to place a positive or negative value on certain characteristics and behaviors. This learning forms the foundation for the attitudes that children develop and for the decisions that they make about how to interact with people with disabilities.

Parents as Teachers   For most young children, parents are the most important source of information about people with disabilities. Parents directly teach children information that shapes the cognitive component of their developing attitudes. This exchange of information can be initiated by parents or can be communicated in response to children's questions (Brightman, 1977).

Young children also learn from observing parents and from the ongoing flow of social exchanges in the family and in other social contexts. Bricker (1995) provided examples of adults' interacting with children with and without disabilities, sending unintentional messages to the children that have the potential to cumulatively affect the attitudes of the participating children. Children can learn about attitudes and values in subtle ways, through body language, vocal inflection, "and the absence of certain groups in their environment" (Ramsey, 1987, p. 64). The message, though subtle, is often pervasive. Thus, parents overtly teach children about people with disabilities, and they also teach children through their own behavior and through the family environment that they create and promote. Table 5.1 lists the ways that parents influence children's attitudes. The table is organized around the three attitude components posited by Triandis (1971): cognition, affect/emotion, and behavioral intent. The following sections elaborate on the paths of influence presented in this table.

Teaching Children to Discriminate and Label Differences Triandis (1971) argued that a cognitive representation of a referent is a minimal condition for having an attitude. If a young child does not perceive a disability in a classmate, then that child cannot have a positive or negative attitude toward the classmate's disability. If a child does not discriminate the difference between a peer who has mental retardation and a peer who has typical intellectual development, then that child cannot have formed an attitude that relates to peers with mental retardation. Children learn about their social

universe by classifying individuals and events into categories (Tajfel, 1981). Children and adults do not share similar cultural knowledge; children may view as important some characteristics of people that adults ignore (Holmes, 1995). Young children tend to focus on superficial characteristics and differences among people. In addition, children's categorizations of people are more concrete and idiosyncratic than adult classification schemes. Ramsey (1987) suggested that children's perceptions of different groups of people are more a function of their cognitive abilities than of their prejudices. Parents teach their children to identify, classify, and label groups of people in ways that are consistent with the parents' world view. As this process unfolds, children are taught about people with disabilities.

As children grow and develop, they detect a greater number of ways in which people differ. Skin color, presence of freckles or dimples, hair color, gender, height, weight, and presence of a disability are just a few of the differences that children begin to notice during early childhood. Children do not assign meaning to these differences. It is the adults

Table 5.1.   Ways that parents influence children's attitudes toward peers with disabilities

Parents teach children about disability
   Discriminating important differences and labeling children
   Characteristics of children with disabilities
   Causes of disability
   Attributions about the meaning of behavior
   Values concerning children with disabilities
Parents control children's access to experience
   Family members, kin, family friends
   Children's peer contacts and friendships
   Books, toys, and play materials
   Media
Parents transmit emotional response to disability
Parents socialize children's behavior
   Altruism, empathy, and other prosocial behavior
   Teaching children how to behave toward children with disabilities
   Role relationships

surrounding the child (and sometimes other children) who teach the young child which differences are important, how different classes of people are labeled, and which differences are valued or devalued. Over time, children are taught to align their attitudinal categorizations with those of their parents. A child may notice that a neighbor child has a crooked finger. Parents quickly let their children know that the shape of the child's finger is irrelevant and not to be used to categorize the child. There is no English word to label groups of children with crooked fingers. At another time, the child may notice that a child sits in a chair with wheels. Parents label this child has having a physical disability or as having cerebral palsy. The child learns from the parent that this difference is important, that it is used to categorize people, and that it is worthy of naming.

Teaching Children about the Characteristics of Children with Disabilities   In addition to categorizing and naming certain groups of people, parents teach children about the characteristics of those groups. Parents teach their children what it means to have a disability. Parents teach that a child who is blind cannot see and that he or she may use a cane or a guide dog to help him or her get around. Children are taught that a child who has cerebral palsy makes unusual movements with her arms or legs and may use braces or a wheelchair. This basic information teaches the child about the disability and helps the child understand the effects that the disability has on the child's ability to play or learn. Innes and Diamond (1999) found that mothers of preschool children made more comments and asked more questions about pictures of children with physical disabilities as compared with pictures of children with Down syndrome. Many of their comments focused on the adaptive equipment used by the children with physical disabilities (e.g., wheelchair, braces).

Similarly, Innes (1999) found that mothers were more likely to explain the disability and emphasize the child's capability when telling stories about a picture of a child with physical disabilities as compared with a child with Down syndrome.

Stoneman, Rugg, and Rivers (1996) studied how 152 parents of typically developing children responded to a series of questions that might be asked by young children who are seeking information about peers with mental retardation, cerebral palsy, and aggressive and hyperactive behavior. Both mothers and fathers overwhelmingly taught their children about the limitations accompanying disability in their responses to children's questions. Fewer than 20% of the parents mentioned both strengths and limitations, and almost no parents (fewer than 1%) focused only on strengths or positive qualities of the child with a disability. Mothers were more likely to include information about strengths and capabilities in their answers than were fathers; strengths were most frequently mentioned for children with mental retardation and cerebral palsy.

Teaching Children about the Causes of Disability   Ronald (1977) found that the most common question that children wanted answered about disability was, "How did it happen?" In a question-and-answer study (Stoneman et al., 1996), parents overwhelmingly described constitutionally based causes, such as organic or brain damage, sickness, or injury to explain what caused cerebral palsy. When explaining mental retardation, approximately half of the parents mentioned constitutionally based causes; the remaining parents explained that the child was experiencing a learning problem that was assumed to be temporary and time-limited. High activity in children was described as being caused by constitutional factors and by emotion or temperament. Causes cited for aggression were more varied, including poor parenting or discipline, inability to control emotions, temperament, lack of personal effort, and family problems, in addition to temporary or learning and constitutionally based causes.

Attributions: Teaching Children to Interpret the Meaning of Behavior Maas, Marecek, and Travers defined social attribution as "the process by which people impute situational, emotional, motivational, and dispositional causes to the behavior of others" (1978, p. 146). People are motivated to understand why other people behave as they do (Heider, 1958; Kelley, 1971). Grusec (1991) suggested that positive character attributions about the good behavior/personality of a child are a strong means used by parents to socialize empathic concern about other children. Attribution theorists (e.g., Weiner, 1974) suggest that responses to success that is believed to be caused by internal, controllable factors, such as personal effort and hard work, are more positive than responses to success that is attributable to external factors, such as luck, fate, or the efforts of others. In addition, people tend to be more sympathetic to the failure of others when that failure is attributed to causes beyond the person's control than when it is attributed to factors that are controllable by the individual, such as laziness or lack of effort. Katz (1981) suggested that people form opinions about different disabilities' attributions that vary in the extent to which the possessor is held responsible for his or her situation. Stoneman and colleagues (1996) found that parents were more likely to attribute the behavior of a child with aggressive behavior to a cause internal to the child and under the child's control, whereas attributions concerning children with cerebral palsy were more likely to be external, out of the control of the child.

Teaching Children Values Concerning Children with Disabilities Wolfens-berger (1972) suggested that after individuals detect differences among people, society informs the observer as to whether the difference is positively or negatively valued. For young children, society speaks in the voice of parents. Some have argued that children with disabilities provide an opportunity to teach children important values about being human. Stratford, for example, wrote that children with intellectual disabilities can help people learn that intelligence is not the most important human characteristic, "love and human relationships are far more important" (1994, p. 12). In the United States, great societal value is placed on successfully struggling to overcome barriers and limitations (Scheier, Carver, Schulz, Glass, & Katz, 1978). Phillips (1985) stated that society assigns value to people with disabilities when they try hard to overcome obstacles. Parents use conversations about children with disabilities as important teaching opportunities to transmit basic values to their children.

One very positive approach that parents take to teaching values is to point out similarities between their child and the child with a disability, stressing that the children are "more alike than different." Stoneman and colleagues (1996) found that parents described similarities more than twice as often for children with cerebral palsy or mental retardation than for children with aggressive behavior or attention-deficit/hyperactivity disorder. Brown and Turner (1981) noted that social categorization theory suggests that acceptance is caused by increasing the salience of similarities between two social groups. This is the potential outcome of this teaching strategy. "Thus, it is possible to teach children about the commonalities human beings share, as well as to appreciate the differences among us" (Holmes, 1995, p. 109). An example comes from a mother of a 4-year-old child, who explained

It is hard for some kids to learn. You know how you had a hard time learning to cut with scissors? Well, some kids have a hard time learning to talk or follow directions. They have to practice really hard—just like you practice really hard to try to learn to use scissors. (Stoneman et al., 1996)

Another positive approach is to teach children that differences among children are to be celebrated and valued. In a question–answer study (Stoneman et al., 1996), parents stressed the importance of valuing differences more than 10 times more frequently for children with mental retardation than for children with the other disabilities studied. One mother of a 4-year-old explained mental retardation to her child: "People are different, just like flowers. We have different kinds of flowers in this world. So some people learn fast, some people learn slow. Some people run fast, some people run slow." The message taught by this mother is that all children are valuable, and differences among children are to be enjoyed and appreciated.

Values are not absolute; what one person considers to be a positive value may be considered offensive by another. Phillips (1990) wrote that people with disabilities were generally considered by society as "damaged goods" and placed in a "sick role." Although society may think that making disability synonymous with illness is a positive view, people with disabilities often find this pairing abhorrent. In our study of parents' responses to children's questions about disability (Stoneman et al., 1996), many parents equated disabilities, particularly cerebral palsy, with illness. For example, a father of a 3-year-old explained cerebral palsy to his child by commenting, "She has an illness. The disease causes her the difficulty." It is likely that this father believed that he was teaching his child a positive value, whereas many advocates with physical disabilities would cringe at his answer.

Children with disabilities often evoke strong feelings of sympathy and altruism (Söder, 1990), which can lead to pitying or paternalistic attitudes. Wolfensberger wrote of a "there but for the Grace of God go I" attitude (1972, p. 20). Ebert (1977) warned that an unintended effect of inclusionary programs may be that typically developing children learn to gain a feeling of satisfaction about themselves for being "nice" and for playing with "poor, unfortunate" children with a disability. She suggested that this attitude is a child's version of *noblesse oblige,* "I am nice to you because one is nice to people like you" (p. 79). Rose wrote that, at times, people with disabilities can "become a project, a vehicle for others to fulfill their acts of kindness" (1997, p. 399). Van Der Klift (1995) captured these patronizing attitudes in her comment, "You are some kind of somebody to be a friend of theirs!" A mother of a 3-year-old in a question–answer study (Stoneman et al., 1996) encouraged her child to be a friend to a child with a disability because she "could probably use a friend." Attitudes based on patronizing beliefs are potentially as harmful, if not more so, than blatantly negative attitudes (Leonard & Crawford, 1989; Rose, 1997; Stoneman, 1993).

Children Who Belong to Multiple Devalued Groups   The processes through which parents teach young children about peers with disabilities are very similar to the manner in which parents teach children about race (Holmes, 1995; Ramsey, 1987). These two teaching processes converge when children are taught about children of different ethnicities who also have disabilities. Leung and Wright argued that people with disabilities who are also members of minority groups face "double discrimination and a double disadvantage in our society" (1993, p. 1). Others have termed this convergence *double oppression* (Stuart, 1992).

Minorities with disabilities are overrepresented among children with disabilities; many are also poor (Walker, Asbury, Maholmes, & Rackley, 1991). "Disability, poverty, and minority status are linked" (Fujiara & Yamaki, 1997, p. 293). Facing cumulative attitudinal disadvantage, these children have the added obstacle of being subjected to greater negative attitudes by the majority in society than are other minority or disability groups. They are doubly marginalized, perhaps even triply marginalized if poverty is added to minority status and disability as marginalizing forces. Thus, as one considers how parents teach children attitudes concerning peers with disabilities, it is informative to think about how this teaching converges with parental transmission of attitudes about race and poverty.

Controlling Young Children's Access to Experience

Children learn by experiencing the world around them. The extent to which young children have the opportunity to learn about people with disabilities varies depending on the information that the children are given and the experiences that they have. For some children, interacting with people with disabilities is a familiar part of everyday life. For other children, seeing people with disabilities is an uncommon occurrence, eliciting curiosity and interest.

Parents as Gatekeepers of Young Children's Everyday Experiences Young children have very little control over their own lives. Decisions about the people with whom young children spend time, the places they visit, the toys and materials with which they play, and other important aspects of their daily lives are largely controlled by adults. Parents and other adults act as gatekeepers, selecting the people, events, activities, and things that young children will and will not experience. By managing the experiences

that young children encounter, parents can powerfully shape young children's attitudes and beliefs.

Family Members, Kin, and Family Friends with Disabilities One way that parents shape the experiences of young children is by making decisions concerning their own social contacts. When a parent invites an adult friend over to visit, that adult usually interacts with the child as well as the parent in the household. Similarly, when a parent goes to visit an adult friend and takes his or her child along, the child gets to know the parent's friend. If the parent's friendship network includes people with disabilities, the child will become acquainted with adults with disabilities in positive, friendly contexts, including the child's own home. If the parent has a co-worker with a disability and invites the office staff over for dinner, then the child meets the person with a disability and learns about his or her role as an employee and co-worker of the parent. Conversely, when the social networks of parents are devoid of people with disabilities, children never have the experience of getting to know adults with disabilities in a social context. "The people [children] see [or do not see] among their parents' friends, in their neighborhoods, and in the media convey information about who is valued and who is not" (Ramsey, 1987, p. 64).

Many children have at least one person with a disability as a member of their extended family. For these children, the experience of interacting with individuals with disabilities can occur frequently, as the family gets together for visits, reunions, celebrations, and social gatherings. If the person with a disability lives close to the child's family, then contact can happen even more frequently. A smaller number of children have a member of their nuclear family who has a disability. This person can be a sibling, a parent, a grandparent, or other relative who resides in the child's home. These children have daily experience with living with a person with a disability and have attitudes and beliefs about people with disabilities shaped by their personal experiences.

Even in families that contain a member with a disability, parents can decide to limit the child's contact with that family member. It was not long ago that one of the primary reasons that children with disabilities were placed in institutions or in other out-of-home placements was to "spare" typically developing children in the family from having ongoing contact with a sibling with a disability. Parents can shield children from extended family members who have disabilities, deciding to leave the children at home when visits are made or failing to invite the person with a disability to the family's home for visits. Conversely, parents can model the inclusion of people with disabilities by supporting the family member with a disability to play important roles in the child's life.

In the community, parents can either model interactions with people with disabilities or model avoidance/ignoring of these individuals. Okagaki, Diamond, Kontos, and Hestenes (1998) found that parents who reported that they would model interactions with a child with a disability in response to a set of vignettes had children who were more likely to spend time with peers with disabilities in a classroom environment. Thus, the decisions that parents make about exposing their children to family members and family friends with disabilities reflect parent attitudes toward people with disabilities and shape the attitudes of children. Similarly, the presence or absence of people with disabilities in the parents' social network can send a powerful message to young children about the attitudes that their parents hold toward this group of people.

Children's Peer Contacts and Friendships   Young children are almost totally dependent on adults, particularly parents, for access to peers and friends. Very young children can visit friends or spend time with other children only if adults are willing to arrange for these visits, provide transportation, and supervise the play of the children as they spend time together. Even older preschool children are highly dependent on adults for their peer contacts. Children who have young children as neighbors may have more freedom to play spontaneously, without adult intervention, but even then the frequency and location of play is often defined by adults. Most parents directly manage their children's contacts with other children (Ladd, 1992; Ladd & Golter, 1988; Ladd & Hart, 1992; Ladd, Profilet, & Hart, 1992). This involvement in children's friendship development has been demonstrated to have positive outcomes. Preschool children whose parents are actively involved in arranging their contacts with other children have a larger network of playmates and have more consistent play partners than do children with less involved parents (Ladd & Golter, 1988; Ladd & Hart, 1992). These children interact in more prosocial ways with peers and spend less time in nonconstructive solitary activity (Ladd & Hart, 1992). Parents play an important role in determining opportunities for their child to establish contact and develop friendships with children with disabilities (Guralnick, 1997; Rosenbaum, Armstrong, & King, 1987; Stoneman, 1993).

Disability researchers have tended to focus their efforts on understanding the interactions between children with disabilities and their typically developing peers in the context of the classroom. Until recently, little attention has been paid to the social world of children with disabilities outside the classroom environment (Stoneman, 1993). There is only limited research focused on the peer contacts of children with and without disabilities outside the preschool/child care context (e.g., Beckman et al., 1998; Guralnick, 1997; Rugg & Stoneman, 1988). The minimal data that exist, however, suggest that many typically developing young children have little or no contact with children with disabilities in their homes, neighborhoods, and communities.

In an inclusive preschool program, a parent survey revealed that only 1 child of more than 100 typically developing children who attended the program had ever invited 1 of the 12 classmates with disabilities to their home to play or had ever visited the home of one of the children with disabilities (Rugg & Stoneman, 1988). Most of the typically developing children in the program, however, had visited the homes of four to five of their classmates and had invited a similar number of school friends over to their own homes to play. This finding is particularly striking because the program implemented intensive classroom interventions to facilitate social play between preschool children with and without disabilities. Even though positive interactions between these children increased in the classroom context, there was no carryover to the children's lives outside the preschool environment.

More recently, Guralnick (1997) found that preschool boys with mild delays see friends less often and are less likely to interact with preschool peers after the school day ends than are typically developing children. Fewer than 8% of the typically developing children in the study had a friend with a disability. This is consistent with other research on preschool and elementary school children with mental retardation that showed very low rates of peer involvement for these children after the school day ends (Stoneman, Brody, Davis, & Crapps, 1988, 1991). It is also consistent with the work of Lewis, Feiring, and Brooks-Gunn

(1988), who found that the social networks of preschool children with disabilities are composed disproportionately of adults and relatives, with limited contact with typically developing peers.

Guralnick (1999) presented a model depicting factors that are thought to influence the social integration of young children with mild disabilities in inclusive environments. In the "Prior Expectations" section of this model, he included experiences that typically developing children have with peers with disabilities before entering child care. He posited that some children enter inclusive environments with an expectation that they will establish social relationships with children with disabilities because they have established similar relationships before entering preschool. These expectations are modified during the time the child spends in the inclusive environment, in part by ongoing management of home and community peer contacts by parents.

It is clear that parents of typically developing young children play an important role in determining the degree to which their children have contact with peers with disabilities. It is also clear that, for many children, the out-of-school contact that they have with children with disabilities is either extremely limited or nonexistent. It seems probable that the attitudes held by the parents of typically developing children are at least partially responsible for this situation, leading parents either to overlook peers with disabilities as possible playmates for their children or to actively prefer that their children spend time with typically developing peers.

Access to Books, Toys, and Play Materials   Toys, books, and play materials are the substance of childhood. Through these materials, children explore their world, try on new roles, and learn to share and play constructively with others. Toys and play materials shape the nature of children's play. Some play materials are more conducive to positive play experiences than others (Quilitch, Christophersen, & Risley, 1977; Quilitch & Risley, 1973). Different toys bring forth different types of play and different play themes. Similarly, certain toys have been found to facilitate social interactions between children with and without disabilities (Beckman & Kohl, 1984; Stoneman, Cantrell, & Hoover-Dempsey, 1983). Although children ask for certain toys and play materials, parents control the materials that are available to young children. Children may strongly desire certain toys, but parents and other adults make important decisions about which toys to purchase for their children.

Toys depicting children with disabilities were once available primarily from preschool specialty catalogs, which are marketed to teachers. Toys with a disability theme are now available in the general toy market. Such toys include dolls with wheelchairs, braces, seeing eye dogs, and other adaptive equipment; ramps; and wheelchair-accessible toy vehicles. Perhaps the most publicized of these toys has been Mattel's "Share a Smile Becky," who uses a wheelchair and is the "friend" of the popular Barbie doll. When parents purchase disability-related toys, they encourage their children to incorporate children with disabilities into their fantasy play, thereby potentially increasing the children's comfort and familiarity with children with disabilities. These toys can provide important opportunities for learning. This is particularly true when parents use the toys as a vehicle for talking to their children and teaching their children disability-related values.

In addition to toys, books can shape children's attitudes and beliefs (Oskamp, Kaufman, & Wolterbeek, 1996; Turner & Traxler, 1997). Books are an important source of socialization for preschool children. Children's literature is one way to develop awareness about individuals with disabilities (Turner & Traxler, 1997). In the 1990s, children's books underwent major changes in the frequency with which characters with disabilities were represented in stories and pictures. In addition, the themes of books about characters with disabilities have become less stereotyped and more positive. An increasing number of books portray positive images of people with disabilities with which the young reader can identify (Turner & Traxler, 1997). Favazza and Odom (1997) provided books about children with disabilities to families as part of a comprehensive program to foster acceptance of people with disabilities among kindergarten children. They cited the importance of family activities such as book reading in developing children's positive attitudes about people with disabilities. As parents comment on the content of books, they convey their attitudes and beliefs to their children.

Access to Media   Parents control the access that young children have to media. Preschool children do not rent their own videos or purchase their own computer software. They do not go to movies by themselves. Parents have the ability to control what children watch on television, choosing programs that are consistent with their values and beliefs. Some families carefully control the media that their children experience; other parents allow children free access to television programs and other media available in the home (Charren & Sandler, 1983). Thus, family rules concerning the young child's access to media constitute one method that parents use to socialize their children's attitudes, including attitudes toward people with disabilities.

Media, including television, exert strong socialization influences on young children (Palmer & Dorr, 1980). These influences are sometimes planned by the developers of media, such as the careful thought that goes into the production of some children's shows (e.g., *Sesame Street*). The effects of television on children, however, are often unplanned. Attitudes and beliefs abstracted and learned by children may not be what television producers intend to teach, but they are very powerful nonetheless (Berry, 1998). For example, television is an important social influence in young children's development of racial attitudes and beliefs (Holmes, 1995). Berry (1998) argued that television's depiction of African American family life unintentionally teaches children that these families are marginalized in American society. Other television programs, such as cartoons, teach gender stereotypes: boys are violent and active and girls are domestic, interested in boys, and concerned with appearances (Thompson & Zerbinos, 1997).

Popular programs, such as *Sesame Street* and *Mr. Rogers' Neighborhood*, have sensitively included children with disabilities in program segments and have provided young viewers with information about specific disabling conditions (Berstein, Hayes, & Shauble, 1977). Other programs have story lines centered around lead characters with disabilities, showing those characters as meaningful participants in their families and communities. Many television programs, however, either exclude characters with disabilities or portray those with disabilities in a negative light (Phillips, 1990). By exerting positive control over the media experienced by young children, parents can control the influences of television, video, and other media, ensuring that these media teach positive rather than negative or exclusionary attitudes about people with disabilities, as well as about other social groups (Charren & Sandler, 1983). The attitudes of parents will determine the media content that they deem appropriate for their children.

Transmitting Emotional Response to Disability

Ronald (1977) suggested that the young child's reaction to disability generally is curiosity and exploration. When this interest is met by embarrassed parents who avoid questions, the child learns to respond to the person with a disability with discomfort and unease. The transmission of a negative emotional response is occasioned. Affect, the second attitude component posited by Triandis (1971), refers to the emotional reaction elicited by the referent. A young child with physical stigmata may elicit discomfort and anxiety from an observer. A child with a physical disability may elicit pity or sadness. Some affective responses make people want to help and get to know specific children; other responses underlie the desire for segregation and social distancing. It is likely that children learn emotional responses by observing adults and duplicating their affective reactions. Fear, disgust, warmth, sadness, love, and other emotions are mirrored by the children who observe them in their parents and in other significant adults.

Socializing Children's Behavior

Socializing children to behave in ways that are consistent with cultural norms and expectations is one of the most important parenting responsibilities. As children develop, they learn to shape their everyday behavior to please their parents and to avoid negative sanctions. Parents socialize general behaviors, such as altruism, that can influence children to interact with people with disabilities. Parents also teach children how to treat individuals with disabilities.

Altruism, Empathy, and Other Prosocial Behavior   Children learn prosocial behavior from their families. Parents teach their children values such as helpfulness, sensitivity, altruism, generosity, and kindness; stimulate role taking and empathy; and teach children about the consequences that their behavior has for the feelings and well-being of others (Eisenberg & Mussen, 1989). Parents socialize in young children concern for others through ongoing daily social exchanges, although the absolute frequency of these teaching events is not high (Grusec, 1991). Diamond, Hestenes, Carpenter, and Innes (1997) found that children's acceptance of classmates with disabilities was related to their general inclination to be accepting of typically developing peers; socially accepting children were accepting of all other children, including children with disabilities. Thus, families that socialized their children in such a way as to emphasize acceptance and prosocial behavior had children who generalized that prosocial teaching to children with disabilities. Similarly, Okagaki and colleagues (1998) found that parents who had more realistic expectations for age-appropriate prosocial behaviors had typically developing children who interacted more with classmates with disabilities.

Teaching Children How to Behave Toward Children with Disabilities
In addition to socializing general prosocial behavior patterns, some parents teach their children specific ways to interact with children with disabilities. A question–answer study (Stoneman et al., 1996) suggested that parents teach different behavioral strategies for interacting with children with different disabilities. Parents were most likely to encourage prosocial behavior (e.g., be a friend, play together) in response to questions about children with mental retardation, although prosocial strategies were taught in response to questions about children with all four disabilities. Children were instructed to ignore the behavior of very active children and to cope with aggressive behavior by going to a teacher, being careful, avoiding the child, not modeling the behavior, and being kind. Children were also instructed not to make fun of children with disabilities and not to call them names.

Söder (1990) concluded from findings of sociometric studies that avoidance seems to be typical in meetings between people with and without disabilities. In the study by Stoneman and colleagues (1996), avoidance was infrequently mentioned by parents as a strategy that they wanted their children to use, and, when mentioned, avoidance was specifically targeted toward children with aggressive behavior. In general, typically developing children were encouraged by their parents to interact with and be friends with peers with disabilities.

Role Relationships   Social relationships involve the enactment of roles, which are organized patterns of behavior that define equality or dominance relationships between people (Sarbin, 1954). Roles are socially useful because they allow individuals to develop expectations about the behavior and interaction patterns of others. It has been suggested that satisfaction with interpersonal relationships is, in part, a function of the ability of the participants to negotiate mutually acceptable roles and to enact those roles in a quality manner (Burr, Leigh, Day, & Constantine, 1979). Parents teach children about roles through the informal communication of expectations for behavior and through direct assignment of specific social roles (e.g., help your brother). These social exchanges occur during ongoing daily interactions between parents and children. From these social encounters, children extract important information about the roles they are expected to perform and the contexts in which those role enactments are appropriate. In addition to parent-ascribed roles, children experiment with roles on their own and create novel ways of interacting that meet the needs and desires of both social participants. Through trial and error and informed by social feedback, children create spontaneous reciprocal roles that define power relationships and that facilitate mutually enjoyable social exchanges.

Grusec (1991) suggested that spontaneously helping others is one of the most frequent forms of prosocial behavior in young children, providing children with a way to initiate and maintain pleasant social interactions with other children. Younger or less competent children are especially likely to elicit helping behavior from their playmates (Stoneman et al., 1988, 1991). In a question–answer study (Stoneman et al. 1996), parents frequently suggested that children provide help to peers with mental retardation. When children serve as "helpers" or "teachers" to others, the ensuing role relationship between the children is hierarchical rather than equalitarian. Friendships, conversely, are rooted in equalitarian role relationships (Hartup, 1979). This does not imply that helping and teaching are not part of the interactions between friends. Rather, roles between friends tend to be symmetrical, in that both children sometimes assume the role of helper or teacher. When one child has a disability, particularly a cognitive disability or a disability that limits the child's verbal expression, the helper and teacher roles tend not to be reciprocal. The typically developing child is dominant, and the child with a disability is in a submissive, nondominant role as the recipient of help or teaching.

Adults with disabilities are clear in their desire for symmetrical, equalitarian role relationships with peers without disabilities. Parents of typically developing children play an important role in teaching their children to interact with peers with disabilities, either as friends or in hierarchical, dominant role relationships. The attitudes and beliefs held by parents are one factor that determines the roles they teach their children to assume. These roles, in turn, define the meaning of the relationships between typically developing children and peers with disabilities.

CONCLUSION

Children learn from their parents about the meaning of different disabilities, and they learn values and behaviors that assist them in relating to children with disabilities when they encounter those children in inclusionary preschool environments, as well as in other community contexts. Parents create interactive social contexts that either include adult friends and family members with disabilities or are devoid of people with disabilities. Parents act as gatekeepers who regulate the experiences that young children have, managing their contacts with peers; choosing toys, books, and play materials; and controlling access to media. In addition, parents directly influence preschool programs through their selection of a program for their children and through their influence on policies and practices once their child is enrolled in a center. Thus, through multiple paths of influence, the attitudes of parents of typically developing children affect the success of preschool inclusion programs. Of course, parents are only one source of influence on young children. As children venture beyond the confines of the home environment, preschool teachers, religious educators, and many other sources of social influence help to shape the child's attitudes and beliefs. Parents, however, are the first source of influence for most children and remain a powerful socializing influence throughout childhood.

The book's title includes the phrase "focus on change." People's basic attitudes and beliefs go to the core of who those people are, what they think about the world in which they live, and what they value. Beliefs that are so deeply rooted in each of us are extremely resistant to change, yet there is cause for optimism. Triandis wrote,

When we think about people whom we know very little. . ., we tend to adopt the beliefs of other people. . .On the other hand, when we think of persons we know very well. . ., we rely mostly on our own experience. (1971, p. 104)

Most adults know very little about people with disabilities and do not have people with disabilities as close friends or as colleagues at work. Similarly, most adults have spent very little time interacting with children with disabilities. As a result, the attitudes discussed in this chapter are relatively fluid and subject to change on the basis of direct experience.

This relative fluidity of attitudes offers a great opportunity, along with substantial risk. The opportunity comes from the ability to influence positively the attitudes of parents of typically developing children by providing them with direct experience with high-quality inclusionary preschool programs. As parents see inclusion succeed, to the benefit of all children involved, they might be expected to change their attitudes and become supporters of inclusion. The risk, however, is great. The primary concern that parents have about inclusion is that providers lack the training and the resources to conduct high-quality programs. Unfortunately, many preschool programs that include children with disabilities are not of high quality. Parents of typically developing children want what is best for their children. If we can succeed in creating a system of inclusive preschool programs that meet the needs of all children, then parents of typically developing children will respond by becoming advocates for inclusionary programs.

If we include children with disabilities in programs that are already of questionable quality or in programs in which staff are not trained to support the needs of these children, then parents of typically developing children will solidify their concerns and their negative attitudes. Once parents have personal experience with unsuccessful inclusion that they perceive as harming their child's emotional or developmental growth, they become a strong force opposed to inclusion. If parents believe that their children are being harmed by going to school with children with disabilities, not even legal mandates such as ADA will guarantee that children with disabilities will continue to be included in preschool programs. This places great responsibility on those who implement inclusionary programs. If we are complacent and accept low-quality services, then parents of typically developing children can be expected to exert their influence and compromise the future of inclusionary programs. It is important that we develop inclusionary programs that are of high quality, providing facilitative learning environments for all children. If we succeed at this task, then the potential barriers to inclusion posed by parents of typically developing children will fall and these parents will become supporters of inclusion.

REFERENCES

Ajzen, I., & Fishbein, M. (1980). *Understanding attitudes and predicting social behavior.* Upper Saddle River, NJ: Prentice Hall.

Ajzen, I., Timko, C., & White, J.B. (1982). Self-monitoring and the attitude–behavior relation. *Journal of Personality and Social Psychology, 42,* 426–435.

Allport, G.W. (1954). *The nature of prejudice.* Reading, MA: Addison Wesley Longman.

Americans with Disabilities Act (ADA) of 1990, PL 101-336, 42 U.S.C. §§ 12101 *et seq.*

Bailey, D.B., McWilliam, R.A., Buysse, V., & Wesley, P.W. (1998). Inclusion in the context of competing values in early childhood education. *Early Childhood Research Quarterly, 13,* 27–47.

Bailey, D.B., & Winton, P.J. (1987). Stability and change in parents' expectations about mainstreaming. *Topics in Early Childhood Special Education, 7,* 73–88.

Barnett, W.S. (1986). Definition and classification of mental retardation: A reply to Zigler, Balla, and Hodapp. *American Journal of Mental Deficiency, 91,* 111–116.

Barsch, R.H. (1964). The handicapped ranking scale among parents of handicapped children. *American Journal of Public Health, 54,* 1560–1567.

Beckman, P.J., Barnwell, D., Horn, E., Hanson, M.J., Gutierrez, S., & Lieber, J. (1998). Communities, families, and inclusion. *Early Childhood Research Quarterly, 13,* 125–150.

Beckman, P.J., & Kohl, F.L. (1984). The effects of social and isolate toys on the interactions and play of integrated and nonintegrated groups of preschoolers. *Education and Training of the Mentally Retarded, 19,* 169–174.

Berry, G.L. (1998). Black family life on television and the socialization of the African American child: Images of marginality. *Journal of Comparative Family Studies, 29,* 233–242.

Berstein, L., Hayes, L., & Shauble, L. (1977). Experimenting with "Sesame Street" for mentally retarded children. In M. Harmonay (Ed.), *Promise and performance: Children with special needs* (pp. 65–77). Cambridge, MA: Ballinger.

Blacher, J., & Turnbull, A.P. (1982). Teacher and parent perspectives on selected social aspects of preschool mainstreaming. *The Exceptional Child, 29,* 191–199.

Bowd, A.D. (1992). Integration and mainstreaming in cultural context: Canadian and American approaches. *International Journal of Disability, Development & Education, 39,* 19–31.

Bricker, D.D. (1995). The challenge of inclusion. *Journal of Early Intervention, 19,* 179–194.

Brightman, A.J. (1977). "But their brain is broken": Young children's conceptions of retardation. In M. Harmonay (Ed.), *Promise and performance: Children with special needs* (pp. 59–64). Cambridge, MA: Ballinger.

Brooks, P.H., & Baumeister, A.A. (1977). A plea for consideration of ecological validity in the experimental psychology of mental retardation: A guest editorial. *American Journal of Mental Deficiency, 81,* 407–416.

Brown, R.J., & Turner, J.C. (1981). Interpersonal and intergroup behavior. In J.C. Turner & H. Giles (Eds.), *Intergroup behavior.* Oxford, England: Basil Blackwell Publishers.

Burr, W.R., Leigh, G.K., Day, R.D., & Constantine, J. (1979). Symbolic interaction and the family. In W.R. Burr, R. Hill, F.I. Nye, & I.L. Reiss (Eds.), *Contemporary theories about the family* (Vol. 2, pp. 42–111). New York: The Free Press.

Buysse, V., Wesley, P., Keyes, L., & Bailey, D.B., Jr. (1996). Assessing the comfort zone of child care teachers in serving young children with disabilities. *Journal of Early Intervention, 20,* 189–203.

Charren, P., & Sandler, M.W. (1983). *Changing channels: Living (sensibly) with television.* Reading, MA: Addison Wesley Longman.

Danseco, E.R. (1997). Parental beliefs on childhood disability: Insights on culture, child development, and intervention. *International Journal of Disability, Development & Education, 44,* 41–52.

Diamond, K.E., Hestenes, L.L., Carpenter, E.S., & Innes, F.K. (1997). Relationships between enrollment in an inclusive class and preschool children's ideas about people with disabilities. *Topics in Early Childhood Special Education, 17,* 520–536.

Diamond, K.E., & LeFurgy, W.G. (1994). Attitudes of parents of preschool children toward integration. *Early Education and Development, 5,* 69–77.

Ebert, S. (1977). Paying deference to differences: A child's version of *Noblesse Oblige?* In M. Harmonay (Ed.), *Promise and performance: Children with special needs* (pp. 78–80). Cambridge, MA: Ballinger.

Eisenberg, N., & Mussen, P.H. (1989). *The roots of prosocial behavior in children.* New York: Cambridge University Press.

Eiserman, W.D., Shisler, L., & Healey, S. (1995). A community assessment of preschool providers' attitudes toward inclusion. *Journal of Early Intervention, 19,* 149–167.

Farber, B., & Rowitz, L. (1986). Families with a mentally retarded child. In N.R. Ellis & N.W. Bray (Eds.), *International review of research in mental retardation* (Vol. 14, pp. 201–224). San Diego: Academic Press.

Favazza, P.C., & Odom, S.L. (1997). Promoting positive attitudes of kindergarten-age children toward people with disabilities. *Exceptional Children, 63,* 405–418.

Fishbein, M., & Ajzen, I. (1975). *Belief, attitude, intention, and behavior: An introduction to theory and research.* Reading, MA: Addison Wesley Longman.

Fujiara, G.T., & Yamaki, K. (1997). Analysis of ethnic variations in developmental disability prevalence and household economic status. *Mental Retardation, 35,* 286–294.

Furnham, A., & Akande, A. (1997). Cross-cultural differences in attributions for overcoming specific psychological problems. *Journal of Social Behavior & Personality, 12,* 727–742.

Gething, L. (1991). Generality vs. specificity of attitudes towards people with disabilities. *British Journal of Medical Psychology, 64,* 55–64.

Gottlieb, J., Corman, L., & Curci, R. (1984). Attitudes toward mentally retarded children. In R.L. Jones (Ed.), *Attitudes and attitude change in special education: Theory and practice* (pp. 143–156). Reston, VA: The Council for Exceptional Children.

Gottlieb, J., & Siperstein, G.N. (1976). Attitudes toward mentally retarded persons: Effects of attitude referent specificity. *American Journal of Mental Deficiency, 80,* 376–381.

Green, A.L., & Stoneman, Z. (1989). Attitudes of mothers and fathers of nonhandicapped children. *Journal of Early Intervention, 13,* 292–304.

Grusec, J.E. (1991). Socializing concern for others in the home. *Developmental Psychology, 27,* 338–342.

Guralnick, M.J. (1994). Mothers' perceptions of the benefits and drawbacks of early childhood mainstreaming. *Journal of Early Intervention, 18,* 168–183.

Guralnick, M.J. (1997). Peer social networks of young boys with developmental delays. *American Journal on Mental Retardation, 101,* 595–612.

Guralnick, M.J. (1999). The nature and meaning of social integration for young children with mild developmental delays in inclusive settings. *Journal of Early Intervention, 22,* 70–86.

Hartup, W.W. (1979). The social worlds of childhood. *American Psychologist, 34,* 944–950.

Heider, F. (1958). *The psychology of interpersonal relations.* New York: John Wiley & Sons.

Holmes, R.M. (1995). *How young children perceive race.* Newberry Park, CA: Sage Publications.

Innes, F.K. (1999, April). *What mothers say to their young children about disabilities.* Presented at the Society for Research in Child Development, Albuquerque, NM.

Innes, F.K., & Diamond, K.E. (1999). Typically developing children's interactions with peers with disabilities: Relationships between mothers' comments and children's ideas about disabilities. *Topics in Early Childhood Special Education, 19,* 103–111.

Jones, R.L. (1974). The hierarchical structure of attitudes toward the exceptional. *Exceptional Children, 40,* 430–435.

Katz, I. (1981). *Stigma: A social psychological analysis.* Mahwah, NJ: Lawrence Erlbaum Associates.

Kelley, H.H. (1971). *Attribution in social interaction.* Morristown, NJ: General Learning.

Klein, T.P. (1995, March). *Parental pathways of influence on children's peer relationships: Social framing and meaning construction.* Paper presented at the Society for Research on Child Development, Indianapolis, IN.

Ladd, G.W. (1992). Themes and theories: Perspective on processes in family–peer relationships. In R.D. Parke & G.W. Ladd (Eds.), *Family–peer relationships: Modes of linkage* (pp. 1–34). Mahwah, NJ: Lawrence Erlbaum Associates.

Ladd, G.W., & Golter, B.S. (1988). Parents' management of preschoolers' peer relations: Is it related to children's social competence? *Developmental Psychology, 24,* 109–117.

Ladd, G.W., & Hart, C.H. (1992). Creating informal play opportunities: Are parents' and preschoolers' initiations related to children's competence with peers? *Developmental Psychology, 28,* 1179–1187.

Ladd, G.W., Profilet, S.M., & Hart, C.H. (1992). Parents' management of children's peer relations: Facilitating and supervising children's activities in the peer culture. In R.D. Parke & G.W. Ladd (Eds.), *Family–peer relationships: Modes of linkage* (pp. 215–254). Mahwah, NJ: Lawrence Erlbaum Associates.

Leonard, R., & Crawford, J. (1989). Two approaches to seeing people with disabilities. *Australian Journal of Social Issues, 24,* 112–125.

Leung, P., & Wright, T.J. (1993). Introduction: Minorities with disabilities. In T.J. Wright & P. Leung (Eds.), *Meeting the unique needs of minorities with disabilities: A report to the President and the Congress.* Washington, DC: National Council on Disability.

Lewis, M., Feiring, C., & Brooks-Gunn, J. (1988). Young children's social networks as a function of age and dysfunction. *Infant Mental Health Journal, 9,* 142–157.

Maas, E., Marecek, J., & Travers, J. (1978). Children's conceptions of disordered behavior. *Child Development, 49,* 146–154.

Marchant, C. (1995). Teachers' views of integrated preschools. *Journal of Early Intervention, 19,* 61–73.

McCollum, J.A., & McBride, S.L. (1997). Ratings of parent–infant interaction: Raising questions of cultural validity. *Topics in Early Childhood Special Education, 17,* 494–519.

Miller, L.J., Strain, P.S., Boyd, K., Hunsicker, S., McKinley, J., & Wu, A. (1992). Parental attitudes toward integration. *Topics in Early Childhood Special Education, 12,* 230–246.

Mink, I.R. (1997). Studying culturally diverse families of children with mental retardation. In N.W. Bray (Ed.), *International review of research in mental retardation* (Vol. 20, pp. 75–98). San Diego: Academic Press.

Okagaki, L., Diamond, K.E., Kontos, S.J., & Hestenes, L.L. (1998). Correlates of young children's interactions with classmates with disabilities. *Early Childhood Research Quarterly, 13,* 67–86.

Oskamp, S.I., Kaufman, K., & Wolterbeek, L.A. (1996). Gender role portrayals in preschool picture books. *Journal of Social Behavior & Personality, 11,* 27–39.

Palmer, E.L., & Dorr, A. (1980). *Children and the faces of television: Teaching, violence, selling.* San Diego: Academic Press.

Peck, C.A., Carlson, P., & Helmstetter, E. (1992). Parent and teacher perceptions of outcomes for typically developing children enrolled in integrated early childhood programs: A statewide survey. *Journal of Early Intervention, 16,* 53–63.

Peck, C.A., Hayden, L., Wandschneider, M., Peterson, K., & Richarz, S. (1989). Development of integrated preschools: A qualitative inquiry into sources of resistance among parents, administrators, and teachers. *Journal of Early Intervention, 13,* 353–364.

Phillips, M.J. (1985). Try harder: The experience of disability and the dilemma of normalization. *Social Science Journal, 22,* 45–57.

Phillips, M.J. (1990). Damaged goods: Oral narratives of the experience of disability in American culture. *Social Science and Medicine, 30,* 849–857.

Quilitch, H.R., Christophersen, E.R., & Risley, T.R. (1977). The evaluation of children's play materials. *Journal of Applied Behavior Analysis, 10,* 501–502.

Quilitch, H.R., & Risley, T.R. (1973). The effects of play materials on social play. *Journal of Applied Behavior Analysis, 6,* 573–578.

Ramsey, P.G. (1987). Young children's thinking about ethnic differences. In J.S. Phinney & M.J. Rotheram (Eds.), *Children's ethnic socialization: Pluralism and development* (pp. 56–72). Newberry Park, CA: Sage Publications.

Reichart, D.C., Lynch, E.C., Anderson, B.C., Svobodny, L.A., DiCola, J.M., & Mercury, M.G. (1989). Parental perspectives on integrated preschool opportunities for children with handicaps and children without handicaps. *Journal of Early Intervention, 13,* 6–13.

Ronald, L. (1977). "How did it happen?": Children's reactions to physical differences. In M. Harmonay (Ed.), *Promise and performance: Children with special needs* (pp. 23–34). Cambridge, MA: Ballinger.

Rose, A. (1997). "Who causes the blind to see": Disability and quality of religious life. *Disability & Society, 12,* 395–405.

Rosenbaum, P.L., Armstrong, R.W., & King, S.M. (1987). Parental attitudes toward children with handicaps: New perspectives with a new measure. *Developmental and Behavioral Pediatrics, 8,* 327–334.

Rugg, M., & Stoneman, Z. (1988, June). *Project CEEI: A demonstration program for mainstreaming special needs young children.* Presented at the Gulf Coast Conference on Early Intervention, Point Clear, AL.

Sarbin, T.R. (1954). Role theory. In G. Lindzey (Ed.), *Handbook of social psychology* (Vol. 1, pp. 223–258). Reading, MA: Addison Wesley Longman.

Scheier, M.G., Carver, C.S., Schulz, R., Glass, D.C., & Katz, I. (1978). Sympathy, self-consciousness, and reactions to the stigmatized. *Journal of Applied Social Psychology, 6,* 270–282.

Selway, D., & Ashman, A.F. (1998). Disability, religion and health: A literature review in search of the spiritual dimensions of disability. *Disability & Society, 13,* 429–439.

Söder, M. (1990). Prejudice or ambivalence? Attitudes toward persons with disabilities. *Disability, Handicap & Society, 5,* 227–241.

Stoiber, K.C., Gettinger, M., & Goetz, D. (1998). Exploring factors influencing parents' and early childhood practitioners' beliefs about inclusion. *Early Childhood Research Quarterly, 13,* 107–124.

Stoneman, Z. (1993). The effects of attitude on preschool integration. In C.A. Peck, S.L. Odom, & D.D. Bricker (Eds.), *Integrating young children with disabilities into community programs: Ecological perspectives on research and implementation* (pp. 223–248). Baltimore: Paul H. Brookes Publishing Co.

Stoneman, Z. (1997, May). *The Comfort Scale.* New York: American Association on Mental Retardation.

Stoneman, Z., Brody, G.H., Davis, C.H., & Crapps, J.M. (1988). Child care responsibilities, peer relations, and sibling conflict: Older siblings of mentally retarded children. *American Journal of Mental Retardation, 93,* 174–183.

Stoneman, Z., Brody, G.H., Davis, C.H., & Crapps, J.M. (1991). Ascribed role relations between children with mental retardation and their younger siblings. *American Journal of Mental Retardation, 95,* 537–550.

Stoneman, Z., Cantrell, M.L., & Hoover-Dempsey, K. (1983). The association between play materials and social behavior in a mainstreamed preschool: A naturalistic investigation. *Journal of Applied Developmental Psychology, 4,* 163–174.

Stoneman, Z., Rugg, M., & Rivers, J. (1996, December). *How do young children learn about peers with disabilities? Examining the role of parents as teachers of values, attitudes, and prosocial behavior.* Presented at the Division for Early Childhood, Council for Exceptional Children, Phoenix, AZ.

Stratford, B. (1994). Down syndrome is for life. *International Journal of Disability, Development & Education, 41,* 3–13.

Stuart, O.W. (1992). Race and disability: Just a double oppression? *Disability, Handicap & Society, 7,* 177–188.

Tajfel, H. (1981). *Human groups and social categories.* New York: Cambridge University Press.

Thompson, T.L., & Zerbinos, E. (1997). Television cartoons: Do children notice it's a boy's world? *Sex Roles, 37,* 415–432.

Triandis, H.C. (1971). *Attitude and attitude change.* New York: John Wiley & Sons.

Triandis, H.C., Adamopoulos, J., & Brinberg, D. (1984). Perspectives and issues in the study of attitudes. In R.L. Jones (Ed.), *Attitudes and attitude change in special education: Theory and practice* (pp. 21–40). Reston, VA: The Council for Exceptional Children.

Turnbull, A.P., Winton, P.J., Blacher, J., & Salkind, N. (1983). Mainstreaming in the kindergarten classroom: Perspectives of parents of handicapped and nonhandicapped children. *Journal of the Division for Early Childhood, 6*, 14–20.

Turner, N.D., & Traxler, M. (1997). Children's literature for the primary inclusive classroom: Increasing understanding of children with hearing impairments. *American Annals of the Deaf, 142*, 350–355.

Van Der Klift, E. (1995, March). *Friendships.* Presented at Better All Together II, Visions and Strategies for Inclusive Education, Athens, GA.

Walker, S., Asbury, C., Maholmes, V., & Rackley, R. (1991). Prevalence, distribution and impact of disability among ethnic minorities. In S. Walker, F.Z. Belgrave, R.W. Nicholls, & K.A. Turner (Eds.), *Future frontiers in the employment of minority persons with disabilities* (pp. 10–24). Washington, DC: President's Committee on Employment of People with Disabilities.

Weiner, B. (1974). *Achievement motivation and attribution theory.* Morristown, NJ: General Learning Press.

Whiteman, M., & Lukoff, I.F. (1965). Attitude toward blindness and other physical handicaps. *Journal of Social Psychology, 66*, 135–145.

Wolfensberger, W. (1972). *Normalization.* Toronto, Ontario, Canada: National Institute on Mental Retardation.

Yuker, H.E. (1983). The lack of a stable order of preference for disabilities: A response to Richardson and Ronald. *Rehabilitation Psychology, 28*, 93–103.

ELIZABETH J. ERWIN

LESLIE C. SOODAK

PAMELA J. WINTON

ANN TURNBULL

6

"I Wish It Wouldn't All Depend on Me"

Research on Families and Early Childhood Inclusion

This chapter is framed by the underlying value of families as partners in early intervention. This basic principle has guided service delivery for young children with disabilities and their families since the 1980s. Despite the presence of parents' participation in a few model programs in the early 1970s, parents' participation was not seriously encouraged until the passage of the Education for All Handicapped Children Act (PL 94-142) in 1975 (Bricker, 1989). The implementation of the Education of the Handicapped Act Amendments (PL 99-457) in 1986 strengthened the commitment to and practices of working collaboratively with families. Because families are the primary source of nurturing for very young children, the family has been recognized as one of the most important influences in a young child's life. Family and professional partnerships are essential in promoting the development, health, and well-being of young children with disabilities.

Given the growing attention to including young children with disabilities in natural environments with their age-peers, the need for parent–professional partnerships remains a priority. The limited availability of or accessibility to inclusive environments for some parents (Erwin & Soodak, 1995; Hanson et al., 1998), however, suggests that parents may be assuming roles and responsibilities for securing an inclusive placement that make the partnership seem unbalanced. Understanding parents' experiences with inclusive education from their own perspectives can provide an invaluable insight into the issues, challenges, and practices of educating young children with disabilities successfully in inclusive environments.

This chapter addresses the impact of perceptions and experiences of families on their participation in their young child's inclusive education. To address families' perspectives, this chapter is organized to accomplish the following three purposes: 1) provide a summary of research on family perspectives on inclusive education since the 1980s, 2) describe a comprehensive framework of parents' perspectives on their participation in inclusive education, and 3) present an agenda for strengthening family–professional partnerships associated with inclusive education for young children with disabilities.

RESEARCH ON FAMILY PERSPECTIVES ON INCLUSION

The body of research on the perspectives and experiences of parents with young children with disabilities can provide a unique and critical context for understanding inclusive education.

During the 1980s

The first study in the literature in the early 1980s focused on the perspectives of mothers who had made a placement decision for their child with a disability in either an inclusive or a specialized early childhood environment (Turnbull & Winton, 1983; Winton, 1981). These mothers addressed the factors that influenced their 1) placement choice of preschool program, 2) perceived benefits and drawbacks for themselves and their children regarding placement, and 3) satisfaction with placement. The 31 children (ages 3–5) included in this study were described as having mild or moderate disabilities. Approximately two thirds of the children were Caucasian, and one third were African American. The definition of *inclusion* adopted by this study was spending at least 6 hours per week in an educational placement with children without disabilities. A multimethod approach to gathering information was used. First, in-depth interviews were conducted with the 31 mothers. Second, the analyzed interview data served as the basis for generating a survey questionnaire that the 31 mothers also completed.

In terms of factors that influenced their choices of preschool programs, mothers described an interaction of both child and parent needs. The child need

mentioned by the greatest number of mothers in both groups was selecting a preschool that would enhance their child's general developmental progress. The mothers who selected an inclusive placement tended to believe that typical peer interaction would be a major catalyst for developmental growth, whereas the mothers who selected a specialized placement believed that developmental progress would be accentuated by peers with similar needs. Regarding mothers' perspectives on their own needs, mothers who chose inclusive and specialized placements both had concerns related to their children's peer group. Some of the mothers who chose specialized environments worried about their child's being teased or rejected by children who were typically developing; alternatively, mothers who chose inclusive placements did not want their child associated with a disability that had a greater stigma than the particular disability that their child experienced (e.g., a child with a physical disability attending a special preschool that had "mental retardation" in the preschool's name). Several mothers of children who chose specialized placements emphasized their own parental need of having an environment in which they believed that their child's special needs would be addressed without their having to feel the constant pressure of working with their child.

The mothers described the major child benefits of inclusive environments as exposure to real-world experiences and interaction with typical peers, whereas they described the major drawbacks to be inadequate special services, lack of individual attention, and inappropriately trained staff. They expressed the most significant concerns about children with autism and mental retardation being part of inclusive classrooms. In terms of mothers' perceptions of benefits and drawbacks for themselves related to their child's placement, the major difference between the inclusive and specialized groups was that a greater number of mothers in the specialized group mentioned professional involvement so that they could relax and not worry about their child. The majority of parents in both groups did not identify any drawbacks for themselves at their child's current preschool placement.

On the topic of parent satisfaction with placement, parents reported that approximately half of their child's needs were met at the current placement and approximately half of their own needs were met. It is interesting that mothers reported that inclusive preschools resulted in more benefits, fewer drawbacks, and a higher percentage of needs met for their child. They also reported more benefits, fewer drawbacks, and a higher percentage of needs met for parents in specialized preschools.

After this early study, a number of investigators asked parents of children without disabilities about their perspectives toward early childhood inclusion (Bailey & Winton, 1987; Green & Stoneman, 1989; Reichart et al., 1989; Winton, Turnbull, Blacher, & Salkind, 1983), as well as the perspectives of parents of children with disabilities. These studies tended to focus primarily on the benefits and drawbacks of inclusion from the perspectives of parents (see Chapter 5). Results generally indicated a high level of agreement between both sets of parents about the greatest benefits of inclusion. These benefits were related to social outcomes (e.g., exposure to the real world, opportunity to learn from children without disabilities). The greatest drawbacks were related to instructional issues (e.g., qualified teachers, special materials, intensive therapies). Bailey and Winton (1987) conducted the first longitudinal study on the topic of parent perspectives on early childhood inclusion.

They reported data collected from parents of preschoolers with and without disabilities who attended an inclusive child care program. The ages of the children ranged from 6 weeks to 5 years. The authors did not describe the program's definition of inclusion. Data were collected in late summer, approximately 2 weeks before the enrollment of nine children with disabilities, and again 9 months later.

Benefits and drawbacks of inclusion remained highly consistent with previous research, with benefits focusing on the fact that inclusion provides exposure to the real world and opportunities for increased community acceptance; drawbacks concentrated more on teacher competency as related to instructional effectiveness. They reported that some of the families' initial expectations (e.g., learning more about typical child development, having opportunities to interact with parents whose children do not have disabilities) did not come to fruition over the 9-month period. The authors concluded that parents perceived that inclusion worked better for children than it did for themselves. They also emphasized the variability across parents that underscored the importance of individualizing in light of the perspectives of each family.

As a follow-up to research findings indicating concern about how inclusion was working for families, two studies investigated the interactions that occur between parents (as contrasted to interactions between children) whose children have disabilities and those whose children do not have disabilities (Blacher & Turnbull, 1982; Bailey & Winton, 1989). Bailey and Winton conducted the most comprehensive analysis on the friendship and acquaintance patterns of parents whose children attended an inclusive child care program. They collected data both at the beginning of the inclusive preschool and 9 months after children had been attending this program. Participants in this study were the same as those previously described in Bailey and Winton's (1987) longitudinal study of parent perspectives on early intervention.

Parents of preschoolers with disabilities reported that they tended to interact with equal frequency with parents of children with disabilities and parents of children without disabilities. On the contrary, the majority of parents of preschoolers without disabilities indicated that they were more likely to interact with other parents of children without disabilities. The parents of children with disabilities reported being less satisfied with their knowledge of other families as contrasted to parents of children without disabilities. These data raise the issue of the extent to which parents perceive that they experience inclusion for *themselves* in environments in which most of the children and their families were not part of the disability world.

In reflecting on this body of research from the perspective of 20-year hindsight, the results across studies are consistent. For example, all of the research on parent perspectives on child benefits and drawbacks highlighted identical variables—benefits associated with social variables and drawbacks associated with instructional variables. Also consistent were findings on how parents viewed their own inclusion with parents of children without disabilities, indicating that they interacted more frequently with other parents of children without disabilities as contrasted to parents of children with disabilities. The research conducted throughout the 1980s primarily incorporated the parent questionnaire that was developed in the original study by Winton (1981) and Turnbull and Winton (1983). Perhaps the use of this questionnaire, which was solidly grounded in parents' experiences (items were generated from a content analysis of in-depth interviews), was one reason that findings have been consistent across studies.

One of the laments one sometimes hears about a systemic educational change such as inclusion is that it cannot be accomplished "overnight" but rather requires years of implementation. When the research results are analyzed across the entire decade of the 1980s, we can soundly conclude that the concerns that parents expressed at the beginning of the decade were still being expressed at the end of the decade. Did this trend continue across the 1990s, or were parental concerns more successfully addressed?

During the 1990s

The early 1990s brought further confirmation of parents' perspectives on the benefits and drawbacks of inclusion for their children with disabilities. Guralnick (1994), who conducted a study of mothers' perspectives on the benefits and drawbacks of early childhood inclusion, expanded the knowledge base by including a much larger sample of children whose disabilities were categorized into four different conditions: cognitive delays, communication disorders, physical disabilities, and children at risk. The sample of children with disabilities included 222 children who ranged in age from 48 to 71 months. The sample of children without disabilities included 59 children of similar ages. In terms of the definition of inclusion, the author reported that "programs considered as mainstreamed, reverse-mainstreamed, and those containing planned integration experience with typical children were all placed in the integration category" (Guralnick, 1994, p. 172). This study also used a variation of the questionnaire originally developed by Winton (1981) and Turnbull and Winton (1983).

Guralnick reported similar findings to the early studies, including that parents believed that it was beneficial for their child to have real-world learning that would more likely lead to acceptance in the community and participation in interesting and creative activities. On the downside, he found, similar to the studies in the 1980s, that parents had major concerns regarding the availability of special help, special services, and qualified personnel in addition to concern about the potential social rejection of their child.

His more in-depth study added to the knowledge base in noting that the mothers' perspectives were not related to their child's developmental status, current placement, or almost all of the child characteristics measured in the investigation (age, gender, ethnicity, IQ score, and language development). Although the severity of the child's disability did not influence mothers' perspectives, mothers whose children had behavior problems were substantially more concerned about the drawbacks of inclusion as contrasted to mothers whose children did not have behavior problems.

Diamond and LeFurgy (1994) conducted a study at approximately the same time as Guralnick's (1994). They reported on the attitudes of 23 parents of preschool children with disabilities and 80 children without disabilities. The children ranged in age from 3 to 4 years. The children with disabilities were described as having neurological disorders and developmental disabilities in the mild to moderate range. The authors characterized the inclusive programs attended by the children as embedding individualized goals within developmentally appropriate practice and curriculum, in addition to also offering appropriate therapies. These researchers administered a questionnaire at the beginning and end of the school year. They concluded that parents of young children typically hold positive attitudes toward inclusion and that their attitudes may be positively influenced by their child's participation in an inclusive program.

An analysis of the research since the mid-1990s reveals new information from both quantitative and qualitative methodologies. Stoiber, Gettinger, and Goetz (1998) reported quantitative data from 150 parents of children with disabilities, 260 parents of children without disabilities, and 128 practitioners. Children ranged in age from 3 to 5 years. There was a broad range of disabilities represented; the most frequent categories were speech/language delays, cognitive delays, and behavior disorders. There was also a wide range of program models represented, including Head Start, child care centers, and a university-affiliated private preschool. The definition of inclusion used by the various programs was not provided. Results indicated that parent demographic variables were associated with their particular perspectives toward inclusion. Some of these findings indicated that 1) parents with high or middle incomes reported more positive inclusion perspectives than did parents with lower incomes, 2) parents with a college education had more positive beliefs than parents with a high school education, 3) parents with one or two children had more positive beliefs than did parents with four or more children, 4) married parents had more positive beliefs than did single parents, and 5) no differences were found in inclusion perspectives by parents from urban, suburban, and rural environments.

Two studies by Bennett and colleagues (Bennett, DeLuca, & Bruns, 1997; Bennett, Lee, & Lueke, 1998) provide an extremely comprehensive analysis of family perspectives toward inclusive experiences. In the first study, Bennett and colleagues (1997) used a combination of surveys and interviews with 84 teachers and 48 parents. The 48 parents had 60 children with disabilities who ranged in age from "preschool-age" through 7 years. A broad range of disabilities were included; almost two thirds of the children were classified as having cognitive delays or behavior disorders. The authors did not provide a definition of inclusion. Findings included the following: 1) Parents reported strong endorsement of the benefits of inclusion for their child and indicated that their experiences with inclusion generally had been positive, 2) the most frequently reported benefit was the availability of typical behavior role models, 3) teachers were less supportive of the concept of inclusion for all children than were parents, 4) parents reported that the most important ingredients of successful inclusion were collaboration among all parties, facilitation of friendships, and parental contributions, 5) teachers reported that the most important ingredients were availability of support staff, assistance with instructional adaptation, sufficient time for planning, and smaller class size, and 6) teachers indicated less positive regard for instructional assistants as contrasted to parental viewpoints. This study was unique in comparing parent and teacher perspectives. The differences in their perspectives are noteworthy.

The study by Bennett and colleagues (1998) involved in-depth interviews of 18 parents of children with a disability. A unique aspect of this study was that interviews were conducted with eight couples composed of both a husband and a wife, with an additional one mother and one father interviewed without his or her spouse. Thus, it seems that this was the first study that made a consistent effort to include the perspectives of fathers. The 11 children in this study ranged in age from 3 to 6 years; approximately half of the children had a developmental disability. Children in this study were placed in a range of specialized and inclusive environments (no definition provided). Approximately half of the children were enrolled dually in both types of programs. Some children attended only specialized programs,

and others attended only inclusive programs.

Three broad themes emerge from the qualitative data. First, with respect to the theme of "expectations and world view of mothers and fathers," placement decisions were influenced by the parents' unique beliefs and expectations about what was important for their child. In addition, the educational beliefs and values interacted with factors such as professional expectations, age of child, type of disability, and educational placement decisions.

With respect to the second theme, a "broad view of inclusion," the following points were expressed: 1) Parents were concerned with inclusion in all areas of life (e.g., religious activities, community recreation, neighborhood playgroups) and across the full life span, 2) parents recognized the need to have the child exposed to a typical environment but also to have related services and intensive therapies, 3) parents spoke of the benefits of real-world exposure and opportunity to interact with typical models, and 4) parents' concerns about inclusion were lack of attention from teachers, concern about the quality of services available, and the possibility of their child's being ridiculed or rejected by peers.

Finally, for the theme of "parent involvement in child's education," parent perspectives can be summarized as follows: 1) Most of the families expressed overall satisfaction with their professional interactions, 2) the involvement of mothers and fathers tended to be along similar lines (mothers tended to be more concerned with socialization and fathers with overall development; these different concerns were complementary in contributing to the child's overall development), 3) parents expressed the need for professionals to teach them intervention strategies that they could implement at home, and 4) parents expressed preferences for informal communication.

Research from these past 2 decades underscores parents' preferences for informal communication and their priority for collaborative planning. Regarding parent perspectives, there is a striking similarity between the first studies reported in the 1980s (Turnbull & Winton, 1983; Winton, 1981) and the last one in the 1990s (Bennett et al., 1998). Inclusion decisions typically are based on a complex interaction of parental beliefs, child characteristics, and other factors (e.g., availability of therapy). Often, parents do not segment inclusion as solely a school issue; rather, they want inclusion in multiple aspects of life—neighborhood, recreational activities, and religious community.

Looking back over the 1990s research findings, it seems that the more things change, the more they stay the same. The same trend persists—the benefits of inclusion tend to be in the social arena (e.g., availability of typical models), and the drawbacks relate to instructional issues (e.g., individualized attention, quality of services). The literature suggests that there are a number of studies that essentially report similar findings. Unfortunately, there is no indication that problems noted in the early 1980s have been resolved. Nevertheless, new problems are emerging, requiring new solutions. For those who believe that systemic change must be looked at on the basis of decades rather than of years, the conclusion from this research on parent perspectives is that inclusion is far from fully implemented. In particular, there remain significant parental concerns that instructional support and services are not adequately in place in typical early childhood environments.

The research agenda is shifting, however, and that shift should be supported. The majority of studies during the past 2 decades have focused on parents' perspectives on the benefits and drawbacks of inclusion from a child-centered per-spective. Clearly, one of the areas of significant progress in the 1990s was the conceptualization and implementation of family-centered approaches in early childhood (Bailey & McWilliam, 1990; Dunst, Johanson, Trivette, & Hamby, 1991; Shelton, Jeppson, & Johnson, 1987; Turbiville, Turnbull, Garland, & Lee, 1996). The goal of family-centered intervention is to enhance the well-being of the family as a whole, in addition to the well-being of the child.

Thus, the research agenda is broadening not only to include the perspectives of families about the inclusion of their children but also to concentrate more directly on the perspectives of families on a broad range of topics. These topics include families' own roles and responsibilities associated with inclusion, as well as inclusion outcomes for the family as a whole. As is discussed in the following section, the participation of parents in inclusive early education environments is influenced by multiple interrelated factors. Given the individuality of each family, the nature and degree of participation most likely will vary from parent to parent. There is, however, a central theme that unifies parents' experiences. Parents generally want to be involved in their child's inclusive education but do not necessarily want to be responsible for creating it or ensuring its success. The next section presents a contemporary view of the myriad variables that must be considered in taking a broader family-centered perspective.

MULTIPLE INFLUENCES ON FAMILY–PROFESSIONAL PARTNERSHIPS IN INCLUSIVE EARLY EDUCATION

Since the early 1980s, research has focused primarily on parents' perspectives on the benefits and drawbacks of early childhood inclusive education. As inclusion becomes more of a reality for a greater number of families, there is growing interest in understanding *how* parents participate in their child's education. There is limited understanding of the conditions that influence parent–professional partnerships in inclusive environments. The research highlighted in this section explores parents' perspectives on their own participation in inclusive environments to understand how effective parent–professional partnerships emerge.

The experiences of two parents, Mary and Anita, are highlighted in this chapter. These parents were participants in a qualitative study conducted by Soodak and Erwin (2000) of 10 parents of young children with significant disabilities who attended inclusive educational environments. The experiences and perspectives shared by each of the parents were analyzed to understand what parents desire in their interactions with school personnel and the factors that shape their participation. This study is highlighted here because it is one of a few to provide a close look at the multiple and complex factors that influence parents' participation as well as the formation of effective parent–professional partnerships in inclusive environments. This

study contributes to a small but growing body of research (Bennett et al., 1997; Bennett et al., 1998; Hanson et al., 1998; Janko, Schwartz, Sandall, Anderson, & Cottam, 1997) that explores how family-centered approaches can be implemented within inclusive environments and how numerous factors interact in shaping parents' participation.

Portraits of Two Parents Who Chose Inclusive Education for Their Young Children with Disabilities

Mary's and Anita's experiences, which are representative of others' in the study, are used to illustrate the major themes that emerged from this research. Both women lived in or around large cities in the northeast. Demographic information about these women and their children is presented in Table 6.1.

These women were similar in that they were both working mothers in two-parent families who wanted their children to have typical and meaningful lives. Both women spoke of having a clear "vision" for their child that drove their desire for inclusion. However, despite some similarities, their stories are markedly different in terms of the nature and quality of the experiences they had

Table 6.1. Parent and child demographics

Anita	Mary
Married	Married
African American	Hispanic
Employed full time as human resources analyst	Employed full time as a family support coordinator
Lives in urban environment	Lives in suburbs
Has one child	Has four children
Adam	**Charles**
Age 4	Age 5
African American	Hispanic
Attends inclusive preschool not in own neighborhood	Attends inclusive kindergarten in neighborhood school
Second year in inclusive environment	Fifth year in inclusive environment
Has Down syndrome	Has label of "other health impaired"
Receives in-class and pull-out related services	Receives most of related services in class

with school personnel. In general, Anita had a more satisfying and positive experience than Mary, whose participation was characterized by disharmony and distrust. The stories of these women are presented to provide a contrast in the quality of experiences that can emerge from parent–professional partnerships.

As indicated in Table 6.1, Mary is a Hispanic married mother of four children who were between the ages of 2 and 10 years. Mary's son Charles, who had been classified by the school as "other health impaired," attended an inclusive kindergarten in the suburban neighborhood school that his siblings attended. Charles, who was described by his mother as "half Spanish and half Anglo-American," attended child care programs with typical children since his birth 5 years earlier.

Mary had what she thought was a very positive experience with the preschool program that Charles attended for 2 years before kindergarten. However, she and her husband were shocked when more than half of the team at the preschool recommended that Charles be placed in a self-contained classroom for kindergarten. They were surprised because they had been told for 2 years that Charles was progressing extremely well and learning a great deal from his peers. Mary discussed how she needed to "fight a little bit" to get him included in kindergarten by developing and sharing a vision of what she and her husband wanted for Charles, bringing to their meetings experts and advocates on inclusion, and, finally, threatening litigation.

As a result of his parents' efforts, Charles was placed in an inclusive kindergarten classroom in his neighborhood public school. He received speech-language therapy, occupational therapy, and physical therapy, as well as the support of an inclusion facilitator and a teacher of students with hearing impairments. In the classroom was a full-time

aide who was introduced to the class as "a helper for the whole class." Most services were provided to Charles in the classroom or other natural environments with the exception of his being pulled out for 30 minutes a week for speech-language therapy.

Mary made sure that she was included "every step of the way" in her son's education, yet she did not feel accepted fully by all personnel with whom she interacted. She was generally satisfied with her son's teachers and acknowledged the efforts of the instructional staff to educate all children in the classroom:

> They're all just wonderful teachers. And I think that all the kids are benefiting from Charles being in the classroom. They have this aide now that not only helps Charles but helps everyone. They have this wonderful occupational therapist coming in and doing activities for all the kids.

Mary did not have the same feelings about her involvement with district-level personnel. She believed that she was kept informed of changes in her son's education by the administration primarily as a result of her own insistence (and the district's fear of litigation). For example, she threatened to call the state's Protection and Advocacy office when the school surprised her with a change in her child's placement, and she requested an additional team meeting when she was not provided with pertinent information before a decision was made. She frequently had to remind the administration that she is part of the decision-making team, and she often felt like a "thorn in their side." Mary described herself as an active and involved parent; perhaps more than she wishes to be. "I wish that I would not have to be such a police woman. I just wish that it would happen without me having to put so much time into it. Because it is exhausting." Her wish that "it would happen without me" suggests that she did not want such intensive involvement and would have preferred that Charles's education be facilitated and coordinated by school personnel instead of by her.

Anita is a married African American woman living in an urban environment. She wanted her only child, Adam, in an inclusive early childhood environment from the time he had entered a center-based, self-contained early intervention program. Adam, an African American 4-year-old boy with Down syndrome, had been in an inclusive child care center for 2 years.

Adam attended a university-affiliated child care center and received speech-language, occupational, and physical therapies. These services were provided in the classroom and on a pull-out basis. The classroom staff consisted of a special education teacher and general education teacher who team-taught, a full-time classroom aide, and a student teacher. Anita learned of the preschool that her son attended through a friend and enrolled him in the program even though it was not located in her neighborhood. She expressed high satisfaction with the program because personnel were receptive to her and her son's needs.

Anita spoke of advocating for Adam "since he came out of my belly." She also talked about feeling overwhelmed because of the intense involvement from day one.

> The books. The footwork. The interviewing people and talking to people. Talking to parents. And it is like I am just getting comfortable with early intervention and I am fearing the next step which is school age. I really don't want to deal with that, but that is what I am approaching. It's a lot.

Although Anita had a very satisfying and positive experience with school personnel, she felt drained at times by the amount of work (as just described) that has to be done. One of her concerns was about the future public school district that Adam would be attending. She already secured an "attorney in the wings" and seriously considered relocating to a school system that is more "progressive."

A Multidimensional Perspective of Parents' Participation in Inclusive Early Education

The experiences and perspectives of Mary and Anita illustrate the factors that shape involvement that were identified in the study conducted by Soodak and Erwin (2000). In this study, 10 parents were interviewed individually about their perspectives on their participation in the inclusive education of their child with disabilities. Each interview was transcribed and analyzed. The parents who were interviewed represented diverse ethnic, cultural, socioeconomic, and geographic backgrounds. It was not the intent to exclude fathers from this study; however, mothers typically were identified as potential study participants by supporters of inclusive education in the field. All of the parents had children with significant disabilities (ages 4–8) who attended inclusive environments. Inclusive environments were characterized as 1) age appropriate or within 1 year of the child's chronological age, 2) the child with a disability was assigned as a full-time member of the class, and 2) at least two thirds of the class composition was typically developing children. For a more detailed description of the participants, methodology, and results, see Soodak and Erwin (2000).

On the basis of the stories of Mary, Anita, and eight other parents, several factors that affect the quality of parents' participation in inclusive environments were identified: 1) the nature and quality of children's entry experiences into inclusive education, 2) the overall school climate, 3) parents' personal perspectives, and 4) the nature and quality of the parent–professional partnerships that evolved over time. These factors interacted in shaping parents' participation, although each environment provided a unique set of conditions that influenced parents' involvement. Because of the space constraints of this chapter, only the most salient themes within the previously mentioned factors are discussed. Mary's and Anita's stories were selected because of differences in their children's placements (preschool versus kindergarten), their geographic location (urban versus suburban), and the quality of their overall experiences with school personnel. Both stories illustrate themes that were representative of the other parents interviewed.

Entry Experiences into Inclusive Education   For many parents, the way in which parents and children entered an inclusive environment has a lasting effect on their interactions with school personnel. These experiences, also referred to as entry experiences, either can be a source of great anxiety and frustration or can be supportive and positive.

Mary was one of several parents who experienced a painful and difficult entry. She was shocked when the majority of the team at her child's inclusive preschool recommended a self-contained classroom for her son. Although Mary remained open-minded and visited the class that the team had recommended, she "knew that it was not [for] Charles and it was not his home school." She was concerned not only because the proposed school was across town and he would have to be bused and separated from his siblings and neighborhood children but also because there was no acknowledgment or support for her family's vision of what was important for Charles's life. As part of their vision, they wanted Charles to develop a strong network of friends and be an active participant, with the necessary supports, in his school. They wanted his classmates to view him as a valued and able member of the class.

Mary became very focused in her struggle to get Charles included in the local school that would be attended by his siblings and other children in the neighborhood. She brought to meetings people who knew Charles and were knowledgeable about inclusive education. She and her husband developed a clear vision statement of what they wanted for Charles in an effort to demonstrate that this was not a decision they took lightly. At the final meeting of the year, Mary threatened to contact the Protection and Advocacy office. She remembers, "I think they knew that I knew my rights and that I knew the law." Mary's son was finally included in a general education kindergarten. This initial experience with the district shaped her future interactions with district and school personnel.

Anita, conversely, did not have to fight for her son to be included. Although Adam had been attending a self-contained program for 2 years, Anita wanted an inclusive environment for him because she believed that he was "limited in the special education environment because everyone had a disability and there was no one to model or imitate." Anita had frequently observed Adam with his typical cousins and noted how he learned and imitated appropriate behavior from the other children. Anita had been researching inclusive environments when a friend told her about a university-affiliated program that included children with and without disabilities. Anita remembered that the administrator of the program was extremely helpful, accessible, and responsive to her request for information. Adam, like all prospective students in this program, participated in an admissions process that involved child observations, parent interviews, and a waiting period in which decisions were made. Anita recalled the joy she felt 2 years earlier when she returned from the grocery store just after the interview and received a telephone message from the school about enrolling Adam in the program. The way in which parents gain access to an inclusive environment provides a strong and lasting first impression for parents.

In the Soodak and Erwin study (2000), the majority of parents expended a great deal of time and energy locating a school that was willing to accept their child. Only three of the other parents were offered the option of an inclusive environment for their child, and two of these parents were told that they would have to pay tuition. (In both cases, the district was willing to pay tuition for the self-contained environment.) Although this may be because of the geographic region in which these parents live or perhaps because of the nature or severity of the children's disabilities, the availability and accessibility of inclusive early childhood environments remains a key ingredient in shaping parents' perspectives about their participation. All of the parents who had to find and secure a placement for their child spoke about their exhaustion and difficulty in finding a program that was willing to accept their child.

Mary and Anita had similar expectations that their children would be educated alongside their age-appropriate typical peers; however, they had dramatically different experiences with finding opportunities to realize these dreams. For many parents, including Mary and Anita, these initial experiences have a long-lasting effect on their perceptions of being welcome, their trust in service providers, and, ultimately, their interactions with school personnel.

School Climate Parents often described their participation as being shaped by qualities of the school, in general, in addition to individual people within the school. These comments were coded into a category called school climate. *School climate* can be thought of as the culture or pulse of a school and is composed of the formal and informal structures that operate within a school (Peterson & Deal, 1998). Specifically, the school's policies and practices related to parents' participation and to the inclusion of children with disabilities reflect aspects of the school climate that play a significant role in shaping parents' participation. The ways in which school or program personnel view parents will most likely be reflected in how parents are treated. In addition, parents have preconceptions about future school placements based on the experiences of other parents.

Parents' perceptions about their participation in their child's education were shaped by the invitations and opportunities for participation offered by the school. In the preschool that Anita's child attended, there was an "open door" policy, which enabled parents to visit anytime they wanted. This reassured Anita that nothing secretive was being done to her son, Adam. The school's openness to parents was further evident to Anita in their forwarding information to her before team meetings, inquiring about her ideas regarding her child's education, and providing her with the teachers' and therapists' home telephone numbers.

Mary did not experience the openness that Anita described in her son's school. Mary's experiences with team members and team meetings were quite different. For her, the element of surprise created fear and suspicion:

> They all have information before the meeting, and they have talked to each other. The parent always goes in there and is surprised and bombarded by reports. We were not allowed to have copies of reports even 2 or 3 days before.

In both situations, the school's receptivity to parents was reflected in the school's openness to parents' presence and willingness to share information. Mary pointed out inherent differences in the culture of an early intervention program and school-based programs. She suggested that "birth-to-3 services are very family centered, very nurturing. But school is not. In school, they don't want you there." A strong message was sent to parents about how welcomed (or not) they were by the nature of the opportunities and invitations for parents to participate.

In addition to how parents were received by a school, their perceptions of how their children were treated emerged as an important and consistent theme that represented the culture of the school. Mary, for example, talked about her fear about the school's seeing her child's "disability" and not the "child." Anita, conversely, believed that her son was understood and supported by the teachers in his preschool:

Right now he is in a progressive setting that moves with him. If they see that Adam loves books, they'll read with him. He likes colors, so they will go over the colors with him. So it's like progressing at the speed he is without pushing things on him. And that is what I want for him.

Parents tend to be very aware of the differences in early intervention programs versus public school programs. Anita was aware that not all schools are alike and discussed concerns similar to those of Mary about Adam entering the public school system the following year. She talked about the local school district as being "horrible," that they do not provide all of the services that children need, and that teachers are not receptive to and involved with children. Anita articulated her fears about how the district makes decisions about children even before meeting them and groups children solely on the basis of their diagnosis. The idea that professionals did not see or understand their children was a common fear that parents articulated clearly.

The school climate had a powerful effect on how parents perceived the school's willingness to collaborate with

and, ultimately, include them. For Anita, a positive school climate facilitated the formation of positive relationships and effective partnerships. Mary, conversely, felt the need to be more observant and watchful in a school in which the climate was not fully open, receptive, or understanding.

Personal Perspectives   The perception women had of themselves related to their being women and mothers also emerged as an important factor in shaping their participation in their child's education. One way of better understanding their experiences was to understand them first as women and caregivers. Mary, Anita, and the other mothers interviewed spoke of maintaining balance and harmony in their lives as well as needing to be heard and informed about their child's activities. Acknowledging the personal side of the parents helped to paint a fuller picture of their participation.

Maintaining Balance   Although all of the mothers interviewed spoke with great conviction of their commitment to their children, many struggled to maintain balance among the many demands they experienced in their lives. The issue of balance emerged in different ways for each parent. The issue of balance surfaced for Mary as she worked to balance her family's needs, specifically the unique needs of all four of her children. For Anita, the issue of balancing her career and her participation in Adam's school surfaced:

This year I have not been as involved as I would want to be because my job has been more demanding. I wish I could spend more time with him. I wish I could go to more of his therapy sessions. I wish I could go to school and pick him up. But I can't. I have to make money.

The issue of balancing the needs of family, career, and other responsibilities was similar to challenges that mothers of typical children face. For Mary and Anita, however, the extra responsibilities of their child's therapy and school meetings, among other demands, placed additional pressure and time constraints on them.

Being Heard and Informed   Other themes that emerged from parents' stories were the need to be heard and informed. Not only did these women want to know about their child's progress in general, but they also wanted to know about their day. For Mary and Anita, it was a matter of simply knowing what was happening with their children in their absence. Mary also spoke of needing information to provide consistency and carryover at home:

> I demand a lot of communication with this school. If there is something happening, they better be talking to me. If they are teaching him a number, they need to tell me how they are teaching him so I can do the same at home, so we are not doing two different things.

Although both parents communicated with the school with a communication "book" or "log," Mary noted that the content and frequency of the communication needed to be useful and informative. She recalled that

> A whole year has gone by and I don't have a clear understanding what [the therapist] is doing. She does not send me a note. She attaches a sheet of paper that she has done with Charles to the [home–school] journal. This means nothing to me. But she still does not use the journal to write back and forth and does not read what I write or what the teacher writes. She is doing her own thing.

Being kept informed as they desired was not a simple matter. Mary believed that she was kept informed primarily because she was "always in their face." Anita insisted that regularly scheduled meetings between her and Adam's team be written directly into her son's individualized education program.

In addition to wanting to be informed, these women wanted to be heard. The need to be heard, which was directly related to the level of trust that parents felt toward the school, is discussed further in the following section. Anita noted that she felt satisfied with her involvement in her child's program because the school was "very receptive" to her. Mary suggested that she would feel more confident if the school respected her and took into account what was important to her family. Mary, who directly linked the idea of being heard with the level of trust she felt, commented, "If the school has not heard what I have said, why should I trust what they can do for my child?" For Mary and Anita, the need for their priorities and concerns to be heard by school and district personnel was a critical factor in how they perceived their participation.

Maintaining Harmony   The desire to maintain harmony (even when there was disagreement) is another key issue in understanding parents' perspectives on participation. The issue of maintaining harmony surfaced more for Mary than for Anita, perhaps because Mary experienced greater conflict with the school administration and team members. Although she believed that it was best to be honest and straightforward, Mary frequently spoke of not wanting to hurt anyone's feelings. In her attempts to maintain harmony, Mary talked about the challenge of not being confrontational and often accepted compromises to achieve that end. For example, at times when Mary was upset about a number of issues, she learned to focus on only one primary issue. Mary was also aware of acknowledging the positive side of others even in difficult situations. Another strategy that Mary used to achieve harmony was through her role as nurturer. She often brought food to meetings and was very cognizant of providing compliments whenever possible:

I'm always very aware to compliment them when I feel that they have done something positive, even if it is a little thing. I just write it in the notebook or I write a little note. Because I think we tend to get stuck on the things that are not working all the time.

The need to maintain harmony even in the face of confrontation was very important in creating an environment in which parents felt comfortable.

The personal perspectives of Mary and Anita were important in understanding their experiences in their child's education. The specific themes that were identified in the Soodak and Erwin study (2000), such as balancing a variety of roles, the need to be heard and informed about their children, and the desire to maintain harmony in their interactions with others, may reflect these women's needs as women, primary caregivers, and/or parents of children with disabilities. Because only women were interviewed in this study, the extent to which these issues are unique to women is not clear. However, many of the personal attributes and ways of interacting that were identified have been explored in research on the psychology of women (e.g., Chadorow, 1978; Gilligan, 1982).

Perhaps what should be learned from the themes that were identified from the stories of Mary, Anita, and the other women in this study is that each woman or parent has individual needs, desires, and ways of interacting that influence her participation. What these women valued in themselves and others played an important role in shaping their relationships with school personnel.

Parent–Professional Partnerships

The relationships that parents had with school personnel were a key factor in understanding their participation. Parents developed relationships with many individuals at various levels within the structure of the school or program, including the district administration,

school administration, and teaching and related services personnel. The instructional staff members typically were referred to as the team. It was not uncommon for parents to have more positive relationships with team members than with district administrators. Perhaps parents attributed unreceptive school policies and difficult entry experiences more to administrators than to the instructional staff. It is also possible that parents, such as Mary, tried to maintain harmony with those closest to their children.

Many themes were identified from parents' descriptions of their relationships with school and district personnel. These themes included trust, shared vision, and communication.

Trust   The issue of trust was perhaps the single most significant indicator of how parents perceived their relationships with school personnel. Mary described her thoughts about the relationship between herself and the district administrator in this way:

> She is bright and very intelligent, and I respect her for that. But she is devious, so I am very cautious when I am with her. But I also know she can add to our lives. She has a lot of power in her role. I am very honest with her and I say that I don't want to walk on eggshells. I am just going to say the way I feel.

Mary had talked about being hurt by this administrator after she had used information that Mary had shared with her to prevent Mary from getting what she had requested for her son. Trust with this individual had become complex. Mary, although recognizing that she must work with this woman because of her authority to make important decisions, felt no trust in their relationship.

Conflicts between the parent and the school or district that the child attended were a problem because of parents' fear of reprisal. In a situation in which Mary disagreed with one of Charles's therapists, Mary compromised because "I knew that she probably would hate me and hate my child forever if I said that." The fear of reprisal against themselves or their children was a threat to parents who did not feel that trust was present in the relationship. It is ironic that parents must let those whom they do not trust make decisions about and assume responsibility for the most important people in their lives—their very own children.

Mary regulated her involvement on the basis of her trust of others. She made a connection between having confidence and a reduced need for participation:

> If I feel you respect me and are taking into account what is important to my family, I am going to have that confidence. If I have that level of confidence with the team, then I don't need to talk to them that much because I know that they know me and my child.

Similarly, as Anita's trust in school personnel increased, she was more confident in their decisions and, thus, found herself in school less frequently. Anita attributed her growing confidence to the school's responsiveness to her:

> Any little thing that I felt was important to make him comfortable, they said "bring it to the school, tell us how to do it, write down the information." So I didn't have to crop up unexpectedly and observe my son anymore. He was okay, he was really comfortable.

In discussing her relationships with school personnel, Anita characterized them as "comrades" and "allies" because she felt as though she had trusted and could continue to trust them. She spoke of the school as a great source of support to both her and her husband. In addition, Anita noted the importance of parent-to-parent networking in her own life and credited the school for providing her with the opportunity for obtaining support from other parents:

> The school is a great support system because I can pick up the phone and call a parent if I feel like it. They do the same with me. You don't feel like you are out there by yourself in an isolated situation.

Based on the experiences of Mary and Anita, trust in how information is used, how parents are supported, and how their children are treated by school personnel are key ingredients to forming positive parent–professional partnerships. Furthermore, schools in which there was trust among parents and professionals were also schools that encouraged relationships among parents.

Shared Vision   Trust was most common in situations in which there was a shared vision about schooling. Shared vision, or synergy, is the degree to which school or district personnel share the same ideas and beliefs as the families they serve. It involves being able to see things in the same way. It does not mean that there is agreement 100% of the time, but it does imply that there are mutually agreed-on ideas about outcomes and processes and the ability to respect the perspective of the other party when disagreements arise.

The beliefs about children and education that school or district personnel hold may or may not be consistent with parents' views. Anita believed that the school supported and shared her vision for her son:

> It is a team effort, I think because myself, my husband, the grandparents, aunts and uncles, and the school are working together. It is like everybody is working for the best of Adam. They are all so supportive of me and my husband. It makes such a difference.

As discussed previously, the support that parents received was important not only in developing trust but also in developing a meaningful and appropriate education program for their child. Anita noted that the suggestions she had were often the same as those of the therapists. Although Mary generally was satisfied with her son's program, she and the speech-language therapist had very different expectations for Charles. Mary believed that the therapist did not share her vision of her son:

So that was what made me think that she has absolutely no clue of who my child is. She has been with him for a year and she really does not know the spirit of this child.

The degree to which the parents and school personnel had shared beliefs about education affected the development of parent–professional relationships beginning with the child's entry into an inclusive environment. However, the experiences of Mary and Anita suggest that the existence of a shared philosophy continues to shape parent involvement well into the early years of schooling.

Communication   Parents viewed the way in which communication occurs as an important influence on the quality of the partnerships that emerge. Mary, Anita, and the other parents interviewed spoke of being most satisfied when communication was open, ongoing, and informal.

Both Mary and Anita spoke of open rather than restricted communication with school personnel. Mary referred to it as "speaking from the heart," and Anita called it "a back-and-forth kind of thing." For most of the parents interviewed, unrestricted communication meant that they could have frequent and unscheduled contact that for most parents extended beyond the school day. Anita noted her satisfaction with unrestricted communication: "The lines of communication are great. I have the therapists' and teachers' home numbers. They give you all of that in the beginning of the year. And I use them."

Both Mary and Anita spoke of not holding back or censoring what was said, although neither had fully realized this goal. Mary's concern was whether her message was received as she meant it to

be: "I will ask questions and I think they view that as criticism. I would love to ask a question without [the teachers] feeling like I am questioning their integrity." One strategy that Mary used to avoid being misunderstood (or ignored) was to locate and present research that supported her ideas. She found that her son's therapist was more receptive to her suggestions when the therapist could see that "it's research, it's not what a mother is saying."

For both parents, communication worked best when there were frequent interactions and multiple methods of communication. Mary talked about meeting informally once a week so that "nothing at those [formal] meetings was a surprise to me." Anita, who spoke about the positive lines of communication as a result of the frequency and the opportunity to meet, explained, "Any time I feel like we need to meet, it is no problem." The nature, frequency, and opportunity for interactions contributed to the quality of communication between home and school. Trust, shared vision, and communication interacted in shaping the relationships that these parents developed with school personnel.

Summary   Parents' participation in inclusive early childhood environments can be shaped by multiple factors, such as entry experiences, school climate, personal perspectives, and parent–professional partnerships. These factors interact with one another and influence the nature and quality of parents' participation in their child's education. Although mere presence can constitute parent participation at a very minimal level, meaningful parent participation occurs in an inclusive school when the parent feels like a valued member of the school community. The nature and degree of participation will most likely vary from parent to parent; however, the contextual factors identified previously make a difference in how parents understand their own participation.

Both Anita and Mary have shared their personal journeys in a meaningful way that provides a unique perspective on inclusive early childhood education. Although parents clearly want to be involved in their child's education, they do not want to work so hard in creating and monitoring it. Parents want the schools to assume responsibility, take the initiative, and maintain a commitment to providing for their child an education that is built on shared goals. It is interesting that the higher the satisfaction and trust that parents feel toward school personnel, the lower their need for participation. Parents want to be seen as a resource and an important voice in decisions and planning. They also want to be kept informed about their child's progress and their day. The idea that parents felt strongly about having no surprises or secrets from the school suggests that the sharing of knowledge and information in a respectful and timely way is vital to parents' sense of comfort and security. Parents wanted to be treated with respect. Their stories suggest that parents have made many strides in creating inclusive education for their children but that some of the very same struggles that were faced 20 years ago still exist.

AN AGENDA FOR STRENGTHENING PARENT–PROFESSIONAL PARTNERSHIPS IN EARLY CHILDHOOD INCLUSION

The themes that emerged from the family research on early childhood inclusion across the 1980s and 1990s are remarkably consistent. These themes emphasize the importance that families place on the following: 1) program entry (the importance of families' having information, easy access, and a smooth transition to quality inclusive options), 2) program or school climate (families and children feeling welcomed and included into the

program and feeling that diversity is valued), and, most critical, 3) the importance of competent, caring staff who value family input, appreciate individual differences, and are skilled at working with children and establishing and maintaining effective communication with families. Using these three themes as an organizing framework, the next section describes important accomplishments and identifies what remains to be accomplished for each theme. The final topic that is addressed in this section is recommendations for achieving systemic change in the implementation of the proposed agenda.

Program Entry

I won't ever forget when the infant program Christy had been in suggested that I find a regular preschool for her, and I started calling around. I called one preschool that was near us at the Methodist church. The director was wonderful. She said that they wanted to see Christy and that she would talk to the teacher of 4-year-olds about taking Christy. And then she called me back up and said that the teacher refused to see Christy and that she couldn't have a child with Down syndrome. She was labeling Christy. And I sat down and I just cried and thought, "She won't even give my child a chance." It wouldn't hurt if she had seen Christy and said, "I don't think it's going to work out," because I wasn't sure it was going to work out. It was a test situation. I didn't know if Christy could cope with it. But they could have given her a chance to try. (Winton, Turnbull, & Blacher, 1984, pp. 78–79)

This voice from almost 20 years ago illustrates some of challenges still faced by families seeking inclusive programs. Table 6.2 highlights some of the accomplishments related to program entry. Because of the Americans with Disabilities Act (ADA) of 1990 (PL 101-336), it is unlawful to deny a child entry into a preschool program on the basis of disability. However, the Soodak and Erwin (2000) study documented that parents are still struggling with finding inclu-

Table 6.2.   Accomplishments related to program entry

The number of inclusive program options has increased, meaning that families have more inclusive options from which to choose when searching for an early childhood program.

OSEP data indicate increases in number of children served in inclusive settings (U.S. Department of Education, 1996).

The reauthorization of Part C of IDEA emphasis on "natural environments" will ensure additional attention by states and communities to creating and supporting inclusive program options (U.S. Department of Education, 1997).

Innovative initiatives in communities are increasing access to inclusive options (Bailey, McWilliam, Buysse, & Wesley, 1998). Examples include the following: a) some communities have used co-location strategies whereby specialized preschool programs and Head Start have co-located to provide families with easier access to inclusion options, b) some states are requiring that a portion of child care subsidies be targeted for young children with disabilities who are being served in general early childhood environments, and c) some agencies are redefining early childhood specialists' roles so that they are engaged in outreach to general early childhood programs that serve young children with disabilities.

Transition planning and practices have received increased attention, meaning that families have more support as they move from one environment to another.

Transition planning is a component of the IFSP as mandated in the early intervention legislation.

The early intervention legislation mandates interagency coordinating councils at community and state levels whose purpose is to ease transitions between programs and support families in accessing programs and services (U.S. Department of Education, 1997).

OSEP has funded model demonstration, in-service, and outreach grants that have developed models and strategies that enhance community-based, family-centered transition planning and interagency coordination (NECTAS, 1998).

sive programs that are welcoming, that assistance with these challenging transition points is not handled well uniformly, and that first impressions can be lasting and formative.

What Remains to Be Accomplished   *Increase the number and quality of early childhood inclusive programs available, especially for children with significant disabilities, so that families have more options from which to choose.* Data indicate that most generic early childhood programs are of poor to mediocre quality (Cost, Quality, and Child Outcomes Study Team, 1995). There is no federal mandate or agency whose mission includes the improvement of early childhood programs. Basically, the early childhood system is a "nonsystem": It is fragmented, market driven, and underregulated. In addition, there are no agreed-on quality standards for inclusive programs. Such standards could assist parents in identifying programs and could be used for program monitoring and enhancement purposes (see Chapter 10). Efforts to develop standards are under way (Aytch, Cryer,

Bailey, & Selz, 1999), and these efforts need to be supported and continued. Making improvements and gaining public support for quality early childhood education is critical for broad-based inclusion to work for young children and families.

Improve interagency coordination and transition policies and practices in ways that provide support to families during transition points. Families of young children with disabilities often face numerous transition points (hospital to home, entry into early intervention, entry into preschool, entry into kindergarten), and these transitions are challenging. Local interagency coordinating councils (LICCs) are in the position to create positive changes in transition policies and support individual families as they deal with transition events. However, LICCs often operate without the benefit of public financial support. Because they are the responsibility of no one agency, they sometimes have to "beg" for human and fiscal resources. They are mandated to have parent membership; however, they sometimes struggle to sustain parent interest (Rosenkoetter, Shotts, Streufert, & Rosenkoetter, 1995). Increasing support and guidance to LICCs is one strategy for improving families' access to information about inclusive programs and improved transition practices.

Mobilize parent organizations to help improve transition. There are several national parent organizations with statewide networks that could serve as potential sources of information for families about inclusive early childhood/ child care options. These include the following: Parent Training and Information Centers (National Early Childhood Technical Assistance System, 1998), which are federally funded and located in every state, whose primary purpose is to provide educational support to families; the Parent-to-Parent Networks (Santelli, Turnbull, Marquis, & Lerner, 1997), which are located in most states, whose primary purpose is to match parents with other parents for support; and the Grassroots Consortium on Disabilities (Turnbull, Blue-Banning, Turbiville, & Park, 1999), a network of 15 programs in culturally and linguistically diverse communities that focus on providing generic support to families. These organizations could serve an important role by compiling a list of programs that have accepted children with disabilities in the past and include contact names of parents who are willing to share information about their experiences in the programs with other parents. This information could be disseminated through LICCs or perhaps through local child care resource and referral agencies whose purpose is to share child care information with parents.

Involve public schools in improving transitions. A survey of kindergarten teachers indicated that very few plan or implement practices that support children's and families' transitions into kindergarten (Pianta, Cox, Taylor, & Early, 1999). The reasons cited by teachers were

for the most part related to school policies (e.g., absence of classroom lists before the beginning of the school year, lack of resources and time). Even though children with disabilities are mandated to have a transition plan in place, the absence of schoolwide policies and practices that support school entry makes it unlikely that strategies that welcome children and families to their new environment are uniformly in place. The perception of the discrepancy between early intervention and public school in terms of responsiveness to families' and children's individual needs, noted by parents in the Soodak and Erwin (2000) study, is one of the byproducts of the absence of supportive transition policies.

School or Program Climate

Research on successful inclusive programs has highlighted the importance of school or program climate. According to this research, a climate that is supportive of inclusion is characterized by underlying values and beliefs related to acceptance of human diversity and each person's belonging and participating in the school community (Hanson et al., 1998; Janko et al., 1997; Lieber et al., 1998; Peck, Furman, & Helmstetter, 1993; Schwartz, 1996). Table 6.3 provides an overview of the accomplishments related to school or program climate. Odom (1998), in synthesizing 5 years of research implemented under the auspices of the Early Childhood Research Institute on Inclusion, stated that programs, not children, have to be "ready for inclusion" and that beliefs about inclusion influence how it is enacted. Schools and programs that view inclusion as the starting point for every child and value and believe in diversity are more likely to provide effective inclusive options for children and families. The Soodak and Erwin (2000) study illustrates the tension created for parents when the school climate is not supportive of diversity and inclusion.

Table 6.3.   Accomplishments related to school or program climate

Innovative projects at the national, community, and state levels have been funded for the purpose of enhancing the readiness of early childhood programs for including children with disabilities. Examples of such programs at each level include the following:

At the national level, the Hilton/Early Head Start Training Project (co-funded by the Hilton Foundation and the Head Start Bureau) is providing training and ongoing support related to serving children with significant disabilities to all Early Head Start programs in the country (California Institute on Human Services, 1997).

At the state level, the Partnerships for Inclusion Project in North Carolina is an effective strategy for providing statewide technical assistance to a large number of early childhood programs across the state to enhance their capacity to serve young children with disabilities (Wesley & Buysse, 1996).

McGregor and Vogelsberg (1998) described a number of initiatives that have achieved success in enhancing inclusion at building and/or district levels.

What Remains to Be Accomplished   Integrate inclusion reforms with general reform efforts. "Fixing schools" has been an ongoing, well-funded federal initiative since 1983. McGregor and Vogelsberg (1998) concluded from their analysis of inclusion efforts that projects to support inclusion are most successful when they move beyond a small group of "target students" or exemplary classrooms and focus on larger contexts. They cited the work of Salisbury and her colleagues (Salisbury, Gallucci, Palombaro, & Peck, 1995; Salisbury, Wilson, Swartz, Palombaro, & Wassel, 1997) as an exemplar of buildingwide change that emphasized a shared vision, collaborative decision making, and a climate of communication and reflection. They noted that one of the effective strategies used by Salisbury was to embed her efforts to enhance inclusion within the school reform initiative. Turnbull, Turnbull, Shank, and Leal (1999) provided information on strategies for addressing school-age inclusion within the context of general school reform. Research on the change process (Fullan, 1993) supports the wisdom of building on existing initiatives when instigating change. This suggests that efforts to improve early childhood programs, promote inclusion, and reform general education need to be coordinated so that resources can be leveraged and maximized (see Chapter 2).

Use innovative staff development strategies. The traditional approach for introducing new ideas and promoting change—changes in policy at administrative levels followed by the episodic, one-shot workshop designed to change attitudes and skills at the individual level—is clearly inadequate for creating school climates that support family participation in early childhood inclusive programs. The approaches developed in model projects, such as the one implemented by Salisbury, especially those that use parents as partners in a systemic, team-based approach to the change process (Bailey, McWilliam, & Winton, 1992; Winton, McWilliam, Harrison, Owens, & Bailey, 1992) need to be replicated, evaluated, and disseminated more broadly.

Effective Family–Professional Partnerships

A consistent finding in the early intervention literature is the importance that families place on working with competent, caring professionals. Trust is often described as the linchpin in cementing the partnership, and effective communication is the attribute that professionals must have to be able to create the partnerships. The Soodak and Erwin (2000) study illustrates the unique challenges to communication and trust that are inherent in inclusive environments; however, communication and trust have been shown to be central in any kind of early intervention context. The Soodak and Erwin (2000) study also illustrates the effort that parents often make in maintaining relationships and the stress that is created when partnerships are not working. Table 6.4 highlights some of the major accomplishments related to family–professional partnerships.

What Remains to Be Accomplished Close the gap between the philosophy that supports a family-centered approach and the daily practices of most practitioners. Research documents that most intervention efforts are "child centered" (Harbin, McWilliam, & Gallagher, 1998; Kochanek & Brady, 1995; McWilliam, Tocci, & Harbin, 1995). Even though practitioners think and say that they are working with and modeling strategies for parents, observations reveal that this is not the case (McBride & Peterson, 1997).

Increase the diversity of the early intervention work force. Demographic data indicate that the majority of practitioners are Euro-American and a large number of the families and children they are serving are not (American Speech-Language-Hearing Association, 1998; Division for Early Childhood, 1997). A nationwide survey of teachers showed that only 20%

of the teachers currently serving diverse children feel comfortable and prepared to work with children who are bilingual and ethnically diverse (Lewis et al., 1999). The challenges to communication when professionals and families do not speak the same language are myriad. Increasing the diversity of the early intervention work force and providing the existing work force with knowledge and skills to work effectively with ethnically and linguistically diverse children and families are critical needs.

Increase the quality of higher education programs. Despite a number of innovative training programs, most entry-level practitioners in the key early intervention disciplines do not have direct experience with working with families or interdisciplinary training experiences (see Chapter 8). Training programs with an interdisciplinary focus have been shown to revert to a unidisciplinary focus when federal funding ends (Rooney, 1995). Continued and increased support for cross-disciplinary, family-centered training in the early intervention disciplines is key. Increased attention to communication,

Table 6.4.   Accomplishments related to family–professional partnerships

The early intervention legislation requires that family needs, concerns, and priorities be included on IFSPs (U.S. Department of Education, 1997). A family-centered approach is now a "given," and few professionals would say that they do not subscribe to the philosophy.

Accumulated research has clearly demonstrated the impact of parent involvement on child outcome in the general education literature (Rutherford, Anderson, & Billig, 1997), meaning that more than ever before, schools and programs are paying attention to parents and trying to involve them.

Research has also delineated a clearer understanding of effective family support practices (Dunst, Trivette, & Deal, 1988; Turnbull, Turbiville, & Turnbull, 2000). This research has guided the development of training materials and curricula that have been used to help practitioners improve their ability to develop effective partnerships (Catlett & Winton, 2000; Winton, McCollum, & Catlett, 1997).

OSEP has funded model personnel preparation, demonstration, in-service, and outreach grants that have developed models and strategies that enhance community-based, family-centered intervention practices. As a result, innovative interdisciplinary and blended training programs have been developed across the United States (Rosenkoetter & Stayton, 1997). Creative strategies for promoting family–professional partnerships, such as creating family practica experiences so that students get direct experience with families (Capone, Hull, & DiVenere, 1997) and involving families as co-instructors (McBride & Brotherson, 1997; Winton & DiVenere, 1995), have been developed as part of these initiatives. In addition, faculty are being supported in their efforts to upgrade their knowledge and skills in preparing students in family-centered, interdisciplinary content and skills (Winton, 1995; Winton et al., 1997).

Parent networks such as the Parent Training and Information centers, the Parent-to-Parent Networks, and the Grassroots Consortium for Disabilities have received federal and state funding to support parents' efforts to be involved in their child's education and to partner with professionals for that purpose.

consultation, and conflict resolution skills is needed so that families do not feel the burden to maintain harmony. Families can and should be involved in preparation of students in education and related fields at the university level.

Improve the ways that families are introduced to early intervention services. The research findings that most intervention services and plans are child centered and that families have expressed high levels of satisfaction with those child-centered services (Kochanek & Brady, 1995; McWilliam, Lang, et al., 1995) have been difficult to interpret. McWilliam, Tocci, and colleagues (1995) raised the question, "Is this a reflection of what parents want, or does this reflect what they are offered and expect?" The Soodak and Erwin (2000) study suggests that families may be working very hard to create programs that support their children's optimal development. With these efforts taking so much energy, perhaps parents feel reluctant to ask for more or do not believe that programs could do more. The comment by the parent in the Soodak and Erwin (2000) study that as her feelings of confidence in her child's program grew, she felt that she could relax and spend less time being involved in the program is telling. These mirror a quote from the original study in which a parent (a nurse by training) stated:

> You've got to have a staff that is smarter than you when it comes to your child's handicap. I'm not a genius; I mean, my background is giving enemas. But you've got to know that the people that are teaching your child know their stuff. Now I drop off Sam in the morning and I feel like, whew, people more competent than I are taking care of him, and that's a great feeling. (Winton et al., 1984, p. 29)

This supports the view that a critical component of family support is listening to and respecting family values and beliefs about their child and implementing pro-

gram activities that reflect those values. As long as that is in place, some families do not expect or want more from the system. Again, this indicates the importance of program entry and the need to support families in their search for programs that are "in sync" with their particular value and belief system.

Ensure adequate support for teachers and children in inclusive environments. An interesting point raised by Bailey and his associates (Bailey, McWilliam, Buysse, & Wesley, 1998) relates to times when a parent's values and beliefs are in conflict with the current emphasis on inclusion. Some parents might believe that a specialized program is the optimal environment for their children. Some of the reasons that parents value specialized programs, according to research cited previously in this chapter, were related to perceived lack of specialized services and specialized training for teachers in inclusive environments. Research suggests that many early childhood teachers are uncomfortable with serving young children with disabilities, especially when those disabilities are significant or involve challenging behaviors (California Institute on Human Services, 1997; Wesley & Buysse, 1996). The professional training programs for early childhood teachers are unlikely to have prepared them adequately to serve children with disabilities (Morgan et al., 1993). The amount of training that early childhood teachers have has been linked to outcomes for young children (Cost, Quality, and Child Outcomes Study Team, 1995; Phillips & Howes, 1987), yet most states have minimal training requirements for early childhood teachers. In some states, all that is required is having a driver's license, being 18 years old, and passing a criminal record check. Creating higher standards for child care programs in general is an important component to increasing the quality of inclusive options.

Child care teaching staff earn unacceptably low salaries, often not receiving any benefits or paid vacation (Whitebook, Howes, & Phillips, 1990). The high staff turnover rates (Cost, Quality, and Child Outcomes Study Team, 1995; Whitebook et al., 1990) reflect the wages and quality-of-life issues that are endemic to the field. Research has documented that inclusion will not work without adequate supportive services for children and teachers (Odom, 1998). Making sure that training, personnel, materials, planning time, and ongoing consultation are available to inclusive programs is key (Odom, 1998). One could question whether an environment can be defined as "inclusive" when these resources are missing. Having a range of high-quality inclusive options from which to choose, providing continued support to the early childhood community through preservice education and innovative staff development around significant disability issues, and supporting families to make informed choices should be goals for all communities. Building public support for increasing the wages and benefits of the early childhood work force is critical to parents' feeling comfortable with the quality of inclusive options in their community.

AGENDA FOR CHANGE

A number of program changes that are supportive of family participation in inclusive environments have been suggested in this chapter: 1) improving community-based service coordination and transition practices, 2) enhancing school and program climates so that diversity is respected and each individual child and family feels appreciated, and 3) supporting the early childhood work force so that they are capable of effectively serving children and building family partnerships in inclusive environments.

As stated in this chapter, accomplishments have been made in each of these areas; however, it should be noted that

similar recommendations have been made consistently for more than a decade (Fowler, 1982; Fowler, Chandler, & Johnson, 1988; Rosenkoetter, Hains, & Fowler, 1994; Winton et al., 1984). Making suggestions is the easy part; instituting systemic changes has proved difficult for a number of reasons, even with the presence of strong, supportive federal legislation.

Complexity of the Problem

What is most challenging about dealing with change in an area as complex as family participation in inclusion is the knowledge that a solution to one set of problems is likely to create new challenges and new sets of problems. For instance, moving toward a family-centered inclusionary approach to service delivery has meant that early interventionists need to develop new competencies, such as integrative therapy, family–professional collaboration, and collaborative consultation. This has created demands for new kinds of preservice training programs, licensure requirements, staff development models, and so forth.

Implementation is further complicated by the nature of inclusive environments for infants, toddlers, and preschool-age children. For the most part, public schools do not provide preschool education; therefore, the potential "inclusion partners" run the gamut of Head Start, private preschools, for-profit and not-for-profit child care programs, family day care homes, Even Start literacy programs, and so forth. With the inclusion mandate has come larger territory to improve and change, territory that does not have strong federal legislation protecting the rights of children and families to early education and care. The emphasis on family-centered approaches that has emerged in the early intervention community has not necessarily been adopted by the early childhood community (Powell, 1999).

Need for Systemic Approaches to Change

Inertia and status quo may be the biggest barriers to enhancing family participation in inclusive environments. That parents of young children with disabilities have the same struggles today—finding inclusive programs that welcome their child and family, are responsive to their individual needs and priorities, value their input, and succeed at building partnerships—that they had 20 years ago is testimony to the sluggish pace of change when issues and problems are complex.

Given the complexity of the task for the early intervention community, a systemic approach to change is imperative. It is important to look to the research and knowledge base on systems change for guidance (Fullan, 1993). A list of change principles for early intervention programs has been generated by Winton (1990), based on this literature:

- Top-down and bottom-up approaches are needed.
- Key stakeholders need opportunities and support for building a shared knowledge and values base.
- Families are an integral part of the stakeholder group and must be supported in their participation in critiquing programs and building a change agenda.
- New ideas must build on existing structures.
- Stakeholders must examine the discrepancy between what is and what is desired.
- Action plans that involve small, manageable steps must be generated.
- Ongoing support, follow-up, and reflection are needed. Fullan (1993) described the importance of "learning communities" that take responsibility for continuous improvement as part of their daily practices.

- Evaluation needs to be part of every step; strategies for recognizing and celebrating successes and learning from mistakes are needed.

Gallagher and Rooney (1999) developed a decision-making model that encourages decision makers and policy analysts to weigh the pros and cons of various options on complex early childhood issues such as inclusion. Their decision-making tool includes variables such as cost, personnel needs, track record, public acceptance, administrative feasibility, and agency acceptance that must be considered when developing solutions to problems.

Learn from Other Change Initiatives

As the field moves into the next decade of trying to construct the best possible service system for young children and families, it is important to draw lessons from other change initiatives. Deinstitutionalization is one that has some parallels. It emerged in the 1960s as a politically popular approach both to saving money, by closing down expensive specialized programs or institutions, and to promoting the normalization of individuals who learned or behaved differently by including them in the fabric of society (Bruininks, Meyers, Sigford, & Lakin, 1981). Within a brief time span, a large number of individuals were released from institutions into the care of their families or, in cases in which no family members could be found who were capable of the responsibility, into communities. Part of the initiative was the promise that the money saved through deinstitutionalization would be redirected toward community-based programs that would provide the support necessary for individuals to succeed in the mainstream. Unfortunately, these programs fell short of the promise. Edgerton's (1967) classic book *The Cloak of Competence* painted a vivid portrait of individuals who were marginalized rather than included by society and experiencing a quality of life that could be described as lower than their lives in institutions. The support and follow-up to make deinstitutionalization succeed have been lacking; the care of adults who have be deinstitutionalized has fallen to families and communities that were not prepared or ready. Unfortunately, blame is often placed on the individuals with disabilities and mental illness and their families rather than on the systems that have failed to support them.

Inclusion could suffer a similar fate. Children, families, and local schools and programs have already been compromised and will continue to suffer unless careful thought is given to how this policy will be supported. The fear is that, as happened in the case of deinstitutionalization, a large change will occur in the service delivery system, and because the change is politically popular, people will think that their work is done. Unless careful examination is made of the degree to which alternative service delivery systems are successful at promoting the education, development, and quality of life of the individuals who experience the change, and efforts are made to constantly improve the alternative service delivery systems, then no real progress has been made.

Need for New Research Partnerships

At this juncture, all key groups with a strong interest in promoting the quality of life for young children and families in natural environments must be participants in a research agenda. The well-documented research-to-practice gap in human services has received increased attention from funding agencies whose support for research is critical (Carnine, 1997; Malouf & Schiller, 1995), and inclusion is an example of a failure in this regard. The conditions that make inclusion effective are known; unfortunately, those conditions are not in place in most

programs and communities. We need either a set of more realistic and manageable conditions or more sustained efforts to reform programs and communities. Building partnerships with the constituents, such as families, who are the beneficiaries of the research findings, and teachers and administrators, who are the implementers of inclusion, has been described as one way to ensure that the research conducted is relevant and the findings are applied to making changes. Parent–researcher partnerships in participatory action research (PAR) has been described in the literature as a way of promoting family-centered practices through a research agenda (McTaggart, 1991; Turnbull, Friesen, & Ramirez, 1998). This approach has been encouraged through federal initiatives (Bruyere, 1993). As a result, some research centers have institutionalized a PAR approach in their research efforts. For instance, the Beach Center on Families and Disability at the University of Kansas has formed partnerships with grass roots parents groups who participate in the design and implementation of their research agenda. This model for conducting research needs to be evaluated and further disseminated.

Accountability Issues

History of the disability field clearly attests to the success of parents in advocating for improved services and supports. Why is it that parents have had this very important role? In our research with parents over a number of different studies, a clear theme is that parents often report that they have taken on this role because there has been a major professional *void* in advocacy for systems change. Parents have been so successful in many of their systems change efforts that now many professionals may have become dependent on them to envision new directions, push for legislation, work to redirect funding streams, and constantly question the system. We sense a degree of learned helplessness in professionals in "passing the buck of accountability" to parents to continue this advocacy role. Often, professionals lament, "It's only parents who can be successful in pushing for change." We beg to disagree with that perspective.

CONCLUSION

The clear theme from our analysis of nearly a quarter of a century of research on inclusion is that families are expressing the same concerns in research at the beginning of the 21st century that they were expressing in the early 1980s. The major message from parents is that they want to rebalance the systems change scales—they want the tremendous investment in professional resources, time, and opportunities to result in enhanced outcomes for their children and themselves. They see that they and their children are the *intended beneficiaries* of research, training, and service delivery efforts, and they want to start reaping the dividends of those efforts.

What needs to change in the professional world for it "all to not depend on parents"? Every constituency who has responsibility needs to rethink its roles in ensuring that its contributions lead to enhanced outcomes for children and families. Three key groups whose efforts could make a tremendous difference for children and families are researchers, trainers, and service providers.

In terms of researchers, a key issue that must be addressed is not only the *production* of knowledge but also the *utilization* of knowledge. What benefits have come to children and families from the past 20 years of research on family issues (reviewed in this chapter) associated with inclusion? In our view, not many. Many people respond that researchers do not have time and resources to consider the utilization of their findings—they are not knowledgeable in these areas—and that

their responsibility is to produce knowledge and other people must assume the role of using it. Those in the research community must rethink and expand their roles so that the knowledge that they produce has a much greater likelihood of being useful in producing positive outcomes for children and families. These are questions that we hope the field will address:

- How do researchers enhance their motivation and knowledge/skills not only to disseminate their findings but also to work on the utilization of findings to enhance outcomes for children and families?
- What are researchers' responsibilities in helping to ensure that research findings are utilized to enhance outcomes for children and families?
- What do federal agencies need to do to hold researchers accountable for increased research utilization to enhance outcomes?
- How does the peer review process need to change to recognize the importance of enhanced outcomes for children and families?
- Ultimately, how does systems change apply to the roles of researchers?

A second constituency that has key roles in rebalancing the advocacy scale for systems change is trainers at preservice and in-service levels. What curricula and instructional methods are being used in training programs across the United States to prepare educators to be change agents as well as to deliver services in the particular role in which they are developing expertise? One of the issues for consideration is the extent to which the faculty and providers of preservice and in-service training have had experience themselves in systems change efforts and have the necessary motivation and knowledge/skills to train the next generation.

If this expertise does not sufficiently exist for faculty members today, then part of a national effort to enhance the quality of inclusion will be to ensure that faculty members have the opportunity to participate as collaborators in systems change efforts in their communities and states as a "learning laboratory" for imparting this knowledge to students. Regarding trainers, these are the questions that we hope the field will address:

- How do trainers enhance their motivation and knowledge/skills to keep abreast of research-based recommended practices and to prepare students/trainees to be systems change agents?
- What are trainers' responsibilities in helping to ensure that training leads to enhancement of outcomes for young children and their families?
- What do federal and state agencies need to do to hold trainers accountable for enhanced outcomes for children and families?
- Ultimately, how does systems change apply to the roles of trainers?

The third key constituency to ensure that "it doesn't all depend on parents" is service providers. Service providers sometimes report that they fear that they might lose their jobs if they advocate too strongly for changes within the current system. In our work with service providers, we have noted a clear trend for service providers to be frustrated with the system but not to perceive that they have the capacity to bring about change. Also, many service providers clearly are overextended and perceive that they do not have the time and energy to take on the major responsibilities associated with changing systems, including reading the research literature. In fact, it would be interesting to have data on the extent to which service providers read inclusion research published in journals, much less

take the research findings and seek to put them into practice. This is not because they are not committed or do not have good intentions for helping children, but it is that they perceive that much research is not presented in a way that is comprehensible and applicable to their service delivery context. Here are some of the questions that we hope the field will reflect on regarding the roles of service providers:

- How do service providers enhance their motivation and knowledge/skills to implement research-based recommended practices as a way to enhance outcomes for children and families?
- What are service providers' responsibilities in helping to ensure that research-based practices lead to systems change to enhance outcomes for children and families?
- What do local and state agencies need to do to hold service providers accountable for incorporating research-based practices to change systems for the benefit of children and families?
- Ultimately, how does systems change apply to the roles of service providers?

Time is overdue for researchers, trainers, and service providers to be accountable for systems change related to enhancing the outcomes for young children and their families. We cannot afford another 20 years of so much work being accomplished with so little benefit for the intended beneficiaries. Thus, the chapter authors call on every individual in the field to reflect on his or her individual responsibility and accountability in creating systems change. By so doing, the bottom-line message of parents from this chapter will not only be heard but heeded: "I wish it wouldn't all depend on me." Professionals must enhance their own empowerment to rebalance advocacy for systems change—

taking more responsibility for systems change to enable families to be collaborators but not to require them to be instigators.

REFERENCES

Americans with Disabilities Act (ADA) of 1990, PL 101-336, 42 U.S.C. §§ 12101 *et seq.*

American Speech-Language-Hearing Association. (1998). ASHA membership grows to nearly 93,000. *ASHA Leader, 3*(7), 5.

Aytch, L.S., Cryer, D., Bailey, D.B., & Selz, L. (1999). Defining and measuring quality in early intervention programs for infants and toddlers with disabilities and their families. *Early Education and Development, 10*(1), 7–23.

Bailey, D.B., & McWilliam, R.A. (1990). Normalizing early intervention. *Topics in Early Childhood Special Education, 10*(2), 33–47.

Bailey, D.B., McWilliam, R.A., Buysse, V., & Wesley, P.W. (1998). Inclusion in the context of competing values in early childhood education. *Early Childhood Research Quarterly, 13*, 27–47.

Bailey, D.B., McWilliam, R.A., & Winton, P.J. (1992). Building family-centered practices in early intervention: A team-based model for change. *Infants and Young Children, 5*, 73–82.

Bailey, D.B., & Winton, P.J. (1987). Stability and change in parents' expectations about mainstreaming. *Topics in Early Childhood Special Education, 7*, 73–88.

Bailey, D.B., & Winton, P.J. (1989). Friendship and acquaintance among families in a mainstreamed day care center. *Education and Training in Mental Retardation, 24*, 107–113.

Bennett, T., DeLuca, D., & Bruns, D. (1997). Putting inclusion into practice: Perspectives of teachers and parents. *Exceptional Children, 64*, 115–131.

Bennett, T., Lee, H., & Lueke, B. (1998). Expectations and concerns: What mothers and fathers say about inclusion. *Education and Training in Mental Retardation and Developmental Disabilities, 33*, 108–122.

Blacher, J., & Turnbull, A.P. (1982). Teacher and parent perspectives on selected social aspects of preschool mainstreaming. *The Exceptional Child, 29*, 191–199.

Bricker, D.D. (1989). *Early intervention for at risk and handicapped infants, toddlers, and preschool children* (2nd ed.). Palo Alto, CA: VORT Corp.

Bruininks, R.H., Meyers, C.E., Sigford, B.B., & Lakin, K.C. (Eds.). (1981). *Deinstitutionalization and community adjustment of mentally re-tarded people.* Washington, DC: American Association on Mental Deficiency.

Bruyere, S. (1993). Participatory action research: An overview and implications for family members of individuals with disabilities. *Journal of Vocational Rehabilitation, 3*, 62–68.

California Institute on Human Services. (1997). *Hilton/Early Head Start Training Program Quarterly Report.* Rohnert Park, CA: Sonoma State University.

Capone, A., Hull, K.M., & DiVenere, N.J. (1997). Parent–professional partnerships in preservice and in-service education. In P.J. Winton, J.A. McCollum, & C. Catlett (Eds.), *Reforming personnel preparation in early intervention: Issues, models, and practical strategies* (pp. 435–451). Baltimore: Paul H. Brookes Publishing Co.

Carnine, D. (1997). Bridging the research-to-practice gap. *Exceptional Children, 63*, 513–521.

Catlett, C., & Winton, P. (2000). *Resource guide to exemplary family-centered interdisciplinary early intervention training materials* (9th ed.). Chapel Hill: The University of North Carolina Press, Frank Porter Graham Child Development Center.

Chadorow, N. (1978). *The reproduction of mothering.* Berkeley: University of California Press.

Cost, Quality, and Child Outcomes Study Team. (1995). *Cost, quality, and child outcomes in child care centers: Public report.* Denver: University of Colorado–Denver, Economics Department.

Diamond, K.E., & LeFurgy, W.G. (1994). Attitudes of parents of preschool children toward integration. *Early Education and Development, 5*, 69–77.

Division for Early Childhood (DEC). (1997). *DEC membership report.* Reston, VA: Author.

Dunst, C.J., Johanson, C., Trivette, C., & Hamby, D. (1991). Family-oriented early intervention policies and practices: Family-centered or not? *Exceptional Children, 58*, 115–126.

Dunst, C.J., Trivette, C., & Deal, A. (1988). *Enabling and empowering families: Principles and guidelines for practice.* Cambridge, MA: Brookline Books

Edgerton, R.B. (1967). *The cloak of competence: Stigma in the lives of the mentally retarded.* Berkeley: University of California.

Education for All Handicapped Children Act of 1975, PL 94-142, 20 U.S.C. §§ 1400 et seq.

Education of the Handicapped Act Amendments of 1986, PL 99-457, 20 U.S.C. §§ 1400 *et seq.*

Erwin, E.J., & Soodak, L.C. (1995). I never knew I could stand up to the system: Families' perspectives on pursuing inclusive education. *Journal of The Association for Persons with Severe Handicaps, 20*, 136–146.

Fowler, S.A. (1982). Transition from preschool to kindergarten for children with special needs. In K.E. Allen & E.M. Goetz (Eds.), *Early childhood education: Special problems, special solutions* (pp. 229–242). Gaithersburg, MD: Aspen Publishers.

Fowler, S.A., Chandler, L.K., & Johnson, T.E. (1988). *It's a big step: A manual for planning transitions from preschool to kindergarten.* Lawrence: University of Kansas, Bureau of Child Research.

Fullan, M. (1993). *Change forces: Probing the depths of educational reform.* Philadelphia: Taylor & Francis Publishers.

Gallagher, J., & Rooney, R. (1999). Policy options for early childhood: A model for decision making. *Early Education & Development, 10,* 69–83.

Gilligan, C. (1982). *In a different voice: Psychological theory and women's development.* Cambridge, MA: Harvard University Press.

Green, A.L., & Stoneman, Z. (1989). Attitudes of mothers and fathers of nonhandicapped children. *Journal of Early Intervention, 13,* 292–304.

Guralnick, M.J. (1994). Mothers' perceptions of the benefits and drawbacks of early childhood mainstreaming. *Journal of Early Intervention, 18,* 168–183.

Hanson, M.J., Wolfberg, P., Zercher, C., Morgan, M., Gutierrez, S., Barnwell, D., & Beckman, P.J. (1998). The culture of inclusion: Recognizing diversity at multiple levels. *Early Childhood Research Quarterly, 13,* 185–210.

Harbin, G., McWilliam, R., & Gallagher, J. (1998). *Service to young children with disabilities: A descriptive analysis.* Chapel Hill, NC: Early Childhood Research Institute, Service Utilization.

Janko, S., Schwartz, I.S., Sandall, S., Anderson, K., & Cottam, C. (1997). Beyond microsystems: Unanticipated lessons about the meaning of inclusion. *Topics in Early Childhood Special Education, 17,* 286–306.

Kochanek, T., & Brady, A. (1995). *Maternal satisfaction with infant/toddler and preschool services: Components, outcomes and correlates.* Chapel Hill, NC: Early Childhood Research Institute, Service Utilization.

Lewis, L., Parsad, B., Carey, N., Bartfai, N., Farris, E., & Smerdon, B. (Project Officer: B. Greene). (1999). *Teacher quality: A report on the preparation and qualifications of public school teachers* (National Center for Education Statistics [NCES] no. 1999-080). Washington, DC: Government Printing Office.

Lieber, J., Capell, K., Sandall, S.R., Wolfberg, P., Horn, E., & Beckman, P.J. (1998). Inclusive preschool programs: Teachers' beliefs and practices. *Early Childhood Research Practices, 13,* 87–106.

Malouf, D.B., & Schiller, E.P. (1995). Practice and research in special education. *Exceptional Children, 61,* 414–424.

McBride, S., & Peterson, C. (1997). Home-based intervention with families of children with disabilities: Who is doing what? *Topics in Early Childhood Special Education, 17,* 209–233.

McBride, S.L., & Brotherson, M.J. (1997). Guiding practitioners toward valuing and implementing family-centered practices. In P.J. Winton, J.A. McCollum, & C. Catlett (Eds.), *Reforming personnel preparation in early intervention: Issues, models, and practical strategies* (pp. 253–276). Baltimore: Paul H. Brookes Publishing Co.

McGregor, G., & Vogelsberg, R.T. (1998). *Inclusive schooling practices: Pedagogical and research foundations: A synthesis of the literature that informs best practices about inclusive schooling.* Allegheny University of the Health Sciences, Consortium on Inclusive Schooling Practices. (Available from Paul H. Brookes Publishing Co., Baltimore.)

McTaggart, R. (1991). Principles for participatory action research. *Adult Education Quarterly, 41,* 168–187.

McWilliam, R., Lang, L., Vandiviere, P., Angell, R., Collins, L., & Underdown, G. (1995). Satisfaction and struggles: Family perceptions of early intervention services. *Journal of Early Intervention, 19,* 43–60.

McWilliam, R., Tocci, L., & Harbin, G. (1995). *Services are child-oriented and families like it that way. . .but why?* Chapel Hill, NC: Early Childhood Research Institute, Service Utilization.

Morgan, G., Azer, S., Costley, J., Genser, A., Goodman, I., Lombardi, J., & McGimsey, B. (1993). *Making a career of it.* Boston: The Center for Career Development in Early Care and Education at Wheelock College.

National Early Childhood Technical Assistance System. (1998). *1997–1998 directory of selected early childhood programs sponsored by OSERS.* Chapel Hill, NC: Author.

Odom, S. (1998, December). *Early Childhood Research Institute on Inclusion: Synthesis points.* Presentation at the Frank Porter Graham Child Development Center, Chapel Hill, NC.

Peck, C.A., Furman, G.C., & Helmstetter, E. (1993). Integrated early childhood programs: Research on the implementation of change in organizational contexts. In C.A. Peck, S.L. Odom, & D.D. Bricker (Eds.), *Integrating young children with disabilities into community programs: Ecological perspectives on research and implementation* (pp. 187–205). Baltimore: Paul H. Brookes Publishing Co.

Peterson, K.D., & Deal, T.E. (1998). How leaders influence the culture of schools. *Educational Leadership, 56,* 28–30.

Phillips, D., & Howes, C. (1987). Indicators of quality child care: Review of the research. In D.A. Phillips (Ed.), *Quality child care: What does research tell us? Monograph of the National Association of the Education of Young Children, Vol. 1.* Washington, DC: National Association for the Education of Young Children.

Pianta, R.C., Cox, M.J., Taylor, L., & Early, D.M. (1999). Kindergarten teachers' practices related to the transition into school: Results of a national survey. *The Elementary School Journal, 100*(1), 71–86.

Powell, D. (1999, January). *Designing responsive parenting programs for low-income families: What have we learned from recent approaches?* Presentation at the University of South Florida Symposium on the Essential Value of Parent Involvement & Family Support, Tampa, FL.

Reichart, D.C., Lynch, E.C., Anderson, B.C., Svobodny, L.A., DiCola, J.M., & Mercury, M.G. (1989). Parental perspectives on integrated preschool opportunities for children with handicaps and children without handicaps. *Journal of Early Intervention, 13,* 6–13.

Rooney, R. (1995, May). *Implementation of interdisciplinary personnel preparation programs for early intervention.* Paper presented at the annual Comprehensive System for Personnel Development (CSPD) meeting, Washington, DC.

Rosenkoetter, S.E., Hains, A.H., & Fowler, S.A. (1994). *Bridging early services for children with special needs and their families: A practical guide for transition planning.* Baltimore: Paul H. Brookes Publishing Co.

Rosenkoetter, S.E., Shotts, C.K., Streufert, C., & Rosenkoetter, L.I. (1995). Local interagency coordinating councils as infrastructure for early intervention: One state's implementation. *Topics in Early Childhood Special Education, 15,* 264–280.

Rosenkoetter, S.E., & Stayton, V.D. (1997). Designing and implementing innovative, interdisciplinary practica. In P.J. Winton, J.A. McCollum, & C. Catlett (Eds.), *Reforming personnel preparation in early intervention: Issues, models, and practical strategies* (pp. 453–474). Baltimore: Paul H. Brookes Publishing Co.

Rutherford, B., Anderson, B., & Billig, S. (1997). *Studies in education reform: Parent and community involvement in education.* Washington, DC: U.S. Department of Education, Office of Educational Research and Improvement.

Salisbury, C.L., Gallucci, C., Palombaro, M.M., & Peck, C.A. (1995). Strategies that promote social relations among elementary students with and without severe disabilities in inclusive schools. *Exceptional Children, 62,* 125–137.

Salisbury, C.L., Wilson, L., Swartz, T., Palombaro, M., & Wassel, J. (1997). Using action research to solve instructional challenges in inclusive elementary school settings. *Education and Treatment of Children, 20,* 21–39.

Santelli, B., Turnbull, A.P., Marquis, J., & Lerner, E. (1997). Parent-to-parent programs: A resource for parents and professionals. *Journal of Early Intervention, 21*(1), 73–83.

Schwartz, I.S. (1996). Expanding the zone: Thoughts on social validity and training [Invited commentary]. *Journal of Early Intervention, 20,* 204–205.

Shelton, T.L., Jeppson, E.S., & Johnson, B.H. (1987). *Family-centered care for children with special health care needs* (2nd ed.). Alexandria, VA: Association for the Care of Children's Health.

Soodak, L.C., & Erwin, E.J. (2000). Valued member or tolerated participant: Parents' experiences in inclusive early childhood settings. *Journal of The Association for Persons with Severe Handicaps, 25,* 29–41.

Stoiber, K.C., Gettinger, M., & Goetz, D. (1998). Exploring factors influencing parents' and early childhood practitioners' beliefs about inclusion. *Early Childhood Research Quarterly, 13,* 107–124.

Turbiville, V.P., Turnbull, A.P., Garland, C.W., & Lee, I.M. (1996). Development and implementation of IFSPs and IEPs: Opportunities for empowerment. In S.L. Odom & M.E. McLean (Eds.), *Early intervention/early childhood special education: Recommended practices* (pp. 77–100). Austin, TX: PRO-ED.

Turnbull, A.P., Blue-Banning, M., Turbiville, V., & Park, J. (1999). From parent education to partnership education: A call for a transformed focus. *Topics in Early Childhood Special Education, 19*(3), 164–172.

Turnbull, A.P., Friesen, B.J., & Ramirez, C. (1998). Participatory action research as a model for conducting family research. *Journal of The Association for Persons with Severe Handicaps, 23,* 178–188.

Turnbull, A.P., Turbiville, V., & Turnbull, H.R. (2000). Evolution of family-professional partnership models: Collective empowerment as the model for the early 21st century. In S.J. Meisels & J.P. Shonkoff (Eds.). *Handbook of early intervention* (pp. 640–650) New York: Cambridge University Press.

Turnbull, A., Turnbull, R., Shank, M., & Leal, D. (1999). *Exceptional lives: Special education in today's schools* (2nd ed.). Westerville, OH: Glencoe/McGraw-Hill.

Turnbull, A., & Winton, P. (1983). A comparison of specialized and mainstreamed preschools from the perspectives of mothers of handicapped children. *Journal of Pediatric Psychology, 8,* 57–71.

U.S. Department of Education. (1996). *Eighteenth annual report to Congress on the implementation of the Individuals with Disabilities Education Act.* Washington, DC: Author.

U.S. Department of Education. (1997). *The Individuals with Disabilities Education Act Amendments of 1997.* Washington, DC: Author.

Wesley, P.W., & Buysse, V. (1996). Supporting early childhood inclusion: Lessons learned through a statewide technical assistance project. *Topics in Early Childhood Special Education, 16,* 476–499.

Whitebook, M., Howes, C., & Phillips, D. (1990). *Who cares? Child care teachers and the quality of care in America: Final report, National Child Care Staffing Study.* Oakland, CA: Child Care Employee Project.

Winton, P.J. (1981). *Descriptive study of parents' perspectives on preschool services: Mainstreamed and specialized* [Doctoral dissertation] (University of North Carolina, Chapel Hill, 1981). Dissertation Abstracts International, 42, 3562A. (University Microfilms No. 42-08).

Winton, P.J. (1990). A systemic approach for planning in-service training related to Public Law 99-457. *Infants and Young Children, 3,* 51–60.

Winton, P.J. (1995). A model for supporting higher education faculty in their early intervention personnel preparation roles. *Infants and Young Children, 8,* 56–67.

Winton, P.J., & DiVenere, N. (1995). Family–professional partnerships in early intervention preparation: Guidelines and strategies. *Topics in Early Childhood Special Education, 15,* 296–313.

Winton, P.J., McCollum, J.A., & Catlett, C. (Eds.). (1997). *Reforming personnel preparation in early intervention: Issues, models, and practical strategies.* Baltimore: Paul H. Brookes Publishing Co.

Winton, P., McWilliam, P., Harrison, T., Owens, A., & Bailey, D. (1992). Lessons learned from implementing a team-based model of change. *Infants and Young Children, 5,* 49–57.

Winton, P.J., Turnbull, A.P., & Blacher, J. (1984). *Selecting a preschool: A guide for parents of handicapped children.* Baltimore: University Park Press.

Winton, P.J., Turnbull, A.P., Blacher, J.B., & Salkind, N. (1983). Mainstreaming in the kindergarten classroom: Perspectives of parents of handicapped and nonhandicapped children. *Journal of the Division of Early Childhood, 6,* 14–20.

7

KAREN E. DIAMOND

FIONA K. INNES

The Origins of Young Children's Attitudes Toward Peers with Disabilities

Sarah is a 3-year-old with cerebral palsy who attends a local preschool with other children from her neighborhood. She uses a wheelchair. Her teachers are help-ing her to use a communication board to talk with her classmates. Colin is a 4-year-old with Down syndrome. He enjoys playing with children his age, but he still has trouble understanding how to play "make-believe." Colin and Sarah are the two children with identified disabilities in their class of fifteen 3- and 4-year-olds. Their parents hope that their children will make friends at school. This goal is shared by their teachers and by the par-ents of the other children in the class. What will school be like for Sarah and Colin? Will they be accepted by their classmates? What can their parents and teachers do to encourage acceptance and friendships?

Questions about acceptance of and friendships between children with and without disabilities are becoming more salient as inclusive programs become more common across the United States. In inclusive classrooms, classmates with-out disabilities are an important part of

the learning environment for a child with a disability. Because out-of-school peer networks often are limited for children with disabilities (Guralnick, 1997; Lewis, Feiring, & Brooks-Gunn, 1987), interac-tions with classmates offer opportunities for children to develop and expand their repertoire of peer-related social skills. In a study of parents' and teachers' percep-tions of the benefits of inclusive pro-grams for children with disabilities, Peck, Carlson, and Helmstetter (1992) found that parents strongly agreed that inclusive experiences for typically developing chil-dren generally were positive. Parents and teachers reported that children became more accepting of human differences, became more aware of the needs of oth-ers, displayed less discomfort with people with disabilities, were less prejudiced, had fewer stereotypes about people who are different, and were more responsive and helpful to other children after their enrollment in an inclusive program.

Research on inclusive playgroups has consistently demonstrated that, as a group, children with disabilities are

The authors thank Dr. William LeFurgy for his helpful comments on earlier drafts of this chapter.

included in social interactions with their peers much less than are children without disabilities (e.g., Guralnick & Groom, 1987). In general, the social play of preschool-age children with disabilities is less sophisticated than that of peers of the same chronological or developmental age (Guralnick, 1999). However, interactions between children with disabilities and their typically developing peers have been reported to occur "with considerable frequency" (Guralnick, Connor, Hammond, Gottman, & Kinnish, 1996, p. 375). Although varying with the type of disability, the majority of children with disabilities who are enrolled in inclusive preschools are reported by their parents to have at least one mutual friend (Buysse, 1993; Guralnick, Connor, & Hammond, 1995). Taken together, these results suggest that children with disabilities are included in some activities in the preschool classroom. At the same time, because children with disabilities participate in social play less often and in less sophisticated ways, their social experiences in preschool are likely to be different from those of typically developing children (see Chapter 1).

By definition, inclusion of children with disabilities in classroom activities requires the involvement of typically developing children. The degree to which a child with a disability is socially integrated is likely to depend on typically developing children's ideas and expectations (cf. Diamond, 1993; Ramsey & Myers, 1990). These ideas and expectations form the basis for the development of attitudes toward people with disabilities. Social psychologists have established that attitudes toward and perceptions of others are learned (Allport, 1954). For people with disabilities, negative attitudes may be just as effective as physical, architectural barriers in limiting opportunities to participate fully in schools and communities (Stoneman, 1993).

THE DEVELOPMENT OF CHILDREN'S ATTITUDES

Attitudes have been defined as cognitive schema that represent groups of individuals or ideas with some degree of positive or negative evaluation (Eagly & Chaiken, 1993). When children have a cognitive schema that represents a group (e.g., boys or girls), they come to identify whether a particular child or adult is a group member. Research suggests that preschool-age children have well-developed cognitive schema for gender and race. For example, Fagot and Leinbach (1993) found that infants as young as 12–15 months begin to categorize individuals on the basis of gender. Most children can reliably use gender to identify others by the time they are 2½ years old. Similarly, Katz (1976) found that 3- and 4-year-old children reliably recognize differences in skin color. Segregation into same-race playgroups has been observed in some preschools (Ramsey & Myers, 1990), and self-initiated segregation by race is a common experience during the elementary years (Katz, 1976; Schofield, 1981). What do we know about children's understanding of different disabilities and their abilities to categorize classmates by whether they have a disability or not?

Cognitive Development

Research suggests that preschool children's awareness of and explanations for specific disabilities are related to their own cognitive/developmental abilities. In a study of children's expressed awareness of different disabilities, Conant and Budoff (1983) found that preschool children had a beginning awareness of only sensory and physical disabilities. These same young children had considerable difficulty understanding the concepts of mental retardation and emotional disturbance. An understanding of these disabilities appears in later childhood and early adolescence. Although physical disabilities are not uncommon and are often represented in media and children's books, hearing impairment and vision loss are relatively uncommon, low-incidence disabilities. It is unlikely that children's awareness of these disabilities was related to their own observations. Rather, Conant and Budoff suggested, young children may be more aware of disabilities that include a salient, observable feature (e.g., wheelchair) or to which they can relate their own experiences (e.g., not being able to see in the dark).

When Diamond (1993) examined preschool-age children's awareness of disability in their peers, she found that children were most often aware of disabilities that affected motor and language skills. When asked to explain what might have caused a child's disability, children most often referred to age or immaturity ("He can't do it because he's a baby"), specific equipment ("She can't walk because she has braces"), classroom placement ("He can't talk because he's in that class"), or accident or trauma ("She can't walk because she broke her leg").

The explanations for disability that were offered by the children in this study are similar to those offered by children in a study by Favazza and Odom (1996). They asked kindergarten-age children, "What does it mean to be handicapped?" Content analysis suggested that children's responses could be categorized into six areas: 1) physical attributes, prosthesis, or equipment; 2) ability or inability (similar to Diamond's category of age or immaturity); 3) alternative terminology; 4) named a specific individual; 5) class enrollment; and 6) specific or general description. Like the children in Diamond's (1993) study, these children used concrete features (e.g., equipment) or things that they already knew about (e.g., accidents) to explain what it means to be handicapped.

It seems that children organize and structure their cognitions about people with disabilities by assimilating new information into cognitive structures that already exist. That is, they use knowledge that they already possess (e.g., that you can be hurt in an accident) to explain something they are only beginning to understand (a child's disability). Children seem to focus on one or two salient features in determining whether a child has a disability. A child may use this awareness to judge how similar or dissimilar a child with a disability is to him- or herself. This, in turn, may be a factor that influences the choice of a child who has a disability as a playmate (Diamond, 1993).

It is possible that children assume that a child with a disability who has difficulty performing one type of developmental task (e.g., walking, for a child with a physical disability) will have difficulty on all developmental tasks. If this is the case, then the child with the disability may be less valued as a friend. Diamond (1994) explored this issue in a study that examined the likelihood that children would generalize from a child's disability-related delays in one developmental area to assume that the same child would be less competent on other developmental tasks (e.g., delayed language skills for a child who uses a wheelchair). She found that children were sensitive to differences in their peers' abilities across different developmental domains; that is, children with mental retardation were rated as less competent than children without mental retardation in all three developmental domains (cognition, language, and physical ability). However, children with physical disabilities were judged as less competent than their typically developing peers only within the physical competence domain (Diamond, 1994).

Diamond and Hestenes (1996) used photographs of unfamiliar children with disabilities to examine preschool-age children's understanding of sensory and physical disabilities and Down syndrome. Children made the most disability-related comments about a photograph of a child with a physical disability, followed by a child with a visual impairment and a child with a hearing impairment. No child commented about the disability of the photographed child with Down syndrome. Explanations for physical disability and visual impairment most often involved equipment (e.g., braces, thick glasses), whereas the majority of children were unable to explain why a child who had a hearing impairment could not hear. In addition, children differentiated among the competencies of children with different disabilities; that is, the child in the wheelchair was rated as significantly less competent on motor tasks than were children who had sensory disabilities. The child who used hearing aids was rated as significantly less competent on language tasks than were any of the other children with disabilities. There were no differences in ratings given to the child with Down syndrome and to the child without disabilities. When children were asked to sort the photographs into groups of children "who belong together," approximately 25% of children consistently used disability as the basis for grouping children. The results provide additional evidence that preschool-age children recognize that children with different disabilities may perform differently on the same task and that disability is a salient social category for some preschool-age children. In addition, these findings suggest that preschool-age children do not recognize someone with Down syndrome as having a disability (Diamond & Hestenes, 1996). In contrast, Goodman (1989) found that third graders relied on facial stigmata in identifying photographs of children as "retarded" or "not retarded." This suggests that awareness of the facial characteristics typically seen in children with Down syndrome may develop in the early elementary years. Unlike older children, preschool-age children enrolled in inclusive classrooms initially may be unaware of the disabilities of some of their classmates, particularly if the classmate uses no specialized equipment.

Katz and Kofkin (1997) suggested that four important developmental components in children's early understanding of race and gender are awareness, identity, preferences, and stereotypes. A similar developmental progression can be applied to young children's understanding of disabilities. By the time children leave preschool, they are aware of and are able to identify individuals who do or do not have a physical or sensory disability. External cues, such as equipment, may be important in children's awareness of these disabilities. There is no evidence, however, that preschool-age children are aware that children with mental retardation (including children with Down syndrome) or behavior problems belong to a group of people who have disabilities. In fact, research suggests that young children are not even aware of the possibility that someone might have a disability that is related to difficulties in thinking, such as mental retardation or emotional disturbance (Conant & Budoff, 1983; Diamond & Hestenes, 1996). There is also evidence that some preschool-age children prefer to play with peers without disabilities (cf. Diamond, LeFurgy, & Blass, 1993; Guralnick, 1999). Not surprising, children are aware of whether classmates have difficulties talking (Diamond, 1993), but this may not be linked with the concept of disability.

There is some evidence that children's attitudes toward people with disabilities are influenced by type of disability. Sigelman, Miller, and Whitworth (1986) examined reactions to potentially stigmatizing physical attributes in a group of 119 Caucasian children in nursery school through third grade. They hypothesized that children's reactions would become more negative with time for some individual differences, such as obesity, but more positive for other differences, such as disabilities. They found that children were likely to offer sympathy to those who were physically different through no fault of their own (e.g., children with physical disabilities) but that children often stigmatized others who were perceived to have had control over their particular "difference" (e.g., an obese child). Older children's evaluations generally were more positive than were the evaluations of young children. In a follow-up study, Sigelman and Begley (1987) explored the influence of causal information (i.e., the controllability of a condition/disability) and the nature of the problem on developmental changes in children's evaluative reactions to those who were physically or behaviorally different. Ninety-six children (in kindergarten through fifth grade) were randomly assigned to three experimental conditions: low responsibility (i.e., controllability for the condition is low), high responsibility (i.e., controllability for the condition is high), and control group (i.e., children were not given information about the cause of the condition). In general, children's evaluations of a child became increasingly negative as the child's perceived responsibility for the characteristic increased.

Although Eagly and Chaiken (1993) emphasized the important role played by cognition in attitudes, cognitive-developmental capabilities are not the only critical component in the development of children's attitudes toward others. There is evidence that the environment plays a role in shaping children's awareness and evaluations of particular individual attributes. Bem (1970) argued that the social environment plays a critical role in determining which attributes of the individual become a basis for discrimination. In particular, he suggested that when a particular category of salient features (e.g., gender) is associated with different treatment by adults (e.g., when teachers consistently respond more promptly to boys than to girls), this can be a critical factor in the formation of attitudes that are relevant to the particular social category (e.g., boys are more valued than girls at school). To the extent that a child's disability becomes a basis for adults' responses, these responses may influence the development of children's attitudes toward people with disabilities.

Social Environment

Although cognitive-developmental capabilities play an important role in attitude development, children's specific experiences have a complementary influence on the development of children's attitudes. In particular, there is evidence that parents' attitudes, children's experiences, and the strategies that teachers use to support inclusion in inclusive preschool classrooms have the potential to influence children's attitudes toward people with disabilities.

Teacher Behaviors There are many salient, readily apparent individual characteristics (or attributes) that children can use in categorizing others. Some are used quite often (e.g., race, gender), whereas discrimination that is based on other attributes (e.g., eye or hair color) rarely occurs. As noted previously, there is evidence that preschool-age children use social categories such as race and gender in thinking about themselves and others. Children's attitudes toward members of these social groups are related both to perceptions of within-group similarities (i.e., how members of one's own social group are alike) and to between-group differences (i.e., how members of different social groups are different). Thus, it is not uncommon to hear even young children making evaluative comments about same- or opposite-sex peers (see Paley, 1984).

Bigler, Jones, and Lobliner (1997) examined the effects of teachers' use of a novel social category ("blue" or "yellow" T-shirts) on the formation of intergroup attitudes in 6- to 9-year-old children. Teachers in the experimental group were asked to make use of color dichotomies in the physical environment as well as in verbal categorization, although they were told to treat each group equally. For example, teachers "routinely asked children to perform tasks by color group" (Bigler et al., 1997, p. 534) and used blue/yellow color dichotomies on bulletin boards. Although children in control classrooms wore the same blue or yellow T-shirts, teachers were instructed to ignore the color groups in their classes. After 4 weeks, children who were enrolled in classrooms in which teachers made functional use of T-shirt color in creating social groups gave significantly higher ratings to members of their own in-group (i.e., children who wore the same color T-shirt). There was little evidence of group differences in the control classrooms. Bigler and her colleagues suggested that when teachers make functional use of social categories, even in the absence of explicit training concerning that attribute as in this study, they communicate to children "that a particular attribute is uniquely important for understanding individuals and their behavior" (1997, p. 539).

In research conducted at a boys' summer camp in the 1950s, Sherif and his colleagues (Sherif, Harvey, White, Hood, & Sherif, 1961) demonstrated that once social groups are formed, children (and adults) develop consistent biases in favor of members of their own group and that these biases can be remarkably resistant to change. There is evidence that intergroup attitudes, including biases about gender (Powlishta, 1995), race (Doyle & Aboud, 1995), age (Seefeldt, 1989), and attractiveness (Langlois & Downs, 1979), emerge during the pre-school years. When children use social categories such as these in relation to their peers, they will be more likely to hold positive attitudes toward peers whom they see as part of their group (i.e., members of the in-group) and more negative attitudes toward children in the out-group. Bigler's research provides evidence that adults can exert an important influence on the attributes that children use in categorizing their peers as members of the in-group or out-group and that this categorization is associated with differences in attitudes toward in-group and out-group members. Following this line of research, one might speculate that if environmental factors such as the administrative structure of the early childhood program and the ways in which teachers plan and implement curriculum result in dividing children into groups on the basis of whether they have a disability, then this may have important influences on the development of children's attitudes toward classmates with disabilities. According to theory, adult behaviors and program-related structures that have the effect of removing children with disabilities from the classroom group, either physically or psychologically, should foster children's identification of their classmates with disabilities as "different" (i.e., members of an out-group). Although grouping children by disability may be based on important goals from the adults' perspective (e.g., individualizing learning opportunities), children's perceptions of their experiences may be quite different from those of their teachers and parents (Peck, 1993). Experiences that lead children to categorize their classmates on the basis of disability may provide a foundation for the development of negative attitudes toward classmates who are in the out-group (i.e., different from the typically developing children).

In one of the first studies that examined this issue, Schnorr (1990) focused on typically developing first-graders' perceptions of Peter, a child with Down syndrome, who was included in their class for part of each school day. Schnorr found that although teachers and parents perceived this part-time inclusion as successful for Peter, his classmates interpreted many of the educational practices that separated Peter from the group as indicating that he was not really a member of their class. The experiences that these children identified as being important in making Peter different included typical interventions such as leaving the classroom for specialized services, having "different" work, and riding a different bus. Janko and her colleagues (Janko, Schwartz, Sandall, Anderson, & Cottam, 1997) identified practices in inclusive early childhood programs that resulted in separating children with disabilities from their classmates. For instance, they described one school district in which children with disabilities were transported to school by a district school bus, whereas children without disabilities were transported by their families (a common practice in many programs). They described the children as noticing and questioning "the difference between the 'car kids' and the 'bus kids'" (p. 293) who not only rode a bus but also stayed at school for lunch. It was clear that for these children, whether you rode a bus was a salient social characteristic that divided them into groups of children with disabilities (bus kids) and children without disabilities (car kids). Conversely, a child care classroom in which each child had an assigned chair, not just the child with Down syndrome whose chair had been modified by the physical therapist, provides evidence of ways in which teachers meet individual children's needs (i.e., one child's need for a chair that provided more support) without differentiating the child from the rest of the group.

Bronson, Hauser-Cram, and Warfield (1997) identified specific classroom variables that were associated with social behavior for preschool-age children with disabilities. They found that children with disabilities displayed "clear benefits" in the quality of their social interactions with peers when they were enrolled in classrooms that were most similar to early childhood environments designed primarily for children without disabilities. Specifically, 5-year-old children with disabilities displayed higher levels of social play in classrooms in which fewer than 50% of children had identified disabilities, class size was larger than eight children, there was no more than one teacher for every four children, and less time was devoted to one-to-one instruction. These relationships remained significant even after accounting for the child's intellectual abilities. Earlier observations of these same children when they were 3 years old revealed that children in more inclusive environments (i.e., environments with a smaller proportion of children with identified disabilities and a more normalized teacher:child ratio) engaged in more peer interaction, both in initiations and responses, and were more independent and less controlled by adults (Hauser-Cram, Bronson, & Upshur, 1993). In addition, children with disabilities who were enrolled in classrooms in which they had more choice of activities engaged in more and higher levels of peer interaction. It seems that children with disabilities were less likely to be singled out when they were enrolled in classrooms in which adult control and one-to-one instruction were less common. To the extent that children with disabilities remained a part of the classroom group in the more inclusive classes, their classmates may have been less likely to see them as substantially different from themselves. If normalized classroom experiences promote more opportunities for all children to work and play together and fewer opportunities for children with disabilities to be seen as members of an out-group who are "not like me," then such experiences may also promote the development of more positive attitudes toward classmates who are different (including classmates with disabilities).

Parents' Attitudes and Behaviors
There is evidence that children can learn positive or negative cultural attitudes or stereotypes about others without being able to describe reliably who belongs in this stereotyped group. For example, Bar-Tal (1996) provided evidence that preschool-age Israeli children held negative attitudes toward people who were identified as "Arabs," even when the child could not reliably identify whether a particular individual was an "Arab." This suggests that the information that children learn about people with disabilities may influence their attitudes, even when they are unable to identify reliably whether someone has a disability. Okagaki, Diamond, Kontos, and Hestenes (1998) found that parents' beliefs about socializing their children in situations involving children with disabilities and their beliefs about the appropriate age at which to teach prosocial behaviors were positively related to children's attitudes about people with disabilities. In addition, parents' beliefs were related to the frequency with which their child had close contact with a classmate with a disability.

Stoneman, Rugg, and Rivers (1996) examined the role of parents as the teachers of values and related concepts about disability (see also Chapter 5). Participants were the parents (70 mothers and 50 fathers) of 3½- to 5-year-old children attending an inclusive preschool. Parents read vignettes about cerebral palsy, mental retardation, attention-deficit/hyperactivity disorder, and aggression and then indicated how they would respond to their child's questions about specific disability-associated behaviors. Parents were more likely to include positive comments and comments regarding the strengths of children with disabil-

ities in their responses to the vignettes about children with mental retardation and cerebral palsy. In addition, parents were more likely to point out similarities between their children and children with mental retardation and cerebral palsy. Children with cerebral palsy were less likely to be blamed for their disability (i.e., parents attributed the disability to an external factor over which the child and family had little control), and this was communicated to their children (Stoneman et al., 1996).

In a study that examined the ways in which parents talk with their children about people with disabilities, Innes and Diamond (1999) asked mothers of typically developing children enrolled in inclusive preschool classrooms to talk with their children about photographs of children with Down syndrome and children with physical disabilities. They found that mothers and their children talked more about children with physical disabilities than about children with Down syndrome during the storytelling task and that mothers' and children's comments about each of these disabilities were positively related.

In contrast to these results, Aboud and Doyle (1996), in a study of parents' influences on children's racial attitudes, found no relationship between parents' and children's attitudes toward people who were of a different race than themselves. This suggests that children experience adults' attitudes about race or disability through specific adult behaviors that may or may not reflect acceptance of people who are different from themselves.

Children's Experiences Stoneman (1993) suggested that children's experiences in inclusive preschool classes may have an important influence on their attitudes toward people with disabilities, with negative experiences leading to the development of negative attitudes. Diamond and her colleagues (Diamond, Hestenes, Carpenter, & Innes, 1997) examined relationships among children's understanding of physical and sensory disabilities and their ideas about social acceptance of children with disabilities as a function of enrollment in an inclusive preschool or a preschool for typically developing children only. The participants were 29 preschool-age children from a preschool program for typically developing children only and 31 preschool-age children from an inclusive preschool program. Although there were no differences in children's basic knowledge about these disabilities, children who were enrolled in the inclusive class had a better understanding of the long-term nature of a physical disability than did children who were enrolled in a preschool class that did not include peers with disabilities. In addition, children in the inclusive classes gave significantly higher social acceptance ratings for children with disabilities than did the children who were enrolled in the preschool class with only typically developing classmates (Diamond et al., 1997).

There is some evidence to suggest that children's attitudes toward people with disabilities are related to the frequency with which they have contact with classmates with disabilities. Okagaki and her colleagues (1998) examined relationships among parents' ideas about social interaction, preschool children's acceptance of people with disabilities, and the frequency of children's contact with classmates with disabilities. The results of the study revealed a significant positive relationship among the frequency of children's contact with their classmates with disabilities during free play at school, children's acceptance of people with disabilities, and parents' beliefs about socializing their children.

Summary

Research suggests that children's attitudes toward people with disabilities are closely associated with children's awareness of disability; the ways in which teachers and parents foster the inclusion of children with disabilities in school and community environments; and the quality, extent, and character of children's interactions with classmates with disabilities during the early school years. Because children's attitudes toward people with disabilities are linked to their understanding of disabilities, it appears that there may be different pathways for the development of children's attitudes toward people with physical disabilities and people with mental retardation/behavior disorders. It may be that young children's attitudes toward people with physical and sensory disabilities develop from their understanding of these obvious disabilities, with their understanding of these disabilities influencing their interactions with classmates. Young children understand that a child with a physical disability can participate fully in some classroom activities (e.g., art, an accessible dramatic play activity). A child's ability to participate in play activities, along with children's understanding of those abilities, may make it more likely that a child with a physical disability will be included in a variety of classroom activities. The chapter authors suspect, however, that young children's attitudes toward people with "hidden" disabilities (e.g., Down syndrome) may develop from their own experiences with classmates with these disabilities and from their observations of adults' interactions. When a group of young children prefer to play with some classmates but not others, group socialization theory suggests that these children will develop negative attitudes toward the group of children with whom they did not play (Harris, 1995; Sherif et al., 1961). Thus, excluding a child with Down syndrome from play activities may serve as an initial step in children's identification of people with Down syndrome as members of an out-group of children who differ from the child's friends. Attitudes toward people with "hidden" disabilities may have their beginnings in this type of differential play during the preschool years.

AGENDA FOR CHANGE: PROMOTING POSITIVE ATTITUDES TOWARD CHILDREN WITH DISABILITIES

Promoting positive attitudes toward and acceptance of people who are different is much more successful than trying to change negative attitudes and evaluations (cf. Sherif et al., 1961). It is during the preschool and early elementary years that children become both more sensitive to cues associated with disabilities and more likely to encounter children with disabilities in their classes. Because these years seem to be a critical period for the development of children's attitudes toward people with disabilities, it is during this time that interventions that promote children's positive attitudes toward people with disabilities may be especially effective. On the basis of theories of attitude development (e.g., Eagly & Chaiken, 1993) and intergroup relations (e.g., Sherif et al., 1961; Tajfel, 1969), the chapter authors have suggested that children's attitudes toward people with disabilities develop out of their understanding of disabilities and their ideas about who "belongs" and who does not (their cognitions), as well as from their experiences with people with disabilities. It is likely that children's attitudes about people with disabilities, in general, as well as about specific classmates, are shaped by the ways in which parents and teachers behave toward and communicate about people who are different from themselves (cf. Bigler et al., 1997; Okagaki et al., 1998). Interventions that are designed to promote the development of positive attitudes toward people with disabilities in young children may be most successful

when they address the cognitive and behavioral components of attitude development. An agenda for change is presented next.

Adult Behaviors and Interventions

In inclusive classes, teachers enact their ideas about children's class membership and belonging when they arrange the classroom environment, encourage children's participation, and assign children to classroom groups (Lieber et al., 1998). Bigler and colleagues (1997) demonstrated that when teachers group children in their classrooms on the basis of a particular social attribute, they communicate to children that this particular attribute is a uniquely important one, even in the absence of explicit training. Adult behaviors and program-related structures that have the effect of removing children with disabilities from the classroom group, either physically or psychologically, should foster children's identification of their classmates with disabilities as different (i.e., members of an out-group). To the extent that teachers intervene in the ways in which children with disabilities participate in classroom groups, they may influence the development of children's attitudes toward classmates with disabilities. What, specifically, might teachers do to moderate children's social participation in preschool?

An important aspect of promoting group participation and group membership is providing opportunities for children to participate in similar classroom activities and routines. Corsaro (1988) suggested that for preschool-age children, the peer culture is tied almost exclusively to behavior routines—to doing things together. He suggested that it is through repeated productions of routine activities, in a variety of environments, that preschool-age children come to understand what it means to be a peer and to see themselves as members of a peer group. This has important implications for the ways in which inclusive classes are organized to meet the individual needs of children with disabilities. Current models of therapeutic and educational intervention for children with disabilities suggest that integrating specialized therapies or instructional strategies within the routines of the classroom reflects important principles of normalization, developmentally appropriate practices, individualization, and collaboration (McWilliam, 1996). Schnorr (1990) provided evidence that educational practices that separated a child with a disability from the classroom group, including leaving the classroom for specialized services, were important in children's identification of the peer with a disability as someone who was different and "not one of us." Although we do not know the consequences of specific models of integrated therapy or intervention for children with disabilities and their classmates, it appears that when integrated in-class therapies consistently result in the removal of children from peer interaction, the child with a disability has fewer opportunities to participate in classroom routines (cf. Corsaro, 1988) and is more likely to be seen as someone who does not really belong (cf. Bigler et al., 1997; Janko et al., 1997). Thus, the chapter authors suggest that teachers and therapists be especially sensitive to the ways in which specialized interventions offer the child with a disability opportunities to continue to participate as part of a group of peers. Recently developed interventions such as activity-based intervention (Bricker, 1998), milieu teaching (Kaiser & Hester, 1994; Warren, 1992), and responsive intervention (Mahoney, Boyce, Fewell, Spiker, & Wheeden, 1998) provide models for implementing specialized instruction or therapy within the context of children's ongoing play. This may mean, for instance, that interventions that are designed to promote a child's language skills are implemented

in the context of a playgroup or small-group activity that includes classmates without disabilities. It may be more difficult to provide some therapies (e.g., physical or occupational therapy) for an individual child while that child is engaged in a group activity. However, the chapter authors have observed therapists who, when they are working individually with a child with a disability, invite one or two of that child's classmates to participate in or help with the therapy. This has included encouraging child–child conversations during passive stretching, teaching peers strategies that they can use to encourage a classmate to move independently from the floor to a wheelchair, and teaching children how to use a child's communication board to interact with that classmate. Identifying therapeutic interventions that address a child's specific needs while allowing the child to continue to participate as part of a classroom group (even with only one or two other children) is likely to reduce the inclination of classmates to see the child with a disability as someone who is different and does not belong.

Helping children understand and appreciate differences—including differences in age, gender, race, economic level, and ability—is an important task for teachers (and other adults). In the course of a preschool day, teachers have opportunities to determine the composition of groups of children (e.g., which children are assigned to a small-group activity, who sits at each table for snacks or meals) as well as individual partners (e.g., partners on a field trip or for a music activity). Such groupings foster children's interactions with all of their classmates (cf. Ramsey, 1991, 1998). Teachers need first to observe the children as they play in self-identified playgroups, usually during a free play period. A variety of strategies (e.g., keeping maps of where each child is playing, anecdotal records of playgroup activities) can be used to identify children who may be more or less involved in social playgroups, as well as a child's more preferred (or less preferred) play partners. This information then can be used to help a teacher form new groups of children for specific activities. Carefully structured groupings provide opportunities for children to learn more about each of their classmates, including classmates whom they may not have chosen as a play partner. Obviously, when teachers determine the membership of classroom groups for specific activities, those activities need to be planned so that all children have opportunities to participate in and contribute to the group.

Research has demonstrated that the ways in which teachers organize their classrooms to include children with disabilities in all aspects of the school day are important in children's developing ideas about who belongs to their peer group. Providing children with disabilities the same opportunities as their typically developing peers to participate in classroom groups is important, although there is little research about the consequences of this type of intervention for children's attitude development. Being part of a group, however, is likely to be insufficient by itself in promoting positive attitudes toward peers with disabilities. Next, specific interventions are addressed that are designed to promote children's understanding of disabilities and promote children's social relationships.

Interventions that Address Preschool Children's Understanding of Disabilities

Preschool children have only a basic understanding of sensory and physical disabilities. Children really begin to understand disabilities such as mental retardation and behavior disorders in the middle of elementary school, when they are 9 or 10 years old (Goodman, 1989). Interventions that are designed to pro-

vide children with information about specific disabilities and the ways that the disability influences a child's participation in typical activities may be most effective when applied during the preschool years and when the focus begins with disabilities that children can understand.

A number of investigators and practitioners have suggested that children's books are an effective tool for promoting positive attitudes toward people with disabilities. As the Carnegie Corporation noted, "In books, children find characters with whom they identify and whose aspirations and actions they might one day try to emulate; they discover, too, a way of perceiving those who are of a different color, who speak a different language or live a different life" (1974, p. 1). In one of the few studies that has examined the effectiveness of children's books in influencing attitudes toward people with disabilities, Salend and Moe (1983) reported positive changes in the attitudes of third-grade children after the use of classroom books that focused on children with disabilities. Later, Gross and Ortiz (1994) and Blaska and Lynch (1998) provided strategies for using books that include children with disabilities, although they have not provided data that demonstrate the effectiveness of this intervention strategy. Children's literature may be most effective when the book emphasizes competence and participation of children with disabilities in ways that are salient and understandable.

Diamond, Cooper, and Pezen (1997) developed a series of classroom activities designed to encourage the development of preschool-age children's positive attitudes toward people with physical disabilities. These activities reflected early childhood practices that emphasize the importance of providing children with opportunities for learning through exploration and provided specific, guided opportunities for children to practice using a wheelchair at school. Activities were implemented in a week-long small group and were designed to be more or less difficult (e.g., getting a drink from the water fountain, rolling the wheelchair up the sloped sidewalk to the building). Some activities were designed to encourage a child to ask for assistance (e.g., picking materials up off the floor), whereas others were designed to be completed independently (e.g., getting a drink from an accessible water fountain). All of these activities were designed to promote children's understanding of the reasons that someone in a wheelchair might (or might not) have difficulty performing a specific activity and the ways in which someone might help. Interviews with children after the group intervention suggested that they had a better appreciation for the difficulties associated with using a wheelchair and more ideas about how they might be able to assist a classmate.

Although these activities promote young children's understanding of and sensitivity to sensory and physical disabilities, they may be less effective in fostering children's understanding and appreciation of disabilities associated with language or cognition. In addition to helping children understand disabilities, it is critical for teachers and parents to help children learn to appreciate the capabilities and contributions of each child in the classroom. Derman-Sparks and colleagues (Derman-Sparks & the A.B.C. Task Force, 1989) offered a variety of strategies for encouraging children's appreciation for individual differences—including racial, ethnic, and gender differences—as well as disabilities. Strategies such as these, which encourage children to appreciate individual differences and similarities, are likely to foster more positive attitudes toward classmates with disabilities that children do not readily understand (e.g., mental retardation, language delays). Edwards (1986) also offered classroom-based strategies for encouraging children to appreciate oth-

ers. One approach that may be particularly appropriate in helping children to develop positive social and moral values related to people with disabilities involves "thinking games." A thinking game is a story situation that poses a social-cognitive problem and that is presented to children (in either a small or large group) for discussion. Children discuss possible solutions for which they need to offer a justification. The use of probing questions by teachers provokes children's "closer consideration of the underlying moral or social problems posed by the game" (Edwards, 1986, p. 23). In inclusive preschool classrooms, one of the important social (and moral) issues is that children with disabilities often are not included in peer-directed play. This classroom dilemma can serve as the source of thinking games that encourage children to think about the ways in which all children in their class are included in or excluded from play activities. For example, a thinking game that focuses on children's ideas about mental retardation might present a situation in which only one more child could join a group of girls who are playing with dolls in the housekeeping area of the classroom. One girl who wants to join the group is good at playing with dolls, but she has had many opportunities to be part of the group earlier in the day. Another girl (who has Down syndrome) would really like to play with the dolls and has not had a chance to play with them in several days. This child needs help playing with the dolls, however, because she does not talk very much and sometimes has difficulty understanding what she should do. The conflict that is posed is which child the group of girls should invite to play with them. Questions about fairness, equal access to play activities, responsibilities of classmates for each other, and strategies for making the play activity enjoyable for all of the children might serve as a beginning for this thinking game. Activities that encourage children to appreciate classmates' unique characteristics will promote the development of positive attitudes toward peers with disabilities that preschool-age children do not yet understand. Additional strategies for promoting children's social experiences are offered in the next section.

Interventions that Target Children's Social Experiences

A number of studies have examined changes in children's attitudes toward people with disabilities after their participation in an inclusive school program. Results of this research are mixed. Esposito and Reed (1986) reported that contact with age-mates with disabilities was associated with long-lasting positive gains in young children's attitudes toward people with disabilities (with attitudes assessed through a brief interview). Helmstetter, Peck, and Giangreco (1994) reported positive outcomes of inclusion for high school students who participated in programs with age-mates with disabilities, and Kishi and Meyer (1994) found that teenagers' attitudes were more positive and accepting of people with disabilities if they had participated in mainstreamed school-based activities during elementary school. In addition, students from both the contact and exposure groups reported that they presently had more social contact with people with physical disabilities and people with mental retardation than did students from the control group (Kishi & Meyer, 1994). Diamond and colleagues (1993) reported, however, that preschool-age children became significantly less likely to say that they would like to play with a classmate with a disability over the course of a school year. The results of this study are also consistent with other studies that used sociometric assessment strategies for documenting children's acceptance of their peers (e.g., Guralnick et al., 1996).

In a series of studies with elementary school–age children, Salisbury and her colleagues (Salisbury, Evans, & Palombaro, 1997; Salisbury, Gallucci, Palombaro, & Peck, 1995) described two specific classroom strategies, collaborative problem solving and cooperative learning, that were designed to promote greater inclusion of children with disabilities in the life of the classroom. In collaborative problem solving, teachers or students identified specific outcomes that reflected ways that individual children could participate more fully with their classmates (e.g., active participation for one child on the playground). Once an outcome was identified, children and teachers generated potential solutions, identified ones that were feasible and that promoted the goal of greater inclusion (e.g., providing a helmet to provide protection from injury, showing children specific ways that they could provide assistance), implemented the strategies that were identified as most appropriate and feasible, and then evaluated the outcome. Cooperative learning activities were ones in which the classroom teacher divided the students into groups for specific projects. They were designed so that all of the members of the group were closely involved with and shared responsibility for the achievement goals of the other group members (cf. Johnson & Johnson, 1994). Research in inclusive elementary and middle school classrooms suggests that, over the course of the school year, children who participate with classmates with disabilities in cooperative learning groups tend to perceive their peers with disabilities as more desirable work partners in May than they had in October. In contrast, children who participated in traditionally taught classes tended to perceive their special education classmates as undesirable partners, and their perceptions remained unchanged from October to May (Putnam, Markovchick, Johnson, & Johnson, 1996).

Favazza and Odom (1997) used a variety of interventions to promote positive attitudes toward peers with disabilities among a group of kindergarten children. The children in the intervention groups in this study attended one of two elementary schools in which children with disabilities were enrolled in special education classes but participated in lunch, recess, music, and library times with the other children in the school. Children in a no-contact control group attended a school that included no children with disabilities. For the high-contact group, 15 kindergarten children participated in a 9-week program that included storytime and discussions about children with disabilities in their classroom, a 15-minute structured free play activity with age-mates with disabilities 3 days each week, and home reading activities. Fifteen children in the low-contact group saw children with disabilities during daily school activities (e.g., recess) but participated in none of the interventions, and 16 children in the no-contact group had no daily contact with children with disabilities. The attitudes of children in the high-contact group were significantly more positive at the end of the intervention than they had been at the beginning. In addition, children in the high-contact group held significantly more positive attitudes toward people with disabilities in general than did children in the low- and no-contact groups. These data suggest that minimal amounts of contact with children with disabilities (the experience of children in the low-contact group) have little influence on children's attitudes. Anecdotal evidence suggested that the storytime activities at school and the home learning component were valuable, although the extent to which each of these components affected children's attitudes is unclear. The chapter authors suspect that the effectiveness of each of these interventions is related to the ways in which they provided adults an opportunity for modeling positive attitudes about people with disabilities and encouraged children to think about the social and moral aspects of inclusion of all children in classroom activities.

CONCLUSION

Attitudes reflect an individual's underlying belief system and may be enacted through a variety of different behaviors. As the research reviewed in this chapter demonstrates, young children have disability-related ideas about individuals with physical and sensory disabilities. Many preschool-age children believe that classmates with physical or sensory disabilities are just as likely to have friends as any other child (e.g., Diamond et al., 1997). These ideas may or may not be reflected in children's behaviors, although this question has not been examined in research studies. Research consistently demonstrates that preschool-age children do not hold disability-related beliefs about individuals with mental retardation, behavior problems, or language delays. However, differences in interaction patterns with classmates with mental retardation or behavior problems may serve as a precursor for the later development of beliefs about and attitudes toward individuals with those disabilities.

Understanding the ways in which a child's interactions with his or her classmates contribute to children's ideas about people with disabilities and to the later development of children's attitudes is an important research goal. In addition, it is important to recognize that attitudes can be enacted in a variety of different contexts and through a variety of different behaviors. When children accept the responsibility for ensuring that a classmate with a disability is included in classroom activities (Salisbury & Palombaro, 1998), wait for a classmate in a wheelchair to "catch up" with the group (Janney & Snell, 1996), or offer assistance to a classmate (Richardson & Schwartz, 1998), these behaviors reflect children's beliefs about and attitudes toward classmates with disabilities. Salisbury and Palombaro suggested that "there is a need to reexamine traditional markers of friendship and propose broader ground rules for describing relationships among students with and without disabilities" (1998, p. 101). Similarly, we need to develop a variety of strategies for understanding the beliefs that are critical in the development of children's attitudes toward people with disabilities. This is a crucial step, for if children with disabilities "are to take their rightful place in the community, they must be participants of the community, and others must see them and acknowledge them as full members" (Kliewer, 1999, p. 153).

REFERENCES

Aboud, F.E., & Doyle, A.B. (1996). Parental and peer influences on children's racial attitudes. *International Journal of Intercultural Relations, 20,* 371–383.

Allport, G. (1954). *The nature of prejudice.* Reading, MA: Addison Wesley Longman.

Bar-Tal, D. (1996). Development of social categories and stereotypes in early childhood: The case of "The Arab" concept formation, stereotype and attitudes by Jewish children in Israel. *International Journal of Intercultural Relations, 20,* 341–370.

Bem, D.J. (1970). *Beliefs, attitudes, and human affairs.* Pacific Grove, CA: Brooks/Cole Publishing.

Bigler, R.S., Jones, L.C., & Lobliner, D.B. (1997). Social categorization and the formation of intergroup attitudes in children. *Child Development, 68,* 530–543.

Blaska, J.K., & Lynch, E.C. (1998). Is everyone included? Using children's literature to facilitate the understanding of disabilities. *Young Children, 53*(2), 36–39.

Bricker, D. (1998). *An activity-based approach to early intervention* (2nd ed.). Baltimore: Paul H. Brookes Publishing Co.

Bronson, M.B., Hauser-Cram, P., & Warfield, M.E. (1997). Classrooms matter: Relations between the classroom environment and the social and mastery behavior of five-year-old children with disabilities. *Journal of Applied Developmental Psychology, 18,* 331–348.

Buysse, V. (1993). Friendships of preschoolers with disabilities in community-based child care settings. *Journal of Early Intervention, 17,* 380–395.

Carnegie Corporation. (1974). Racism and sexism and children's books. *Carnegie Quarterly, 22*(4), 1–8.

Conant, S., & Budoff, M. (1983). Patterns of awareness in children's understanding of disability. *Mental Retardation, 21,* 119–125.

Corsaro, W. (1988). Peer culture in the preschool. *Theory into Practice, 27*(1), 19–24.

Derman-Sparks, L., & the A.B.C. Task Force. (1989). *Anti-bias curriculum: Tools for empowering young children.* Washington, DC: National Association for the Education of Young Children.

Diamond, K. (1993). Preschool children's concepts of disability in their peers. *Early Education and Development, 4,* 123–129.

Diamond, K. (1994). Evaluating preschool children's sensitivity to developmental differences. *Topics in Early Childhood Special Education, 14,* 49–63.

Diamond, K., Cooper, D., & Pezen, C. (1997). *Teaching preschool children about physical disabilities.* Unpublished program manual. West Lafayette, IN: Purdue University.

Diamond, K., & Hestenes, L. (1996). Preschool children's conceptions of disabilities: The salience of disability in children's ideas about others. *Topics in Early Childhood Special Education, 16,* 458–475.

Diamond, K., Hestenes, L.L., Carpenter, E., & Innes, F. (1997). Relationships between enrollment in an inclusive class and preschool children's ideas about people with disabilities. *Topics in Early Childhood Special Education, 17,* 520–536.

Diamond, K., LeFurgy, W., & Blass, S. (1993). Attitudes of typical preschool children toward their peers with disabilities: A year-long study in four integrated classrooms. *Journal of Genetic Psychology, 154,* 215–222.

Doyle, A.B., & Aboud, F. (1995). A longitudinal study of white children's racial prejudice as a social-cognitive development. *Merrill-Palmer Quarterly, 41,* 209–228.

Eagly, A., & Chaiken, S. (1993). *The psychology of attitudes.* New York: Harcourt.

Edwards, C.P. (1986). *Promoting social and moral development in young children: Creative approaches for young children.* New York: Teachers College Press.

Esposito, B.G., & Reed, T.M. (1986). The effects of contact with handicapped persons on young children's attitudes. *Exceptional Children, 53,* 224–229.

Fagot, B.I., & Leinbach, M.D. (1993). Gender-role development in young children: From discrimination to labeling. *Developmental Review, 13,* 205–224.

Favazza, P.C., & Odom, S.L. (1996). Use of the Acceptance Scale to measure attitudes of kindergarten-age children. *Journal of Early Intervention, 20,* 232–248.

Favazza, P., & Odom, S.L. (1997). Promoting positive attitudes of kindergarten-age children toward people with disabilities. *Exceptional Children, 63,* 405–418.

Goodman, J. (1989). Does retardation mean dumb? Children's perceptions of the nature, cause, and course of mental retardation. *Journal of Special Education, 23,* 313–329.

Gross, A.L., & Ortiz, L.W. (1994). Using children's literature to facilitate inclusion in kindergarten and primary grades. *Young Children, 49*(3), 32–35.

Guralnick, M.J. (1997). The peer social networks of young boys with developmental delays. *American Journal on Mental Retardation, 101,* 595–612.

Guralnick, M.J. (1999). Family and child influences on the peer-related social competence of young children with developmental delays. *Mental Retardation and Developmental Disabilities Research Reviews, 5,* 21–29.

Guralnick, M.J., Connor, R., & Hammond, M. (1995). Parent perspectives of peer relations and friendships in integrated and specialized programs. *American Journal on Mental Retardation, 99,* 457–476.

Guralnick, M.J., Connor, R., Hammond, M., Gottman, J.M., & Kinnish, K. (1996). Immediate effects of mainstreamed settings on the social interactions and social integration of preschool children. *American Journal on Mental Retardation, 100,* 359–378.

Guralnick, M.J., & Groom, J.M. (1987). The peer relations of mildly delayed and nonhandicapped preschool children in mainstreamed playgroups. *Child Development, 58,* 1566–1572.

Harris, J.R. (1995). Where is the child's environment? A group socialization theory of development. *Psychological Review, 102,* 458–489.

Hauser-Cram, P., Bronson, M., & Upshur, C. (1993). The effects of the classroom environment on the social and mastery behavior of preschool children with disabilities. *Early Childhood Research Quarterly, 8,* 479–497.

Helmstetter, E., Peck, C.A., & Giangreco, M.F. (1994). Outcomes of interactions with peers with moderate or severe disabilities: A statewide survey of high school students. *Journal of The Association for Persons with Severe Handicaps, 19,* 263–276.

Innes, F., & Diamond, K. (1999). Typically developing children's interactions with peers with disabilities: Relationships between mothers' comments and children's ideas about disabilities. *Topics in Early Childhood Special Education, 19,* 103–111.

Janko, S., Schwartz, I., Sandall, S., Anderson, K., & Cottam, C. (1997). Beyond microsystems: Unanticipated lessons about the meaning of inclusion. *Topics in Early Childhood Special Education, 17,* 286–306.

Janney, R.E., & Snell, M.E. (1996). How teachers use peer interactions to include students with moderate and severe disabilities in elementary general education classrooms. *Journal of The Association for Persons with Severe Handicaps, 21,* 72–80.

Johnson, R.T., & Johnson, D.W. (1994). An overview of cooperative learning. In J.S. Thousand, R.A. Villa, & A.I. Nevin (Eds.), *Creativity and collaborative learning: A practical guide to empowering students and teachers* (pp. 31–44). Baltimore: Paul H. Brookes Publishing Co.

Kaiser, A.P., & Hester, P.P. (1994). Generalized effects of enhanced milieu teaching. *Journal of Speech and Hearing Research, 37,* 1320–1340.

Katz, P. (1976). The acquisition of racial attitudes in children. In P.A. Katz (Ed.), *Towards the elimination of racism* (pp. 125–154). New York: Pergamon Press.

Katz, P.A., & Kofkin, J.A. (1997). Race, gender, and young children. In S.S. Luthar & J.A. Burack (Eds.), *Developmental psychopathology: Perspectives on adjustment, risk, and disorder* (pp. 51–74). New York: Cambridge University Press.

Kishi, G.S., & Meyer, L.H. (1994). What children report and remember: Six-year follow-up of the effects of social contact between peers with and without severe disabilities. *Journal of The Association for Persons with Severe Handicaps, 19,* 277–289.

Kliewer, S. (1999). Seeking the functional. *Mental Retardation, 37,* 151–154.

Langlois, J.H., & Downs, A.C. (1979). Peer relations as a function of physical attractiveness: The eye of the beholder or behavioral reality? *Child Development, 50,* 409–418.

Lewis, M., Feiring, C., & Brooks-Gunn, J. (1987). The social networks of children with and without handicaps: A developmental perspective. In S. Landesman & P. Vietze (Eds.), *Living environments and mental retardation* (pp. 377–400). Washington, DC: American Association on Mental Retardation.

Lieber, J., Capell, K., Sandall, S.R., Wolfberg, P., Horn, E., & Beckman, P. (1998). Inclusive preschool programs: Teachers' beliefs and practices: *Early Childhood Research Quarterly, 13,* 87–106.

Mahoney, G., Boyce, G., Fewell, R.R., Spiker, D., & Wheeden, C.A. (1998). The relationship of parent–child interaction to the effectiveness of early intervention services for at-risk children and children with disabilities. *Topics in Early Childhood Special Education, 18,* 5–17.

McWilliam, R.A. (1996). A program of research on integrated versus isolated treatment in early intervention. In R.A. McWilliam (Ed.), *Rethinking pull-out services in early intervention: A professional resource* (pp. 71–102). Baltimore: Paul H. Brookes Publishing Co.

Okagaki, L., Diamond, K., Kontos, S., & Hestenes, L. (1998). Correlates of young children's interactions with classmates with disabilities. *Early Childhood Research Quarterly, 13,* 67–86.

Paley, V.G. (1984). *Boys & girls: Superheroes in the doll corner.* Chicago: University of Chicago Press.

Peck, C.A. (1993). Ecological perspectives on the implementation of integrated early childhood programs. In C.A. Peck, S.L. Odom, & D.D. Bricker (Eds.), *Integrating young children with disabilities into community programs: Ecological perspectives on research and implementation* (pp. 3–15). Baltimore: Paul H. Brookes Publishing Co.

Peck, C.A., Carlson, P., & Helmstetter, E. (1992). Parent and teacher perceptions of outcomes for typically developing children enrolled in integrated early childhood programs: A statewide study. *Journal of Early Intervention, 16,* 53–63.

Powlishta, K.K. (1995). Gender bias in children's perceptions of personality traits. *Sex Roles, 32,* 17–28.

Putnam, J., Markovchick, K., Johnson, D.W., & Johnson, R.T. (1996). Cooperative learning and peer acceptance of students with learning disabilities. *Journal of Social Psychology, 136,* 741–752.

Ramsey, P.G. (1991). *Making friends in school: Promoting peer relationships in early childhood.* New York: Teachers College Press.

Ramsey, P.G. (1998). *Teaching and learning in a diverse world* (2nd ed.). New York: Teachers College Press.

Ramsey, P.G., & Myers, L.C. (1990). Salience of race in young children's cognitive, affective, and behavioral responses to social environments. *Journal of Applied Developmental Psychology, 11,* 49–67.

Richardson, P., & Schwartz, I.S. (1998). Making friends in preschool: Friendship patterns of young children with disabilities. In L.H. Meyer, H.-S. Park, M. Grenot-Scheyer, I.S. Schwartz, & B. Harry (Eds.), *Making friends: The influences of*

culture and development (pp. 65–80). Baltimore: Paul H. Brookes Publishing Co.

Salend, S., & Moe, L. (1983). Modifying nonhandicapped students' attitudes toward their handicapped peers through children's literature. *Journal for Special Educators, 19*(3), 22–28.

Salisbury, C.L., Evans, I.M., & Palombaro, M. (1997). Collaborative problem-solving to promote the inclusion of young children with significant disabilities in primary grades. *Exceptional Children, 63,* 195–209.

Salisbury, C.L., Gallucci, C.L., Palombaro, M., & Peck, C. (1995). Strategies that promote social relations among elementary students with and without severe disabilities in inclusive schools. *Exceptional Children, 62,* 125–137.

Salisbury, C.L., & Palombaro, M.M. (1998). Friends and acquaintances: Evolving relationships in an inclusive elementary school. In L.H. Meyer, H.-S. Park, M. Grenot-Scheyer, I.S. Schwartz, & B. Harry (Eds.), *Making friends: The influences of culture and development* (pp. 81–104). Baltimore: Paul H. Brookes Publishing Co.

Schnorr, R. (1990). "Peter? He comes and goes. . .": First graders' perspectives on a part-time mainstream student. *Journal of The Association for Persons with Severe Handicaps, 15,* 231–240.

Schofield, J. (1981). Complementary and conflicting identities: Images and interactions in an interracial school. In S.R. Asher & J.M. Gottman (Eds.), *The development of children's friendships* (pp. 53–90). New York: Cambridge University Press.

Seefeldt, C. (1989). Intergenerational programs: Impact on attitudes. *Journal of Children in Contemporary Society, 20,* 185–194.

Sherif, M., Harvey, O.J., White, B.J., Hood, W.R., & Sherif, C.W. (1961). *Intergroup cooperation and competition: The Robbers Cave experiment.* Norman, OK: University Book Exchange.

Sigelman, C.K., & Begley, N.L. (1987). The early development of reactions to peers with controllable and uncontrollable problems. *Journal of Pediatric Psychology, 12,* 99–115.

Sigelman, C.K., Miller, T.E., & Whitworth, L.A. (1986). The early development of stigmatizing reactions to physical differences. *Journal of Applied Developmental Psychology, 7,* 17–32.

Stoneman, Z. (1993). The effects of attitude on preschool integration. In C.A. Peck, S.L. Odom, & D.D. Bricker (Eds.), *Integrating young children with disabilities into community programs: Ecological perspectives on research and implementation* (pp. 223–248). Baltimore: Paul H. Brookes Publishing Co.

Stoneman, Z., Rugg, M., & Rivers, J. (1996, December). *Parents as teachers of attitudes and values about peers with disabilities.* Presented at the International Early Childhood Conference on Children with Special Needs, Phoenix, AZ.

Tajfel, H. (1969). Cognitive aspects of prejudice. *Journal of Social Issues, 25*(4), 79–97.

Warren, S.F. (1992). Facilitating basic vocabulary acquisition with milieu teaching procedures. *Journal of Early Intervention, 16,* 235–251.

8

VIRGINIA BUYSSE

PATRICIA W. WESLEY

HARRIET ABLE-BOONE

Innovations in Professional Development

Creating Communities of Practice to Support Inclusion

Changes brought about by the "philosophical and technical challenges of inclusion" (Guralnick, 1993, p. ix) have required a corresponding set of changes in the way in which we prepare professionals to work with young children and families. For both professional development efforts and the field in general, the philosophical challenge exists as a result of a paradigm shift in the way early intervention services are designed and delivered—from a segregated stimulation or remediation model to one that promotes competence and supports full inclusion and participation in the community. Dramatic changes in where services are delivered, who delivers them, and the nature of the services have resulted in new professional roles for personnel in general early childhood environments as well as for early interventionists traditionally associated with specialized programs for children with disabilities. The move to serve children and families in the least restrictive and most natural environments also has resulted in a proliferation of new techniques, strategies, and models that

professionals are required to know to implement effective practices that support inclusion. For example, relatively recent innovations such as activity-based intervention, the consulting teacher model, and milieu teaching all have come about in large measure as a direct result of early childhood inclusion (Bricker, 1998; File & Kontos, 1992; Hart & Rogers-Warren, 1978; Warren & Bambara, 1989).

In addition to the philosophical and technical challenges associated with inclusion, professional development programs have responded to several other important changes in the field. All of these changes are related to policies and practices associated with inclusion and reinforce them, although there are challenges associated with each one. The first is the movement to adopt family-centered practices (Bailey, 1996; Bailey, Buysse, Edmondson, & Smith, 1992). The assumptions that underlie a family-centered philosophy (e.g., families as decision makers, families' competence in setting and achieving their own goals,

179

family priorities driving early intervention services) are now widely accepted tenets of early intervention practice (Bailey, McWilliam, Buysse, & Wesley, 1998). At the same time, learning how to respond to families' needs and priorities, identify family supports, and view parents as partners in all aspects of early intervention has redefined the ways in which parents and professionals work together. Moreover, implementing a family-centered approach has required professionals to learn new skills in communicating and negotiating with families from a variety of cultural and ethnic backgrounds.

The second change that has influenced professional roles is the move to integrate therapy and special services into children's daily routines and activities (McWilliam, 1996). As a recommended practice, integrated therapy has required that professionals understand how to individualize within a developmentally appropriate practice framework, learn how to work as a consultant, expand their concept of teaming to include new community partners (e.g., child care teachers) as well as families, and coordinate a wide range of community services from a variety of agencies and programs.

The unification of two fields, early childhood education and early childhood special education, represents yet a third change that has influenced professional development programs (Kemple, Hartle, Correa, & Fox, 1994; Stayton & Miller, 1993). Developing coursework and field-based experiences that combine two sets of professional competencies—general early childhood and early childhood special education—presents significant logistical challenges, particularly in states that do not offer a single licensure. One of the primary difficulties in developing "blended" professional development programs has been the lack of consensus about what constitutes recommended practices that ideally are integrated across

different sets of competencies. The lack of a common educational enterprise is reinforced by the existence of separate professional organizations, journals designed primarily for either general or special early childhood audiences, and two sets of recommended practices. In other words, the philosophies, policies, and underlying assumptions within general and special education have not been completely aligned and sometimes conflict.

A fourth change concerns the recent commitment to ensuring that early care and intervention services that are provided to young children and families are of high quality (Bailey, Aytch, Odom, Symons, & Wolery, 1999; Buysse, Wesley, Bryant, & Gardner, 1999). Although a number of factors have been shown to influence children's early care and education experiences, perhaps the single most important determinant of quality programming is the quality of the personnel who staff these programs (Cost, Quality, and Child Outcomes Study Team, 1995). Inclusion has helped to focus attention on the need for improved quality largely because the limited availability of high-quality early childhood programs has served as a significant barrier to implementing inclusion (Bailey et al., 1998; Buysse et al., 1999; Buysse, Wesley, & Keyes, 1998; Smith & Rose, 1993). Because previous research has demonstrated that teacher education and training are linked inextricably to program quality and child outcomes (Cost, Quality, and Child Outcomes Study Team, 1995), developing quality inclusive programs and services requires a careful examination of existing approaches to professional development.

How should designers of professional development programs respond to these forces? Fenichel and Eggbeer (1991) identified four elements of professional development that are essential in preparing all personnel who work with young children and families. First, the authors noted the critical need to create a knowledge base built on a framework of concepts that are common to all disciplines affiliated with young children and families. Although this effort will require broad-based support as well as a significant investment of resources and expertise, it is important that professionals from related fields begin to recognize the need for common core concepts that underlie sound practice in areas such as human development, environmental arrangements, and relationship-based interventions with families.

Second, Fenichel and Eggbeer (1991) pointed out the critical need to create meaningful opportunities for direct observation and involvement with young children and families from diverse cultural and ethnic backgrounds as well as with an array of programs that serve them. Ideally, this should include a wide range of experiences that include working with teenage parents, parents who have developmental disabilities, and families who are homeless. Without this experiential base, it is difficult for professionals to learn how to apply theory to practice in a manner that is responsive to the individual needs and competencies of young children and families from different backgrounds in a variety of contexts.

Individualized supervision and collegial support that begin during formal preparation and continue throughout one's professional life are the third and fourth critical components of professional development programs (Fenichel & Eggbeer, 1991). Developing with an experienced mentor and other colleagues relationships that involve opportunities to reflect on all aspects of work with young children and families can help a professional acquire self-knowledge that may sustain more formal professional development and training experiences. Although emphasis on supervision and collegial support is less common in the early childhood and intervention fields than it is for

other disciplines (e.g., mental health, allied health), there is a growing awareness of the importance of encouraging professionals to assume greater responsibility for their own professional growth and change through reflective practice techniques used in supervision and mentorship (Duff, Brown, & Van Scoy, 1995; Fenichel, 1991; Gallacher, 1997).

In his assessment of how professional development programs should be fundamentally restructured to respond to inclusion, Bailey (1996) took a slightly different approach. First, he argued that professional development programs must build a philosophical base to provide a framework for responding to conflicting values held by families and other professionals. Second, he suggested that professional development designers integrate content related to inclusion and family-centered practices into other core content areas (e.g., child development, assessment and intervention methods, teaming), rather than teaching this content in isolation. Third, he recommended that blended professional development programs include faculty from other departments and offer interdisciplinary field experiences. Finally, to enhance problem-solving skills among professionals who face many ethical challenges in their work with young children and families, he suggested using case method instructional approaches (see, e.g., Snyder & McWilliam, 1999) augmented by supervision.

COMMUNITIES OF PRACTICE: A MODEL FOR PROFESSIONAL DEVELOPMENT

The community-of-practice framework is yet another approach that should be considered in restructuring professional development programs. Although somewhat unfamiliar to the early childhood and intervention fields, the use of communities of practice as a model of professional development is well documented in the teacher education literature (Englert & Tarrant, 1995; Marshall & Hatcher, 1996; Rogoff, 1994; Stamps, 1997; Westheimer & Kahne, 1993). A community of practice can be defined as a group of professionals and other stakeholders in pursuit of a shared learning enterprise. As a framework for supporting professional growth, a community of practice challenges the one-sided view of learning in which researchers are perceived as experts and "knowledge generators" and practitioners are considered novices and "knowledge translators." Rather, teaching and learning are viewed as bidirectional; both groups contribute equally to the professional community's knowledge base.

Originally, the notion of a community of practice was used to identify the way in which meaning was negotiated and reflected in the practices of specific groups (e.g., architects, physicians, performing artists). In education, the emphasis has shifted from describing various communities of practice to creating communities for the purpose of *improving* practice as a model of professional development (Palincsar, Magnusson, Marano, Ford, & Brown, 1998). Communities of practice were created in response to several barriers to professional development that exist in the culture of American schooling. The first is the lack of general agreement about what constitutes "recommended" or "best" practice. Palincsar and colleagues argued that although there are principles in education that are widely accepted, there is not consensus about how to translate these principles into practice. They illustrated this point by noting that even though there is general agreement about constructivism in principle, there are many different constructivist views that may translate into practice in different ways. The second barrier to professional development is the private, personal, and isolated nature

of teaching. This isolation also exists in the early childhood and intervention fields and contributes to a lack of collegiality, intellectual stimulation, and professional support. In contrast to a field such as science, in which the work of individual scientists contributes to a larger body of knowledge, teachers are only peripheral participants in the professional education community.

Barriers to professional development also may exist within the very universities and institutions of higher learning that are designed to prepare professionals to work with young children and families. Not only does research tend to be separated from practice in many universities, it is also captured by its own agenda, which may or may not yield useful professional knowledge (Schön, 1987). Furthermore, students are expected to apply research-based knowledge to the problems of everyday practice with only very limited opportunities for practicum and field experiences.

How might the early childhood and intervention fields begin incorporating a community-of-practice framework into existing professional development programs to overcome these obstacles? First, it is important to note that there is much to learn about the specific mechanisms by which traditional professional development programs (where practitioners are viewed as recipients of knowledge) might be transformed into learning communities (where practitioners are viewed as co-producers of knowledge; Englert & Tarrant, 1995). Palincsar and colleagues (1998) suggested that designers of professional development programs begin by building a community of practice from the ground up—bringing together people with diverse expertise (e.g., parents, university faculty, researchers, policy makers, administrators, service providers) and introducing them to an inquiry-based approach that first explores the meaning of a community of practice. The purpose of this initial inquiry into the nature of a community of practice is to reveal the tools, language, images, roles, procedures, understandings, assumptions, and shared world views concerning professional practice related to work with young children and families. Over time, the goal is to develop practices that are reflective of a specific orientation to early education and intervention (e.g., inclusive, family-centered, culturally sensitive, individually and developmentally appropriate) by encouraging members of the community to be interactive and interdependent on the basis of trust and mutual commitment to the process. Another important goal is to share new knowledge and products that emerge from constructing a community of practice with the broader early education and intervention community.

The vision for early education and intervention is for communities of practice to take many different forms to support inclusion. A group of early education and intervention professionals could use the Internet to engage in on-line discussions about the meaning and definition of natural environments for infants and toddlers. Parents could present their experiences with inclusion in college classrooms, participate in state and national conferences, work as consultants or advisors on research projects, and serve as mentors to university students who are preparing to work in a variety of community environments. University faculty and practitioners could co-teach a methods course on assessment and intervention practice. Students, university faculty, family members, and field supervisors could meet monthly to discuss relevant topics, concerns, or questions defining what it means to individualize inclusion. Child care staff and program consultants could meet with a researcher to view videotapes and reflect on strategies for improving classroom or home-visiting practices.

The next sections extend this notion of building a community of practice to transform professional development first by examining new and emerging professional roles that serve as the foundation for professional practice, second identifying strategies for creating communities of practice within existing professional development efforts, and finally by describing some of the challenges that the field must overcome to change and improve the way in which professionals are prepared to work with young children and families in the future.

PROFESSIONAL GOALS AND ROLES: A FOUNDATION FOR PRACTICE

The construct of role is the primary way to organize conceptually the various responsibilities of professionals in the field of early intervention and education. By defining professional roles and identifying their interrelatedness, one can form a more cohesive picture of the nature of our work than by considering professional competencies, education and training, or job functions alone. New and changing roles are a barometer of the profession's response to innovations in philosophy and practice. Effective professional development models prepare individuals with both the knowledge and the skills needed to do their jobs and an understanding of roles as a framework within which to reference their actions to the field as a whole.

Traditional frameworks for conceptualizing professional roles in early intervention have focused almost exclusively on the direct service component of the early interventionist's job, emphasizing one-to-one work with the child and family (Bailey, 1989; Bricker, 1989). The evolution to inclusive practices has stimulated a reconceptualization of roles for both general early childhood educators and specialists to reflect increased collaboration with personnel of different disciplines and the expectation of filling multiple roles in a variety of contexts (Buysse & Wesley, 1993; File & Kontos, 1992; Hanson & Widerstrom, 1993; Winton, McCollum, & Catlett, 1997). As early interventionists broaden their scope of work to include indirect services, for example, delivering consultation to other care providers, the new roles they experience parallel changes in teacher roles created by school reform (Buysse & Wesley, 1993). These roles emphasize building at the individual, program, and systems levels relationships that are characterized more by equality than by dominance and expert authority (Murphy, 1991). They rely on a set of skills related to effective communication, planning, and problem solving (Buysse & Wesley, 2000).

Although professional roles have undergone considerable transformation over a short period of time, a shared sense of professional responsibility toward collaborative inquiry for the purpose of contributing to a common core of knowledge in the field is still missing. Practices may be evolving and improving, but in what way do the lessons learned by practitioners and families drive professional development? Opportunities for learning and teaching, practice and research, family perspectives, and policy to inform each other are isolated and infrequent, a situation that practitioners and constituents often feel powerless to change. It is ironic that, as a field, we have embraced as basic tenets natural and interactive processes of how children learn to interact, negotiate, collaborate, and guide inquiry, yet this perspective stands in stark contrast to the direct instruction that dominates traditional methods of teacher preparation.

As a framework for professional development, a community of practice in education offers an orientation that reflects the spirit of inquiry and advocacy and that recognizes the link between professional development and improving outcomes for children, families, and the field as a whole. The emphasis is on high interaction and interdependence among people with diverse expertise, including higher education, research, and direct services (Palincsar et al., 1998). Faculty, practitioners, and families work together closely to tackle challenges in which they have mutual interests, and they share the responsibility and authority to advance professional knowledge about practice. In this way, communities of practice are different from professional development activities in which knowledge is delivered to learners by experts or in which learners acquire knowledge through self-instruction (Rogoff, 1994).

Figure 8.1 represents three broad professional goals that provide a framework for considering the multiple roles of the early interventionist: designing, implementing, and evaluating intervention; promoting high-quality inclusion; and promoting professional development and the advancement of the field. At the heart of our work is the desire to enhance the quality of life for children and families. This value is shared across disciplines and organizations and, for many of us, is the reason we chose a profession in the field. The goal most traditionally and closely associated with this mission is the design, delivery, and evaluation of intervention to the child and family. The other two goals also are familiar to professionals, but they require greater attention than ever before. Preparing professionals for roles that are related to actively promoting high-quality inclusion and engaging in self-directed and collaborative inquiry will require more than restructuring professional development activities. It will demand a "reculturation" of the profession, involving a change of norms, values, incentives, skills, and relationships (Fullan, 1998). The design of professional development contexts such as communities of practice may be one step toward such reculturation. The following

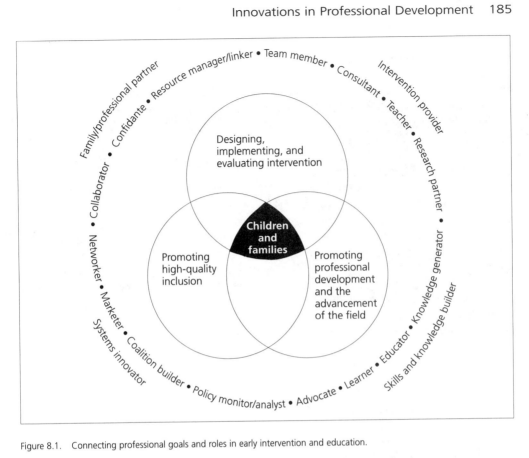

Figure 8.1.   Connecting professional goals and roles in early intervention and education.

sections offer a brief rationale for each of the three broad professional goals.

Professional Goals

This section presents a brief rationale for each of the three broad professional goals. Collaboration with families and other professionals provides the foundation for work in each area.

Designing, Implementing, and Evaluating Early Intervention   There is widespread acceptance of the value of early childhood intervention for children in groups at high risk, including those who are economically disadvantaged and those who have developmental disabilities or delays. Efforts to provide direct services to young children are based on the belief that the early years are a critical period in which interventions have the best chance of achieving long-term benefits for children and families.

Many challenges confront the effective design, implementation, and evaluation of early intervention services. First, our work involves a multidisciplinary and ecological approach that takes into account the development of the "whole child" and the family's influential role in the child's development. Working with the child and family requires forming partnerships with service providers from many disciplines and theoretical orientations, including medicine, education, speech-language pathology, physical therapy, occupational therapy, nursing, public health, social services, psychology, and child care. Early interventionists must become comfortable with such professional pluralism and develop competence in providing a range of services in a variety of environments. In addition to the challenges and benefits of shared decision making are those associated with providing both direct services to the child and family and indirect services through consultation with other care providers. Moreover, early interventionists are faced with the need to provide services that are sensitive to the needs of families from many cultures. Finally, new technologies not only advance the early identification and survival of children with disabilities but also provide a range of rapidly changing innovations to assist them in daily life. Now, more than ever, early interventionists need a flexible menu of professional development opportunities designed to address the multiple demands of service delivery.

Promoting High-Quality Inclusion   Providing services in inclusive community-based environments is considered by many to be a linchpin of improving outcomes for children and families. As families and professionals work together to serve children with special needs in child care programs, evidence about the lack of quality in early childhood programs and the barrier that this presents to inclusion is mounting (Buysse et al., 1999; Buysse et al., 1998; Cost, Quality, and Child Outcomes Study Team, 1995). Consultation has been used as a strategy to provide teachers with new knowledge, skills, and support to facilitate inclusion (Buysse & Wesley, 1993; File & Kontos, 1992; Hanson & Widerstrom, 1993; West, Idol, & Cannon, 1988). Consultation has also been demonstrated to be effective in enhancing global program quality in early childhood environments as a critical first step to promoting successful inclusion (Palsha & Wesley, 1998; Wesley, 1994). As more and more interventionists deliver services in community child care environments, an expansion in their collaboration with other professionals to address not only the needs of individual children but also issues related to the overall program quality is anticipated.

A new and progressive direction for early intervention and education professionals is to work at the systems level to define and implement high-quality inclusion, including extending opportunities for inclusion and intervention beyond the school day. Although on a case-by-case level advocacy such as this is familiar ground for professionals in the field, growth in the scope and number of roles related to moving systems of services toward inclusion for the benefit of all is predicted. Such roles may include working with recreation directors or public librarians to expand and improve community activities for young children with special needs.

Promoting Professional Development and the Advancement of the Field   Professional development is paramount to our work; to be effective, it must be ongoing and include multiple approaches. Efforts by early intervention and education professional organizations to develop joint personnel standards and competencies reflect a new era in which professionals must be open to new ways of learning that depend on collaboration and partnerships. At the same time, innovations in training formats and models such as distance learning and self-instructional software increase the potential to individualize the learning experience and require professionals to assume greater responsibility for the direction of their own development. Although well established in the fields of social work and mental health, the responsibility to seek individual supervision and mentorship for the purpose of supporting inquiry and reflective practice is underemphasized in early intervention and education. Because early intervention work concentrates so much on meeting the needs of others, it may seem uncomfortable at first for professionals to take the time and give themselves permission to focus on their own progress and skills, yet the intellectual process of planning, enacting, and reflecting on one's work is essential to improving practice (Schön, 1987) and is a first step to developing the disposition, tools, and commitment needed for lifelong learning.

Reflection and self-evaluation can be effective keys to professional development when they occur in the context of collaborative inquiry (Fenichel, 1991; Palincsar, 1998; Schön, 1987). For example, a community of practice that investigates child guidance techniques to address challenging behaviors not only serves to advance individual knowledge and skills but also contributes to the collective "know-how" of the group (see, e.g., Englert & Tarrant, 1995; Palincsar et al., 1998; Schifter, 1996). Rapid changes in early intervention and education practices and contexts pose concerns that the gap will widen between what universities teach and what practitioners need to know. By viewing the development of individual and collective knowledge and skills as a professional goal, practitioners have the potential to contribute to the relevance of academic research and instruction.

Key Professional Roles and Activities

Key roles performed by professionals in the early intervention and education field include family–professional partner, intervention provider, systems innovator, and skills and knowledge builder. The collaborative and dynamic nature of this work demands that professionals be willing and able to fill several roles at one time and be open to changes in roles as they develop and evolve. The following section examines each role and related activities as they apply to work across the major goal areas.

Family–Professional Partner   A positive and respectful relationship with the family and child is the cornerstone for work in early intervention. As family partners, professionals must be skilled in human relations and able to communicate confidently, effectively, and confidentially with families from different backgrounds who have different expectations. The focus on family concerns, priorities, and resources and the emphasis on natural environments as a context for services have required early interventionists to become knowledgeable about and link families to an array of local and state resources. For example, a family whose toddler has fragile X syndrome could benefit from learning about a new initiative at a nearby university devoted to the early identification and treatment of this genetic disorder. A family with a young child who has autism might be encouraged to investigate a new model demonstration program providing inclusive services that targets children with autism. Indeed, collaboration among a number of disciplines and professions is essential to providing comprehensive, coordinated services to children and families.

The roles of confidante, resource linker, and collaborator epitomize the supportive rather than competitive approach that best serves the family–professional partner. Interdependence among professionals and families has replaced the professional's exclusive control of decision making and requires new knowledge, skills, and attitudes related to building trust and relationships, resolving problems and conflicts, and strategic planning.

Intervention Provider   Although the basic responsibility to conduct assessments and design, implement, and evaluate intervention for individual children and families is not new, the way professionals perform these activities has changed drastically since the 1990s. The complexity of the task is enormous: We strive to provide appropriate, coordinated, and nonduplicative transdisciplinary therapeutic and educational services that are integrated within the child's and family's typical routines and activities and that make use of their natural supports. To accomplish this goal, the professional may participate in numerous committees and teams and be faced with the increasingly complicated task of managing time and fiscal resources to allow for travel and planning. Although the professional's ability to function as a collaborative generalist is often demanded by the role of team member and contributor, the role of expert is also needed as new content is required to serve very young children with an ever-increasing range of disabilities.

At a time when professionals are adjusting to the roles of team member and resource manager, new attention to outcomes and accountability in early intervention at the state and federal levels has sparked programs to reexamine the way early interventionists classify and document activities. Complex and changing billing systems require thorough and sometimes creative record keeping by professionals and families to describe activities within definitions of billable services. The perspectives of practitioners as well as their paperwork are important contributions to program evaluation efforts.

Effective practices in the field have always profited from the application of relevant research findings, and to that end early intervention and education professionals have played an important translation role. Increased focus on the community as the context for research and new interest in qualitative methods offer enriched opportunities for professionals to expand their activities related to research. For example, researchers may invite early educators to assist in identifying potential study participants and to collect data or participate in focus groups or surveys themselves. Partnerships between institutions of higher education and community programs also may create opportunities for practitioners and

families to participate in setting the research agenda and implementing the study.

Systems Innovator   National news has provided numerous potent catalysts for expanding professional roles to work at a systems level to influence the development of services and policy. Foremost among them is the increasing need for child care in the United States and, related to that, research confirming the importance of the early years in brain development. The lack of quality in early childhood programs and the link among quality and child development (Cost, Quality, and Child Outcomes Study Team, 1995), the reauthorization and strengthening of legislation that supports inclusion, and the need to define and increase access to high-quality inclusive programs, especially for children with severe and multiple disabilities, have created new energy and focus in early education and intervention. In the role of systems innovator, professionals recognize the responsibility to be a catalyst for change as the natural next step of viewing the child and family in the context of the sociopolitical factors that affect them. That is, if we accept in early intervention an ecological perspective that recognizes the transactional relationships between individuals and their environments (Bronfenbrenner, 1979), then we must extend our view of our jobs to include active participation in the promotion and preservation of services and policies that benefit the children and families we serve.

Effecting Services   Many early intervention and education professionals already view their work with individual children and families in the broader context of social change. For example, one reason to observe and note specific positive impacts of inclusion on individual children and families is to be able to share success stories with others who may be considering inclusion for the first time. In this way, professionals play an important role as marketers of inclusion (Buysse & Wesley, 1993). The philosophy of early childhood inclusion not only has changed the way professionals design and deliver educational services to children but also has extended their interest in strategies that promote full community inclusion for the family. Professionals today must be willing to investigate and expand resources for inclusion in all aspects of community life. Ideally, the ability to do this effectively is a natural extension of their interactions and experiences with other adults as active community members. Some practitioners find that over the years they have become experts on the local "inclusion landscape" by developing an awareness of barriers and supports to inclusive opportunities. Although this sort of system-level savvy is especially valuable as professionals collaborate with individual families to achieve inclusion, it may also lead to a broader interest and more active roles in identifying gaps in community services and developing plans to fill them.

One of the most innovative and important new challenges in the field is to expand our focus to include not only the development of the child and family but also the development of the community. For example, some local interagency groups are forming or expanding their memberships and activities to address systems planning issues in an effort to increase efficiency of and access to early childhood services (Smart Start Evaluation Team, 1998). Because advocates for children with disabilities participated in these planning efforts, the definition of improved access to early childhood services has expanded to include activities such as the hiring of additional personnel to provide integrated classroom therapies and facility enhancements to improve physical accessibility. The perspectives and participation of early intervention and education professionals in facilitating broad-based

public participation in systemwide planning are important for at least two reasons. First, they may be aware of parents and other key players in the community who are interested in developing or improving comprehensive services for children and families. Early intervention and education professionals already create important links between the general early childhood and early childhood special education fields. They are in a position to promote awareness and coalition among people who typically are not a part of service coordination, such as recreation organizers, community librarians, and summer camp directors. Second, the experiences and skills of early intervention and education professionals in collaborating with adults who represent different interests, disciplines, and professional affiliations provide a valuable foundation on which to build their own leadership skills.

Effecting Policy   The roles of legislative watchdog, policy analyst, public speaker, and advocate are not new in our profession. We are faced with opportunities to fill these roles with broader purpose, however, as a result of inclusion and the new recognition of the importance of quality programming. General early childhood issues such as child care standards, policy, and professional compensation now directly affect children with special needs and their families. Professionals and families must contribute to and advocate for the development of strong early childhood program standards and adequate funding. Their perspectives and participation continue to be critical in promoting flexibility in the way early intervention program eligibility and funding criteria are defined and in standards review processes to remove impediments to the implementation of early childhood inclusion. The perspectives of families and professionals can inform policy on the basis of their daily implementation and actual experiences with policy.

As early childhood and early intervention issues converge, early intervention and education providers have new opportunities to join professional organizations that represent both fields and to participate in state and national activities that are related to unifying personnel development systems, including certification and licensure. Through attending and speaking at conferences, serving on state and national task forces, actively contributing to the development of professional standards, and participating in collaborative inquiry and research, practitioners can expand their professional identity and enjoy an impact beyond the children and families they serve directly.

Skills and Knowledge Builder

To an extent, early intervention and education professionals have been managing their own professional development for some time. As delivering services to children and families has become increasingly a collaborative process, professionals have had to acquire skills on the job, including consultation, teaming, and technical assistance, to help them work effectively with a variety of adults (Buysse & Wesley, 1993; Buysse & Wesley, in press; File & Kontos, 1992). In the role of skills and knowledge builder, practitioners engage in activities at multiple levels to improve outcomes for children and families. These include the following:

- Self-evaluation and reflection for the purpose of assessing and acting on the need for new knowledge, skills, and attitudes to enhance one's own job performance and enjoyment

- Participation as an educator or mentor to promote professional development opportunities for others

- Collaborative inquiry for the purpose of contributing to the continued expansion and relevance of a common core of knowledge to drive practice in the field

Essential to the practitioner's continued ability to do effective work in a rapidly changing field is the perspective that staff development is more than the acquisition of isolated knowledge and skill sets. Rather than view professional competence as something that one possesses or masters, a more holistic perspective views professional development as a career-long process that evolves through the interplay of maturation and experience, self-reflection, and collaborative problem solving. The role of skills and knowledge builder begins with the responsibility for directing one's own inquiry and progress and the habit of measuring one's own performance against the standard for the profession. In contrast to the learner who waits for the right training opportunity to come along, the skills and knowledge builder charts a plan of action to ensure participation in the most appropriate learning opportunities. Through regular reflection on practices, relationships, and career goals, practitioners engage in a productive and empowering approach to professional growth (Duff et al., 1995). Creating an atmosphere that fosters such an approach may require major changes in how supervision and personnel preparation are conducted.

Increased recognition of mutual support among colleagues as a format for professional development invites practitioners to consider their role as providers as well as beneficiaries of staff development opportunities. As professionals develop interagency relationships that are necessary to implement effective early childhood inclusion, they may find both formal and informal opportunities to offer training, supervision, coaching, and consultation to others and, thus, begin to see their individual work as contributing to the professional community as a whole. For example, an early interventionist who is collaborating with a child care provider in one classroom to serve a child with special needs also may be asked to provide technical assistance related to preparing other classrooms to enroll additional children with disabilities. A physical therapist who integrates therapy into classroom experiences for children may be asked to participate as a practicum supervisor for a graduate student who is seeking community experiences. The development of community-based training innovations (Wesley & Buysse, 1997) and the emerging flexibility between higher education and the community (McCollum & Catlett, 1997) provide numerous opportunities for professionals to serve as educators and promote training needs assessments and staff development opportunities that cut across agencies, disciplines, and institutions.

Extensive dialogue among professionals in both general and special early childhood education has begun to lay the foundation for improvement in the quality of staff preparation by focusing on the framework and content for a comprehensive professional development system (Bredekamp & Willer, 1993). To accomplish this goal requires us to accept our responsibility to develop not only the professional but the profession, to create a collective knowledge base and a common understanding about what constitutes recommended practices. As knowledge builders, we view professionalism broadly to encompass activities related to just such collaboration and reform as a part of our jobs. This new role of early intervention and education professionals challenges traditional practices that support the belief that knowledge making occurs only in academia and is a call for a reexamination of the epistemology of professional practice in our field. By incorporating a community-of-practice approach, knowledge generation becomes a collaborative enterprise that involves practitioners, families, higher education faculty, and students.

STRATEGIES FOR CREATING COMMUNITIES OF LEARNING WITHIN EXISTING PROFESSIONAL DEVELOPMENT EFFORTS

Before a community of practice is implemented to transform professional development, it is helpful to examine traditional approaches to personnel preparation and training. In general, a comprehensive system of professional development in early education and intervention has encompassed an array of learning opportunities (e.g., structures, events, activities) that are designed to equip professionals with the knowledge and skills that they need to work effectively with young children and families. The professional development curriculum (i.e., training content and process) historically has been divided into preservice and in-service training, with the assumption being that recipients of preservice training generally are novice practitioners, whereas recipients of in-service training are experienced professionals. Within institutions of higher learning, professional development opportunities at the preservice level generally have concentrated on a combination of coursework (to teach new knowledge) and field experiences (to apply new knowledge to the problems of everyday practice); continuing education for experienced practitioners in the field has been more disjointed, typically providing limited exposure to a wide range of topics through workshops, staff development activities, and professional conferences.

In early education and intervention, this distinction between preservice and in-service training is beginning to blur, largely because of broad changes in recommended practices and the increase in complexity of professionals' roles as a result of inclusion (McCollum & Catlett, 1997). According to McCollum and Catlett (1997), it is appropriate to examine critically training content and processes during periods in which new practices are emerging in order to determine the compatibility of existing training approaches with the new professional roles. The need to incorporate new training approaches is particularly important when professionals are required to learn the art of handling situations of uncertainty and change (e.g., problem solving, collaboration, values clarification, negotiation) in addition to new technical skills (e.g., portfolio development, positioning techniques to facilitate social interaction and play). An added challenge is that new roles and skills that reflect the art of effective practice are often difficult to organize by content areas within specific courses but must be embedded throughout the curriculum (McCollum & Catlett, 1997).

By incorporating a community-of-practice perspective into existing training programs, designers of professional development programs can create an overall climate of intellectual inquiry to develop professional identity during periods of transition and change. In many ways, we have already begun to apply some of the community-of-practice principles to professional development efforts to support inclusion, even though the field lacks a grounded theory and common vocabulary to understand and describe these efforts. For example, we demonstrate the value of diverse expertise in our move toward interdisciplinary preservice education, as illustrated by the collaboration across university departments to offer courses that bring together students from education, allied health, and related disciplines. Another way we demonstrate this is by providing university and college students with an array of field experiences, including meaningful opportunities to interact with families from a variety of backgrounds and cultures. In addition, many college and university courses in early intervention now

routinely offer diverse perspectives through presentations and guest lectures from family members, service providers, administrators, and policy makers. Recognition of the value of ongoing reflection and inquiry now is reflected in professional competencies that are promoted by national professional organizations in both early education and intervention. As a field, we have acknowledged the need to close the gap between institutions of higher learning and community-based practice as illustrated by efforts to integrate in-service and pre-service training, perhaps best demonstrated by the professional development school model (The Holmes Group, 1986, 1990). However, these reforms exist as isolated examples. They are present in some universities and states but not others. Because these efforts are not part of a systematic, integrated philosophy of how best to prepare professionals, they do not reflect a true community-of-practice approach. More important, the field has not acknowledged fully the value of involving families and practitioners as co-constructors of knowledge. We have opened the door to include the experiences and perspectives of families and practitioners, but we have not yet determined an effective way to use these perspectives to build the knowledge base and improve practice.

An ideal professional development system in early education and intervention would encompass not only professional competencies and a philosophical base as these currently exist but also mechanisms for shared inquiry and learning to identify new and emerging professional competencies in response to change. It would expand Fenichel and Eggbeer's (1991) notion of the need to create a common foundation for practice across all disciplines by providing a blueprint for how to achieve this monumental task. It would extend Bailey's (1996) recommendation to foster interdisciplinary education by including diverse members of the early education and intervention community outside of academia. Finally, an ideal professional development system would transcend the goal of reflection for one's *own* professional growth to include the shared responsibility and authority of the broader community to build the knowledge base and improve practice for the field as a whole.

Strategies and Scenarios

How should designers of professional development programs begin to build communities of practice to support inclusion? Drawing on lessons outlined by Englert and Tarrant (1995) in forming communities of learning to promote early literacy and the chapter authors' own attempts to incorporate this approach into existing professional development activities, several suggestions for how to get started are offered. These suggestions are followed by some scenarios that illustrate more fully the application of these ideas to personnel development efforts in early education and intervention.

Identify areas that could benefit from communities of practice. The first step is to identify areas in which communities of practice would assist in accomplishing specific goals. Obviously, some activities lend themselves to this approach more so than others. For example, it may be reasonable to use a community-of-practice approach to develop an inclusive early childhood curriculum, but it may not be practical to use this framework to identify community resources to support inclusion or provide follow-up training strategies to individual practitioners to reinforce new classroom practices. A related issue is determining how much participation in various communities of practice can be effective at any one time. In one university, a community of practice that involved students, faculty, and practitioners was established to redesign the master's program in early intervention to create more meaningful field experiences and to make the requirements more consistent with other graduate degree programs within the School of Education. This effort, though productive, entailed many meetings and detailed records over many months. It is unrealistic to expect effective participation and institutional support for multiple communities of practice that involve many of the same players from within the same organization.

Build relationships and negotiate new roles to achieve diverse expertise. Achieving diverse expertise requires building new relationships with families, practitioners, and other nontraditional stakeholders in professional development efforts. Before a community-of-practice approach is implemented, it is necessary to rethink the learning hierarchy and to negotiate new roles for families, practitioners, and students, generally considered the recipients of knowledge. Obviously, this will require a fundamental change in how the field conceptualizes institutions of higher learning and the roles of faculty and researchers from knowledge generators and translators to knowledge co-contributors and organizers. Fortunately, movements that are under way to change the way in which we view and involve participants in research studies (i.e., participatory action research) and recent efforts to connect research findings to practices in working with children and families (i.e., professional development schools) make the timing for adopting this orientation particularly good. Underpinning the effectiveness of identifying new roles for nontraditional stakeholders is the value of achieving diverse expertise in professional development efforts. Everyone who is involved in professional development must understand that each member brings a unique perspective and set of questions and concerns that invite new questions, further inquiry, an articulation of beliefs, and, ultimately, a shared orientation about the best way to serve children and families (Englert & Tarrant, 1995). Unless families, teachers, and other practitioners make decisions about issues that matter to them, well-intended efforts to identify and teach recommended practices cannot succeed.

Establish a discourse among community members. Once a community has been assembled, the next step is to begin a dialogue about issues that are relevant to community members. Englert and Tarrant (1995) identified some of the issues and benefits of establishing such a dialogue. First, it is important to note that establishing trust and a discourse about professional roles and practices must be allowed to evolve gradually over time. Members of a learning community should be encouraged to take risks, offer innovative ideas, and work out their differences of opinion within a safe forum. Second, the examples of instructional strategies and children's experiences offered by service providers and families that emerge from daily practice enrich the discussion and help students make connections between their coursework and field experiences. University faculty members contribute to the discourse by identifying ideas from the broader professional community and the research knowledge base. The ultimate goal is that the discourse within a community of practice will lead to deep and lasting changes that improve services for young children and families rather than to an introduction of new ideas that produce only superficial and short-lived innovations. Finally, a productive discourse that results in lasting program improvements may lead to new roles for practitioners and families, who may be invited to help other communities of practice identify more effective practices.

Develop mechanisms for making decisions and sharing new ideas. The notion that new ideas that emanate from communities of practice should be documented and disseminated is perhaps the least developed

aspect of this approach. Englert and Tarrant (1995) created among classroom teachers and university faculty a community of practice that constructed new literacy meanings that eventually were incorporated into a curriculum. But what is the best way for communities of practice in early education and intervention to disseminate their findings and build support for this process? Unfortunately, the research literature offers few suggestions. It will take additional research funding and experience before the field can provide answers. In the meantime, we suggest that newly established communities of practice begin by considering dissemination strategies that are both practical and relevant. Designers of professional development programs could begin by modifying their existing curricula to incorporate new activities or field experiences that are based on ideas that emerge from working with parents, practitioners, and students to promote quality inclusive practices. These approaches for enhancing professional development should be disseminated to the broader professional community in the form of grant proposals and publications in peer-reviewed journals. Practitioners, students, families, and university faculty should consider co-authoring articles about their experiences in constructing a community of practice in magazines and newsletters that target families and practitioners. New ideas that emerge from communities of practice could be reflected in co-authored monographs, cracker-barrel sessions at professional conferences, and web sites. Ultimately, there is a need to create mechanisms whereby individual communities that exist as models of professional development might contribute new knowledge to the broader professional community.

The following scenarios provide examples of how communities of practice can enhance professional development and improve inclusive practices.

Scenario 1 An early childhood faculty member who had been involved in preservice education for 10 years took a 12-month sabbatical to work as a teacher in a center-based early intervention program. During her sabbatical, she engaged program staff (the director, teachers, teaching assistants, and speech-language and physical therapists) in an ongoing dialogue for the purpose of developing specific activity or routine-based instructional strategies to support inclusion. The faculty member had previously taught her graduate students the principles of activity-based intervention as a method for incorporating children's individualized education program and individualized family service plan goals and outcomes into children's daily routines and natural environments, but she felt disconnected from actually implementing these practices. The early intervention staff had been introduced to these strategies at a statewide conference that they attended, but not all of them had used these strategies with individual children in natural environments. In time, several family members and graduate students joined the group and were invited to share their perspectives about implementing activity- and routine-based interventions. The faculty member and the more experienced staff shared their knowledge and offered practical advice to less experienced staff and students. At the end of the faculty member's sabbatical, the group submitted a proposal to present at a statewide early education and intervention conference on their ideas about activity-based intervention.

Scenario 2 At one university, a summer practicum involves graduate students from different departments—early childhood intervention, speech-language pathology, and school psychology. The students are assigned to work in interdisciplinary student teams, and each team is placed in an inclusive community-based environment. Each student team works jointly with a team of early intervention professionals who are affiliated with the community program. Together with the university faculty who supervise the students' practicum experience, the students and early intervention team meet on a regular basis to discuss current team practices and strategies for change to support inclusion for individual children and families. Embedded in these discussions is content related to promoting social interaction and play, with particular emphasis on organizing the physical and social environment. The students are required to record their reflections and experiences in daily journal entries. The university faculty analyze these written reflections to consider how they might change or improve future summer practica.

Scenario 3 The lead agency for Infant Toddler Programs of IDEA (Part C) developed a statewide mentorship network for early intervention professionals from different backgrounds and disciplines. The network consists of experienced practitioners who have completed a college course on supervision and mentorship and now serve as mentors to novice early intervention professionals. The mentors offer regular support and feedback to their mentees as well as provide a forum for critical observation and reflection about their work with young children and families. With assistance from university faculty and support from the Part C lead agency, the mentors and mentees have decided to conduct several focus groups across the region to learn more about how mentorship is being used to support inclusion and to identify effective strategies to promote this practice. Focus group findings will be published in several early intervention newsletters and a magazine that target child care teachers and directors.

Scenario 4 An early intervention practitioner is seeking culturally appropriate methods for assessing young

Latino children who are new, permanent residents of her community. She identified in the community other colleagues who share the same need and interest, such as family members, specialists from a local developmental evaluation center, a public health agency director, two early intervention graduate students, a researcher, and a community college instructor who is Latino. They meet together monthly, engaging in a process of inquiry and problem solving to identify culturally sensitive assessment strategies. The practitioners share challenges and dilemmas from their experiences in working with Latino families. The graduate students, researcher, and community college instructor offer new ideas from their coursework and research regarding the use of portfolio assessment and strategies to involve families in the assessment process. The group agrees to develop a resource guide that lists assessment instruments, strategies, and other Spanish-language materials that are appropriate for working with Latino families in early intervention.

Scenario 5 A university professor who researches the role and process of consultation to support early childhood inclusion wants to identify effective skills and processes in providing supervision to consultants. He recognizes that the preservice preparation of early interventionists as consultants is limited and knows from his experience in supervising consultative practica the challenges in providing adequate and meaningful supervision. He forms a working group of interdisciplinary faculty, two current students who have completed the consultation course and practicum, a preschool teacher, and several families whose children receive consultative services to assist him in planning a summer institute focused on consultation. This institute will be conducted in a community-based program and will engage diverse participants from the university and community.

The purpose of the institute is to revise and refine the university consultation course and practicum sequence and to develop a course sequence to meet practitioners' as well as preservice students' needs.

AGENDA FOR CHANGE: CHALLENGES AND NEW DIRECTIONS FOR THE FIELD

A professional development system within a community-of-practice framework is multifaceted and designed to *inform* as well as *reform* practices to improve the quality of services for young children and families. The overarching goal of a community-of-practice approach is to create an environment for collaborative inquiry to transform professional development from *individual* to *multiple* perspectives, from *isolated* to *shared* practice, from *behavioral goals and objectives* to *deep knowledge and learning*, and from *routinized practice* to *reflective discourse* (Digisi, Morocco, & Shure, 1998). Achieving these reforms in professional development efforts to support inclusion will not be easy. We envision a number of challenges and new directions for the field if a community-of-practice orientation is adopted.

First and foremost, the challenge lies in transforming existing professional development approaches from emphasizing the transmission of knowledge to promoting the construction of knowledge. Fostering communities of practice within college classrooms and community-based environments requires a shift in power and philosophy and the creation of a common language to communicate new ideas so that students, families, and practitioners, along with faculty from institutions of higher learning, become co-producers of knowledge. As the field moves in this direction, a number of questions must be addressed. Some of these questions have been articulated by

Englert and Tarrant (1995); others derive from the chapter authors' own experiences and inquiry in this area.

How will professional development activities within communities of practice be recreated and sustained over time? As new members join the community, it will become necessary to orient them to the process and re-create it by inviting them to participate with more experienced members. To sustain communities of practice over time, it is necessary to identify the capacity of the organization to support this kind of work. This involves gaining administrative support, accessible places for meetings, release time for program staff and families, clerical support, and other resources.

What is the optimal size of a community of practice to support inclusion and promote professional development? Although it may seem desirable to restrict the number of members to promote mutual trust and active participation, there is also a need for larger communities of practice, for example, to launch a new statewide early childhood initiative.

What are the most effective strategies for promoting tolerance for ambiguity and divergent perspectives? It is likely that many potential members of a community of practice in early education and intervention may lack the skills to deal with uncertainty and conflict, particularly in the face of sweeping change. As a result, designers of professional development programs should identify competencies that are related to group formation and dynamics, methods for establishing ground rules for productive dialogues, and strategies for managing conflict and divergent views.

A second challenge for professional development programs is the need to shift the emphasis from teaching technical skills that apply a set of rules to a well-defined problem with the assumption that there is one right answer to the art of practice, which involves helping practi-

tioners acquire the skills that they need to be competent in "indeterminate zones" of practice (Schön, 1987). Schön noted that professional practice consists of technical skills in part but also requires one to be research-like and inquiry driven. Professional practice is also deeply personal because it involves incorporating a set of professional values into one's own value and belief system. In the field's efforts to prepare practitioners to work with young children and families in least restrictive and natural environments, we have recognized the need to prepare professionals to deal with uncertain or unique situations, yet we are uncertain about the best way to do this. Schön (1987) identified two approaches for promoting the artistry of professional practice that seem particularly promising for early education and intervention. The first is mentorship, commonly described as a relationship for learning that provides regular opportunities for less experienced and more experienced professionals to reflect together about their work (Fenichel, 1991). This is a familiar but underused approach for promoting professional growth in our field. The second approach, parallel practice, is a less widely known technique in which a mentor helps a mentee gain insight into his or her emotional responses to working with individual children and families. Both approaches represent positive new directions for helping professionals acquire the artistry of practice to support inclusion.

A final challenge for future professional development programs is to develop mechanisms for communicating new ideas that emerge from individual communities of practice to the field at large. Englert and Tarrant (1995) reported that six categories of topics characterized their community-of-practice discussions: 1) principles of the particular project being undertaken, 2) description of current teaching practices, 3) problem solving about particular concerns, 4) the effects of new practices on children and families, 5) comparisons among teacher practices, and 6) case examples to illustrate the effects of new practices on specific children. Perhaps newly established communities of practice in early education and intervention could use these six categories as a starting point for developing strategies for making decisions and sharing new ideas. The chapter authors encourage the field to think about other ways of sharing new knowledge. Conference planners should consider offering a community-of-practice track devoted to describing community-of-practice experiences and findings at professional conferences. Perhaps the field could establish a "practice to theory" journal to offer an alternative to publications that emphasize a "theory to practice" orientation. Ultimately, the field's success in sharing new discoveries with the broader community hinges on our ability to find a common language to communicate effectively with a diverse group of stakeholders. It is no longer acceptable for researchers to write exclusively for other researchers. Co-learning and co-discovery demand co-production of knowledge as the most effective tool for disseminating new ideas.

CONCLUSION

Although creating communities of practice to support inclusion seems to be a daunting task, there is evidence to suggest that the field is already moving in this direction. Many programs of professional development in early education and intervention are being redesigned to transcend disciplinary boundaries and more fully involve families, practitioners, and nontraditional stakeholders from within and outside academia. Communities of practice can make an important contribution by providing a process for shared inquiry and learning to build the knowl-edge base and improve services for children and families.

REFERENCES

Bailey, D.B. (1989). Issues and directions in preparing professionals to work with young handicapped children and their families. In J.J. Gallagher, P.L. Trohanis, & R.M. Clifford (Eds.), *Policy implementation and PL 99-457: Planning for young children with special needs* (pp. 97–132). Baltimore: Paul H. Brookes Publishing Co.

Bailey, D.B. (1996). Preparing early intervention professionals for the twenty-first century. In M. Brambring, H. Rauh, & A. Beelman (Eds.), *Early childhood intervention: Theory, evaluation, and practice* (pp. 488–503). Hawthorne, NY: Walter de Gruyter.

Bailey, D.B., Aytch, L.S., Odom, S.L., Symons, F., & Wolery, M. (1999). Early intervention as we know it. *Mental Retardation and Developmental Disabilities, 5,* 11–20.

Bailey, D.B., Buysse, V., Edmondson, R., & Smith, T. (1992). Creating family-centered services in early intervention: Perceptions of professionals in four states. *Exceptional Children, 58,* 298–309.

Bailey, D.B., McWilliam, R.A., Buysse, V., & Wesley, P.W. (1998). Inclusion in the context of competing values in early childhood education. *Early Childhood Research Quarterly, 13,* 27–47.

Bredekamp, S., & Willer, B. (1993). Professionalizing the field of early childhood education: Pros and cons. *Young Children, 48,* 82–84.

Bricker, D.D. (1989). *Early intervention for at-risk and handicapped infants, toddlers, and preschool children.* Glenview, IL: Foresman.

Bricker, D. (1998). *An activity-based approach to early intervention* (2nd ed.). Baltimore: Paul H. Brookes Publishing Co.

Bronfenbrenner, U. (1979). *The ecology of human development: Experiments by nature and design.* Cambridge, MA: Harvard University Press.

Buysse, V., & Wesley, P.W. (1993). The identity crisis in early childhood special education: A call for professional role clarification. *Topics in Early Childhood Special Education, 13,* 418–429.

Buysse, V., & Wesley, P.W. (2000). Models of collaboration for early intervention: Laying the foundation. In P. Blasco (Ed.), *Early intervention services for infants, toddlers, and their families.* Needham Heights, MA: Allyn & Bacon.

Buysse, V., Wesley, P.W., Bryant, D., & Gardner, D. (1999). Quality of early childhood programs in inclusive and noninclusive settings. *Exceptional Children, 65,* 301–314.

Buysse, V., Wesley, P.W., & Keyes, L. (1998). Implementing early childhood inclusion: Barrier and support factors. *Early Childhood Research Quarterly, 13*, 169–184.

Cost, Quality, and Child Outcomes Study Team. (1995). *Cost, quality, and child outcomes in child care centers: Public report.* Denver: University of Colorado–Denver.

Digisi, L., Morocco, C., & Shure, A. (1998). *A framework of stages to understand the development of teams into a schoolwide community of practice.* Washington, DC: Education Development Center.

Duff, R.E., Brown, M.H., & Van Scoy, I.J. (1995, May). Reflection and self-evaluation: Keys to professional development. *Young Children,* 81–88.

Englert, C.S., & Tarrant, K.L. (1995). Creating collaborative cultures for educational change. *Remedial and Special Education, 16,* 325–336.

Fenichel, E.S. (1991). Learning through supervision and mentorship to support the development of infants, toddlers, and their families. *Zero to Three Bulletin, 12,* 1–8.

Fenichel, E.S., & Eggbeer, L. (1991). Preparing practitioners to work with infants, toddlers, and their families: Four essential elements of training. *Infants and Young Children, 4,* 56–62.

File, N., & Kontos, S. (1992). Indirect service delivery through consultation: Review and implications for early intervention. *Journal of Early Intervention, 16,* 221–234.

Fullan, M. (1998). Leadership for the 21st century: Breaking the bonds of dependency. *Educational Leadership, 55*(7), 6–10.

Gallacher, K.K. (1997). Supervision, mentoring, and coaching: Methods for supporting personnel development. In P.J. Winton, J.A. McCollum, & C. Catlett (Eds.), *Reforming personnel preparation in early intervention: Issues, models, and practical strategies* (pp. 191–214). Baltimore: Paul H. Brookes Publishing Co.

Guralnick, M.J. (1993). Foreword. In C.A. Peck, S.L. Odom, & D.D. Bricker (Eds.), *Integrating young children with disabilities into community programs: Ecological perspectives on research and implementation* (pp. ix–x). Baltimore: Paul H. Brookes Publishing Co.

Hanson, M.J., & Widerstrom, A.H. (1993). Consultation and collaboration: Essentials of integration efforts for young children. In C.A. Peck, S.L. Odom, & D.D. Bricker (Eds.), *Integrating young children with disabilities into community programs: Ecological perspectives on research and implementation* (pp. 149–168). Baltimore: Paul H. Brookes Publishing Co.

Hart, B., & Rogers-Warren, A. (1978). A milieu approach to teaching language. In R. Schiefelbusch (Ed.), *Language intervention strategies* (pp. 193–235). Baltimore: University Park Press.

The Holmes Group. (1986). *Tomorrow's schools.* East Lansing, MI: Author. (ERIC Document Reproduction Service No. ED 270 454).

The Holmes Group. (1990). *Tomorrow's schools.* East Lansing, MI: Author. (ERIC Document Reproduction Service No. ED 328 533).

Kemple, K.M., Hartle, L.C., Correa, V.I., & Fox, L. (1994). Preparing teachers for inclusive education: The development of a unified teacher program in early childhood and early childhood special education. *Teacher Education and Special Education, 17,* 38–51.

Marshall, S.P., & Hatcher, C. (1996, March). Promoting career development through CADRE. *Educational Leadership,* 42–46.

McCollum, J.A., & Catlett, C. (1997). Designing effective personnel preparation for early intervention: Theoretical frameworks. In P.J. Winton, J.A. McCollum, & C. Catlett (Eds.), *Reforming personnel preparation in early intervention: Issues, models, and practical strategies* (pp. 105–125). Baltimore: Paul H. Brookes Publishing Co.

McWilliam, R.A. (Ed.) (1996). *Rethinking pull-out services in early intervention: A professional resource.* Baltimore: Paul H. Brookes Publishing Co.

Murphy, J. (1991). *Restructuring schools: Capturing and assessing the phenomena.* New York: Teachers College Press.

Palincsar, A.S. (1998). Social constructivist perspectives on teaching and learning. *Annual Review of Psychology, 49,* 345–375.

Palincsar, A.S., Magnusson, S.J., Marano, N., Ford, D., & Brown, N. (1998). Designing a community of practice: Principles and practices of the GIsML community. *Teaching and Teacher Education, 14,* 5–19.

Palsha, S.A., & Wesley, P.W. (1998). Improving quality in early childhood environments through on-site consultation. *Topics in Early Childhood Special Education, 18,* 243–253.

Rogoff, B. (1994). Developing understanding of the idea of communities of learners. *Minds, Culture and Activity, 1,* 209–229.

Schifter, D. (1996). *Reconstruction of professional identities.* New York: Teachers College Press.

Schön, D.A. (1987). *Educating the reflective practitioner: Toward a new design for teaching and learning in the professions.* San Francisco: Jossey-Bass Publishers.

Smart Start Evaluation Team. (1998). *Smart Start and local inter-organizational collaboration.* Chapel Hill: The University of North Carolina Press.

Smith, B.J., & Rose, D.F. (1993). *Administrator's policy handbook for preschool mainstreaming.* Cambridge, MA: Brookline Books.

Snyder, P., & McWilliam, P.J. (1999). Evaluating the efficacy of case method of instruction: Findings from preservice training in family-centered care. *Journal of Early Intervention, 22,* 114–125.

Stamps, D. (1997). Communities of practice: Learning is social. Training is irrelevant? *Training, 34,* 34–42.

Stayton, V.D., & Miller, P.S. (1993). Combining early childhood education and early childhood special education standards in personnel preparation programs: Experiences in two states. *Topics in Early Childhood Special Education, 13,* 372–387.

Warren, S., & Bambara, L. (1989). An experimental analysis of milieu language intervention: Teaching the action-object form. *Journal of Speech and Hearing Disorders, 54,* 448–461.

Wesley, P.W. (1994). Providing on-site consultation to promote quality in integrated child care programs. *Journal of Early Intervention, 18,* 391–402.

Wesley, P.W., & Buysse, V. (1997). Community-based approaches to personnel preparation. In P.J. Winton, J.A. McCollum, & C. Catlett (Eds.), *Reforming personnel preparation in early intervention: Issues, models, and practical strategies* (pp. 53–80). Baltimore: Paul H. Brookes Publishing Co.

West, J.F., Idol, L., & Cannon, G. (1988). *Collaboration in the schools: Communicating, interacting, and problem solving.* Austin, TX: PRO-ED.

Westheimer, J., & Kahne, J. (1993). Building school communities: An experience based model. *Phi Delta Kappan, 75,* 324–328.

Winton, P.J., McCollum, J.A., & Catlett, C. (Eds.). (1997). *Reforming personnel preparation in early intervention: Issues, models, and practical strategies.* Baltimore: Paul H. Brookes Publishing Co.

III

Programs

9

MARY BETH BRUDER

Inclusion of Infants and Toddlers

Outcomes and Ecology

The Education for All Handicapped Children Act of 1975 (PL 94-142) (reauthorized in 1990 as the Individuals with Disabilities Education Act [IDEA; PL 101-476]) mandated preschool services for children with disabilities and provided an opportunity for states to develop statewide systems of services for eligible children from birth to age 3 and their families. Congress delineated five reasons for needing such systems, including the need to maximize children's development and to enhance the capacity of families to meet the special needs of their children (42 U.S.C. § 671[a]). As a result, all states provide for children from birth to 3 a system of services and supports that complies with requirements under Part C of IDEA, most notably to provide quality early intervention services (42 U.S.C. § 671[b][3]).

One requirement of early intervention systems under IDEA first articulated in 1986 was the need for services to be delivered in a child's natural environment: the home or in places in which other children participate—that is, those places that are natural or normal for children who do not have disabilities

(§ 634[16][A]). One reason for this emphasis was to ensure that children with disabilities and their families would be included in everyday home and community activities and that early intervention services would not be delivered in places that would isolate the child with disabilities or his or her family from everyday life (Federal Register, 54[11a], p. 26313).

The inclusion of young children with disabilities into programs with children without disabilities has a history that began during the 1960s through federal discretionary programs such as the Handicapped Children's Early Education Program (PL 90-538) and Head Start (Bricker, 2000). The rationale for this practice has been articulated (cf. Bailey, McWilliam, Buysse, & Wesley, 1998; Bricker, 1978; see also Chapter 1), and research documenting its effectiveness began in the 1970s (Guralnick, 1978). Although schools question the appropriateness of inclusive practices for children ages 5–21, inclusion in natural environments is an accepted practice in the field of early childhood intervention (Guralnick, 1990; Odom & Diamond, 1998) as reflected by the position statement adopted by the Division for Early Childhood (DEC), Council for Exceptional Children (the major professional organization for the field); see Table 9.1 and the position statement adopted by the IDEA Part C Coordinators Association (Council for Exceptional Children, Division for Early Childhood, 2000; IDEA Infant and Toddler Coordinators Association, 2000). Nonetheless, the field of early intervention is still struggling with issues surrounding the delivery of services in inclusionary settings, most notably with the definition and implementation of natural group environments for infants and toddlers with disabilities (Bailey, McWilliam, Buysse, et al., 1998).

On July 1, 1998, additional amendments to IDEA went into effect that reemphasized the need for early intervention to be provided in natural environments such as the home, community, or formalized programs such as child care, Gymboree, and so forth. These amendments require a justification on a child's individualized family service plan (IFSP) for any early intervention service not provided in the natural environment (34 C.F.R. § 303.344[d][iv]). As a result of the need for IFSP justification, early interventionists and early intervention programs are struggling with the development and payment of service delivery models that meet the criteria of natural environments (M. Greer, personal communication, March 31, 2000). These struggles have resulted, in part, from service models that were developed by professionals (across multiple disciplines) who were trained to provide intervention from a discipline-specific focus in places such as clinics or rehabilitation facilities (Kilgo & Bruder, 1997). Furthermore, difficulties are related to the fact that early intervention has traditionally used a deficit model in which assessments and interventions isolate the skills that a child has not yet mastered across the developmental domains of fine and gross motor, receptive and expressive language, cognition, social,

Table 9.1. Division for Early Childhood (DEC) position on inclusion

Inclusion, as a value, supports the right of all children, regardless of abilities, to participate actively in natural settings within their communities. Natural settings are those in which the child would spend time had he or she not had a disability. These settings include, but are not limited to home, preschool, nursery schools, Head Start programs, kindergartens, neighborhood school classrooms, child care, places of worship, recreational (such as community playgrounds and community events) and other settings that all children and families enjoy.

DEC supports and advocates that young children and their families have full and successful access to health, social, educational, and other support services that promote full participation in family and community life. DEC values the cultural, economic, and educational diversity of families and supports a family-guided process for identifying a program of service.

As young children participate in group settings (such as preschool, play groups, child care, kindergarten) their active participation should be guided by developmentally and individually appropriate curriculum. Access to and participation in the age appropriate general curriculum becomes central to the identification and provision of specialized support services.

To implement inclusive practices DEC supports: (a) the continued development, implementation, evaluation, and dissemination of full inclusion supports, services, and systems that are of high quality for all children; (b) the development of preservice and inservice training programs that prepare families, service providers, and administrators to develop and work within inclusive settings; (c) collaboration among all key stakeholders to implement flexible fiscal and administrative procedures in support of inclusion; (d) research that contributes to our knowledge of recommended practice; and (e) the restructuring and unification of social, educational, health, and intervention supports and services to make them more responsive to the needs of all children and families. Ultimately, the implementation of inclusive practice must lead to optimal develomental benefit for each individual child and family.

From the Council for Exceptional Children, Division of Early Childhood. (2000). *Position on inclusion.* Available: http://www.dec-sped.org/positions/inclusio.html.

and self-care (Bruder, 1997b; Hanft & Feinberg, 1997; Hanft & Pilkington, 2000). These developmental needs are incorporated into an IFSP and translated into individual services (e.g., occupational therapy, physical therapy, speech-language therapy) that may or may not be delivered within a child's natural environment (Bruder, Staff, & McMurrer-Kaminer, 1997). Last, cost has proved to be a struggle for state systems of early intervention intent on moving from a service reimbursement model into a more integrated model utilizing community resources (Cavallaro, Haney, & Cabello, 1993; Roberts, Innocenti, & Goetze, 1999).

PURPOSE

The purpose of this chapter is to provide a framework for early intervention for children with disabilities from birth to age 3, as delivered under Part C of IDEA. This framework is predicated on the notion that the enhancement of a child's development by his or her family and others should happen only in natural environments as described by law: the home or in places in which typical children can also participate. Early intervention then can provide the foundation for families as they pursue inclusionary home and community (including school) activities as their children age out of early intervention.

Infants and toddlers with disabilities and their families may in fact receive services under a variety of formal structures (e.g., Early Head Start, Healthy Families), as well as participate in a number of informal activities (see Chapter 4). This chapter, however, focuses only on the challenges inherent in the Part C early intervention service system and, in particular, the provision of services in natural environments in order to address, in depth, the opportunities presented by this requirement of Part C service

delivery systems; a requirement that has the potential to create a vision for early intervention that represents inclusion in both philosophy and practice. To lay out the intended framework, the chapter begins with an overview of early intervention, provides information about service delivery in natural environments, describes recent research on children's learning within natural environments, and provides recommendations for the field so that children will be provided with opportunities to learn in a variety of natural environments, including those environments that include same-age peers without disabilities.

EARLY INTERVENTION

The rich history of the field of early intervention spans many disciplines and fields of study. The health, child development, early childhood education, and special education fields have collectively influenced the design and delivery of early intervention in the United States. Early intervention is aimed at minimizing the impact of the child's disability or risk factors, strengthening the family, and establishing the foundation for subsequent development and competence (Guralnick, 1997a, 1998). Conceptualized from an ecological model of human learning and development (Bronfenbrenner, 1992), early intervention views child, parent, and family functioning as complex. The processes that influence early learning and development are produced by the interaction of the environments experienced by a child and the characteristics of the people (including the developing child) within these environments (Dunst, Trivette, & Jodry, 1997; Garbarino, 1992; Garbarino & Abramowitz, 1992). A number of characteristics have been associated with early intervention programs under Part C of IDEA. Four of the most important are further described.

Family-Centered Orientation

The family context and the experiences provided within this context are extremely critical to a child's development (Dunst, 1999b; Guralnick, 1998, 1999). The importance of families has been acknowledged by the field of early intervention for many years, and family-centered models are a logical expansion of practices that aim to maximize intervention efforts. Besides the obvious fact that the child's family is usually the constant over the child's life span, it should also be acknowledged that a family spends the most time with the child. Even in the rare examples in which a toddler receives up to 20 hours of structured interventions per week (e.g., recommended for a child with autism), this represents only 20% of a child's waking time. Because most children in early intervention receive far fewer service hours than this (Bruder & Staff, 1998; Kochanek & Buka, 1998), it is obvious that a family (or other caregiver) has the opportunity to provide the greatest influence on a child's developing competence. The family has ultimate responsibility for caregiving, supporting the child's development, and enhancing the quality of the child's life. Thus, the family must be seen as the primary unit for service delivery (Bruder, 2000).

Just as the population of children served in early intervention is heterogeneous, so too are their families. This diversity can be challenging to early interventionists as they try to provide information, education, and support to families who differ along a number of dimensions that influence child development and competence. For example, parents' education level, socioeconomic status, and home environment have been related to child development (Garbarino, 1990; Werner, 1990), and in early intervention, these characteristics have related to service delivery patterns (Bruder et al.,

1997; Kochanek & Buka, 1998; Sontag & Schacht, 1993). Other factors that have been identified as contributing to child development include parent–child interaction patterns and parents' ability to follow intervention recommendations for facilitating child development (Bricker, Bruder, & Bailey, 1982; Kaiser, Hancock, & Hester, 1998; Kaiser et al., 1996; Mahoney, Boyce, Fewell, Spiker, & Wheeden, 1998; McCollum & Hemmeter, 1997). An additional contributing factor to child development is the availability of social supports for families, in particular informal support networks. A review of the literature pertaining to the role of social supports in early intervention concluded that social supports have direct, mediating, and moderating influences on the behavior and development of children with disabilities and their families (Dunst et al., 1997).

Parents' attitudes and belief systems are also important variables that enhance child development (Guralnick, 1999). These variables include parents' beliefs about child social competence (Guralnick, 1997b; Mills & Rubin, 1992; Mize, Pettit, & Brown, 1995) and about their child's need for early intervention (Affleck et al., 1989). Emphasis has also been placed on the cultural belief systems of families (Chen, Brekken, & Chan, 1997; Turnbull, Blue-Banning, Turbiville, & Park, 1999), as beliefs about how children learn and about parental roles are associated with ethnicity and both acculturation and enculturation (Dunst, Trivette, Hamby, Raab, & Bruder, 2000; Leyendecker & Lamb, 1999). Another parent variable that influences child competence and development is family orchestrated learning experiences that occur in the home and community (Dunst, Bruder, Trivette, Raab, & McLean, 1998; Guralnick, 1998).

The importance of parents to their child's development underscores the need for early intervention to provide to families a sense of confidence and competence about their children's current and future learning and development (Bailey, McWilliam, Darkes, et al., 1998; Turnbull & Turnbull, 1997). In particular, it has been suggested that parents should be given information in a way that supports their ability to parent their child and facilitate learning without threatening self-confidence and cultural, religious, or familial traditions (Dunst, 2000). Family diversity and the reciprocal nature of the relationship between family members and service providers should be the foundation of early intervention (Bruder, 2000). Intervention delivered in this way is termed *family centered* and is a cornerstone of early intervention philosophy and practice.

Accordingly, family-centered practices include treating families with dignity and respect; being culturally and socioeconomically sensitive to family diversity; providing choices to families in relation to their priorities and concerns; fully disclosing information to families so that they can make decisions; focusing on a range of informal, community resources as sources of parenting and family supports; and using help-giving practices that are empowering and competency enhancing (Dunst, 1999a). Considerable literature has been amassed on the individual and collective use of these practices, as they add value to early intervention (cf. Dunst, 2000; Dunst, Brookfield, & Epstein, 1998; Dunst, Trivette, Boyd, & Hamby, 1996; Mahoney & Bella, 1998; McWilliam, Tocci, & Harbin, 1998; Thompson et al., 1997; Trivette & Dunst, 1998) by contributing to improved family and child outcomes.

Team-Based Service Delivery

Infants and young children with disabilities may require the combined expertise of numerous professionals who provide specialized services. For example, personnel who have medical expertise, therapeutic expertise, educational/developmental expertise, and social services expertise traditionally have been involved in the provision of services to infants and young children with disabilities and their families. The coordination of both people and services is frequently overwhelming. Each of these service providers may represent a different professional discipline and a different philosophical model of service delivery. In fact, each discipline has its own training sequence (some require undergraduate, whereas others require graduate degrees), licensing and/or certification requirements (most of which do not require age specialization for young children), and treatment modality (e.g., occupational therapists may focus on sensory integration techniques) (Bruder, 1994). In addition, many disciplines have their own professional organization that encompasses the needs of people across the life span, unlike organizations that focus on a single age group (e.g., National Association for the Education of Young Children). Nonetheless, as services for young children with disabilities continue to grow, so too does the need for professionals.

To improve the efficiency of the individuals who provide early intervention, it has been suggested that services be delivered through a team approach (Sexton, Snyder, Lobman, Kimbrough, & Matthews, 1997). A group of people become a team when their purpose and function are derived from a common philosophy with shared goals (Bruder, 1995). The type of team approach that has been recommended for service delivery models for infants and toddlers with disabilities is the transdisciplinary model (Garland & Linder, 1994; McGonigel, Woodruff, & Roszmann-Millican, 1994). This approach was conceived as a framework for professionals to share important information and skills with primary caregivers (Hutchinson, 1978) and integrates a child's developmental needs across the major developmental domains as it requires team members to share roles and systematically cross discipline boundaries. The primary purpose of the approach is to pool and integrate the expertise of team members so that more efficient and comprehensive assessment and intervention services may be provided. The communication style in this model involves continuous give and take between all members (especially the parents) on a regular, planned basis. Professionals from different disciplines teach, learn, and work together to accomplish a common set of intervention goals for a child and his or her family (McWilliam, 1996). The role differentiation between disciplines is defined by the needs of the situation, as opposed to discipline-specific characteristics (Hanft & Pilkington, 2000). Assessment, intervention, and evaluation are carried out jointly by designated members of the team, and different members of the team may be used to provide direct services at times, though collaborative consultation remains a strong component of the service model (Bruder, 1996). This model facilitates the delivery of appropriate interventions across developmental domains, as opposed to having a specific speech time, fine motor time, gross motor time, and so forth. Other characteristics of this team approach are joint team effort and joint staff development to ensure continuous skill development among members (Bruder, 1995). This does not mean that early interventionists stop providing direct services to children. In reality, for early interventionists to be effective, they need to maintain direct contact with the child, family, and other caregivers. The transdisciplinary approach has been strongly recommended as a mechanism to ensure effective inclusionary practices in early intervention (Bruder, 1994, 1995).

Curricula and Instructional Practice

A curriculum provides a basis for the intervention that is delivered to children and their families. In particular, curriculum addresses the content of the intervention, the teaching/learning strategies, and the means for assessing intervention (Bailey, Jens, & Johnson, 1983). Dunst defined curriculum for infants and young children with disabilities as consisting of:

> A series of carefully planned and designed activities, events, and experiences intentionally organized and implemented to reach specified objectives and goals, and which adhere and ascribe to a particular philosophical and theoretical position, and whose methods and modes of instruction and curriculum content are logically consistent with the psychological perspective from which it has been derived. (1981, p. 9)

Most curricula in early childhood intervention have a developmental focus, utilizing developmental skills in domain-specific categories. This is not surprising, because most eligibility criteria for early childhood intervention emphasize the discrepancy between a child's chronological age and developmental abilities. Indeed, Part C of IDEA requires assessment information across major developmental domains. This focus results in an overreliance on developmental descriptions of children according to developmental discipline area, as opposed to a holistic integration of a child's strengths and abilities (Berkeley & Ludlow, 1992; Mallory, 1992). Although not negating the influence and necessity of a developmental framework and foundation, recent efforts to reconceptualize curricula have resulted in a fresh examination of constructs felt to be important to a child's ability to negotiate his or her environment (Bruder, 1997a; Guralnick, 1997b).

The most widely used descriptor of early childhood curriculum is developmentally appropriate practice. This approach refers to a set of guidelines established to articulate appropriate practices for the early education of young children (Bredekamp, 1987). Two core beliefs within these guidelines are age appropriateness and individual appropriateness; the latter is most important for children with disabilities. Within early intervention, curriculum models that emphasize developmentally appropriate practices are usually insufficient without the adoption of adaptations and teaching techniques individually tailored to a child's needs (Carta, 1994; Carta, Schwartz, Atwater, & McConnell, 1991; Johnson, 1993; Wolery & Bredekamp, 1994).

Activity-based instruction has been used to describe a model of curriculum development for infants and young children with disabilities. This model embeds individual teaching/learning objectives into ongoing child-initiated activities that cross developmental domains and occur throughout a classroom session. The objectives are derived from a child's developmental assessment, and the activities represent age-appropriate developmentally referenced activities. This curriculum model has been recommended for use in inclusionary settings (Bricker, 1995), though data collected thus far on the effectiveness of this approach are sparse and not favorable (Grisham-Brown & Hemmeter, 1998; Lamorey & Bricker, 1993). This may be due in part to methodological issues encompassed in these studies (Hemmeter, 2000).

Despite a lack of evidence supporting certain curricular approaches for use with infants and toddlers with disabilities, two intervention mechanisms that must be kept in mind are the use of intervention objectives (usually carried out in conjunction with the IFSP/individualized education program [IEP]) and responsive teaching methods across developmental domains (including therapy-dominated areas). Objectives represent learning expectations and are based on a child's strengths, needs, and preferences. Each objective should be written so that there is no doubt of the intervention target. Responsive teaching methods include a variety of instructional systems that can be used to enhance a child's learning, for example, incidental teaching, time delay, mand-model, systematic commenting, and milieu teaching (Hemmeter, 2000; Wolery & Gast, 2000). The key to using these procedures in responsive teaching situations lies in tailoring intervention to the needs of each child, using the least intrusive strategies to promote the learning of skills, and embedding instruction within developmentally appropriate routines and activities such as play. Most notable, all early interventionists must collaboratively implement responsive intervention strategies across intervention objectives that are integrated across developmental domains (Bruder, 1997a).

Service Delivery Settings

A variety of factors influence the decision about the optimum service setting for an infant or young child with disabilities. These include where the family lives (urban versus rural), the needs of the child, the transportation resources of the family and program, and the preference of the intervention team and the family. Early intervention can be provided in a neonatal intensive care unit (cf. Als, 1997), a child care setting (a center, family day care home, or baby sitter's house) (Bruder et al., 1997; see also Chapter 10), the home (Roberts, Behl, & Akers, 1996), and community activities (Umstead, Boyd, & Dunst, 1995; see also Chapter 14). Not all interventions have to be provided at the same location, and the settings may change over time as the needs of the family and child change (Hanft & Feinberg, 1997). Clearly, there is no standard setting in which to provide early intervention. Under the law, these settings must be in places in which the child would participate if he or she did not have a disability. This has resulted in a move away from group settings that serve only children with disabilities.

Early childhood inclusion is the provision of early intervention services in group settings with children without disabilities (Peck, Odom, & Bricker, 1993). A more recent definition includes the terms *physical membership* and *critical mass* (Brown, Odom, Li, & Zercher, 1999). As a concept, the field of early intervention agrees with the potential benefits of inclusive intervention models (Bailey, McWilliam, Buysse, et al., 1998). However, as previously noted, concerns about the feasibility and quality of inclusive programs continue to surface (Bricker, 2000; Cavallaro, Ballard-Rosa, & Lynch, 1998). Although early childhood programs are proliferating because of government initiatives (e.g., Early Head Start, state-funded prekindergarten programs) and the growing need for programs by working parents (e.g., child care), quality inclusive early childhood options for all young children with disabilities remain an elusive goal for the field of early intervention (see Chapter 1).

Much has been written about the barriers to implementing inclusive early childhood services (Bailey, McWilliam, Buysse, et al., 1998; Bricker, 1995, 2000; Odom, 2000). Among the barriers cited are attitudes, staff skills, administrative structures, support systems, fiscal resources, and competing values (e.g., quality, intensity, and family choice versus inclusive programs). Unfortunately, these barriers have been prevalent within early intervention systems that focus on location alone as the description for a natural environment.

NATURAL ENVIRONMENTS AS SETTINGS FOR INTERVENTION: RESEARCH FINDINGS

The focus on natural environments for infants and toddlers with disabilities has created multiple opportunities for children with disabilities to participate in a variety of home and community activities as environments for learning. Home activities are events that occur on either a regular or periodic basis in a child's primary living setting (e.g., getting dressed, taking a bath), and community activities include a wide range of informal (e.g., visits to the park, going to McDonalds, taking walks) and formal (e.g., storytime at the library, child care, Gymborees) experiences provided by community people, groups, organizations, and so forth (Trivette, Dunst, & Deal, 1997). Unfortunately, the field does not have much research to support the provision of early intervention in the home or in places (in the community) in which typical children participate. In addition, most research on setting (and variables including typical peers within the setting) as a variable in early childhood programs with children with disabilities has been conducted with preschool-age children (cf. Hyson, Diamond, Hart, Avery, & Odom, 1998). The following is a brief description of research conducted within early intervention programs that serve infants and toddlers and their families in natural environments as defined by Part C.

Research on Home Settings

The field of early childhood intervention has a rich history of using the home as a source of learning (Bromwich, 1981). Home visiting has been used as a strategy to provide support, information, and education to parents and their children who have developmental delays and those who are at risk for developmental delays (Klass, 1996). A plethora of home-visiting models have focused on both parent and child competence, and these models span the fields of health, education, and social services (cf. Behrman, 1999). In fact, most children who receive services through Part C programs receive them in the home (Cavallaro et al., 1998; M. Greer, personal communication, March 31, 2000). Despite the frequency of home interventions, only a few studies have examined Part C services delivered in this setting. For example, an extensive study of home visiting for children eligible for Part C services was conducted by Roberts, Akers, and Behl (1996) and involved 193 programs that serve children who are eligible for Part C. It was found that a major focus of the home visits was direct services for children and families and on assisting families to coordinate and integrate additional services needed from other agencies and resources. This service coordination function filled approximately 40% of home visitors' time; the remainder of the time was used for enhancing parenting skills and enhancing child development skills, direct services to children, and informal family counseling.

McBride and Peterson (1997) performed a comprehensive analysis of early intervention delivered during home visits with 28 families. During 160 home visits (average 6 per family), observational data were taken by a research assistant using a code that examined four categories: individuals present, interaction partners, content addressed during the interaction, and the role of the home interventionist during the interaction. A parent, the child, and the home interventionist were always present at the home visits; siblings were present for 33% of visits, and other professionals (19%) and neighbors or friends of the family (19%) were also present. During the observed home visits,

almost half of the home interventionist's time was in joint interactions with the parent or another professional and the child; the remainder of the time was split between home interventionist's interacting alone with children (26%), home interventionist's interacting with parents (21%), and parents' interacting with the child without the home interventionist (3%). The content of the home visits was overwhelmingly child focused, consisting of activities relating to child development or caregiving (89%). This suggested that the interventionists were not guided by a family systems framework that emphasizes attention to both family and child needs with an emphasis on parent–child interaction; that is, the interventionists provided a model of early intervention that was not oriented to a family systems model.

Research on Community Settings

Another application of natural environments is the provision of early intervention within community settings and activities. Two applications of community settings are discussed next.

Community Groups   Although a number of community options for infants and toddlers with disabilities exist, little research has been conducted on the use of community settings as intervention sites. One example of this type of option is the Parents Interacting with Infants (PIWI) program. This model is an example of an inclusionary, formal, community playgroup for infants and toddlers with disabilities and their parents. The model was designed in 1986 for training preservice professionals in the implementation of inclusive, family-centered services. The PIWI philosophy supports sensitive, responsive relationships between adults and infants and among adults. The intervention (for all children) is based on eight program components, and the playgroups are staffed with two to four interdisciplinary students from the University of Illinois. Each group has a maximum of 10 parent–infant dyads of which one to two children have disabilities. The groups meet for 90 minutes weekly for 13 weeks in a room with age-appropriate materials, equipment, and activities.

A qualitative analysis of 12 parents who participated in PIWI suggested four unifying evaluative themes (Appl, Fahl-Gooler, & McCollum, 1997). The first was the goals that the parents had for their children and themselves: Most parents shared similar goals for their children related to socialization with other children. The second was the benefits identified by parents, again identified as increased opportunities for their child to socialize. A third theme that emerged was difficulties experienced by parents in regard to participation. These themes included seeing the differences between their child and others who were typically developing. However, many parents reported that these difficulties were mitigated by the support that the parents received in the groups, which was the fourth theme. In particular, parents' sense of belonging was enhanced when they felt accepted, respected, and appreciated in regard to their individual differences, and this was more likely to occur when the focus was on strengths rather than on weaknesses. Unfortunately, no outcome data on child or family change were provided.

Child Care   There are more data on the use of formal community programs such as child care and nursery schools as early intervention settings for infants and toddlers with disabilities, though this option is also underused by Part C systems (Cavallaro et al., 1998; see Chapter 10). For example, Connecticut, Delaware, and Massachusetts reported on model early intervention programs within community child care settings developed during the 1980s (Bruder,

Deiner, & Sachs, 1990). Each used a combination of federal and state funds to provide a variety of services to enrolled children, families, and child care staff. A variety of supports to enable this model to flourish were provided in each state. These included training to child care staff and early interventionists on inclusive practices, flexible funding streams to pay for additional supports for children attending child care, and policy development to facilitate the implementation of this model. Each state used a comprehensive evaluation plan to document the impact of this model, though child/family outcome data were not provided.

One model demonstration project, the Community Integration Project (Bruder, 1993a, 1993b), used community early childhood programs (nursery schools, child care programs) to provide intervention to toddlers and preschool-age children with a range of disabilities and developmental profiles. The model required an intensive commitment by program staff to develop new service delivery methods and roles for specialized staff. Twelve school districts and four early intervention projects participated in the model. Thirty children, 23 of whom were preschool-age and 7 of whom were toddler-age children, participated in the project. Results revealed that statistically significant gains on standardized developmental scores were achieved for all children during project enrollment (2 years). During the project, a number of service delivery characteristics were identified as necessary for the effective implementation of inclusionary, community-based early childhood settings, including existence of an inclusive philosophy, a system for family involvement, staff training, and so forth.

Project BLEND (Beginning Learning Experiences in Developmentally Inclusive Child Care and at Home) provided an inclusive model of early intervention services for 35 children younger than 3 years of age (Brown, Horn, Heiser, & Odom, 1996). Three interrelated components composed the model: service coordination, family–childcare–BLEND partnerships, and transition services. A number of indices suggested the model's effectiveness. First, in comparison with a similar group of children in segregated settings, Project BLEND children were as actively engaged, received similar levels of adult assistance, and spent significantly more time interacting with peers. Second, the itinerant model of service delivery was effective in improving the developmental competence of children (again in comparison with a comparable group of same-age peers). Third, children made progress in attaining goals as measured by goal attainment scaling. Fourth, parents and child care providers demonstrated satisfaction with the model. A cost analysis was conducted to demonstrate that the model was comparable to other service delivery options.

Last, an examination of placement in either inclusionary child care settings or segregated toddler programs was conducted to document whether the developmental progress of children varied as a function of service setting (Bruder & Staff, 1998). Thirty-seven children ages 2–3 years were participants in this 1-year study. The two groups of children were comparable on indices of child development and family background, though service characteristics varied between the settings. Children in the segregated settings received a higher intensity and frequency of related services, and children in the child care classrooms (no more than two children with disabilities in a group/child care class) attended class for slightly more hours per week than those in the segregated settings. After 1 year of intervention in these settings, there was no difference in developmental progress between the groups on three separate standardized developmental assessments, suggesting that children who received

early intervention in child care programs progressed at the same rate as children in the segregated settings.

Implications for Practice

The field of early intervention for infants and toddlers is encouraged by law to provide services within the home or in places in which typically developing children participate. Unfortunately, data on these service settings and what happens within them are sparse. What is known is that services are increasingly being provided in these environments. In fact, in 1997–1998, 63% of early intervention services were delivered in the home, child care settings, or nursery schools under Part C as opposed to segregated centers or clinics, according to the U.S. Department of Education (J. Holt, personal communication, January 27, 2000). What and how services are being provided, reimbursed, and evaluated within these "natural environments" is still open to question at the beginning of the 21st century.

It should also be noted that the sparseness of data is not limited to service settings (or natural environments); there is also a paucity of data on other early intervention characteristics such as curriculum (Bruder, 1997a) and team-based models of service delivery (cf. Sexton et al., 1997; Winton, McCollum, & Catlett, 1997). This is one of the many reasons that Guralnick (1997b) called for an adoption of more rigorous research designs in early intervention as a means of documenting efficacy. These designs are referred to as second-generation designs, and they call for an acknowledgment of the complexity of early intervention. In particular, Guralnick proposed that early intervention efficacy studies be designed to examine the interactions of the influence of program features (e.g., settings), child and family characteristics, and the specific outcomes or goals of early intervention (e.g., learning and development).

NATURAL ENVIRONMENTS: BEYOND SETTING AND LOCATION

The Increasing Children's Learning Opportunities Through Families and Communities Early Childhood Research Institute (Bruder & Dunst, 2000; Dunst et al., 1998) has been identifying and cataloging naturally occurring learning opportunities experienced by children from birth to age 6 years with identified disabilities and delays, those at risk for developmental delays, and those who are typically developing. These activities have been done in collaboration with families. Co-principal investigators Dunst and Bruder have been examining how different locations and settings within those locations are sources of development-enhancing experiences and opportunities for children. The institute is also engaging children in learning opportunities in natural environments and evaluating the development-enhancing qualities and consequences of these kinds of experiences. All of its research has been developed to meet the criteria for second-generation research (Guralnick, 1997b).

Sources of Children's Learning Opportunities

Children's lives are made up of many different kinds of learning experiences and opportunities that have the potential to enhance their development. The ecological model of learning and development suggests that behavior exists and is best understood contextually. Infants and toddlers participate in a number of contexts, such as the family context, the community context, and program context (see Chapter 14). The family context includes a mix of people and places that support a variety of different kinds of child learning opportunities. These include experiences

such as eating during mealtime, splashing water during bath time, listening to stories, and learning greeting skills at family get-togethers. The same kinds of opportunities occur in the community context and include the people and places that are experienced on neighborhood walks and at a children's park, children's festivals, nature centers, and so forth. The early childhood context includes child care programs, early intervention, and other early childhood experiences provided by professionals. These contexts support a variety of subcontexts that can be used to describe the experiences and opportunities given children as part of daily living. They include child and family routines, family rituals, and family and community celebrations and traditions. Termed *activity settings* for purpose of analysis (Gallimore, Goldenberg, & Weisner, 1993; Gallimore, Weisner, Bernheimer, Guthrie, & Nihira, 1993), these units are important features of any planned interventions for children and their families (Roberts, 1999).

Importance of Activity Settings Families almost universally consider different activity settings as the primary contexts for defining important aspects of family life (Bernheimer & Keogh, 1995; Ehrmann, Aeschleman, & Svanum, 1995; Floyd & Gramann, 1993; Gallimore, Weisner, et al., 1993; Harrison, Wilson, Pine, Chan, & Buriel, 1990; Hughes, Seidman, & Williams, 1993; O'Donnel, Tharp, & Wilson, 1993; Schuck & Bucy, 1997). Activity settings include both the psychological (including cultural) and physical components of the interactions, tasks, and routines of a family (Roberts, 1999). "They are the 'common stuff' of family life. . .and reflect a mix of personal and cultural values and parents' beliefs about their children and families" (Bernheimer & Keogh, 1995, p. 420). Activity settings include but are not limited to family mealtimes, reading children books at bedtime, participation in storytelling, family rituals and traditions, and community festivals and celebrations (Dunst et al., 1987; Kellegrew, 1994). These activity settings are similar in the sense that they all provide child development opportunities and experiences, but they may differ in terms of their purposes, functions, demands, and expectations. In addition, it is now known that the particular activity settings that define family life are ones to which families ascribe special meaning, again including but not limited to experiences that parents desire for their children in order to promote development, skills, and values that are consistent with their cultural belief systems (Dunst et al., 2000). These commonalities have been found in studies of children with (Ehrmann et al., 1995; Gallimore, Weisner, Kaufman, & Bernheimer, 1989) and without (Gallimore, Goldenberg, et al., 1993; O'Donnel et al., 1993) disabilities.

The learning activities that occur in activity settings either can be planned (with specific goals and purposes) or can happen as the result of opportunities and experiences that do not have predetermined goals and purposes. Library storytimes, baby exercise classes, and swimming lessons are examples of planned learning activities. Serendipitous learning activities are ones that occur by being in "the right place at the right time." These include "going along" to a ball game with an older sibling, going food shopping with a parent, visiting a neighbor, and so forth. All of these are likely to include experiences that have development-enhancing effects. Both kinds of learning opportunities (planned and serendipitous) are important for promoting and enhancing child competence and development.

Findings from the Increasing Children's Learning Opportunities Through Families and Communities Early Childhood Research Institute (e.g.,

Dunst, 1997; Dunst, Bruder, et al., 1998; Trivette, Dunst, Boyd, & Hamby, 1996; Umstead et al., 1995) indicate that young children with and without disabilities and delays participate in many different kinds of natural social and nonsocial learning environments every day, on certain days of the week, at different times of the year, and as part of different kinds of family and community celebrations and traditions. Activity settings involve the active participation of a child in learning, and they serve to strengthen existing capabilities as well as promote and enhance new competencies. Activity settings occur in a variety of different locations within the home and the community and in places in which typical children participate. Natural learning environments can be described in terms of activity settings because activity settings provide the context for everyday, typically occurring learning opportunities.

Family-Identified
Natural Learning Environments

Two surveys, one on family life as a source of children's learning opportunities and the other on community life as a source of children's learning opportunities, were developed through the Increasing Children's Learning Opportunities Through Families and Communities Early Childhood Research Institute (Dunst, Hamby, Trivette, & Raab, 1999). Each survey included 50 different kinds of activity settings and sources of learning opportunities. The items were identified from an extensive review of the literature with an emphasis on activity settings that occur across families and communities that represent many different racial, ethnic, and cultural backgrounds in the United States and its jurisdictions. Participants were recruited through Part C early intervention programs in 46 states; Part B early childhood special education programs in 39 states; Early Head Start and Head Start programs in all 50 states, Puerto Rico, and the Federated State of Yap in Micronesia; and 140 American Indian Head Start, early intervention, and early childhood programs in 29 states. A family completed a survey of either family or community life as a source of their child's learning opportunities. Specifically, they were asked to indicate the extent to which different activity settings (natural environments) were places where their child(ren) learned desired behavior.

The parents and other caregivers who completed either a family survey (N = 1,723) or a community survey (N = 1,560) were predominantly the biological mothers (89%) of the children receiving early intervention. The largest majority of respondents were between 20 and 40 years of age, high school graduates, and married or living with a partner, although there was considerable variability among the study participants in these variables. Approximately half (54%) of the respondents identified their ethnicity as other than Caucasian. Except for people with Asian or Middle Eastern roots, the study participants were diverse in their cultural and ethnic backgrounds. Family economic status was reported by the majority of the respondents as borderline to economically strained.

The ages of the respondents' children were varied and ranged from birth to 6 years. The children were equally divided in terms of having an identifiable disability/developmental delay or being at risk for poor outcomes. Most children were involved in center-based programs or a combination of center- and home-based programs. One fourth of the children (26%) received 2 or fewer hours of services per week, whereas 43% of the children received 10 or more hours of services per week.

Findings indicated that family and community life together were sources of 22 kinds of natural learning environ-

ments (e.g., child routines, family celebrations, literacy activities). Table 9.2 lists these sources of family learning environments and includes examples of activities in each category (see Table 14.2 in Chapter 14 for the community examples). These findings make obvious the possibilities for providing children varied development-enhancing learning opportunities within and across the 22 different kinds of natural learning environments. Moreover, because these are real-life learning contexts, it is likely that children will acquire functional skills (for more information on the survey, see Dunst et al., 2000).

Natural Learning Environments for Individual Children

A second line of research initiated by the institute used a case study methodology to study the natural learning environments and learning opportunities within a diversity of families. A total of 119 families in eight states were followed to identify and clarify the ecology of children's learning opportunities and experiences across a broad range of child and family characteristics (Dunst, Bruder, et al., 1998). The families were carefully recruited so that they were diverse in terms of their cultural, ethnic, and socioeconomic backgrounds; parent and child ages (birth to 6); diagnosis and severity of child's disability; and place of residence.

The findings of this line of research suggested that where a family lived made a big difference in the specific types of learning opportunities given an individual child; however, most children, irrespective of their disability or severity of delay, experienced multiple kinds of learning opportunities wherever they lived. For example, findings indicated that young children experienced learning opportunities, on average, in approxi-

Table 9.2. Categorization of home and family activities serving as sources of children's learning opportunities

Family routines

Household chores
Cooking/preparing meals
Caring for pets/animals
Running errands
Food shopping

Parenting routines

Child's bath time
Child's bedtime/naptime
Child's wake-up times
Mealtimes
Fixing/cutting child's hair

Child routines

Brushing teeth
Washing hands/face
Cleaning up room
Picking up toys
Toileting
Dressing/undressing

Literacy activities

Reading/looking at books
Telling stories

Bedtime stories

Taking walks/strolls
Adult–child playtime
People "coming and going" (hellos and goodbyes)
Cuddling with child

Physical play

Riding bike/in wagon
Playing ball/games
Water play/swimming

Play activities

Art activities/drawing
Board games
Video games

Dancing/singing

Listening to music
Watching television/videos
Playing alone

Family rituals

Family talks
Saying grace at meals
Religious/spiritual readings
Praying
Family meetings

Family celebrations

Holiday dinners
Family members' birthdays
Decorating home for holidays

Socialization activities

Family gatherings
Picnics
Having friends over to play
Visiting neighbors
Sleepovers

Gardening activities

Doing yard work
Planting trees/flowers
Growing a vegetable garden

mately 15 different home locations and 23 different community locations. These locations, in turn, supported an average of 87 and 76 home and community activity settings or natural learning environments, respectively. These learning environments, in turn, resulted in an average of 113 and 106 learning opportunities in the child's home and community, respectively. Consequently, an individual child could be expected to experience 200 or more learning opportunities in the context of his or her family and commu-

nity life beyond those provided as part of a child's involvement in an early intervention or preschool program.

A number of measures were used to document a range of family and child behaviors, attitudes, belief systems, and child opportunities for learning: 79% of the families believed that interventions embedded within parent-identified activity settings had strong benefits for their children, and 74% believed that these also had strong benefits for them. Consequently, 98% of the families expressed a preference for interventions embedded in family-identified activity settings that occur in family life (home), and 90% also expressed preference for interventions embedded in family-identified activity settings in the community. This was as opposed to interventions delivered in any way. One last point of interest and some dismay was an analysis conducted on the participating children's IFSPs or IEPs. Unfortunately, only 1.3% of outcomes and objectives on IFSPs and 0.4% of goals and objectives on IEPs were described partially or entirely within a learning context. Using less stringent criteria, 17% of the IFSP outcomes and objectives and 31% of the IEP goals and objectives promoted some child participation in family or community activity settings. The Increasing Children's Learning Opportunities Through Families and Communities Early Childhood Research Institute is completing a series of intervention studies. These are designed to examine outcomes related to child and family goals and objectives when comparing interventions embedded within child/family activity settings and interventions using a variety of methods currently in use within early intervention (e.g., routine- and activity-based interventions).

Thus far, the findings from the Increasing Children's Learning Opportunities Through Families and Communities Early Childhood Research Institute have helped clarify the meaning of natural learning environments, the learning opportunities available to young children in these learning environments, and the variety of learning opportunities that are likely to occur for individual children and families. Rather than equate location as a descriptor of natural environments, our research suggests that we should consider locations as sources of activity settings and activity settings as sources of learning opportunities that can be expanded on or enhanced by early intervention.

AGENDA FOR CHANGE

Promoting and enhancing child learning and development are primary goals of early intervention practice (Dunst, 1996). Both theory and research indicate that children's competence is optimized when children experience learning opportunities that have development-enhancing qualities. These opportunities occur as part of daily living, child and family routines, family rituals, and family and community celebrations and traditions. They either are planned or happen serendipitously, and they constitute the life experiences of a developing child (Bronfenbrenner, 1979). Although formal, planned learning opportunities have been the foundation of early intervention and early childhood special education, legislation and recommended practice suggest a new emphasis on natural environments: the home or in places in which typical children participate. Natural learning environments are the places where children experience everyday, typically occurring learning opportunities that promote and enhance behavioral and developmental competencies.

Advances in understanding the kinds of natural learning environments that occur as part of family and community life provide a basis for broadening the meaning of early intervention. Two things can be said about learning in natural environments. First, to the extent that a child's participation in natural environments provides learning opportunities that have development-enhancing consequences, the learning opportunities can be said to have functioned as early intervention. Second, learning in the context of natural environments ought to be a practice of choice in instances in which the development-enhancing qualities of natural learning environments are known and therefore can be used as a basis for optimizing child benefits. What is especially appealing about natural learning environments as the contexts for promoting and enhancing child competence is that they are readily available and easily used as sources of children's learning opportunities. In addition, this model lends itself to a clarification and enhancement of early intervention program characteristics, such as those described in the beginning of this chapter.

First, the practice of using family-identified learning opportunities is inherently family centered. The case study methodology used to generate the previously described findings relied primarily on "listening" to families. The families were approached to help us understand what was important to them, in which home and community activity settings they and their child participated, in which activity settings they wanted to participate in the near and distant future, and what learning opportunities occurred within these activity settings for their child. The information was collected in a manner best described as "relationship based" in that the priority was on establishing a reciprocal, respectful, and mutually informative collaboration (Bruder, 2000).

As part of the Increasing Children's Learning Opportunities Through Families and Communities Early Childhood Research Institute, child behavior was assessed within this relationship. This was done, however, only in the context of the activity settings that were identified and prioritized by the families. It should be noted that Part C services are dependent on an evaluation of a child's development and then on further developmental assessment if the child is eligible for participation. This does not preclude using family-centered practices throughout this process and conducting such assessments under a family's guidance (Hanft & Pilkington, 2000); that is, a child's evaluation/assessment should be family driven in terms of the examination of a child's participation in activity settings through observations and parent report.

A primary purpose of Part C of IDEA is to enhance the capacity of the family to meet the special needs of their child. A model of early intervention that emanates from family-identified activity settings provides the foundation for this to occur and capitalizes on research findings about the importance of family attitudes and beliefs, family social support networks, and family-orchestrated learning experiences to child development and competence. An important family factor that can influence child learning and development is parents' awareness and use of the learning opportunities that occur within their activity settings.

Second, the emphasis on learning through everyday learning opportunities has repercussions for all personnel who serve children in early intervention. Not only do personnel have to understand learning theory, they also have to understand basic principles such as the integration of development across domains (Bruder, 1997a), family-centered practices (see previous section), effective evidence-based intervention strategies (Bruder, 2000), and collaborative consultation models (Palsha & Wesley, 1998; Stayton & Bruder, 1999). The prime requirement of providing early intervention through a model that promotes learning through family-identified opportunities and experiences is the retirement of the model of service delivery that uses discipline-specific people who focus on one developmental domain. Many in the field have been calling for a move away from this deficit-driven model into a more asset-based (Dunst, 2000) and functional model (Hanft & Pilkington, 2000) to meet child and family needs. Although not negating the need for the technical expertise that specialists (including therapists) have in regard to domain-specific behaviors, this model requires that interventions and therapies be incorporated as supports to families and children as they participate in activity settings (cf. Hanft & Pilkington, 2000). Indeed, Part C of IDEA requires as the general role of service providers to 1) consult with parents, other service providers, and representatives of appropriate community agencies to ensure the effective provision of services in that area; 2) train parents and others regarding the provision of those services; and 3) participate in the team's assessment of a child and the child's family and in the development of integrated goals and outcomes for the IFSP (303.12[c]). Thus, the law itself calls for a move away from isolated discipline-specific interventions.

Much has been written about the need for initial and ongoing staff support to facilitate inclusive options for infants and toddlers and their families (Bricker, 1995; Bruder, 1995; Odom, 2000; Palsha & Wesley, 1998). Unfortunately, much has also been written about the inability of preservice training programs to appropriately prepare personnel within and across disciplines to appropriately serve infants and toddlers and their families as required by law (Hanft & Pilkington, 2000; Kilgo & Bruder, 1997). This has created a huge barrier to the implementation of interventions in natural learning environments—a barrier that needs to be overcome by those in both higher education who prepare professionals at the preservice level and state systems that provide in-service support to service providers. Only when training systems and those within them take on the responsibility to meet the needs of infants and toddlers and their families through the use of evidence-based practices will personnel be able to provide quality supports and services across a range of natural learning environments.

Third, family-identified sources of learning opportunities can provide the context and content for early intervention curricula. The kind of learning that takes place in natural environments is best described as situated learning (Lave & Wenger, 1991). Situated learning is learning that is embedded in everyday, natural environments that emphasize the acquisition of competence that is functional and makes possible increased child participation in those environments, both social and nonsocial. Situated learning is the acquisition of knowledge and skills that have real-life meaning and significance for a developing child. An important characteristic of situated learning is that participation in both social and nonsocial natural learning environments is often a sufficient condition to evoke desired child competence. Natural learning environments that have development-enhancing effects provide the opportunity to facilitate a child's development through the use of a variety of naturalistic response-contingent and response-elaboration instructional strategies (cf. Wolery & Gast, 2000; Wolery & Sainato, 1996). Naturalistic instructional strategies reinforce a child for engaging in (desired) behavior and for attempting something new or more complex. These kinds of teaching practices are designed to keep a child engaged in production of situated behavior and to promote and enhance the development of new skills and competence.

Although this orientation may be criticized by many in the field who perceive that this model is a restatement of a curriculum model for children with severe disabilities that has its roots in the 1970s and 1980s (Brown, Holvoet, Guess, & Mulligan, 1980; Wilcox & Bellamy, 1987; Williams & Gotts, 1977) and was most recently adapted to early childhood as activity-based instruction (Bricker, 1998), important distinctions must be made. The curriculum development process derived from the Increasing Children's Learning Opportunities Through Families and Communities Early Childhood Research Institute has two important features. First, the content of the intervention is determined solely by the identification and expansion of family-identified activity settings and learning opportunities. This can be supplemented by caregivers who also spend time with the child (e.g., child care, extended family). Second, the purpose of the intervention is to facilitate learning through the expanded and/or enhanced participation of the child in the activity setting, using responsive intervention methodology (Wolery & Gast, 2000). Developmentally appropriate intervention objectives then can be developed from the contexts of the activity settings and the expectations for participation within them, and intervention methodology can be used to promote and enhance this participation. Thus, this curriculum model can easily be applied by all of the early intervention personnel (across disciplines) in the child's and family's life, a recommendation made in regard to early intervention curricula (Bruder, 1997a) and most recently applied to therapy-based interventions (Hanft & Pilkington, 2000).

A last implication from the findings of the institute is the one on which this chapter is based: the setting of early intervention. As previously stated, a natural environment is more than just location. The field of early intervention must go beyond the superficial notion that placement alone as an early intervention feature will provide more effective outcomes for families and children. The emphasis across the United States on compliance with the natural environment mandate of IDEA has resulted in a situation in which ineffective and inappropriate intervention practices are still occurring, the difference being that they are now happening in family homes, child care centers, and other locations deemed "natural" (M. Greer, personal communication, March 31, 2000).

An expectation from the Increasing Children's Learning Opportunities Through Families and Communities Early Childhood Research Institute is that a renewed focus will be placed on maximizing children's development and learning and on enhancing the family's capacity to meet the special needs of their child through early intervention systems that use home and community activity settings and learning opportunities. Emphasis should be placed on learning in the contexts that are most appropriate to families. These contexts have been identified through surveys and case studies to include a wide range of experiences that are inclusive as a means (e.g., learning) as opposed to an end (placement) and individualized to each family. This framework, if adopted, could result in a much more functional and achievable vision for inclusion than is currently happening under the requirements for natural environments.

MOVING THE AGENDA

Early intervention can be an exciting time for families and their children and those who serve them. This excitement stems from the opportunities that abound to maximize a child's learning potential in the context of family and community life. Possibilities are endless, especially when recognizing the impact that early interventionists can have on a family's belief system about their child and the child's assets and about their own abilities. However, a paradigm shift must occur within early intervention. This shift must embrace the inherent appeal of natural environments as a mechanism to facilitate child and family inclusion in home and community activities that have development-enhancing potential, as opposed to the current emphasis on terminology (e.g., natural environments) that has been misinterpreted, exclusionary, and representative of location only.

Though research has provided evidence for the feasibility of such a shift in emphasis to natural learning environments, the practice of enhancing children's learning and participation in family-identified home and community activity settings is far from prevalent. This seems to be because the majority of those in early intervention continue to address the natural environments concept as a setting or placement issue only, thus dooming it to failure as many of the barriers identified for preschool- and school-age inclusion will be extended downward to the infant and toddler age group. To prevent this outcome, a strong recommendation to the field is to shift its thinking and adopt new "mental models" for the delivery of supports and services to infants and toddlers and their families.

The concept of mental models (Senge, 1994; Senge et al., 1999) identifies two things (at a minimum) that facilitate the adoption of innovations or new ways of doing things: the development of learning communities and the concept of shared leadership. Learning communities are composed of five types of learning disciplines—lifelong programs of study and practice (Senge, 1994). These include personal mastery, mental models, shared vision, team learning, and systems thinking. Learning communities use a refined strategic planning process that allows a group or individual to develop a model to solve a current practice problem (see Senge, 1994). The steps to do this are as follows: 1) identify the symptoms of the problem, 2) map all of the quick fixes, 3) identify the undesirable impacts on all levels of a system, 4) identify fundamental solutions, 5) map addictive side effects of quick fixes, 6) identify interconnections to fundamental loops, and 7) identify high-leverage actions. At each step, appropriate training content is identified by the learner as necessary to proceed to develop the model. Learning communi-

ties continue with follow-up provided both individually through technical assistance (phone, e-mail), in dyads via mentorship models, or in groups. This model lends itself well to state and local early intervention programs that wish to address natural learning environments as the context for the delivery of services that are effective for children's learning and development. In particular, the collective development of mental models and a shared vision for what constitutes early intervention should guide the field into the adoption of more appropriate and effective models for children and their families—models that embrace inclusion in development-enhancing home and community activity settings.

A second concept recommended to shift the emphasis of early intervention services toward natural learning environments is shared leadership. Shared leadership is a concept that proposes that all members of an organization take responsibility for its values, governance, and results. Part C programs, unfortunately, have been structured to rely more on managers than leaders (Bruder, 2000). Certainly, the complexity of the system in regard to compliance with regulations, reimbursement rates, and timelines seems to have overshadowed a quest for effective models of intervention that occur within the context of family lives in homes and communities. Although good management is a component of leadership, leadership establishes higher standards of operation by focusing on values, vision, effectiveness, and results (Covey, 1991). Leaders must establish and maintain a number of essential working principles that become inherent to the organization that they are leading (DePree, 1992). These include a rational environment, a clear statement of the values of the organization, openness to change and innovation, maturity, space for people to grow, momentum, effectiveness, and, most important, stewardship (Block, 1996). In the field of early intervention, we all must begin to take responsibility to display the leadership necessary to create and lead rational, value-driven, and innovative organizations that function to maximize a child's learning and development in natural learning environments.

CONCLUSION

In closing, it is appropriate to highlight the values inherent in Part C of IDEA. These values emanate from the statements made by Congress as to the purpose of Part C programs: most important, maximizing children's development and enhancing the family's capacity to meet the special needs of their child. These statements provide the foundation for Part C services, and research strongly suggests that these two purposes can, and should, be met within the context of family-identified activity settings and natural learning environments. By using the learning opportunities embedded within these contexts, we will have no reason to exclude children from participating in home and community activities with their typically developing peers.

REFERENCES

Affleck, G., Tennen, H., Rowe, J., Roscher, B., Walker, L., & Higgins, P. (1989). Effects of formal support on mothers' adaptation to the hospital-to-home transition of high risk infants: The benefits and costs of helping. *Child Development, 60,* 488–501.

Als, H. (1997). Earliest intervention for preterm infants in the newborn intensive care unit. In M.J. Guralnick (Ed.), *The effectiveness of early intervention* (pp. 47–76). Baltimore: Paul H. Brookes Publishing Co.

Appl, D.J., Fahl-Gooler, F., & McCollum, J.A. (1997). Inclusive parent–child play groups: How comfortable are parents of children with disabilities in the group? *Infant-Toddler Intervention, 7*(4), 235–249.

Bailey, D.B., Jr., Jens, K., & Johnson, N. (1983). Curricula for handicapped infants. In S. Garwood & R. Fewell (Eds.), *Educating handicapped infants* (pp. 387–415). Gaithersburg, MD: Aspen Publishers.

Bailey, D.B., Jr., McWilliam, R.A., Buysse, V., & Wesley, P.W. (1998). Inclusion in the context of competing values in early childhood education. *Early Childhood Research Quarterly, 13*(1), 27–47.

Bailey, D.B., Jr., McWilliam, R.A., Darkes, L.A., Hebbeler, K., Simeonsson, R.J., Spiker, D., & Wagner, M. (1998). Family outcomes in early intervention: A framework for program evaluation and efficacy research. *Exceptional Children, 64*(3), 313–328.

Behrman, R.E. (Ed.). (1999). Home visiting: Recent program evaluations. *The Future of Children, 9*(1).

Berkeley, T.R., & Ludlow, B.L. (1992). Developmental domains: The mother of all interventions; or, the Subterranean early development blues. *Topics in Early Childhood Special Education, 11*(4), 13–21.

Bernheimer, L.P., & Keogh, B.K. (1995). Weaving interventions into the fabric of everyday life: An approach to family assessment. *Topics in Early Childhood Special Education, 15,* 415–433.

Block, P. (1996). *Stewardship: Choosing service over self interest.* San Francisco: Berrett-Koehler Publishers.

Bredekamp, S. (Ed.). (1987). *Developmentally appropriate practice in early childhood programs serving children from birth through age 8.* Washington, DC: National Association for the Education of Young Children.

Bricker, D. (1978). Rationale for the integration of handicapped and nonhandicapped preschool children. In M. Guralnick (Ed.), *Early intervention and the integration of handicapped and nonhandicapped preschool children* (pp. 3–26). Baltimore: University Park Press.

Bricker, D. (1995). The challenge of inclusion. *Journal of Early Intervention, 19*(3), 179–194.

Bricker, D. (1998). *An activity-based approach to early intervention* (2nd ed.). Baltimore: Paul H. Brookes Publishing Co.

Bricker, D. (2000). Inclusion: How the scene has changed. *Topics in Early Childhood Special Education, 20*(1), 14–19.

Bricker, D., Bruder, M., & Bailey, E. (1982). Developmental integration of preschool children. *Analysis and Intervention in Developmental Disabilities, 2,* 207–222.

Bromwich, R. (1981). *Working with parents and infants: An interactional approach.* Baltimore: University Park Press.

Bronfenbrenner, U. (1979). *The ecology of human development: Experiments by nature and design.* Cambridge, MA: Harvard University Press.

Bronfenbrenner, U. (1992). Ecological systems theory. In R. Vasta (Ed.), *Six theories of child development: Revised formulations and current issues* (pp. 187–249). London: Jessica Kingsley Publishers.

Brown, F., Holvoet, J., Guess, D., & Mulligan, M. (1980). The Individualized Curriculum Sequencing model (III): Small group instruction. *Journal of The Association for the Severely Handicapped, 5*(4), 352–367.

Brown, W.H., Horn, E.M., Heiser, J.G., & Odom, S.L. (1996). Project BLEND: An inclusive model of early intervention services. *Journal of Early Intervention, 20*(4), 364–375.

Brown, W.H., Odom, S.L., Li, S., & Zercher, C. (1999). Ecobehavioral assessment in inclusive early childhood programs: A portrait of preschool inclusion. *The Journal of Special Education, 33,* 148–153.

Bruder, M.B. (1993a). Early childhood community integration: An option for preschool special education. *OSERS News in Print, V*(3), 38–43.

Bruder, M.B. (1993b). The provision of early intervention and early childhood special education within community early childhood programs: Characteristics of effective service delivery. *Topics in Early Childhood Special Education, 13*(1), 19–37.

Bruder, M.B. (1994). Working with members of other disciplines: Collaboration for success. In M. Wolery & J.S. Wilbers (Eds.), *Including children with special needs in early childhood programs* (pp. 45–70). Washington, DC: National Association for the Education of Young Children.

Bruder, M.B. (1995). Early intervention. In J.W. Wood & A.M. Lazzari (Eds.), *Exceeding the boundaries: Understanding exceptional lives* (pp. 534–569). New York: Harcourt.

Bruder, M.B. (1996). Interdisciplinary collaboration in service delivery. In R.A. McWilliam (Ed.), *Rethinking pull-out services in early intervention: A professional resource* (pp. 27–48). Baltimore: Paul H. Brookes Publishing Co.

Bruder, M.B. (1997a). The effectiveness of specific educational/developmental curricula for children with established disabilities. In M.J. Guralnick (Ed.), *The effectiveness of early intervention* (pp. 523–548). Baltimore: Paul H. Brookes Publishing Co.

Bruder, M.B. (1997b). Inclusion for preschool age children: A collaborative services model. *First steps: Stories on inclusion in early childhood education* (pp. 111–122). Paris, France: Unified Nations Educational, Scientific, and Cultural Organization.

Bruder, M.B. (2000). Family centered early intervention: Clarifying our values for the millennium. *Topics in Early Childhood Special Education, 20*(2), 105–115.

Bruder, M.B., Deiner, P., & Sachs, S. (1990). Models of integration through early intervention/child care collaboration. *Zero to Three Bulletin, 10*(3), 14–17.

Bruder, M.B., & Dunst, C.J. (2000). Expanding learning opportunities for infants and toddlers in natural environments: A chance to reconceptualize early intervention. *Zero to Three Bulletin, 20*(3), 34–36.

Bruder, M.B., & Staff, I. (1998). A comparison of the effects of type of classroom and service characteristics on toddlers with disabilities. *Topics in Early Childhood Special Education, 18*(1), 26–37.

Bruder, M.B., Staff, I., & McMurrer-Kaminer, E. (1997). Toddlers receiving early intervention in childcare centers: A description of a service delivery system. *Topics in Early Childhood Special Education, 17*(2), 185–208.

Carta, J.J. (1994). Developmentally appropriate practices: Shifting the emphasis to individual appropriateness. *Journal of Early Intervention, 18*(4), 342–343.

Carta, J.J., Schwartz, I.S., Atwater, J.B., & McConnell, S.R. (1991). Developmentally appropriate practice: Appraising its usefulness for young children with disabilities. *Topics in Early Childhood Special Education, 11,* 11–20.

Cavallaro, C.C., Ballard-Rosa, M., & Lynch, E.W. (1998). A preliminary study of inclusive special education services for infants, toddlers, and preschool-age children in California. *Topics in Early Childhood Special Education, 18*(3), 169–182.

Cavallaro, C.C., Haney, M., & Cabello, B. (1993). Developmentally appropriate strategies for promoting full participation in early childhood settings. *Topics in Early Childhood Special Education, 13*(3), 293–307.

Chen, D., Brekken, L.J., & Chan, S. (1997). Project CRAFT: Culturally responsive and family-focused training. *Infants and Young Children, 10*(1), 61–73.

Council for Exceptional Children, Division of Early Childhood. (2000). *Position on inclusion.* Available: http://www.dec-sped.org/positions/inclusio.html.

Covey, S.R. (1991). *Principle-centered leadership.* New York: Simon & Schuster.

DePree, M. (1992). *Leadership jazz.* New York: Random House.

Dunst, C. (1981). *Infant learning: A cognitive-linguistic intervention strategy* (Vol. 4). New York: McGraw-Hill Education & Professional Publishing Group.

Dunst, C.J. (1996). Early intervention in the USA: Programs, models, and practices. In M. Brambring, H. Rauh, & A. Beelmann (Eds.), *Early childhood intervention: Theory, evaluation, and practice* (pp. 11–52). Hawthorne, NY: Walter de Gruyter.

Dunst, C.J. (1997). Conceptual and empirical foundations of family-centered practice. In R. Illback, C. Cobb, & J.H. Joseph (Eds.), *Integrated services for children and families: Opportunities for psychological practice* (pp. 75–91). Washington, DC: American Psychological Association.

Dunst, C.J. (1999a). *An integrated framework for studying the influences of environmental factors on child, parent and family functioning: Implications for investigating and practicing early intervention and family support.* Submitted for publication.

Dunst, C.J. (1999b). Placing parent education in conceptual and empirical context. *Topics in Early Childhood Special Education, 19*(3), 141–146.

Dunst, C.J. (2000). Revisiting "rethinking early intervention." *Topics in Early Childhood Special Education, 20*(2), 95–104.

Dunst, C.J., Brookfield, J., & Epstein, J. (1998). *Family-centered early intervention and child, parent and family benefits.* Asheville, NC.

Dunst, C.J., Bruder, M.B., Trivette, C.M., Raab, M., & McLean, M. (1998). *Increasing Children's Learning Opportunities Through Families and Communities Early Childhood Research Institute.* Year 2 Progress Report submitted to the U.S. Department of Education. Asheville, NC.

Dunst, C.J., Hamby, D., Trivette, C.M., & Raab, M. (1999). *Sources of naturally occurring children's learning opportunities in the context of family and community life.* Submitted for publication.

Dunst, C.J., Lesko, J.J., Holbert, K.A., Wilson, L.L., Sharpe, K.L., & Liles, R.F. (1987). A systemic approach to infant intervention. *Topics in Early Childhood Special Education, 7*(2), 19–37.

Dunst, C.J., Trivette, C.M., Boyd, K., & Hamby, D. (1996). Family-oriented program models, helpgiving practices, and parental control appraisals. *Exceptional Children, 62,* 237–248.

Dunst, C.J., Trivette, C.M., Hamby, D., Raab, M., & Bruder, M.B. (2000). Family ethnicity, acculturation and enculturation, and parent beliefs about child behavior, learning methods and parenting roles. *Journal of Early Intervention, 23*(3).

Dunst, C.J., Trivette, C.M., & Jodry, W. (1997). Influences of social support on children with disabilities and their families. In M.J. Guralnick (Ed.), *The effectiveness of early intervention* (pp. 499–522). Baltimore: Paul H. Brookes Publishing Co.

Education for All Handicapped Children Act Amendments of 1986, PL 99-457, U.S.C. 20, §§ 1471 *et seq.*

Ehrmann, L., Aeschleman, S.R., & Svanum, S. (1995). Parental reports of community activity patterns: A comparison between young children with disabilities and their nondisabled peers. *Research in Developmental Disabilities, 16,* 331–343.

Floyd, M.F., & Gramann, J.H. (1993). Effects of acculturation and structural assimilation in resource-based recreation: The case of Mexican Americans. *Journal of Leisure Research, 25,* 6–21.

Gallimore, R., Goldenberg, C.N., & Weisner, T.S. (1993). The social construction and subjective reality of activity settings: Implications for community psychology. *American Journal of Community Psychology, 21,* 537–559.

Gallimore, R., Weisner, T.S., Bernheimer, L.P., Guthrie, D., & Nihira, K. (1993). Family responses to young children with developmental delays: Accommodation activity in ecological and cultural context. *American Journal on Mental Retardation, 98,* 185–206.

Gallimore, R., Weisner, T.S., Kaufman, S.Z., & Bernheimer, L.P. (1989). The social construction of ecocultural niches: Family accommodation of developmentally delayed children. *American Journal of Mental Deficiency, 94,* 216–230.

Garbarino, J. (1990). The human ecology of early risk. In S.J. Meisels & J.P. Shonkoff (Eds.), *Handbook of early childhood intervention* (pp. 78–96). New York: Cambridge University Press.

Garbarino, J. (Ed.) (1992). *Children and families in the social environment* (2nd ed.). Hawthorne, NY: Aldine de Gruyter.

Garbarino, J., & Abramowitz, R. (1992). The ecology of human development. In J. Garbarino (Ed.), *Children and families in the social environment* (2nd ed., pp. 11–33). Hawthorne, NY: Walter de Gruyter.

Garland, C.W., & Linder, T.W. (1994). Administrative challenges in early intervention. In L.J. Johnson, R.J. Gallagher, M.J. LaMontagne, J.B. Jordan, J.J. Gallagher, P.L. Hutinger, & M.B. Karnes (Eds.), *Meeting early intervention challenges: Issues from birth to three* (2nd ed., pp. 133–166). Baltimore: Paul H. Brookes Publishing Co.

Grisham-Brown, J., & Hemmeter, M.L. (1998). Writing IEP goals and objectives: Reflecting an activity-based approach to instruction for children with disabilities. *Young Exceptional Children, 1*(3), 2–10.

Guralnick, M.J. (Ed.). (1978). *Early intervention and the integration of handicapped and nonhandicapped preschool children.* Baltimore: University Park Press.

Guralnick, M.J. (1990). Major accomplishments and future directions in early childhood mainstreaming. *Topics in Early Childhood Special Education, 10,* 1–27.

Guralnick, M.J. (Ed.). (1997a). *The effectiveness of early intervention.* Baltimore: Paul H. Brookes Publishing Co.

Guralnick, M.J. (1997b). Second-generation research in the field of early intervention. In M.J. Guralnick (Ed.), *The effectiveness of early intervention* (pp. 3–20). Baltimore: Paul H. Brookes Publishing Co.

Guralnick, M.J. (1998). Effectiveness of early intervention for vulnerable children: A developmental perspective. *American Journal on Mental Retardation, 102*(4), 319–345.

Guralnick, M.J. (1999). Family and child influences on the peer-related social competence of young children with developmental delays. *Mental Retardation and Developmental Disabilities Research Reviews, 5,* 21–29.

Handicapped Children's Early Education Program, PL 90-538, 20 U.S.C §§ 621 *et seq.*

Hanft, B.E., & Feinberg, E. (1997). Toward the development of a framework for determining the frequency and intensity of early intervention services. *Infants and Young Children, 10*(1), 27–37.

Hanft, B.E., & Pilkington, K.O. (2000). Therapy in natural environments: The means or end goal for early intervention? *Infants and Young Children, 12*(4), 1–13.

Harrison, A.O., Wilson, M.N., Pine, C.J., Chan, S.Q., & Buriel, R. (1990). Family ecologies of ethnic minority children. *Child Development, 61,* 347–362.

Hemmeter, M.L. (2000). Classroom-based interventions: Evaluating the past and looking toward the future. *Topics in Early Childhood Special Education, 20*(1), 56–61.

Hughes, D., Seidman, E., & Williams, N. (1993). Cultural phenomena and the research enterprise: Toward a culturally anchored methodology. *American Journal of Community Psychology, 21,* 687–703.

Hutchinson, D. (1978). The transdisciplinary approach. In J. Curry & K. Peppe (Eds.), *Mental retardation: Nursing approaches to care* (pp. 65–74). St. Louis, MO: Mosby.

Hyson, M.C., Diamond, K.E., Hart, C.H., Avery, C.S., & Odom, S. (Eds.). (1998). Inclusion in early childhood settings [Special issue]. *Early Childhood Research Quarterly, 13*(1).

Individuals with Disabilities Education Act (IDEA) of 1990, PL 101-476, 20 U.S.C. §§ 1400 *et seq.*

IDEA Infant and Toddler Coordinators Association. (2000, April). *Position paper on the provision of early intervention services in accordance with federal requirements on natural environments.* Indianapolis, IN: Author.

Johnson, C.B. (1993). Developmental issues: Children infected with human immunodeficiency virus. *Infants and Young Children, 6*(1), 1–10.

Kaiser, A.P., Hancock, T.B., & Hester, P.P. (1998). Parents as co-interventionists: Research on applications of naturalistic language teaching procedures. *Infants and Young Children, 10*(4), 36–45.

Kaiser, A.P., Hemmeter, M.L., Ostrosky, M.M., Fischer, R., Yoder, P., & Keefer, M. (1996). The effects of teaching parents to use responsive interaction strategies. *Topics in Early Childhood Special Education, 16*(3), 375–406.

Kellegrew, D.H. (1994). *The impact of daily routines and opportunities on the self-care skill performance of young children with disabilities.* Unpublished doctoral dissertation, University of California, Santa Barbara.

Kilgo, J.L., & Bruder, M.B. (1997). Creating new visions in institutions of higher education: Interdisciplinary approaches to personnel preparation in early intervention. In P.J. Winton, J.A. McCollum, & C. Catlett (Eds.), *Reforming personnel preparation in early intervention: Issues, models, and practical strategies* (pp. 81–101). Baltimore: Paul H. Brookes Publishing Co.

Klass, C.S. (1996). *Home visiting: Promoting healthy parent and child development.* Baltimore: Paul H. Brookes Publishing Co.

Kochanek, T.T., & Buka, S.L. (1998). Patterns of service utilization: Child, maternal, and service provider factors. *Journal of Early Intervention, 21*(3), 217–231.

Lamorey, S., & Bricker, D.D. (1993). Integrated programs: Effects on young children and their parents. In C.A. Peck, S.L. Odom, & D.D. Bricker (Eds.), *Integrating young children with disabilities into community programs: Ecological perspectives on research and implementation* (pp. 249–270). Baltimore: Paul H. Brookes Publishing Co.

Lave, J., & Wenger, E. (1991). *Situated learning: Legitimate peripheral participation.* New York: Cambridge University Press.

Leyendecker, B., & Lamb, M.E. (1999). Latino families. In M.E. Lamb (Ed.), *Parenting and child development in "nontraditional" families* (pp. 247–262). Mahwah, NJ: Lawrence Erlbaum Associates.

Mahoney, G., & Bella, J.M. (1998). An examination of the effects of family-centered early intervention on child and family outcomes. *Topics in Early Childhood Special Education, 18*(2), 83–94.

Mahoney, G., Boyce, G., Fewell, R.R., Spiker, D., & Wheeden, C.A. (1998). The relationship of parent–child interaction to the effectiveness of early intervention services for at-risk children and children with disabilities. *Topics in Early Childhood Special Education, 18*(1), 5–17.

Mallory, B. (1992). Is it always appropriate to be developmental? Convergent models for early intervention practice. *Topics in Early Childhood Special Education, 11*(4), 1–12.

McBride, S.L., & Peterson, C. (1997). Home-based early intervention with families of children with disabilities: Who is doing what? *Topics in Early Childhood Special Education, 17*(2), 209–233.

McCollum, J.A., & Hemmeter, M.L. (1997). Parent–child interaction intervention when children have disabilities. In M.J. Guralnick (Ed.), *The effectiveness of early intervention* (pp. 549–576). Baltimore: Paul H. Brookes Publishing Co.

McGonigel, M.J., Woodruff, G., & Roszmann-Millican, M. (1994). The transdisciplinary team: A model for family-centered early intervention. In L.J. Johnson, R.J. Gallagher, M.J. LaMontagne, J.B. Jordan, J.J. Gallagher, P.L. Hutinger, & M.B. Karnes (Eds.), *Meeting early intervention challenges: Issues from birth to three* (2nd ed., pp. 95–131). Baltimore: Paul H. Brookes Publishing Co.

McWilliam, R.A. (Ed.). (1996). *Rethinking pull-out services in early intervention: A professional resource.* Baltimore: Paul H. Brookes Publishing Co.

McWilliam, R.A., Tocci, L., & Harbin, G.L. (1998). Family-centered services: Service providers' discourse and behavior. *Topics in Early Childhood Special Education, 18*(4), 206–221.

Mills, R.S.L., & Rubin, K.H. (1992). A longitudinal study of maternal beliefs about children's social behaviors. *Merrill-Palmer Quarterly, 38,* 494–512.

Mize, J., Pettit, G.S., & Brown, E.G. (1995). Mothers' supervision of their children's peer play: Relations with beliefs, perceptions, and knowledge. *Developmental Psychology, 31,* 311–321.

Odom, S.L. (2000). Preschool inclusion: What we know and where we go from here. *Topics in Early Childhood Special Education, 20*(1), 20–27.

Odom, S.L., & Diamond, K.E. (1998). Inclusion of young children with special needs in early childhood education: The research base. *Early Childhood Research Quarterly, 13*(1), 3–26.

O'Donnel, C.R., Tharp, R.G., & Wilson, K. (1993). Activity settings as the unit of analysis: A theoretical basis for community intervention and development. *American Journal of Community Psychology, 21,* 501–520.

Palsha, S.A., & Wesley, P.W. (1998). Improving quality in early childhood environments through on-site consultation. *Topics in Early Childhood Special Education, 18*(4), 243–253.

Peck, C.A., Odom, S.L., & Bricker, D.D. (Eds.). (1993). *Integrating young children with disabilities into community programs: Ecological perspectives on research and implementation.* Baltimore: Paul H. Brookes Publishing Co.

Roberts, R.N. (1999). Supporting families where children live: Community principles in action. In R.N. Roberts & P.R. Magrab (Eds.), *Where children live: Solutions for serving young children and their families* (pp. 31–72). Stamford, CT: Ablex.

Roberts, R.N., Akers, A.L., & Behl, D.D. (1996). Family-level service coordination within home visiting programs. *Topics in Early Childhood Special Education, 16*(3), 279–301.

Roberts, R.N., Behl, D.D., & Akers, A.L. (1996). Community-level service integration within home visiting programs. *Topics in Early Childhood Special Education, 16*(3), 302–321.

Roberts, R.N., Innocenti, M.S., & Goetze, L.D. (1999). Emerging issues from state level evaluations of early intervention programs. *Journal of Early Intervention, 22*(2), 152–163.

Schuck, L.A., & Bucy, J.E. (1997). Family rituals: Implications for early intervention. *Topics in Early Childhood Special Education, 17*(4), 477–493.

Senge, P.M. (1994). *The fifth discipline: The art and practice of the learning organization.* New York: Random House.

Senge, P., Kleiner, A., Roberts, C., Ross, R., Roth, G., & Smith, B. (1999). *The dance of change: The challenges to sustaining momentum in learning organizations.* New York: Random House.

Sexton, D., Snyder, P., Lobman, M.S., Kimbrough, P.M., and Matthews, K. (1997). A team-based model to improve early intervention programs: Linking preservice and inservice. In P.J. Winton, J.A. McCollum, & C. Catlett (Eds.), *Reforming personnel preparation in early intervention: Issues, models, and practical strategies* (pp. 495–526). Baltimore: Paul H. Brookes Publishing Co.

Sontag, J.C., & Schacht, R. (1993). Family diversity and patterns of service utilization in early intervention. *Journal of Early Intervention, 17*(4), 431–444.

Stayton, V., & Bruder, M.B. (1999). Early intervention personnel preparation for the new millennium: Early childhood special education. *Infants and Young Children, 12*(1), 59–69.

Thompson, L., Lobb, C., Elling, R., Herman, S., Jurkiewicz, T., & Hulleza, C. (1997). Pathways to family empowerment: Effects of family-centered delivery of early intervention services. *Exceptional Children, 64*(1), 81–98.

Trivette, C.M., & Dunst, C.J. (1998, December). *Family-centered helpgiving practices.* Presentation made at the 14th Annual Division for Early Childhood International Conference on Children with Special Needs, Chicago, IL.

Trivette, C.M., Dunst, C.J., Boyd, K., & Hamby, D.W. (1996). Family-oriented program models, helpgiving practices, and parental control appraisals. *Exceptional Children, 62,* 237–248.

Trivette, C.M., Dunst, C.J., & Deal, A.G. (1997). Resource-based approach to early intervention. In S.K. Thurman, J.R. Cornwell, & S.R. Gottwald (Eds.), *Contexts of early intervention: Systems and settings* (pp. 73–92). Baltimore: Paul H. Brookes Publishing Co.

Turnbull, A., & Turnbull, H. (1997). *Families, professionals and exceptionality: A special partnership* (3rd ed.). Upper Saddle River, NJ: Prentice Hall.

Turnbull, A.P., Blue-Banning, M., Turbiville, V., & Park, J. (1999). From parent education to partnership education: A call for a transformed focus. *Topics in Early Childhood Special Education, 19*(3), 164–172.

Umstead, S., Boyd, K., & Dunst, C.J. (1995). Building community resources: Enabling inclusion in community programs and activities. *Exceptional Parent, 25*(7), 36–37.

Werner, E.E. (1990). Protective factors and individual resilience. In S.J. Meisels & J.P. Shonkoff (Eds.), *Handbook of early childhood intervention* (pp. 97–116). New York: Cambridge University Press.

Wilcox, B., & Bellamy, G.T. (1987). *A comprehensive guide to The Activities Catalog: An alternative curriculum for youth and adults with severe disabilities.* Baltimore: Paul H. Brookes Publishing Co.

Williams, W., & Gotts, E.A. (1977). Selected considerations on developing curriculum for severely handicapped students. In E. Sontag, J. Smith, & N. Certo (Eds.), *Educational programming for the severely and profoundly handicapped* (pp. 221–236). Reston, VA: Division on Mental Retardation, The Council for Exceptional Children.

Winton, P.J., McCollum, J.A., & Catlett, C. (Eds.). (1997). *Reforming personnel preparation in early intervention: Issues, models, and practical strategies.* Baltimore: Paul H. Brookes Publishing Co.

Wolery, M., & Bredekamp, S. (1994). Developmentally appropriate practices and young children with disabilities: Contextual issues in the discussion. *Journal of Early Intervention, 18*(4), 331–341.

Wolery, M., & Gast, D.L. (2000). Classroom research for young children with disabilities: Assumptions that guided the conduct of research. *Topics in Early Childhood Special Education, 20*(1), 49–55.

Wolery, M., & Sainato, D.M. (1996). General curriculum and intervention strategies. In S. Odom & M. McLean (Eds.), *Recommended practices in early intervention/early childhood special education* (pp. 125–158). Austin, TX: PRO-ED.

10

MARION O'BRIEN

Inclusive Child Care
for Infants and Toddlers

A Natural Environment for All Children

Nonmaternal child care for infants and toddlers became more common than exclusive maternal care for U.S. families beginning in the early 1990s (U.S. Department of Labor, Bureau of Labor Statistics, 1994; Zigler & Gilman, 1993). Although many politicians and columnists continue to describe a nostalgic ideal of family life with mother at home caring for young children, the reality in the year 2000 is that most mothers return to work before their infants are 6 months old (National Institute of Child Health and Human Development [NICHD] Early Child Care Research Network, 1997). Furthermore, the majority of new mothers express a preference for working, at least part time. In a nationwide sample of 1,277 mothers who had 6-month-old children and who were asked their preference regarding working or attending school versus staying at home full time, 674 (53%) reported a preference for part-time work or school and

another 175 (14%) for full-time work (O'Brien, Peyton, Roy, Huston, & Hughes, 2000). Thus, policies to allow new mothers to stay at home full time will not meet the needs of two thirds of U.S. families.

Given that care for infants and toddlers is here to stay and is likely to continue to be a part of the early experience of a substantial majority of U.S. children, it is somewhat surprising that relatively little attention has been paid to the organization of child care services for our youngest children or to the quality of the care that children receive (Carnegie Corporation of New York, 1996). In 1991, a long-term longitudinal study of the effects of early child care and home experiences on children's development was initiated by the NICHD. The NICHD Study of Early Child Care is the most comprehensive investigation of child care that has yet been conducted (NICHD Early Child Care Research Network, 1994).

BENEFITS OF CHILD CARE FOR INFANTS AND TODDLERS AND THEIR FAMILIES

The observations of infants and toddlers in child care environments that were conducted as part of the NICHD Study of Early Child Care (NICHD Early Child Care Research Network, 1996, 1999) confirm other reports that describe care quality as mediocre at best when matched against professional standards (Cost, Quality, and Child Outcomes Study Team, 1995; Galinsky, Howes, Kontos, & Shinn, 1994; Whitebook, Howes, & Phillips, 1990). Nevertheless, results from the first phase of the NICHD study, in which children's developmental status was evaluated at age 3, indicate that, overall, children's development is not adversely affected by attending child care environments and that, in fact, some aspects of development seem to be enhanced by exposure to non-maternal care (NICHD Early Child Care Research Network, 1998a, 2000b). A particularly consistent finding from other studies as well is that high-quality care is associated with positive outcomes in social and cognitive development (Burchinal, Roberts, Nabors, & Bryant, 1996; Galinsky et al., 1994). Thus, it is clear that out-of-home care is not inherently "bad" for children. By contrast, when that care is of high quality, research has shown that it is beneficial to children. It is equally evident that most parents, especially mothers, see child care as a benefit to themselves as well. The availability of reliable, affordable, and high-quality child care provides parents with opportunities to pursue their personal educational and career goals and offers families increased financial stability and therefore less stress related to making ends meet. In addition, when children are enrolled in a child care program that includes other young children, their parents' social networks are expanded and they are brought into contact with other families who have similar-age

children and with child care providers who may offer support and information about child rearing. Like the system of early intervention services, child care, when it is of good quality, provides a helpful resource for parents as well as increased learning opportunities for children. These positive factors, which are part of the everyday experience of most U.S. families, provide a counterpoint to the often-expressed view that the increased use of child care is a sign of social problems in the United States (e.g., Adelson, 1997; Brownlee & Miller, 1997; Olsen, 1999).

CHILD CARE FOR INFANTS AND TODDLERS WITH SPECIAL NEEDS

There is one group of parents in the United States who are much less likely than others to use out-of-home child care: parents of children with disabilities. Booth and Kelly (1998) conducted an extensive study of 166 families of 1-year-old children identified as having disabilities or being at medical risk for developmental delays or having chronic health care needs, compared with 139 parents of typically developing children. They found that fewer mothers of children with special needs were employed full time and that more were employed or in school for fewer than 10 hours a week than those in the comparison sample. This was the case even though the two groups were comparable in their employment rates before the child's birth. Furthermore, the children with special needs began nonmaternal care later and spent fewer hours in care up to 15 months of age. The care received by the children with special needs was more often provided by a relative and less often by a child care center or child care home. Approximately one quarter of the parents reported finding care for their child to be a problem because of their child's special needs. In another study of the work force participation and child care needs of parents of children with disabilities, Landis (1992) reported that although approximately half of the mothers had out-of-home jobs, most of the child care that they arranged was in their own homes, and in approximately 50% of the families, fathers were the care providers. To make this child care arrangement work, one or the other parent was usually employed part time or during irregular shifts. No national statistics on the availability of out-of-home care for children with special needs are available. However, in the NICHD Study of Early Child Care, which includes nine states spread across the United States, center directors and home care providers who were caring for the children in the study were asked whether they cared for children with special needs. Of the 278 centers in which study children were enrolled as infants or toddlers, approximately half (148 [53.2%]) reported that they did have a child with special needs enrolled. Of the 664 child care homes surveyed, only 82 [12.3%] reported caring for a child with special needs. Thus, it seems that many parents of children with special needs have limited options for out-of-home child care and may be denied the benefits that organized child care provides to the majority of children and families.

This chapter examines issues surrounding the provision of quality infant and toddler care and the inclusion in these care environments of children with special health care needs, developmental delays, and disabilities. Because most children who do not have developmental delays or disabilities now spend time in child care environments, these environments have become a natural environment for all children and therefore a potentially valuable part of the early intervention system. In a high-quality child care environment, children have many opportunities for social interaction with other children and adults and

receive the kinds of play and language stimulation that promote development of social and cognitive skills (Bronson, Hauser-Cram, & Warfield, 1997; Hauser-Cram, Bronson, & Upshur, 1993). Center-based care is usually considered more "educational" than other types of care, and most inclusion demonstration programs have used centers as their program model; however, many parents of infants and toddlers with and without disabilities choose child care homes rather than centers (Kontos, 1988; NICHD Early Child Care Research Network, 1997). The smaller group of children and the home environment are seen by some parents as better suited to the needs of their children. Thus, home-based care must also be considered a natural environment for infants and toddlers with special needs.

The principle of inclusion of infants and toddlers with special needs in child care programs of all types is supported by federal law, which specifies that child care environments are public facilities and therefore open to all (Craig & Haggart, 1994; Rab & Wood, 1995). In addition, current social trends encourage the full participation of all individuals at every level of society (Bailey, McWilliam, Buysse, & Wesley, 1998). Infants and toddlers are no exception to these laws and policies.

Educational practice at the beginning of the 21st century supports the inclusion of children with special needs in natural environments that are appropriate for all children. This standard of practice has emerged from a growing understanding that children with disabilities are, first and foremost, *children,* with many more similarities to typical children than differences (Fewell, 1993). Observations in classrooms have clearly shown that child care centers that serve all children afford a broader range of opportunities for learning than do specialized classrooms or individual therapy sessions held in a clinic (Bricker, 1995). There is also considerable evidence that child care environments provide a more developmentally appropriate environment for young children than do segregated classrooms. Inclusive programs offer more choices of play activities and less teacher direction than do specialized programs (Bruder & Brand, 1995; Bruder & Staff, 1998). In addition, many parents and professionals report experiences with behavior change of children with disabilities, who seem to be more active and engaged (i.e., more "typical") when in the company of peers without disabilities (Kontos, 1988). For families, inclusion offers an opportunity to normalize their lives. Dropping off children at child care in the morning and picking them up in the evening is what most families of young children do these days; taking children to special therapy sessions three times a week is not. Finally, educational policy has been influenced by a widespread belief that inclusion ultimately will lead to greater community acceptance of all individuals with disabilities, in all sectors of society (Siegel, 1996).

CHARACTERISTICS OF SUCCESSFUL INCLUSIVE CHILD CARE ENVIRONMENTS

In child care environments, *inclusion* means caring for children with disabilities or special health care needs along with children who are typically developing (Cavallaro, Ballard-Rosa, & Lynch, 1998; Odom & Diamond, 1998). Fully including children with special needs involves considerably more than simply placing them in a care environment, however (Bricker, 1995). The necessary characteristics of an inclusive care environment have been identified by Odom and colleagues (1996) as active involvement of all children in all activities, focus on individual differences and provision of services to meet individual learning and developmental goals, emphasis on collab-

oration with parents and special service providers, and tracking developmental progress. The following sections describe some aspects of inclusive care environments that help to contribute to the successful implementation of these characteristics.

Program Focus

In an inclusive program, children with disabilities, developmental delays, or special health care needs are active participants in all of the activities of the child care environment. Thus, children's special needs for care are accommodated within the daily routines that are experienced by all children, and play and learning activities are organized to encourage full participation, regardless of ability or developmental level. For example, an infant with a gastrostomy tube is fed in the company of other infants in the feeding area, not alone in her crib where it is more convenient to provide special care. A nonmobile toddler goes to the playground sharing a ride in a wagon with whatever playmate has been lucky enough to get his turn to ride that day. The nonmobile child is not kept inside, where it is "safe," or carried by a teacher but is given opportunities to have experiences similar to those of the other toddlers.

Inclusion is readily fostered in infant-toddler care environments that place activities of daily living at the center of the curriculum (Bricker, 1995; O'Brien, 1997). For these very young children, the routine events that happen in predictable sequence every day—getting dressed, going to the bathroom, washing hands, eating pudding with a spoon—are priorities. In their participation with adults and other children in these activities, infants and toddlers learn the basics of communication, practice fine and large motor skills, gain direct experience with cause–effect relationships, and have opportunities to use and expand their memory and problem-solving abilities. And they get all of these learning opportunities while doing something functional! These daily living tasks are just as important for children with disabilities as they are for children who are typically developing. Often, children with disabilities or delays need more time and more help from adults to complete daily living activities successfully. When the program focus is on practice of functional skills, care providers are encouraged to devote time to routine activities, not to rush through them to get to "more important" academic-type activities.

Another program characteristic that fosters inclusion is an emphasis on individualization in all activities. All infants and toddlers need some type of special care on the basis of their own idiosyncrasies or their families' individual or cultural preferences. It is not uncommon for each infant in a child care center to have his or her own menus that may include soy formula, puréed organic vegetables, or ethnic foods or that completely exclude certain foods. The inclusion of another child with special feeding needs is not a major departure from the usual practice in infant-toddler care. Because quality child care means individualized care, incorporating children with developmental delays or special health care needs into individualized child care environments for infants and toddlers requires relatively little adjustment on the part of teachers and care providers with regard to the organization of daily care.

Space

The physical and social environment in child care can help facilitate all children's active involvement in learning activities. One important environmental characteristic is space. The space that is available to children and teachers must be large enough to accommodate all of the children who will use the space without crowding. Dividing space into clearly

defined activity areas—defined by function, such as feeding and diapering, and by type of play, such as building or active play—is helpful. However, areas are best divided by low barriers that allow adult supervision and communication or by visual barriers, such as foam blocks or area rugs, that do not restrict movement or access (Bailey & Wolery, 1984). Most child care environments for infants and toddlers do not need a lot of remodeling or physical changes to accommodate a wide range of individual differences; however, often the environments become more appropriate when they are opened up by removing pieces of furniture that serve as barriers to children with movement limitations or sensory disabilities. When special equipment, such as positioning devices, adapted toys and learning materials, and assistive technology devices, are added to an infant or toddler classroom, they provide learning opportunities for all children.

Grouping Children

Quality infant-toddler child care environments can readily include children with special needs because they are already organized around the individual differences of every child. Within any group of infants or toddlers, *typical* developmental levels vary widely. The "expected" age for children to begin walking, for example, ranges anywhere from 9 to 15 months. Similar ranges exist for most other, less visible markers of development. Thus, grouping of infants and toddlers with their age-mates rather than defining groups on the basis of motor skills or other developmental milestones is most effective for all children. Until the 1990s, it was common for children who were not walking to be limited, by state regulations, to enrollment in infant programs. Most states now recognize that these regulations are inappropriate for children with developmental delays or disabilities, whose educational progress demands that they be grouped along with their age-mates. Home-based programs typically serve children from a wide range of ages and are therefore highly individualized. Mixed-age grouping seems to be an effective strategy for preschool inclusion (Blasco, Bailey, & Burchinal, 1993; Roberts, Burchinal, & Bailey, 1994) but has not been examined for infants and toddlers.

Successful inclusive programs also incorporate more than one child with special needs into a classroom. When one child is viewed by care providers as "special," he or she is more likely to be singled out for treatment that has the effect of removing the child from the peer group. The inclusion of several children with varying types or levels of delay or disability normalizes the experience for care providers and makes exclusion almost impossible.

Play Materials and Activities

Infants and toddlers appreciate both variety and predictability. Thus, play activities in a child care environment afford the greatest opportunities for learning when the two are mixed: old favorite toys and activities given a new twist through a teacher's imagination or the unique combination of materials to stimulate creative play. In inclusive care environments, toys must also be selected for their adaptability to a wide range of play behaviors. Trucks can be used in sensory play (the feel of the rolling wheels on the child's skin), art (making wheel prints), or hide and seek (partially wrapping the truck in a scarf for easy discovery) as well as functionally. Toys that have only one use are less appropriate in inclusive care.

Organizing activities for inclusion also means giving consideration to children's positioning during play. If a child with disabilities needs to spend time resting on her stomach on a foam wedge, then several other foam wedges should be placed around the teacher who is

leading storytime, for use by the rest of the participating children. Critical to successful inclusion is the active involvement of adults with the children during play (Mahoney & Wheeden, 1999). Teachers serve as motivators, as models, and as playmates. Children with special needs, who often require a higher level of stimulation to become involved themselves, are even more dependent on adult participation than are typical children. It is never enough for care providers to watch and supervise; successful infant-toddler teaching means active participation and enthusiastic involvement.

Teaching Approaches

In general, all infants and toddlers prefer relatively unstructured play activities. Although these young children need a lot of adult support in their play, they typically do not respond well to extensive adult direction. Until close to age 3, children are not invested in final products, such as block towers, but want to be actively involved in the process, including both building and knocking down the blocks, over and over again. Teachers of infants and toddlers are most effective when they take advantage of the children's own interests and focus of attention, using opportunities provided by the children to elaborate, extend, and enhance learning. This technique has been labeled "responsive teaching" (O'Brien, 1997) and is based on what is known about effective parent–child interactions (e.g., Mahoney, 1988; Mahoney, Robinson, & Powell, 1992). Children with developmental delays and disabilities also learn through responsive teaching approaches but often need additional support from adults initially to become involved with toys or play activities (Bricker, 1998; Linder, 1993; Mahoney & Wheeden, 1999).

Because infants and toddlers are learning so much about everything and each activity of the day offers potential as a learning opportunity, effective infant-toddler teachers also encourage and foster effort and involvement rather than reward achievement. Emphasis on trying rather than succeeding, on the act of doing rather than the final result, is the appropriate focus for all infants and toddlers and allows for a very wide range of ability and disability within a group of children.

Effective teachers also make use of naturally occurring opportunities to foster social interaction among infants and toddlers (Odom & Brown, 1993). Even the most socially and communicatively skilled 1-year-old has a limited repertoire of social initiations and responses. When that 1-year-old is interacting with another child of similar skill, it is easy to understand why communication breaks down! Teachers can facilitate the beginnings of social play by interpreting the communicative attempts of one child to another ("Jamie wants to touch that"), by helping children initiate social exchanges ("Give the little block to Dora"), and by pointing out areas of commonality between children ("Darcie and Jed both have blue sandals"). These interventions are appropriate for all infants and toddlers and can be particularly effective in promoting the inclusion of children with disabilities. In addition, communication skills are fostered in inclusive care by the everyday use of basic sign language, along with spoken words, for routine activities and requests. Children begin to recognize and use simple signs by 9 months of age, and sign language provides a useful bridge to communication for children with speech and language delays.

Staffing

Provision of individualized, inclusive care requires that there be enough adults available to meet the needs of every child. Regulatory and accrediting bodies typically describe child care center staff needs in terms of ratios, or the number of children per adult in the environment. Although ratios are important, it is also necessary in designing inclusive care to consider the *minimum* number of adults present. When fewer than three adults are available to manage the needs of a group of infants or toddlers of any size, quality will suffer. Individual, one-to-one care—in feeding for infants, in diaper changing, in providing kisses and care for a scraped finger—is frequently needed in infant-toddler care environments. If there is only one adult, then the other children are left unsupervised during this time. If two adults are present, then the second adult becomes responsible for the entire remaining group of children—some of whom may need to be fed or diapered and all of whom require supervision and adult involvement. When three adults are present, that individual care can be provided while there are still two care providers available to meet the needs of the rest of the group. Thus, a staff size of three teachers for a group care situation is the minimum, especially when children with special needs are included in a group. In home-based care, where there typically is one care provider, it is important to keep the group size small and have backup support available when needed.

A second consideration with regard to staffing is the organization of teacher responsibilities. When children with special needs are included in a child care program, some centers add a staff person who is responsible for that child's care. The additional staff member may be a paraprofessional or a certified special educator (Bruder & Staff, 1998). In these cases, the added staff person usually shadows the child with developmental delay or disability, meeting that child's individual needs on a one-to-one basis. Given the standard that inclusion requires full participation of all children in all activities, this type of staff arrangement does not truly meet the definition of inclusion. A more effective alternative is to add the staff member but divide the responsibilities for caring for the child with special needs among all program staff, just as the care for typical children is divided. This way, each teacher assumes responsibility for including all children in whatever activities he or she is leading, but the addition of a teacher allows more time for meeting individual needs, thus benefiting all children. When each teacher has a clearly defined responsibility at all times and teachers alternate among the different tasks of care (e.g., feeding, diapering, organizing play in an infant care center) throughout the day, the process of inclusion for children with disabilities becomes a natural part of every staff member's duties. The child is not isolated by having an adult always hovering nearby but is supported and cared for by all of the teachers.

Training

In the United States, most child care workers have minimal training in child development or early childhood education and no training or experience in working with children who have developmental delays or disabilities (Wolery et al., 1994). This situation is not likely to change in the early years of the 21st century. Thus, if inclusion is to become a standard in the field as well as an ideal standard of practice, then in-service training of child care staff will be the primary way that care providers learn to provide quality care for all children. In this regard, it is important to remember that most parents of children with disabilitites have no formal knowledge of special education. Parents who have never encountered disability become extremely competent caregivers and teachers when the occasion arises. Child care providers are in a similar situation and can be effective teachers of children with special needs, given appropriate sup-

port and training (Jones & Meisels, 1987; Kontos, 1988; Wesley, 1994).

Often, the best trainers of teachers are the child's parents, who have learned to respond to their child's needs and who are the best and most effective advocates for their child and themselves. Arranging opportunities for teachers to learn about children directly from their parents—at individualized family service plan (IFSP) meetings, informally in the child's classroom, through daily conversations and telephone calls, and in specially planned in-service training sessions—is probably the best method of training teachers. Parents can communicate the important details about their child that special service providers often overlook but that make so much difference in daily care. Without even trying, parents can also provide encouragement to teachers who are fearful of handling a child whom they perceive as fragile; when teachers see that parents are comfortable with the child in a variety of positions, they become more confident themselves. Because parents and teachers work so closely together in providing care for the child, these training sessions also promote communication that will enhance the child's care in the long run.

Special service providers also play a role in training child care workers to provide special care. Often, a special service provider can help parents with their training session or may provide follow-up training that emphasizes the developmental needs or health care practices that are appropriate for an individual child. The important point is that training for care providers is directed toward helping them address the needs of *this individual child.* Training is not geared toward making the care provider into a special educator or occupational therapist's assistant. Most experienced child care providers, even without formal training or degrees in early childhood education, are knowledgeable about children and the environments in which children learn. Special service providers can build on this knowledge to help child care staff make changes in the environment and their teaching practices to meet the individual needs of all children, including those who have delays or disabilities. Just as parents are not expected to know everything there is to know about child development, teachers in child care environments do not need to become experts in all aspects of disability to provide quality inclusive care. What they do need is a willingness to learn, a commitment to the well-being of all of the children in their care, and the support and consultation of parents and professionals.

Collaboration

When children with disabilities are included in child care environments, the care providers automatically become part of the child and family intervention team. This means that the child care environment becomes a focus for collaboration with parents and special service providers on behalf of the child (Hanson & Widerstrom, 1993). Typically, ongoing evaluation of developmental progress is a part of an inclusive program and will be supplemented by more extensive assessments carried out by special service providers. Sharing of these evaluations on a regular basis leads to more effective care and intervention.

Open and frequent communication between the child care environment and parents is of the utmost importance (Bennett, DeLuca, & Bruns, 1997). Parents who visit frequently and participate actively in their child's care environment as well as at home will provide valuable information and support to child care staff. In turn, child care staff have the responsibility to provide support and information to all parents, even those who are not so fully or willingly involved.

Collaboration with special service providers is a new experience for many child care centers. Child care has long been the bottom rung in the ladder of child and family services. Its care providers often are not professionally trained, and even if they are, their considerable skills—their knowledge about child development, the organization of learning environments, and the presentation of activities that engage children—typically are not recognized by specialists. Thus, becoming a full member of an intervention team requires advocacy and self-promotion on the part of the child care staff. The goal in an inclusive child care program is for all teachers to use intervention approaches with all of the children all of the time. For this to happen, special service providers must be willing to share the information that they have gained through long years of higher education. If service providers come to the child care environment, interact only with their client child, and communicate only by writing a few brief sentences in a log or on a report form, then they are not participating as members of a team. If teachers are content to let the service providers "do their thing" without interference or questions, then they are not participating as members of a team. The two sets of service providers must be willing to communicate with and teach the other and must allow ample time for this to occur if true collaboration is to be achieved (Peck, Furman, & Helmstetter, 1993).

CURRENT STATUS

Despite our knowledge about what is needed for successful inclusive care and our beliefs in the importance of inclusion for children and their families, most child care in the United States at the beginning of the 21st century is not fully inclusive. Child care program directors typically report a willingness to include children with chronic illness (asthma, epilepsy, diabetes), speech-language delays, and minor sensory impairments but not children with more severe physical or sensory impairments, autism, or mental retardation (Crowley, 1990). Few data are available on the proportion of child care home providers who are willing to take responsibility for the care of children with special needs; however, from the results of Booth and Kelly (1998), it seems that many parents rely on relatives for home-based care for their children with disabilities. Although there has been an increase in the number of child care environments that are enrolling children with disabilities, the children included typically are *not* those with multiple disabilities or impairments of motor or sensory development. Furthermore, in many areas, special services for infants and toddlers are still provided primarily in children's homes, even when children receive out-of-home care (Cavallaro et al., 1998).

In this section, the barriers and difficulties that prevent full inclusion of infants and toddlers in child care are described. In addition, a brief survey of research into and clinical experience with inclusive care, its outcomes for children and families, and its impact on programs are presented to identify how some of the existing barriers to inclusion may be overcome.

Concerns About Inclusion

Issues related to the enrollment of children with disabilities or developmental delays in community-based child care centers have been raised by parents of children with special needs, parents of typically developing children, teachers, program directors, and special service providers. Each of these groups has a different perspective on inclusion, and each has expressed concerns related to that perspective.

Concerns of Parents of Children with Disabilities Although many parents of children who have developmental

delays or disabilities express positive attitudes about inclusive child care programs, others express fears regarding such placements (Bailey & Winton, 1987; Guralnick, 1994). Of primary concern to many parents are the qualifications of the care providers and their child's health and safety (Bricker, 1995; Guralnick, 1994). Quality of care providers and health and safety issues top the list of factors that *all* parents cite as important to them in choosing child care (Pungello & Kurtz-Costes, 1999); in this regard, parents of children with special needs are no different. If the child has special health care needs or has a disability that makes the child susceptible to frequent illness, however, issues regarding health and safety may be of particular concern. In addition, parents report worries that their child may be perceived as different by the other children and therefore not be accepted as a friend and social partner (Guralnick, 1994; Guralnick, Connor, & Hammond, 1995). Finally, parents express concern as to whether their child will receive enough help and teacher attention in a group of largely typically developing children (Guralnick, 1994).

Concerns of Parents of Typical Children When their child care provider proposes to accept a child with special needs or when making choices about care for their own child, parents of typically developing children also express concerns regarding inclusive care. Parents worry that the needs of children with disabilities will be so great that the amount of teacher attention that their own child receives will be diminished (Guralnick, 1994). Some parents express concern that too much emphasis will be placed on health care, with a concomitant reduction in the quality or level of stimulation and learning activities available. Furthermore, there are parents who fear negative consequences for their own child—a concern that the disability of the included child may somehow be "catching" or lead to an unwelcome change in their own child's behavior.

Concerns of Care Providers Because of their lack of training or experience in caring for children with special needs, many child care workers express fear or trepidation about their own ability to care for children who have disabilities or need special health care (Dinnebeil, McInerney, Fox, & Juchartz-Pendry, 1998; Kontos, 1988). Of particular concern is whether they will be able to find time to provide for the included child's special needs as well as all of the other children's needs. Others admit to feeling uncomfortable in talking with and building a relationship with parents of the child who has a disability (Dinnebeil et al., 1998). The teachers may feel pity for the parents and child and be uncertain about how to communicate without conveying this emotion. Many teachers and care providers are concerned about handling challenging behavior of children with special needs and creating activities to teach these children (Dinnebeil et al., 1998).

Some child care providers are uncomfortable with opening their classroom or home to special service providers. Teachers typically have considerable authority within their own classrooms, and child care home providers may have chosen the profession to be independent and in charge. Thus, care providers may be unwilling to have "outsiders" come into their environment and possibly want to make changes. Teachers and care providers who have had experience with special service providers may be aware of the negative attitudes about child care held by many specialists. In general, the skills and knowledge of early childhood educators, including degreed teachers and paraprofessionals, with regard to the management of safe and healthy learning environments are not recognized by specialists. The perception of not being treated as an equal may lead some child care workers to resist the collaborative demands of inclusion.

Concerns of Program Directors Those who administer child care centers express concerns at the regulatory and financial level. Many directors cite difficulties with meeting licensing requirements for inclusive care without incurring such expenses as to make provision of care financially impossible. Of primary concern are staffing issues (Chang & Teramoto, 1987; Crowley, 1990). In addition, many directors believe that extensive remodeling and physical changes need to be made to make classrooms accessible for all children (Crowley, 1990).

Concerns of Special Service Providers Special service providers have invested in years of schooling to gain skills and credentials in their fields. When asked to provide services in an inclusive child care environment, they often express dissatisfaction with "giving away" their hard-won knowledge and express fears about whether the typical child care worker is capable of implementing intervention approaches (Kontos, 1988). Also, the demands that inclusive care places on special service providers to communicate with care providers from a wide range of educational backgrounds and with varying experience can be daunting (Kontos, 1988). In addition, specialists who are accustomed to having children brought to them by parents may find that inclusion requires them to travel to a number of child care centers each day. These logistical issues raise concerns about time management and uncertainty regarding liability, insurance, and reimbursement.

Furthermore, most specialists who work in early intervention have been trained in clinic-based models of service delivery (Bricker & LaCroix, 1996). Many of the intervention approaches that specialists learned during their clinic-based training may be inappropriate for use in the context of child care. As true inclusion requires that services be delivered within the natural classroom environment and not in a "pull-out" session, therapists must evaluate their interventions and adapt them for wider use. Some specialists may be unpleasantly surprised to find that child care staff do not see the utility of intervention approaches that do not address functional skills that the child can use in the child care environment. These differences in values and perceptions can add to the communication difficulties among members of the child's intervention team.

Outcomes of Inclusion

Relatively little research has been conducted to describe the experiences that children have in inclusive care environments or the outcomes for all children (Kontos, Moore, & Giorgetti, 1998). What research has been done has primarily involved preschool-age children, not infants and toddlers, and has focused to a great extent on child development outcomes, not on changes in the attitudes, perceptions, or behavior of care providers or specialists. Most of the reports that are available have identified positive effects of inclusion, but the sparse research makes it difficult to draw firm conclusions. The following sections summarize what is reported in the research literature and what has been observed in the author's experience with inclusive care environments (see also Chapter 1).

Gains for Children Analyses of the developmental progress of children with special needs who attend inclusive child care environments have found gains in cognitive, language, and motor domains that match those of children in specialized programs (e.g., Bruder & Staff, 1998; Buysse & Bailey, 1993; Lamorey & Bricker, 1993). In addition, inclusion seems to promote social interactions beyond what would be expected

of children who receive services in special classrooms or in a home or clinic environment (Guralnick et al., 1995). Of importance to many parents of children with disabilities is that children in inclusive environments show increases in alertness and involvement when there are typically developing peers and a range of play and learning activities available to them (Kontos, 1988). Most of these studies have observed children of preschool age (3 years) or older, not infants and toddlers. Nevertheless, they suggest a pattern of increased involvement leading to learning and skill building at a rate at least equal to that of children in special classrooms.

For typically developing children, the learning environment of an inclusive classroom also seems to be equal to that of other child care environments (Odom, DeKlyen, & Jenkins, 1984). The few studies of changes in children's attitudes have found preschool and kindergarten children with experience in inclusive classrooms to have more positive attitudes about individuals with disabilities than children without such experience (Diamond, Hestenes, Carpenter, & Innes, 1997; Favazza & Odom, 1997; Okagaki, Diamond, Kontos, & Hestenes, 1998; see also Chapter 7).

Perceptions of Parents of Children with Disabilities Once they have had experience with inclusion, parents of children with special needs tend to support the participation of their child in an environment with typical children, believing that it prepares the child for the "real world" (Bailey & Winton, 1987; Guralnick, 1994; see also Chapter 6). Parents report that their children develop friendships, often with children who are typically developing (Buysse, 1993; Guralnick et al., 1995), and that they gain an ability to play, share toys, and cooperate with others (Bennett et al., 1997; Guralnick et al., 1995). In addition, parents of children with special needs often comment on what their child has learned by watching and imitating other children (Bennett et al., 1997; Guralnick, 1994). Some parents are also able to develop close relationships with their child's teachers in an inclusive care environment and use them as a major source of support for parenting and child rearing (Bennett et al., 1997), whereas others find the team approach to early intervention confusing (Wesley, Buysse, & Tyndall, 1997).

Perceptions of Parents of Typically Developing Children   Parents of typically developing children who have had experience with inclusive care also report that their own children gain from the exposure to children with special needs. Frequently, parents mention the gains in sensitivity to others and acceptance of differences that they observe in their children (Guralnick, 1994; Peck, Carlson, & Helmstetter, 1992). In addition, parents see clearly that their children do not experience any negative effects in terms of their learning and development when children with disabilities are cared for in the same child care environment (Odom et al., 1984; see also Chapter 5).

Perceptions of Care Providers   Caregivers with experience in working with children who have special needs typically feel confident and capable in assuming this responsibility, whereas those with no experience do not (Dinnebeil et al., 1998). Most teachers also believe that children in inclusive environments become more accepting of differences and that children with special needs benefit from their exposure to other children (Lieber et al., 1998). Teachers also report positive experiences with parents and use parents as resources to help in caring for children with special needs in their classroom (Bennett et al., 1997). Teachers who have received some training in working with children who have disabilities are more positive about inclusion than those who have not (Bennett et al., 1997). Some

teachers in inclusive care environments find that they gain in teaching skills because they have opportunities to learn about a variety of different teaching approaches through their contacts with special service providers (Kontos, 1988). One possible result of this perception of increased skill may be a more professional outlook and a greater emphasis on team approaches to child care and intervention. Such a change in attitude would be likely to result in higher job satisfaction and lower turnover of child care workers, although such programmatic effects of inclusion have not been studied directly. Unfortunately, experience with inclusion does not relieve teachers of their concerns about time pressures and how to make time to provide adequately for all children's needs (Bennett et al., 1997). This concern is a major one to teachers, and the realities of child care make it a difficult one to address.

Perceptions of Program Directors   For administrators, there are several potential benefits to inclusive care, including increased involvement of families in child care, opportunities for teachers to gain skill and competence through in-service training related to provision of care for children with special needs, and greater overall emphasis on training and professionalism. None of these outcomes of inclusion has been examined systematically. Financial concerns are always at the top of the list of administrators' worries in child care. When children with special needs are enrolled, program directors often become aware of new sources of support for their care, thus expanding the financial base of the program. In general, child care programs that offer inclusive care are more involved with the community network of child and family services and therefore have more connections with other agencies and service providers.

Perceptions of Special Service Providers   Specialists who deliver services within inclusive child care programs are challenged to change their view of development from a narrow focus that fits their specialty to an understanding of the whole child and how the therapeutic techniques they use fit into the daily life of the child, the child care center, and the child's family. Through work in inclusive environments, special service providers have opportunities to gain skill in consulting and collaboration through their work with child care staff (Gallagher, 1997). For specialists, inclusive care does not come without some loss, however. Many special service providers have difficulty giving up their hard-won role as "expert" in exchange for a consultant role, and others cite reduced personal involvement with families as a disadvantage from their viewpoint (Gallagher, 1997; Wesley et al., 1997). As with teachers in child care classrooms, the press of time continues to be a problem, and it is exacerbated by the logistical difficulties of providing services in a large number of different locations.

Summary

The research that has been done on the difficulties and benefits of inclusive child care is limited in scope. Little research addresses issues directly related to infant-toddler care, and few investigators have examined program outcomes, focusing instead on child developmental progress. There are substantial perceived barriers to inclusion in child care, particularly with regard to staff time and training, but what research exists suggests strongly that inclusion also offers benefits to children, families, child care workers and administrators, and special service providers.

AGENDA FOR CHANGE

During the last 30 years of the 20th century, concepts of inclusion of all people in all aspects of society moved from hopes and dreams of a few to recommended practice throughout all of education and community living. The task of the early years of the 21st century is to continue this progress by making inclusion a reality at all age levels, including the environments that serve the youngest children.

Historical Background of Child Care and Early Intervention Services

Child care services for working parents and early intervention services for children with disabilities historically have been completely separate service systems. Traditionally, child care was considered to be the primary task of mothers who were expected to stay at home. If they held out-of-home jobs, mothers found substitutes to provide care, usually within their own family. Most child care was informal and family based until social change and economic demands beginning in the 1980s led large numbers of women—both mothers and the female relatives who formerly had helped provide substitute care—to enter the work force. For the most part, however, child care continues to be a private matter, funded by fees paid by parents, with relatively little regulation by the public sector.

The potential for early education to help children from environments that place them at risk was recognized in the mid-1960s with the creation of Head Start as part of the War on Poverty. Although not intended to be child care, Head Start is widely viewed by the public as filling a need for care for children whose parents are poor. Several comprehensive intervention programs have also been implemented for infants and toddlers, and their evaluations show generally positive effects on children's cognitive development (e.g., Campbell & Ramey, 1994; Gross, 1993). Early educational interventions for 3- and 4-year-olds are considered to be an effective way of helping children whose early experiences place them in jeopardy for being "ready to learn" at school entry and have been implemented by many private and public agencies around the United States, including an increasing number of school districts. In the 1990s, an emphasis on development in the first 3 years of life led to an expansion of programs for infants and toddlers and their families, including Early Head Start. Since the 1970s, Head Start has required that 10% of the children enrolled be identified as having developmental delays or disabilities, thus ensuring inclusion. However, the ideals of publicly funded programs such as Head Start have not been applied to the provision of quality care and learning opportunities for *all* children, including those whose parents are not poor.

Unlike parents seeking child care, who often express feelings of guilt or dismay about placing their child in someone else's care, parents of children with disabilities have actively and publicly advocated for the provision of quality services for their children. Vocal and politically effective parents have joined with professionals to fight for the legally mandated provision of school-based services for preschool-age children (Safford & Safford, 1996). Parents have been active advocates for the expansion of services to infants and toddlers with special needs as well. As a result, by the mid-1990s, all U.S. states had implemented a system of early intervention for infants and toddlers with identified disabilities, and these services were required to be provided at no cost to parents.

Although the histories of these three types of services—child care, early childhood education, and early intervention for children with disabilities—are only briefly sketched here, it is evident that the three systems are perceived very differently by society. Child care is considered to be the responsibility of children's own parents; parents cannot rely on public funding or legislation to assist them in their search for affordable and high-quality care. The pervasive view remains that mothers would do well to stay at home with their young children. Early childhood education for children whose families are poor has wide public support and public funding, and its contributions to the well-being of children are extensively reported. The message seems to be that mothers who live in poverty should *not* stay home with their young children. Early intervention services for children with special needs are considered a necessity and are legally guaranteed. Services are mandated to be provided in the child's natural environment, which is left open for definition by the child's family. Because the same social trends and financial pressures affect families whose children have disabilities as those who have typically developing children, child care environments will increasingly be *the* natural environment for infants and toddlers with disabilities (Fewell, 1993). The task that early educators face is how to merge all three of these systems into one effective set of services that affords quality care and educational benefits to *all* children, from rich to poor, at all levels of ability, with all types of individual health care needs.

Questions for Research

As mentioned previously, very little research has been conducted on early inclusive care environments. Much of what we know about effective inclusion comes from clinical experience of individuals who have organized and operated inclusive care programs for infants, toddlers, and preschool-age children. (Descriptions of some of these programs can be found in Bagnato, Kontos, & Neisworth, 1987; Bruder, Deiner, & Sachs, 1990; Fewell, 1993; and O'Brien, 1997.) As a result, many important questions remain unanswered.

What characteristics of inclusive care programs for infants and toddlers are most beneficial to which children? Basic questions about aspects of inclusive care environments that enhance the development of children with special needs have not been addressed in the research literature. We do not know whether factors that promote the development of typically developing children in infant-toddler child care environments (sensitive caregiving, child-focused attitudes of care providers, much language stimulation [NICHD Early Child Care Research Network, 1996]) are equally important for children with special needs. Furthermore, we do not know whether level of impairment or nature of disability interacts with quality indicators to produce different outcomes for different children. We also do not fully understand the role of family factors, including ethnic and cultural differences, in affecting children's development in inclusive care environments (see Chapter 18).

Is the health of children with disabilities affected by experience in child care environments? Exposure to more children increases illness rates of infants and toddlers in child care (NICHD Early Child Care Research Network, 1998b). When children's health is already compromised because of neonatal illness or disability, increased illness rates could be detrimental. However, Gross (1993) reported no differences in the frequency of serious health conditions for premature infants who attended high-quality child care programs from 12 to 36 months of age as compared with a similar group of infants who were cared for at home. Furthermore, more frequent illness among typically developing children in child care in the first 2 years seems to be offset to some degree by a reduction in the rate and severity of illness in the third year (NICHD Early Child Care Research Network, 1998b) and fewer allergies in later life (Kramer, Heinrich, & Wjst, 1999). It is therefore possible that if early illness is not debilitating, it may have advantages in promoting health over time. The health risks and potential benefits for children in inclusive care envi-

ronments need to be evaluated closely for appropriate recommendations for individual children to be made.

Does inclusion in the infant-toddler period help children with disabilities adapt to future inclusive placements? Because the disabilities and developmental delays of infants and toddlers often are less noticeable in the early years than they will become later and because of the developmental limitations and needs for individual care of *all* infants and toddlers, inclusion is relatively easy to implement at this stage. It also may be that experience in an inclusive care environment before age 3 offers children with special needs benefits in the form of skills needed to adapt to preschool environments. In infant-toddler care, children learn the rudiments of getting along with others, following daily care routines, and participating in group play. If some of these skills are transferred to the preschool environment, then children with this early experience may be better prepared to participate fully in inclusive care environments as preschoolers. Of particular interest is whether early experience in inclusive infant-toddler care facilitates social interaction among children with and without disabilities at a later point in time.

Is full-day care in a high-quality inclusive program equal to, better than, or less beneficial than combining specialized intervention with part-day care? Many U.S. children of toddler and preschool age attend a part-day intervention program in a specialized environment and spend the remainder of the day in a home- or center-based child care environment. In these cases, the child care environments are usually not focused on caring for children with special needs and do not implement intervention practices (Dinnebeil et al., 1998). When early intervention is delivered in a full-day inclusive child care environment, children are expected to receive services from therapists in the care environment and receive intervention provided by child care providers all day long. In theory, this should be a more effective service delivery model. However, no studies have yet been conducted to compare these two approaches.

Does training and collaboration related to inclusion of children with disabilities enhance the professionalism and competence of child care workers? Staff who work in child care programs that have included children with special needs and child care home providers who have participated in inclusion training models have reported that they have gained teaching skill through their exposure to special service providers (Kontos, 1988). However, there have been few observational studies to quantify such a change in performance by child care staff, and no investigators have measured other aspects of professionalism. Furthermore, it is often suggested that attitudes toward individuals with disabilities are affected by experience with such individuals, but no studies have been conducted to examine the role that caring for children with special needs plays in attitude change.

What are the benefits of quality inclusive child care to families? For families of children with special needs, early intervention services are intended to provide a range of services, including resource supports, social supports, and information, as well as child-centered services (Guralnick, 1997, 2000). For families of typically developing children, child care that is of high quality also provides a number of supports: It is a source of information about child rearing and child health, encourages a widening of the social network by bringing young parents in contact with each other, and relieves stress associated with work–family conflict. It would be useful to investigate the role of child care in families when a child has a disability to determine whether it serves a supportive function similar to or different from that of early

intervention services. The extent to which cultural background affects families' involvement with the child care environment and the nature of support parents receive from inclusive care staff is another important topic for investigation.

Recommendations for Policy Changes

The inclusion of infants and toddlers with special needs into child care programs that serve typically developing children and merging these services with early educational intervention programs has potential advantages to all children and families. In addition, inclusion itself and increased collaboration across service systems offer opportunities for professional development and personal growth to child care program staff and specialists alike. For these benefits to be realized, however, policies regarding child care and early intervention services will need to be examined and revised. Some of the policy issues that are of immediate importance are described in this section.

Provide Additional Resources for Child Care   Quality child care cannot be achieved without additional funding from a source other than young children's parents. The "true cost" of child care is much higher than the fees that parents now pay (Culkin, Helburn, & Morris, 1990). A cost is also being paid by child care workers who earn minimum wage—not enough to support themselves, much less a family. A long-term cost is also being paid by society, in that the children who attend low-quality child care centers are negatively affected across all developmental domains. Young parents, at the start of their careers, cannot afford to pay for the high-quality care that children deserve without support from the rest of society.

Child and family services provide benefits to all segments of the community. Funding for child care that would serve all children, including children with special needs, should therefore come from all segments of the community. Partnerships among governmental, business, educational, medical, child care, and early intervention agencies need to be formed and strengthened with a focus on ensuring that every child receives quality education and care from birth onward.

Make Child Care Environments Accountable for Quality Funding alone will not ensure quality care, but funding will permit the implementation of higher standards of quality within child care programs and increased requirements for education, training, and job performance of teachers. These standards should be expanded to include requirements for care for children with special needs and be applied to all child care environments. Opponents of tighter regulation of child care often cite the increased costs that would result (Scarr, 1998). If adequate funding were available, the child care standards published by professional organizations (American Public Health Association and American Academy of Pediatrics, 1992; National Association for the Education of Young Children, 1991) could be widely applied, to the benefit of all children and families.

Modify Training Programs and Accreditation Standards for Early Childhood Personnel A commitment to inclusion requires that all preservice and in-service training programs in early childhood education and early childhood special education be merged. All individuals who are trained to work with young children must be knowledgeable about the full range of abilities and needs that they may encounter and also about family issues (Miller & Stayton, 1998). In most states, reimbursable early intervention services can be delivered only by certified special educators or other specialists, yet essentially all child care is provided by paraprofessionals and early childhood educators. Children may spend 8 or 10

hours a day in the care of these individuals. True inclusion requires that child care workers be recognized as the primary teachers, next to parents, of young children. When child care providers receive specialized training or work in collaboration with specialists, they should be able to be certified to deliver special instruction to make inclusive care a reality for more children with special needs and their families. Such certification would be an incentive to child care workers to obtain additional training and participate more actively as members of early intervention teams.

Recognize Quality Inclusive Child Care as a Family-Focused Intervention Service As of 2000, laws covering services for infants, toddlers, and preschool-age children with disabilities do not mention childcare, even though child care is reported as a need by many parents of children with special needs (Bailey, Blasco, & Simeonsson, 1992). School districts typically organize part-day services for preschool-age children, and in many locations, infant-toddler services are individually scheduled with families by therapists. When parents work, they are on their own to find care for the rest of the child's day. Many parents must work out shared care arrangements between spouses, thereby requiring them to work part time or at odd hours (Landis, 1992). Others are able to place children in child care centers or family child care homes (Kontos, 1988), but often these care environments do not receive support and consultation to provide for children's special needs (Cavallaro et al., 1998). In these cases, the effects of the relatively brief early intervention services that children receive are likely to be minimal compared with the effects of spending many hours in a care environment that is not truly inclusive. Thus, a recognition of the reality of the child care needs of most families would result in enhancement of early intervention's effectiveness as well as placing increased emphasis on family support services.

Provide Support for Training, Consultation, and Collaboration Early intervention law requires collaboration, but funding streams often do not support collaboration time. Effective service delivery requires consultation and training of all care providers, but there is often no provision for reimbursement of professionals for training time, and child care centers cannot afford to pay workers to attend extra training sessions. Professionals who provide family service coordination frequently do so without funding. A great deal of volunteer time now goes into the delivery of early intervention services. These functions must be recognized and supported as integral parts of the service system.

The Future of Infant-Toddler Child Care as a Natural Environment for All Children

Child care environments are well established as natural environments for children. Fully 68% of the more than 1,200 children participating in the NICHD Study of Early Child Care were spending more than 20 hours a week in a child care environment by 24 months of age (NICHD Early Child Care Research Network, 2000a). Children with disabilities use child care at a much lower rate, however (Booth & Kelly, 1998).

Despite the widespread dependence on child care by young families, society continues to hold a negative view of other-than-mother care. This view is not supported by research with typically developing children, showing that they thrive in care that is of high quality (NICHD Early Child Care Research Network, 1997, 1998a, 2000b). At least in part because of this inaccurate and negative view of child care, society is missing an opportunity to build a system of

quality care and early intervention that would provide widespread benefits to children and families (Kagan & Cohen, 1997). Most parents of young children go to their child's care environment twice a day. This frequent presence of parents with their children provides an unparalleled opportunity to use child care as an environment for the delivery of comprehensive child and family services. Child care centers, in collaboration with other community agencies, could serve as the environment for well-child health care and immunizations, adult literacy programs, prenatal classes, parenting support and education, and family counseling. Of particular interest in this chapter is the potential for inclusion in child care programming of intervention approaches for children with special needs and their families and the use of child care environments as the primary focus for child and family service coordination, information, and support when children have disabilities. Because most child care programs serve children from infancy to school age, the use of child care environments for early intervention service delivery could also promote increased coordination of services from Part C to Part B (Guralnick, 2000).

Employers have begun to recognize the importance of stable and positive families to the provision of a consistent and reliable work force (Chung, 1998; Hall & Parker, 1993). Employers, too, could collaborate with child care centers to offer programs related to reducing work–family conflict and enhancing parenting skills. In turn, child care professionals could help employers design workplace policies that promote the dual roles of worker and parent.

Finally, a collaboration between child care and education agencies, especially the public schools, is long overdue (Zigler & Gilman, 1993). After being required to provide services to 3- and 4-

year-olds with special needs, many school systems have begun to support classrooms for 4-year-olds who are at risk for poor school performance. In general, however, the schools have developed their own programs for both children with special needs and those at risk with little input from the early child care professionals in their communities.

CONCLUSION

Childhood is a continuum. Children are not "ready to learn" at age 6 because of a year spent in a school-based preschool at age 4. Instead, the child's learning and motivation to learn begin at (or before) birth. Coordination of curriculum approaches and models, collaboration across different levels of early education, and communication among school and child care staff would work to the benefit of children, families, the schools, and the community.

REFERENCES

Adelson, J. (1997). What we know about day care. *Commentary, 104*, 52.

American Public Health Association and American Academy of Pediatrics. (1992). *Caring for our children—National health and safety performance standards: Guidelines for out-of-home child care programs.* Washington, DC, and Elk Grove Village, IL: Author.

Bagnato, S.J., Kontos, S., & Neisworth, J.T. (1987). Integrated day care as special education: Profiles of programs and children. *Topics in Early Childhood Special Education, 7,* 28–47.

Bailey, D.B., Jr., Blasco, P.M., & Simeonsson, R.J. (1992). Needs expressed by mothers and fathers of young children with disabilities. *American Journal on Mental Retardation, 97,* 1–10.

Bailey, D.B., Jr., McWilliam, R.A., Buysse, V., & Wesley, P.W. (1998). Inclusion in the context of competing values in early childhood education. *Early Childhood Research Quarterly, 13,* 27–47.

Bailey, D.B., Jr. & Winton, P.J. (1987). Stability and change in parents' expectations about mainstreaming. *Topics in Early Childhood Special Education, 7,* 73–88.

Bailey, D.B., Jr., & Wolery, M. (1984). *Teaching infants and preschoolers with handicaps.* Westerville, OH: Glencoe/McGraw-Hill.

Bennett, T., DeLuca, D., & Bruns, D. (1997). Putting inclusion into practice: Perspectives of teachers and parents. *Exceptional Children, 64,* 115–131.

Blasco, P.M., Bailey, D.B., Jr., & Burchinal, M.R. (1993). Dimensions of mastery in same-age and mixed-age integrated classrooms. *Early Childhood Research Quarterly, 8,* 193–206.

Booth, C.L., & Kelly, J.F. (1998). Child-care characteristics of infants with and without special needs: Comparisons and concerns. *Early Childhood Research Quarterly, 13,* 603–621.

Bricker, D. (1995). The challenge of inclusion. *Journal of Early Intervention, 19*(3), 179–194.

Bricker, D. (1998). *An activity-based approach to early intervention* (2nd ed.). Baltimore: Paul H. Brookes Publishing Co.

Bricker, D., & LaCroix, B. (1996). Training practices. In D. Bricker & A. Widerstrom (Eds.), *Preparing personnel to work with infants and young children and their families: A team approach* (pp. 43–64). Baltimore: Paul H. Brookes Publishing Co.

Bronson, M.B., Hauser-Cram, P., & Warfield, M.E. (1997). Classrooms matter: Relations between the classroom environment and the social and mastery behavior of five-year-old children with disabilities. *Journal of Applied Developmental Psychology, 18,* 331–348.

Brownlee, S., & Miller, M. (1997). Five lies parents tell themselves about why they work. *U.S. News & World Report, 122,* 58–61.

Bruder, M.B., & Brand, M. (1995). A comparison of two types of early intervention environments serving toddler-age children with disabilities. *Infant-Toddler Intervention, 5,* 207–218.

Bruder, M.B., Deiner, P., & Sachs, S. (1990). Models of integration through early intervention/child care collaboration. *Zero to Three Bulletin, 10*(3), 14–17.

Bruder, M.B., & Staff, I. (1998). A comparison of the effects of type of classroom and service characteristics on toddlers with disabilities. *Topics in Early Childhood Special Education, 18,* 26–37.

Burchinal, M., Roberts, J.E., Nabors, L.A., & Bryant, D. (1996). Quality of center child care and infant cognitive and language development. *Child Development, 67,* 606–620.

Buysse, V. (1993). Friendships of preschoolers with disabilities in community-based child care settings. *Journal of Early Intervention, 17,* 380–395.

Buysse, V., & Bailey, D.B., Jr. (1993). Behavioral and developmental outcomes in young children with disabilities in integrated and segregated settings: A review of comparative studies. *Journal of Special Education, 26,* 434–461.

Campbell, F.A., & Ramey, C.T. (1994). Effects of early intervention on intellectual and academic achievement: A follow-up study of children from low-income families. *Child Development, 65,* 684–698.

Carnegie Corporation of New York. (1996). *Years of promise: A comprehensive strategy for America's children.* New York: Author.

Cavallaro, C.C., Ballard-Rosa, M., & Lynch, E.W. (1998). A preliminary study of inclusive special education services for infants, toddlers, and preschool-age children in California. *Topics in Early Childhood Special Education, 18*(3), 169–182.

Chang, A., & Teramoto, R. (1987). Children with special needs in private day care centers. *Child & Youth Care Quarterly, 16,* 60–67.

Chung, B.G. (1998). Accounting for changing times: Aligning human resource practices to employees' non-work lives. *Marriage and Family Review, 28,* 143–152.

Cost, Quality, and Child Outcomes Study Team. (1995). *Cost, quality, and child outcomes in child care centers: Public report* (2nd ed.). Denver: University of Colorado at Denver, Economics Department.

Craig, S.E., & Haggart, A.G. (1994). Including all children: The ADA's challenge to early intervention. *Infants and Young Children, 7,* 15–19.

Crowley, A.A. (1990). Integrating handicapped and chronically ill children into day care centers. *Pediatric Nursing, 16,* 39–44.

Culkin, M.L., Helburn, S.W., & Morris, J.R. (1990). Current price versus full cost: An economic perspective. In B. Willer (Ed.), *Reaching the full cost of quality in early childhood programs* (pp. 9–26). Washington, DC: National Association for the Education of Young Children.

Diamond, K.E., Hestenes, L.L., Carpenter, E.S., & Innes, F.K. (1997). Relationships between enrollment in an inclusive class and preschool children's ideas about people with disabilities. *Topics in Early Childhood Special Education, 17,* 520–536.

Dinnebeil, L.A., McInerney, W., Fox, C., & Juchartz-Pendry, K. (1998). An analysis of the perceptions and characteristics of childcare personnel regarding inclusion of young children with special needs in community-based programs. *Topics in Early Childhood Special Education, 18,* 118–128.

Favazza, P.C., & Odom, S.L. (1997). Promoting positive attitudes of kindergarten-age children toward people with disabilities. *Exceptional Children, 63,* 405–418.

Fewell, R.R. (1993). Child care for children with special needs. *Pediatrics, 91,* 193–198.

Galinsky, E., Howes, C., Kontos, S., & Shinn, M. (1994). *The study of children in family child care and relative care: Highlights of findings.* New York: Families and Work Institute.

Gallagher, P.A. (1997). Teachers and inclusion: Perspectives on changing roles. *Topics in Early Childhood Special Education, 17,* 363–386.

Gross, R. (1993). Day care for the child born prematurely. *Pediatrics, 91,* 189–191.

Guralnick, M.J. (1994). Mothers' perceptions of the benefits and drawbacks of early childhood mainstreaming. *Journal of Early Intervention, 18,* 168–183.

Guralnick, M.J. (1997). Second-generation research in the field of early intervention. In M.J. Guralnick (Ed.), *The effectiveness of early intervention* (pp. 3–20). Baltimore: Paul H. Brookes Publishing Co.

Guralnick, M.J. (2000). The early intervention system and out-of-home child care. In D. Cryer & T. Harms (Eds.), *Infants and toddlers in out-of-home care* (pp. 207–234). Baltimore: Paul H. Brookes Publishing Co.

Guralnick, M.J., Connor, R.T., & Hammond, M. (1995). Parent perspectives of peer relations and friendships in integrated and specialized programs. *American Journal on Mental Retardation, 99,* 457–476.

Hall, D.T., & Parker, V.A. (1993). The role of workplace flexibility in managing diversity. *Organizational Dynamics, 22,* 5–18.

Hanson, M.J., & Widerstrom, A.H. (1993). Consultation and collaboration: Essentials of integration efforts for young children. In C.A. Peck, S.L. Odom, & D.D. Bricker (Eds.), *Integrating young children with disabilities into community-based programs: Ecological perspectives on research and implementation* (pp. 149–168). Baltimore: Paul H. Brookes Publishing Co.

Hauser-Cram, P., Bronson, M.B., & Upshur, C. (1993). The effects of the classroom environment on the social and mastery behavior of preschool children with disabilities. *Early Childhood Research Quarterly, 8,* 479–497.

Jones, S., & Meisels, S. (1987). Training family day care providers to work with special needs children. *Topics in Early Childhood Special Education, 7,* 1–12.

Kagan, S.L., & Cohen, N.E. (1997). *Not by chance: Creating an early care and education system for America's children.* New Haven, CT: Yale University Press, The Bush Center in Child Development and Social Policy.

Kontos, S. (1988). Family day care as an integrated early intervention setting. *Topics in Early Childhood Special Education, 8,* 1–14.

Kontos, S., Moore, D., & Giorgetti, K. (1998). The ecology of inclusion. *Topics in Early Childhood Special Education, 18,* 38–48.

Kramer, U., Heinrich, J., & Wjst, M. (1999). Age of entry to day nursery and allergy in later childhood. *Lancet, 353,* 450–454.

Lamorey, S., & Bricker, D. (1993). Integrated programs: Effects on young children and their parents. In C.A. Peck, S.L. Odom, & D.D. Bricker (Eds.), *Integrating young children with disabilities into community-based programs: Ecological perspectives on research and implementation* (pp. 249–270). Baltimore: Paul H. Brookes Publishing Co.

Landis, L.J. (1992). Marital, employment, and childcare status of mothers with infants and toddlers with disabilities. *Topics in Early Childhood Special Education, 12,* 496–507.

Lieber, J., Capell, K., Sandall, S., Wolfberg, P., Horn, E., & Beckman, P. (1998). Inclusive preschool programs: Teachers' beliefs and practices. *Early Childhood Research Quarterly, 13,* 87–106.

Linder, T.W. (1993). *Transdisciplinary play-based intervention: Guidelines for developing a meaningful curriculum for young children.* Baltimore: Paul H. Brookes Publishing Co.

Mahoney, G.J. (1988). Enhancing the developmental competence of handicapped infants. In K. Marfo (Ed.), *Parent–child interaction and developmental disabilities: Theory, research, and intervention* (pp. 203–219). Westport, CT: Praeger Publishers.

Mahoney, G.J., Robinson, C., & Powell, A. (1992). Focusing on parent–child interaction: The bridge to developmentally appropriate practices. *Topics in Early Childhood Special Education, 12,* 105–120.

Mahoney, G.J., & Wheeden, C.A. (1999). The effect of teacher style on interactive engagement of preschool-aged children with special learning needs. *Early Childhood Research Quarterly, 14,* 51–68.

Miller, P.S., & Stayton, V.D. (1998). Blended interdisciplinary teacher preparation in early education and intervention: A national study. *Topics in Early Childhood Special Education, 18,* 49–58.

National Association for the Education of Young Children. (1991). *Accreditation criteria and procedures of the National Academy of Early Childhood Programs.* Washington, DC: Author.

National Institute of Child Health and Human Development Early Child Care Research Network. (1994). Child care and child development: The NICHD Study of Early Child Care. In S.L. Friedman & H.C. Haywood (Eds.), *Developmental follow-up: Concepts, domains, methods* (pp. 377–396). San Diego: Academic Press.

National Institute of Child Health and Human Development Early Child Care Research Network. (1996). Characteristics of infant child care: Factors contributing to positive caregiving. *Early Childhood Research Quarterly, 11,* 269–306.

National Institute of Child Health and Human Development Early Child Care Research Network. (1997). Child care in the first year of life. *Merrill-Palmer Quarterly, 43,* 340–360.

National Institute of Child Health and Human Development Early Child Care Research Network. (1998a). Early child care and self-control, compliance, and problem behavior at 24 and 36 months. *Child Development, 69,* 1145–1170.

National Institute of Child Health and Human Development Early Child Care Research Network. (1998b, May). *In sickness and in health: Results from the NICHD Study of Early Child Care.* Paper presented at the SEED Conference, National Institutes of Health, Bethesda, MD.

National Institute of Child Health and Human Development Early Child Care Research Network. (1999). Child outcomes when child care center classes meet recommended standards for quality. *American Journal of Public Health, 89,* 1072–1077.

National Institute of Child Health and Human Development Early Child Care Research Network (2000a). Characteristics and quality of child care for toddlers and preschoolers. *Applied Developmental Science, 4,* 116–135.

National Institute of Child Health and Human Development Early Child Care Research Network. (2000b). The relation of child care to cognitive and language development. *Child Development, 71,* 960–980.

O'Brien, M. (1997). *Inclusive child care for infants and toddlers: Meeting individual and special needs.* Baltimore: Paul H. Brookes Publishing Co.

O'Brien, M., Peyton, V., Roy, C., Huston, A.C., & Hughes, K. (2000). *Mothers' employment preferences and actual employment: Effects on family well-being.* Unpublished manuscript, University of Kansas, Lawrence.

Odom, S.L., & Brown, W.H. (1993). Social interaction skill training for young children with disabilities in integrated settings. In C.A. Peck, S.L. Odom, & D.D. Bricker (Eds.), *Integrating young children with disabilities into community-based programs: Ecological perspectives on research and implementation* (pp. 39–64). Baltimore: Paul H. Brookes Publishing Co.

Odom, S.L., DeKlyen, M., & Jenkins, J.R. (1984). Integrating handicapped and nonhandicapped preschoolers: Developmental impact on the non-handicapped children. *Exceptional Children, 51,* 41–49.

Odom, S.L., & Diamond, K.E. (1998). Inclusion of young children with special needs in early childhood education: The research base. *Early Childhood Research Quarterly, 13,* 3–25.

Odom, S.L., Peck, C.A., Hanson, M., Beckman, P.J., Kaiser, A.P., Lieber, J., Brown, W.H., Horn, E.M., & Schwartz, I.S. (1996). Inclusion at the preschool level: An ecological systems analysis. *SRCD Social Policy Report, 10,* 18–30.

Okagaki, L., Diamond, K.E., Kontos, S.J., & Hestenes, L.L. (1998). Correlates of young children's interactions with classmates with disabilities. *Early Childhood Research Quarterly, 13,* 67–86.

Olsen, D. (1999). Should government stay out of child care? *USA Today, 127,* 10.

Peck, C.A., Carlson, P., & Helmstetter, E. (1992). Parent and teacher perceptions of outcomes for typically developing children enrolled in early childhood programs: A statewide survey. *Journal of Early Intervention, 16,* 53–63.

Peck, C.A., Furman, G.C., & Helmstetter, E. (1993). Integrated early childhood programs: Research on the implementation of change in organizational contexts. In C.A. Peck, S.L. Odom, & D.D. Bricker (Eds.), *Integrating young children with disabilities into community-based programs: Ecological perspectives on research and implementation* (pp. 187–205). Baltimore: Paul H. Brookes Publishing Co.

Pungello, E.P., & Kurtz-Costes, B. (1999). Why and how working women choose child care: A review with a focus on infancy. *Developmental Review, 19,* 31–96.

Rab, V.Y., & Wood, K.I. (1995). *Child care and the ADA: A handbook for inclusive programs.* Baltimore: Paul H. Brookes Publishing Co.

Roberts, J.E., Burchinal, M.R., & Bailey, D.B., Jr. (1994). Communication among preschoolers with and without disabilities in same-age and mixed-age classes. *American Journal on Mental Retardation, 99,* 231–249.

Safford, P.L., & Safford, E.J. (1996). *A history of childhood and disability.* New York: Teachers College Press.

Scarr, S. (1998). American child care today. *American Psychologist, 53,* 95–108.

Siegel, B. (1996). Is the emperor wearing clothes? Social policy and the empirical support for full inclusion of children with disabilities in the preschool and early elementary grades. *SRCD Social Policy Report, 10,* 2–17.

U.S. Department of Labor, Bureau of Labor Statistics. (1994). *1993 Handbook on women workers: Trends and issues.* Washington, DC: U.S. Government Printing Office.

Wesley, P.W. (1994). Providing on-site consultation to promote quality in integrated child care programs. *Journal of Early Intervention, 18,* 391–402.

Wesley, P.W., Buysse, V., & Tyndall, S. (1997). Family and professional perspectives on early intervention: An exploration using focus groups. *Topics in Early Childhood Special Education, 17,* 435–456.

Whitebook, M., Howes, C., & Phillips, D. (1990). *Who cares? Child care teachers and the quality of care in America* (Final report). National Child Care Staffing Study. Oakland, CA: Child Care Employee Project.

Wolery, M., Martin, C.G., Schroeder, C., Huffman, K., Venn, M.L., Holcombe, A., Brookfield, J., & Fleming, L.A. (1994). Employment of educators in preschool mainstreaming: A survey of general early educators. *Journal of Early Intervention, 18,* 64–77.

Zigler, E., & Gilman, E. (1993). Day care in America: What is needed? *Pediatrics, 91,* 175–178.

11

SAMUEL L. ODOM

DON BAILEY

Inclusive Preschool Programs

Classroom Ecology and Child Outcomes

Inclusive preschool classrooms are dynamic and complex environments. They consist of physical space and materials that teachers arrange in colorful, attractive, and stimulating ways; classmates who differ in appearance, developmental level, gender, and ethnicity; and adults who vary in number (during the day), responsibilities, and ways in which they communicate with children in the classroom. These features of the classroom create environments that affect young children's development and learning, and they constitute the *ecology* of the preschool classroom.

This chapter examines the ecological features of inclusive preschool environments for young children with and without disabilities and reports linkages between ecological features of the classroom and behavioral and developmental outcomes for children. First is a discussion of the meaning of classroom ecology and then a brief examination of the organizational and philosophical contexts within which inclusive preschool classrooms exist. Next, the features of high-quality early childhood education programs and the level of quality that seems to occur in inclusive environments for preschool-age children with disabilities are discussed. Research addressing the physical (e.g., classroom activities, community) and social (e.g., teacher behavior, social interaction) ecological features of inclusive preschools is reviewed. Elements of high-quality inclusive classroom environments are summarized, and barriers to implementing such high-quality environments are identified. Finally, future directions for research and practice are proposed.

ECOLOGY OF EARLY CHILDHOOD EDUCATION ENVIRONMENTS

Ecology, as applied to children and classrooms, is an elusive term that can apply to multiple aspects of the environment. The ecological psychologists of the 1960s and 1970s described the features of environ-

Preparation of this chapter was supported by Grant No. H024K960001 from the U.S. Department of Education, Office of Special Education Programs and Office of Educational Research and Improvement.

ments such as classrooms and assessed the extent to which environments influenced the behavior of adults and children (Barker, 1968; Barker & Gump, 1964). Initially, this research was based on a set of unidirectional assumptions about how environments affect human behavior. Later, researchers extended this perspective by examining the interdependence that occurs between features of the classroom ecology and individual behavior (Patterson, 1976); that is, within classroom environments, changes in one feature may well have effects on other aspects of the classroom or behavior of children (Rogers-Warren & Wedel, 1980). For example, when a teacher rearranges the room, space might be reduced in several play areas. This reduced space may result in children's spending greater amounts of time in social interaction with peers when in that area. For some children, increases in positive social interaction with peers might in turn lead to the development of positive relationships and increased interactions in other environments. This, in turn, may influence how much time and attention the teacher directs to the child to promote social play with peers. Such reciprocal effects have rarely been examined in inclusive environments, but in interpreting the often unidirectional findings and conclusions that come from most studies, it is important to recognize the transactional nature of ecology and behavior. Not only does environment affect behavior, but behavior affects environment.

A broader ecological systems theory proposed by Bronfenbrenner and colleagues (1979; Bronfenbrenner & Morris, 1998) has been applied by several researchers (Guralnick, 1982; Odom et al., 1996; Peck, 1993) to examine the research on and implementation of inclusive preschool programs. Bronfenbrenner argued that human development is best described as "the progressive, mutual accommodation,

throughout the lifespan, between a growing human organism and the changing immediate environments in which it lives" (1977, p. 514). He suggested an ecological systems model that contains four levels. For the purpose of this chapter, this model would classify a preschool classroom as a *microsystem* (an environment in which the child with disabilities and other individuals participate). The microsystem is seated within more distal systems, termed the *mesosystem* (interactive influences with other microsystems in which the child participates, such as the family), the *exosystem* (factors that influence the microsystem coming from environments in which the child or teacher does not participate, such as policymaking bodies), and the *macrosystem* (the cultural context of the community or society). This chapter focuses on events within the classroom (i.e., the microsystem) while acknowledging the important and sometimes critical influences that occur from other "layers" of the ecological system (Odom, Horn, et al., 1999).

Organizational Contexts

Although this chapter focuses primarily on the microsystem as evident in inclusive preschool classrooms, two dimensions of the broader context within which the classrooms exist must be acknowledged: organizational and philosophical contexts. One central feature that is likely to affect the classroom ecology is the organizational context in which the inclusive preschool classroom is located. In an examination of 16 inclusive preschool programs across the United States, Odom, Horn, and colleagues (1999) found that inclusive classrooms exist in a wide range of organizational contexts. These include *community-based programs* (i.e., private or not-for-profit child care and preschool programs operating in the community), *Head Start programs* operating outside the public school organization, and *public school programs* (programs for children at risk for disabilities, Head Start programs for which public schools are the sponsoring agency, and tuition-based programs). In interpreting research on classroom ecology (or any other dimension of preschool inclusion), it is important to understand that the nature of preschool inclusion may differ substantially across these organizational contexts. Inclusion in child care, Head Start, and a public school prekindergarten program are likely to constitute qualitatively different inclusion experiences. This differing nature may well be reflected in the ecological features of the classroom, but this has not been studied systematically. An important direction for future research is to examine the variation in classroom ecology across organizational contexts and determine the extent to which this variation affects child behavior and development.

Philosophical Contexts

Classroom ecologies are also affected by prevailing philosophies about appropriate care for young children. Developmentally appropriate practice (DAP), as defined by the National Association for the Education of Young Children (NAEYC), is the guiding philosophy for most early childhood education in the United States and as such can be seen as a global ecological feature of inclusive preschool environments. DAP is based on "current knowledge about child development and learning. . .the strengths, interests, and needs of each individual child in the group. . .(and) the social and cultural context in which children live" (Bredekamp & Copple, 1997, p. 9). In developmentally appropriate classrooms, teachers plan engaging and responsive classroom environments, use a range of teaching strategies to promote children's learning, construct appropriate curricula, assess children's learning, and establish

positive relationships with families (Bredekamp & Copple, 1997). The quality of the physical environment for children is fundamental to the implementation of DAP, and specific guidelines for environmental provisions are provided by the NAEYC.

Prevailing philosophies about preschool ecologies are also reflected in environmental or ecological measurement tools. One of the most frequently used assessments is the Early Childhood Environment Rating Scale (ECERS; Harms & Clifford, 1980), which was revised (ECERS-R; Harms, Clifford, & Cryer, 1998). The ECERS-R provides a general overall rating of quality as well as subscale ratings on specific aspects of the classroom environment (e.g., Space and Furniture, Personal Care Routines, Activities). Using a 7-point Likert-type scale, mean ratings of 5 or above are considered to be "good," mean ratings in the middle range (3–4) are considered "mediocre," and ratings below 3 are considered "poor." Based on the same format, the Infant-Toddler Environment Rating Scale (ITERS; Harms, Cryer, & Clifford, 1987) is designed to assess classes for infants and toddlers. A similar rating scale developed by other researchers is the Assessment Profile for Early Childhood Programs (Abbott-Shim & Sibley, 1987). A comparison of these three scales by Scarr, Eisenberg, and Deater-Deckard (1994) found that they measure very similar aspects of the classroom environment. Using direct observation rather than a rating scale to collect information about environments, Hyson, Hirsh-Pasek, and Rescorla (1990) designed the Classroom Practices Inventory to directly assess the use of DAP for 4- and 5-year-old children. All of these assessments can provide information about the quality of the general early childhood education environment in which children with disabilities are included.

GLOBAL CLASSROOM QUALITY

Using the ECERS, previously described, researchers have examined the quality of early childhood environments containing only typically developing children and also classroom environments in which children with disabilities participate.

Quality in Child Care and Preschool Programs

Since the mid-1980s, much effort has been directed toward describing the global quality of child care and preschool programs for young children and determining the effects of variations in global quality on child behavior and development. Most of this research has focused on typically developing children from a variety of socioeconomic levels. Five general conclusions can be drawn from this work. First, there is general agreement about what constitutes quality and that global dimension of the preschool ecology can be assessed in a reliable and valid fashion using scales such as the ECERS. Second, the quality of child care and preschool programs in the United States may best be characterized as "mediocre," and a number of such programs are of poor quality, especially programs that serve infants and toddlers (e.g., Bryant, Burchinal, Lau, & Sparling, 1994; Burchinal, Roberts, Nabors, & Bryant, 1996; Helburn, 1995; Phillips, Voran, Kisker, Howes, & Whitebook, 1994). Third, higher quality child care environments lead to better developmental and behavioral outcomes for children (Bryant et al., 1994; Burchinal et al., 1996; Cost, Quality, and Child Outcomes Study Team, 1995; Dunn, 1993; Howes, Phillips, & Whitebook, 1992). Fourth, broader ecological variables seem to influence quality, among which are state regulations, cost and resources invested in child care, background of the program supervisor, and the training/degree credentials of staff who work in child care

and preschool programs (e.g., Burchinal, Cryer, & Clifford, in press; Cost, Quality, and Child Outcomes Study Team, 1995). Finally, quality seems to make a difference for all children, but the differential effects of variation in quality are especially evident in the case of children whose mothers have low levels of education (Peisner-Feinberg et al., 1999).

Quality in Programs for Preschool-Age Children with Disabilities

The research on typical child care and preschool programs has important implications for both policy and practice in the care of typically developing children. It also raises important questions about the appropriateness of some inclusive environments for preschool-age children with disabilities. Clearly, it is not desirable for inclusion to occur in a mediocre- or poor-quality environment; thus, parents and professionals must pay special attention to global quality indicators in potential inclusive environments (Bailey, McWilliam, Buysse, & Wesley, 1998).

In comparison with the general child care literature, only a limited amount of research has examined global levels of quality in programs that serve children with disabilities. In the first study to assess qualitative differences in special education and early childhood education environments, Bailey, Clifford, and Harms (1982) used the ECERS to compare preschool education environments for children with disabilities in special education environments with those for typically developing children in general early childhood education environments. They found that special education environments had significantly lower scores on the ECERS than early childhood education environments. Using an ecobehavioral observational assessment, Odom, Skellenger, and Ostrosky (1993) observed children with disabilities who were enrolled in special education classes and typically developing children who were enrolled in NAEYC-accredited child care centers and found significant differences in the types of activities provided for children in those environments. In the early childhood education classrooms, play occurred significantly more often; in the special education environments, preacademic activities occurred significantly more often. These data suggest that substantial differences occur in the early childhood education and special education environments; the early childhood education environment exhibits features that are more consistent with the NAEYC's definition of DAP. However, these studies did not examine quality in inclusive environments.

Using both the ECERS and the Classroom Practices Inventory, La Paro, Sexton, and Snyder (1998) observed early childhood education quality in inclusive preschool programs and segregated special education programs. They reported that the two types of programs did not differ significantly on overall quality, nearly half of the programs in each sample had the equivalent of "good quality," and no programs had poor quality. In their examination of programs for toddlers, however, Bruder and Brand (1995) used the ITERS to assess program quality and found that inclusive center-based programs scored significantly higher on the full-scale score than did nonintegrated early childhood education environments. In their sample of inclusive preschool programs in North Carolina, Buysse, Wesley, Bryant, and Gardner (1999) found that the majority of programs received ECERS scores of at least mediocre quality; the inclusive programs actually received significantly higher scores. Few programs in this sample received ratings of poor quality. Together, these three studies suggest that the overall quality of the early childhood education environment in inclusive programs for young children may be mediocre to good and at least equivalent

to or better than the quality in either special education or nonintegrated general early childhood education programs.

CLASSROOM ECOLOGICAL VARIABLES

Ecological features of inclusive preschool classrooms can be defined as both physical and social in nature. *Physical ecology* refers to relatively static characteristics of a classroom (Carta, Sainato, & Greenwood, 1988). The physical space of the classroom, organization of the space in the classroom, toys or play materials available, number of children in the classroom, and teacher–child ratio all could be identified as part of the physical ecology of a classroom. The *social ecology* of a classroom refers to the interactions that occur between adults and children, interactions that occur between peers, and characteristics of the adults or children that affect those interactions. These variables are relatively more dynamic in nature in that their form may change more quickly than the physical ecology features (Carta et al., 1988). Physical ecology and social ecology variables often are not independent of each other, and most global rating scales include both dimensions. This section, however, distinguishes between the two and explores research on specific components of each dimension.

Physical Ecology of Inclusive Classrooms

Specific instructional techniques used by teachers in inclusive environments are discussed in Chapter 22, although the chapter authors acknowledge that instruction is very much a part of the social and physical ecology of the classroom. For this chapter, ecological features of the classroom represent the setting events for instruction (Sainato & Carta, 1992) or contexts within which instruction occurs. *Instruction* refers to specific techniques that teachers use to promote the individual learning outcomes identified for specific children in their classrooms. It is a generally accepted axiom in early intervention and early childhood special education that participation in typical early childhood education classroom environments is important for young children with disabilities, but many children may need additional instruction to address individual goals and objectives (Carta, Schwartz, Atwater, & McConnell, 1991; Wolery, Strain, & Bailey, 1992).

Space for Activities   The space allotted for activities in early childhood education environments is one specific feature of the physical environment that has been investigated. It seems that in early childhood education classrooms, well-defined space for activities may lead to smaller groupings of children and greater engagement with materials (Pollowy, 1974; Sheehan & Day, 1975). Also, the size of the space for activities may affect children's participation. DeLong, Tegano, Moran, and Brickley (1994) found that typically developing children spent more time in relatively more complex forms of play when the space provided for the activity was reduced. When examining the number of children within a specific space, however, Carta and colleagues (1988) proposed that the way in which more or less dense classroom environments are established affects children's responses. When density increases through adding children to a fixed amount of space, children are more likely to maintain their distance from peers and become more aggressive. If density increases as a result of decreasing the space for a fixed number of children, then children may engage in less physical contact and aggression. For children in Head Start, Smith and Dickinson (1994) found that classrooms with larger numbers of children (i.e., more diversity at a classroom level) had lower quality teacher–child interactions than did class-

rooms with smaller numbers of students and shorter days.

Number of Activity Materials and Toys   The number of play materials available for children is a second dimension of the physical environment that has been investigated in early childhood education environments. A range of studies have indicated that when the number of toys available for children is relatively low, more disruption and conflict among children occurs (see Carta et al., 1988, for a historical review of the research). However, having a large number of toys or play materials available may lead to children's being more engaged with materials and less engaged with peers (Chandler, Fowler, & Lubeck, 1992). Depending on the objective of the activity, there seems to be a trade-off between the number of play materials available and the behavior of children. For example, Gillespie, Pelren, and Twardosz (1998) experimentally examined the effects of the number of books available in a book area on the voluntary book use of typically developing children. When relatively few books were available, a greater percentage of the books in the area were used, but when more books were available, a larger number of different books were used. Book rotation did not seem to affect overall book use but rather the way in which books were used.

Types of Play Materials and Nature of the Activity   There has been a long history of research about the effects of play materials on the social cognitive play of young typically developing children. Generally, children tend to be involved in solitary play when materials such as blocks, puzzles, playdough, clay, and books are available (Quilitch & Risley, 1973; Shure, 1963); parallel play when sand, water toys, and crayons are available (Rubin, 1977); and social play when dolls, housekeeping, and dress-up materials are available (Rubin, 1977). Some activities seem to affect the cognitive competence that typically developing children exhibit in play. Kontos and Wilcox-Herzog (1997) found that children engaged in more cognitively competent play when in activities that Hadeed and Sylva (1995) identified as "high yield" activities (i.e., activities requiring concentration, "stretch," and perseverance—art, blocks, sociodramatic play) than when they were participating in "low yield" activities (e.g., gross motor, books, games with rules). Research also suggests that when teachers organize an activity around a theme rather than simply provide materials in an activity area (i.e., clothes in a dress-up area versus a pretend shopping theme), typically developing children will engage in more complex levels of play (Bagley & Klass, 1998).

The research on the effects of play materials and activities on typically developing children has been extended to children with disabilities. In an early study, Beckman and Kohl (1984) systematically observed the effects of "isolate" and "social" toys on the interaction for children with disabilities in inclusive and noninclusive playgroups. Social interactions among children in both environments occurred more frequently when social toys were available, whereas nonsocial toy play occurred more often when isolate toys were available. Using this information, Kohl, Beckman, and Swenson-Pierce (1984) taught children with disabilities to use toys for which typically developing children had shown a preference, resulting in increases in social interactions between children with and without disabilities for two of the four playgroups in the study. In a similar study, Stoneman, Cantrell, and Hoover-Dempsey (1983) examined different amounts of play that occurred among children with and without disabilities in different activities and found that social interaction among children occurred more frequently in activities that required

cooperative play (e.g., blocks and vehicles, housekeeping).

The "structure" (i.e., clarity of the roles) of play activities also seems to affect social interaction among peers in inclusive environments. DeKlyen and Odom (1989) examined a range of play activities that occurred in inclusive classrooms and found more social interaction among peers in activities that had a relatively high structure (e.g., doctor, shoe store) than low structure (e.g., water table, painting) activities. Most of the high-structure activities were sociodramatic in nature and had clear roles that required cooperative and social play. Using an experimental design to compare the effects of isolate (e.g., puzzles, peg boards) and social (e.g., housekeeping, puppets) toys on social interaction, Martin, Brady, and Williams (1991) observed children with disabilities in inclusive and noninclusive playgroups; social interaction among peers occurred significantly more often in the inclusive playgroups in which social toys were available.

The type of classroom activity in which children with disabilities participate also affects the types of play and may affect opportunities for the communication in which they engage. McCabe, Jenkins, Mills, Dale, and Cole (1999) assigned children with disabilities in inclusive and noninclusive playgroups to activities designed to foster functional, constructive, and dramatic play. In each type of activity, children with disabilities engaged more frequently in the type of play anticipated (e.g., functional play occurring most often in functional activities), suggesting that the specific play activity planned has a major effect on the type of play that will occur for children. However, in a similar study, this group of researchers (McCabe et al., 1996) did not find that the different play activities had an effect on communication among children with disabilities or peers. In contrast, O'Brien and Bi (1995) found significant differences in teachers' communication with toddlers with disabilities in three different types of activities (dollhouse, blocks, trucks, large motor—in descending order of teacher interaction). Children's communication in the three activities was also significantly different. The differences between the McCabe et al. (1996) and O'Brien and Bi (1995) findings may be attributable to the differences in the ages of children and the level of participation by adults allowed by the researchers.

Class Schedules   Schedules specify in advance the order and amount of time devoted to routines and activities during the day. They provide classroom environments with a degree of predictability that may help some children with disabilities more independently make transitions between activities (Sainato, 1990). Early research on the sequencing of scheduled activities indicated that the activity level of children in one activity will affect the level of physical activity in the next activity (Krantz & Risley, 1977). For example, when an outdoor activity is followed by a storytime activity, there will be more physical activity among the children than would have occurred if a manipulative (i.e., quiet) activity had preceded storytime. In that NAEYC guidelines also recommend that there be a sequence of active and quiet activities in schedules for young children, the Krantz and Risley data suggest that teachers be aware of the spillover in physical activity that may occur across routines and activities in the schedule.

One problem with both conducting research on schedules and using teacher schedules to plan instruction is that the written schedule for the classroom may not correspond to what actually happens in the classroom. Both Ostrosky, Skellenger, Odom, McConnell, and Peterson (1994)—in a study of children with disabilities in noninclusive special education environments—and Smith and Dickinson (1994)—in a study of Head Start environments—had teachers provide their daily schedules and then observed activities that occurred in the classroom. They found little agreement between the two sources of information; Smith and Dickinson concluded that class schedules may represent an idealized projection of what the teacher would like to have happen in the classroom.

Ratio of Students to Teachers   A commonly accepted adage about programs for young children is that a lower student to teacher ratio is more beneficial to students than is a higher ratio. For preschool programs, the NAEYC recommends that there be no more than sixteen 3-year-olds per two adults and twenty 4-year-olds per two adults. If there are children with disabilities who require an instructional assistant, then an even lower ratio might be needed. In one study conducted in inclusive preschool classrooms, Hauser-Cram, Bronson, and Upshur (1993) found that lower ratios of children to adults resulted in children's spending less time in social interaction with peers. The lower ratio may have led to more opportunities for adult–child interaction, which, as is discussed in a subsequent section, may have led to decreased peer interaction.

Ratio of Children with and without Disabilities   Questions about the appropriate ratio of children with disabilities to typically developing children in inclusive classrooms have existed for many years (Guralnick, 1982). However, there has been little systematic research that examined the effects of different ratios of children. In their study of 16 inclusive preschool programs, Odom, Horn, and colleagues (1999) found that programs varied widely on the ratio of children with and without disabilities. From their observations in a range of inclusive programs, Hauser-Cram and colleagues (1993) found a positive relationship between degree of inclusion of children with disabilities (i.e., degree assessed as the ratio of typically developing children to children with disabilities in the inclusive classrooms) and the degree of social engagement. In their study of programs with different ratios of children with and without disabilities, Mills, Cole, Jenkins, and Dale (1998) found that relatively higher performing children seemed to benefit more (on measures of cognitive and language development) from integrated special education programs (ratio, 4:8), whereas lower performing children benefited more from inclusive (ratio, 8:4) and noninclusive special education programs.

Accessibility of Space and Materials
A final dimension of the physical ecology that is relevant to children with disabilities is the accessibility of space and materials. The Americans with Disabili-ties Act (ADA) of 1990 (PL 101-336) requires that reasonable accommodations be made to ensure that public facilities are accessible to people with a range of disabilities, including those with motor or sensory impairments. This applies to child care and preschool programs as well, and certainly accessibility of the physical environment is critical for inclusion to be successful. However, very little research has been conducted on the issue of accessibility of environments for preschool-age children with disabilities. Conducting such research is a challenge, because accessibility is a phenomenon that varies according to each individual child. General guidelines for accessibility include considerations such as ramps for building entry and exit, entrances to buildings and rooms of sufficient size to accommodate wheelchairs, support bars and sinks of appropriate height in bathrooms, and braille symbols for children with visual impairments. In the case of children with physical impairments, however, the specific nature of modifications needed may vary widely depending on the nature and amount of impairment, the child's cognitive level, the adaptive equipment that the child uses, and the preferences of the child and the family. This variability is likely to occur with most children; thus, early childhood education programs must conduct individualized assessments of accessibility. Research is needed to define accessibility in the context of inclusive programs, describe the level of accessibility currently available in inclusive classroom environments, and examine the relationship between accessibility and outcomes for children with disabilities.

Social Ecology of Inclusive Preschool Classrooms

The physical ecology of inclusive classrooms provides an environment and structure in which a more dynamic set of social interchanges may occur among adults, between adults and children, and among the children themselves. These interchanges make up the social ecology of the preschool classroom. Other important interchanges occur in inclusive preschool programs, most notably the interactions between family members and teachers. However, this chapter describes the social ecology of the classroom environment itself as a microsystem.

Characteristics of the Peer Group
The other children in the classroom constitute the most obvious dimension of the social ecology of a preschool classroom. Historically, children with disabilities have been served in segregated environments only with other children with disabilities. This volume reflects the major shift that has occurred since the early 1980s toward inclusive programs, although currently only approximately half of the preschool-age children with disabilities are served in inclusive environments (U.S. Department of Education, 1999). The research on what happens when one's peers have or do not have a disability is reviewed thoroughly in other chapters of this book.

This chapter assumes that there will be typically developing peers in the classroom and raises the question of whether the age and developmental capabilities of those peers are an important consideration in planning inclusive preschool programs.

One logical way to group children is by age. With this model, children with disabilities are placed in classrooms with children of their own chronological age. This has the advantage of normalization (i.e., most typically developing children are in classes with same-age peers), but it means that peers at times may be involved in activities that may be too advanced for the child with a disability. Matching children on the basis of developmental age is an alternative approach. This offers the advantage of greater comparability of interests and skills but means that children with disabilities might be placed in classrooms with much younger children.

Research on typically developing children suggests that children's social and cognitive play does indeed vary as a function of the age and developmental level of their peers. In general, this research shows that young children may benefit developmentally from playing with older children (Brownell, 1990; Howes & Farver, 1987; Lougee, Grueneich, & Hartup, 1977) but that older children who are paired with younger playmates may not benefit as much (Brownell, 1990; Goldman, 1981). A study by Bailey, Burchinal, and McWilliam (1993) provided longitudinal documentation of this phenomenon and demonstrated that children in mixed-age environments tended to score higher on developmental assessments at younger ages, but these average differences decreased over time and had disappeared by 5 years of age. Burchinal, Bailey, and Snyder (1994) replicated the earlier Bailey and colleagues (1993) findings with a small group of children with disabilities, suggesting that characteristics of peers may in fact be important for children with disabilities as well.

Earlier research in both the animal and human literature is also relevant to this issue. Suomi and Harlow (1972) demonstrated that isolate-reared monkeys that exhibited severe social skills deficits gained social skills when paired with immature, younger playmates but not with same-age playmates. Furman, Rahe, and Hartup (1979) then paired typically developing children who exhibited low rates of peer interaction with either same-age or younger playmates. Both groups increased their social interaction skills, but the children who were paired with younger partners made the most gain. Roberts, Burchinal, and Bailey (1994) found that children with disabilities in mixed-age environments took more turns in conversations and received more turns from partners than did children in same-age environments. In contrast, Guralnick and Groom (1987) found that children with mild delays exhibited higher rates of social interaction with same-age peers as compared with younger typically developing peers.

These findings suggest that the age and developmental status of peers are salient variables in inclusive classrooms but that more research needs to be conducted to determine the factors that relate to these influences. The question is a complicated one and will likely have a complex answer that varies by age of the child with a disability and the activities in which he or she is involved.

Social Interaction Among Peers
Examination of the social interaction patterns of young children with disabilities and their typically developing peers constitutes the largest literature on preschool inclusion. This literature is summarized in greater detail in Chapters 1 and 21 and is addressed only briefly here. A primary rationale for inclusive preschool pro-

grams is that they will provide an environment in which children with disabilities may engage in positive, playful, and developmentally important interchanges with socially competent peers (Bricker, 1978; Guralnick, 1990; Strain, 1990). When children with disabilities are socially integrated into the peer group and classroom, these interactions are thought to represent a powerful dimension of the social ecology.

Mixed evidence exists about the degree to which children with disabilities are well integrated into inclusive classrooms. The work of Guralnick and colleagues as well as others has documented the unique pattern of difficulties that children with disabilities have with engaging in social interaction with peers in comparison with typically developing children and that typically developing peers prefer interacting with other typically developing children (e.g., Guralnick, 1980, 1999; Guralnick, Connor, Hammond, Gottman, & Kinnish, 1996; Guralnick & Groom, 1988; Kopp, Baker, & Brown, 1992). For some children with disabilities, this pattern of interaction may lead to social isolation or rejection in the preschool programs, but other children with disabilities are well accepted (Odom, Zercher, Li, Marquart, & Sandall, 1998). In addition, it seems that children with disabilities, when in inclusive classes, spend more time in groups with typically developing children than in groups that contain only peers with disabilities or in solitary activities (Brown, Odom, Li, & Zercher, 1999).

Inclusion in play activities and programs with typically developing children seems to affect directly the social and communicative behavior of children in those environments. Without instruction or teacher prompts, typically developing children adjust their communication with children with disabilities (Guralnick & Paul-Brown, 1977), which may facilitate language development for the children

with disabilities (Guralnick, 1981). Across studies of children with developmental delays, hearing impairments, and visual impairments, it seems that children with disabilities engage in more social interactions with peers when participating in inclusive environments than when enrolled in nonintegrated environments or playgroups (Erwin, 1993; Guralnick et al., 1996; Hauser-Cram et al., 1993; Levine & Antia, 1997), although there have been some notable exceptions to this finding (Hundert, Mahoney, Mundy, & Vernon, 1998). Also, when involved in play activities with typically developing children, children with developmental delays and hearing impairments engage in more advanced forms of play than occurs when participating in play with other children with disabilities (Guralnick et al., 1996; Levine & Antia, 1997; Pickett, Griffith, & Rogers-Adkinson, 1993). Also, Guralnick (1981) found that children with severe delays engage in less inappropriate play when in playgroups with typically developing children than when in groups with other children with disabilities. For children with autism, Strain (1983) found that participation in playgroups with typically developing children facilitated generalization of social behavior learned in intensive interventions to occur in other nonintervention environments. In summary, although children with disabilities as a group may not experience the same degree of social integration into the peer group as do typically developing children, their participation in inclusive classrooms and playgroups seems to have positive effects on their social and play behavior.

Teacher Interaction In addition to being orchestrators of the physical ecology, teachers have a direct effect on learning and development. It seems that as a group, teachers tend to interact with children with disabilities more frequently than with typically developing children in inclusive environments. Relative to typically developing children, File (1994) found that teachers were more facilitative of cognitive play for children with disabilities, Brown and colleagues (1999) found that teachers provided significantly more adult support for children with disabilities, and Quay (1993) found that teachers directed a greater amount of attention to children with disabilities. An exception to this general trend is a study by Kontos, Moore, and Giorgetti (1998) in which teachers in inclusive programs were more likely to ignore and less likely to be involved with children with disabilities. Also, Hundert, Mahoney, and Hopkins (1993) found that resource teachers were more likely than classroom teachers to interact with children with disabilities.

In general, it seems that teachers' interactions have a substantial effect on children's social and task mastery behavior. Across a number of studies, it seems that teachers' interactions with children are negatively related to social interaction with peers (Chandler et al., 1992; Hauser-Cram et al., 1993; Hundert et al., 1993; Kontos et al., 1998; McWilliam & Bailey, 1995). Undoubtedly, specific types of teacher behavior have different effects on the social interaction of children. Nabors, Badawi, and Cheney (1997) found that children with disabilities were more likely to play with teachers than with peers during teacher-led playgroups; however, when teachers or assistant teachers provide verbal prompts, children with disabilities are more likely to engage in social interaction with peers (Hundert & Hopkins, 1992; Sontag, 1997). For typically developing children, Kontos and Wilcox-Herzog (1997) found that teacher responsiveness, when in a play environment with children, was likely to support peer interactions. Also, it does seem that teacher interaction with children with disabilities may be facilitative of cognitive play (File, 1994), which might provide a context for positive interactions with peers. The implication of this research

is that when teachers wish to intervene to promote social interaction among peers, they should strategically select the way they interact with children. Commenting to and playing with children may direct children's interactions away from peers. Verbally prompting, responding to children, and redirecting social initiations from children to peers may be effective strategies for promoting interaction.

Teacher Beliefs   To the extent that beliefs and attitudes about inclusion may affect the nature of the learning environment for children, teacher beliefs could be viewed as a feature of the social ecology of the classroom. In general, early childhood education and early childhood special education teachers have fairly positive attitudes toward inclusion of children with disabilities in early childhood education environments (Eiserman, Shisler, & Healey, 1995), especially if they are in center-based rather than family child care environments (Dinnebeil, McInerney, Fox, & Juchartz-Pendry, 1998). Teachers seem to feel more competent and more positive about including children with relatively mild disabilities than children with severe disabilities (Buysse, Wesley, Keyes, & Bailey, 1996; Gemmell-Crosby & Hanzlik, 1994). When asked, teachers identify a number of benefits of inclusion for children with disabilities (Buysse et al., 1996) and typically developing children (Marchant, 1995; Peck, Carlson, & Helmstetter, 1992). However, it seems that teachers may have different philosophies about or definitions of inclusion, and their specific definitions affect the way inclusive programs are implemented in the classroom (Lieber et al., 1998).

Professional Collaboration   The nature of the interactions that occur between adults in inclusive environments also constitutes a dimension of the social ecology. In their examination of a co-teaching approach in inclusive

Head Start environments, McCormick, Noonan, and Heck (1998) found that cohesive teacher behaviors (i.e., consistent across teachers) were related to children's engagement in the inclusive environment; this cohesion occurs through collaboration among professionals. Such collaboration is based on an effective and consistent mode of communication (Donegan, Ostrosky, & Fowler, 1996), a shared philosophy about education and inclusion (Lieber et al., 1997), shared "ownership" of children with disabilities (Lieber et al., 1997), and joint participation in program development (Peck, Furman, & Helmstetter, 1993). In their study of inclusive programs that were discontinued after a period of implementation, Peck and colleagues (1993) found that the primary factor associated with discontinuation was the poor relationships that developed among the adults in the program, often characterized by acrimony rather than respect. Professional relationships cast a positive or negative affective valence across the social ecology of preschool classrooms that undoubtedly affects the learning environment for children and the existence of the programs themselves.

CLASSROOM ECOLOGY AND OUTCOMES FOR CHILDREN

Several difficulties confront the reader who is interested in understanding the relationship between features of the classroom ecology and outcomes for children. First, different types of outcomes exist for children. Some outcomes reflect the *process* that is thought to lead to learning and development for children, such as engagement in developmentally appropriate activities, task mastery, or more advanced level of play. *Summative* outcomes reflect more global or perhaps enduring changes in children's learning, development, or attitudes. A second issue is whether one can infer a causal rela-

tionship between outcomes and the specific ecological feature. Only a few studies have used experimental designs; most have examined co-occurring relationships. In the latter cases, inferences can be made, but this should be done cautiously.

Process Outcomes

Throughout the previous sections, process outcomes have been noted in descriptions of ecological features:

1. Children with disabilities participate in more social interactions with peers when they are in programs or playgroups with typically developing peers than when they are in nonintegrated programs or playgroups.

2. Children with disabilities display more cognitively mature forms of play in programs or playgroups with typically developing children.

3. Social interaction among peers occurs more frequently in play activities that have more structured activities (e.g., sociodramatic) than in activities with less structure.

4. General teacher interaction with peers is negatively related to social interaction with peers.

5. Teachers' beliefs about inclusion influence the way in which inclusion is implemented in the classroom.

6. Collaboration among adults affects the classroom ecology and learning environment for children.

Child Engagement as a Process Outcome   *Child engagement* refers to the active physical participation of children in activities or routines in the classroom. It is through such active participation in the physical and social ecologies of the classroom that learning and development are thought to occur. McWilliam, Trivette, and Dunst (1985) proposed that child engagement be considered as one measure of effectiveness for early childhood education programs. Engagement in inclusive preschool classrooms seems to be determined by several features. Hauser-Cram and colleagues (1993) found a positive relationship between the degree of inclusion (i.e., operationalized as the ratio of typically developing children to children with disabilities) and engagement in task mastery. They also noted that the amount of choice by children was associated positively with time spent in social interactions with peers, higher rates of engaging peers, and higher levels of persistence on tasks. Similarly, for typically developing children in early childhood education classrooms, Tegano, Lookabaugh, May, and Burdette (1991) noted that children's constructive play increased when children imposed structure on the play situation and decreased when the teacher imposed structure. These findings suggest a relationship between children's choice of and engagement in an activity.

To examine the relationship between child choice and engagement, Odom, Favazza, Brown, and Horn (2000) assessed child engagement in teacher- and child-initiated activities in two sets (in different years) of inclusive and noninclusive early intervention programs (i.e., children were 15–36 months old). They examined the conditional probabilities of engagement when children with and without disabilities initiated (or chose) activities and when teachers initiated activities (see Figure 11.1). In six of the seven conditions that occurred over the two sets of classroom environments, child engagement was greater in child-initiated conditions. In a study of preschool-age children enrolled in 16 classrooms that employed a range of inclusive approaches, Odom, Brown, Li, and Zercher (1999) found a similar relationship between engagement and activity initiator.

Summative Outcomes

Although there have been studies of the outcomes associated with preschool inclusion, few investigators have examined the specific effects of physical or social ecological features (i.e., independent of instruction occurring in the classroom) on more summative outcomes for children. For typically developing children, participation in high-quality early childhood education environments (as

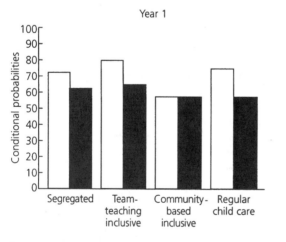
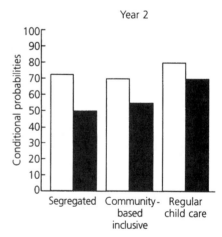

Figure 11.1.   Conditional probability for engagement given teacher-initiated or child-initiated activities. (□, child-initiated; ■, adult-initiated.) (From Odom, S.L., Favazza, P.C., Brown, W.H., & Horn, E.M. [2000]. Approaches to understanding the ecology of early childhood environments for children with disabilities. In T. Thompson, D. Felce, & F.J. Symons [Eds.], *Behavioral observation: Technology and applications in developmental disabilities* [p. 210]. Baltimore: Paul H. Brookes Publishing Co.; reprinted by permission.)

defined by the ECERS) is linked to on-going and long-term developmental progress (Howes, 1997). In a stratified random sample of 400 programs in four states, the Cost, Quality, and Child Outcomes Study Team (1995) found a significant relationship between program quality and both social and cognit-ive developmental outcomes (Peisner-Feinberg & Burchinal, 1997). For a smaller group of Head Start programs in North Carolina, Bryant and colleagues (1994) found that children in higher quality programs scored significantly higher on measures of achievement and preacademic skills. These studies have been conducted with typically developing children, and although one would expect that the same benefits of high-quality early childhood education would accrue for children with disabilities, that rela-tionship has not been documented.

As noted briefly in a previous sec-tion, there is some evidence that the ratio of typically developing children to chil-dren with disabilities may affect summa-tive outcomes for children. Mills and col-leagues (1998) assigned children to noninclusive, integrated special educa-tion (11 children with disabilities and 3 typically developing children), and inclu-sive (5 children with disabilities and 9 typ-ically developing children) classrooms. Assessing cognitive and language devel-opment at the beginning and end of the year, they found that relatively higher per-forming children with disabilities made more progress in the integrated special education classrooms on the cognitive measures and the relatively lower per-forming children with disabilities made more progress in the inclusive and non-integrated special education classrooms. No differences were found for language development. These data suggest that the ratio of children with and without disabil-ities may affect cognitive outcomes for children with disabilities. However, the authors advised caution in applying these results because of the relatively small amount of variance explained by the dif-ferences between classroom conditions.

One proposed benefit of preschool inclusion for typically developing chil-dren is the formation of positive attitudes that may come about through their con-tact and interactions with children with disabilities (see Chapter 7). In a series of studies, Diamond and Hestenes (1994, 1996) found that typically developing children acquire knowledge of physical disabilities and hearing impairments as a result of being in inclusive classrooms with children with those impairments, although they are less aware of issues related to Down syndrome. Also, typically developing children in inclusive class-rooms give higher acceptance ratings to children with disabilities described in hypothetical situations than do typically developing children enrolled in nonin-clusive early childhood education pro-grams (Diamond, Hestenes, Carpenter, & Innes, in press). Okagaki, Diamond, Kontos, and Hestenes (1998) found a positive relationship between typically developing children's attitudes toward children with disabilities and the amount of social interaction directed toward chil-dren with disabilities. In summary, there seems to be increasing evidence to sug-gest that typically developing children's participation in inclusive preschool pro-grams has at least short-term effects on understanding and attitudes toward chil-dren with disabilities.

Experimental Studies

Although rare, several researchers have used experimental designs to examine changes that come about when the behav-ioral ecology of preschool classrooms is altered. It should be noted that most nat-uralistic intervention approaches arrange classroom activities or routines in ways that set the occasion for a desired behav-ior to occur for children with disabilities (Rule, Losardo, Dinnebeil, Kaiser, & Rowland, 1998), and considerable experimental research has examined the effects of these naturalistic approaches (see Chapter 22). Nordquist, Twardosz, and McEvoy (1991) examined the effects of changing three ecological features (increasing play materials available, rearranging the classroom furniture and space, and reorganizing the schedule) on children with autism and teachers in two classrooms. They documented increases in adults' smiling and affectionate words and children's use of play materials and compliance with adult instructions.

To support children's social interactions with peers in inclusive environments or activities, researchers have used environmental arrangement or social integration activities. These activities combine the ecological features of space (i.e., activity is in a confined area), peer group (i.e., socially competent peer and peers with special needs), and play theme (i.e., activities that have roles that allow interaction to occur). In a comparison of this procedure with other types of social interaction interventions, Odom, McConnell, et al. (1999) found environmental arrangements to produce greater increases in peer ratings (as given by children with classmates with disabilities in special education classrooms) than other interventions. Jenkins, Odom, and Speltz (1989), using a group design, and Frea, Craig, Odom, and Johnson (1999), using a single-subject design, found the environmental arrangement activities to be effective for promoting interaction among children with and without disabilities. However, for some children, it seems that other interventions (e.g., peer-mediated, group friendship activities) may be equally or more effective in promoting interaction than environmental arrangement activities (Frea et al., 1999; Odom, McConnell, et al., 1999).

To support the transition of children with disabilities in Head Start to kindergarten programs, Ager and Shapiro (1995) used an observational ecobehavioral measure to assess the ecological features of kindergarten classrooms. They then reorganized one Head Start class so that it contained several of the important ecological characteristics of the kindergarten classes, while two other classes remained unchanged (i.e., contrast classrooms). When children in these classroom were observed the next year in kindergarten, the children who had been in the reorganized classroom had fewer competing behaviors (e.g., acting out) and required less prompting from the teachers during independent seat work than did children who had been in the two contrast classrooms. From this range of experimental studies, it seems that changing ecological features can have an impact on children's and teachers' behavior; however, the experimental literature on effects of ecological intervention is somewhat limited.

BARRIERS TO ESTABLISHING HIGH-QUALITY INCLUSIVE PRESCHOOL ENVIRONMENTS

Although evidence exists about the features of inclusive preschool environments that affect young children's development and learning, program providers may encounter barriers in establishing high-quality environments. These barriers are related to availability of high-quality early childhood education environments, training for staff, and collaboration between early childhood education and specialized professional staff.

High-Quality Early Childhood Education Environments

Inclusive preschool programs often operate in community-based child care programs or Head Start programs operating outside the public schools. Although there is evidence that the quality of inclusive preschool programs does not seem to differ from programs that do not contain children with disabilities (Buysse et al., 1999; La Paro et al., 1998), there is also considerable evidence that the general quality of child care in the community may be mediocre at best and in some cases poor. Such qualitative features of early childhood education programs are affected by several factors. In their examination of Head Start programs, Smith and Dickinson (1994) found lower quality, as measured by the ECERS, in programs that had longer days and larger numbers of children. To examine the effects of ratio of students to teachers, Russell (1990) observed children and teachers in high-ratio (11:1), average-ratio (9:1), and low-ratio (7:1) conditions. Children in high-ratio conditions exhibited more problem behaviors and were less absorbed in classroom activities. A parallel circumstance exists for itinerant collaboration special education teachers who have large case loads of children (Lieber et al., 1998).

Training

In their study of child care in the United States, the Cost, Quality, and Child Outcomes Study Team (1995) noted that training and education was one factor related to the quality of the early childhood education program. Similarly, in Head Start centers, Smith and Dickinson (1994) found that teachers with a higher level of training had classes that received higher ECERS scores. In a study of the factors that affect quality in early childhood education programs in Florida, Howes, Smith, and Galinsky (1995) found that teacher preparation was significantly related to quality and also children's play with objects and peers.

In addition to overall early childhood education quality, training seems to be a major barrier to inclusion of children with disabilities. In their survey of service providers in North Carolina, Buysse, Wesley, and Keyes (1998) found that lack of training was noted as a primary barrier to inclusion. This general reaction from teachers in inclusive environments, especially when asked about including children with more severe disabilities, has been reported in a range of studies that use different samples and methodologies (Buysse et al., 1996; Dinnebeil et al., 1998; Eiserman et al., 1995; Gemmell-Crosby & Hanzlik, 1994; Wesley, Buysse, & Tyndall, 1997).

Professional Relationships and Support

To plan a high-quality inclusive program for children with disabilities, early childhood education teachers often require the support of and collaboration with specialized staff (e.g., itinerant special education teachers, speech pathologists; Odom, Horn, et al., 1999). A major barrier often identified is the establishment of effective working relationships among professionals (Peck et al., 1993). Several factors seem to stand in the way of establishing positive relationships. At times, staff may have differing philosophies concerning early childhood education and teaching (Buysse et al., 1998; Lieber et al., 1997). Also, in the busy day of a teacher, there may not be time for planning or discussing children's progress (Lieber et al., 1997). In addition, a primary barrier to establishing positive professional relationships is communication that may or may not occur among professionals (Donegan et al., 1996).

AGENDA FOR CHANGE

This chapter is based on the assumption that the ecology of preschool classrooms—the physical and social contexts in which inclusion occurs—is a salient variable that is likely to affect the success of inclusion efforts. In contrast with the extensive research described elsewhere in this book on the role of adults in supporting positive outcomes in inclusive environments, however, there has been a relatively small amount of research on the classroom ecology and how manipulations of that ecology could be used, either independently or in conjunction with instructional interventions, to promote positive outcomes. The research that has been conducted is relatively piecemeal in nature and generally is not tied to a broader model of ecological influences.

Nonetheless, the research affirms the key role of the classroom ecology in promoting behavior and development. Research with typically developing children clearly demonstrates that global ratings of the quality of the preschool environment are correlated with better outcomes for typically developing children. This is assumed to be the case for children with disabilities, but the factors that promote successful inclusion may not be limited to those ecological features that promote successful development in typically developing children. Six key areas that might serve to guide future research efforts are discussed next.

Develop a more comprehensive understanding of the national level of quality in inclusive environments. A number of large-scale studies have documented the variation in quality in general early childhood education programs. Although no study has included a nationally representative sample of programs, the size and geographic distribution of the studies, combined with the consistency of findings across these studies, lead to some confidence in general statements about quality in early childhood education environments from a national perspective. Several studies have described quality in a small number of inclusive environments, but there is not nearly enough research to make any conclusions about the general level of quality in inclusive environments in the United States. This will require a larger set of more geographically distributed studies, conducted in a

sufficient range of program contexts (e.g., child care, Head Start, public school preschool programs), to assess the extent to which program context and state policies and regulations contribute to variability in quality of inclusive environments.

Document the relationship between global classroom quality and outcomes for children with disabilities. Numerous studies have provided strong evidence of this relationship for typically developing children. Outcomes for children with disabilities in inclusive environments need to be identified, and the relationship between global quality and the extent to which these outcomes are achieved needs to be documented.

Identify and validate aspects of quality of the classroom ecology for preschool-age children with disabilities that extend beyond those for typically developing children. Much of the debate over DAP versus early childhood special education has focused on the role of instruction in inclusive early childhood education programs. A comparable set of discussions and research efforts needs to focus more specifically on the classroom ecology to determine the extent to which the environment (as opposed to adult instructional efforts) needs to be modified to support the appropriate development and behavior of young children with disabilities. The research and discussion need to include not only the physical environment but also the social environment, with a continued examination of the effects of specific peer characteristics (e.g., age, developmental status, gender) on children's development and behavior.

Conduct experimental studies to determine whether changes in the ecology result in changes in outcomes. Most of the general early childhood education research on the relationship between quality and outcomes has been correlational in nature. The next generation of research in inclusive environments needs to include experimental studies in which environments are manipulated to determine more precisely whether efforts to change environments will indeed have the desired results. Although some of this research can be of a short-term nature, there is also a significant need for longitudinal research that follows children over time to determine the lasting impact of varying ecological conditions.

Identify more systematically the factors that are likely to improve quality. More research is needed documenting the barriers to and facilitators of high-quality environments for inclusion of young children with disabilities. This likely will require a series of studies and efforts at multiple levels of the ecology, beginning with state rules and regulations and moving down to local programs and the individuals who work in those environments. Strategies for improving practices and ensuring that improvements are maintained in individual classrooms need to be proposed and studied.

Develop models for individualizing classroom ecologies. Although research will be able to identify a number of characteristics of the preschool ecology that are generally applicable to young children with disabilities, when teachers are faced with individual children in their own classrooms, there is likely to be considerable variation in what individual children need. Teachers and researchers need methods and tools by which these individual needs can be assessed and classroom ecologies can be modified to meet those unique needs.

CONCLUSION

The physical and social ecology of inclusive preschool environments have major effects on children with and without disabilities. The research to date has documented, primarily in a descriptive manner, how aspects of the classroom environment may promote desired outcomes for children. Such information may guide teachers in designing classroom environments that set the context for important learning experiences and social interchanges for children. The next step in this research is to determine more precisely how features of the classroom ecology produce desired outcomes for children and use this information to build effective inclusive programs for children with and without disabilities.

REFERENCES

Abbott-Shim, M., & Sibley, A. (1987). *Assessment profile for early childhood programs.* Atlanta, GA: Quality Assist.

Ager, C.L., & Shapiro, E.S. (1995). Template matching as a strategy for assessment of and intervention for preschool students with disabilities. *Topics in Early Childhood Special Education, 15,* 187–219.

Americans with Disabilities Act (ADA) of 1990, PL 101-336, 42 U.S.C, §§ 12101 *et seq.*

Bagley, D.M., & Klass, P.H. (1998). Comparison of the quality of preschoolers' play in housekeeping and thematic sociodramatic play centers. *Journal of Research in Childhood Education, 12,* 71–77.

Bailey, D.B., Burchinal, M.R., & McWilliam, R.A. (1993). Age of peers and early child development. *Child Development, 64,* 848–862.

Bailey, D.B., Clifford, R.M., & Harms, T. (1982). Comparison of preschool environments for handicapped and nonhandicapped children. *Topics in Early Childhood Special Education, 2*(1), 9–20.

Bailey, D.B., McWilliam, R.A., Buysse, V., & Wesley, P.W. (1998). Inclusion in the context of competing values in early childhood education. *Early Childhood Research Quarterly, 13,* 27–48.

Barker, R.G. (1968). *Ecological psychology.* Stanford, CA: Stanford University Press.

Barker, R.G., & Gump, P.V. (1964). *Big school, little school.* Stanford, CA: Stanford University Press.

Beckman, P.J., & Kohl, F.L. (1984). The effects of social and isolate toys on the interactions and play of integrated and nonintegrated groups of preschoolers. *Education and Training of the Mentally Retarded, 19,* 169–174.

Bredekamp, S., & Copple, C. (1997). *Developmentally appropriate practice in early childhood programs* (Rev. ed.). Washington, DC: National Association for the Education of Young Children.

Bricker, D.D. (1978). A rationale for the interaction of handicapped and nonhandicapped preschool children. In M. Guralnick (Ed.), *Early intervention and the integration of handicapped and nonhandicapped children* (pp. 3–26). Baltimore: University Park Press.

Bronfenbrenner, U. (1977). Toward an experimental ecology of human development. *American Psychologist, 32,* 513–531.

Bronfenbrenner, U. (1979). *The ecology of human development: Experiments by nature and design.* Cambridge, MA: Harvard University Press.

Bronfenbrenner, U., & Morris, P.A. (1998). The ecology of developmental process. In R. Lerner (Ed.), *Handbook of child psychology: Theoretical models of human development* (5th ed., Vol. 1, pp. 993–1028). New York: John Wiley & Sons.

Brown, W.H., Odom, S.L., Li, S., & Zercher, C. (1999). Ecobehavioral assessment in inclusive early childhood programs: A portrait of preschool inclusion. *Journal of Special Education, 33,* 138–153.

Brownell, C.A. (1990). Peer social skills in toddlers: Competencies and constraints illustrated by same-age and mixed-age interaction. *Child Development, 61,* 838–848.

Bruder, M.B., & Brand, M. (1995). A comparison of two types of early intervention environments serving toddler-age children with disabilities. *Infant-Toddler Intervention, 5,* 207–217.

Bryant, D.M., Burchinal, M., Lau, L.B., & Sparling, J.J. (1994). Family and classroom correlates of Head Start children's developmental outcomes. *Early Childhood Research Quarterly, 9,* 289–304.

Burchinal, M.R., Bailey, D.B., & Snyder, P. (1994). Using growth curve analysis to evaluate child change in longitudinal investigations. *Journal of Early Intervention, 18,* 403–423.

Burchinal, M.R., Cryer, D., & Clifford, R.M. (in press). Caregiver training and classroom quality in childcare centers. *Early Childhood Research Quarterly.*

Burchinal, M.R., Roberts, J.E., Nabors, L.A., & Bryant, D.M. (1996). Quality of center child care and infant cognitive and language development. *Child Development, 67,* 606–620.

Buysse, V., Wesley, P.W., Bryant, D.M., & Gardner, D. (1999). Quality of early childhood programs in inclusive and noninclusive settings. *Exceptional Children, 65,* 301–314.

Buysse, V., Wesley, P., & Keyes, L. (1998). Implementing early childhood inclusion: Barriers and support factors. *Early Childhood Research Quarterly, 13,* 169–184.

Buysse, V., Wesley, P., Keyes, L., & Bailey, D.B. (1996). Assessing the comfort zone of child care teachers in serving young children with disabilities. *Journal of Early Intervention, 20,* 189–203.

Carta, J.J., Sainato, D.M., & Greenwood, C.R. (1988). Advances in ecological assessment of classroom instruction for young children with handicaps. In S.L. Odom & M.B. Karnes (Eds.), *Early intervention for infants and children with handicaps: An empirical base* (pp. 217–239). Baltimore: Paul H. Brookes Publishing Co.

Carta, J.J., Schwartz, I.S., Atwater, J.B., & McConnell, S.R. (1991). Developmentally appropriate practice: Appraising its usefulness for young children with disabilities. *Topics in Early Childhood Special Education, 11*(1), 1–20.

Chandler, L.K., Fowler, S.A., & Lubeck, R.C. (1992). An analysis of the effects of multiple setting events on the social behavior of preschool children with special needs. *Journal of Applied Behavior Analysis, 25,* 249–262.

Cost, Quality, and Child Outcomes Study Team. (1995). *Cost, quality, and child outcomes in child care centers: Executive summary.* Boulder: University of Colorado.

DeKlyen, M., & Odom, S.L. (1989). Activity structure and social interaction with peers in developmentally integrated play groups. *Journal of Early Intervention, 13,* 342–351.

DeLong, A.J., Tegano, D.W., Moran, J.D., & Brickley, J. (1994). Effects of spatial scale on cognitive play in preschool children. *Early Education and Development, 5,* 237–246.

Diamond, K., & Hestenes, L. (1994). Preschool children's understanding of disability: Experiences leading to the elaboration of the concept of hearing loss. *Early Education and Development, 5,* 301–309.

Diamond, K., & Hestenes, L. (1996). Preschool children's conceptions of disabilities: The salience of disability in children's ideas about others. *Topics in Early Childhood Special Education, 16,* 458–475.

Diamond, K., Hestenes, L., Carpenter, E., & Innes, F. (in press). Relationships between enrollment in an inclusive class and preschool children's ideas about people with disabilities. *Topics in Early Childhood Special Education.*

Dinnebeil, L.A., McInerney, W., Fox, C., & Juchartz-Pendry, K. (1998). An analysis of the perceptions and characteristics of childcare personnel regarding inclusion of young children with special needs in community-based programs. *Topics in Early Childhood Special Education, 18,* 118–128.

Donegan, M.M., Ostrosky, M.M., & Fowler, S.A. (1996). Children enrolled in multiple programs: Characteristics, supports, and barriers to teacher communication. *Journal of Early Intervention, 20,* 95–106.

Dunn, L. (1993). Proximal and distal features of day care quality and children's development. *Early Childhood Research Quarterly, 8,* 167–192.

Eiserman, W.D., Shisler, L., & Healey, S. (1995). A community assessment of preschool providers' attitudes toward inclusion. *Journal of Early Intervention, 19,* 149–167.

Erwin, E.J. (1993). Social participation of young children with visual impairment in specialized and integrated environments. *Journal of Visual Impairments and Blindness, 87,* 138–142.

File, N. (1994). Children's play, teacher–child interactions, and teacher beliefs in integrated early childhood programs. *Early Childhood Research Quarterly, 9,* 223–240.

Frea, W., Craig, L., Odom, S.L., & Johnson, D. (1999). Differential effects of structured social integration and group friendship activities for promoting social interaction with peers. *Journal of Early Intervention, 22,* 230–242.

Furman, W., Rahe, D.F., & Hartup, W.W. (1979). Rehabilitation of socially withdrawn pre-school children through mixed-age and same-age socialization. *Child Development, 50,* 915–922.

Gemmell-Crosby, S., & Hanzlik, J.R. (1994). Preschool teachers' perceptions of including children with disabilities. *Education and Training in Mental Retardation and Developmental Disabilities, 29,* 279–290.

Gillespie, C.W., Pelren, S.L., & Twardosz, S. (1998). An ecological perspective on voluntary book use of 2- and 3-year-olds in day care. *Early Education and Development, 9,* 283–306.

Goldman, J.S. (1981). Social participation of preschool children in same- versus mixed-age groups. *Child Development, 52,* 644–650.

Guralnick, M.J. (1980). Social interaction among preschool handicapped children. *Exceptional Children, 46,* 248–253.

Guralnick, M.J. (1981). Peer influences on the development of communicative competence. In P. Strain (Ed.), *The utilization of classroom peers as behavior change agents* (pp. 31–68). New York: Kluwer Academic/Plenum Publishers.

Guralnick, M.J. (1982). Mainstreaming young handicapped children: A public policy and ecological systems analysis. In B. Spodek (Ed.), *Handbook of research in early childhood education* (pp. 456–500). New York: The Free Press.

Guralnick, M.J. (1990). Social competence and early intervention. *Journal of Early Intervention, 14,* 3–14.

Guralnick, M.J. (1999). The nature and meaning of social integration for young children with mild developmental delays in inclusive settings. *Journal of Early Intervention, 22,* 70–86.

Guralnick, M.J., Connor, R.T., Hammond, M.A., Gottman, J.M., & Kinnish, K. (1996). Immediate effects of mainstreamed settings on the social interactions and social integration of preschool children. *American Journal on Mental Retardation, 100,* 359–377.

Guralnick, M.J., & Groom, J.M. (1987). Dyadic peer interactions of mildly delayed and nonhandicapped preschool children. *American Journal of Mental Deficiency, 92,* 178–193.

Guralnick, M.J., & Groom, J.M. (1988). Friendships of preschool children in mainstream playgroups. *Developmental Psychology, 24,* 595–604.

Guralnick, M.J., & Paul-Brown, D. (1977). The nature of verbal interactions among handicapped and nonhandicapped preschool children. *Child Development, 48,* 254–260.

Hadeed, J., & Sylva, K. (1995, September). *Behavioral observations as predictors of children's social and cognitive progress in day care.* Paper presented in the Fifth European Early Childhood Education Research Association on the Quality of Early Childhood Education, Paris.

Harms, T., & Clifford, R.M. (1980). *Early Childhood Environment Rating Scale.* New York: Teachers College Press.

Harms, T., Clifford, R.M., & Cryer, D. (1998). *Early Childhood Environment Rating Scale, Revised Edition.* New York: Teachers College Press.

Harms, T., Cryer, D., & Clifford, R. (1987). *The Infant-Toddler Environmental Rating Scale.* Chapel Hill: The University of North Carolina Press, Frank Porter Graham Child Development Center.

Hauser-Cram, P., Bronson, M.B., & Upshur, C.C. (1993). The effects of the classroom environment on the social and mastery behavior of preschool children with disabilities. *Early Childhood Research Quarterly, 8,* 479–497.

Helburn, S. (Ed.). (1995). *Cost, quality, and child outcomes in child care centers: Technical report.* Denver: University of Colorado at Denver, Center for Research in Economic and Social Policy, Department of Economics.

Howes, C. (1997). Children's experiences in center-based child care as a function of teacher background and adult–child ratio. *Merrill-Palmer Quarterly, 43,* 404–425.

Howes, C., & Farver, J. (1987). Social pretend play in 2-year-olds: Effects of age of partners. *Early Childhood Research Quarterly, 2,* 305–314.

Howes, C., Phillips, D.A., & Whitebook, M. (1992). Thresholds of quality: Implications for the social development of children in center-based childcare. *Child Development, 63,* 449–460.

Howes, C., Smith, E., & Galinsky, E. (1995). *The Florida quality improvement study: Interim report.* New York: Families and Work Institute.

Hundert, J., & Hopkins, B. (1992). Training supervisors in a collaborative team process to promote peer interaction of children with disabilities in integrated preschools. *Journal of Applied Behavior Analysis, 25,* 385–400.

Hundert, J., Mahoney, B., & Hopkins, B. (1993). The relationship between the peer interaction of children with disabilities in inclusive preschools and resource and classroom teacher behaviors. *Topics in Early Childhood Special Education, 13,* 328–343.

Hundert, J., Mahoney, B., Mundy, F., & Vernon, M.L. (1998). A descriptive analysis of developmental and social gains of children with severe disabilities in segregated and inclusive preschools in southern Ontario. *Early Childhood Research Quarterly, 13,* 49–65.

Hyson, M.C., Hirsh-Pasek, K., & Rescorla, L. (1990). The Classroom Practices Inventory: An observation instrument based on NAEYC's guidelines for developmentally appropriate practice for 4- and 5-year-old children. *Early Childhood Research Quarterly, 5,* 475–494.

Jenkins, J.R., Odom, S.L., & Speltz, M.L. (1989). Effects of integration and structured play on the development of handicapped children. *Exceptional Children, 55,* 420–428.

Kohl, F.L., Beckman, P.J., & Swenson-Pierce, A. (1984). The effects of directed play on functional toy use and interactions of handicapped preschoolers. *Journal of the Division for Early Childhood, 8,* 114–118.

Kontos, S., Moore, D., & Giorgetti, K. (1998). The ecology of inclusion. *Topics in Early Childhood Special Education, 18,* 38–48.

Kontos, S., & Wilcox-Herzog, A. (1997). Influences on children's competence in early childhood classrooms. *Early Childhood Research Quarterly, 12,* 247–262.

Kopp, C.B., Baker, B.L., & Brown, K.W. (1992). Social skills and their correlates: Preschoolers with developmental delays. *American Journal on Mental Retardation, 96,* 357–367.

Krantz, P., & Risley, T.R. (1977). Behavior ecology in the classroom. In K.D. O'Leary & S. O'Leary (Eds.), *Classroom management: The successful use of behavior modification* (2nd ed., pp. 349–366). New York: Pergamon.

La Paro, K.M., Sexton, D., & Snyder, P. (1998). Program quality characteristics in segregated and inclusive early childhood settings. *Early Childhood Research Quarterly, 13,* 151–168.

Levine, L.M., & Antia, S.D. (1997). Th effects of partner hearing status on social and cognitive play. *Journal of Early Intervention, 21,* 21–35.

Lieber, J., Beckman, P.J., Hanson, M.J., Janko, S., Marquart, J.M., Horn, E., & Odom, S.L. (1997). The impact of changing roles on relationships between professionals in inclusive programs for young children. *Early Education and Development, 8*(1), 67–82.

Lieber, J., Capell, K., Sandall, S.R., Wolfberg, P., Horn, E., & Beckman, P. (1998). Inclusive preschool programs: Teachers' beliefs and practices. *Early Childhood Research Quarterly, 13,* 87–105.

Lougee, M.D., Grueneich, R., & Hartup, W.W. (1977). Social interaction in same- and mixed-age dyads of preschool children. *Child Development, 48,* 1353–1361.

Marchant, C. (1995). Teachers' views of integrated preschools. *Journal of Early Intervention, 19,* 61–73.

Martin, S.S., Brady, M.P., & Williams, R.E. (1991). Effects of toys on the social behavior of preschool children in integrated and nonintegrated groups: Investigation of a setting event. *Journal of Early Intervention, 15,* 153–161.

McCabe, J.R., Jenkins, J.R., Mills, P.E., Dale, P.S., & Cole, K.N. (1999). Effects of group composition, materials, and developmental level on play in preschool children with disabilities. *Journal of Early Intervention, 21,* 283–293.

McCabe, J.R., Jenkins, J.R., Mills, P.E., Dale, P.S., Cole, K.N., & Pepler, L. (1996). Effects of play group variables on language use by preschool children. *Journal of Early Intervention, 20,* 329–340.

McCormick, L., Noonan, M.J., & Heck, R. (1998). Variables affecting engagement in inclusive preschool classrooms. *Journal of Early Intervention, 21,* 160–176.

McWilliam, R.A., & Bailey, D.B. (1995). Effects of classroom social structure and disability on engagement. *Topics in Early Childhood Special Education, 15,* 123–147.

McWilliam, R., Trivette, C.M., & Dunst, C.J. (1985). Behavior engagement as a measure of the efficacy of early intervention. *Analysis and Intervention in Developmental Disabilities, 5,* 33–45.

Mills, P.E., Cole, K.N., Jenkins, J.R., & Dale, P.S. (1998). Effects of differing levels of inclusion on preschoolers with disabilities. *Exceptional Children, 65*(1), 79–90.

Nabors, L., Badawi, M., & Cheney, S. (1997). Factors related to teacher-directed play between preschool-aged children with special needs and their typical peers. *Early Education and Development, 8,* 407–417.

Nordquist, V.M., Twardosz, S., & McEvoy, M.A. (1991). Effects of environmental reorganization in classrooms for children with autism. *Journal of Early Intervention, 15,* 135–152.

O'Brien, M., & Bi, X. (1995). Language learning in context: Teacher and toddler speech in three classroom play areas. *Topics in Early Childhood Special Education, 15,* 148–163.

Odom, S.L., Brown, W.H., Li, S., & Zercher, C. (1999, April). *Ecobehavioral analysis of engagement of preschool children with and without disabilities in teacher- and child-initiated activities.* Paper presented at the Biennial Meeting of the Society for Research on Child Development, Albuquerque, NM.

Odom, S.L., Favazza, P.C., Brown, W.H., & Horn, E.M. (2000). Approaches to understanding the ecology of early childhood environments for children with disabilities. In T. Thompson, D. Felce, & F.J. Symons (Eds.), *Behavioral observation: Technology and applications in developmental disabilities* (pp. 193–214). Baltimore: Paul H. Brookes Publishing Co.

Odom, S.L., Horn, E.M., Marquart, J., Hanson, M.J., Wolfberg, P., Beckman, P., Lieber, J., Li, S., Schwartz, I., Janko, S., & Sandall, S. (1999). On the forms of inclusion: Organizational context and service delivery models. *Journal of Early Intervention, 22,* 185–199.

Odom, S.L., McConnell, S.R., McEvoy, M.A., Peterson, C., Ostrosky, M., Chandler, L.K., Spicuzza, R.J., Skellenger, A., Creighton, M., & Favazza, P.C. (1999). Relative effects of interventions supporting the social competence of young children with disabilities. *Topics in Early Childhood Special Education, 19,* 75–91.

Odom, S.L., Peck, C.A., Hanson, M., Beckman, P.J., Lieber, J., Brown, W.H., Horn, E.M., & Schwartz, I.S. (1996). Inclusion at the preschool level: An ecological systems analysis. *Social Policy Report: Society for Research in Child Development, 10*(2–3), 18–30.

Odom, S.L., Skellenger, A., & Ostrosky, M. (1993, March). *Ecobehavioral analysis of engagement and child initiation for children with and without disabilities.* Presentation at the Biennial Meeting of the Society for Research on Child Development, New Orleans, LA.

Odom, S.L., Wolery, R., Lieber, J., Sandall, S., Hanson, M.J., Beckman, P.J., Schwartz, I., & Horn, E. (2000). *Preschool inclusion: A review of research from an ecological systems perspective.* Submitted for publication.

Odom, S.L., Zercher, C., Li, S., Marquart, J., & Sandall, S. (1998, May). *Social relationships of preschool children with disabilities in inclusive settings.* Paper presented at the Conference on Research Innovations in Early Intervention, Charleston, SC.

Okagaki, L., Diamond, K.E., Kontos, S.J., & Hestenes, L.L. (1998). Correlates of young children's interactions with classmates with disabilities. *Early Childhood Research Quarterly, 13,* 67–86.

Ostrosky, M.M., Skellenger, A.C., Odom, S.L., McConnell, S.R., & Peterson, C. (1994). Teachers' schedules and actual time spent in activities in preschool special education classes. *Journal of Early Intervention, 18,* 25–33.

Patterson, G.R. (1976). The aggressive child: Victim and architect of a coercive system. In L. Hamerlynk, L. Handy, & E. Mash (Eds.), *Behavior modification and families: Theory and research* (Vol. 1, pp. 267–316). Levittown, PA: Brunner/Mazel Publishing.

Peck, C.A. (1993). Ecological perspectives on the implementation of integrated early childhood programs. In C.A. Peck, S.L. Odom, & D.D. Bricker (Eds.), *Integrating young children with disabilities into community programs: Ecological perspectives on research and implementation* (pp. 3–15). Baltimore: Paul H. Brookes Publishing Co.

Peck, C.A., Carlson, P., & Helmstetter, E. (1992). Parent and teacher perceptions of outcomes for typically developing children enrolled in integrated early childhood programs: A statewide survey. *Journal of Early Intervention, 16,* 53–63.

Peck, C.A., Furman, G.C., & Helmstetter, E. (1993). Integrated early childhood programs: Research on implementation of change in organizational contexts. In C.A. Peck, S.L. Odom, & D.D. Bricker (Eds.), *Integrating young children with disabilities into community programs: Ecological perspectives on research and implementation.* (pp. 187–205). Baltimore: Paul H. Brookes Publishing Co.

Peisner-Feinberg, E.S., & Burchinal, M.R. (1997). Relations between preschool children's child-care experiences and concurrent development: The Cost, Quality, and Outcomes Study. *Merrill-Palmer Quarterly, 43,* 451–477.

Peisner-Feinberg, E.S., Burchinal, M.R., Clifford, R.M., Yarzgian, N., Culkin, M.L., Zelazo, J., Howes, C., Byler, P., Kagan, S.L., & Rustici, J. (1999). *The children of the Cost, Quality and Outcomes Study go to school.* Chapel Hill: The University of North Carolina Press, Frank Porter Graham Child Development Center.

Phillips, D.A., Voran, M., Kisker, E., Howes, C., & Whitebook, M. (1994). Child care for children in poverty: Opportunity or inequity? *Child Development, 65,* 472–492.

Pickett, P.L., Griffith, P.L., & Rogers-Adkinson, D. (1993). Integration of preschoolers with severe disabilities into day care. *Early Education and Development, 4,* 54–58.

Pollowy, A.M. (1974). The child in the physical environment: A design problem. In G. Coates (Ed.), *Alternative learning environments* (pp. 370–382). Stroudsburg, PA: Downden, Hutchinson, and Ross.

Quay, L.C. (1993). Social competence in nonhandicapped, low interacting, and five handicapped groups of preschoolers. *Early Education and Development, 4,* 89–98.

Quilitch, H.R., & Risley, T.R. (1973). The effects of play materials on social play. *Journal of Applied Behavior Analysis, 6,* 575–578.

Roberts, J.E., Burchinal, M.R., & Bailey, D.B. (1994). Social communication interactions of children with developmental delays in integrated settings: An exploratory study. *Topics in Early Childhood Special Education, 18,* 239–242.

Rogers-Warren, A., & Wedel, J.W. (1980). The ecology of preschool classrooms for the handicapped. *New Directions for Exceptional Children, 1,* 1–24.

Rubin, K.H. (1977). The social and cognitive value of preschool toys and activities. *Canadian Journal of Behavioral Sciences, 9,* 382–385.

Rule, S., Losardo, A., Dinnebeil, L., Kaiser, A., & Rowland, C. (1998). Translating research on naturalistic instruction into practice. *Journal of Early Intervention, 21,* 283–293.

Russell, A. (1990). The effects of child–staff ratio and child behavior in preschools: An experimental study. *Journal of Research in Childhood Education, 4*(2), 77–90.

Sainato, D.M. (1990). Classroom transitions: Organizing environments to promote independent performance in preschool children with disabilities. *Education and Treatment of Children, 13,* 288–297.

Sainato, D.M., & Carta, J.J. (1992). Classroom influences on the development of social competence in young children with disabilities. In S.L. Odom, S.R. McConnell, & M.A. McEvoy (Eds.), *Social competence of young children with disabilities: Issues and strategies for intervention* (pp. 93–109). Baltimore: Paul H. Brookes Publishing Co.

Scarr, S., Eisenberg, M., & Deater-Deckard, K. (1994). Measurement of quality in child care programs. *Early Childhood Research Quarterly, 9,* 131–151.

Sheehan, R., & Day, D. (1975). Is open space just empty space? *Day Care and Early Education, 3,* 10–13.

Shure, M.B. (1963). The psychological ecology of the nursery school. *Child Development, 34,* 979–992.

Smith, M.W., & Dickinson, D.K. (1994). Describing oral language opportunities in Head Start and other preschool classrooms. *Early Childhood Research Quarterly, 9,* 345–366.

Sontag, J.C. (1997). Contextual factors influencing sociability of preschool children with disabilities in integrated and segregated classrooms. *Exceptional Children, 63,* 389–404.

Stoneman, Z., Cantrell, M.L., & Hoover-Dempsey, K. (1983). The association between play materials and social behavior in a mainstreamed preschool: A naturalistic investigation. *Journal of Applied Developmental Psychology, 4,* 163–174.

Strain, P.S. (1983). Generalization of autistic children's social behavior change: Effects of developmentally integrated and segregated settings. *Analysis and Intervention in Developmental Disabilities, 4,* 163–171.

Strain, P. (1990). LRE for preschool children with handicaps: What we know, what we should be doing. *Journal of Early Intervention, 14,* 291–296.

Suomi, S.J., & Harlow, H.F. (1972). Social rehabilitation of isolate-reared monkeys. *Developmental Psychology, 6,* 487–496.

Tegano, D.W., Lookabaugh, S., May, G.E., & Burdette, M.P. (1991). Constructive play and problem solving: The role of structure and time in the classroom. *Early Child Development and Care, 68,* 27–35.

U.S. Department of Education. (1999). *To assure the free appropriate public education of all children with disabilities: 21st annual report to Congress on the implementation of the Individuals with Disabilities Education Act.* Washington, DC: Author.

Wesley, P.W., Buysse, V., & Tyndall, S. (1997). Family and professional perspectives on early intervention: An exploration using focus groups. *Topics in Early Childhood Special Education, 17,* 435–456.

Wolery, M., Strain, P.S., & Bailey, D.B. (1992). Reaching potentials of children with special needs. In S. Bredekamp & T. Rosegrant (Eds.), *Reaching potentials: Appropriate curriculum and assessment for young children* (Vol. 1, pp. 92–113). Washington, DC: National Association for the Education of Young Children.

12

BARBARA SCHWARTZ

MARIE E. BRAND

Head Start and the Inclusion of Children with Disabilities

Head Start was established in 1965 as a comprehensive child development and family support program to interrupt the cycle of poverty within communities (Zigler & Anderson, 1997). It was built on a foundation of research on the benefits of early intervention (see Hess, 1967, and Guralnick, 1997, for related historical information). Head Start is acknowledged as the largest provider of inclusive environments for young children with disabilities and may be the only early childhood program operating in the United States that has always been inclusive.

To understand the extent to which Head Start has been inclusive and has met the needs of children with disabilities from birth to age 5 years in its community-based programs, a historical framework of Head Start is necessary. Only by reviewing this history from 1965 to the present, the conception of the program, the program's plan to set aside 10% of enrollment opportunities for children with disabilities, and the research that assessed the impact of Head Start on children and families that live in poverty can the con-

text for Head Start today be understood. This context provides a framework for understanding how the Head Start programs of the future will provide an even more secure environment for meeting the needs of children with disabilities and their families.

HEAD START: DEVELOPMENT AND DESIGN

The Economic Opportunity Act of 1964 (PL 88-452) established Head Start as a child development intervention to stimulate intellectual growth and development while attending to the nutritional health and developmental needs of the child and working to support the independence of the family (Zigler & Valentine, 1997). Sargent Shriver, then Director of the Office of Economic Opportunity (OEO), commissioned a panel of 14 child development experts, chaired by pediatrician Robert Cooke, to develop a plan of intervention to meet the needs of preschool-age children who were living in poverty. They recommended the creation of a

The authors thank Dinah Heller, former Director of the New York University Quality Improvement Center for Disabilities, for her assistance.

comprehensive community-based program to break the cycle of poverty and that would develop the child's social competence, improve the child's cognitive processes and skills with particular attention to conceptual and verbal skills, establish patterns and expectations of success within the child, guarantee that each child received adequate nutrition, ensure that the child's physical health needs were addressed, strengthen the family's ability to relate positively to the child, support the family to be ready to meet the challenge of work, and link the family to health care options (Califano, 1997; Tjossem, 1976).

Begun as an 8-week summer program in 1965 projected to serve 50,000 children, it actually enrolled 561,000 3- to 5-year-old children who were economically disadvantaged. As a result of its huge success during the summer of 1965, Head Start shifted to a year-long program emphasizing early education, parent involvement, comprehensive service delivery, and local control.

In 1969, Head Start was moved from OEO to the Office of Child Development in the Department of Health, Education, and Welfare (HEW) and began to serve the children of migrant workers beginning with infants as young as 6 weeks (Valentine, 1997). Head Start has remained in this organizational structure since that time, reflecting its core role as a human services program. (HEW later became the Department of Health and Human Services, and the Office of Child Development became the Administration on Children, Youth, and Families.)

HEAD START: SERVICES TO CHILDREN WITH DISABILITIES

From the earliest years of Head Start, some programs believed that serving income-eligible children within their community included serving children with disabilities (King-Elkan & Fink,

n.d.). It was not unusual to find many examples of Head Start programs, rural and urban alike, that included children with spina bifida, cerebral palsy, missing limbs, visual impairments, or Down syndrome (Heller, 1985). Head Start's health and developmental screenings routinely identified many typical children within classrooms who were in need of referral for comprehensive professional evaluation beyond the scope of the standard services available in Head Start.

Although many believed that Head Start would be the "early intervention" for children with disabilities, it was apparent that for some children, more specialized services would be needed than the child development opportunities provided by Head Start staff. Without mandates or designated fiscal support, an array of strategies were implemented, such as hiring professional speech-language, physical, and occupational therapists; collaborating with local medical or special education providers; establishing special education classrooms; and "sharing" children with special education programs while providing part-day or alternate-day programs at Head Start. The Economic Opportunity Act Amendments of 1972 (PL 92-424) specified that the Secretary of HEW ensure that 10% of enrollment was "reserved for handicapped" and that these children must be receiving adequate treatment through the Head Start program opportunities for children with disabilities (Ackerman & Moore, 1976). This amendment was issued in response to the outcomes of a series of court cases in the early 1970s challenging the segregation of children with disabilities in separate schools (see Chapters 2 and 4). The federal government turned to its only national program for children, Head Start, to demonstrate its willingness to respond to court-mandated changes and include children with disabilities alongside typically developing children (i.e., guaranteeing their civil rights [P. Coughlin, personal communication, October 15, 1999]). In 1973, after only 1 year of mandated enrollment, 13.2% of the children in Head Start met criteria for a range of disability categories (Zigler & Valentine, 1997). This proportion remained fairly constant over the years.

To ensure that services were implemented consistently across Head Start programs, the Head Start Bureau issued a series of Transmittal Notices from 1972 to 1975 providing guidelines for serving children with disabilities, including clearly delineated diagnostic criteria. Specifically, Head Start programs were to

- Implement developmental screening for *all* children as part of comprehensive health screening
- Refer children who were identified as a result of screening, observation, or other concerns to licensed professionals to determine whether they met diagnostic criteria
- Develop individualized education programs (IEPs), including goals for families, in addition to the provision of individualized education services expected for all Head Start children
- Form collaborations with local community organizations and school districts to obtain in-kind or low-fee related services
- Identify and, if necessary, hire specialized consultants to meet the needs of children with disabilities
- Designate a handicapped services coordinator to ensure that children were appropriately screened, assessed, evaluated, and diagnosed and, if diagnosed, ensure that the child received the necessary services

As might be expected, Head Start agencies were concerned about their ability to provide these services adequately, knowing that they lacked fiscal resources and specialized expertise to work with children with disabilities. To ensure targeted support for special supplemental costs that were required for effective implementation of efforts to include children with disabilities, the Head Start Bureau allocated an additional funding track to Head Start budgets. These funds were to be used by Head Start to pay for direct services to children with disabilities, including the expansion and improvement of services already available, and training opportunities for staff. Eventually, these funds were incorporated in the overall Head Start budget with the expectation that Head Start programs would continue to provide the same "maintenance of effort" for children with disabilities.

The fiscal burden was further lessened for Head Start programs in some states by the implementation in 1975 of the Education for All Handicapped Children Act (PL 94-142). This legislation, which provided support for the participation of children older than 5 years in the least restrictive environment (LRE), was of some help to Head Start. In some cases, local education agencies (LEAs) or special education programs in the community made "shared" placements possible—a child attended Head Start part of the day/week and a special education preschool as well. In other instances, direct support was provided at Head Start programs for children with diagnosed disabilities. In either case, the fiscal impact to Head Start was beginning to be relieved. These arrangements were made possible by the development of state-level Memorandums of Understanding (MOU) between Departments of Education/Special Education and Head Start.

Additional support for Head Start's "mainstreaming" of children with disabilities was provided by the Head Start Bureau in its funding in 1976 of a technical assistance support system, the

Resource Access Projects (RAPs).[1] RAPs were funded across the country to provide training and technical assistance to Head Start programs in each of the federal regions and to provide support to Migrant and American Indian Head Start programs. Their role was to assist Head Start staff in providing services to children with disabilities and their families through "mainstreaming" conferences, cluster training sessions, developing and introducing training resources (e.g., the widely known series "Mainstreaming Preschoolers: Children with. . ."[2]), technical assistance, sharing of resources and information, and the development of state-level MOU with Departments of Education to act as a foundation for the development of LEA agreements. Annual evaluation studies in the first 10 years of the work of the RAPs found that the RAPs provided a clear beneficial impact by enhancing the capacity of staff and families in understanding the needs and provision of services to children with disabilities.

With the passage of the Education of the Handicapped Act Amendments of 1986 (PL 99-457) and the mandates to provide a free appropriate public education (FAPE) in the LRE to all children from ages 3 to 21 and the option to serve children from birth, Head Start finally had a means to provide the full range of services for children with disabilities but at public expense. The Head Start community cheered and waited for LEAs and special education providers to seek out Head Start programs. Head Start knew that it was one of the few programs to which LEAs could turn to provide FAPE in the LRE to preschool-age children. The impact of PL 99-457 and subsequent revisions and reauthorizations of the

Individuals with Disabilities Education Act (IDEA) (PL 101-476, PL 102-119, PL 105-17) has in fact brought about changes. Since 1986, increasing numbers of children in Head Start have received their services through IEPs developed and supported by the LEAs. Proportionately fewer Head Start dollars are required to support special education and related services.

In January 1993, Head Start Program Performance Standards for Children with Disabilities (45 C.F.R. Part 1308) were issued specifying the requirements by which Head Start programs were to deliver services to preschool-age children with disabilities. These standards were developed to be consistent with IDEA and state-level special education regulations.

Head Start Expansion

Although Head Start funding increased slowly during the 1970s and 1980s, actual enrollment declined as Head Start programs offset increased the cost of services with changes in program design (e.g., increased length of day, increased number of program days). However, from 1989 to 1993, expansion occurred at an unprecedented rate with almost one third more additional children being served. The growing pains were evident. The quality of services suffered, and programs questioned whether what they were doing was truly effective. The Head Start Bureau affirmed in 1993 its commitment to children with disabilities when its commissioner, Mary Jo Bane, convened a "Blue Ribbon Panel" to examine the impact of expansion on the quality of services offered (U.S. Department of Health and Human Services, 1993). The report of the panel emphasized a

---

[1] Renamed Disabilities Services Quality Improvement Centers (DSQICs) in 1997, training and technical assistance continues to be available to all Head Start programs in support of their efforts to include children with disabilities. (For a list of DSQICs and other Head Start information, go to http://www.acf.dhhs.gov.)

[2] This series of eight guides on specific disabilities was developed by the Head Start Bureau for teachers, parents, and others.

renewed support for Head Start as a provider of services to children with disabilities and recommended that Head Start 1) revise Head Start Program Performance Standards, 2) expand Head Start's role as a "prevention program" through a renewed effort to serve pregnant women and children younger than 3 years of age, 3) develop strategies to improve the quality of classroom staff, and 4) implement a research agenda. The Blue Ribbon Panel also recommended increased collaboration between the Head Start Bureau and the Office of Special Education and Rehabilitative Services (OSERS).

Even with additional support from special education legislation, staff and parents reported increasing numbers of children who were "difficult to manage," "out of control," and "challenging." Were the children now entering Head Start in the 1990s different from before? Was Head Start experiencing the impact of the "crack epidemic?" Or were the staff, hired to meet the needs of expansion, lacking the skills necessary to address the child development issues of preschool children? In response to meeting the needs of these children, the RAP network, with the support of the Head Start Bureau, developed *Child to Child: Maximizing Opportunities for Social Integration* (National Network of Resource Access Projects for Head Start, 1993). This training guide was built on a foundation of current field-based knowledge regarding intervention strategies known to support the development of improved peer social relations. It was designed to support inclusion of children with more challenging and significant disabilities by offering strategies for teaching staff, administrators, and parents. Field-test results indicated that as a result of participation, teachers had a greater awareness

of how their attitudes affected the acceptance of children with disabilities and were better able to recognize when to implement intervention strategies and how to integrate their strategies into ongoing classroom activities (Johnson & LaMontagne, 1992).

Acknowledging the need for ongoing staff support for effective quality Head Start services, the Head Start Bureau in 1994 funded a series of national contractors to develop sets of training guides related to each of the Head Start service areas. The contract for the development of materials to support disability-related services was awarded to the Educational Development Corporation.[3] All guides in the series were based on extensive field testing and incorporated the best and most effective principles of adult learning (that learning is most effective when it includes opportunities for active participation and the components of "coaching" and mentoring).

Early Head Start

Another recommendation of the Blue Ribbon Panel was the creation of a renewed and expanded program to serve Head Start children and families before age 3. The Head Start Reauthorization Act of 1994 (PL 103-252) established a new Early Head Start (EHS) program. Even though Head Start served children younger than 3 years since 1967 through Parent Child Centers (PCCs) and Migrant Head Start, the new model of services to pregnant women, infants, and toddlers had a new orientation (supporting the early parent–child relationship while maintaining high-quality comprehensive services for the entire family, including pregnant women). EHS is expected to set aside 10% of enrollment opportunities for infants and toddlers who were diagnosed with disabilities by

---

[3]From 1994 through 1997, five guides were developed: *Setting the Stage: Including Children with Disabilities in Head Start; Leading the Way: A Guide for the Head Start Management Team; Supporting Children with Challenging Behavior: Relationships Are Key; Translating the IEP into Everyday Practice;* and *Including Children with Significant Disabilities.*

their state's early intervention Part C system and to have a collaborative relationship in place with their Part C agency. At the beginning of the 21st century, there are almost 500 funded programs. As part of President Clinton's Child Care initiative of 1999, the number of children in EHS is proposed to double over 5 years (Administration for Children and Families, 2000).

The establishment of the first EHS programs in 1995 brought with it new challenges. For Early Head Start programs, the 10% allocation of enrollment opportunities is only for children who have received diagnoses through the state's Part C system. At the time of funding, they are expected to have in place a linkage with their local Part C system. IDEA's emphasis on early intervention and related services within the "natural environment' has been an easy fit, as EHS programs are designed to reflect the needs of their communities and families that they serve. With the 1997 reauthorization of IDEA (PL 105-17) and the key placement of Head Start on state and federal interagency coordinating councils, the voice of Head Start and Early Head Start is now fully within the early intervention community.

In support of the unique needs of infants and toddlers with disabilities, the Disabilities Services Quality Improvement Centers (DSQICs) added an Infant/Family Specialist and the Head Start Bureau provided two additional training and technical assistance supports. The Early Head Start National Resource Center (EHS NRC) was funded by the Head Start Bureau to address the overall needs of establishing programs to serve pregnant women, infants, and toddlers, including many innovative models. Support for EHS to enroll infants and toddlers with more significant disabilities was enhanced through the Hilton/Early Head Start Training Program funded through Sonoma State University's Cali-

fornia Institute on Human Services. This grant provides for a series of four annual state-of-the-art week-long "SpecialQuest" intensive training sessions to EHS teams composed of a parent, EHS administrators, and early intervention community partners, in each of five regional hubs. A learning coach accompanies the teams and provides two follow-up sessions to help the teams meet their goals. The results of the second year of the program evaluation indicated improved progress toward goals and demonstrated increases in the number of children with disabilities who were identified and for whom services were provided.

Quality of Programs

As Head Start was looking at quality within its programs, there was a parallel level of analysis of the cost and quality of child care occurring on several levels. The major National Institute of Child Health and Human Development (NICHD) study found that programs with teachers who had either bachelor's degrees or a child care credentials, as well as other measures of higher quality, were associated with children's being better prepared for school (NICHD Early Child Care Research Network, 1999). With respect to Head Start, Bryant, Burchinal, Lau, and Sparling (1994) examined the relative effect of the quality of the environment, level of teacher education, and effects of home environment on student outcomes. As with the NICHD study, children in higher quality programs performed better on child outcome measures. However, in this study, in which 91% of Head Start teaching staff had an associate's degree or higher, the mean rating on the 37-item Early Childhood Environment Rating Scale (ECERS; Harms & Clifford, 1980) was 4.24. This was slightly below the criterion of 5 that would place classrooms in the "good" range for quality. In addition, there was no correlation between level of teacher education and quality of classrooms.

Head Start's assessment of program quality is expanding on the work of Bryant and colleagues (1994) and others in the form of the multisite Family and Child Experience Study (FACES). FACES is assessing a set of performance measures in a nationally representative sample of 2,400 children and families in 40 Head Start programs (U.S. Department of Health and Human Services, 1998). The first FACES results, as measured by the ECERS scale, indicated that 61% of Head Start programs were of good quality, scoring a 5 on the overall 7-point scale, with a mean rating of 4.9. Parallel to this was the rating of outcomes for children. Children scored higher on early literacy measures when they experienced teacher–child interactions that were rich in language learning opportunities and embedded in an environment that was well equipped with learning resources. Moreover, FACES demonstrated positive educational outcomes, with 4-year-olds in the sample demonstrating knowledge and skills in early literacy and numeracy, as well as social skills signifying readiness to learn in kindergarten. The initial results were promising; none of the 403 classrooms assessed with the ECERS scored in the minimal quality range, 68% of the teaching staff had some college experience or a college degree, and teacher–child ratios averaged 5.6 per child. These findings that reflected a national sample were more positive than those of Bryant and colleagues (1994) that had been conducted in only one state, which is encouraging. Unfortunately, little is mentioned in the preliminary report regarding services to children with disabilities except for the extent to which programs were able to deliver services. Within the sample studied, 88% of children with diagnosed disabilities were found to have IEPs in place. These findings underscore the need for Head Start to continue to address the issue of "quality" by supporting an improved level of professional development for Head Start teaching staff.

HEAD START'S EFFECTIVENESS: TRAINING AND RESEARCH

Children with disabilities have been part of Head Start from its inception; as programs served their communities, they served their children with special needs. Throughout the years, increased federal funding of special education and related services has reduced the fiscal burden initially incurred by Head Start and created opportunities for greater flexibility of supports for children with disabilities within Head Start. Guralnick (1999), in assessing the outcomes of social integration in inclusive environment, concluded that the outcomes for preschool children with disabilities will be limited without comprehensive child-, family-, and community-focused intervention.

Impact of Inclusive Practices on Children and Staff

At first glance, it seems that as a comprehensive child-, staff-, family-, and community-based program, Head Start programs are operating well within the realm of expectations. However, many barriers remain.

The Early Period As Head Start began to include children with disabilities, it readily became apparent that mere placement of children with disabilities was not sufficient. Fortunately, these concerns coincided with the funding of the first Handicapped Children's Early Education Program (HCEEP), which was designed to provide services through demonstration projects and outreach training programs (Ackerman & Moore, 1976). Two of the many programs that directly provided supports to Head Start were the project established by Sanford at Chapel Hill (Grossi, Pinkstaff, Henley, & Sanford, 1975) and the Infant, Toddler, and Preschool Program at the New York University Medical Center, Rusk Institute of Rehabilitation Medicine (see Tjossem, 1976, for examples of other HCEEP projects).

Head Start programs across the nine states that compose Federal Region IV (southeastern United States) were concerned that only one sixth of teachers were certified, and therefore substantial numbers of teachers lacked the necessary skills to support the specialized education needs of children with disabilities (Grossi et al., 1975). Survey results indicated that teachers, even with a lack of expertise, enjoyed their opportunity to work with children with disabilities, and they acknowledged that to be more effective in this work they required substantial training. The Chapel Hill Training Program provided intensive outreach from 1972 to 1975 to nearly 1,750 staff from 223 agencies who acknowledged the positive benefits of training that had improved their skills in identifying and referring children for specialized services. It was outcomes such as this that provided support for the RAP/DSQIC network that has provided ongoing training and technical assistance to Head Start since 1976.

The program at the Rusk Institute provided intensive training to more than 100 Head Start education staff during a 3-year period through workshops provided by the preschool's special education staff, on-site training at the Head Start agencies, and/or "miniplacements" of 1-week periods in the preschool classroom at Rusk (Gordon & Schwartz, 1976). With staff at Head Start acquiring these skills, it was then possible to help children make the transition from special education programs into classroom environments where Head Start staff had developed specialized skills.

The extent to which the transition of children with disabilities into inclusive Head Start programs was successful was examined in a study by Schwartz, Gordon, Ezrachi, and Lawrence (1978). This study focused on differences of social behaviors of children with physical disabilities participating in Head Start classrooms as opposed to those who were enrolled in special education preschools. Relative to their typical peers, children with disabilities in Head Start decreased their peer involvement and social behavior during the course of the year. The results of the experience in the Head Start classrooms were more positive for the teachers than for the children. As a result of including children with physical disabilities, teaching staff learned that improvement and change occurred on an individual child-by-child basis, not necessarily disability related. The outcome for parents was favorable; parents of children with and without disabilities viewed the practice of mainstreaming as positive. However, parents of children with disabilities in both inclusive and specialized environments voiced concerns regarding the ability of general education teachers to provide the specialized supports and services that were needed (see Chapter 6). Staff and parents were optimistic that secondary effects would occur (i.e., that the typically developing children would in the long term be able to accept individuals with disabilities in the "real world"). Finally, teachers in this study believed that if there had been greater support and consultation, they would have been more effective in supporting the needs of the child with a disability.

Findings   These findings are similar to what has occurred since the early 1990s, as more children with disabilities are fully included in Head Start and other community-based environments (that mere proximity, without planned intervention, is not a sufficient condition for improving social skills and peer engagement [Guralnick, 1999]). Indeed, Schwartz (1987) found that in Head Start and child care environments in which children with disabilities and typically developing peers were left to engage in play without teacher supports, there was limited evidence of peer-to-peer engagement. If Head Start is to make effective changes in improving the social outcomes for children, including engagement with typically developing peers, then more must be done than just ensuring that adequate support services are offered as specified in IEPs.

The limitations in implementing the necessary level of skill development are highlighted in a study by Innocenti, Kim, and Gutschall (1996) that assessed the impact of training on activity-based intervention (ABI) with 17 Head Start paraprofessional staff working with 83 children with diagnosed disabilities. Eight staff were provided in-service education in ABI, and nine received no direct training. Paraprofessional staff who received the training were more likely to implement the intervention and use more verbal prompts. The children with disabilities were more likely to become the activity leader. Unfortunately, as a result of the intervention, children with disabilities were not found to participate more with typically developing peers, and the paraprofessional staff were not able to develop the skills to implement ABI correctly. The authors concluded that the intensity of intervention training needed to create change was far beyond what could reasonably be accommodated in Head Start programs.

With both a DSQIC network in place and supplemental training guides available, more intensive training on targeted interventions by skilled staff and an enhanced teacher–child ratio may be needed to demonstrate adequate change in children. Bennett, DeLuca, and Bruns (1997) found that the degree to which

Head Start and other child care teachers were supportive of inclusion was affected by the teachers' perceptions of their own skills and resources. That is, teaching staff who perceived that they had increased skills would therefore view their experience of including children with disabilities in a more positive light.

Of necessity, all staff involved should hold positive attitudes toward individuals with disabilities, be trained in inclusive educational practices, and have current knowledge of the positive benefits of such an inclusive approach (Buscemi, Bennett, Thomas, & DeLuca, 1995). This is underscored by the findings of an extensive review by Scruggs and Mastropieri (1996) of 28 studies. They identified a number of variables that teachers stated should be included if they are to be more effective in educating children with disabilities alongside their typical peers: 1) sufficient time for meetings to plan, 2) preservice, in-service, and extended supported consultation, 3) additional support staff to ensure that the child's goals are being met on a daily basis, and 4) reduction of class size, particularly with regard to the nature and severity of the child's disability. Ideally, Head Start programs should consider the extent that these factors can be accommodated in program design.

Concerns regarding skills and quality of staff expertise in Head Start are not surprising. The lack of highly trained staff to provide necessary interventions for children with disabilities is echoed in concerns that the Head Start Bureau raised in earlier days and that were addressed by the 1998 Head Start reauthorization, which specified that by 2003, 50% of all Head Start teachers are to have at minimum an associate's degree. Funding to provide professional training and salary enhancements at the attainment of degrees was provided to Head Start programs. It would be beneficial for Head Start agencies, in planning a career ladder and professional development for individual staff members and the agency as a whole, to encourage staff to enroll in courses in early childhood special education or programs that support inclusive training models.

Impact of Inclusive Practices on Families and Communities

The role of the parent is essential in services to children with disabilities (Guralnick, 1998). A key component that differentiates Head Start from other early childhood education programs is the primary role of the family. Head Start families have always played a significant role in screening, decisions about referral for early intervention or special education, ongoing assessment, program planning and intervention, and transition (Heller, 1985; Phillips & Cabrera, 1996).

Research has found that Head Start parents are significantly more involved than parents in other publicly funded preschool options (Marcon, 1999). From its inception, Head Start had a legislative mandate for "maximum feasible participation" in all programmatic efforts. Highlights of the research underscore the value of Head Start for the parent as much as for the child. For example, a concerted 5-year assessment of the impact of parental involvement in urban Head Start programs found that a parent's involvement in Head Start improved family life and parent–child relationships, enhanced home learning environments, supported greater social competence, increased parent self-efficacy, and led to greater involvement of the parent at the elementary school level (Parker et al., 1997). These are not isolated findings.

The continued satisfaction of Head Start parents as consumers of services is outstanding. Their satisfaction ratings exceeded consumer satisfaction of services provided by any other government agen-

cies and by private corporations (Barr, 1999). Earlier research cited by Schwartz and colleagues (1978) highlighted the positive views that families of children with disabilities had regarding their child's experience in Head Start. Anecdotal evidence points to parents' satisfaction with the ability of Head Start to provide a "normalized" environment (Bonnelli, 1998; Demerest, 1983). Nevertheless, qualitative and quantitative research on families of Head Start children with disabilities is not available.

Early Head Start is likely to have an even more profound impact on services to families in general and especially for infants and toddlers with disabilities. By design, Part C services are offered in collaboration with the EHS program. In addition, EHS provides prevention and intervention beginning at pregnancy. It is also hoped that in some communities there will be a reduction in infant mortality, high-risk pregnancies, and premature births. In many Early Head Start programs across the United States, strategies are being implemented that may ultimately reduce many of the risk factors associated with high-risk births and early infant–parent relationship problems (e.g., prenatal home visits, training to support infant–parent relationships, lactation intervention to support breastfeeding and quality nutrition, training on risks of birth defects provided by the March of Dimes, linkages of infant and family with primary care health providers).

In addition to Head Start's impact on the family, one of the key outcomes of Head Start research has been Head Start's positive long-term change in community social agencies (McKey et al., 1985). Greater community-based merging of resources frequently resulted in integrated seamless services for families and their children, as well as increased development of family support services and teacher empowerment. With renewed emphasis on community partnerships in the 1995 revision of Head Start Program Performance Standards 1304 and the emphasis on community building for Early Head Start, expectations for the future are even more optimistic. For children with disabilities, this is well established through the formal collaborative arrangements as part of IDEA at the federal, state, and local levels.

LOOKING TO THE FUTURE: CONCERNS AND NEW DIRECTIONS

With the incidence of disability rising in families that live in poverty (Fujiara & Yamaki, 2000), Head Start in the coming years will be called upon to serve an ever-increasing number of children and families. Whereas Head Start was at one time the only preschool intervention model for children from low socioeconomic backgrounds, it is now one of numerous models and programs that serve young children and families from the prenatal period through the early years of public school (Kagan, 1991). Head Start established itself as an "inclusion" model before the language to describe its community-based efforts existed. With different inclusion models available in the general community (see Chapter 1), it is evident that Head Start will never be one model but will be many models.

The creators of Head Start were careful to have individual communities define what best met their needs and to give parents a role in each aspect of the program. Head Start became a program that could, when represented at its highest quality, truly act as the most effective model to meet the needs of the child with disabilities.

As Head Start begins a course of planned research and evaluation, it has an opportunity to demonstrate its impact and success in meeting the needs of all children and families it serves, including children with disabilities. Looking forward to the next century of Head Start, there continues to be a large unmet need for Head Start services. However, in many communities, Head Start, public schools, and other early childhood programs and providers operate in isolation from one another, each without adequate resources, planning, and coordination. There continues to be a strong need to ensure quality and strive to attain excellence in every local program. Programs must respond flexibly to the needs of today's children and families, including those currently unserved. Head Start continues to forge new partnerships at the community, state, and federal levels and renew and recraft these partnerships to fit the changes in families, communities, and state and national policy.

Quality Improvement

Head Start is at the beginning of a new era. The 1994 Head Start reauthorization called for sweeping improvements in the quality of programs, including funding to support the increase in the proportion of licensed, credentialed teachers, as well as the development of a sound, well-designed research agenda. For children with disabilities, this will truly be advantageous. In addition, the 1996 revision of Head Start Program Performance Standards finally established clear guidelines for developing and implementing quality services for infants and toddlers with disabilities.

Guralnick examined the many factors that lead to positive outcomes of social integration for children with mild disabilities. He noted that one constant is the emphasis on contexts that provide the highest quality early childhood environment and "exemplify inclusive principles and values by promoting full participation of all children in social and non-social activities" (1999, p. 70). The standard for including children with disabilities cannot be an environment that is adequate; it must be the highest quality environment, in which teachers are skilled in providing the ongoing individualized planning of activities, the support of the child's interactions with peers, and the materials that will maximize the opportunities for the child with disabilities (Odom et al., 1999).

Collaborative Efforts

By maximizing its collaborations with community school districts and providers of special education, Head Start is in a unique position to provide supports and services with reduced barriers to optimum service delivery. Collaborations with special education bring to Head Start the benefits of special education staff and related service providers with the level of skills and expertise needed. These collaborations also bring with them problems that emerge when the two spheres—early childhood and special education, with their varying foundations and theoretical orientations—come together (Wolery & Bredekamp, 1994). Head Start staff at times find that their implementation of a developmentally appropriate early childhood curriculum is at odds with the strategies and activities that are brought into the Head Start classrooms by special educators and therapists. The conclusions found in the extensive review of staff issues by Scruggs and Mastropieri (1996) emphasize the need for greater time for staff to meet and plan together. In some communities, local school districts have been able to add a special education team within the Head Start program; in other instances, it may be necessary for Head Start programs to consider the addition of a special educator/early interventionist as a program-based consultant—someone familiar with the workings of Head Start/Early Head Start's developmentally appropriate services and also familiar with the expectations of specialists who enter the Head Start environment. This would be in addition to the disabilities services specialist who would continue to work within the agency to ensure that systems and services are in place. Clearly, it is time for some rethinking of the problems for both the Head Start world and the special education community.

Outcome Research

In October 1999, the Head Start Advisory Panel issued its report in response to the federal mandate to conduct outcome research. Unfortunately, not one point specifically targeted the impact of the services on children with disabilities. It is hoped that the research agenda will be expanded to provide some substantive data regarding the largest program in the United States that includes children with disabilities and their families. Head Start, as it undertakes its research mantle, has a unique opportunity to learn from the problems of previous research on children who live in poverty and to address some focused questions with regard to the impact of Head Start for children with disabilities. A thorough analysis of the problems that are endemic to research that addresses the long-term impact of intervention programs, noted by Bryant and Maxwell (1997), points to the need for carefully controlled, well-designed studies to determine more than short-term gains.

With regard to children with disabilities, the one finding that needs to be addressed is the proportion of children who enter special education in elementary school and beyond. Little is known, except anecdotally, about whether children who received special education services within Head Start go on to special education services. An even more important question is to determine to what extent children with disabilities become fully included in the social framework of the school and their peer group.

AGENDA FOR CHANGE

There are many questions that can be incorporated into research designs to determine whether Head Start and Early Head Start are effective for young children with disabilities. Scruggs and Mastropieri (1996), in their analysis of teachers' attitudes regarding mainstreaming/inclusion from 1958 to 1995, found that across the years, elementary school teachers supported inclusion in principle, but they indicated that they lacked sufficient expertise and time to be effective. Although Head Start has provided a training and technical assistance support system since 1976, only a small number of Head Start education staff are fully licensed. With Head Start regulations requiring that 50% of all Head Start education staff have an associate's or a bachelor's degree by 2003, it is hoped that many Head Start agencies will begin to look toward training and degree-granting programs that will provide teachers with coursework on including children with disabilities. An important research question is, "Will there be greater acceptance of and improved outcomes for inclusion of children with disabilities as greater numbers of Head Start staff obtain early childhood and related degrees?"

For Head Start to meet the challenges that lie ahead, there must be a strong commitment to quality, expanded enrollment opportunities for children with disabilities, enhanced service delivery, greater collaboration with early intervention and special education systems, and well-designed research to address issues of importance. For Head Start outcomes to be maximized, factors that are predictive of positive outcomes for children with and without disabilities must be implemented and family patterns that provide quality parent–child interaction, family-orchestrated experiences for the child, and a healthy and safe environment must be established (Guralnick, 1997, 1998).

CONCLUSION

Head Start programs at the beginning of the 21st century are addressing many of the same issues that most American early childhood programs encounter: changes in families because of dual earners and divorce, decreases in public safety, and differing concepts of kindergarten readiness across communities (Graue, 1993). Head Start is the largest American program with a primary commitment to enrolling children from low-socioeconomic backgrounds, including children with disabilities. It can be the most effective, but substantive training and research as well as a refocusing of some aspects of the program must be implemented. The underlying factor that will ensure that Head Start can move from the largest provider of inclusive programs to the most effective program for children and families is the full implementation of high-quality services by skilled staff who believe that their role and their skills will and can make a difference for very young children with disabilities.

REFERENCES

Ackerman, P., & Moore, M. (1976). Delivery of educational services to preschool handicapped children. In. T. Tjossem (Ed.), *Intervention strategies for high risk infants and young children* (pp. 669–688). Baltimore: University Park Press.

Administration for Children and Families. (2000, February 24). Fact sheet—Head Start. Available:http://www.acf.dhhs.gov/programs/opa/fact/headst.htm

Barr, S. (1999, December 13). Customers rate U.S. services positively. *The Washington Post*, p. A1.

Bennett, T.C., DeLuca, D.A., & Bruns, D. (1997). Putting inclusion into practice: *Perspectives of teachers and parents. Exceptional Children, 64,* 115–131.

Bonnelli, D. (1998). Letter to Head Start. In Education Development Center (Ed.), *Setting the stage: Including children with disabilities in Head Start* (p. viii). Washington, DC: U.S. Department of Health and Human Services.

Bryant, D., Burchinal, M., Lau, L.B., & Sparling, J.J. (1994). Family and classroom correlates of Head Start children's development outcomes. *Early Childhood Research Quarterly, 9,* 289–309.

Bryant, D., & Maxwell, K. (1997). The effectiveness of early intervention for disadvantaged children. In M.J. Guralnick (Ed.), *The effectiveness of early intervention* (pp. 23–46). Baltimore: Paul H. Brookes Publishing Co.

Buscemi, L., Bennett, T., Thomas, D., & DeLuca, D. (1995). Head Start: Challenges and training needs. *Journal of Early Intervention, 20,* 1–13.

Califano, J. (1997). Leadership within the Johnson administration. In E. Zigler & J. Valentine (Eds.), *Project Head Start: A legacy of the war on poverty* (2nd ed., pp. 76–77). Alexandria, VA: National Head Start Association.

Demerest, E. (1983, January–February). Mainstreaming: A parent's view. *Children Today,* 22–23.

Economic Opportunity Act Amendments of 1972 (PL 92-424).

Economic Opportunity Act of 1964, PL 88-452, 42 U.S.C. §§ 2701 *et seq.*

Education for All Handicapped Children Act of 1975, PL 94-142, 20 U.S.C. §§ 1400 *et seq.*

Education of the Handicapped Act Amendments of 1986, PL 99-457, 20 U.S.C. §§ 1400 *et seq.*

Fujiara, G.T., & Yamaki, K. (2000). Trends in demography of childhood poverty and disability. *Exceptional Children, 66,* 187–199.

Gordon, R., & Schwartz, B. (1976). Infant, toddler, preschool research and intervention project. In T. Tjossem (Ed.), *Intervention strategies for high risk infants and young children* (pp. 467–508). Baltimore: University Park Press.

Graue, M.E. (1993). *Ready for what? Constructing meaning of readiness for kindergarten.* Albany: State University of New York.

Grossi, J., Pinkstaff, D., Henley, C., & Sanford, A. (1975). *Chapel Hill study of the impact of mainstreaming handicapped children in Region IV Head Start.* Chapel Hill, NC: Lincoln Center.

Guralnick, M.J. (Ed.). (1997). *The effectiveness of early intervention.* Baltimore: Paul H. Brookes Publishing Co.

Guralnick, M.J. (1998). The effectiveness of early intervention for vulnerable children: A developmental perspective. *American Journal on Mental Retardation, 102,* 319–345.

Guralnick, M.J. (1999). The nature and meaning of social integration for young children with mild developmental delays in inclusive settings. *Journal of Early Intervention, 22,* 70–86.

Harms, T. & Clifford, R.M. (1980). *Early Childhood Environment Rating Scale.* New York: Teachers College Press.

Head Start Reauthorization Act of 1994, PL 103-252, 42 U.S.C. §§ 9831 *et seq.*

Heller, D. (1985, August). Head Start—20 years later. *Journal of the NYS School Boards Association,* 8–11.

Hess, R.D. (1967). Early education as socialization. In R.D. Hess & R.M. Bear (Eds.), *Early education: Current theory, research, and action* (pp. 1–8). Chicago: Aldine Publishing Company.

Individuals with Disabilities Education Act Amendments of 1991, PL 102-119, 20 U.S.C. §§ 1400 *et seq.*

Individuals with Disabilities Education Act Amendments of 1997, PL 105-17, 20 U.S.C. §§ 1400 *et seq.*

Individuals with Disabilities Education Act (IDEA) of 1990, PL 101-476, 20 U.S.C. §§ 1400 *et seq.*

Innocenti, M.S., Kim, Y.U., & Gutschall, N. (1996). Disability focused training in Head Start: Effectiveness and implementation issues. In *Proceedings of the Head Start Third Annual Research Conference* (pp. 354–355). Washington, DC: Administration for Children, Youth and Families, Administration for Families, U.S. Department of Health and Human Services.

Johnson, L., & LaMontagne, M. (1992, July). *Evaluation report: Child to Child Project.* Cincinnati, OH: University of Cincinnati, Evaluation Team.

Kagan, S.L. (1991). Moving from here to there: Rethinking continuity and transitions in early care and education. In B. Spodek & O.N. Saracho (Eds.), *Yearbook in early childhood education: Vol. 2. Issues in early childhood curriculum* (pp. 132–151). New York: Teachers College Press.

King-Elkan, S., & Fink, E. (n.d.). *Where they are now: A follow-up study of Head Start children with special needs.* Cooperstown, NY: Opportunities for Otsego, Inc.

Marcon, R.A. (1999). *Impact of parent involvement on children's development and academic performance: A three-cohort study.* (ERIC ED427880).

McKey, R.H., Condelli, L., Ganson, H., Barrett, B.J., McConkey, C., & Plantz, M.C. (1985). *The impact of Head Start on children, families, and communities* (DHHS Publication No. OHDS 85-31193). Washington, DC: Government Printing Office.

National Network of Resource Access Projects for Head Start. (1993). *Child to child: Maximizing opportunities for social integration.* Newton, MA: Education Development Center.

NICHD Early Child Care Research Network. (1999). Cost, quality, and outcomes study. *American Journal of Public Health, 89,* 1072–1077.

Odom, S., Horn, E.M., Marquart, J.M., Hanson, M.J., Wolfberg, P., Beckman, P., Lieber, J., Li, S., Schwartz, I., Janko, S., & Sandall, S. (1999). On the forms of inclusion: Organizational context and individualized service models. *Journal of Early Intervention, 22,* 185–199.

Parker, F., Piotrkowski, C., Kessler-Sklar, S., Baker, A., Peay, L., & Clark, B. (1997). *The impact of parent involvement in Head Start on parents and children. Final report [and] executive summary.* New York: National Council of Jewish Women.

Phillips, D.A., & Cabrera, N.J., (Eds.). (1996). *Beyond the blueprint: Directions for research on Head Start's families.* Washington, DC: National Academy Press.

Richards, A. (1998). Different solutions to the same problem. *Children and Families, 17,* 10–6.

Schwartz, B. (1987). *An examination of the social skills of preschool delayed and non-delayed children in mainstreaming settings.* Unpublished doctoral dissertation, New York University, New York.

Schwartz, B., Gordon, R., Ezrachi, O., & Lawrence, A. (1978). *Pilot study of the efficacy of mainstreaming-integrating handicapped children* (Rehabilitation Monograph No. 58). New York: New York University Medical Center, Rusk Institute of Rehabilitation Medicine.

Scruggs, T.E., & Mastropieri, M.A. (1996). Teacher perceptions of mainstreaming/inclusion, 1958–1995: A research synthesis. *Exceptional Children, 63,* 59–74.

Tjossem, T. (1976). Early intervention: Issues and approaches. In T. Tjossem (Ed.), *Intervention strategies for high risk infants and young children* (pp. 3–36). Baltimore: University Park Press.

U.S. Department of Health and Human Services. (1993). *Creating a 21st century Head Start: Final report of the advisory committee for Head Start quality and expansion.* Washington, DC: Head Start Bureau.

U.S. Department of Health and Human Services; Administration on Children, Youth and Families; Research, Demonstration and Evaluation Branch; and the Head Start Bureau. (1998, June). *Head Start program performance measures: Second progress report.* Washington, DC: Author.

Valentine, J. (1997). Program development in Head Start: A multifaceted approach to meeting the needs of families and children. In E. Zigler & J. Valentine (Eds.), *Project Head Start: A legacy of the war on poverty* (2nd ed., pp. 349–366). Alexandria, VA: National Head Start Association.

Wolery, M., & Bredekamp, S. (1994). Developmentally appropriate practices and young children with disabilities: Contextual issues in the discussion. *Journal of Early Intervention, 18*(4), 331–341.

Zigler, E., & Anderson, K. (1997). An idea whose time had come: The intellectual and political climate. In E. Zigler & J. Valentine (Eds.), *Project Head Start: A legacy of the war on poverty* (2nd ed., pp. 3–20). Alexandria, VA: National Head Start Association.

Zigler, E., & Valentine, J. (Eds.) (1997). *Project Head Start: A legacy of the war on poverty* (2nd ed.). Alexandria, VA: National Head Start Association.

13

DIANE M. SAINATO

REBECCA S. MORRISON

Transition to Inclusive Environments for Young Children with Disabilities

Toward a Seamless System of Service Delivery

One approach to understanding the world inhabited by young children and their families is the ecological perspective, in which children and their families interact with and are acted on by their environment (Bronfenbrenner, 1979). All children and their families may encounter numerous ecological environments at home, in schools, or in the community. These encounters may happen simultaneously among home, school, and community at any given time (horizontally), or they may occur across time as children progress from preschool- to school-age programs (vertically) (Kagan & Neuman, 1998; Mangione & Speth, 1998). The continuity of experiences that children have between periods and between spheres of their lives has been defined as *transition* (Kagan & Neuman, 1998; Zigler & Kagan, 1982).

Children with disabilities are likely to experience circumstances that require specialized planning to ensure continuity of services across a variety of programs and environments (Atwater, Orth-Lopes, Elliot, Carta, & Schwartz, 1994). For example, young children from birth to age 3 years may receive early intervention services both in the home and in community-based centers. These same children may make the transition at age 4 to early childhood special education classrooms or to environments with their typically developing peers. In the latter case, these inclusive environments may provide many benefits to young children with disabilities, including the presence of competent peer models from whom to learn appropriate social and adaptive behavior skills (Wolery & Wilbers, 1994). Along with the benefits of inclusion, how-

The authors gratefully acknowledge the contributions of Susan A. Fowler, Ph.D., of the University of Illinois for her assistance during the preparation of this chapter.

ever, come the challenges of providing a seamless system of service delivery.

This chapter presents a framework for developing such a system, noting first the challenges to developing a seamless system of service delivery and then presenting possible solutions for meeting those challenges.

TOWARD A SEAMLESS
SYSTEM OF SERVICE DELIVERY

In the Individuals with Disabilities Education Act (IDEA) Amendments of 1997 (PL 105-17), the change in the legislative language emphasizing a move from providing separate early intervention programs to "a system that provides early intervention services" (§ 631[b][1][4]) is a clear attempt to address the issue of continuity of services and promote a seamless system of services for young children with disabilities and their families. With regard to children's transitions into inclusive environments, several factors provide the framework for success.

Indicators of Successful Transitions

There are common elements identified in both the general and special education literature regarding successful transitions. The idea of continuity was approached by Mangione and Speth (1998) in terms of agencies' and programs' developing comprehensive and responsive partnerships with families, sharing leadership responsibilities among themselves, and evaluating partnership success. Pianta, Cox, Taylor, and Early (1999) suggested that positive parental attitudes are crucial for successful transitions. Therefore, families should be supported in their efforts to act as partners in their children's learning. This involves linking families, programs, and communities to demonstrate sensitivity and respect for individual differences and cultures.

Wolery (1999) proposed that continuity of services is needed to minimize

disruptions to families. He noted that this may be accomplished when agencies and programs help families adapt to future changes and ensure that children are able to function in receiving programs. In this context, continuity of services is evaluated on the basis of family involvement and support, coordination among agencies and programs, and, ultimately, the child's successful participation in the receiving program (Bruder & Chandler, 1996; Rous & Hallam, 1999).

Challenges to a Systems Approach

The challenges to developing a seamless system of service delivery to young children with disabilities are numerous. Continuity can be elusive in view of changing legislation, major responsibilities shared among regulatory systems, direct-service programs challenged by differing philosophies and locations, diversely trained early childhood educators, and vastly defined expectations for individual children's performance (Fowler, Schwartz, & Atwater, 1991; Kagan & Neuman, 1998; Wolery, 1999). Achieving continuity to promote a seamless system approach depends on the field's responsiveness to each of these areas.

There is structural complexity in the delivery of services for young children with disabilities because of the multidimensional roles of regulatory systems and providers of early intervention services. The overriding element is the legal mandate requiring specific collaborative action from state and local agencies to oversee transitional services within early intervention. Stemming from this regulatory level of state and local agencies is the element of transitional services delivered directly to children and their families via programs and early childhood educators (Rosenkoetter, Hains, & Fowler, 1994).

Changing Legislation   The term *transition services*, as stated in IDEA 1997, refers to a coordinated set of activities that are developed and implemented to support children with disabilities during changes in services and programs. In an attempt to regulate action in this area, legislation described in Part C mandates a written age 3 transition plan. A transition plan must include designation of a local "lead" agency, communication with the family's local education agency 90 days before the child's third birthday, and family involvement.

Other aspects of IDEA 1997 present challenges to providing continuity of services. One of these issues relates to the child's eligibility for special education services. IDEA allows states to determine eligibility for preschool-age children with disabilities under the category of developmental delay. This category is not sufficient, however, for the same children in school-age programs. School-age programs continue to require specific categories of disabilities for service provision.

Another eligibility challenge is the less specific criteria used to determine eligibility for service provision for children from birth to 3 years compared with those of children 3 to 6 years. In the younger group, children need only to be "at risk for future deficits" to meet eligibility requirements for early intervention services. Some children who receive early intervention services according to the "at risk" criterion may no longer receive services after their third birthday. This is particularly troubling when the conditions that placed the child in the "at risk" category in the first place still exist. Families are likely to experience a loss of support and continuity as a result of the discrepancies within the legislative requirements (Shotts, Rosenkoetter, Streufert, & Rosenkoetter, 1994; Wolery, 1999).

Although legal mandates exist for age 3 transitions, this is not the case with children who are making the transition from early intervention to school-age programs (Wolery, 1999). Children who are making the transition into school-age programs and their families are subject to

transition services developed at the discretion of their local agencies and programs. In some situations, the result is an absence of transition planning and support for children who are entering school-age programs. For successful transition planning to occur, regulatory systems and programs must form successful partnerships not only with families but also among themselves to give as much attention to transition into school-age programs as they do with age 3 transitions (Rosenkoetter et al., 1994).

One issue for families is the loss of continuity and services when changing from an individualized family service plan to an individualized education program on the child's third birthday. Moving from a legal document that focuses on the needs of the family to one that focuses solely on the needs of the child is certain to impair the continuity of services for families that desire the same level of family involvement.

IDEA states that children in early intervention programs should experience a smooth and effective transition to preschool or other appropriate services. "Other appropriate services" becomes important in view of recent legislative changes in the U.S. welfare program.

Welfare Reform   Although the issue of quality child care has been debated at length, there is a greater urgency in response to welfare reform and young children with disabilities (Kagan & Neuman, 1998; see also Chapter 10). Welfare reform is certain to affect services for young children with disabilities and their families in terms of transition planning and involvement, service quality, and placement selections (Ohlson, 1998; Rimm-Kaufman & Pianta, 1997).

For young children with disabilities whose families are affected by welfare reform, transitions from home to outside child care environments present a variety of challenges. Young children with disabilities are overrepresented among families from low socioeconomic backgrounds, suggesting the eventual need for continuation and extension of early intervention and early childhood special education services (Kagan & Neuman, 1998). The movement of young children with disabilities from home to community environments may be hindered by the availability of placement options, competency of the staff who provide transition services to children with disabilities, and family involvement from parents who encounter a variety of new demands upon entering the work force (Ohlson, 1998). Families of young children with disabilities that receive welfare will be affected by the involvement and collaboration of even more regulatory systems such as the Department of Human Services, Department of Health, and Department of Education.

Challenges for Regulatory Systems: Statewide Implementation of Services

Early intervention collaboration often involves participation from various governmental departments and large operating agencies that oversee service provision. In some states, the Department of Health is responsible for services that are delivered to children from birth to 3 years, whereas the Department of Education is responsible for services for children 3 through 6 years. The transition difficulties that arise for families under this framework transcend direct service transition planning. It involves the coordination and collaboration of large state departments and agencies that serve as regulatory systems for service provision.

Some states have responded by developing local interagency coordinating councils (LICCs), which develop written interagency agreements. These councils are responsible for coordinating policies, programs, and services for children and their families during age 3 transitions across different regulatory systems

and agencies (Wischnowski, Fowler, & McCollum, in press). Another manner in which states have responded is to expect informal collaboration among agencies. In either case, transition services for families and their young children with disabilities are an enormous task that involves numerous working entities. The establishment of responsive LICCs and written interagency agreements is therefore essential for developing a seamless system approach to early intervention services.

Challenges for Direct Services Delivery

At a local level, individual agencies and programs are responsible for coordinating services among sending and receiving programs. This may involve the active solicitation of family involvement, the identification of possible receiving programs, and the support needed to transfer children's skills with minimal disruption (Bruder & Chandler, 1996).

Family involvement is determined by a number of factors, often reflecting the unique characteristics of the family. Programs are responsible for supporting families in achieving the goals they have for their children. Transition planning embraces families' priorities for their children and attempts to prepare families for the receiving program. Accessibility of collaborative meetings and transportation, the interest and comfort levels of families, and time availability often determine the extent of family involvement (Odom & Chandler, 1990). Geographic boundaries and transportation needs may dictate where and when services are provided, further influencing the amount of family involvement (Rimm-Kaufman & Pianta, 1997). Dynamic approaches and promoting cultural pluralism are necessary for determining family involvement and services during transitions (Odom & Chandler, 1990).

The partnership between families and programs is certainly influenced by the type of collaboration at the state department and agency level. The extent that this collaboration enhances or detracts from the relationship between families and programs is further shaped by the transition planning efforts at the direct services level. Moving toward a comprehensive view of family–program relationships that place families at the center of an equal partnership promotes continuity of services (Mangione & Speth, 1998).

Early education and child care programs are often characterized by their philosophies and practices. Transition between programs with differing or opposing philosophies can create barriers for continuity (Kagan & Neuman, 1998). Receiving programs may not identify and build on skills that children have learned in previous environments (Love, Lougue, Trudeau, & Thayer, 1992), citing incompatible philosophies and inadequate curricula. Pedagogical discontinuity should not excuse disruption in services for families and their young children with disabilities or prevent the placement of young children with disabilities in inclusive environments.

In 1998, the National Education Goals panel suggested factors that contribute to "ready schools." In this model, the education panel identified characteristics of ready schools, three of which related to transition. "Ready schools" were noted to focus on a smooth transition between home and school; strive for continuity of services between early childhood services and school-age services; and be committed to serving families, children, and the community (Pianta et al., 1999). Schools and programs need to adopt a level of responsibility for preparing for children from sending programs (Mangione & Speth, 1998). This concept of "ready schools" would support the efforts of all those concerned with helping young children and their families enter more inclusive education environments.

Challenges for Educators

There are many important issues that encompass the roles early childhood educators, kindergarten teachers, child care staff, and early childhood special educators play when providing services to young children with disabilities in inclusive environments. The competencies of untrained staff in addressing the transition needs of young children with disabilities is an important consideration. An additional concern is the delineation of responsibilities that early childhood special educators hold in the inclusion process before, during, and after important transitions.

The reauthorization of IDEA in 1997 and the Welfare Reform Act (i.e., HR 3734, the Personal Responsibility and Work Opportunity Reconciliation Act of 1996) are increasing opportunities for young children with disabilities to participate in inclusive environments. The resulting changes create unique challenges for preparing early childhood educators and child care staff to effectively support the transition of young children with disabilities into their classrooms.

Studies suggest that the majority of general and special early childhood service providers indicate inclusion placements are beneficial for young children with disabilities (Buysse, Wesley, Keyes, & Bailey, 1996; Dinnebeil, McInerney, Fox, & Juchartz-Pendry, 1998; Gallagher, 1997). Transition into these programs, however, can prove to be challenging for staff, families, and children. Early childhood service providers feel less confident about meeting the needs of young children with disabilities because of their lack of specialized training (Buysse et al., 1996; Dinnebeil et al., 1998). To promote continuity of services, a system of supports and training that extends beyond individual placement is needed for adults who provide direct services to young children with disabilities during transition periods.

Challenges for Children

For young children with disabilities, the successful transition from early intervention programs to preschool- or school-age programs is a critical factor in inclusion, often ensuring continued access to inclusive environments. Transition has typically been approached on the basis of children's performance. Skill level has sometimes been viewed as a predictor of the child's potential for success (Atwater et al., 1994). Functional, social, and behavior skills are identified by kindergarten teachers as more important for successful transition than academic skills (Atwater et al., 1994; Rous & Hallam, 1999; Wolery, 1999). Readiness skills, language competence, self-care skills, appropriate social behavior, and independent performance during group activities are sometimes considered as prerequisites to inclusive placements. Focusing on skills to increase the likelihood of the child's success during transitions is important but should not be used to prevent young children with disabilities from participating in inclusive placements (Salisbury & Vincent, 1990).

The overarching goal of early intervention, to reduce present problems and prevent future difficulties, emphasizes intervention to heighten children's development. Placement in inclusive environments should not deter early interventionists from embracing the fundamental goals of the field. Inclusion is not an adequate goal in and of itself; rather, participating with one's peers in an environment in which intervention is delivered is of consequence. Whether the inclusive environment is an appropriate environment for the delivery of services should be individually assessed for each child and should be considered in the context of child and family goals. Children's development is the focus of early intervention and should serve to determine the most appropriate and least restrictive environment in which growth and development can occur. In this manner, inclusion is an outcome of the overall determination of what will benefit the child and the priorities of the family.

AGENDA FOR CHANGE

The chapter authors have noted significant challenges faced by regulatory systems, those involved in direct services delivery, educators, and children with regard to children's transition to inclusive environments. Presented next is a framework for change to address these factors. The following scenario is representative of one child's experience in the transition to an inclusive environment.

Katie is 6 years old and is spending her first week in kindergarten. She was diagnosed at birth as having cerebral palsy and attended early intervention services as an infant. The early intervention program with which her family was involved was operated by the state Department of Health. On Katie's third birthday, she moved to an inclusive early childhood special education preschool that was operated in her local school district by a contract agency. Although she can walk, Katie continues to struggle with an unsteady gait and unintelligible speech.

Katie's early intervention service providers worked diligently to establish a system of gestures for Katie to use to communicate. When Katie made the transition into an early childhood special education classroom, the teachers did not understand Katie's gesture system, which frustrated Katie and her parents. The early childhood special education service providers, however, taught Katie to use a photographic communication system by the end of her first year. Although her parents believed that Katie spent most of the school year without a communication system in place, they were relieved when their daughter was again able to express herself.

Later, during the kindergarten placement conference, Katie's parents expressed their concern regarding the support that Katie would need to be able to use her photographic communication system when she made the transition into the new kindergarten room. They were assured that their daughter would be supported during her transition into a general kindergarten. Katie's parents met with her kindergarten teacher, special education teacher, occupational therapist, and physical therapist 1 month after Katie entered kindergarten. Katie's team expressed concern over her inclusion in the kindergarten classroom with 25 other children and the amount of instructional time she lost as a result of pull-out services such as physical therapy. They found that Katie was unable to answer questions, interact with peers, or follow directions to complete tasks. Her communication board was available, but she did not use it in the classroom.

For Katie, success during the transition into an inclusive kindergarten was heavily influenced by her inability to communicate. The inability of her kindergarten team to understand Katie's unique use of her communication system resulted in a collapse of support for Katie to transfer the only communication system she had into the new classroom. Direct collaboration was absent between Katie's early childhood special education team and her kindergarten team. In part, this was because the early childhood education staff worked for a contract agency and not directly for the school district, as did the kindergarten team. This is an all-too-common scenario for young children with disabilities.

Children and families need to be supported during critical transitions. Loss of services for families or the loss of skill on the part of the child should not be an acceptable standard in a field that is dedicated to enhancing children's performance and supporting families. Change

needs to occur at all levels to move toward a seamless system of services for young children with disabilities and their families.

Systems Changes

Two levels of change need to be addressed with regard to structural bureaucracy. The first is the collaboration and coordination among regulatory bodies such as state departments and administering agencies. The second is the support needed for direct service providers.

Developing and implementing a framework for interagency collaboration has been recognized as a foundational component for successful continuity of early intervention services (Wischnowski et al., in press). Written interagency agreements define such factors as bureaucratic structures, fiscal responsibilities, shared resources, and differing policies and processes among agencies (Harbin & McNulty, 1990). Details about these factors form the basis of a system's overall coordination and collaboration, thereby enhancing continuity of services delivered to families and their children at the direct service level.

The dynamic nature of early intervention and early childhood special education services demands a certain level of expertise on the part of families. Vocabulary, policies, procedures, and practices are often complex and novel for families of children with disabilities. Without a working knowledge of the complexities of service delivery, families are dependent on existing bureaucratic collaboration to advocate for them and their children. Ineffective collaboration may result in a loss of support networks and continuity of services for their children over time and across environments. The concept of family-centered practice has been evaluated in several studies (Bailey, 1994).

Identifying and providing the appropriate level of support and information for families during transitions is a step toward a seamless system of services. In this manner, families are equipped to advocate for their children during transitions and to serve as a constant and consistent source of information over time and across environments. In this role, families must be informed about expectations for themselves and for their children in future placements. During transitions, it is as important not only for children to adjust to new placements but also for families to adjust and determine a comfortable level of cooperation and interaction with the receiving program (Atwater et al., 1994).

Changes for Direct Services Delivery

The emphasis during transition should be for child care sites to participate in practices to adjust to families and children from sending programs (Wolery, 1999). The idea of schools' needing to be ready for the child, however, is not enough to ensure continuity of services (Mangione & Speth, 1998). Although theoretically different philosophies and practices exist among programs, the notion of developmentally appropriate practice (DAP) may bridge the continuum of services for young children with disabilities from one environment to another and across early childhood special and general education environments (Wolery & Bredekamp, 1994).

Developmentally appropriate practices are a published set of guidelines related to appropriate curriculum and instructional practices for early education programs (Bredekamp & Rosegrant, 1992). Controversy occurs when appropriate practice statements are applied universally to the education of all children (Wolery & Bredekamp, 1994). The framework of DAP, however, is based on relevant decisions that must be made across environments and populations and may be used by transition-planning direct services providers to support continuity

(Wolery & Bredekamp, 1994). Borrowing this idea from DAP, participants of transition planning among programs can begin to evaluate different philosophies and practices and how they may have an impact on the successful transition of young children with disabilities into inclusive environments.

Pertinent dimensions for consideration are appropriateness, effectiveness, efficacy, empirical determination of behavior changes, and social validity of implemented philosophies and practices (Wolery & Bredekamp, 1994). Under this scrutiny, programs and practices are evaluated by performance outcomes for families and children while providing a general guide about appropriate practice. Examination of these dimensions of appropriate practice and their impact on early intervention service provision during transitions may provide a common bridge for promoting continuity of services among different service providers.

Changes for Educators

One pervasive challenge to continuity is staff preparation. Those who provide services to young children with disabilities and their families hail from a variety of child care or preschool environments, with different levels of experience and training and implementing diverse sets of philosophies and practices for young children. In-service training is often inadequate to address the skills needed to help young children with disabilities make the transition into inclusive programs. Teaching methods and models presented in traditional, lecture-type staff development situations do not transfer well into classroom practice (Carnine, 1992; Showers & Joyce, 1996). A tactic that may prove fruitful in the preparation of staff is peer coaching.

Peer coaching is an adult instructional strategy in which colleagues systematically model new skills and observe each other to provide feedback and support in the acquisition, maintenance, and generalization of their instructional skills (Ackland, 1991; Kohler, Crilley, Shearer, & Good, 1997; Showers & Joyce, 1996). The need to provide specialized services that are directly interactive with both the child and the classroom teacher in the natural environment warrants the development of a peer coaching strategy for preparation of personnel who work in inclusive environments. Using teachers to coach teachers avoids the authoritarian problems associated with supervision models and offers an effective way for teachers to observe the implementation of effective practices and gain feedback about their own performance (Kohler, 1993; Showers & Joyce, 1996).

Expert and consultant peer coaching is based on the premise that professionals who have specific expertise observe service providers in natural environments and provide peer-oriented feedback (Ackland, 1991). Peer coaching roles may include providing expert information and modeling effective intervention before, during, and after the child's placement (File & Kontos, 1992). Vail, Tschantz, and Bevill (1997) described the process that an early childhood special educator used to implement a combination "expert–reciprocal" peer coaching model in three inclusive Head Start classrooms. Teacher satisfaction of the intervention was very high and was referred to by the teachers as "beneficial," "nonintrusive," and a model that "they wished to continue" (Vail et al., 1997, p. 13).

Support and guidance to help service providers develop competent skills are essential. Peer coaching is one strategy that might provide the level of support and training needed for promoting successful transitions for families and their young children with disabilities. Planning becomes crucial for promoting the successful transition of a child with a disability into an inclusive environment. Although typical instructional practices

used in early childhood environments are appropriate for many children, adaptations in intervention techniques are often necessary to meet the needs of children with disabilities (Buysse et al., 1996; see also Chapter 22). If these intervention techniques are not in place during the transitional period, then inclusion is not as likely to be successful.

Changes for Children

Determining what constitutes successful transitions into inclusive environments for young children with disabilities is a complex and difficult task. When service providers in receiving programs are asked what is important for them when including children with disabilities in their classrooms, they commonly cite the presence of functional skills and independent performance by the children (Buysse et al., 1996; Rous & Hallam, 1999). Preparing young children with disabilities for the transition into inclusive environments requires addressing the issue of independent performance and generalization of independent performance into the receiving environment (Sainato, Strain, Lefebvre, & Rapp, 1990).

Child engagement and independent performance have long been identified as necessary ingredients for children's successful participation in a variety of early childhood education environments (McWilliam & Bailey, 1995; Sainato et al., 1990). The National Association for the Education of Young Children (Bredekamp & Rosegrant, 1992) further noted the importance of programs' facilitating the active engagement of young children. McWilliam defined *engagement* as "the amount of time a child spends in developmentally and contextually appropriate behavior" (1991, p. 42). The successful participation of children in one environment is not enough to ensure the active engagement and independent performance of children in future environments. Careful transition planning and support are needed to prepare young children with disabilities for transitions, therefore becoming a critical element for direct service providers.

The ability of children to demonstrate skills in one environment and use those skills under a variety of conditions is referred to as *generalization* (Cooper, Heron, & Heward, 1987). When this does not occur, all children are vulnerable to disruptions in learning, particularly children with disabilities. Generalization should be viewed as an active process that must be taught directly (Cooper et al., 1987).

Periods of transition place children at an increased risk for skill loss and may be especially detrimental for children who have slower learning acquisition rates and who are already socially or academically behind their peers. A vital issue becomes preparing the child not only for present learning and success but also for future learning and success (Pianta et al., 1999). To promote successful transitions and identify the type and amount of support needed, the focus must be on evaluating the success of a program on the basis of the ability of the child to make the transition successfully into the next environment.

Research suggests that children with disabilities do not often generalize skills without direct intervention (Cooper et al., 1987). The emphasis moves from striving for equal services to focusing on equal outcomes for young children with disabilities in inclusive environments (Walzer, 1983). Teaching for generalized outcomes is one way to foster this concept. Specifically, skills are not taught in isolation; rather, they are taught with the intention of supporting the transfer of children's skills and independent performance into new environments, with new people, and over time.

The relevant dimensions of promoting generalized outcomes are helping children contact natural reinforcement that is already in the environment, teaching enough examples, and developing self-management skills. Attention to these components focuses the efforts of direct service providers on preparing children for receiving programs.

McGee, Almeida, Sulzer-Azaroff, and Feldman stated, "When generalization occurs, it is probably derived from teaching multiple examples of behavior within ongoing stimulus conditions, which are the same conditions under which responses later will be cued and reinforced" (1992, p. 118). For children who are making transitions to other environments, this might include interventions based on environmental arrangements, learning materials, adult prompts, or social cues. Teaching children to identify common cues likely to be present in receiving programs will eventually assist them in gaining skills that will bring them into contact with natural reinforcement already available in the environment. For example, teaching children to follow routine directions, watch the other children for cues about what to do, and learn to listen to adults in the classroom all are skills that may generalize to the next environment under similar conditions (Zanolli, Daggett, & Adams, 1996). These types of skills promote successful participation in the classroom and increase the likelihood that the child will be reinforced for his or her behavior. Knowing how to contact natural reinforcement helps children to maintain and generalize important skills to new environments.

Researchers have explored the relationship between the generalization of children's performance to instruction that occurs in the natural environment. This relationship is sometimes referred to as *naturalistic instruction* (Koegel, Koegel, & Surratt, 1992; Santos & Lignugaris-Kraft, 1997; Zanolli et al., 1996). The concept behind naturalistic instruction provides a possible framework for planning and supporting children's transitions into a variety of inclusive environments.

Naturalistic instruction occurs within contexts that encourage application, including intervention that is delivered during routine events (Rule, Losardo, Dinnebeil, Kaiser, & Rowland, 1998). Children seem more motivated to use language, for example, when it is necessary to get what they want to eat or drink (Koegel et al., 1992). When conditions do not exist to support behaviors across transitions from one environment to another, important behaviors might eventually disappear (Baer & Wolf, 1967). Baer and Wolf recommended that direct support be identified to maintain behavior change across activities and environments. For young children with disabilities, this might include intervention delivered during multiple experiences with small- and large-group instruction, peer interaction, and independent completion of learning tasks.

Other intervention strategies to promote generalization are those that examine the effects of self-management strategies on children's academic achievement, social interactions, generalization of skills, and inclusion in preschool environments (Sainato et al., 1990). One self-management strategy that may support children's performance during transitions is the use of photographic activity schedules. In many cases, activity schedules promote increased engagement and self-management skills, as well as the transfer of skills from one environment to another (Frazier, 1997; Morrison, 1999; Odom, Chandler, Ostrosky, McConnell, & Reaney, 1992; Valk & Schwartz, 1997).

Photographic activity schedules supplement verbal instructions that sometimes serve to increase adult dependence, particularly with children who are experiencing auditory processing difficulties (Schwartz, Garfinkle, & Bauer, 1998). Activity schedules provide a tool for transferring assistance from the teacher to another set of cues that represent natural elements in the environment, thereby reducing adult involvement. Activity schedules are cost- and time-efficient, transferable across environments, and a viable support option for helping young children with disabilities maintain and generalize self-direction and self-management skills during transitions (McClannahan & Krantz, 1999).

Morrison (1999) used photographic activity schedules to increase children's engagement during free play in an inclusive environment. Four children with autism, ages 4 and 5, learned to make play selections, interact appropriately with materials, and make the transition from one activity to another without adult assistance alongside typically developing peers. This strategy was used to help three of the four children maintain and generalize their play skills as they made the transition into a new classroom with a new teacher. Strategies that focus on the generalization of skills across environments and people and over time are valuable in the movement toward a seamless system of services.

CONCLUSION

Providing a seamless system of service delivery is a daunting but not impossible task. Challenges faced at the systems level by regulatory agencies, at the direct service level by educators, and by children and families in the transition process are readily identified. Building on previous research may reveal many viable and effective approaches to the challenges faced by those who strive to provide services to young children and their families during transitions to inclusive environments. Future efforts should focus on refining coordination procedures and agreements by agencies and programs and identifying efficient and effective strategies to promote the generalization of children's behavior across inclusive environments. The goal for the provision of these services should be continuity for children and families as they make the transition throughout early intervention services into school-age programs.

REFERENCES

Ackland, R. (1991). A review of the peer coaching literature. *Journal of Staff Development, 12*(1), 22–27.

Atwater, J.B., Orth-Lopes, L., Elliot, M., Carta, J.J., & Schwartz, I.S. (1994). Completing the circle: Planning and implementing transitions to other programs. In M. Wolery & J.S. Wilbers (Eds.), *Including children with special needs in early childhood programs* (pp. 167–188). Washington, DC: National Association for the Education of Young Children.

Baer, D.M., & Wolf, M.M. (1967). The entry into natural communities of reinforcement. In R. Ulrich, T. Stachnick, & J. Mabry (Eds.), *Control of human behavior* (Vol. 2, pp. 319–324). Glenview, IL: Scott Foresman-Addison Wesley School Publishing Group.

Bailey, D.B., Jr. (1994). Working with families of children with special needs. In M. Wolery & J.S. Wilbers (Eds.), *Including children with special needs in early childhood programs* (pp. 23–44). Washington, DC: National Association for the Education of Young Children.

Bredekamp, S., & Rosegrant, T. (1992). *Reaching potentials: Appropriate curriculum and assessment for young children* (Vol. 1). Washington, DC: National Association for the Education of Young Children.

Bronfenbrenner, U. (1979). *The ecology of human development: Experiments by nature and design.* Cambridge, MA: Harvard University Press.

Bruder, M.B., & Chandler, L.K. (1996). Transition. In S.L. Odom & M.E. McLean (Eds.), *Early intervention/early childhood special education: Recommended practices* (pp. 287–307). Austin, TX: PRO-ED.

Buysse, V., Wesley, P., Keyes, L., & Bailey, D.B., Jr. (1996). Assessing the comfort zone of child care teachers in serving young children with disabilities. *Journal of Early Intervention, 20*(3), 189–203.

Carnine, D. (1992). Expanding the notion of teachers' rights: Access to tools that work. *Journal of Applied Behavior Analysis, 25*(1), 13–19.

Cooper, J.O., Heron, T.E., & Heward, W.L. (1987). *Applied behavior analysis.* Columbus, OH: Merrill.

Dinnebeil, L.A., McInerney, W., Fox, C., & Juchartz-Pendry, K. (1998). An analysis of the perceptions and characteristics of childcare personnel regarding inclusion of young children with special needs in community-based programs. *Topics in Early Childhood Special Education, 18*(2), 118–128.

File, N., & Kontos, S. (1992). Indirect service delivery through consultation: Review and implications for early intervention. *Journal of Early Intervention, 16*(3), 221–233.

Fowler, S.A., Schwartz, I., & Atwater, J. (1991). Perspectives on the transition from preschool to kindergarten for children with disabilities and their families. *Exceptional Children, 58*(2), 136–145.

Frazier, J. (1997). *The effects of correspondence training and picture schedules on the choice making and individual engagement of developmentally delayed preschool children during playtime.* Unpublished master's thesis, The Ohio State University, Columbus.

Gallagher, P.A. (1997). Teachers and inclusion: Perspectives on changing roles. *Topics in Early Childhood Special Education, 17*(3), 363–386.

Harbin, G., & McNulty, B. (1990). Policy implementation: Perspectives on service coordination and interagency cooperation. In S.J. Meisels & J.P. Shonkoff (Eds.), *Handbook of early childhood intervention* (pp. 700–721). New York: Cambridge University Press.

Individuals with Disabilities Education Act Amendments of 1997, PL 105-17, 20 U.S.C. §§ 1400 *et seq.*

Kagan, S.L., & Neuman, M.J. (1998). Lessons from three decades of transition research. *The Elementary School Journal, 98*(4), 366–379.

Koegel, R.L., Koegel, L.K., & Surratt, A. (1992). Language intervention and disruptive behavior in preschool children with autism. *Journal of Autism and Developmental Disorders, 22*(2), 141–153.

Kohler, F.W. (1993). Designing a comprehensive and sustainable innovation by blending two different approaches to school reform. *Education and Treatment of Children, 16*(4), 382–400.

Kohler, F.W., Crilley, K.M., Shearer, D.D., & Good, G. (1997). Effects of peer coaching on teacher and student outcomes. *The Journal of Educational Research, 90*(4), 240–250.

Love, J.M., Lougue, M.E., Trudeau, J.V., & Thayer, K. (1992). *Transitions to kindergarten in American schools. Final report of the National Transition Study.* Portsmouth, NH: RMC Research Corp.

Mangione, P.L., & Speth, T. (1998). The transition to elementary school: A framework for creating early childhood continuity through home, school, and community partnerships. *The Elementary School Journal, 98*(4), 381–397.

McClannahan, L.E., & Krantz, P. (1999). *Activity schedules for children with autism.* Bethesda, MD: Woodbine House.

McGee, G.G., Almeida, M.C., Sulzer-Azaroff, B., & Feldman, R.S. (1992). Promoting reciprocal interactions via peer incidental teaching. *Journal of Applied Behavior Analysis, 25*(1), 117–126.

McWilliam, R.A. (1991). Targeting teaching at children's use of time: Perspectives on preschoolers' engagement. *Teaching Exceptional Children, 24,* 42–43.

McWilliam, R.A., & Bailey, D.B., Jr. (1995). Effects of classroom social structure and disability on engagement. *Topics in Early Childhood Special Education, 15*(2), 123–147.

Morrison, R. (1999). *The effects of correspondence training and activity schedules on the play behavior of preschoolers with autism in an inclusive classroom.* Unpublished doctoral dissertation, The Ohio State University, Columbus.

Odom, S.L., & Chandler, L.K. (1990). Transition to parenthood for parents of infants with chronic health care needs. *Topics in Early Childhood Education, 9*(4), 43–54.

Odom, S.L., Chandler, L.K., Ostrosky, M., McConnell, S.R., & Reaney, S. (1992). Fading teacher prompts from peer-initiation interventions for young children with disabilities. *Journal of Applied Behavior Analysis, 25*(2), 307–317.

Ohlson, C. (1998). Welfare reform: Implications for young children with disabilities, their families, and service providers. *Journal of Early Intervention, 21*(3), 191–206.

Personal Responsibility and Work Opportunity Reconciliation Act of 1996, HR 3734.

Pianta, R.C., Cox, M.J., Taylor, L., & Early, D. (1999). Kindergarten teachers' practices related to the transition to school: Results of a national survey. *The Elementary School Journal, 100,* 71–86.

Rimm-Kaufman, S.E., & Pianta, R.C. (1997). *Perspectives on the transition to kindergarten.* Manuscript under review.

Rosenkoetter, S.E., Hains, A.H., & Fowler, S.A. (1994). *Bridging early services for children with special needs and their families: A practical guide for transition planning.* Baltimore: Paul H. Brookes Publishing Co.

Rous, B., & Hallam, R.A. (1999). Easing the transition to kindergarten: Assessment of social, behavioral, and functional skills in young children with disabilities. *Young Exceptional Children, 1*(4), 17–26.

Rule, S., Losardo, A., Dinnebeil, L., Kaiser, A., & Rowland, C. (1998). Translating research on naturalistic instruction into practice. *Journal of Early Intervention, 21*(4), 283–293.

Sainato, D.M., Strain, P.S., Lefebvre, D., & Rapp, N. (1990). Effects of self-evaluation on the independent work skills of preschool children with disabilities. *Exceptional Children, 56*(6), 540–549.

Salisbury, C.L., & Vincent, L.J. (1990). Criterion of the next environment and best practices: Mainstreaming and integration 10 years later. *Topics in Early Childhood Special Education, 10*(2), 78–89.

Santos, R.M., & Lignugaris-Kraft, B.L. (1997). Integrating research on effective instruction with instruction in the natural environment for young children with disabilities. *Exceptionality, 7*(2), 97–129.

Schwartz, I.S., Garfinkle, A.N., & Bauer, J. (1998). The picture exchange communication system: Communicative outcomes for young children with disabilities. *Topics in Early Childhood Special Education, 18*(3), 144–159.

Showers, B., & Joyce, B. (1996). The evolution of peer coaching. *Educational Leadership, 53*(6), 12–16.

Shotts, C.K., Rosenkoetter, S.E., Streufert, C.A., & Rosenkoetter, L.I. (1994). Transition policy and issues: A view from the states. *Topics in Early Childhood Special Education, 14,* 395–411.

Vail, C.O., Tschantz, J.M., & Bevill, A. (1997). Dyads and data in peer coaching. *Teaching Exceptional Children, 30*(2), 11–15.

Valk, J.E., & Schwartz, I. (1997, May). *Using a progressive time delay procedure to implement photographic schedules during a free choice period.* Poster session presented at the 23rd annual Association for Behavior Analysis conference, Chicago.

Walzer, M. (1983). *Spheres of justice: A defense of pluralism and equality.* New York: Basic Books.

Wischnowski, M.W., Fowler, S.A., & McCollum, J.A. (in press). Supports and barriers to writing an interagency agreement on the preschool transition. *Journal of Early Intervention.*

Wolery, M. (1999). Children with disabilities in early elementary school. In R.C. Pianta & M.J. Cox (Eds.), *The transition to kindergarten* (pp. 253–280). Baltimore: Paul H. Brookes Publishing Co.

Wolery, M., & Bredekamp, S. (1994). Developmentally appropriate practices and young children with disabilities: Contextual issues in the discussion. *Journal of Early Intervention, 18*(4), 331–341.

Wolery, M., & Wilbers, J.S. (Eds.) (1994). *Including children with special needs in early childhood pro-*

grams. Washington, DC: National Association for the Education of Young Children.

Zanolli, K., Daggett, J.M., & Adams, T. (1996). Teaching preschool-age autistic children to make spontaneous initiations to peers using priming. Journal of Autism and Developmental Disorders, 26(4), 407–422.

Zigler, E., & Kagan, S.L. (1982). Child development knowledge and educational practice: Using what we know. In A. Lieberman & M. McLaughlin (Eds.), Policy making in education. Eighty-first yearbook of the National Society for the Study of Education (pp. 80–104). Chicago: University of Chicago Press.

14

CARL J. DUNST

Participation of Young Children with Disabilities in Community Learning Activities

The life course of a developing child is paved with vast numbers of experiences and opportunities that have either development-instigating or development-impeding characteristics and consequences (Bronfenbrenner, 1992; Hunt, 1979). Life experiences that have development-enhancing characteristics and consequences constitute the focus of this chapter. According to activity theory (Farver, 1999), these kinds of experiences and opportunities provide the sociocultural context for children's participation in everyday activity-promoting and -sustaining interactions with people and objects. These interactions, in turn, provide a basis for knowledge acquisition; skill development and use; and learning social expectations and cultural rules, roles, and routines, among other developmental consequences. Research and practice

are used as the foundation for describing and explaining how everyday life experiences and opportunities afforded young children with disabilities can and do promote learning and development.

A simple but useful way of conceptualizing the life experiences of a developing child is to think of them as occurring in the context of family life, community life, and early childhood education programs (broadly conceived). Family life includes a mix of people, places, activities, and opportunities that provide a child with experiences in the context of parent, family, and child routines; child and parent–child play; family rituals, celebrations, and traditions; and other kinds of family activities. Community life also includes a mix of people and activities that provide a child with experiences in the context of family outings, running

The work described in this chapter was supported, in part, by grants from the U.S. Department of Education, Office of Special Education Programs (# HO24B60119, # HO24B40020, # HO24596008), and the Pennsylvania Department of Public Welfare, Office of Mental Retardation, Children's Services Division, which are greatly appreciated. Special thanks are extended to the staff of the Building Community Resources Project; my colleagues and staff of the Increasing Children's Learning Opportunities Through Families and Communities Early Childhood Research Institute; and the parents, children, and community members who have been my sources of learning opportunities for the model, strategies, and practices described in this chapter. Appreciation is also extended to Tharesa Owenby for typing the manuscript and Lisa Noack for preparing the references.

errands, neighborhood and community places, community programs and organizations, neighborhood and community celebrations, and other community activities. Early childhood education program experiences include learning opportunities afforded young children (and their parents) in the context of early intervention programs, Early Head Start and Head Start, child care programs, family day care homes, preschool programs, early childhood special education programs, parent–child play groups, and so forth.

As one might expect, family, community, and early childhood activities are not independent sources of environmental influence and consequence. Figure 14.1 shows one way of depicting the relationship among the three sources of learning experiences and opportunities. As shown in the figure and as described in detail next, the many different activities that make up the fabric of children's lives constitute the experiences, events, and so forth that serve as the contexts for learning and development. Overlaps in the spheres of influence can be expected and

do occur when sociocultural influences in one sphere translate into experiences in another sphere (e.g., family spiritual beliefs result in community activity such as church attendance [e.g., Hill, 1999] or ceremonial spirit dancing [e.g., Jilek, 1982]). These overlaps also can be expected to be bidirectional and transactional. For example, family participation in a community activity such as a fair or social gathering is likely to provide a topic for discussion during family mealtimes (Blum-Kulka, 1997). This, in turn, is likely to result in plans for subsequent family outings and activity.

The learning opportunities afforded by family, community, and early childhood activity over the course of the life span constitute the life experiences of developing children. The extent to which these activities promote participation and learning depends on the characteristics of the activities themselves and the people (parents, family members, community members) involved in the activities with the children (Bronfenbrenner, 1993, 1999). Activities that have development-instigating and development-enhancing

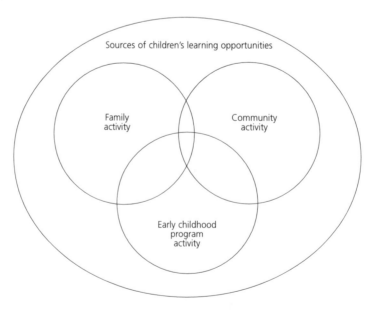

Figure 14.1.   Major sources of infant, toddler, and preschool-age children's learning opportunities.

qualities are described in this chapter as *participatory learning opportunities (PLOs)*. PLOs provide children the contexts to express interests and capabilities, strengthening functioning in ways that promote competence and a greater sense of child self-efficacy. Environmentally supportive PLOs "provide opportunities for children to participate meaningfully in cultural activities, to use their knowledge and experience in order to achieve [desired outcomes]. . .where children's own interests and sense-making processes are a [central feature] of supportive environments" (Guberman, 1999, p. 207). The focus of this chapter is PLOs that occur in the context of the community experiences and opportunities of children from birth to 6 years of age. Consequently, the learning experiences and opportunities that constitute the focus of the chapter are a subset of the rich array of PLOs that a child experiences as part of everyday life in other settings (see Figure 14.2).

The content of this chapter provides a broad-based perspective for defining and identifying the many different person and environmental experiences that serve as contexts for children's learning opportunities. As illustrated, despite being a subset of everyday learning opportunities, community life is made up of hundreds of possibilities that generally go unrecognized and therefore nonactualized in the context of more traditional early intervention and early childhood education program practices.

It is worth taking the time to describe some points of departure between this chapter and many other chapters in this book and elsewhere with regard to young children's learning opportunities (e.g., Guralnick, 1999; Noonan & McCormick, 1993; Odom & Diamond, 1998; Wolery & Wilbers, 1994). First, learning experiences that are afforded by inclusion are considered an important but nonetheless very small sub-

set of community-based PLOs (see Figure 14.2). In contrast to inclusion that is defined as participation of both children with and without disabilities in early childhood education programs as well as in the broader-based community (see Chapter 1), community-based PLOs encompass a broader range of environmental experiences that would not necessarily include other children yet would provide children with learning opportunities that have development-enhancing qualities (Dunst & Bruder, 1999a; Dunst, Hamby, Trivette, Raab, & Bruder, 2000a). Figure 14.2 shows the relationship among the universe (U) of children's learning experiences, the subset of community-based learning experiences (A), learning experiences that occur in places other than children's communities (Ā), and inclusion as a subset of community-based learning experiences.

Second, everyday community life—in particular, child, parent, and family community routines—is not viewed as a setting in which early intervention, preschool practices, and therapy are embedded or conducted (Beckman et al., 1998; Koegel, Koegel, Kellegrew, & Mullen, 1996; Noonan & McCormick, 1993). Rather, everyday community learning opportunities are considered a viable form of early childhood intervention in and of themselves. Research and practice has found that the community (as well as family) experiences afforded children do have development-enhancing qualities when learning opportunities mirror the characteristics known to promote learning and development (Dunst & Bruder, 1999a).

Third, in contrast to contentions that the community (and family) lives of children with disabilities are less rich and varied (Ehrmann, Aeschleman, & Svanum, 1995) and more troublesome to parents (Harris & McHale, 1989) than the lives of children without disabilities, recent research indicates that in fact this

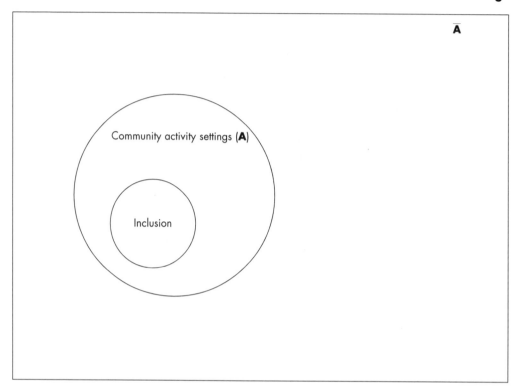

Figure 14.2.   Venn diagram depicting community activity settings as a subset of the universe of children's life experiences and inclusion as a subset of community-based learning opportunities. (Key: U = the universe of children's learning experiences; A = the subset of community-based learning experiences; Ā = learning experiences that occur in places other than children's communities.)

generally is not the case (Dunst, Bruder, Trivette, Raab, & McLean, 1998). There are many examples from research that indicate that children with disabilities have lives that are rich in everyday community activity. Furthermore, contrary to contentions that child and parent characteristics account for differences in the participation patterns of children with and without disabilities in their communities, research indicates that these differences in many instances are attributable to the professional demands that are placed on parents of young children with disabilities (Dunst, Bruder, et al., 1998). There also are many instances in which parenting time is consumed by therapy appointments, conducting professionally prescribed interventions, and other demands that leave little or no time for other family activity. As one mother said, "We used to have a family life and a community life, but now [that my child has a disability] we have mostly a professional life" (Dunst, Faris, et al., 1998) This kind of life situation has led to a call for a better balance between traditional and nontraditional kinds of early childhood learning opportunities.

Fourth—and certainly the most controversial—the term *participatory learning opportunity* is preferred over *inclusion* as the descriptor of community-based involvement because inclusion, despite its generally accepted adoption and use, emphasizes disability rather than ability as the basis for social participation, learning, and development (Lipsky &

Gartner, 1996). According to Danforth and Rhodes (1997), the term *inclusion* can and often does have stigmatizing and negative connotations and consequences because it calls attention to differences and communicates inability rather than ability, at least in certain instances. Terminology and practice that are based on differences and disability are by definition characteristics of a deficit-based approach to and model of early intervention (Dunst & Trivette, 1997). As described next, using PLOs to promote learning and development is derived from an alternative perspective of intervention (Dunst, Trivette, & Thompson, 1990) in which ability, assets, and strengths form the foundation for using community life as sources of children's learning opportunities.

CONCEPTUAL FOUNDATIONS

Both the thesis and premise of this chapter are that a family's community life and environment are sources of children's learning opportunities and experiences and that children's participation in social and nonsocial activities that strengthen existing child competence and promote new abilities are principal contexts for learning and development. The conceptual foundations for PLOs are ecological systems theory (Bronfenbrenner, 1979, 1992, 1993, 1999) and a number of congruent perspectives of human development, including activity theory (Farver, 1999; Leont'ev, 1981; Wertsch, 1985, 1991), individuals as producers of their own behavior (Brandtstädter & Lerner, 1999), social support theory (Dunst, Trivette, & Jodry, 1997), and a resource-based perspective of child and family learning and development (Dunst, Trivette, & Deal, 1994a; Trivette, Dunst, & Deal, 1997).

According to Bronfenbrenner (1992, 1993), learning and development are a joint function of person and environment characteristics and the *processes* that mediate interactions and transactions between a developing child, other people, and the nonsocial environment (Bronfenbrenner, 1992, 1999). Operationally, person characteristics include but are not limited to child interests, abilities, preferences, and so forth that encourage participation in and interaction with the social and nonsocial environments (Scarr & McCartney, 1983). Environment characteristics include but are not limited to the physical, social, and psychological features of everyday activity that encourage and sustain (or impede and prevent) a child's engagement with people and objects. Processes that mediate a child's engagement in learning activities include but are not limited to parents' and community members' attitudes, beliefs, and behaviors that make possible child participation in community activity and these individuals' interaction styles that support or discourage a child's engagement, exploration, and other kinds of learning and development. As described next, processes that are deliberately implemented and manipulated, regardless of whether they have anticipated or serendipitous consequences, are viewed as a form of early childhood intervention.

Activity Settings

The contention that the community life of a developing child and his or her family is made up of many different kinds of PLOs has its foundation in different but compatible conceptual and theoretical frameworks (Bronfenbrenner, 1979, 1992; Cole, 1996; Hobbs et al., 1984; Kretzmann & McKnight, 1993; Rappaport, 1981, 1987; Sarason, Carroll, Maton, Cohen, & Lorentz, 1977; Wertsch, 1985). In the context of ecological systems theory (Bronfenbrenner, 1979, 1992), everyday community (as well as family and early childhood) life is viewed as the source and context of learning experiences and opportunities that can and often do have development-enhancing characteristics and consequences. Activity settings generally are recognized as major and principal sources of young children's learning experiences and opportunities (Göncü, 1999). An activity setting is an everyday event, experience, or opportunity that provides a context for children's learning and development (Dunst & Bruder, 1999a).

Research (Dunst et al., 2000a; Lancy, 1996; Rogoff, Mistry, Göncü, & Mosier, 1991; Tudge et al., 1999) indicates that an everyday activity that has development-enhancing characteristics and consequences includes a combination of planned and unplanned, structured and unstructured, and intentional and incidental PLOs. Activity settings include such things as car or bus rides, neighborhood walks, swimming, feeding ducks bread crumbs, visiting an animal shelter, listening to storytellers, and so forth. Community activity settings provide children with a rich mix of PLOs through involvement in adult-oriented activities (e.g., camping), family-oriented activities (e.g., picnics), child-oriented activities (e.g., climbing on a jungle gym), social-oriented activities that bring children in contact with other children and adults (e.g., Sunday school), children's attractions (e.g., nature center activities), community events (e.g., festivals), and recreation and sports activities (e.g., T-ball). Factors that are associated with the specific kinds of activity settings and PLOs experienced by individual children are discussed later in the chapter. Suffice it to say that any one activity setting is likely to be the source of both planned and serendipitous PLOs. Take, for example, a nature trail hike with a young child who is just mastering walking. A parent may foresee that this activity will provide her child an opportunity to practice and perfect ambulation. Along the trail, the child

and parent may happen upon a field of flowers that becomes a context for other, unanticipated activity (e.g., picking flowers, carrying them home, and placing them in a vase).

As part of a study to identify activity settings that serve as sources of PLOs, Dunst, Bruder, and colleagues (1998) collected data about the numbers and types of learning opportunities afforded young children in their neighborhoods and communities. The participants were children with disabilities and children who were at risk for poor developmental outcomes from birth to 6 years of age and their parents in seven states (Alaska, California, Connecticut, Hawaii, New Mexico, North Carolina, Wisconsin). Parents were interviewed about their family's community life, completed a survey about participation in community activities, and were observed with their children in different community activity settings. Findings indicated, regardless of a child's disability or severity of delay, that most children experienced many different kinds of PLOs. On average, the children studied were participants in activity settings in approximately 25 different community locations. These locations, in turn, were the contexts for approximately 75 different kinds of activity settings. These activity settings, in turn, were the sources of more than 100 different parent- and investigator-identified PLOs. Results from this study indicate that various community locations are sources of multiple kinds of activity settings, and activity settings are sources of many different kinds of PLOs.

Asset-Based Learning Opportunities

Individuals possess many different traits and characteristics that foster or impede self-development and action (Brandt-städter & Lerner, 1999; Lerner & Busch-Rossnagel, 1981; Wachs, 2000). One important but sometimes overlooked domain of development-instigating individual characteristics is people's strengths and assets (Chen, Krechevsky, Viens, & Isberg, 1998; Kretzmann & McKnight, 1993; Scales & Leffert, 1999). Children's assets include but are not limited to their existing and emerging capabilities, interactive competencies, interests, preferences, talents (e.g., "showing off"), and so forth that bring them in contact with people and objects and that are often used by parents and other caregivers as the basis for providing different kinds of PLOs. According to Guberman (1999), children's interests and existing capabilities are often overlooked in understanding the development-enhancing characteristics and consequences of activity settings. (The same is often the case for parents and families [Dunst et al., 1994a] and community members and groups [Kretzmann & McKnight, 1993].)

An asset-based approach to PLOs uses children's assets, and especially their interests, as a condition for engaging children in activity settings that have competency-strengthening and competency-enhancing characteristics and consequences. Figure 14.3 shows the relationship among activity settings, child interests, and child competence, and how activity settings that have development-instigating characteristics set in motion a cycle of interest-based participation (Haith, 1972; Watson, 1972) in activity settings that engage children in competence production (Appleton, Clifton, & Goldberg, 1975; Hunt, 1979), strengthening their sense of mastery motivation (MacTurk & Morgan, 1995). Interests are things that children like to do, things that motivate them to do something, things that "turn them on," things that they find exciting, things that are fun and enjoyable to do, and so forth. Competencies are the knowledge, skills, capabilities, and so forth that are strengthened and learned from activity setting–based

PLOs. Accordingly, PLOs matching a child's interests lead to engagement in desired activities; displays of competence in the activities strengthen functioning; enhanced competence promotes an increased sense of mastery; and mastery motivates continued interest, engagement, competence, and so forth. The framework shown in Figure 14.3 is based on more than 25 years of child development research on the characteristics and consequences of child-initiated learning opportunities (e.g., Appleton et al., 1975; Fogel, 1997; Gewirtz & Pelaez-Nogueras, 1992; Goldberg, 1977; Hunt, 1979; Lipsitt & Werner, 1981; MacTurk & Morgan, 1995; Rovee-Collier, 1987; Schaeffer, 1971; Wachs, 2000) and on research and practice using child assets (abilities, interests, etc.) as the basis for promoting learning and development.

Parenting assets, parenting styles, and (self-efficacy) beliefs that have facilitative functions serve an important role in providing optimal development-enhancing consequences for PLOs. Research investigating everyday community (as well as family) life as sources of children's learning opportunities finds that certain kinds of parenting strategies are effective more often than others in promoting children's learning in the context of activity settings (see especially Gauvain, 1999). These include guided participation (Rogoff, Mistry, Göncü, & Mosier, 1993), situated learning/instruction (Lave & Wenger, 1991), apprenticeship (Rogoff, 1990), and caregiver responsiveness (Field, 1978; Goldberg, 1977; Schaffer, 1977). Guided participation includes the many different kinds of actions taken by parents (as well as other caregivers) to provide children with PLOs, engage children in desired activity, and provide assistance and guidance as needed (e.g., Wertsch, 1985, 1991). Situated learning constitutes a strategy whereby children intentionally or

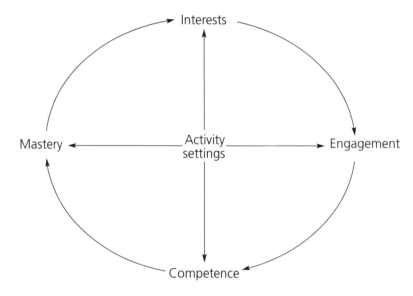

Figure 14.3.   Activity settings as the context for expressing children's interests, engagement in activity, competence strengthening and enhancement, and sense of mastery.

by happenstance are provided opportunities to observe experienced community members (including peers) participating in a desired activity, providing a standard for expectant behavior (Clark, 1998; Lancy, 1996). Apprenticeship "involves close and active coordination of an expert and a novice in the course of learning an activity" or desired behavior (Gauvain, 1999, p. 179). Parent responsiveness involves physical, social, and verbal attention to child interests and competence, which functions as a reinforcer to maintain and promote child behavior (Mahoney, 1988). These (instructional) procedures have a high probability of producing child-initiated learning (Wolery & Sainato, 1996; Wolery & Wilbers, 1994) in which a child develops a sense of his or her own competence and abilities (Goldberg, 1977; Lamb, 1981; MacTurk & Morgan, 1995).

Community-Based Learning Activities as Early Intervention

Historically, early intervention and early childhood education were all about children's learning and development and the

environmental conditions best suited for affecting behavior change (Dunst, 1996). The experiences afforded by activity settings and their participants constitute person and environmental factors (Bronfenbrenner, 1992, 1993, 1999) that have growth-producing influences and effects. As conceptualized here, community-based PLOs are considered early intervention inasmuch as they are sources of learning experiences that have development-enhancing characteristics and consequences. This conceptualization of early intervention is based on theory and research (see Dunst, 1985, 2000), indicating that the environmental experiences afforded young children, regardless of whether they are deliberately manipulated (Horowitz, 1994), function as a form of early intervention. Accordingly, child participation in activity settings and both intended and serendipitous PLOs experienced by the child in these settings are viewed as environmental opportunities that provide a context for learning and development. The remainder of this chapter covers the operationalization of this approach to early childhood intervention and the person, environment, and process factors that are associated with development-instigating and development-enhancing PLOs in community activity settings. As previously noted, community-based PLOs are but one set of broader-based learning opportunities in addition to those afforded by family activity settings and early childhood activity settings.

OPERATIONAL FRAMEWORK

Dunst (1985) proposed a social support definition of early intervention that became the foundation for a family systems intervention model (Dunst, Trivette, & Deal, 1988, 1994b) and a resource-based approach to early childhood intervention and family support (Dunst et al., 1994a; Trivette et al., 1997). The resource-based approach to early childhood intervention viewed communities as sources of information, experiences, opportunities, and so forth that provide supportive opportunities for influencing child as well as parent and family functioning. Operationalization of this approach to early childhood learning experiences and opportunities was accomplished through a number of model-demonstration projects and research studies, several of which are described next.

Earlier research and practice culminated in two lines of work—a model-demonstration project (Dunst, 1997) and an early childhood research institute (Dunst & Bruder, 1999b; Dunst, Bruder, et al., 1998)—that have permitted considerable advancement in understanding the methods and strategies for identifying and using community activity settings as sources of children's learning opportunities. Research that investigated and practice that promoted children's participation in community learning activities led to the development of the model shown

in Figure 14.4. The three components of the model are 1) sources of community-based learning opportunities, 2) identifying (mapping) community-based activity settings, and 3) the capacity-building strategies used to promote participation in learning activities. Sources of learning opportunities include the community people, places, events, and so forth that are contexts for development-instigating and development-enhancing activity settings. Community mapping is a process used to identify, catalog, and inform parents and other family members about the kinds of learning experiences and opportunities that are available in a target community. Capacity-building strategies are the methods and procedures used with children, parents, other family members, and community people to increase children's participation in activity settings.

Sources of Children's Learning Opportunities

Two approaches have been used to collect and catalog information about children's community-based learning opportunities. One is to gather and compile information (see the section "Activity Setting Mapping") about the community places, programs, organizations, events, and people who are sources of learning opportunities (Dunst, 1997). The other is to administer a parent questionnaire for purposes of categorizing the makeup of community life (Dunst, Hamby, et al., 2000a). Both approaches have yielded findings that indicate that community life provides infants, toddlers, and preschool-age children with a rich array of learning experiences and opportunities.

Community Activity Listing Efforts to identify, compile, and categorize information about the community places, people, groups, organizations, events, and so forth that serve as sources of children's learning opportunities were first carried out in two communities in

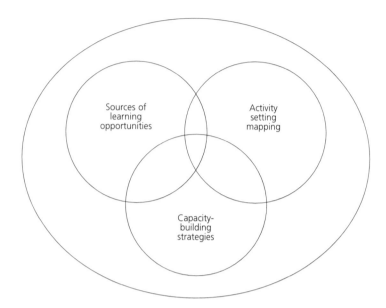

Figure 14.4.   Components of a model for identifying, mapping, and promoting the use of community-based activity settings as sources of children's learning opportunities.

Pennsylvania (Cranberry and Pottstown) and in one community in North Carolina (Asheville/Buncombe County). The procedures were subsequently replicated in two communities in North Carolina (Burke County and Henderson County) and in one community in Vermont (Burlington/Chittenden County). A lesson learned very early in the activity-identification process (within 6 months of initiating the effort) was that parents of young children with disabilities and community people did not think about or describe community learning opportunities in terms of developmental domains or specific behavioral achievements, as is often the case among specially trained professionals. Rather, they described community activities in terms of the opportunities and experiences they afforded. This led to a categorization of community learning opportunities into 10 different sources of activity settings. The categories and examples of sources of learning opportunities in each are shown in Table 14.1. The particular categories to which activities are assigned in some cases is arbitrary and in other cases

depends on the function of the activity and the kind of child participation in the activity. The actual database of activities has some activities assigned to multiple categories depending on the kinds of experiences and learning opportunities afforded by the settings, programs, organizations, and so forth.

Development of procedures to identify community learning opportunities was begun in Cranberry and Pottstown, Pennsylvania. In each community, nearly 400 different sources of learning activities were located that potentially constituted places where young children from birth to 6 years of age could experience learning opportunities. This initial effort focused primarily on more formal kinds of learning opportunities, such as Water Babies, Gymboree, playgroups, library story hours, horseback riding, and so forth. Although the number of activities identified was impressive, it became apparent that informal kinds of learning activities such as those afforded at duck ponds, neighborhood walks, lakes and streams, playgrounds, and so forth were sometimes overlooked. When these kinds of community activities were included in the mix of learning opportunities, many more sources of learning opportunities were discovered. In Asheville/Buncombe County, North Carolina, for example, more than 1,000 activities were located and identified, and in Burlington/ Chittenden County, Vermont, more than 600 activities were found. The number of activities identified in mostly rural Henderson County, North Carolina, was almost 700, and in rural Burke County, North Carolina, more than 1,000 activities were located.

Clarification and explanation are needed to provide a fuller understanding of the contexts of the sources of learning opportunities shown in Table 14.1. Some of the sources are the contexts for activities in which a child is the target of participation, and his or her involvement is the focus of PLOs (e.g., a parent and her toddler going to pajama storytime at a local library). Many other activities simply occur as a function of children's opportunities afforded by different contexts, conditions, situations, and so forth. One example found over and over is a younger child's going along to activities when an older sibling is the target of participation. In one case, a young boy just about 1 year of age was observed in a playpen at his older sister's softball game. During the game, he accidentally dropped one of his toys on the ground. A passerby picked up the toy and handed it back to the child. The child then began a game of getting people's attention by intentionally dropping toys over the side of the playpen so that people would retrieve them, which in turn resulted in considerable gratification in his accomplishments. Research and practice confirm that a good number of children's learning experiences are the result of these kinds of serendipitous learning opportunities.

The Categorization of Community Activity   A national survey of more than 1,500 parents and other caregivers in 48 states and Puerto Rico provides additional information about community life as a source of everyday learning opportunities (Dunst et al., 2000a). The survey included 50 different learning activities and opportunities identified from an extensive literature review and the kind of information shown in Table 14.1. Parents of young children from birth to 6 years of age involved in Part C early intervention programs, Part B (Section 619 of IDEA) early childhood special education programs, Early Head Start and Head Start programs, and other early childhood programs were asked how often each activity was a place or setting in which child learning took place. Exploratory and confirmatory factor analysis was used to portray the landscape of learning opportunities that affect child behavior functioning. Table 14.2 shows the final categorization scheme. Findings indicated that community activity could be grouped into 11 categories, providing rich and varied kinds of PLOs. (Note that the scale items are only a very small subset of the multitude of possible activity settings in each category.) As can be seen, the activity categories are much like those shown in Table 14.1, providing credence to the ways in which community activity has been organized. More important, the findings from the analysis of the survey data confirmed what is found in practice; namely, community life is in fact made up of a mix of formal and informal, structured and unstructured, and planned and naturally occurring learning opportunities.

Activity Setting Mapping

Knowledge about and awareness of sources of children's learning opportunities is a necessary (though not sufficient) condition for increasing children's PLOs. A procedure called activity setting mapping has been developed to identify, compile, map, and mobilize community learning opportunities. Activity setting mapping involves four steps: 1) identifying the kinds of PLOs to be mapped, 2) gathering information about the sources of PLOs, 3) developing an informational database about PLOs and their characteristics, and 4) using maps as informational tools for involving children in PLOs.

Kinds of Learning Opportunities
Activity setting mapping begins by deciding which kinds of activities are to be used as PLOs. This can be as broad based

Table 14.1.   Examples of sources of community-based participatory learning opportunities

Amusements and attractions	Heritage festivals	**Outdoor activities**
Amusement parks	Historic	Biking
Aquariums	reenactments/celebrations	Bird watching
Arcades	Holiday festivals (hay rides,	Boating/canoeing
Aviaries, bird sanctuaries	light shows)	Camping
Displays and attractions	Local/county/regional fairs	Fishing
Farms: seasonal/holiday	Parades	Gardening
activities	Picnics	Hiking
Planetariums	**Family outings**	Horseback riding
Play lands	Church/synagogue	Kite flying
Science centers	Circus, Ice Capades	Skating/sledding/skiing
Train rides	Family reunions	Walks/races
Zoos and wildlife preserves	Holiday gatherings	**Parks and recreation**
Arts and culture activities	Movies	Open/family gym time
Children's museums	Picnics	Organized activities
Historic sites	Pumpkin patches, tree farms	Parks
Museums	Shopping, eating out	Playgrounds
Musicals/plays/ballets	Special family celebrations	Swimming pools
Outdoor concerts	**Learning and education**	Summer camps
Performing arts for children	**activities**	**Parent and child activities**
Regional attractions	Afterschool programs	Baby/toddler gym (e.g.,
Clubs and organizations	Art	Gymboree)
4-H	Book store story hours	Neighborhood games
Big Brothers/Big Sisters	Ceramics	(dodgeball, kickball, etc.)
Community centers	Children's museum activities	Pajama storytime, read to me
Ethnic heritage clubs	Creative movement	(public library)
Family centers	Dance	Playful parenting
Hobby/activity clubs	Child care/preschools	Playgroups
MOMS clubs	Drama classes	Time for Mommy and Me
Playgroups	Enrichment classes	Water Babies
Scouting/Camp Fire Girls/	Gymnastics/tumbling	**Sports activities**
Indian Guides	Library storytimes, movies and	Baseball/T-ball
Service clubs	activities	Basketball
Toy lending libraries	Lunch bunch for toddlers	Bowling
YMCA / YWCA	Magic shows	Football
Youth groups	Music	Golf/miniature golf
Community celebrations	Nature center activities	Ice skating
Block parties	Parent education classes	Karate
Children's festivals	Puppet shows	Roller skating/blading
Church festivals	Religious education	Soccer
Community days	Science center activities	Softball
Farm shows	Storytellers	Swimming
Folk festivals		Tennis
		Track and field

as the approach used to generate the 10 categories listed in Table 14.1, more circumscribed such as only arts and culture or parks and recreation activities, or as specific as only one kind of learning opportunity (e.g., literacy PLOs). In addition, a decision needs to be made as to whether formal learning opportunities (e.g., Water Babies swimming classes) or informal learning opportunities (e.g., "open" swimming pool times) or both are going to be used as PLOs. The more encompassing approach opens up more possibilities for young children and their parents.

Gathering Information   After the kinds of learning opportunities to be mapped are identified, the information-gathering process is begun. This is accomplished by collecting information from existing written sources, talking to key informants, and compiling information from existing computer databases. The kind of information gathered is purposely kept simple. The name (program, organization, place, or person), street address, city, county, state, zip code, telephone number, activity (e.g., swimming), and activity category (e.g., Table 14.1) are sufficient. The idea is to have enough information to promote awareness of an activity and to begin the process of activity participation. Other information, such as hours, days, and months of operation, costs (if any), ages of children served, availability of scholarships, and so forth, that is useful for informed choices is collected as access to activities is gained.

Key informants generally include community people who are responsible for or providing child learning opportunities (e.g., swimming instructors), community members with a vested interest in informing customers of available community resources (e.g., parks and recreation staff), and consumers of community resources (e.g., parents). Many different sources of information have been found to be useful for identifying

community learning activities, including visitor guides, libraries, brochure displays at motels and hotels, and chambers of commerce. In communities that are child and family friendly, realty company staff often compile information about a broad range of community activities, places, and events that "entice" prospective buyers to purchase homes in those communities. The "information packets" that they put together can be helpful in the information-gathering stage of activity setting mapping.

Particularly useful sources of information about community activities are the ProCD Select Phone computerized telephone directories (Select Phone Deluxe, 1999). Directories are available for all 50 United States and Canada and include in addition to names, addresses, and telephone numbers the Standard Industrial Classification (SIC; U.S. Department of Commerce, 1987) codes for entries identified as businesses. SIC codes, for example, identify child care centers, churches, scout troops, performing arts classes, martial arts programs, swimming pools and programs, amusement parks, children's attractions, and so forth. Select Phone has been used as a first step for identifying sources of learning opportunities in a target county and all of its contiguous counties as a way of beginning to compile an informational database (see next section).

In addition to databases such as Select Phone, the Internet is becoming a primary source of information about community learning opportunities. For example, LaPierre (1997) provided the addresses for 11 web sites of national, state, and local parks throughout the United States. In instances in which activity setting mapping is being done in communities where parks are located, these data sources can be helpful in identifying sources of PLOs.

Gathering information about community activity settings and sources of

Table 14.2.   Categorization of 50 community-based participatory learning opportunities

Family excursions	Recreational activities
Family activities	Fishing
Weekend activities	Recreation/community centers
Car rides/bus rides	Swimming
Running errands	Ice skating/sledding
Family outings	Horseback riding
Eating out	**Children's attractions**
Going shopping/mall	Animal farms/petting zoos
Visiting friends/neighbors	Parks/nature preserves
Family reunions	Zoos/animal preserves
Play activities	Pet stores/animal shelters
Outdoor playgrounds	Nature centers
Indoor playgrounds	**Art/entertainment activities**
Child playgroups	Children's museums/science centers
Video/arcade games	Music concerts/children's theatre
Parent–child classes	Library/book mobiles
Community activities	Storytellers
Community celebrations	Music activities
Children's festivals	**Church/religious activities**
County/community fairs	Religious activities
Parades	Going to church
Hay rides	Sunday school
Outdoor activities	**Organizations/groups**
Hiking	Children's clubs (4-H, Indian Guides)
Nature trail walks	Karate/martial arts
Boating/canoeing	Scouting
Camping	Gymnastics/movement classes
Community gardens	**Sports activities**
Rafting/tubing	Baseball/basketball
Hunting	Soccer/football

children's learning opportunities is a lot like detective work. Pursuing all leads can yield highly informative and useful compilations of PLOs. It is also helpful if broader-based lenses are used for surveying the landscape of possible learning opportunities (Dunst & Trivette, 1997; Dunst et al., 1994a; Trivette et al., 1997).

Building a Database   Microsoft Access, FoxPro, or any other data management software program can be used to build a database of sources of community learning opportunities. A number of "lessons learned" in compiling information about community activities in a computerized database system need to be fol-

lowed at this step of activity setting mapping. First, street addresses are necessary for the locations of the activities to be easily geocoded and for the geographic information system (GIS) software (step 4) used for mapping the locations of the activities. Assigning geographic coordinates (longitudes and latitudes) to individual activities (see next section) is simplified when street addresses are compiled following the convention that number, name, and type of thoroughfare (e.g., street, road, avenue) all are entered in the same data field (e.g., 3421 Western Boulevard). Other street-related information (e.g., office number, post office box) should always be entered in a separate data field (typically designated Address 2). If an activity setting has no address (e.g., neighborhood park, fish pond), then an address as close as possible to the location is assigned to the activity. For example, if the "real" addresses on either side of a fish pond were 78 Trout Road and 86 Trout Road, then the fish pond would be assigned the address 82 Trout Road.

Second, to make the database user friendly, everyday language used by parents and other community members should be used to describe the activities. The more customary the language used to describe the activities, the easier it is to use everyday language as "search terms" for locating desired activities. This may mean having to attend to regional and cultural variations in the words used to describe community activities. Especially flexible information databases include as many related words as needed to "capture" the full range of descriptive terms for an activity (e.g., a swimming pool having such search words as swimming, swimming pool, water play, water sport, aquatics, swimming lessons). When this is done, using any one of these search terms will result in the location of swimming pools.

Geographic Information System Mapping   Using GIS software (e.g., ARCVIEW, Maptitude) facilitates identification of community learning activities by producing computer-generated maps of the locations of one or more kinds of PLOs. GIS is a "constellation of hardware and software that integrates computer graphics with an [informational] database for the purposes of managing and [mapping] data about geographic locations" (Garson & Biggs, 1992, p. 3). Maps are especially useful tools because all people construct spatial images of where they live and where different things are located in relation to their domicile.

People who drive or use public transportation learn different routes to get to and from different places and locations. Similarly, most people use maps (e.g., bus routes, road maps) to orient themselves to their surroundings by using streets, landmarks, and so forth to provide guidance as to where things are located and how to get from place to place. In the author's experience, maps (as opposed to resources guides and other written materials) are the preferred method for learning about the location of community activities.

For GIS software to produce maps of the locations of community activities, the addresses of the activities first need to be geocoded. Geocoding is a procedure for assigning longitude and latitude coordinates to street addresses so that mapping software can locate the coordinates on a map and represent (locate) the activity using designated symbols. EZLocate is a good means for geocoding addresses (http://www.etak.com). A database is submitted to EZLocate via the Internet, and geocodes are assigned to addresses that can be located through a process that systematically uses all available data to assign longitudes and latitudes. For a variety of reasons, some addresses cannot be located. These are assigned geocodes by using an internal GIS software feature that permits assignment of coordinates by "clicking" on the location of an entity.

A useful feature of the mapping procedure developed by Dunst, Herter, Shields, and Bennis (in press) is the use of an international system of icons for representing different activities (e.g., swimming, playgrounds, horseback riding) (Caliper Corporation, 1999). (In instances in which symbols are not available, those found in other sources are adapted.) In this way, reading requirements are minimized and the display of the locations of a desired activity is easily understood (e.g., an "open book" icon indicates the locations of storytimes at libraries, book stores, family resource centers).

The process and procedure for using an activity setting database (and mapping software if desired) for promoting children's participation in community learning opportunities are straightforward once information is compiled and coded in the ways described previously. Parents are made aware of the information through any number of means: they can make a request for information as part of their participation in early childhood programs, the kinds of activities available in a target community can be highlighted in newsletters, the databases can be integrated into public library community information packets, and so forth. Lists or maps of activities can be used by parents to locate possible sources of learning opportunities for their children. Children's interests (as well as other factors [see next section]) can be used for choosing target activities. Finally, steps are taken to involve children in PLOs, and the capacity-building strategies described next are used to promote learning and development.

Capacity-Building Strategies

The KISS principle (**K**eep **I**t **S**ituational and **S**imple) has been a standard for guiding efforts to learn about the best ways to build people's capacity to include children with disabilities in PLOs. A lesson learned is to use people's (e.g., children, parents, siblings, community members) assets as the foundation for supporting and strengthening competence and for parents and caregivers to do so *without* communicating a need for them to learn any special techniques and strategies.

The impetus for the approach to using community activities as sources of children's learning opportunities was a

request many years ago by a mother of a 2½-year-old girl with cerebral palsy. She wanted her daughter to learn to swim so that she could be involved in family swimming outings at a community lake. The mother, along with an early childhood practitioner, met with the swimming instructor for the toddler swimming program at the local city recreation program. The mother described her interest in having her daughter take swimming lessons. The instructor's only concern was the child's safety, and the instructor agreed that the daughter could take swimming lessons if there was an extra person in the pool to keep an eye on her, someone who was a proficient swimmer and who was certified in CPR. The high school swim team was approached for a volunteer to help with the swim classes. A senior on the boys' swim team volunteered, and his assistance facilitated the young girl's participation in the swim classes. It was that simple. This initially surprised the practitioner and the parent but has subsequently been replicated hundreds of times.

Different capacity-building strategies like the one just described have been gleaned from research and practice with an eye toward strategies that support and strengthen parents' and community members' competence and confidence. Three such strategies have worked well in efforts to learn about increasing PLOs for young children with disabilities.

Community Members' Assets as a Capacity-Building Strategy Building and strengthening community members' capacity to include children with disabilities in community learning activities has been systematically examined to identify a set of questions and associated activities that have proved useful for using community members' assets as a foundation for providing PLOs to young children with disabilities. The five questions are as follows:

1. What do you find most successful in getting children involved in XYZ activity?

2. What things do you do that work best in helping children participate in and benefit from XYZ activity?

3. When a child is having a difficult time doing XYZ activity, what have you found most helpful in getting the child more involved in the activity?

4. When you have children with disabilities participating in XYZ activity, what do you do to make their involvement successful?

5. What kinds of assistance or advice have you found most useful in terms of what you are trying to accomplish?

All of the questions are asset based. They all focus on what makes participation successful and what knowledge, competence, and resources community members possess and use to involve children in community activities. The story of the young girl in swimming classes is an example of this capacity-building strategy. The extent to which the strategy works best depends on other factors, including but not limited to a positive attitude on the part of community activity staff. A lesson learned is to promote involvement in PLOs with community members whose attitudes, beliefs, and approaches are conducive to successful participation. The following illustrates this concept:

A mother wanted her child with severe disabilities to have literacy experiences at a weekly storytime at a public library. The children's librarian was adamantly opposed to having the child involved because the child was not toilet trained, even though the storytime lasted only approximately 45 minutes and the child's bowel control almost guaranteed no accidents during this time. Nothing the mother said would change the librarian's mind. By happenstance, the mother became aware of a children's story hour at a small community bookstore. She was in the store with her son looking for a book while the store owner was conducting storytime. The store owner invited the mother and child to listen to the story, and this became the source of an ongoing literacy experience for this young boy.

Sometimes there is no better strategy than associating with community members who care, are inviting, and have the opportunity to express their own assets in interactions with young children.

Parents' Assets as a Capacity-Building Strategy Many children's community-based PLOs involve experiences with their parents (and other family members) and do not include or involve community members. Parents' own assets often operate as determinants of the kinds of learning experiences and opportunities that they afford their children. For example, a parent's interest in outdoor activities often provides a context for children's everyday community learning opportunities. Recent work has focused on identifying, building on, and strengthening parents' own confidence, competence, interests, and other assets as sources of children's learning opportunities (Dunst, Bennis, Durant, & Shivers, 1999). People feel most comfortable and most able when doing things that they enjoy and do well. Parents are no exception. A highly effective capacity-building strategy is to use parents' assets as the basis for involving their children in PLOs and supporting parents' confidence and competence by providing encouraging and reinforcing consequences to their efforts and actions.

An example of doing and not doing this happened as part of the model-demonstration project that forms, in part, the context of this chapter. The mother of a 6-year-old boy and a 1½-year-old girl with cognitive and motor delays wanted her daughter to be able to go bike riding with her older son, who had just learned to ride a bike, and thought a bike trailer for her daughter would provide the child an opportunity to be part of family outings. She knew that the county program for people with disabilities had family support funds available to help purchase the bike trailer but needed from a professional an endorsement indicating that the purchase was in fact for a family support activity. The mother met with a staff member from her younger daughter's early intervention program and several days later received this letter:

> Dear Maggie,
> I spoke with both [physical therapist] and [occupational therapist] regarding the bike trailer for Sally. Although the trailer would facilitate family development, it would not facilitate Sally's skill development.
> The recommendation from both [physical and occupational therapists] would be to explore purchasing a piece of equipment that Sally would be able to actively participate with. It is felt that, considering Sally's abilities, this does not seem to be age appropriate for her.
> Please contact me if you have any questions or for possible suggestions regarding equipment for Sally that would facilitate development of her skills/abilities.
> [Early Interventionist]

The letter infuriated the mother and had confidence- and competence-attenuating effects. This was a simple, socioculturally relevant request and proved to be a lost opportunity for the early intervention program staff to support and strengthen the parent's thoughtful way of providing her children with community-based PLOs. As it turned out, the child's pediatrician approved the request, and the activity happened anyway.

Children's Assets as a Capacity-Building Strategy The extent to which parents and community members see children in terms of their abilities rather than disabilities is extremely important for participation in community activities to occur and be successful. The power of an asset-based versus deficit-

based approach to community involvement is illustrated in the following example. In a community in which the author and his colleagues were developing and testing their asset-based model, a state-funded Partnership for Preschool Inclusion project was also implementing procedures for including children with disabilities in community-based programs. Both groups happened to be working with the same staff of a YMCA to promote children's participation in a number of different program activities. More interesting, both groups were working with some of the same children. The Partnership for Preschool Inclusion staff used the children's disabilities as the entrée, emphasized their right to participate on the basis of the Americans with Disabilities Act (ADA) of 1990 (PL 101-336), explained to the staff what they needed to learn to be capable and competent in working with children with disabilities, and asked (actually demanded) that quotas be established for ensuring that children with disabilities were fully included in the YMCA's programs. In contrast, the author's group used children's assets, especially their interests, as the basis for entrée, emphasized children's abilities as a context for describing the children to the YMCA staff, identified and actualized existing staff competence as a basis for supporting participation, and reinforced the YMCA's mission of being a program that is available to all community members. The Partnership for Preschool Inclusion approach evoked resistance, feelings of inadequacy, and an attitude that the children would not be able to successfully be part of YMCA activities. In contrast, the asset-based approach evoked openness, feelings of competence and confidence, and a sense that the children with disabilities were just like any other children participating in the activities. The irony is that these conflicting sets of approaches were used with the same children, attesting to the fact that ability- versus disability-focused approaches matter a great deal in terms of their capacity-building or capacity-impeding consequences.

FURTHER SPECIFICATION OF PARTICIPATORY LEARNING OPPORTUNITIES

The conceptual and operational models described in the previous section are general frameworks for understanding the rationale and approach to using community activities as sources of children's learning opportunities. Many other person and environment factors influence the kinds of activities that children are likely to experience and the likelihood that participation has development-enhancing characteristics and consequences. This section includes further specification and delineation of key factors that are associated with effective PLOs.

Factors that Influence Children's Community Learning Activities

Among all of the possible PLOs available in a given community, an individual child is likely to experience a subset of learning opportunities; some daily, others periodically, and still others at certain times of the year. Many person and environment factors influence the kinds of PLOs that make up the fabric of a child's community life, some of which are highlighted here.

Place of Residence   Where a family lives matters a great deal in terms of a child's PLOs. For example, winter activities such as sledding are more likely to occur for children whose families live in colder climates, whereas summer activities such as playing in the surf are more likely to occur among children whose families live near the ocean. Children who live in urban areas are more likely to experience learning opportunities at children's museums and science centers, and

those who live in rural areas are more likely to experience learning opportunities such as horseback riding, camping, and hiking. A national survey of community life as sources of children's learning opportunities (Dunst et al., 2000a)—as well as extensive case studies of families in seven states—found, despite many commonalities in children's PLOs, considerable specificity depending on place of residence.

Parent Factors   The things that parents themselves enjoyed doing as children are often used as a factor for at least introducing their children to different community learning activities. It is not unusual, for example, for parents to decide to take their children to the zoo, a community wading pool, parades, county fairs, and so forth because these were things that their own parents did with them as children and that they enjoyed. As already noted, parents' own assets (e.g., interests, likes) are often the context for involving their children in community activities. They provide a basis for parents to introduce their children to new experiences and opportunities (e.g., storytelling) and to promote similar interests and talents in their children.

Sociocultural and Personal Beliefs   Culture and personal beliefs and values are the foundation for many parents' decisions about their children's participation in community activities. Parents' strong religious or spiritual beliefs, for example, are likely to promote children's participation in formal religion-related activities. Similarly, cultural customs and practices often are important contexts for PLOs as part of ethnic celebrations, cultural celebrations, and the like.

Personal Social Networks   Parents, friends, neighbors, and other social support network members are often sources of invitations, suggestions, and so forth about community activities. This is especially true when network members have children who are approximately the same ages as those of the parents.

Sibling Influences   Younger children who have older siblings almost always are drawn into the community activity of their siblings. So frequent and powerful are these opportunities that they are called "going along" activities. These kinds of activities involve younger children in situations that give rise to different types of serendipitous learning opportunities. Parents also often use activities that their older children liked as infants, toddlers, and preschoolers as a basis for figuring out whether their youngest child(ren) might also find the activities fun and enjoyable.

Children's Assets   As might be expected, young children's assets (interests, preferences, abilities, etc.) are the foundation for many parent decisions about community PLOs. It is not unusual, for example, for parents to use their children's interests (e.g., liking to play in water) as a basis for seeking out PLOs that permit expression of these interests. The ways in which children's assets translate into community learning opportunities are described previously in this chapter, and additional examples follow.

Factors Associated with Competency-Strengthening and -Enhancing PLOs

Community learning activities that are judged by parents and community members to be effective in terms of positive influences on child functioning are consistently associated with the same or similar person and environment characteristics. Particularly important and salient characteristics are reviewed here to further facilitate an understanding and appreciation of children's participation in community-based activity settings and the characteristics of development-enhancing PLOs.

Child Characteristics   Age and both existing and emerging capabilities

influence the kinds of community activities that preschool-age children experience. The kinds of experiences afforded young children in community contexts would therefore be expected to be different at different ages. Research indicates that participation in different community activities does increase as children become older and more capable. This is illustrated with data on participation patterns in the 11 categories of community activity (Table 14.2) identified in a national survey of community life as sources of children's learning opportunities (Dunst, Hamby, Trivette, Raab, & Bruder, 2000b). A series of 11 repeated measures analysis of variance for the community activities in Table 14.2 with 12 age groupings (birth–6, 6–12, . . ., 60–66, and 60–72 months) as between factors and the activities in categories as within (repeated) measures each produced highly significant age effects in every analysis and significant age X activity interactions for 10 of the 11 analyses. Participation patterns in 4 of the 11 categories of community activity revealed that in nearly all instances, percentage of participation was higher at older ages (age effects) and participation patterns within categories differed as a function of activity setting (interaction effects).

Parent Characteristics   A number of parent characteristics have emerged as important determinants and mediators of children's participation in community activities. The first and perhaps the most important is also the most difficult about which to be precise. Parent attitudes and beliefs matter a great deal in whether children become involved in community activity. Many parents have a "can-do" attitude toward and are positive about their children's being involved in their communities. Regardless of a child's disability, severity of delay, or level of functioning, many children become part of community activities because parents believe that it is an important part of life experiences.

In contrast, other parents have an attitude that their children cannot or should not be involved in community activities. These parents believe that it will or might be detrimental to their children's health and well-being. This belief, at least in some cases, is influenced by professionals who advise parents against child involvement in community activities. It is surprising how many parents are discouraged by professionals from involving their children in their communities. Fortunately, many parents ignore this advice and promote participation in PLOs.

A number of other parent characteristics have emerged as important factors that contribute to children's PLOs. Persistence is one factor. Parents who have a sense that their children might enjoy or benefit from PLOs do not give up even if the first few attempts to promote participation are not successful. In most cases, they "back off" and let their children take the lead and decide when and how they become involved in PLOs. It is not unusual, for example, for a parent to take her child swimming and it takes four, five, or even more visits before the child decides that he or she wants to be in the water.

Another factor is related to the consequences of parents' efforts to provide their children PLOs. When parents derive enjoyment and gratification from seeing their children involved in community activities and judge participation to have positive child benefits (of any kind), there is a higher probability that the parents will continue to involve their children in PLOs.

Parents' sense of confidence about community members' abilities to work with their children also matters in whether they continue to involve children in PLOs. When community members are perceived as kind, considerate, able, and dedicated and parents judge their children's interactions with community members as positive, parents are more likely to continue their children's involvement in the PLOs.

Community Member Characteristics Parents have repeatedly indicated that when community members warmly greet parents and their children and have an attitude that child and family participation is welcomed because they are community members, it is more likely that participation will continue. Flexibility, a willingness to make necessary accommodations, and a "can-do" attitude on the part of community members also contribute to successful participation. For example, a preschool-age child with a visual impairment was able to play ice hockey because the team coach fitted a puck with bells so that the child was able to follow its location and placed gymnastic mats along the inside walls of the rink so that the child would not hurt himself.

Community members who use children's interests and assets as a basis for participation and who see children in terms of their abilities rather than disabilities are more likely to make participation successful. One particularly vivid example happened when a parent discovered her child's musical abilities. This young boy was born with only one arm, and his arm had only a thumb and a forefinger. The child accompanied his mother to visit a friend, who was playing the piano when they arrived. The mother and friend retreated to the kitchen, and suddenly they heard the piano. The little boy, with a single finger, was repeating from memory note by note the song that he had heard. Unbeknownst to the parent, her son had a musical talent that until that time had gone unexpressed. The mother used this asset as a basis for involving her son in a variety of different musical activities. When the boy started kindergarten, he had the opportunity to play musical instruments as part of music classes. He showed an interest and knack for playing the bells and chimes and was able to repeat almost every song he heard with uncanny accuracy. His abilities became the talk of the school, and he was invited to be a guest performer at concerts with the high school band. His music teacher and the high school band leader, as well as audiences, came to see this boy for his talents, and never was there any reference to his physical limitations.

Multiple and Cumulative Influences   Activity setting and child, parent, and community member characteristics that coalesce in mutually beneficial ways contribute to highly successful PLOs. The interactions and transactions between different factors are the rule rather than the exception in children's participation in development-instigating and development-enhancing PLOs. The following example best illustrates this phenomenon.

A 2½-year-old girl had cerebral palsy and was just beginning to pull to stand and bear weight on her feet. She especially liked music, and whether standing or sitting, she bounced up and down whenever music was played. Her mother called this "dancing" and often would join in the activity with her daughter. The child's interest in music became the basis for a search for a community activity that would provide this young girl an opportunity to express her musical interests. A music/dance/gymnastics program was located, and it provided young children an opportunity to learn gymnastics and dance movements in concert with children's songs and other music. The day the mother visited the program, the children were doing exercises on a balance beam. At first, the mother said that she was not sure that this was appropriate for her daughter because she was not yet walking. The instructors (one a music teacher and the other a gymnast) reassured her by explaining that children, no matter how well they are able to stand or walk by themselves, get to hold onto the instructors' hands and that they never let go but let the children decide when they feel confident enough to try

to traverse the balance beam on their own.

The mother decided to try the program and enrolled her daughter in twice-a-week classes that lasted approximately 2 hours each. After the fourth session, the mother called the staff member who was working with the family and exclaimed, "You won't believe what has happened today! My daughter walked down the balance beam all by herself!" The mother described her daughter's success, saying that her child looked forward to going to the classes, smiled and got excited when she saw the other children, tried as hard as she could to walk down the balance beam, tried to do the same movements as the other children, and radiated a sense of enjoyment and success when she finally was able to do it on her own.

This example illustrates the different person and environment factors that contribute to successful PLOs. All of the elements depicted in Figure 14.3 are represented in the example, and the characteristics and consequences of parent and community member attitudes, beliefs, and behavior make clear their contributions to child participation and benefits. But the story doesn't end there. The mother had repeatedly asked the therapists in the early intervention program that was serving her child and family to do the kinds of things that proved successful as part of her child's participation in the gymnastics movement program. She asked the therapist to play music, have other children present, pick things the child liked to do, and so forth, none of which were done. Her daughter disliked therapy so much (because it was uninteresting) that she cried and became upset whenever she entered the therapy room. All of this ran counter to what the music and gymnastics instructors had done to make her daughter's experience enjoyable and beneficial.

Child and Family Benefits

The kinds of contrasting experiences described in the previous section have been expressed by many parents of young children who are trying to facilitate participation in PLOs. Often, parents describe their children's and their own participation in community activities as more relaxing, more enjoyable, and more gratifying than that experienced in early intervention or preschool special education programs. In a parent survey (Dunst, 1997) to evaluate the effects of PLOs, two quality-of-life questions were added to evaluate parents' experiences with community activities. The questions, one about child quality of life and the other about family quality of life, produced unexpected findings. For both measures, parents were asked to indicate whether quality of life was better in the early intervention/preschool program in which their children were enrolled, better in the community activities used as PLOs, or was about the same regardless of setting. Sixty-seven percent of the parents judged child quality of life to be better in community activities (compared with 8% for early intervention/preschool program participation), and 75% of the parents judged family quality of life to be better in community activities (compared with 9% for early intervention/preschool program participation).

To ensure that these findings were not an artifact of the parents' knowledge that project staff were aware of their responses, an independent third-party evaluation was conducted by a research firm in a different state. Families were assured that their responses were confidential and that their identity was protected. In addition, the third-party evaluators were kept blind to the purposes and focus of the project. The survey used to do the evaluation included six measures of child quality of life and five measures of family quality of life. The survey also included six measures of child competence and five measures of the extent to which respondents (all parents) had control over the kinds of PLOs provided to their children, when and how the PLOs were done, and parent participation in the activities. Nearly half (48%) of the parents rated the indicators of child quality of life to be better in community activities (compared with 18% for early intervention/preschool program participation), and 48% of the parents rated the indicators of family quality of life to be better in the community activities (compared with 15% for early intervention/preschool program participation). Forty-six percent of the parents judged child display and acquisition of the different competencies to be better in community activities (compared with 22% for early intervention/preschool program participation), and 59% of the parents judged the five control appraisal indicators to be better in community activities (compared with 12% for early intervention/preschool participation). For all four sets of measures, considerably more parents indicated that participation in community learning activities was associated with better child and parent/family benefits compared with participation in early childhood programs for infants, toddlers, and preschool-age children with disabilities.

These findings were produced as part of the model-demonstration project that provided a foundation for the methods and strategies described in this chapter (Dunst, 1997). Similar results were found as part of case study research (Dunst & Bruder, 1999b; Dunst, Bruder, et al. 1998). Several findings are briefly summarized here. First, for 2,600 child behavior outcomes and objectives on children's individualized family service plans (IFSPs) or individualized education programs (IEPs) and prescribed or recommended by professionals, parents indicated that it was a very good idea to promote the behaviors in the context of community activity settings. For the more than 1,000 behaviors on IFSPs and IEPs, however, fewer than 0.5% were actually implemented in community activity settings. Second, for three child, parent, and family quality-of-life measures, between 50% and 60% of parents indicated that quality of life was better when child learning occurred in everyday community activities, compared with 4%–5% of parents who indicated that quality of life was better when child learning did not occur in community activities. Third, 74% of the parents indicated that their children mostly or always derived positive benefits and consequences from their participation in community activities, compared with 10% who said that their children never benefited or benefited just a little from participation in community activities.

Taken together, findings indicate that parents consider community activities to be important sources of children's learning opportunities and judge participation to be associated with a number of positive benefits but that early intervention and early childhood special education program practices do not use community activities to promote child competence or to produce other desired outcomes (e.g., improved quality of life), at least as evidenced by IFSP and IEP analyses.

CONCLUSION

An activity setting perspective of young children's community-based learning opportunities was the focus of this chapter. Research and practice couched in an ecological social systems framework formed the foundation for the conceptual model, methods, and procedures and for the description of development-instigating and development-enhancing qualities of participatory learning opportunities. The examples in this chapter are real-life experiences that have not been embellished to make a point. They are but a few of the hundreds of vivid examples of successful participation of young children with disabilities in their communities.

Early intervention and early childhood education have always been about children's learning, the experiences that promote learning, and at least for some professionals, strategies for supporting and strengthening parenting confidence and competence. The kinds of community activities that constitute the focus of this chapter provide the context for this perspective of early child learning and parenting supports. Consequently, using community activity as a form of early intervention and early childhood education seems warranted and indicated. There is a paramount caution in doing so. Adoption and use of the kinds of practices described in this chapter require a major paradigm shift in professional views of children, parents, families, and communities. This is especially the case in terms of an asset-based orientation and the recognition that community-based learning opportunities are, in fact, early intervention and early childhood education. In the absence of a shift in perspectives, efforts to conduct early intervention therapy and early childhood education practices in community-based settings may do more harm than good.

REFERENCES

Americans with Disabilities Act (ADA) of 1990, PL 101-336, 42 U.S.C. §§ 12101 *et seq.*

Appleton, T., Clifton, R., & Goldberg, S. (1975). The development of behavior competence. In F. Horowitz (Ed.), *Review of child development* (Vol. 4, pp. 101–186). Chicago: University of Chicago Press.

Beckman, P., Barnwell, D., Horn, E., Hanson, M., Gutierrez, S., & Lieber, J. (1998). Communities, families and inclusion. *Early Childhood Research Quarterly, 13,* 125–150.

Blum-Kulka, S. (1997). *Dinner talk.* Mahwah, NJ: Lawrence Erlbaum Associates.

Brandtstädter, J., & Lerner, R.M. (Eds.). (1999). *Action and self-development: Theory and research through the life span.* Newbury Park, CA: Sage Publications.

Bronfenbrenner, U. (1979). *The ecology of human development: Experiments by nature and design.* Cambridge, MA: Harvard University Press.

Bronfenbrenner, U. (1992). Ecological systems theory. In R. Vasta (Ed.), *Six theories of child development: Revised formulations and current issues* (pp. 187–248). Philadelphia: Taylor & Francis Publishers.

Bronfenbrenner, U. (1993). The ecology of cognitive development: Research models and fugitive findings. In R.H. Wozniak & K.W. Fischer (Eds.), *Development in context: Acting and thinking in specific environments* (pp. 3–44). Mahwah, NJ: Lawrence Erlbaum Associates.

Bronfenbrenner, U. (1999). Environments in developmental perspective: Theoretical and operational models. In S.L. Friedman & T.D. Wachs (Eds.), *Measuring environment across the life span: Emerging methods and concepts* (pp. 3–28). Washington, DC: American Psychological Association.

Caliper Corporation. (1999). *Maptitude user's guide.* Newton, MA: Author.

Chen, J.Q., Krechevsky, M., Viens, J., & Isberg, E. (H. Gardner, D. H. Feldman, & M. Krechevsky, Series Eds.). (1998). *Project Zero frameworks for early childhood education: Vol. 1. Building on children's strengths: The experience of Project Spectrum.* New York: Teachers College Press.

Clark, S. (1998). Learning at the public bathhouse. In J. Singleton (Ed.), *Learning in likely places: Varieties of apprenticeship in Japan* (pp. 239–252). New York: Cambridge University Press.

Cole, M. (1996). *Cultural psychology.* Cambridge, MA: Harvard University Press.

Danforth, S., & Rhodes, W.C. (1997). Deconstructing disability: A philosophy for inclusion. *Remedial and Special Education, 18,* 357–366.

Dunst, C.J. (1985). Rethinking early intervention. *Analysis and Intervention in Developmental Disabilities, 5,* 165–201.

Dunst, C.J. (1996). Early intervention in the USA: Programs, models, and practices. In M. Brambring, H. Rauh, & A. Beelmann (Eds.), *Early childhood intervention: Theory, evaluation, and practice* (pp. 11–52). Hawthorne, NY: Walter de Gruyter.

Dunst, C.J. (1997). *Building Community Resources Project.* Unpublished manuscript.

Dunst, C.J. (2000). Revisiting "Rethinking early intervention." *Topics in Early Childhood Special Education, 20,* 95–104.

Dunst, C.J., Bennis, L.A., Durant, V., & Shivers, S. (1999, August). *Project PAL: Parents accessing learning opportunities for their young children.*

Second year progress report. Asheville, NC: Orelena Hawks Puckett Institute.

Dunst, C.J., & Bruder, M.B. (1999a). Family and community activity settings, natural learning environments, and children's learning opportunities. *Children's Learning Opportunities Report, 1*(2).

Dunst, C.J., & Bruder, M.B. (1999b). Increasing children's learning opportunities in the context of family and community life. *Children's Learning Opportunities Report, 1*(1).

Dunst, C.J., Bruder, M.B., Trivette, C.M., Raab, M., & McLean, M. (1998, May). *Increasing Children's Learning Opportunities Through Families and Communities Early Childhood Research Institute: Year 2 progress report.* Asheville, NC: Orelena Hawks Puckett Institute.

Dunst, C.J., Faris, C., Meehan, T., Valenzuela, N., Russell, A., Mendez, S., Nagurski, L., & Martinez, M. (1998, September). *Culturally based children's learning opportunities.* Presentation made at the Magic Years Conference, Albuquerque, NM.

Dunst, C.J., Hamby, D., Trivette, C.M., Raab, M., & Bruder, M.B. (2000a). Everyday family and community life and children's naturally occurring learning opportunities. *Journal of Early Intervention, 23*(3), 156–169.

Dunst, C.J., Hamby, D., Trivette, C.M., Raab, M., & Bruder, M.B. (2000b). *Young children's participation in everyday family and community activity.* Manuscript submitted for publication.

Dunst, C.J., Herter, S., Shields, H., & Bennis, L. (in press). Mapping community-based natural learning opportunities. *Young Exceptional Children.*

Dunst, C.J., Lesko, J.J., Holbert, K.A., Wilson, L.L., Sharpe, K.L., & Ritchie, F.L. (1987). A systemic approach to infant intervention. *Topics in Early Childhood Special Education, 7*(2), 19–37.

Dunst, C.J., & Trivette, C.M. (1997). Early intervention with young at-risk children and their families. In R. Ammerman & M. Hersen (Eds.), *Handbook of prevention and treatment with children and adolescents: Intervention in the real world* (pp. 157–180). New York: John Wiley & Sons.

Dunst, C.J., Trivette, C.M., & Deal, A.G. (1988). *Enabling and empowering families: Principles and guidelines for practice.* Cambridge, MA: Brookline Books.

Dunst, C.J., Trivette, C.M., & Deal, A.G. (1994a). Resource-based family-centered intervention practices. In C.J. Dunst, C.M. Trivette, & A.G. Deal (Eds.), *Supporting and strengthening families: Methods, strategies and practices* (pp. 140–151). Cambridge, MA: Brookline Books.

Dunst, C.J., Trivette, C.M., & Deal, A.G. (Eds.). (1994b). *Supporting and strengthening families:*

Methods, strategies and practices. Cambridge, MA: Brookline Books.

Dunst, C.J., Trivette, C.M., & Jodry, W. (1997). Influences of social support on children with disabilities and their families. In M.J. Guralnick (Ed.), *The effectiveness of early intervention* (pp. 499–522). Baltimore: Paul H. Brookes Publishing Co.

Dunst, C.J., Trivette, C.M., & Thompson, R.B. (1990). Supporting and strengthening family functioning: Toward a congruence between principles and practice. *Prevention in Human Services, 9*(1), 19–43.

Ehrmann, L.C., Aeschleman, S.R., & Svanum, S. (1995). Parental reports of community activity patterns: A comparison between young children with disabilities and their nondisabled peers. *Research in Developmental Disabilities, 16,* 331–343.

Farver, J.A.M. (1999). Activity setting analysis: A model for examining the role of culture in development. In A. Göncü (Ed.), *Children's engagement in the world: Sociocultural perspectives* (pp. 99–127). New York: Cambridge University Press.

Field, T. (1978). The three R's of infant–adult interactions: Rhythms, repertoires, and responsivity. *Journal of Pediatric Psychology, 3,* 131–136.

Fogel, A. (1997). Information, creativity, and culture. In C. Dent-Read & P. Zukow-Goldring (Eds.), *Evolving explanations of development: Ecological approaches to organism–environment systems* (pp. 413–443). Washington, DC: American Psychological Association.

Garson, G.D., & Biggs, R.S. (1992). *Analytic mapping and geographic databases.* Newbury Park, CA: Sage Publications.

Gauvain, M. (1999). Everyday opportunities for the development of planning skills: Sociocultural and family influences. In A. Göncü (Ed.), *Children's engagement in the world: Sociocultural perspectives* (pp. 173–201). New York: Cambridge University Press.

Gewirtz, J.L., & Pelaez-Nogueras, M. (1992). B.F. Skinner's legacy to human infant behavior and development. *American Psychologist, 47,* 1411–1422.

Goldberg, S. (1977). Social competence in infancy: A model of parent–infant interaction. *Merrill-Palmer Quarterly, 23,* 163–177.

Göncü, A. (Ed.). (1999). *Children's engagement in the world: Sociocultural perspectives.* New York: Cambridge University Press.

Guberman, S.R. (1999). Supportive environments for cognitive development: Illustrations from children's mathematical activities outside of school. In A. Göncü (Ed.), *Children's engagement in the world: Sociocultural perspectives*

(pp. 202–227). New York: Cambridge University Press.

Guralnick, M.J. (1999). The nature and meaning of social integration for young children with mild developmental delays in inclusive settings. *Journal of Early Intervention, 22,* 70–86.

Haith, M. (1972). The forgotten message of the infant smile. *Merrill-Palmer Quarterly, 18,* 321–322.

Harris, V.S., & McHale, S.M. (1989). Family life problems, daily caregiving activities, and the psychological well-being of mothers of mentally retarded children. *American Journal on Mental Retardation, 94,* 231–239.

Hill, S.A. (1999). *African American children: Socialization and development in families.* Newbury Park, CA: Sage Publications.

Hobbs, N., Dokecki, P., Hoover-Dempsey, K., Moroney, R., Shayne, M., & Weeks, K. (1984). *Strengthening families.* San Francisco: Jossey-Bass Publishers.

Horowitz, F.D. (1994). Developmental theory, prediction, and the developmental equation in follow-up research: Introduction. In S.L. Friedman & H.C. Haywood (Eds.), *Developmental follow-up: Concepts, domains, and methods* (pp. 27–44). San Diego: Academic Press.

Hunt, J.M. (1979). Psychological development: Early experience. *Annual Review of Psychology, 30,* 103–143.

Jilek, W.G. (1982). *Indian healing: Shamanic ceremonialism in the Pacific Northwest today.* Surrey, Canada: Hancock House.

Koegel, L.K., Koegel, R.L., Kellegrew, D., & Mullen, K. (1996). Parent education for prevention and reduction of severe problem behaviors. In L.K. Koegel, R.K. Koegel, & G. Dunlap (Eds.), *Positive behavioral support: Including people with difficult behavior in the community* (pp. 3–30). Baltimore: Paul H. Brookes Publishing Co.

Kretzmann, J., & McKnight, J. (1993). *Building community from the inside out.* Evanston, IL: Northwestern University, Center for Urban Affairs and Policy Research.

Lamb, M. (1981). The development of social expectations in the first year of life. In M. Lamb & L. Sherrod (Eds.), *Infant social cognition* (pp. 155–175). Mahwah, NJ: Lawrence Erlbaum Associates.

Lancy, D.R. (1996). *Playing on the mother ground: Cultural routines for children's development.* New York: The Guilford Press.

LaPierre, Y. (1997, July/August). Virtual parks. *National Parks, 71,* 37–39.

Lave, J., & Wenger, E. (1991). *Situated learning: Legitimate peripheral participation.* New York: Cambridge University Press.

Leont'ev, A.N. (1981). The problem of activity in psychology. In J. Wertsch (Ed.), *The concept of activity in Soviet psychology* (pp. 37–71). San Diego: Academic Press.

Lerner, R.M., & Busch-Rossnagel, N.A. (Eds.). (1981). *Individuals as producers of their development: A life-span perspective.* San Diego: Academic Press.

Lipsitt, L., & Werner, J. (1981). The infancy of human learning processes. In E. Gollin (Ed.), *Developmental plasticity* (pp. 101–133). San Diego: Academic Press.

Lipsky, D., & Gartner, A. (1996). Inclusion, restructuring, and the remaking of American society. *Harvard Educational Review, 6,* 762–796.

MacTurk, R.H., & Morgan, G.A. (Eds.). (1995). *Advances in applied developmental psychology: Vol. 12. Mastery motivation: Origins, conceptualizations, and applications.* Stamford, CT: Ablex Publishing Corp.

Mahoney, G. (1988). Enhancing the developmental competence of handicapped infants. In K. Marfo (Ed.), *Parent–child interaction and developmental disabilities: Theory, research, and intervention* (pp. 203–219). Westport, CT: Praeger Publishers.

Noonan, M.J., & McCormick, L. (1993). *Early intervention in natural environments: Methods and procedures.* Pacific Grove, CA: Brooks/Cole Publishing.

Odom, S.L., & Diamond, K.E. (Eds.). (1998). Inclusion in early childhood settings [Special issue]. *Early Childhood Research Quarterly, 13*(1).

Rappaport, J. (1981). In praise of paradox: A social policy of empowerment over prevention. *American Journal of Community Psychology, 9,* 1–25.

Rappaport, J. (1987). Terms of empowerment/exemplars of prevention: Toward a theory for community psychology. *American Journal of Community Psychology, 15,* 121–148.

Rogoff, B. (1990). *Apprenticeship in thinking: Cognitive development in social context.* New York: Oxford University Press.

Rogoff, B., Mistry, J., Göncü, A., & Mosier, C. (1991). Cultural variation in the role relations of toddlers and their families. In M. Bornstein (Ed.), *Cultural approaches to parenting* (pp. 173–183). Mahwah, NJ: Lawrence Erlbaum Associates.

Rogoff, B., Mistry, J., Göncü, A., & Mosier, C. (1993). Guided participation in cultural activities by toddlers and caregivers. *Monographs of the Society for Research in Child Development, 58*(8, Serial No. 236).

Rovee-Collier, C. (1987). Learning and memory in infancy. In J.D. Osofsky (Ed.), *Handbook of infant development* (2nd ed., pp. 98–148). New York: John Wiley & Sons.

Sarason, S.B., Carroll, C., Maton, K., Cohen, S., & Lorentz, E. (1977). *Human services and resources networks: Rationale, possibilities, and public policy.* Cambridge, MA: Brookline Books.

Scales, P.C., & Leffert, N. (1999). *Developmental assets: A synthesis of the scientific research on adolescent development.* Minneapolis, MN: Search Institute.

Scarr, S., & McCartney, K. (1983). How people make their own environments: A theory of genotype–environment effects. *Child Development, 54,* 424–435.

Schaeffer, H.R. (Ed.). (1971). *The origins of human social relations.* San Diego: Academic Press.

Schaffer, R. (1977). *Mothering.* Cambridge, MA: Harvard University Press.

Select Phone Deluxe [CD-ROM]. (1999). Danvers, MA: ProCD.

Trivette, C.M., Dunst, C.J., & Deal, A.G. (1997). Resource-based approach to early intervention. In S.K. Thurman, J.R. Cornwell, & S.R. Gottwald (Eds.), *Contexts of early intervention: Systems and settings* (pp. 73–92). Baltimore: Paul H. Brookes Publishing Co.

Tudge, J., Hogan, D., Lee, S., Tammeveski, P., Meltsas, M., Kulakova, N., Snezhkova, I., & Putnam, S. (1999). Cultural heterogeneity: Parental values and beliefs and their preschoolers' activities in the United States, South Korea, Russia, and Estonia. In A. Göncü (Ed.), *Children's engagement in the world: Sociocultural perspectives* (pp. 62–96). New York: Cambridge University Press.

U.S. Department of Commerce. (1987). *Standard industrial classification (SIC).* Washington, DC: Author.

Wachs, T.D. (2000). *Necessary but not sufficient: The respective roles of single and multiple influences on individual development.* Washington, DC: American Psychological Association.

Watson, J.S. (1972). Smiling, cooing, and the "game." *Merrill-Palmer Quarterly, 18,* 323–339.

Wertsch, J.V. (1985). *Vygotsky and the social formation of mind.* Cambridge, MA: Harvard University Press.

Wertsch, J.V. (1991). *Voices of the mind: A sociocultural approach to mediated action.* Cambridge, MA: Harvard University Press.

Wolery, M., & Sainato, D.M. (1996). General curriculum and intervention strategies. In S.L. Odom & M.E. McLean (Eds.), *Early intervetion/early childhood special education: Recommended practices* (pp. 125–158). Austin, TX: PRO-ED.

Wolery, M., & Wilbers, J.S. (Eds.). (1994). *Including children with special needs in early childhood programs.* Washington, DC: National Association for the Education of Young Children.

IV

Special Groups and Topics

15

PHILLIP S. STRAIN

GAIL G. McGEE

FRANK W. KOHLER

Inclusion of Children with Autism in Early Intervention Environments

An Examination of Rationale, Myths, and Procedures

The inclusion of young children with autism with their preschool-age peers has been the subject of heated debate, a distinguishing feature of early intervention programs, a pivotal issue in litigation, and the occasional subject of scientific inquiry. When an issue generates such controversy, it is not surprising that an abundance of myth and folklore emerges. In large part, the purpose of this chapter is to shed some empirical light on the many myths that have emerged regarding the inclusion of young children with autism, beginning with a discussion of the rationale for inclusionary practices that are specific to children with autism. Following this discussion is an analysis of a number of myths surrounding inclusion options and their relationship to the extant database. The chapter concludes with suggestions for how inclusion options may be optimized to benefit all parties.

WHY INCLUSION FOR CHILDREN WITH AUTISM?

Not unlike the rationale for inclusion practices in general, there are at least four compelling reasons for the establishment of high-quality inclusion options for young children with autism. First, there is a strong argument to be made under federal law, specifically the Individuals with Disabilities Education Act (IDEA) Amendments of 1997 (PL 105-17; see Chapters 3 and 4). The potential legal issues are twofold. Initially, one can make the case that a free appropriate public education (FAPE) could not be achieved for young children with autism, who by definition exhibit significant social relationship deficits with peers, without regular and planned interactions with such peers. Although it has been argued that young children with autism need to be "behaviorally ready" to benefit from inclusion and peer social interaction

337

intervention, there is no direct evidence to support this contention. Alternatively, there are 80 cases of young children with autism developing peer interactions without the benefit of any readiness training (Strain & Kohler, 1998).

The second argument under IDEA 1997 centers around the ability to modify early childhood activities and contexts in such a way that they facilitate the development of young children with autism. Although the complexity of such a task is not discounted and, indeed, a more honest portrayal of the complexities has been argued for (Strain & Kohler, 1998), it is clear that the instructional, curricular, and personnel training technology is available to meet the challenge (McGee, Daly, & Jacobs, 1993; Strain & Cordisco, 1993). Given the state of knowledge, the question is not so much whether an individual child with autism can profit from inclusionary programming but whether the service system in question has put into place the necessary instructional supports to create a high-quality inclusion program.

In addition to a legal rationale, inclusion programs are important as an alternative to the prevailing, developmentally segregated mode of service delivery for young children with autism (U.S. Department of Education, 1998). Simply put, there is a dearth of high-quality inclusion programs across the United States, creating minimal and/or poor choices of services for families. Not only would an expansion of inclusion options result in more legitimate service delivery choices for families, but such a change in prevailing practice might also result in a more contemporary, data-based approach to how services for children with autism are conceptualized.

With few exceptions, services for children with autism have been based on the notion that these children learn in unique ways and, therefore, need unique

services delivered by uniquely trained individuals. However, there is no definitive evidence to support the relationship between a diagnosis of autism and a particular constellation of differentially effective practices. Moreover, the problems with overselective attention, stereotypies, and failure to generalize, once thought to be specific to autism, are actually shared by many children with disabilities (Van Hasselt, Strain, & Hersen, 1988).

Related is that instructional methods that have been effective with children with autism have also been effective with other groups of children; that is, interventions such as discrete trial instruction, incidental teaching, natural language paradigm, peer-mediated instruction, positive behavioral support, and self-control training do not operate uniquely or differentially for children with autism. It is interesting that most of these strategies were *not* initially developed and tested for children with autism. The danger is that "autism only" services may create the conditions under which professionals and families read and think in the most narrow fashion, ignoring, for example, general research on the efficacy of a variety of intervention practices for young children with *and* without disabilities (Strain, Wolery, & Izeman, 1998).

A third compelling reason to support high-quality inclusive practices is that they represent the necessary condition to implement a number of effective intervention practices, including peer-mediated social skills training, peer-based script training for language acquisition, and group individualized instruction for teaching cognitive and preacademic skills. For each of these strategies, typically developing peers are essential agents of intervention. For example, they may initiate and persist in maintaining social contact with a reluctant playmate, they may cue or signal the next word or phrase needed to maintain a dramatic play theme, they may remind one another that everyone has to play, they may model specific behaviors that their classmates will be asked to imitate, and they may expand on or praise what a peer has done or said. By excluding these intervention options, developmentally segregated services not only limit their teaching options but, in the case of peer-mediated social skills intervention, fore-close the choice of what is clearly the most widely replicated tactic for addressing this core behavioral impairment of autism.

A fourth and final rationale for the inclusion of young children with autism concerns the benefits that are unique to this service delivery arrangement. Benefits include enhanced generalization of social skills (Strain, 1982) and more favorable attitudes held by typically developing peers (Strain & Kohler, 1998). Specific to the issue of generalization, there are two studies that have examined the differential effects of developmentally segregated and inclusive generalization environments on children's peer social skills (Strain, 1983, 1984). In both studies, developmentally segregated environments had an immediate toxic effect, with learner behavior rapidly returning to baseline levels of performance. In contrast, inclusive environments, as a consequence of peer responsiveness, resulted in continued behavioral improvement outside the initial teaching environments.

The data specific to the attitudes of typically developing children involve a comparison of preschool-age children who had not been exposed to children with disabilities and typically developing children involved in the LEAP (Learning Experiences—An Alternative Program for Preschoolers and Parents) Preschool (Strain & Cordisco, 1993) model. In this study, 40 children from 20 early childhood programs that did not enroll children with special needs were selected by their teachers as the "social stars" of their class. The attitudes of these 40 children were compared with those of 20 typically developing children in the LEAP program after 1 year of preschool. In general, the social stars as 4- and 5-year olds were highly bigoted in their perceptions of young strangers with purported special needs, suggesting that they "should be punished" for their lack of skill and dismissing their competence as "luck." In sharp contrast, after 1 year in the inclusionary LEAP program, the 20 typically developing participants readily acknowledged the competence displayed by children who purportedly had disabilities and suggested overwhelmingly that they could help them in addressing lack of skill. The early emergence of adult-like bigotry and stereotypic thinking among the social stars should be of profound concern to all those involved with the education and welfare of people with disabilities (see Chapter 7). That carefully orchestrated exposure to peers with autism seems to prevent these stereotypical thought patterns is of general significance to people with disabilities and to the choice of service delivery models at the earliest age.

In presenting this multifaceted rationale for the inclusion of children with autism, it is not suggested that an inclusionary option is always the most appropriate choice of service delivery. Certainly, there are circumstances in which there is a poor match between child needs and the quality of an available inclusionary option. It is suggested, however, that the burden is not on children with autism to get ready to benefit from inclusionary environments; rather, inclusionary environments need to be ready to modify staffing, curriculum, and teaching practices for children whose range and depth of need may exceed that of many other young children with special needs.

MYTHS SUPPORTING DEVELOPMENTALLY SEGREGATED SERVICES

This section addresses several myths that have helped to perpetuate developmentally segregated services for children with autism. Understanding the extent of mythology surrounding early intervention for children with autism is crucial because families and policymakers are making programmatic decisions as if the myths are based on irrefutable empirical evidence. First, it is important to specify what is meant by *myths* and briefly review their historical roots. In general, myths refer to summary conclusions made about early intervention programming for children with autism that 1) have no direct empirical basis, 2) in some cases have extensive data to refute their validity, 3) are based on decades of doing things one way (concluding illogically and erroneously that any success demonstrates the relative superiority of the practice), and 4) are institutionalized and memorialized in the writings of respected professionals, funding patterns, and service delivery policies and procedures. Simply put, the myths can be thought of as long-standing, influential, somewhat impervious to conflicting data, and slow to change. The specific myths include the notions that 1) young children with autism require a "readiness" curriculum to prepare them for more functional instruction to address the core impairments of communicative and peer social skills, 2) one-to-one, tutorial-like instruction is necessary to address the intensity of intervention needed to achieve developmental gains, 3) young children with autism are "overstimulated" in typical classroom environments, and 4) one cannot do the necessary behavioral control procedures directed toward reducing challenging behaviors in typical environments.

The Readiness Myth

Perhaps more pervasive than any other myth, the readiness notion has many manifestations, including 1) an initial curriculum that focuses almost entirely on child compliance in the context of simple motor-imitation tasks, 2) systematic movement of children from developmentally segregated to inclusionary environments based on achieving certain developmental skills in the segregated environments, and 3) always beginning intervention using the most directive, adult-driven teaching methods, followed by more child-initiated tactics. Although these readiness notions may be strongly held and vigorously defended, there is no direct evidence to support their validity. What would this evidence look like if it existed? Three possibilities come to mind: 1) that children with autism have failed to learn important skills without readiness training, 2) that children with autism learn only certain fundamental skills after readiness training has been completed, and 3) that children who have had some readiness training have different and superior long-term outcomes from those who do not. Again, there are *no* examples of these kinds of data. Because children with autism do demonstrate developmental growth in "readiness" models, it does not follow that this approach is mandatory *or* superior to others.

Although the evidence refuting the readiness notion is less than perfect, particularly with regard to high-quality comparative intervention studies, the available database is nonetheless compelling. The most relevant data refuting the readiness notion are as follows:

1. Peer-mediated intervention studies in which all of the young children with autism studied ($N = 80$) have acquired important social skills without any readiness training in the

forms of curricular or teaching tactics (see review by Strain & Kohler, 1998)

2. Self-control interventions conducted by Koegel, Koegel, and Carter (1998) in which 500 behaviors have been brought under the influence of tactics that are independent of readiness training

3. Dozens of language intervention studies (e.g., Kaiser & Hester, 1994; Koegel, Koegel, et al., 1998; Koegel, O'Dell, & Koegel, 1987; McGee, Krantz, & McClannahan, 1985; Prizant, Schuler, Wetherby, & Rydell, 1997; Warren, McQuarter, & Rogers-Warren, 1984; Yoder et al., 1995) in which a variety of child-initiated instructional tactics have proved effective; included are tactics such as the Natural Language Paradigm, incidental teaching, milieu language teaching, and mand-model procedures

4. Direct, behavior-analytic comparison studies in which more incidental, learner-initiated tactics *are equal or superior to* more adult-directed tactics in producing generalized responding and positive affect among teachers and learners (Elliott, Hall, & Sopher, 1991; Koegel, O'Dell, & Dunlap, 1988; McGee et al., 1985; Miranda-Linne & Melin, 1992; Schreibman, Kaneko, & Koegel, 1991)

At this point, the question is not what data support the readiness notion, but how many cases of invalidity are enough to dispel the notion? Or perhaps this is not an issue to be decided by data. In either case, it is important to understand where there are and where there are not data to support this or another early intervention practice for children with autism.

The Tutorial-Like Instruction Myth

Closely tied to the readiness myth is the notion that young children with autism *require* tutorial, one-to-one instruction to learn important developmental skills. Often, the one-to-one instruction notion is thought of as the primary tactic to achieve a high level of intervention intensity. What would the evidence to support the tutorial instruction myth look like if it existed? Three possibilities exist: 1) data to show that children have failed to acquire important skills when provided with alternative instructional methods, 2) data to show that children *only acquire* certain important skills under one-to-one instructional conditions, 3) data to show that children who are exposed to one-to-one instruction have a different and superior developmental course than those who are not. Again, there is no direct evidence to support this myth. The efficacy of tutorial-like instruction is not in question. However, because children learn under this approach, it does not follow that the approach is mandatory *or* superior.

By contrast, there are numerous cases of invalidity that should cause one to question the soundness of the one-to-one myth. The data that contradict the tutorial instruction myth are as follows:

1. Studies in which self-management techniques have been applied successfully in the context of ongoing routines in fully inclusive environments to improve task engagement, appropriate behavior, and academic responses (e.g., Callahan & Rademacher, 1998; Koegel, Harrower, & Koegel, 1998; Sainato, Strain, Lefebvre, & Rapp, 1990)

2. Studies in which adult-mediated behavioral teaching strategies are embedded in ongoing, group-based

class routines to improve cognitive skills, early reading skills, imitation, and a variety of specific individualized education program (IEP) objectives (e.g., Hoyson, Jamieson, & Strain, 1984; Kamps, Barbetta, Leonard, & Delquadri, 1994; Kohler, Strain, Hoyson, & Jamieson, 1997; Venn, Wolery, Werts, et al., 1993)

3. Studies in which typically developing peers have been taught to engage peers with autism in specific social and instructional exchanges during routine, group-based class activities to enhance communicative skills, object use, and toy play skills (e.g., Goldstein, Kaczmarek, Pennington, & Shafer, 1992; Pierce & Schreibman, 1997; Wolfberg & Schuler, 1993)

4. Studies in which high levels of child engagement and many instructional opportunities have been achieved within the context of routine preschool activities involving large numbers of children (e.g., Kohler et al., 1997; Strain, Danko, & Kohler, 1994; Venn, Wolery, Fleming, et al., 1993; Venn, Wolery, Morris, DeCesare, & Cuffs, in press)

The Overstimulation Myth

This overstimulation myth, unlike the previous two, has seldom found its way into the literature. However, it continues to serve as a foundation assumption controlling access to typical environments. In all likelihood, there are multiple origins to the overstimulation myth. For example, 1) the difficulty that some children with autism have with changing activities, 2) that some children with autism are easily distracted from performing requested behaviors, 3) that some children with autism routinely ignore various instructional and social cues, and 4) that some children with autism engage in less challenging behaviors when taught in isolated environments. Although no one can deny

that many children with autism display limited attention to important environmental cues, there is no evidence that these challenges to instruction have a neurobehavioral basis akin to overstimulation. It is also true that many children with autism have unusual sensory preferences and dislikes, yet there are no data to support an overstimulation origin to these unusual behavioral patterns either.

Although there are no data to suggest that children with autism are understimulated in a neurobehavioral sense, there are several data sources that may be viewed as casting suspicion on the overstimulation notion. These data sources are as follows:

1. Studies in which programmed variations or changes in instructional stimuli, choice making, and reinforcer variation (generally speaking, more varied stimulation) lead to higher levels of engagement, appropriate behavior, and developmental outcomes (e.g., Dunlap, 1984; Dunlap et al., 1994; Dunlap & Koegel, 1980)

2. Studies in which chronic, high-amplitude challenging behaviors have been reduced successfully in typical (presumably highly stimulating) environments (Carr et al., 1999; Dunlap & Fox, 1999; Fox, Dunlap, & Philbrick, 1997; Frea & Hepburn, 1999; Vaughn, Clarke, & Dunlap, 1997)

3. Studies of children's social skill acquisition in which "day one" intervention effects co-occur with the onset of increased and more varied social stimuli (e.g., Odom, Strain, Karger, & Smith, 1986; Strain, 1977, 1987; Strain, Kohler, Storey, & Danko, 1994)

4. Studies of older children and adults with autism who have experienced significant reductions in challenging behavior as a result of being provided nonaversive behavioral intervention

and a more varied, stimulating, and independent lifestyle (e.g., Bellamy, Newton, LeBaron, & Horner, 1990; Carr & Carlson, 1993; Carr et al., 1999; Lucyshyn, Olson, & Horner, 1995)

If there was validity to the overstimulation myth, one could point to research in which a reduction in stimulation (a controlled independent variable) led directly to behavioral improvement; however, no such study exists. Taken together, the results of research that points to invalidity suggest the presence of redundant, inappropriate, and uninteresting stimuli in the lives of many young children with autism.

The Behavioral Control Limitation Myth

The behavioral control limitation myth asserts that inclusionary environments do not allow for the types and intensity of interventions that are needed to control the challenging behaviors of children with autism. To some extent, there is truth to this myth; that is, most inclusion programs promote the use of normalized interventions (Wolery, Strain, & Bailey, 1995), restrict or prohibit the use of tactics that are considered disrespectful of children (Council for Exceptional Children, 1993), and generally place more emphasis on skill building versus behavioral redirection (Dunlap, Johnson, & Robbins, 1990). In this sense, it is true that placement in an inclusionary environment may be incompatible, in a sociopolitical fashion, with the use of behavior control tactics that would not be used readily for typically developing preschool-age children. However, the question of fundamental importance is whether, for example, a prohibition on exclusionary time out, physical aversives, overcorrection, and the like deprive children with autism of a necessary and appropriate educational program. On the basis of the extensive and successful use of more normalized, positive strategies, the answer to this question is no. Following are the data sources that support the use of more typical strategies to reduce challenging behaviors:

1. Studies in which a response substitution strategy has been used successfully to reduce challenging behaviors (Carr et al., 1999; Dunlap & Fox, 1999)

2. Studies in which a variety of curricular modifications have been used successfully to prevent or reduce challenging behaviors (Dyer, 1987; Mason, McGee, Farmer-Dougan, & Risley, 1989; Strain & Sainato, 1987)

3. Studies in which children with autism have been taught to self-manage their behavior (Dunlap, Kern-Dunlap, Clarke, & Robbins, 1991; Koegel, Harrower, & Koegel, 1998; Stahmer & Schreibman, 1992)

4. Studies in which various strategies have emerged from ongoing functional analysis and then been applied successfully to reduce challenging behaviors (Blair, Umbreil, & Bos, in press; Durand & Crimmins, 1988; Storey, Lawry, Danko, & Strain, 1994)

Although there are a variety of normalized strategies available to reduce children's challenging behaviors, it is important to recognize that many typical preschool environments and their instructional staff have had limited experience and training in using these tactics (Strain & Hemmeter, 1998). It is also true that profound changes in classroom practices may be needed to prevent challenging behaviors. Examples of such changes include the following:

1. Additional assessment resources devoted to identifying children's preferred activities or reinforcers

2. Supplementing verbal directions with pictorial cues, modeling, and prompting strategies

3. Modifying complex, developmentally sophisticated activities to include many legitimate response opportunities for children with autism

4. Carefully arranging and regulating the physical environment of the classroom to optimize cues for transitions, access to preferred toys and materials, and exposure to appropriate behavior models by peers

The presentation of these myths and the documentation of sources of invalidity are not meant to substitute any myth regarding the absolute supremacy of inclusionary environments and the intervention practices that are common to them. Most of all, the intention is not to perpetuate the myth that equates a placement decision or an environment with a legitimate intervention. What is suggested regarding the myths is as follows:

1. The myths rest on the most shaky, if not absent, empirical grounds. This fact leads to the belief that their purpose and continued recitation function to justify personal preferences for service delivery. As such, it is doubtful that our recitation of sources of invalidity presented herein will change many minds.

2. The myths that are at all related to empirical evidence (e.g., readiness, tutorial instruction) represent leaps of logic and analysis that far exceed the data. For example, because children with autism learn under one-to-one conditions, it does not follow that they learn only under this arrangement or that this arrangement is a necessary precedent to other instructional paradigms. Likewise, because studies show that children learn in a group context, it does not follow that the superiority or necessity of group

procedures is thus proved. The good news is that there are many varied instructional approaches for teaching essential skills to young children with autism.

3. Those who support the myths, at least in part, seem to be suggesting that as a matter of public policy (Green, 1996) one should begin services for young children in a restrictive, one-to-one, adult-initiated learning context. Then, if and only when significant behavioral improvement occurs, an inclusionary environment may be considered. Any factual reading of the entire special education history regarding the "make them normal first" approach must conclude that systems and services that are designed primarily to exclude individuals with disabilities for a lifetime are the consequence. Some children may experience a change to a more normalized environment, but the probability of that happening, once in a restrictive environment, is exceedingly remote (Strain & Smith, 1993). In contrast, IDEA 1997 and the early intervention literature suggest that placement decisions be made *individually* and that inclusion options are at least, if not more, defensible places to begin intervention.

The Final Myth: It's Easy!

Achieving true inclusion for children with autism is not easy. Inclusion proponents who base their commitments on the principles of civil rights often make the "just do it" argument. There is reason to assume that the quality of life will improve as people with disabilities gain access to more normalized environments, at least partially as a result of removing the iatrogenic effects of segregated or institutional environments (Bellamy et al., 1990). However, the goal of improving quality of life is different from the goal of making the social behavior of young children with autism more typical (Risley, 1996, 1997). The nature of autism is such that profound social irregularities preclude significant benefit from typical social learning opportunities, in the absence of early social intervention. By definition, children with autism lack the ability to develop peer friendships, to reciprocate social overtures, to engage in the imaginative play that is occupying their same-age peers, and even to acknowledge peer approaches at the most basic nonverbal level (Schreibman, 1988; Volkmar & Cohen, 1988). In sum, children with autism do not enter intervention with the ability to attract and reward their peers' social approaches, and they do not seem interested in social events.

It may be logical to ask why young children with autism need constant exposure to typically developing peers whom they do not seem to even notice. From a treatment perspective, it is likely that qualitative social improvements can best be achieved when children are as young as possible (McGee, 1988). From a practical perspective, more time can be devoted to changing atypical social behaviors if intervention begins early. It is also easier to blend inclusive social learning experiences into early childhood classrooms, because social goals are the developmentally appropriate agenda for all young children (Guralnick, 1993).

Unfortunately, the social impairments of children with autism do not naturally improve with age (McGee, Feldman, & Morrier, 1997), and treatment-induced improvements in language and other domains do not automatically transfer to social behavior (Guralnick & Groom, 1985; McGee, Daly, et al., 1993). Although there is a growing body of research that documents the possibility of obtaining social gains given planned social intervention, the same literature also outlines the complexity of achieving sustained social improvements (McConnell, Sisson, Cort, & Strain, 1991). In short, there is no empirically based rationale for simply dropping off a child with autism in a child care environment and hoping that he or she will become more social. The very real potential for a child with autism to achieve marked social growth is best realized when "supported inclusion" is implemented (i.e., practices that ensure that social learning opportunities are fully exploited at the earliest possible age).

SUPPORTED INCLUSION

The term *supported inclusion* refers to the provision of resources needed to ensure maximum learning in the context of natural environments. To achieve the maximum feasible benefits of inclusion, there must be active instruction for typically developing peers and children with autism on how to interact with one another.

It is not necessary to sacrifice intervention intensity for inclusion. If supports are adequate, then the number of objectives that can be taught is independent of educational placement. In fact, an approach of supported inclusion requires recognition that numerous skill deficits must be addressed during the early childhood years if the goal is to help a child make the most progress possible. The payoff of successful early autism intervention is the probability that far less intensive supports will be needed in the kindergarten years and beyond.

Key resources that are needed to achieve successful inclusion of young children with autism include sufficient numbers of well-trained teaching staff, preparation of parents in how to maintain their child's inclusion, and administrative support for program innovation. A discussion of the "how to" of direct social instruction is followed by an overview of considerations in arranging supported inclusion of children with autism during the early intervention period.

Promoting Social Learning During Planned Instructional Sessions

A variety of formats for social skills instruction have been shown to be effective in promoting social interactions among children with autism and typically developing peers. Some involve direct teaching of children with autism in how to interact with their peers (Odom, Hoyson, Jamieson, & Strain, 1985), and others involve rehearsal of typically developing peers in how to interact with children with autism (Strain, Hoyson, & Jamieson, 1985; Strain, Kerr, & Ragland, 1979). However, research has shown that a combination of direct instruction for both typically developing peers and children with autism is most effective (Odom & Strain, 1986). An example of a strategy for direct teaching of peer interactions is peer incidental teaching.

Typically developing peers can be taught to do incidental teaching with peers with autism, and research has shown that their interactions will maintain at least in the environment in which they learned to play (McGee, Almeida, Sulzer-Azaroff, & Feldman, 1991). A typically developing peer is selected as a play partner for a child with autism on the basis of an expressed interest in getting a response from the child with autism. The peer may then be directly coached in the "how to" of incidental teaching (McGee et al., 1985) while he or she is playing with the child with autism. Toys that are especially appealing to both the child with autism and the typically developing peer must be preselected, and access to these toys may be reserved for play sessions to maintain novelty. The typically developing peer is coached by a teacher through prompts with a pictorial checklist, which illustrates the basic steps of incidental teaching. Specifically, *a stop sign* signals the peer to wait for an initia-

tion by the child with autism, which consists of reaching for or asking for the toy that the peer is holding. Next, *a question mark* suggests the time to ask a question about the toy that has been requested (e.g., "What do you want?"). Finally, an illustration of *a wrapped present* reminds the peer tutor to give the child with autism a reward in the form of social praise and access to the desired toy. In the beginning, the teacher lavishes praise on the peer tutor when he or she follows the steps of the picture checklist. As the peer tutor becomes proficient with the steps of incidental teaching, the adult teacher begins physically to back away and monitor the session from a few feet away. The physical distance of the adult teacher is gradually increased across sessions, and teacher contact becomes limited to brief approaches to comment on the peer tutor's efforts. At the final stage of fading, the adult teacher simply makes the basket of preferred toys available to the peer tutor at the designated time.

Blending Learning Opportunities into the Preschool Day

The natural environment can be systematically engineered to maintain high levels of child engagement and frequent teaching opportunities. Two means of ensuring that instruction is intensive throughout naturally occurring early childhood activities are to blend specific objectives into particular activities and to prepare teachers to seize upon teaching opportunities that arise throughout the day. Both strategies have certain advantages.

The primary benefit of attaching objectives directly to activities is that a sufficient number of teaching episodes are provided for the child to master a new skill. In the absence of planning, the instructional staff can actively teach all day long and still not produce learning by a child with autism. Consider a situation in which a teacher provides a child with one or two teaching trials on each of 10 new object labels, the paraprofessional actively teaches 10 different action words, and the speech therapist emphasizes use of still other words. By the end of the day, the child may have received 50 trials of vocabulary instruction. Although typically developing children would not learn all new words taught under such circumstances, they would probably learn a reasonable number. However, a child with autism would be unlikely to have practiced any one word enough to master it. In other words, haphazard instruction may be adequate, if not ideal, for typically developing children, but sporadic instruction is a waste of time and effort for children with autism.

Planning when and where to teach a given skill provides a logistical advantage for teaching staff in that teachers begin to view certain teaching times as part of their routine. For example, children may be required to greet and acknowledge their peers upon entry to and exit from every classroom activity. This builds in a routine in which children are motivated to practice greetings to 1) get to the snack in the morning, 2) leave snack to go to free play, 3) get to the water table (or other desired activity), and 4) get to and leave lunch. Teachers are available to prompt at these times, but the child who learns to be independent in greetings gets to the desired areas most quickly. Moreover, teachers do not have to remember to plan a greeting session because it is part of their everyday routine. When a child has mastered this particular skill, a new objective (e.g., looking at friends when talking to them) may be substituted.

An additional advantage of designating certain activities as times for teaching specific skills is accountability. If parents need assurance that their child is actually receiving the instruction promised, then they can view the classroom schedule and their child's plan to determine when to observe a given lesson. If a mother pays a surprise visit to the classroom, she should be able to see that the teaching activity is taking place as planned and perhaps benefit from observational learning on how she might teach that skill at home. Similarly, program administrators can monitor teacher implementation of educational plans if there is a specific schedule rather than rely on vague reports. Assessment is also facilitated, because an independent observer can know exactly when to conduct probes of how well a child is progressing in a given instructional activity.

Conversely, there are benefits of incorporating teaching episodes into unplanned "teachable moments" that occur throughout the day. When a child with autism is learning a new skill, he or she will be able to use that skill in varied situations if teaching has been conducted in multiple environments (Stokes & Baer, 1977). In other words, spreading brief follow-up teaching episodes throughout the day facilitates generalization or transfer from the teaching situation to daily life. Furthermore, there are some potent teaching opportunities that arise at unplanned times. For example, a child who is learning to say, "My turn," during tabletop games can later be prompted to use this phrase to express eagerness for a turn on the playground swings.

Addressing Wide-Ranging Developmental Needs

It is a significant challenge to address the developmental needs of children who are functioning at a wide range of skill levels. One strategy that can be helpful is to post "cue cards" of the general classroom goals in the areas in which they are to be addressed. The teacher's job is further facilitated when classroom goals have been specified to span across developmental levels and when teaching prompts have been posted to indicate how to vary instruction according to children's differing levels. For example, if entry into social groups is targeted during an afternoon free-play period, then children with new language may be taught to bring an attractive toy to a peer, whereas a more advanced child may be learning to suggest a new play activity to a group of desired playmates. If these skill levels are posted on the walls in the free-play area, then the teachers are more likely to adjust their teaching prompts appropriately. In sum, teachers are free to concentrate on the quality of their child interactions when the issue of exactly what to teach has been specified in advance.

In addition, cue cards can be posted to remind teachers of the specific individualized instructional objectives that a particular child needs to work on in a designated activity. This practice is especially helpful when curriculum adjustments are needed because the general activity goal is not a good match for an individual child's needs. Thus, typically developing 4-year-olds have pretty well mastered skills such as cutting, and it would be a waste of their time to sit in an activity that is designed to teach the use of scissors. However, a child with fine motor delays may need extra practice in cutting to prepare for kindergarten. One solution is to provide the child with special needs with an activity that looks like the general classroom activity but in fact has a very different purpose. For example, a science activity may provide typically developing children the opportunity to construct a mobile to teach concepts related to balance. The child with fine motor delays may attend the same activity, and although it does not matter whether he or she learns the concept of balance, the child can get practice in cutting out shapes that will go on the mobile. In this way, the child has the advantage of not being singled out as different, although the individual teaching prompts received

are very different from those provided to the rest of the group.

Maintaining Physical Proximity

The probability that children with autism will observe their peers is increased if they are kept constantly near other children. The procedure for ensuring proximity to typically developing peers is simple for young children, who may be picked up and placed to play near other children. If a child actively seeks to get away, then he or she may be coaxed back by bringing his or her most preferred toys to an area where other children are playing or by attracting peers to the child with autism by setting up a really fun activity in his or her vicinity. Teachers must be vigilant in preventing children with autism from drifting away on their own.

Because close proximity among children with autism often yields undesired side effects of increased self-stimulatory behaviors (Lord & Hopkins, 1986; McGee, Paradis, & Feldman, 1993), it is important to minimize opportunities for inadvertent segregation. For example, children with autism should always be seated between two typically developing peers at snack or lunch. During activities that are conducive to isolated play, such as computers, classroom rules may dictate that children have a buddy with them. When two buddies with autism happen to get together, the teacher may find something more interesting for one to do and prompt the child most interested in the computer to find another buddy.

Inclusive classrooms may need to make accommodations when a child with autism requires one-to-one instructional sessions to learn a particularly difficult skill, such as making comments about ongoing activities. Although an easy solution is to take the child to another room or to a quiet area away from other children in the classroom, there is the cost of limiting the child's access to typically developing peers. Another cost can be that the child learns to make rote statements in the distraction-free environment in which teaching occurs but does not learn how to interject comments into daily conversations. A workable solution is to provide the one-to-one session directly in the classroom free-play area. The child receives the advantage of the extra teaching episodes that are ensured by a one-to-one teaching format without forgoing the benefits of instruction in his or her natural environment.

A red flag for failed inclusion is when the desk of a child with autism is facing a wall in the corner of a classroom. Such arrangements are stigmatizing, and there is no potential for the benefits of inclusion. Supported inclusion requires that children with autism remain in constant physical proximity to typically developing peers so that there are frequent opportunities for social learning to occur. This is a necessary, albeit insufficient, starting point for inclusion.

Specification of Social Objectives

One of the advantages of inclusion is the availability of typically developing peers to inform teachers regarding typical behavior, which helps them to specify age-appropriate objectives. It is one thing for a teacher to remember developmental milestones from a child psychology class in college and quite another to be confronted on a daily basis with the language and social behavior of typically developing children. To illustrate, in special education classrooms, it is not uncommon to find a child working on an eye contact objective defined as "looks at teacher 100% of the time." However, child care providers can tell you that a typically developing child does not stare at them constantly; rather, a child's "looking" varies according to whether the teacher is talking about something of mutual interest, the child is being called in from the playground, or the child is engrossed in working a puzzle.

There are several examples in the literature in which social objectives were specified based on observations of the social behavior of typically developing children (see Chapter 21). The effectiveness of different types of social initiations by children in a preschool (e.g., sharing, organizing play) in securing peer responses was used as the basis for designing a series of peer-mediated interventions (Hendrickson, Strain, Tremblay, & Shores, 1982; Tremblay, Strain, Hendrickson, & Shores, 1981). Similarly, levels of reciprocal peer interactions, as well as the distribution of social behaviors such as observing other children, have been delineated in children without disabilities for the purpose of quantifying benchmarks for desired intervention effects (Greenwood, Walker, Todd, & Hops, 1981; McGee, Almeida, et al., 1991; McGee et al., 1997).

Environmental Arrangements that Promote Engagement and Prevent Problems

Recommended practice for early childhood environments specifies a variety of environmental requirements (Bredekamp, 1987), some of which are rarely attended to in special education classrooms. For example, early childhood environmental surveys monitor issues such as the availability of multicultural books and materials. These issues are more than just a matter of political correctness, because the ethnic familiarity of a doll or a book can be directly related to the interest value of a child with autism. Not only do interesting dramatic play centers serve the purpose of attracting children to areas that may be used to promote peer interactions, but also creatively enriched environments attract parents of typically developing children to enroll their children.

However, there are some concessions that must be made to commonly recommended guidelines for early childhood environments. Thus, children with autism may not be safe or easily supervised in a classroom with a cozy reading loft. A child with autism may use tents or playground tunnels to escape contact with the teacher and peers. If a child enjoys throwing objects, then it may be necessary to temporarily remove hard toys (e.g., a Tonka truck is a dangerous weapon if thrown in a classroom). Children who exhibit pica, the tendency to eat small, inedible objects, require that there be extra monitoring of toys with small pieces. In sum, the behavioral challenges posed by a given child with autism can sometimes require judgments regarding the cost benefit of ready classroom access versus the extra teacher time required for supervision.

Although children with autism by no means corner the market on preschool behavior problems, they do generally have the greatest difficulty in maintaining engagement in learning activities (McGee, Daly, Izeman, Mann, & Risley, 1991). A variety of strategies have been detailed for arranging early childhood environments in such a way as to increase engagement and minimize challenging behaviors (McGee & Daly, 1999). The importance of systematic reinforcer assessment has been outlined in terms of maintaining engagement and prevention of problem behaviors (Mason et al., 1989). The use of hobby boxes has been specified as a means of ensuring that all children in inclusive classrooms have ownership of preferred toys, which may be displayed in ways that create verbal learning opportunities (McGee, Daly, et al., 1991). A schedule for optimal rotation of classroom toys has been shown to decrease negative behaviors in an inclusive classroom (including hitting, spitting, name calling, and tattling) and to increase positive social behaviors such as turn taking and sharing (McGee & Daly, 1999).

A proactive strategy for minimizing behavior challenges also requires attention to commonsense teacher solutions, such as rearranging furniture that is being used in inappropriate ways. For example, if a couch in the book area has become a potentially dangerous mat for diving and sliding, then it can be secured to restrict mobility. Environmental solutions are always preferable to nagging and fussing, which are the common alternatives to prevention plans. Once curriculum planning and environmental arrangements have been accomplished in such a way as to maximize learning opportunities, the next challenge is to prepare teachers to capitalize on those opportunities.

A Supported Inclusion Illustration

As indicated previously, one of the primary concerns is identifying natural and multiple opportunities to provide instruction for children's IEP objectives. Subsequently, teachers address children's IEP skills during the full range of preschool activities that involve children with autism and their peers, such as snack, computer, art, gross motor, sociodramatic play, and so forth. These instructional episodes always entail some exchange between the teacher and the child with autism, which varies according to the individual child, skill to be addressed, and ongoing activity. In some cases, teachers also look for ways to include typically developing peers in the process of addressing children's IEP objectives. This section provides data to illustrate the feasibility of this process as well as its associated effects on child and teacher behavior. These data were collected at LEAP Preschool, an inclusive program that houses multiple one-half day classrooms that contain 3–4 children with autism and 8–10 typically developing peers.

The data presented in this section represent teachers' efforts to address the

IEP objectives of 11 children with autism. Each child had four to five different targeted skills representative of the language/communication, social, cognitive, and motor skills as follows:

1. *Language and communication:* Use pictures or words to request items; name pictures in a book; follow requests to find or get an object; put objects on, beside, inside, behind, and so forth; and answer who, what, or where questions

2. *Social interaction:* Greet others by using their name, take turns with others, hand objects to and receive objects from others, imitate the actions of others upon request, and direct the activities of others

3. *Cognitive:* Match simple shapes; recall past events or experiences; match and/or identify letters, numbers, colors, and so forth; count to 10 using one-to-one correspondence; and sort objects according to size

4. *Motor:* Copy vertical or horizontal strokes; pour liquids; throw and catch a ball with others; copy shapes, letters, and so forth; and cutting skills such as snipping edge of paper, cutting along a line, and so forth

All observational sessions were 10 minutes in duration and focused on teachers' efforts to address the skills of a single child. Research staff videotaped the entire session and then coded various dimensions of teacher and child behavior at a later time. Teachers invited peers to participate in three different ways: modeling the desired IEP skill for the child with autism, providing a verbal antecedent for the behavior (e.g., question or request), or serving as the recipient of the target child's skill.

The results revealed a number of important points. Specifically, the supplement of peer mediation produced an average of 0.75 objectives taught each

minute, and children exhibited the targeted IEP responses in 91% of the episodes. Overall, the teachers were able to incorporate peer mediation into 75% of the episodes conducted with these children. The most common form of peer mediation was having the typically developing child provide the antecedent (63% of peer episodes), followed by "serve as recipient" of the skill (29%). The process of peer modeling was least frequent, occurring in only 4% of the episodes.

For teacher-conducted unstructured episodes, the children received instruction during a range of eight different activities. Snack, table time, and art and sensory contained the highest proportion of teaching episodes (20%–27%) because of their structure, the nature of children's IEP objectives, and ready access to typically developing peers. Conversely, teachers were less likely to embed instruction during classroom transitions, book area, and gross motor play (4%–6%).

These data support several important conclusions about the efficacy of educational inclusion for preschool-age children with autism. First, they suggest that teachers can address children's IEP objectives within the full range of inclusive preschool activities. In essence, activities such as snack, art, and sociodramatic play are more than a structure for typical social interaction and proximity; they provide a context for instruction that is individualized, intensive, and high quality in nature.

A second conclusion pertains to the inclusion of typically developing peers in education programs for children with autism. As noted previously, a common myth is that overstimulation created by typically developing young children may preclude the provision of high-quality and intensive instruction for children with special needs. The data presented here suggest the contrary. Peers not only permit effective instruction but may actually be deployed as resources for this process. Teachers were able to incorporate modeling and related forms of peer mediation into 75% of their instructional episodes. Moreover, these instructional episodes led to correct responding more than 90% of the time.

PREPARING FOR INCLUSION

The following sections discuss in detail the areas that need to be addressed to prepare for inclusion.

Complexities of Training Teachers

Unfortunately, there is little research and few curriculum guidelines on how to train teachers (and other support personnel) to promote inclusion and peer interactions. Moreover, there is no particular discipline or educational specialty that specifically prepares professionals to foster social growth. Kindergarten teachers may be the most effective trainers of social skills, because they are experienced in socializing children with varied histories in interacting with other children. Yet, the social impairments presented by children with autism often defy even the most skillful of social mentors.

One of the procedural challenges is that effective teaching of peer interactions requires a complex series of judgments on when to provide direct instruction and how to fade instructional cues. Thus, the social skills research literature is replete with failures to achieve generalized social gains through systematic instruction in artificially contrived situations. For example, unassertive children can learn social skills through role play and specific skill feedback (Bornstein, Bellack, & Hersen, 1977), but there is very little automatic transfer from teaching situations to daily use of newly acquired social skills (Berler, Gross, & Drabman, 1982). Considering that children with autism have characteristic impairments in pretend play skills, along

with pervasive difficulties in generalization of any skills (Schreibman, 1988), the probability of success through highly structured social instruction seems very limited. Indeed, the social skill literature for children with autism provides abundant documentation that the greatest challenge of social instruction procedures is maintaining and transferring newly learned social skills (McConnell et al., 1991).

The most promising option is for teachers to learn to teach social skills in the environments in which they will be used. However, even teachers who are proficient in teaching children in the context of natural environments must develop teaching repertoires that are vastly different from those needed to promote acquisition of other skills by children with autism. For example, successful incidental teaching of language requires that a teacher constantly look for teachable moments and provide as many prompts as possible for children to expand their language. However, if teachers are eagerly approaching children engaged in social interaction, for the purpose of expanding social skills, the likely result is that the peer interaction will dissolve as children attend to the teacher.

In short, an effective promoter of social interactions must learn a sophisticated series of skills in prompting and fading. The format of social promotion skills may proceed as follows:

1. Set up activities and/or toys that will attract both typically developing peers and children with autism and that are conducive to social interaction.

2. Ensure that children with autism are near typically developing peers.

3. Plan exactly which social objective will be taught at a given time.

4. Directly teach typically developing peers something to say or do to get a

response from the child with autism by showing him or her and then praising his or her efforts.

5. Assist and reward the child with autism for participation in the interaction.

6. As the typically developing peers become proficient in securing responses from the child with autism, gradually withdraw physical presence.

7. Return as needed to ensure that the interaction continues, and unobtrusively praise the continued participation of the typically developing peer (e.g., pat Billy on the shoulder and comment on how nicely he is playing with Ben).

8. Over a period of time, begin to set up the social activity and back up and watch from across the room.

To promote participation in group activities, it is advantageous to have a two-person "tag team" approach. For example, if the goal is for the child with autism to attend to a teacher who is reading a story, then a second teacher ideally will prompt engagement from behind the group. As needed, the inclusion coach should give the most subtle cue necessary to ensure that the child with autism looks in the direction of the classroom teacher, raises his or her hand to ask a question, or stands up to leave when the activity is over. If the coach holds the child with autism in his or her lap or sits next to the child, then the child's attention is likely to be directed toward the coach rather than toward the teacher.

An excellent example of this minimal prompting strategy was observed in a Japanese classroom that included children with autism among a majority of typically developing peers (Roland, McGee, Risley, & Rimland, 1987). Children stood in lines doing exercises, and the goal was for the child with autism to imitate the multiple models of children doing jump-

ing jacks in front of him or her. The teacher coached from behind the child with autism, using the minimal amount of physical prompting necessary to ensure participation. Attention to the relevant models was achieved, and fading to minimal prompting promoted independent imitation of peers.

Virtually all of the procedures for creating social learning opportunities in a preschool can be implemented by families at home and in the community. In fact, the difficulty of improving social abilities in children with autism essentially mandates that both teachers and parents invest significant and regular portions of their child's day in social skills promotion.

Preparing Parents to Support Inclusion

Parent involvement is integral to the concept of early intervention (McCollum & Hemmeter, 1997), and parental expertise is especially crucial to the success of inclusion of children with autism (McGee, Jacobs, & Regnier, 1993). At the simplest level, it is important that parents attend to the physical appearance of their children with autism, who are unlikely to notice the popular dressing trends that become evident to other children (McClannahan, McGee, MacDuff, & Krantz, 1990). Thus, a parent may need to forgo the temptation to send her daughter to kindergarten in the beautiful smocked dress sent by Grandmother and give in to the purchase of the Tarzan T-shirt that is being worn by all of the other children in the class.

At the most complex level, it is helpful when parents develop the sophisticated teaching skills needed to set up, support, and maintain peer interactions. If there are siblings in the home, then the preparation of brothers and sisters to do peer tutoring can serve dual purposes. Siblings can provide additional social learning opportunities for their brother or sister with autism while enjoying positive attention for their efforts.

Parents can also learn to set up regular home visitations with neighborhood children and classmates (Guralnick & Neville, 1997), who may provide further social instruction in environments that promote generalization. Parents should begin with brief visits (no more than 1 hour), and the visitation agenda should be planned to accommodate variety, lots of fun, and delicious snacks for the visitor. As at school, the visiting child must be heavily reinforced for interacting with the child with autism. Competing siblings may need to be engaged in other activities, or they can be brought in periodically to create momentum in running and chase games. As children with autism develop expertise in certain areas (e.g., video games, swimming), it becomes important to showcase these activities during the visitation schedule. For example, one child with autism, who was having difficulty making friends on his block, soon became very popular when it was discovered that he could reach higher levels on the video games than his neighbors could. It turned out that he was the only one who had bothered to read the instruction manual from cover to cover. Nonetheless, his peers interpreted his skill as pure genius.

Even when children are successfully included in preschool or kindergarten, it remains important for their parents to enroll them in structured community activities (Staros & Roberts, 1999; see Chapter 14). Depending on the child's strengths and interests, appropriate selections may range from organized sports (T-ball, soccer, or swim teams) to lessons (karate, ballet, horseback riding) to arts and crafts activities at the YMCA or simply a daily visit to the neighborhood playground. Of course, any child may elect to drop a new activity, so inexpensive options are advisable.

Parents often require considerable encouragement to begin extracurricular activities because of concern regarding their child's potential for failure. However, invaluable lessons can be learned regarding the supports that the child will need in future placements. If a child is doing well in his or her specialized preschool but has great difficulty at choir practice, then the child will likely need higher levels of support in a general kindergarten than are available at the choir. Alternatively, there are often pleasant surprises, and children succeed sometimes when least expected. When the parent has arranged successful community inclusion, the case is strengthened that the school should be able to successfully include the child in a general classroom.

Finally, parent advocacy skills are absolutely essential to ensuring that a child with autism has successful and continued access to supported inclusion. Parents must be knowledgeable of their child's rights to education in natural environments so that their wishes will not be written off as unrealistic. They must be able to articulate how inclusion will benefit their child educationally, and they must be able to discern which of various support plans are likely to be adequate (Nickels, 1996). Parents must also be skillful negotiators, trainers, and supporters of the professionals who work with their children (Turnbull & Turnbull, 1996).

At the early intervention level, increasing numbers of parents are participating as collaborators in their young children's individualized family service plans. It seems probable that these same parents will expect to contribute to their child's lifelong education planning. In sum, parents can be the most dedicated and long-term advocates for their child's access to supported inclusion, and it is critical that they be empowered with the knowledge and skills that will ensure their children's rights to full community participation (Zigler, 1997).

AGENDA FOR CHANGE: CONSIDERATIONS IN DEVELOPING INCLUSIVE PROGRAMS FOR CHILDREN WITH AUTISM

Top-down and bottom-up commitment of administrative, instructional, and support staff is ideal in arranging successful inclusion programs. System barriers are well documented as a primary source of difficulty in developing inclusive programs, because many special education systems were developed with interfering policies, facilities, and financial streams (Smith & Rose, 1993; Strain & Smith, 1993). Most states are deeply invested in the infrastructure of segregated special education services during the elementary school years. With a few exceptions, such as Colorado, the relatively new Part B preschool programs for 3- to 5-year-old children with special needs are also aimed primarily at serving only children with disabilities. There may be more flexibility within the even newer birth-to-3 early intervention programs, which for the most part have been developed as in-home service delivery systems. Several states, including Texas and Georgia, have taken firm stands that restrict early intervention dollars to payment for services provided in natural environments. Sweeping changes are needed by innovative administrators at all levels to provide children with autism with supported inclusion with typically developing peers in quality early childhood programs.

At the local level, early intervention/special education administrators and school principals must be philosophically committed and willing to invest the resources needed to ensure successful inclusion. If a principal or child care director is opposed to the inclusion of children with autism, then teachers'

efforts can be inadvertently punished. In other cases, when resistance comes from the instructional staff, strong administrative support can make clear that effective performance is a job requirement.

In one small town, the paraprofessional staff wrongly perceived that reductions in general education support staff were related to the extra supports provided to two children with autism who were entering general kindergarten. These aides took their case to the local newspaper, and parents of the children with autism feared derisive comments from the community. However, the special education director and school principal did not waver; they made the facts available and proceeded steadfastly according to plans, and the controversy subsided as staff were either won over or left the system. Although this thankfully rare experience posed additional hardship to the parents of the children involved, their anxiety was short lived. It did not take long for parents of all of the children to be reassured when they noticed how the typically developing peers eagerly approached their children with autism at neighborhood restaurants and parks. It is obviously ideal if teachers can be selected on a volunteer basis. Often the first to volunteer are the most experienced and successful teachers, who are excited at the prospect of a new challenge. When teachers are reluctant, their concern usually pertains to whether adequate staffing resources will be made available to them and whether they will be provided with the training to know how to be effective. In short, teachers do not necessarily have to begin the job with a commitment to inclusion, as long as adequate resources are provided to ensure that they will be successful. Given appropriate supports, their conversion nearly always comes easily.

Similarly, instructional support staff can be won over as they gain experience in including children with autism, but it is essential that all school personnel involved receive both motivational and skill-based training. The glitches in inclusive programs are, in fact, most likely to occur from a failure to involve paraprofessionals, speech-language pathologists, occupational therapists, school psychologists, librarians, physical education teachers, cafeteria workers, janitors, bus monitors, and so forth. Behavioral difficulties with children with autism are most likely to occur during times of transition, high noise levels, and the chaos that sometimes accompanies less structure. Similar pitfalls occur in general child care centers, where less experienced caregivers may be watching the children by the end of the day when parents pick up their children. Again, committed administrators will interpret mishaps as a signal that additional training and support are needed to prevent future difficulties rather than as an indication that the child with autism has failed.

Staffing Arrangements

The most important factor regarding the number and arrangement of teachers pertains to child safety. All young children require careful supervision, but extra care is needed to ensure the safety of all in an inclusive early childhood classroom. Some children with autism may dart or run out of the room or may run away on the playground, and a teacher cannot leave other children unsupervised while running off to chase a child with autism. Therefore, there is a need for at least two, ideally more, adult instructors in an inclusive classroom. If training sequences are solid and close supervision is provided, then it is not necessary that all instructors be certified teachers.

There is a clear advantage for children with autism to have more than one teacher. Multiple teachers make it possible for children to learn to use their new skills with a variety of people. When a one-to-one teacher or paraprofessional is assigned as a hovering instructor, many of the advantages of an inclusive classroom can be lost. Children become dependent on what amounts to a full-time caregiver, and peer interactions will not naturally occur if an adult is constantly present to intercept and inadvertently interrupt social bids.

Ideally, multiple instructors are available in an inclusive classroom, and they rotate across varied roles. The lead teacher may conduct a large-group activity while the classroom assistant promotes the engagement of a child with autism from behind the group. After the group instruction, the special education paraprofessional may take the child with autism and other typically developing peers for more focused instruction, which offers additional instructional advantage to the typically developing students in the classroom. Later, the lead teacher may elect to get a good feel for the learning style of a child with autism by conducting a one-to-one session at the classroom's listening center while the special education paraprofessional monitors other activity centers and while the classroom assistant prepares the upcoming art activity.

Although there may be occasions when pull-out therapies are appropriate, it is highly preferable if specialized services for children with autism can be provided in the natural context of the classroom. Many children with autism have difficulty making transitions, and it adds unnecessary challenge to arrange their daily schedules with many changes across rooms and situations. Moreover, if a child needs a certain therapy, then presumably the teacher and assistants need to observe the therapist so that they can buttress the therapy session with additional teaching throughout the day. On-the-job coordination is also important because few programs have the luxury of time for daily interdisciplinary discussions of a child's progress.

Ratios of Children with Autism and Typically Developing Peers

When there are more typically developing children to teach each child with autism, there are more opportunities for social learning. However, the ideal must be balanced against the needs of a young child with autism to have intensive instruction, which requires considerable resources. Therefore, compromises are often needed to ensure that there is an adequate number of adults in a given classroom, so it may be fiscally unrealistic to provide the necessary level of early intervention enrichment to a class that has only one child with autism. If the class size is reduced to a small overall number of students, then each typically developing child must carry a large peer-tutoring burden. If there are not enough typically developing children, then the behavioral momentum of a typical early childhood classroom is jeopardized. Although there are no hard and fast rules, the bottom line is that there must be a majority of typically developing children in an inclusive classroom (see Chapter 1).

As programs gain experience in including children with autism with typically developing peers, there is a tendency to alter ratios gradually in the direction of more typically developing peers to each child with autism (McGee, Paradis, & Feldman, 1993; Strain & Cordisco, 1993). When there is a bare majority of typically developing peers, an epidemic of chicken pox or other childhood illness can sweep the center of typically developing peers, and the program quickly reverts to a specialized classroom. Recruitment of typically developing peers is also easier when there are more typically developing children. Although space, staffing, curriculum, and other factors will set some arbitrary limits on the feasible composition of an inclusive classroom, it is important to establish a minimum ratio. Both public and private programs that build good inclusion reputations are often threatened by an influx of students whose parents are desperate for quality services. As placements are quickly filled, it is important to be prepared to distribute new referrals across other good alternatives so that the advantages of inclusion are not lost to all.

Is Social Inclusion an Alternative?

There is a common assumption that the administrative difficulties of arranging inclusive classrooms and a reluctance to sacrifice the perceived advantages of special education classrooms can be addressed by taking children with autism to visit a classroom of typically developing children. At the most absurd level, one school suggested that such an approach would occur a few times a year during group assemblies. More reasonable is that a school with special education classes may offer a daily plan of inclusion in activities such as lunch, recess, music, and art (social inclusion). These also tend to be the activities during which staffing resources are lowest and noise levels are highest. When there is no one available to teach children with autism and typically developing children how to interact, there are few therapeutic advantages of inclusion.

Another strategy used to deal with the lack of availability of 3-year-olds in public school is to take preschool-age children with autism to visit a kindergarten. At first impression, it may seem that this arrangement works because eager kindergarten girls often smother the child with autism with attention. However, there are limited opportunities for social growth when the child with autism is inevitably assigned a passive or inappropriate role.

The biggest flaw with social inclusion boils down to the lack of regular, sustained social instruction. Even typically developing children have difficulty establishing friendships when they attend a group on a sporadic basis or for brief periods of time. Moreover, the intensive efforts needed to prepare typically developing peers as confederates do not confer full benefit if those peers are available to interact only under limited, circumscribed situations. For children with autism, who face immense social challenges, more rather than less social learning will always be preferable.

CONCLUSION

It has been argued in this chapter that there is both a legal and an empirical basis for the inclusion of young children with autism. Moreover, social intervention must be a key component of early intervention for children with autism, and a sufficient knowledge base is available to make inclusion of young children with autism (at both social and instructional levels) both a feasible and a productive experience. In one sense, it seems ironic that social behavior turned out to be the last domain to be addressed for children with a disorder that was originally identified as a fundamental social disorder (Kanner, 1943). However, now that the complexity of altering social growth has become better understood, it is apparent that the belated priority of social intervention was most likely inevitable.

Also suggested were several myths that serve to limit inclusion options. These myths likely grew out of initial experiences in treating children with autism. The early behavioral demonstrations that children with autism could learn to talk, be toilet trained, and make cognitive gains were indeed revolutionary (Lovaas, 1977; Risley & Wolf, 1967). Perhaps they were so revolutionary that they became "reified," taking on a presumed degree of relative efficacy not supported by the empirical literature. Moreover, the logistics of traditional behavioral intervention required a degree of environmental and procedural control that was not easily obtained in the natural environment. However, as the dozens of empirical studies cited here show, children with autism can learn to talk, be toilet trained, and make developmental progress in inclusive contexts. The myths surrounding autism intervention have outlived any historical utility. There are so many cases of invalidity that the myths may well preclude sound decision making at the individual client and policy level. Discovery of the enormous potential of the early intervention period has made it possible to help children with autism reach traditional intervention goals much more quickly (Fenske, Zalenski, Krantz, & McClannahan, 1985; Lovaas, 1987; Strain & Hoyson, 2000). Dramatic progress during the early intervention period has also increased the likelihood that greater numbers of children with autism will have real and present needs to navigate the social world. Concurrently, the field of early intervention has reached a technical and conceptual point that social intervention can now be a major focus (Guralnick & Neville, 1997). Although much remains to be accomplished in the science of early intervention for children with autism, inclusion-compatible procedures have been developed and refined across more than a decade. There have been demonstrations in model programs that children can be prepared for lifelong inclusion while they spend their early years with typically developing peers. The knowledge, the laws, and the practical guidelines are available to make early inclusive education a reality for young children with autism. The field of autism intervention is now ready for the challenge of "just do it."

REFERENCES

Bellamy, G.T., Newton, J.S., LeBaron, N., & Horner, R.H. (1990). Quality of life and lifestyle outcomes: A challenge for residential programs. In R. Schalock (Ed.), *Quality of life: Perspectives and issues* (pp. 127–137). Washington, DC: American Association on Mental Retardation.

Berler, E.S., Gross, A.M., & Drabman, R.S. (1982). Social skills training with children: Proceed with caution. *Journal of Behavior Analysis, 15,* 41–54.

Blair, K., Umbreil, J., & Bos, C. (in press). Using functional assessment and children's preferences to improve the behavior of young children with behavioral disorders. *Behavioral Disorders.*

Bornstein, M.R., Bellack, A.S., & Hersen, M. (1977). Social skills training for unassertive children: A multiple-baseline analysis. *Journal of Applied Behavior Analysis, 10,* 183–195.

Bredekamp, S. (Ed.). (1987). *Developmentally appropriate practice in early childhood programs serving children from birth through age 8.* Washington, DC: National Association for the Education of Young Children.

Callahan, K., & Rademacher, J.A. (1998). Using self-management strategies to increase the on-task behavior of a student with autism. *Journal of Positive Behavioral Interventions, 1,* 117–122.

Carr, E.G., & Carlson, J.I. (1993). Reduction of severe behavior problems in the community using a multicomponent treatment approach. *Journal of Applied Behavior Analysis, 26,* 157–172.

Carr, E.G., Levin, L., McConnachie, G., Carlson, J.I., Kemp, D.C., Smith, C.E., & McLaughlin, D.M. (1999). Comprehensive multisituational intervention for problem behavior in the community: Long-term maintenance and social validation. *Journal of Positive Behavioral Interventions, 1,* 5–25.

Council for Exceptional Children. (1993). *DEC recommended practices.* Reston, VA: Author.

Dunlap, G. (1984). The influence of task variation and maintenance tasks on the learning and affect of autistic children. *Journal of Experimental Child Psychology, 37,* 41–64.

Dunlap, G., dePerczel, M., Clarke, S., Wilson, D., Wright, S., White, R., & Gomez, A. (1994). Choice making to promote adaptive behavior for students with emotional and behavioral challenges. *Journal of Applied Behavior Analysis, 24,* 505–518.

Dunlap, G., & Fox, L. (1999). A demonstration of behavioral support for young children with autism. *Journal of Applied Behavior Analysis, 1,* 77–87.

Dunlap, G., Johnson, L.F., & Robbins, F.R. (1990). Preventing serious behavior problems through skill development and early intervention. In A.C. Repp & N.N. Singh (Eds.), *Perspectives on the use of nonaversive and aversive interventions for persons with developmental disabilities* (pp. 273–286). Sycamore, IL: Sycamore Press.

Dunlap, G., Kern-Dunlap, L., Clarke, S., & Robbins, F.R. (1991). Functional assessment, curricular revision, and severe behavior problems. *Journal of Applied Behavior Analysis, 24,* 387–397.

Dunlap, G., & Koegel, R.L. (1980). Motivating autistic children through stimulus variation. *Journal of Applied Behavior Analysis, 13,* 619–627.

Durand, V.M., & Crimmins, D.B. (1988). Identifying the variables maintaining self-injurious behavior. *Journal of Autism and Developmental Disorders, 18*(1), 99–117.

Dyer, K. (1987). The competition of autistic stereotyped behavior with usual and specially assessed reinforcers. *Research in Developmental Disabilities, 8,* 607–626.

Elliott, R., Hall, K., & Sopher, H. (1991). Analog language teaching vs. natural language teaching: Generalization and retention of language learning for adults with autism and mental retardation. *Journal of Autism and Developmental Disorders, 21,* 433–447.

Fenske, E.C., Zalenski, S., Krantz, P.J., & McClannahan, L.E. (1985). Age at intervention and treatment outcome for autistic children in a comprehensive intervention program. *Analysis and Intervention in Developmental Disabilities, 5,* 49–58.

Fox, L., Dunlap, G., & Philbrick, L.A. (1997). Providing individualized supports to young children with autism and their families. *Journal of Early Intervention, 21,* 1–14.

Frea, W.D., & Hepburn, S.L. (1999). Teaching parents of children with autism to perform functional assessments to plan interventions for extremely disruptive behaviors. *Journal of Positive Behavioral Interventions, 1,* 112–116.

Goldstein, H., Kaczmarek, L., Pennington, R., & Shafer, K. (1992). Peer-mediated intervention: Attending to, commenting on, and acknowledging the behavior of preschoolers with autism. *Journal of Applied Behavior Analysis, 25,* 289–305.

Green, G. (1996). Early behavioral intervention for autism: What does research tell us? In C. Maurice, G. Green, & S. Luce (Eds.), *Behavioral intervention for young children with autism: A manual for parents and professionals* (pp. 29–44). Austin, TX: PRO-ED.

Greenwood, C.R., Walker, H.M., Todd, N.M., & Hops, H. (1981). Normative and descriptive analysis of preschool free play social interaction rates. *Journal of Pediatric Psychology, 6,* 343–367.

Guralnick, M.J. (1993). Developmentally appropriate practice in the assessment and intervention of children's peer relations. *Topics in Early Childhood Special Education, 13,* 344–371.

Guralnick, M.J., & Groom, J.M. (1985). Correlates of peer-related social competence of developmentally delayed preschool children. *American Journal of Mental Deficiency, 90,* 140–150.

Guralnick, M.J., & Neville, B. (1997). Designing early intervention programs to promote children's social competence. In M.J. Guralnick (Ed.), *The effectiveness of early intervention* (pp. 579–610). Baltimore: Paul H. Brookes Publishing Co.

Hendrickson, J.M., Strain, P.S., Tremblay, A., & Shores, R.E. (1982). Interactions of behaviorally handicapped preschool children: Functional effects of peer initiations. *Behavior Modification, 6,* 323–353.

Hoyson, M., Jamieson, B., & Strain, P.S. (1984). Individualized group instructions of normally developing and autistic-like children: The LEAP curriculum model. *Journal of the Division for Early Childhood, 8,* 157–172.

Individuals with Disabilities Education Act Amendments of 1997, PL 105-17, 20 U.S.C §§ 1400 *et seq.*

Kaiser, A., & Hester, P. (1994). Generalized effects of enhanced milieu teaching. *Journal of Speech and Hearing Research, 37,* 63–92.

Kamps, D.M., Barbetta, P.M., Leonard, B.R., & Delquadri, J. (1994). Classwide peer tutoring: An integration strategy to improve reading skills and promote peer interactions among students with autism and general education peers. *Journal of Applied Behavior Analysis, 27,* 49–61.

Kanner, L. (1943). Autistic disturbances of affective contact. *Nervous Child, 2,* 217–250.

Koegel, L.K., Harrower, J.K., & Koegel, R.L. (1998). Support for children with developmental disabilities in full inclusion classrooms through self-management. *Journal of Positive Behavioral Interventions, 1,* 26–33.

Koegel, L.K., Koegel, R.L., & Carter, C.M. (1998). Pivotal responses and the natural language teaching paradigm. *Seminars in Speech and Language, 19,* 355–372.

Koegel, R., O'Dell, M.C., & Koegel, L.K. (1987). A natural language paradigm for teaching nonverbal autistic children. *Journal of Autism & Developmental Disorders, 17,* 187–199.

Koegel, R., O'Dell, N., & Dunlap, G. (1988). Producing speech use in nonverbal autistic children by reinforcing attempts. *Journal of Autism and Developmental Disorders, 18,* 525–538.

Kohler, F.W., Strain, P.S., Hoyson, M., & Jamieson, B. (1997). Combining incidental teaching and peer-mediation with young children with autism. *Focus on Autism and Other Developmental Disorders, 12,* 196–206.

Lord, C., & Hopkins, M. (1986). The social behavior of autistic children with younger and same-age nonhandicapped peers. *Journal of Autism and Developmental Disorders, 16,* 249–262.

Lovaas, O.I. (1977). *The autistic child.* New York: Irvington Publishers.

Lovaas, O.I. (1987). Behavioral treatment and normal educational and intellectual functioning in young autistic children. *Journal of Consulting and Clinical Psychology, 55,* 3–9.

Lucyshyn, J.M., Olson, D., & Horner, R.H. (1995). Building an ecology of support: A case study of one woman with severe problem behaviors living in the community. *Journal of The Association for Persons with Severe Handicaps, 20,* 16–30.

Mason, S.A., McGee, G.G., Farmer-Dougan, V., & Risley, T.R. (1989). A practical strategy for reinforcer assessment. *Journal of Applied Behavior Analysis, 22,* 171–179.

McClannahan, L.E., McGee, G.G., MacDuff, G.S., & Krantz, P.J. (1990). Assessing and improving child care: A personal appearance index for children with autism. *Journal of Applied Behavior Analysis, 23,* 469–482.

McCollum, J.A., & Hemmeter, M.L. (1997). Parent–child interaction intervention when children have disabilities. In M.J. Guralnick (Ed.), *The effectiveness of early intervention* (pp. 549–576). Baltimore: Paul H. Brookes Publishing Co.

McConnell, S.R., Sisson, L.A., Cort, C.A., & Strain, P.S. (1991). Effects of social skills training and contingency management on reciprocal interaction of preschool children with behavioral handicaps. *The Journal of Special Education, 24,* 473–495.

McGee, G.G. (1988). Early prevention of severe behavior problems. In R. Horner & G. Dunlap (Eds.), *Behavior management and community integration* (pp. 22–40). Washington, DC: U.S. Department of Education, Office of Special Education and Rehabilitative Services.

McGee, G.G., Almeida, M.C., Sulzer-Azaroff, B., & Feldman, R.S. (1991). Promoting reciprocal interactions via peer incidental teaching. *Journal of Applied Behavior Analysis, 25,* 117–126.

McGee, G.G., & Daly, T. (1999). Prevention of problem behavior in preschool-aged children with autism. In A.C. Repp & R.H. Horner (Eds.), *Functional analysis of problem behavior: From effective assessment to effective support* (pp. 171–196). Belmont, CA: Wadsworth Publishing Co.

McGee, G.G., Daly, T., Izeman, S.G., Mann, L., & Risley, T.R. (1991). Use of classroom materials to promote preschool engagement. *Teaching Exceptional Children, 23,* 44–47.

McGee, G.G., Daly, T., & Jacobs, H.A. (1993). The Walden preschool. In S.L. Harris & J.S. Handleman (Eds.), *Preschool education programs for children with autism* (pp. 127–162). Austin, TX: PRO-ED.

McGee, G.G., Feldman, R.S., & Morrier, M.J. (1997). Benchmarks of social treatment for children with autism. *Journal of Autism and Developmental Disorders, 27,* 353–364.

McGee, G.G., Jacobs, H.A., & Regnier, M.C. (1993). Preparation of families for incidental teaching and advocacy for their children with autism. *OSERS News in Print, 5,* 9–13.

McGee, G.G., Krantz, P.J., & McClannahan, L.E. (1985). The facilitative effects of incidental teaching on preposition use by autistic children. *Journal of Applied Behavior Analysis, 18,* 17–31.

McGee, G.G., Paradis, T., & Feldman, R.S. (1993). Free effects of integration on levels of autistic behavior. *Topics in Early Childhood Special Education, 13,* 57–67.

Miranda-Linne, F., & Melin, L. (1992). Acquisition, generalization, and spontaneous use of color adjectives: A comparison of incidental teaching and traditional discrete trial procedures for children with autism. *Research in Developmental Disabilities, 13,* 191–210.

Nickels, C. (1996). A gift from Alex—The art of belonging: Strategies for academic and social inclusion. In L.K. Koegel, R.L. Koegel, & G. Dunlap (Eds.), *Positive behavioral support: Including people with difficult behavior in the community* (pp. 123–144). Baltimore: Paul H. Brookes Publishing Co.

Odom, S.L., Hoyson, M., Jamieson, B., & Strain, P.S. (1985). Increasing handicapped preschoolers' peer social interactions: Cross-setting and component analysis. *Journal of Applied Behavior Analysis, 18,* 3–16.

Odom, S.L., & Strain, P.S. (1986). A comparison of peer-initiation and teacher-antecedent interventions for promoting reciprocal social interaction of autistic preschoolers. *Journal of Applied Behavior Analysis, 19,* 59–71.

Odom, S.L., Strain, P.S., Karger, M.A., & Smith, J.D. (1986). Using single and multiple peers to promote social interactions of preschool children with severe handicaps. *Journal of the Division for Early Childhood, 10,* 53–64.

Pierce, K., & Schreibman, L. (1997). Multiple peer use of PRT to increase social behavior of classmates with autism: Results from trained and untrained peers. *Journal of Applied Behavior Analysis, 28,* 157–160.

Prizant, B.M., Schuler, A.L., Wetherby, A.M., & Rydell, P.J. (1997). Enhancing language and communication: Language approaches. In D. Cohen & F. Volkmar (Eds.), *Handbook of autism and pervasive developmental disorders* (2nd ed., pp. 330–355). New York: John Wiley & Sons.

Risley, T.R. (1996). Get a life! Positive behavioral intervention for challenging behavior through life arrangement and life coaching. In L.K. Koegel, R.L. Koegel, & G. Dunlap (Eds.), *Positive behavioral support: Including people with difficult behavior in the community* (pp. 425–437). Baltimore: Paul H. Brookes Publishing Co.

Risley, T.R. (1997). Family preservation for children with autism. *Journal of Early Intervention, 21,* 15–16.

Risley, T.R., & Wolf, M.M. (1967). Establishing functional speech in echolalic children. *Behaviour Research and Therapy, 5,* 73–88.

Roland, C., McGee, G.G., Risley, T.R., & Rimland, B. (1987). *A description of the Tokyo Higashi Program.* Boston: Boston Trust for Autism.

Sainato, D.M., Strain, P.S., Lefebvre, D., & Rapp, N. (1990). Effects of self-evaluation on the independent work skills of preschool children with disabilities. *Exceptional Children, 56,* 540–551.

Schreibman, L. (1988). *Autism.* Newbury Park, CA: Sage Publications.

Schreibman, L., Kaneko, W., & Koegel, R. (1991). Positive affect of parents of autistic children: A comparison across two teaching techniques. *Behavior Therapy, 22,* 479–490.

Smith, B.J., & Rose, D.F. (1993). *Administrators policy handbook for preschool mainstreaming.* Cambridge, MA: Brookline Books.

Stahmer, A.C., & Schreibman, L. (1992). Teaching children with autism appropriate play in unsupervised environments using a self-management treatment package. *Journal of Applied Behavior Analysis, 25,* 447–459.

Staros, T., & Roberts, G. (1999, June). Address presented at the Emory Autism Resource Center annual conference, Emory University, Atlanta, GA.

Stokes, T.F., & Baer, D.M. (1977). An implicit technology of generalization. *Journal of Applied Behavior Analysis, 10,* 349–367.

Storey, K., Lawry, J., Danko, C., & Strain, P.S. (1994). Functional analysis and intervention for disruptive behaviors of a kindergarten student. *Journal of Education Research, 30,* 8–19.

Strain, P.S. (1977). Training and generalization effects of peer social initiations on withdrawn preschool children. *Journal of Abnormal Child Psychology, 5,* 445–455.

Strain, P.S. (Ed.). (1982). *Social behavior of exceptional children.* Gaithersburg, MD: Aspen Publishers.

Strain, P.S. (1983). Generalization of autistic children's social behavior change: Effects of developmentally-integrated and segregated settings. *Analysis and Intervention in Developmental Disabilities, 3,* 23–34.

Strain, P.S. (1984). Social behavior patterns of nonhandicapped and nonhandicapped-developmentally disabled friend pairs in mainstream preschool. *Analysis and Intervention in Developmental Disabilities, 4,* 15–28.

Strain, P.S. (1987). Comprehensive evaluation of young autistic children. *Topics in Early Childhood Special Education, 7,* 97–110.

Strain, P.S., & Cordisco, L. (1993). LEAP Preschool. In S.L. Harris & J.S. Handleman (Eds.), *Preschool education programs for children with autism* (pp. 127–162). Austin, TX: PRO-ED.

Strain, P.S., Danko, C., & Kohler, F.W. (1994). Activity engagement and social interaction development in young children with autism: An examination of "free" intervention effects. *Journal of Emotional and Behavioral Disorders, 2,* 15–29.

Strain, P.S., & Hemmeter, M.L. (1998). Dealing with challenging behavior. *Young Exceptional Children, 1,* 1–6.

Strain, P.S., & Hoyson, M. (2000). On the need for longitudinal, intensive social skill intervention: LEAP follow-up outcomes for children with autism as a case-in-point. *Topics in Early Childhood Special Education, 20,* 116–122.

Strain, P.S., Hoyson, M., & Jamieson, B. (1985, Spring). Normally developing preschoolers as intervention agents for autistic-like children: Effects on class deportment and social interaction. *Journal of the Division for Early Childhood,* 105–115.

Strain, P.S., Kerr, M.M., & Ragland, E.U. (1979). Effects of peer-mediated social initiation and prompting/reinforcement procedures on the social behavior of autistic children. *Journal of Autism and Developmental Disorders, 9,* 41–54.

Strain, P.S., & Kohler, F.W. (1998). Peer-mediated social intervention for young children with autism. *Seminars in Speech and Language, 19,* 391–405.

Strain, P.S., Kohler, F.W., Storey, K., & Danko, C. (1994). Teaching preschoolers with autism to self-monitor their social interaction. *Journal of Emotional and Behavioral Disorders, 2,* 78–88.

Strain, P.S., & Sainato, D.M. (1987). Preventive discipline in the preschool class. *Teaching Exceptional Children, 19,* 26–30.

Strain, P.S., & Smith, B.J. (1993). Comprehensive educational, social, and policy forces that affect preschool integration. In C.A. Peck, S.L. Odom, & D.D. Bricker (Eds.), *Integrating young children with disabilities into community programs: Ecological perspectives on research and implementa-*

tion (pp. 209–222). Baltimore: Paul H. Brookes Publishing Co.

Strain, P.S., Wolery, M., & Izeman, S. (1998). Considerations for administrators in the design of service options for young children with autism and their families. *Young Exceptional Children, 1,* 1–16.

Tremblay, A., Strain, P.S., Hendrickson, J.M., & Shores, R.E. (1981). Social interactions of normal preschool children: Using normative data for subject and target behavior selection. *Behavior Modification, 5,* 237–253.

Turnbull, A.P., & Turnbull, H.R. (1996). Group action planning as a strategy for providing comprehensive family support. In L.K. Koegel, R.L. Koegel, & G. Dunlap (Eds.), *Positive behavioral support: Including people with difficult behavior in the community* (pp. 99–114). Baltimore: Paul H. Brookes Publishing Co.

U.S. Department of Education. (1998). *Twentieth annual report to Congress on the implementation of the Individuals with Disabilities Education Act.* Washington, DC: U.S. Government Printing Office.

Van Hasselt, V., Strain, P.S., & Hersen, M. (Eds.). (1988). *Handbook of behavioral and physical disabilities.* New York: Pergamon Press.

Vaughn, B.J., Clarke, S., & Dunlap, G. (1997). Assessment-based intervention for severe behavior problems in a natural family context. *Journal of Applied Behavior Analysis, 30,* 713–716.

Venn, M.L., Wolery, M., Fleming, L.A., DeCesare, L.D., Morris, A., & Sigesmund, M.H. (1993). Effects of teaching preschool peers to use the mand-model procedure during snack activities. *American Journal of Speech-Language Pathology, 2*(1), 38–46.

Venn, M.L., Wolery, M., Morris, A., DeCesare, L.D., & Cuffs, M.S. (in press). Use of progressive time delay to teach in-class transitions to preschoolers with autism. *Journal of Autism and Developmental Disorders.*

Venn, M.L., Wolery, M., Werts, M.G., Morris, A., DeCesare, L.D., & Cuffs, M.S. (1993). Embedding instruction in art activities to teach preschoolers with disabilities to imitate their peers. *Early Childhood Research Quarterly, 8,* 277–294.

Volkmar, F.R., & Cohen, D.J. (1988). Classification and diagnosis of childhood autism. In E. Schopler & G.B. Mesibov (Eds.), *Diagnosis and assessment in autism* (pp. 31–59). New York: Kluwer Academic/Plenum Publishers.

Warren, S.F., McQuarter, R.J., & Rogers-Warren, A.K. (1984). The effects of teacher mands and models on the speech of unresponsive language-delayed children. *Journal of Speech and Hearing Research, 49,* 43–52.

Wolery, M., Strain, P.S., & Bailey, D. (1995). Applying the framework of developmentally appropriate practice to children with special needs. In S. Bredekamp (Ed.), *Reaching potentials: Appropriate curriculum for young children* (pp. 65–83). Washington, DC: National Association for the Education of Young Children.

Wolfberg, P.J., & Schuler, A.L. (1993). Integrated play groups: A model for promoting the social and cognitive dimensions of play with children with autism. *Journal of Autism and Developmental Disorders, 23,* 467–489.

Yoder, P.J., Kaiser, A.P., Goldstein, H., Alpert, C., Mousetic, L., Kaczmarek, L., & Gischer, R. (1995). An exploratory comparison of milieu teaching and responsive interaction in classroom applications. *Journal of Early Intervention, 19,* 218–242.

Zigler, M. (1997, June). *Parents empowered as partners.* Address presented at the Emory Autism Resource Center annual conference, Emory University, Atlanta, GA.

16

SHIRIN D. ANTIA

LINDA M. LEVINE

Educating Deaf and Hearing Children Together

Confronting the Challenges of Inclusion

Inclusion for children who are deaf or hard of hearing is a matter of heated discussion; most authors regard the debate as a school-age issue. The literature on inclusion at the preschool level is scanty, and the inclusion issues of preschool-age children are largely ignored. This is an unfortunate omission as early childhood inclusion is a vital matter for all children, irrespective of their needs. Accordingly, this chapter identifies and examines four issues that must be considered when developing inclusive preschool services for children who are deaf or hard of hearing: 1) demographic barriers to service delivery for children with low-incidence disabilities, such as being deaf or hard of hearing, 2) adequate and appropriate access to communication and language within the inclusive environment, 3) social integration issues, and 4) attitudes of parents, professionals, and the Deaf community. Also presented are models of inclusion and recommendations for practice. One of the goals of this chapter is to emphasize that inclusion of children who are deaf or hard of hearing is an unusually difficult task that requires careful planning, adequate resources, and professional expertise.

DEFINITIONS

Physically, hearing loss occurs on a continuum from mild to profound. The term *hearing impaired* is a generic term that refers to children who have any degree of hearing loss. Unfortunately, using a generic term implies that children whose needs may be different can be treated alike. To indicate distinctions between children, professionals have started using the term *deaf or hard of hearing* to refer to the range of children with hearing losses. The distinction between children who are deaf and those who are hard of hearing can be made from an *audiological* or an *educational* perspective. From an audiological perspective, children who are deaf are those with severe and profound hearing losses (averaging 71 decibels [dB] or above in the better ear), whereas children who are hard of hearing are those with mild, moderate, and moderately severe hearing losses (averaging 27–70 dB in the better ear). In educational terms, children who are deaf are those who rely primarily on *vision* to learn language, whereas children who are hard of hearing are those who rely primarily on *hearing* to learn language. Not all children who are deaf learn or use sign language. Some children who are deaf may rely on their vision to learn oral language as their first—and, sometimes, their only—language. Although there is considerable overlap between children who are *audiologically deaf* and those who are *educationally deaf,* the overlap is not complete, because children's use of their residual hearing depends on many factors. Ross, Brackett, and Maxon (1991) referred to the "in-between" child who cannot be categorized neatly as either deaf or hard of hearing. These are children who rely on both hearing and vision to acquire language but the degree to which they rely on these senses may vary depending on the situation. The term *Deaf* (as opposed to *deaf*) is used to identify children who are culturally Deaf (i.e., belong to a Deaf family and learn American Sign Language [ASL] as their first language, from their parents or other family members). In this chapter *deaf or hard of hearing* refers to the range of children who have this disability, and *Deaf* indicates a clear cultural identity with the Deaf community.

DEMOGRAPHIC BARRIERS

Children who are deaf or hard of hearing constitute only 1.8% of the school-age population (Ries, 1994). The 1997–1998 Annual Survey of Deaf and Hard of Hearing Children and Youth conducted by Gallaudet University's Center for Assessment and Demographic Studies (CADS) indicated that there are 4,894 preschool-age children between the ages of 3 and 5 who are deaf or hard of hearing in the United States. This figure is

0.03% of the 555,902 children of the same age who are receiving services for developmental disabilities under the Individuals with Disabilities Education Act (IDEA) Amendments of 1997 (PL 105-17) Preschool Grants Program (Office of Special Education and Rehabilitative Services, 1998). A majority (57%) of preschool-age children reported as receiving services have severe to profound hearing loss. This figure is somewhat higher than the percentage of the school-age population identified as having severe and profound hearing losses, because children with mild and moderate losses are more likely to be identified at later ages. Ninety-five percent of the preschool-age children identified as being deaf or hard of hearing receive special education services. Fifty-two percent receive these services at a general education facility for hearing students. Despite this widespread placement in the public schools, 66% of preschool-age children do not spend any part of the week with hearing children for academic instruction. Only 11% are with hearing children for 16 or more hours a week. It is evident that very few preschool-age children who are deaf or hard of hearing are receiving services in an inclusive educational environment. The most typical service delivery program for preschool-age children is a self-contained, school-based preschool program, a speech and hearing center, or a preschool program at a state school for the deaf.

The need for preschool and infant services has long been recognized among professionals who work with children who are deaf or hard of hearing. Craig (1992), in a 1982 survey of programs, found that 89% of existing educational programs were serving children birth to 4 years of age. A follow-up survey in 1990 indicated that this number had increased to 95%. Although there was a small increase in the number of programs adding early childhood services during this 8-year period, the number of children and the intensity of services offered to children seem to have changed considerably. The number of children served by the surveyed programs more than doubled from 1,602 in 1982 to 3,411 in 1992. In 1982, 34% of children were receiving ½–2 hours of direct services, and 31% were receiving 3–9 hours per week of direct services. By 1992, the number receiving ½–2 hours per week of direct services increased to 61%, but those receiving 3–9 hours per week decreased to 8%. Although the numbers of children served increased, the number of hours of direct services decreased.

Craig (1992) attributed the decrease in direct service to the trend for providing preschool-age children with services in their own home communities. Because children who are deaf or hard of hearing are few and far between, service providers have to travel long distances to reach them. As a result, travel time often exceeds instructional time, although expenses for each child remain high. Thus, when children reach an age at which they can attend preschool, the preferred solution for many districts is to group children together at a single location to increase the amount and efficiency of direct services. When children are at a single location, a mainstreaming model is usually in effect (i.e., children are offered direct services in a segregated classroom environment and may share recess and lunch periods with their hearing peers). Many children who are deaf or hard of hearing may spend part of their day in undocumented child care environments with hearing children, where special services are not provided, but there is almost no information about these kinds of environments.

The primary research need in this field is better demographic data. The Gallaudet Research Institute is likely to undercount the numbers of young children who are hard of hearing in general preschool programs because these children may be identified late (Meadow-Orlans, Sass-Lehrer, & Mertens, 1998) and placed in general preschool programs that are not included in the CADS survey. More detailed surveys need to be conducted, with particular care taken to include children who reside in rural areas and who are more likely to attend inclusive child care programs because of their distance from specialized programs. To obtain an accurate picture of where children attend preschool, surveys need to obtain information from parents as well as professionals.

Another gap in the knowledge concerns why preschool-age children spend so much time in general education facilities but are kept apart from their hearing peers. These data are quite distinct from the data on school-age children that indicate that 40% are placed full time with hearing children (Holden-Pitt & Diaz, 1998). Interviews with parents, program administrators, and teachers may illustrate the reasoning behind such segregated placement.

ACCESS TO COMMUNICATION AND LANGUAGE

The major difficulty faced by children who have a hearing loss is access to oral communication and the oral language of the community. As a result, the main focus of early intervention with children who are deaf or hard of hearing is to enhance language acquisition and development. This, in turn, requires that language and communication be accessible to the child. The following section discusses the issues of language and communication access to sign or spoken language within inclusive preschool environments.

In the area of communication and language learning, the differences between deaf and hard-of-hearing children become most apparent. For children who are deaf, oral language may be learned through speech reading supplemented by audition. Sign language is often considered the "natural" language for these children and is uniquely suited to the visual channel. However, except for some children who are deaf, learning either an oral spoken language or a visual sign language poses problems. The visual channel is very inefficient for learning an oral language, as many aspects of speech are not visible (e.g., back consonants /k/and /g/). Other aspects of speech, such as vowels, are often indistinguishable from each other especially in connected speech. For the young child who is deaf, learning an oral language can be slow and takes exceptional effort on the part of the child and exceptional dedication on the part of parents. Although learning sign language may be easier for the visually oriented child, access to a community of signers usually is not available. In contrast, children who are hard of hearing are able to learn the spoken language of society through their residual hearing. Although Ross and colleagues (1991) characterized these children as more similar to children with normal hearing than to children who are deaf, language acquisition, development, and access remain issues for them during the preschool years.

Issues Surrounding Acquisition of Sign Language

The issues around access to sign language include 1) access to and interaction with skilled signers, 2) "second-hand" language access though an interpreter, and 3) appropriate visual environments.

Access to and Interaction with Skilled Signers   All children learn language through interaction with mature users of the language. Most children who are deaf are born to hearing parents (Marschark, 1993), who usually start

learning sign language when they discover that their child is deaf. Their fluency and comfort with the language are likely to be limited during the child's early years. Some parents may delay learning sign language until their children are in preschool (Spencer & Lederberg, 1997). Typically, home-visitor programs that are the service delivery of choice for infants who are deaf and their families are not intensive enough to allow the families to learn sign language from the professional who visits the home. Frequently, these professionals may not even know sign language (Brown & Yoshinaga-Itano, 1994); in rural areas, they may be local audiologists, speech-language pathologists, and other special educators who are unlikely to have learned sign language as part of their professional preparation. As a result, children who are deaf may enter preschool with delayed language because of their lack of exposure to an accessible language and their lack of interaction with mature language users.

Unlike hearing children, children who are deaf may be dependent on interaction with their preschool teachers for initial language acquisition, making it important that teachers and other adults in the preschool be fluent sign language users. Unfortunately, any preschool teacher who begins to learn sign language to communicate with a child who is deaf or hard of hearing cannot provide a rich language environment immediately for this child. Because of the low incidence of deafness, it is unlikely that a neighborhood preschool will admit more than a few children who are deaf during a 10-year period. Such limited contact with children who are deaf is unlikely to give the preschool staff the motivation to master a second language.

The quality of early interaction between adults and children has a major effect on a child's language learning. In their landmark longitudinal study of hearing children, Hart and Risley (1995) provided evidence that all children need access to such quality features of language as varied vocabulary and sentences, adult responses to children's talk, adult initiations to children, and positive emotional tone of interactions between children and adults. These authors found that (hearing) children who were the recipients of a large amount of adult talk were also the recipients of these quality features of language. Although their research focused on the interaction of children and parents in homes, their findings are equally valid when generalized to teacher–child interactions in the classroom. If, because of the language capabilities of the adults with whom they interact, children who are deaf do not have a large quantity of quality interactions, then they cannot be expected to learn language and communication. Greenberg and Kusche (1993) suggested that parents and teachers who are not fluent signers are likely to have short and simple interactions with children. These authors described a cycle of "linguistic overprotection" of children who are deaf. Because of the adults' lack of skill and insecurity about sign, they reduce the linguistic and cognitive complexity of their communication. Consistent exposure to such simple language results in limited language development in the young child, leading to continuing limited interactions with adults. Although there is not much specific research evidence for this impoverished cycle, several research studies indicate that hearing adults show patterns of interaction with children who are deaf that are unlike those between adults and children who are hearing and adults and children who are deaf (Mather, 1989; Meadow, Greenberg, Erting, & Carmichael, 1981; Spencer & Lederberg, 1997). Some of the mother–child interaction literature indicates that children who are deaf and who have hearing mothers may have fewer opportunities than other

children to engage in lengthy conversational turn taking. Early research by Meadow and colleagues (1981) examined the communication between four groups of adult–child dyads: 1) hearing mothers with hearing children, 2) deaf mothers with deaf children, 3) hearing mothers with deaf children who were in signing preschool programs, and 4) hearing mothers with deaf children who were enrolled in oral preschool programs. The authors found that the hearing mother–deaf child dyads engaged in shorter turn-taking sequences and had higher adult-initiated topics than the other dyads. Spencer and Lederberg (1997), reporting on their longitudinal studies of deaf mother–deaf child and hearing mother–deaf child dyads, found that although both sets of mothers used short signed sentences with their children, the hearing mothers' productions were not as well formed as those of the deaf mothers. The hearing mothers also produced only a few signs during play sessions with their children. Thus, both the quantity and the quality of their sign language seemed to have been constrained.

Mather (1989) described differences between two preschool teachers, one a native deaf signer and the other a teacher who acquired sign language as an adult. She observed these two teachers while they were reviewing a story with preschool-age children who were deaf. In addition to many differences in the instructional use of sign language, she reported that the nonnative signer seemed to ignore the children's contributions and questions frequently, whereas the native signer responded by acknowledging and clarifying the students' utterances. In such observational studies, it is not possible to determine the underlying causes of such interaction patterns, but one likely explanation is the signing competence of the adults. Spencer and Lederberg (1997) suggested that hearing adults without much experience in sign language may be limited in their ability to respond intuitively to young children, as the ability to modify communications for young language learners is closely associated with the adults' own communicative experience. If this is true, even when the hearing adult is a teacher with (presumably) some fluency in sign language, the language experiences of a young deaf child in an inclusive preschool, where the hearing adults are unlikely to know sign language, could be even less facilitative of language learning.

The major reason that most professionals who work with preschool-age children who are deaf recommend segregated programs is that these programs are likely to employ adults (teachers and aides) who are competent users of sign language. Moreover, these programs are more likely to have access to deaf adults who can serve as fluent and mature language models for the children, teachers, and parents. There is some emerging evidence that the presence of deaf adults in parent–infant and preschool programs offers direct benefits to young children who are deaf. Watkins, Pittman, and Walden (1998) completed an exploratory study to examine the effects of visits by deaf mentors on the language and communication development of young children (ages 27–45 months) who were receiving home visits through the widely used SKI*HI program (Clark & Watkins, 1985). Families that participated in the experimental deaf mentor program received additional visits by a deaf adult who taught the family American Sign Language (ASL) and also interacted in ASL with the child. The authors reported that the children in the experimental program had higher rates of language growth than did the control group that had not received such mentoring. Inclusive programs that enroll few children who are deaf are unlikely to include flu-

ent signers among their staff or to include deaf adults.

Despite these problems, there are a few studies that indicate that some of these language barriers can be alleviated. Winter and Van Reusen (1997) studied an inclusive kindergarten program that enrolled 40 hearing children and 7 children who were deaf or hard of hearing. Two kindergarten teachers and one special education teacher of the deaf served these children. The authors interviewed the teachers and kept extensive running records regarding teacher interaction, strategies, and environmental arrangements. They reported that the kindergarten teachers spent time learning sign language from the special education teacher and expressed a belief that learning and using sign language was a way of encouraging membership of all children in the classroom. Antia (1998, 1999) completed a case study of an inclusive program in an elementary school. Two children who were deaf and one who was hard of hearing were enrolled in grades K, 1, and 2, with the support of a special education teacher of the deaf. Interviews and observations concerning the use of sign language indicated that the kindergarten and first-grade teachers learned some signs. They were able to communicate directly with the children who were deaf and to conduct routine classroom activities in sign language. These teachers mentioned that sign language created a beneficial visual environment for all children in the classroom. Antia's findings indicated that teachers who expressed a strong sense of ownership of the child were motivated to learn sign. Other reports of inclusive classrooms of school-age children (Jimenez & Antia, 1999; Kreimeyer, Crooke, Drye, Egbert, & Klein, 2000) also indicate that the adults in these classrooms learned sign language when they co-taught with a full-time special education teacher who could sign.

Learning Language through Inter-
preters   When classroom teachers cannot sign, preschools often hire sign language interpreters. The role of the sign
language interpreter is to facilitate communication between students who are
deaf or hard of hearing and their teachers and peers (Humphrey & Alcorn,
1994). However, there is considerable disagreement as to exactly what constitutes
communication facilitation. Traditionally,
a sign language interpreter's job has been
to translate language interactions between hearing people and those who are
deaf. In such a "mechanical model" of
interpreting (Siegel, 1995), the interpreter is seen as a neutral conduit for all
messages between the teacher and the
student. However, interpreters in preschools cannot be mere translators and
transmitters of information. Seal (1998)
suggested that for young children, the
interpreter's job is to reproduce the
teacher's language in a "helping way"
because the interpreter is a "language
teacher." Unfortunately, the interpreter
cannot be a language teacher in the manner that parents or teachers are language
teachers. Language is learned through
both interaction and exposure; the interpreter can provide only exposure. Thus,
although sign language interpreting can
expose the child to the vocabulary and
sentences that the teacher produces, it
does not substitute for quality interactions with adults in the classroom. The
teacher who works through an interpreter neither responds to the child
directly nor receives direct feedback from
the child. Moreover, the child may not
understand that the interpreter is actually
functioning as the "hands" for the
teacher. The young child may be puzzled
because the interpreter continues interpreting when the child wants to respond
or to initiate communication. Of course,
the interpreter may not always be in a
translating role and may communicate

and interact with the child. Interpreters
may also be instrumental in facilitating
sign language acquisition of the teachers
and children in the classroom (Antia,
Kreimeyer, & Williams, 1998).

Even if the interpreter can function
as a language model for the child, the
skill of the interpreter may exert considerable influence on the child's interactions in the classroom and, subsequently,
on his or her language development. In
one of the few studies on classroom discourse in interpreted situations, Shaw
and Jamieson (1997) observed a child
who was deaf in a third-grade classroom.
They found that the teacher's lessons
were interpreted approximately 60% of
the time. Thus, an interpreter may provide access only to part of the communication interaction in the class. Keeping
up with rapid class talk may become difficult for the interpreter, especially during
discussions, leaving the child ignorant of
what was said by his or her peers. Even
worse, the child may not know that the
interpreter is interpreting for peers and
not for the teacher, leaving the child con-
fused as to the purpose of the classroom
talk. Lag time (i.e., the time between the
teacher's talk and the interpreter's translation) may prevent the child from taking
a turn in the discussion, thus making him
or her a marginal participant in the classroom (Stewart & Kluwin, 1996; Stinson &
Antia, 1999). A skilled interpreter can
alleviate some of these problems. Unfortunately, many educational interpreters
have minimal skills in interpreting, and
even skilled interpreters typically are prepared to interpret for adults and may
have difficulty interpreting in a preschool
classroom.

A final difficulty that can occur when
an interpreter is present is that the
teacher may give ownership and responsibility for the child to the interpreter.
Shaw and Jamieson (1997) found that the
teacher hesitated to initiate interaction

with the child, even through the interpreter. Thus, there may be a severe reduction of opportunity for the child to experience language input and interaction. In some cases, the interpreter's presence and actions can facilitate acceptance and learning of sign language in the classroom. In the previously mentioned case study of young children who were deaf or hard of hearing in an inclusive elementary school (Antia, 1998, 1999; Antia et al., 1998), it was found that the classroom interpreter seemed to be a key player in the inclusion process because she was a sign language resource to the other adults. She taught sign language classes and encouraged the teachers and aides to use sign with the children. As a result, the kindergarten and first-grade teachers and many of the hearing children learned to sign.

Appropriate Visual Environments

For children who are signing, it is important to pay attention to the visual aspects of the environment. The adults in the classroom must think about visual techniques and strategies for attention getting, turn taking, movement activities, transitions, and storytelling (Sass-Lehrer, 1998). The lack of visual strategies may pose several barriers to participation for children who cannot use auditory cues for these activities. For example, during preschool storytelling time, most teachers arrange the environment so that the hearing children can look at the book and pictures at the same time that they are listening to the story. Children who are deaf and rely on an interpreter can give visual attention to only one aspect of the environment; they can watch either the interpreter or the book. If they choose to look at the interpreter, they miss the important visual cues provided by the pictures or the print. Mather (1989) observed a deaf teacher solve this problem by using such strategies as making miniature signs on the book, a strategy that was not used by the hearing, sign-

ing teacher. Hearing teachers, particularly those who are not familiar with children who are deaf or with the visual demands of sign language, may not realize how much they need to restructure their instruction and communication to allow for children's full sequential visual attention (Seal, 1998). Hearing adults and peers may also have trouble accommodating to signing preschool-age children's visual needs and use inappropriate ways of obtaining and holding their attention (Spencer & Lederberg, 1997).

Other aspects of the visual environment may also limit children's access to communication. Visual distractions may be created by shadows on the speaker or signer. Furniture placement may create barriers that block children's visual access to teachers or interpreters (Ross et al., 1991). These problems may lead to visual fatigue and a lack of visual attention.

Some of these concerns can be addressed in inclusive classrooms. Winter and Van Reusen (1997) found that with the help of the special education teacher, the two kindergarten teachers in the inclusive classroom were able to create a good visual environment. Antia (1999) also found that teachers learned visual strategies from the special education teacher and the educational interpreter. They used many of these strategies, especially those that were perceived as benefiting children, both hearing and deaf or hard of hearing.

There is little research on language access and acquisition in inclusive preschool classrooms. Within this framework, there is a specific need to examine the frequency and quality of language interactions between classroom teachers and children who are deaf or hard of hearing. There is no information regarding their direct or interpreted interactions, and there is not much information about the participation of the children in classroom discourse. Examination of the conditions under which teachers in inclusive classrooms learn to sign is also needed. The few studies in this area indicate that the presence of a signing teacher or an interpreter who can teach sign may be important. Investigation into other issues that affect sign language learning and use is also needed, such as how to foster a sense of child ownership in general classroom teachers.

Similarly, there is a need to study discourse patterns in classrooms in which young children use interpreters. There is not much knowledge of how young children perceive their interpreters, whether they understand that the teacher talk is being interpreted, and how interpreters facilitate or inhibit children's classroom participation. Studies that obtain both quantitative and qualitative data about interpreter–child interactions might assist in designing guidelines for interpreters in preschool classrooms. *Quantitative* data would provide information about how much communication is being interpreted and its accuracy, and *qualitative* data would provide information about the perceptions of the interpreter's role by the teacher and other adults. There is also a need to obtain additional information about the manner in which preschool teachers address the visual environment and how consistently they do so, the effects of changes in the environment on the hearing children, and the type of help needed to support change.

Issues Surrounding Access to and Acquisition of Spoken Language

For many children who are deaf or hard of hearing, access to spoken language is crucial for language acquisition. The concerns for these children, who are acquiring the same language spoken by their parents and teachers, are distinct from the concerns for children who are acquiring sign language. Access to spoken language hinges on the ability of the child to hear (and be understood) in the pre-

school environment. Two issues are paramount in the discussion of access to spoken language: 1) the acoustic environment of the classroom and 2) the use and monitoring of appropriate amplification. This section describes some of the barriers posed by acoustic environments and issues of amplification as they relate to inclusion and language acquisition.

Acoustic Environments   It is important for children with any degree of hearing loss to be assured access to oral language through hearing the speech of their teachers and classmates with as much clarity as possible. Unfortunately, the two aspects that most affect classroom acoustics are *noise* and *reverberation,* both of which are prevalent to a large degree in preschool environments.

All preschool classrooms are noisy places. The noise is created by the simultaneous talk of adults and children, the air-conditioning and heating systems, the moving of furniture, and the outside noise (e.g., traffic) that enters the classroom. Many classrooms also have excessive reverberation, which is the prolongation of the speech signal as a result of reflections of sound from the surfaces of walls, ceiling, and floor. Long reverberation times (more than 0.4–0.6 seconds) cause the speech signal to mingle with other signals and to lose clarity. Whereas all children have difficulty hearing in poor acoustic environments, children with hearing loss have significantly greater difficulty than children with normal hearing (Finitzo-Heiber & Tillman, 1978). This difficulty is greatly exacerbated by poor speech perception and is especially salient for children who enter preschool with preexisting language delays.

Listening effort is another within-child variable that is affected by classroom acoustics (DeConde-Johnson, 1998; Ross, 1990). As hearing difficulty increases, the child expends more effort to hear. When the effort becomes intolerable, the child might refuse to participate in activities or to interact with others in the preschool. The more frequently this occurs, the less likely it is that the child will be engaged in learning or in interpersonal interaction.

Certain classroom acoustic conditions can be improved by using carpeting, curtains, and acoustic wall tiles to reduce reverberation and background noise. However, the noise level created by children and teachers who are engaged in movement and interaction is much more difficult to control. Freedom of action and communication is an integral part of early childhood education, but it is this very freedom that compromises language access for children who are hard of hearing. In segregated programs, which typically contain three to five children and one adult, the acoustic environment is more likely to be controlled (and controllable).

Amplification   The use of appropriate amplification devices, which typically are fitted by an audiologist, can significantly affect language access for children who are deaf or hard of hearing and who have some residual hearing. Although a thorough discussion of specific amplification devices is outside the scope of this chapter, it is important to touch on the difficulties faced by teachers and children in the use of personal and environmental devices. The kinds of amplification that are available to children are personal hearing aids (typically worn behind the ear), cochlear implants, FM assistive listening systems, and classroom amplification systems.

The major difficulty with the use of any amplification device is that it can amplify only the sound that reaches it. The farther away children are from the adults or peers who are speaking, the more difficult it will be for them to perceive speech. Even the best personal

hearing aid will not provide good language access to children when the classroom is large and noisy.

An *FM assistive listening system* is one way to solve the problem of distance between children and the speech source. In such a system, speech is transmitted via a radio signal from a microphone worn by the speaker to an FM receiver worn by the child. Because the speech signal is transmitted directly to the child, the impact of poor classroom acoustics can be minimized. The problem of using an FM system is that the child can receive signals only from one individual and loses access to speech input from others in the classroom. Ideally, the FM system should be set up so that the child can hear both teachers and peers, requiring the use of several shared microphones. The system can also be configured to allow access to speech from both the microphone and the environment. Different arrangements for this may have to be provided several times a day according to the activity. As with other types of technology, the benefits derived from an FM system depend on the system's appropriate use. As FM systems require monitoring throughout the day, a teacher who is trained in education of children who are deaf or hard of hearing needs to spend a significant amount of time in the classroom or ascertain that the classroom teachers are well educated in the appropriate use of the system. It is likely that teachers in a busy classroom with many children will forget to use the FM system appropriately, thus creating difficulties for the child who is deaf or hard of hearing.

Classroom amplification systems or *sound field systems* function like wireless FM systems except that the signal is transmitted from the microphone to a receiver/amplifier that transmits the signal to loudspeakers placed throughout the classroom. In this system, the amplified sound is available to all of the children in the classroom, many of whom can benefit from the enhanced signal-to-noise ratio. However, if only the teacher wears the FM microphone, then only the teacher's speech may be accessible to children, depriving them of the benefits of communication with their peers.

Amplification is beneficial only when it is working. Several studies have shown that although children may wear amplification, the devices often function poorly or not at all (Elfenbein, Bentler, Davis, & Niebuhr, 1988; Potts & Greenwood, 1983; Zink, 1972). A survey of functioning amplification devices (both personal hearing aids and FM systems) in Colorado, where educational audiology services are provided to school children in all school districts (DeConde-Johnson, 1998), revealed that only 57% of children had all prescribed amplification devices functioning. Children in segregated classrooms tended to have better functioning amplification than those who were in inclusive classrooms. It is likely that these results are typical and that despite good educational audiology services and amplification monitoring, amplification devices have high rates of malfunctioning. If these malfunctions are not corrected by teachers in a timely manner, then opportunities for learning are lost and children are deprived of crucial language access.

There is little information about how classroom organization and noise levels influence child participation. Needed is research that describes the physical and acoustical characteristics of inclusive classrooms and the participation of children who are deaf or hard of hearing in these environments. Also needed is research on the consistency of amplification use by preschool-age children and the reasons for nonuse, teachers' comfort levels for monitoring amplification systems, and the modifications that teachers are willing to make in their classroom discourse patterns to accommodate amplification systems.

SOCIAL INTEGRATION ISSUES

One of the major goals of inclusion is the social integration of children with special needs into the larger community (see Chapter 1). Although there is little research on the outcomes of language and communication development of young children who are deaf or hard of hearing and enrolled in inclusive programs, there is a reasonable body of research in the area of social integration. This section examines social integration outcomes for young children who are deaf or hard of hearing by examining research on the extent of peer interactions, interpersonal relationships, and accommodations made during interpersonal communication.

Peer Interactions

Social interaction with hearing peers during play is probably the most frequently studied phenomenon among children who are deaf or hard of hearing and enrolled in inclusive programs. Children can have a passive connection with peers by observing their play, by engaging with them in parallel play, or by creating an active connection through engagement in group play (Guralnick, 1999). The research in this area for children who are deaf or hard of hearing is primarily descriptive and is not yet sufficient to tease out the variables that affect the frequency and quality of interaction between children of different hearing status.

The data on play and interaction suggest that although social separation occurs between children who are deaf or hard of hearing and their hearing peers, under certain circumstances such separation can be mitigated or reduced. Esposito and Koorland (1989) compared the play of two preschool-age children with severe to profound hearing losses in self-contained and inclusive environments and found that although both children engaged primarily in parallel play in their self-contained classroom, they engaged in frequent associative play while attending separate inclusive child care programs. Because the inclusive environments consisted only of hearing children and no particular intervention was used, the authors concluded that the presence of hearing children as models and possible partners was successful in promoting interactive play.

Although self-segregation tendencies exist in inclusive environments, positive social interaction between children of different hearing status also occurs occasionally. Minnett, Clark, and Wilson (1994) examined social and nonsocial play and communication of 60 children who attended an inclusive preschool program. They found that all children were more likely to engage in interaction with peers of similar hearing status, although 70% of the children who were hearing and 57% of the children who were deaf or hard of hearing engaged at least once in interaction with peers of opposite hearing status.

There are indications that under certain circumstances, the frequency and quality of interaction between young children of different hearing status can be enhanced. Antia, Kreimeyer, and Eldredge (1994) compared the effects of two interventions on positive peer social interaction and found that both resulted in a small but significant increase in interaction with peers of the opposite hearing status. During the social skills intervention, small integrated groups of young children were taught specific interactive social skills using shared activities, cooperative games, and role plays. During the comparison interaction, children were engaged in activities within similar small groups but were not given any instruction

in specific interaction skills. The authors concluded that providing children of different hearing status the opportunity to interact in small integrated groups over a period of time could increase peer interaction.

In another study, Antia and Ditillo (1998) examined the play of small groups of preschool-age children in integrated free-play situations under conditions that promoted interaction: limited physical space, limited number of materials, interactive toys, familiar peers who were deaf or hard of hearing and hearing, and minimal teacher direction. They found that both hearing children and those who were deaf engaged in similar levels of positive peer interaction; the hearing children engaged in primarily linguistic interactions, and the children who were deaf or hard of hearing engaged in primarily nonlinguistic interaction. Unfortunately, the authors did not record the hearing status of the peer partner, which made it impossible to know how frequently the children engaged with peers of the opposite hearing status. This research suggests that given optimal play conditions, children who are deaf or hard of hearing are not necessarily "noninteractors" as suggested by the results of previous studies (see Antia, 1985, for a review).

It is possible that these studies underestimate the capacity of children who are deaf or hard of hearing to interact with hearing peers. Although the children in the previously mentioned studies were enrolled in the same school, many of the children who were deaf or hard of hearing spent several hours a day in a resource room. Thus, their interactions may not be representative of what occurs in truly inclusive environments in which children attend the general classroom on a full-time basis. Only one investigation has been made of the frequency of peer interaction in an inclusive environment. Spencer, Koester, and Meadow-Orlans

(1994) examined the peer interaction of four children who were deaf and four hearing children enrolled together in an inclusive preschool. The hearing children were taught to sign, and efforts were made to teach all children to communicate with one another. Although both groups of children initiated to peers of the same hearing status at levels significantly higher than those occurring by chance, they also initiated to peers of the opposite hearing status with some frequency. Hearing peers initiated to children who were deaf for 29% of total initiations, whereas children who were deaf initiated to hearing peers for 58% of total initiations. Thus, in inclusive programs in which communication between hearing and deaf children is facilitated through the use of sign language learning, frequency of interaction between the two groups of children is higher than that reported by other authors (Antia et al., 1994). The authors suggested that interaction was facilitated by maintaining a balance in the group according to hearing status.

The Quality of Peer Interactions
There is also a body of emerging research that examines the quality of play and interaction between hearing children and those who are deaf or hard of hearing. Researchers have examined the length of interactions (Hulsing, Luetke-Stahlman, Loeb, Nelson, & Wegner, 1995; Vandell & George 1981), success of initiations and responsiveness to peer initiations (Antia & Ditillo, 1998; Hulsing et al., 1995; Messenheimer-Young & Kretschmer, 1994), the quality of play (Levine & Antia, 1997), and the topics of communication during pretend play (Brown, Prescott, Rickards, & Paterson, 1994).

The length of interactions can be regarded as an index of the ability of children to engage in conversation and to engage in extended associative and cooperative play. Short, functional exchanges with peers may not be sufficient to promote friendship and may be an indicator of mere "acquaintanceship" (Stinson & Antia, 1999). An early study by Vandell and George (1981) observed interaction between dyads of children with different hearing status enrolled in separate, self-contained programs at the same preschool center. The hearing children were taught sign language as part of their program. The researchers compared interactions of dyads with the same hearing status (hearing–hearing; deaf or hard of hearing–deaf or hard of hearing) and different hearing status (deaf or hard of hearing–hearing). The different hearing status dyads interacted less frequently and for shorter duration than did the dyads with similar hearing status. The researchers observed that although the children who were deaf or hard of hearing initiated more frequently than the hearing children did, their initiations were more likely to be rejected or ignored. They also suggested that the shorter length of interaction may have resulted from lack of motivation or of signing skill on the part of the hearing children or from the inability of the children who were deaf or hard of hearing to initiate appropriately. The results may reflect that the children were schoolmates rather than classmates.

In the Antia and Ditillo (1998) study mentioned previously, patterns of initiations and responses were examined in children who were playing in groups that contained children of different hearing status. The children who were deaf or hard of hearing were less successful than the children who were hearing in eliciting positive responses. Both groups of children initiated to peers and received initiations from peers with equal frequency. Both groups also gave and received significantly more positive responses than negative responses to peer initiations. However, the children who were hearing received significantly more positive responses than nonresponses, whereas there was no significant difference between the positive responses and nonresponses received by the children who were deaf or hard of hearing. Because the authors did not record the hearing status of the interaction partners, it is unclear whether it was the partner's motivation or communication skill that was the crucial factor in the response pattern.

In inclusive classrooms, interaction patterns of children of different hearing status seem to be more similar than different. Hulsing and colleagues (1995) examined the interactions of six children: three hearing children, one child who was hard of hearing, and two children who were deaf. Children were enrolled in three different inclusive kindergarten classrooms. They found that the child who was hard of hearing had a higher total number of interactions than did the two who were deaf. However, the number of turns per interaction was similar for all six children, as was the percentage of successful initiations. The authors indicated that differences in classroom atmosphere seemed to influence the rate of peer interaction more than the hearing status of the children did. The differences between children might also be due to the mode of communication, as the child who was hard of hearing used oral communication whereas the other children signed. Differences might also be attributed to the presence of an interpreter for the children who were deaf to facilitate communication and remove the inhibiting effect of sign language skill.

Messenheimer-Young and Kretschmer (1994) also found few differences in successful initiations between a child who was hard of hearing and his hearing peers in an inclusive school environment. Although the teachers perceived that the child who was hard of hearing was not able to gain entry to play activities appropriately, the researchers found that he attempted to get involved in interactive play a total of 76 times during a 5-week period. He used 10 different entry strategies, all of which were similar to those used by other children in the group. His proportion of unsuccessful initiations (82%), though high, was not markedly different from that of the other children in the classroom. The researchers noted that the entry strategy most often prompted by the teachers (verbal request to participate) was one of the least successful strategies for all of the children.

Two studies have examined the quality of play of hearing children and those who are deaf or hard of hearing in integrated groups. Levine and Antia (1997) examined the effect of partner hearing status on the social and cognitive play behaviors of 46 preschool-age children who were deaf or hard of hearing (3–6 years old) and enrolled in various types of program models across the United States. The playgroups were small and contained children of different hearing status; at least two children in each group were deaf or hard of hearing. The authors reported that the children who were deaf or hard of hearing engaged more frequently in group play than in parallel play with all partners and at all age levels. However, the cognitive level of group play (functional, constructive, and dramatic) was affected by partner hearing status. When playing with partners who were deaf or hard of hearing, the children who were deaf or hard of hearing engaged in significantly more constructive than functional or dramatic play. When playing with hearing partners, they engaged in equal levels of functional, constructive, and dramatic play. However, when playing in groups that consisted of partners who were both hearing and deaf or hard of hearing, the children engaged most frequently in dramatic play. The authors suggested that the interactive dramatic play of the children who were deaf or hard of hearing was facilitated by the presence of familiar playmates who were deaf or hard of hearing with whom they could communicate, as well as the presence of hearing playmates who initiated dramatic play and modeled advanced behaviors.

Brown and colleagues (1994) investigated the ability of children to sustain pretend play through verbal communication. They examined the pretend play episodes of four kindergarten children who were deaf or hard of hearing and who communicated orally and compared these with pretend play episodes of four hearing children. The authors reported that the children who were deaf or hard of hearing produced higher proportions of literal object utterances and current action utterances than did the hearing children. Both groups produced equal numbers of role utterances, but the children who were deaf or hard of hearing produced no scripted utterances. No data were available on the effect of partners on the play utterances, so it is unclear whether the talk about play was influenced by hearing or by deaf or hard of hearing partners. The authors suggested that the inability of the children who were deaf or hard of hearing to produce scripted utterances would affect their ability to engage in sustained pretend play with hearing partners.

To summarize, the research on frequency of peer interaction indicates that although children prefer to interact with peers of similar hearing status, they do not ignore peers of different hearing status. The frequency of interaction seems to be enhanced when children are taught to communicate with one another using sign language or are given opportunities to interact with one another during specific activities. Group composition may affect both the quality and the quantity of interaction; small stable groups that consist of both deaf or hard of hearing and hearing children are the best combination. Such groups provide both familiar

deaf or hard of hearing peers for fluent communication and hearing peers who may help in organizing and facilitating advanced play. The degree of inclusion may affect interaction, as children who spend all of their time in inclusive environments seem to interact more frequently with hearing peers than do children who spend part of their day in segregated environments. In terms of the quality of interactions, children who are deaf or hard of hearing seem to initiate interaction frequently but may not have as high a rate of successful initiations as hearing children do. Finally, children who are deaf or hard of hearing may engage in different kinds of talk than their hearing peers during pretend play, making them less attractive playmates for their hearing peers.

There seems to be a need for further examination of the quality rather than the quantity of interactions between children who are deaf or hard of hearing and hearing, to tease out the factors that contribute to successful interactions. Several researchers have reported that children are more likely to engage in nonlinguistic rather than linguistic interactions, most likely because of communication barriers. Further research is needed to investigate whether it is possible for children to sustain nonlinguistic interactions and whether nonlinguistic communications are facilitative of later linguistic communication. It is possible that in their history of peer interaction, children who are deaf or hard of hearing have found that nonlinguistic communication is more successful with most peers than is linguistic communication. However, nonlinguistic communication between children may not sustain play or facilitate advanced levels of play.

Another research area in need of investigation is how children who are deaf or hard of hearing gain access to playgroups and the success rate of various entry strategies. Findings suggest that the presence of more than one child who is deaf or hard of hearing in conjunction with hearing peers within a playgroup is facilitative of more interaction and higher levels of play, but it is not clear how or why this is so. Further in-depth analysis of the dynamics of play and communication within integrated playgroups may enhance the ability to create appropriate environments for interaction to occur. Finally, research is needed concerning interventions that facilitate sign language learning for hearing children.

Interpersonal Relationships

Compared with the research on peer interaction, little research has been conducted on the formation of interpersonal relationships of young children who are deaf or hard of hearing in inclusive environments. A few studies have examined friendship formation through the use of sociometric scales. Cappelli, Daniels, Durieux-Smith, McGrath, and Neuss (1995) compared the social acceptance of 23 children who were deaf or hard of hearing and 23 of their hearing classmates in grades 1–6. At lower grade levels, seven children who were deaf or hard of hearing were rejected by their classmates compared with only two rejected hearing children. Antia and Kreimeyer (1996) used a peer nomination scale before and after a social skills intervention with young deaf or hard of hearing children and their hearing peers. They found that hearing peers labeled the children who were deaf or hard of hearing as less desirable playmates than the other hearing children; they most often reported that they played with them "a little" rather than "not at all." Kluwin and Gonsher (1994) examined an inclusive, team-taught kindergarten in which children who were deaf or hard of hearing and hearing were assigned communication buddies and instruction in sign language was provided to the hearing children. In a co-enrollment model, all

children are members of the same class, which is co-taught by a general education teacher and a teacher of students who are deaf or hard of hearing. Peer nomination data showed that by spring, the nominations of the children who were deaf or hard of hearing were in the moderate or upper range of popularity and were not different from those of hearing peers. In addition, an examination of the classroom social networks showed that whereas in the fall, cliques were separated by hearing status, by spring there were several cliques consisting of children who were deaf or hard of hearing and hearing.

Because the research in this area is so sparse, it is difficult to tease out the factors that might contribute to these disparate results. The results of the Antia and Kreimeyer (1996) study may be explained by the fact that the children were enrolled in the same school but received many services in a segregated environment. However, the differences between the acceptance of children reported by Cappelli and colleagues (1995) and Kluwin and Gonsher (1994) require further explanation. Both groups were enrolled in inclusive programs, but each group had a different mode of communication. Cappelli and colleagues studied children using oral communication, whereas the children in the Kluwin and Gonsher study used signed communication. However, because it is assumed that oral communication is more facilitative of interaction with hearing peers, this difference may not be the sole contributing factor. It is possible that the degree of affiliation with other class members may have been different for the children in the two studies. The children in the Cappelli and colleagues study were the only children who were deaf or hard of hearing in their respective classrooms and received pull-out itinerant services, whereas the children studied by Kluwin and Gonsher were in a co-enrolled class with no pull-out services. Thus, the latter may have been perceived as members of the class and not different in any way. Also, the specific attempts to include the children who were deaf or hard of hearing by teaching sign language to hearing peers and by using buddies may have created more opportunities for reciprocal friendships to develop in the co-enrolled class.

Three studies that produce widely differing results are not sufficient to draw conclusions about friendship formation within inclusive early childhood programs. There is a need for additional intensive, qualitative, ethnographic studies similar to the in-depth investigation of peer relationships and social culture conducted by Corsaro (1985) to deepen the understanding of friendships between children, especially when communication barriers exist.

Accommodations

Successful interaction between hearing children and those who are deaf or hard of hearing requires that the participants adapt to the linguistic characteristics of their partners. One way to accommodate for language differences is for the hearing children to learn sign language. Another accommodation is to rely on nonlinguistic communication. Although the latter adaptation may meet functional communication needs, it may not serve to develop extended interactions or friendships between the two groups of children. Nevertheless, there are some studies that show that children are able to make adaptations to each other's communication needs.

Lederberg, Ryan, and Robbins (1986) compared the dyadic interaction of young children who were deaf or hard of hearing with familiar hearing peers, unfamiliar hearing peers, and peers who were deaf or hard of hearing. The authors found that the children who were deaf or hard of hearing tended to com-municate with signs when with a partner who was deaf or hard of hearing but used object-related behavior and toy play with a hearing partner. They also experienced more success when initiating play with familiar hearing peers and engaged in more pretend play and physical contact with familiar than unfamiliar hearing peers. Familiar hearing peers used more gestures, exaggerated facial expressions, and vocalizations with a familiar than with an unfamiliar peer who was deaf or hard of hearing. Thus, both groups of children were able to make accommodations, particularly with familiar play partners.

A major accommodation that needs to be made by hearing children is the use of sign language to interact with peers who are deaf or hard of hearing. Despite the apparent difficulties that this might create, at least two studies indicate that under the right conditions, many young hearing children become sufficiently fluent in sign language to communicate extensively with their classmates who are deaf. Kluwin and Gonsher (1994), in their examination of the co-enrolled classroom, also examined improvement in sign language for both groups of children by testing them on a standardized receptive sign vocabulary test. They reported that hearing children showed rapid and significant improvement on this test over the course of the school year. They also reported that hearing children who had reciprocal relationships with peers who were deaf or hard of hearing had better sign language skills than did the rest of the group. Antia (1998), in her case study of an inclusive elementary school, reported that the child who was deaf had many linguistic interactions with her peers on the playground. Her first-grade teacher also reported that she had a group of friends who could conduct fluent sign conversations with her. In both of these classes, sign language learning was promoted and the children who were deaf were full-time members of the classroom.

It seems that both hearing children and those who are deaf or hard of hearing are willing and able to make several accommodations, including learning sign language. However, merely teaching hearing children sign language or demonstrating specific accommodations in isolated situations may emphasize differences between children and may not result in interaction (Antia, 1985). Thus, research is needed on how to promote children's learning in interactive situations. Because familiarity seems to facilitate accommodations, it would also be fruitful to investigate how interaction changes within stable groups of children.

ATTITUDES

One of the major issues that influences the development, availability, and evaluation of inclusive programs is the attitudes of parents, professionals, and Deaf people themselves regarding inclusion. With the movement toward full inclusion in schools and preschools, many believe that placement of young children who are deaf or hard of hearing in inclusive environments may be inappropriate for the development of communication and social skills. Professionals are concerned about placing these young children in inclusive programs without the support of teachers and peers who can enhance communication during the course of the entire school day. Although parents are considered pivotal to the intervention process (Harrison, Dannhardt, & Roush, 1996), their opinions may be heard less frequently than are those of professionals. Parents are often under great stress in trying to negotiate the service delivery system, the overwhelming developmental challenges presented by the presence of hearing loss in their child, and the confusion of having to make choices about communication and education. Although many parents perceive the benefits and drawbacks of inclusion without regard to their child's disability (Guralnick, 1994), parents of children who are deaf or hard of hearing may be less likely to perceive inclusion as the most beneficial type of programming for enhancing social, emotional, and communication development. Parents of young children who are deaf or hard of hearing are a small group being pulled in several directions by professionals who disagree about practices that best serve the needs of young children in relation to programming choices, models of service delivery, and development of communication skills. This section describes the attitudes of parents, professionals, and the Deaf community regarding inclusive programs.

Parents' Attitudes

Many factors contribute toward shaping parents' attitudes toward children's placements. Meadow-Orlans and Sass-Lehrer (1995) reported that attitudes may be highly influenced by child factors, particularly age at diagnosis, degree of hearing loss, and the presence of additional disabilities. Attitudes are also influenced by parent characteristics, including hearing status, cultural/linguistic status, and socioeconomic status. Ross (1990) pointed out the complexity involved in the formation of parents' attitudes and related parents' opinions to the age at which the child's hearing loss is discovered and professional services are offered. Early diagnosis of hearing loss allows parents to acclimate to the reality of having a child who is deaf or hard of hearing and to consider various accommodations early in the child's life. Parents' attitudes are not only tempered by parent and child characteristics but also may be affected by the programming options that are offered and the parents' own affiliation or knowledge of the Deaf culture.

Since the early 1990s, federal legislation has extended early intervention to infants and toddlers and support for their families, bringing service delivery to families at earlier stages of their children's lives (Craig, 1992). Although positive developmental gains have resulted from intervention associated with very early identification of hearing loss and from earlier intervention and use of hearing aids (Yoshinaga-Itano, Sedey, Coulter, & Mehl, 1998), controversies in the field concerning appropriate placements for delivery of early intervention services and communication options continue to confuse parents and add to their overall levels of stress (Meadow-Orlans, 1990). For many families, there is a lag of several months between initial suspicion of hearing loss and the diagnosis and again between the diagnosis and the start of intervention services (Meadow-Orlans, Mertens, Sass-Lehrer, & Scott-Olson, 1997). These gaps in identification and service delivery may translate into only 2 years of total early intervention services before the child reaches school age. By the time parents acclimate to the new information about their child, absorb information about available services, and recognize the choices that they must make for their child's future communication needs, their child is ready for school-age services.

The attitudes of both deaf and hearing parents toward the programs that serve their children can be highly influenced by the attitudes, sensitivity, and openness of professionals. Meadow-Orlans and Sass-Lehrer suggested that professionals in the education of children who are deaf or hard of hearing "come from a long tradition of directiveness in prescribing for parents" (1995, p. 318). They reported that educators may enable parents who are deaf by encouraging them to share their experience and expertise with hearing parents or may disenfranchise them by focusing exclusively on the interests of the hearing parents. Similarly, because the concerns of parents who are deaf are different from those of parents who are hearing, hearing parents may feel "left out" of parent groups that include deaf parents (Luterman, 1999). Thus, parents' working relationships with professionals may be a key influence in their attitudes toward specific preschool placements.

Several surveys provide information about parents' attitudes regarding satisfaction with preschool programs. Families of 6- and 7-year-old children who were participating in the 1996 Gallaudet University's Annual Survey of Deaf and Hard of Hearing Children and Youth were surveyed concerning their satisfaction with previously delivered infant and preschool services. Responses were received from 404 parents of children who were deaf (46%) or hard of hearing (54%) who were enrolled in 137 programs in 39 states. Parents were asked to recall information and provide opinions about early intervention services and to describe their children's current developmental status and progress. Early intervention services received highly favorable evaluations and enthusiastic responses from parents, although 40% of the families reported that they had no choice but had to enroll their child in the only program available to them(Meadow-Orlans et al., 1997).

Another national survey of parents' attitudes and satisfaction was conducted by Harrison and colleagues (1996) to obtain information from families of children with hearing loss concerning the effects of the infant-toddler component of Part H of the Education of the Handicapped Act Amendments of 1986 (PL 99-457), specifically about individualized family service plan (IFSP) development and family-centered practices. Responses to the survey were received from 398 families representing 67 programs in 35 states. Additional comments were received from 80% of the families and strongly supported early intervention programs; almost half (47%) of the respondents noted the great concern and care of staff toward them and their child. However, no parent comments specifically addressed inclusive program structure. In general, families were pleased with services, and only 7% of the families that responded cited concerns over a lack of program choice. However, 20% of the families that responded reported that they were not informed by program staff about the effects of deafness on language development, and 30% were not made aware that communication modes and educational environments other than what were being offered were also options for their children.

The few surveys of parents' satisfaction with early childhood services indicate reasonably high levels of satisfaction with available programs. However, the surveys did not ask questions or solicit parents' opinions about inclusive programs. Clearly, there is a need to identify children who are served in inclusive programs and to obtain parents' opinions about placement in such programs and satisfaction with their services. Parents' opinions regarding the desirability of inclusion for their children who are deaf or hard of hearing also need to be obtained, although it may be difficult to obtain these in regard to nonexistent programs. Because of the low incidence of childhood hearing loss, parents usually do not have many program choices within a reasonable geographic range. Also, as indicated by the surveys, parents may not be informed of choices that may be available to them. More in-depth research is needed concerning how and why parents make placement choices and the factors that influence their choices. As mentioned previously, child characteristics such as age at identification of hearing loss and degree of hearing loss are likely to influence the choices that par-

ents make about educational programming.

Another fruitful area of investigation is studying how the characteristics of the parents influence programming choices. Parents who are deaf may be more comfortable with segregated, center-based programs, as these may reflect their own experiences. Conversely, hearing parents may be wary of "giving up" their children to a Deaf community that believes that hearing loss is a sign of community membership rather than a limiting characteristic (Marschark, 1997). Hearing parents may also become concerned at the prospect of "losing" their children to the Deaf culture and may sense discrimination by advocates in the Deaf community who may denigrate the choices that the hearing parents make for their child who is deaf. Such feelings may influence their choice of programs or their satisfaction with preschool services. Parents' socioeconomic status and ethnic membership may also influence attitudes toward inclusion. An early study by Jensema (1977) showed that school-age children from higher socioeconomic backgrounds were less likely to be enrolled in segregated residential and day programs than were children from lower socioeconomic backgrounds.

Finally, the influences of professional advice, information, and working relationships with parents needs to be studied as factors in parents' attitudes toward inclusion. Parents who might be inclined to place their children in inclusive programs may be discouraged by professional advice or attitudes opposing inclusive programs. Professionals are in a position to provide or withhold information and to help or hinder choices made by parents. Research descriptions of the kinds of information that early childhood providers give to parents, the perceived relationships between professionals and parents, and the quality and frequency of communication between parents and professionals are almost nonexistent. The parental voice in the literature on education of children who are deaf or hard of hearing is faint.

Professional Attitudes

Professional educators of children who are deaf or hard of hearing generally have been cautious and occasionally hostile to the movement toward full inclusion. Strong advocacy efforts on the part of organizations that represent educators and the Deaf community have promoted the broadest possible interpretation of federal legislative requirements for providing children with a free appropriate public education (FAPE) in the least restrictive environment (LRE). These efforts have attempted to safeguard the educational rights of deaf children and youth but also clearly illustrate the perceived barriers to inclusion by professionals who work with children who are deaf or hard of hearing.

Recommendations from the 1988 report of the Commission on Education of the Deaf (COED) reflected concern about the unsatisfactory status of the education of people who are deaf and specifically addressed their unique educational and communication needs. Partly as a reaction to the movement of students from schools for the deaf into public school programs, the COED recommendations made strong statements about the importance of schools for the deaf in the continuum of placements available to deaf students. In 1992, then Secretary of Education Lamar Alexander issued a policy document that required state and local education agencies to consider the communication needs and preferred communication modes; linguistic needs; severity of hearing loss; academic level; and social, emotional, and cultural needs, including opportunities for peer interactions and communication, when developing an individualized education program (IEP) for a student who is deaf. The fol-

lowing excerpt from this document addresses the needs of children who are deaf or hard of hearing in relation to appropriate education in the LRE:

> Meeting the unique communication and related needs of a student who is deaf is a fundamental part of providing a free appropriate public education to the child. . . . Any setting, including a regular classroom, that prevents a child who is deaf from receiving an appropriate education that meets his or her needs, including communication needs, is not the LRE for that individual child. . . . The Secretary recognizes that regular educational settings are appropriate and adaptable to meet the unique needs of particular children who are deaf. For others, a center or special school may be the least restrictive environment in which the child's unique needs can be met. (p. 3)

The recognition by the Department of Education of the special circumstances pertaining to the importance of communication development for children who are deaf or hard of hearing is unique to this one category of children with special needs.

As the inclusion movement grows, professionals have felt a strong need to sound an alarm concerning the limitations that inclusion may impose on a child who is deaf. An examination of editorials in *American Annals of the Deaf,* a professional journal and the official organ of two major professional organizations, illustrates some of the thinking in the field by leading educators. The issue of identification with others in the Deaf community and the Deaf culture was presented as a strong argument for the retention of self-contained programs by Vernon (1988), the editor of the journal between 1970 and 1990. Vernon condemned the early mainstreaming movement as detrimental to the Deaf community and a roadblock to identification and maintenance of Deaf cultural identity. His advocacy for continuance of self-contained day/residential schools was based on the argument that young children who are deaf or hard of hearing, especially those who are isolated in public schools in small towns and rural schools, are not fully accepted by those with hearing and experience a "life of loneliness and rejection" growing up without contact with other deaf individuals (Vernon, 1988). Moores, the editor of the journal since 1990, endorsed inclusion programs as appropriate for some children who are deaf or hard of hearing but cautioned that the pendulum has swung too far toward implementation of inclusion as the only approach for all children. He stated that policies formulated in good faith, such as the movement toward normalization, may end up harming those whom they were intended to help. Moores views inclusive environments that do not offer the option of sign language as a vehicle for communication as segregationist for children who are deaf. He believes that inclusive programs may give parents a negative and erroneous message about the value of sign language as an appropriate and essential service for their children (Moores, 1993, 1995, 1996).

A series of articles on full inclusion by educators and administrators (Corson & Stuckless, 1994) illustrates the cautious attitude of professionals toward inclusion of children who are deaf or hard of hearing. Several authors concede that although children who are deaf or hard of hearing may benefit academically, they are likely to be isolated socially (Bunch, 1994; McCartney, 1994; Stinson & Lang, 1994). Other authors (Polowe-Aldersley, 1994) oppose inclusion on the basis of cost, lack of professional expertise, and the likelihood of poor-quality services in inclusive programs, particularly those that serve only a single child. The opinions of many administrators of schools for the deaf is exemplified by Cohen, the superintendent of the Lexington School for the Deaf, who called for maintaining a full continuum of placements for all children but condemned as naïve the view that public schools can develop an environment in which everyone in the school will be able to "communicate directly and proficiently according to the learning styles and needs of all deaf children" (1994, p. 2).

Although many opinion-type articles have been published, research on the attitudes of professionals on inclusion of deaf children is scarce and focuses on the perceptions of teachers of school-age children. A study targeting attitudes of general education teachers, special educators, and teachers of children who are deaf or hard of hearing was conducted in Greece (Lampropoulou & Padeliadu, 1997). The special educators and the teachers of children who are deaf or hard of hearing composed the entire population of those teachers in Greece. The survey targeted attitudes toward inclusion and disability and found that the teachers of the children who were deaf or hard of hearing had less favorable attitudes toward inclusion than did teachers in either of the other groups. The longer these teachers were engaged with children who were deaf or hard of hearing, the more pronounced was this attitude. The researchers believed that these results were based partially on the teachers' knowledge of the social and communication needs of the children and, partially, on their view that these children are "different" rather than "deficient." This opinion seems to be common among deaf educators (Aldridge, Timmins, & Wood, 1995), who regard children who are deaf or hard of hearing as having very specialized needs but not as having a "disability" or an "impairment."

Other studies indicate that many professionals, both teachers of children who are deaf or hard of hearing and those engaged in general education, express positive attitudes if the inclusion program is successful. Afzali-Nomani (1995) investigated the attitudes of 55 educators of children who were deaf or hard of hearing and 48 general educators, long involved in inclusion programs for school-age children who were deaf or hard of hearing. Both groups of teachers indicated that inclusion had a positive impact on the academic achievement, social adjustment, and self-esteem of hearing students and those who were deaf or hard of hearing.

Chorost (1988) published findings concerning the attitudes of 15 general education teachers who had been the homeroom teachers for a group of six deaf or hard of hearing children over a 6-year period as the children moved from preschool environments into the elementary grades. Teachers explored their feelings of anxiety when they learned that their programs would include a child who was deaf or hard of hearing and their subsequent positive feelings after having the child as part of the class. The majority believed that the extra time required to accommodate the children was time well-spent. Several viewed the experience positively, and many felt comfortable with repeating the experience. In general, children who required less than 30 minutes of extra teacher time and attention were regarded as a more positive presence in the classroom than were children whose time needs exceeded 30 minutes of accommodation each day. Children with mild or moderate hearing losses were viewed more positively than were children with severe or profound losses. The teachers who did not feel positively about the experience cited the extra time involved and the lower academic level of the child as the two major drawbacks.

It should be clear that inclusion is considered to be a placement *option,* and not a *goal,* by many professionals and a choice that can be less than advantageous for the child who is deaf or hard of hearing. Despite the large number of school-age children who are deaf or hard of hearing and who are already attending public schools with hearing peers, most opinion pieces written by members of the professional community are extremely cautious in their attitude toward inclusion as the most beneficial option for the majority of children who are deaf or hard of hearing. The placement of children in inclusive environments is to be considered only when the characteristics of the children are such that they can benefit from the services offered by the program. The research gives some indication, however, that teachers who are involved in successful integrated programs support inclusion. Stinson and Antia (1999) drew distinctions between the philosophical approach to inclusion as an obligation to accommodate all children in the general classroom and the pragmatic approach to inclusion, which considers whether such accommodation is actually possible and cost-effective. The professional community comes down on the side of a pragmatic approach to inclusion.

Surveys of special education teachers who have been involved in integrated programming show positive attitudes toward inclusion as a programming philosophy and enthusiasm about the role of the teacher in affecting child change (Gallagher, 1997; Marchant, 1995). Little such research has been completed with teachers of children who are deaf or hard of hearing, particularly those in preschool programs. Attitude surveys targeting preschool teachers who have experience with programs that include children who are deaf or hard of hearing would provide valuable information concerning professional perceptions of the outcomes of inclusion and help uncover the educational conditions that are necessary for successful inclusion to occur. Qualitative research that examines changes in teacher beliefs and attitudes as they work in inclusive preschool environments is also needed to enrich the literature base and allow informed decisions concerning the next steps in crafting appropriate programs.

Attitudes of the Deaf Community

The Deaf community is unique among all of the communities of individuals with disabilities in that it is defined by a common culture and language more than by the physical fact of hearing loss. Fluency in ASL is a defining factor for membership in the community, as are shared experiences, usually in schools for the deaf. These schools are therefore seen by many as the cultural hub of the community. Whereas most children are socialized into their community by their parents, most children who are deaf are socialized into the Deaf community by their schoolmates. Therefore, the Deaf community's argument against inclusive educational programs is as much an argument for keeping separate schools for the deaf as it is about appropriate education (Marschark, 1997).

In 1994, the National Association for the Deaf (NAD) issued a strongly worded position statement that labeled the term *full inclusion* as an ideological movement rather than as a federal mandate. The NAD position statement condemned any interpretation of full inclusion that calls for implementation without regard to disability condition. The NAD stated that full inclusion threatens children's access to intense communication programming and is thus a violation of their rights to reach maximum human potential. The NAD position statement urged a continuation and expansion of the FAPE provision of IDEA for a full continuum of choices and a broad range of services in environments determined to be appropriate for individual children.

It is not necessarily true that dispersing children in public schools rather than concentrating them in separate schools will prevent their membership in the Deaf community. However, Deaf adults need to be involved in children's educational programs. As mentioned previously, the presence of Deaf mentors can have a positive effect on families with children who are deaf or hard of hearing. Once parents have knowledge of and are comfortable with Deaf adults, they may encourage their children to be part of the community. Descriptions of outreach programs by Deaf communities need to be available, and the degree of involvement and membership of children who are deaf or hard of hearing and their parents in the community should be documented.

MODELS OF INCLUSION

Because there are so few preschool-age children who are deaf or hard of hearing, no single school district is likely to have the resources or the professional expertise to serve them adequately, let alone optimally. Cooperative agreements between districts and agencies in some states have produced conditions that lend themselves well to the institution of inclusive programming. Two models that have the potential for success are co-teaching and co-enrollment.

Co-teaching

The co-teaching model can be seen as a variant of traditional itinerant services. In the itinerant model, the child is enrolled in the neighborhood school and served by an itinerant teacher who provides pull-out services several times a week. In the co-teaching model, the itinerant teacher co-teaches the class with the general classroom teacher during the time that she is at the preschool, instead of providing one-to-one service to the child. The co-teaching model can be successful if the itinerant teacher has a small case load and is able to spend substantial time in the classroom. During his or her time there, the itinerant teacher can assist in making the classroom acoustically and visually accessible for the child. She can also model appropriate communication strategies for adults and peers and develop programs to promote social interaction and acceptance. It is unlikely, however, that any visiting teacher can provide the support that is needed for adults and peers in the classroom to learn and use sign language. This model, therefore, is more likely to be successful for children who are hard of hearing and are learning oral language.

A small amount of research on co-teaching has focused on teachers' perceptions of the process. Antia (1998, 1999) studied two children who were deaf and one child who was hard of hearing and enrolled in grades K–2. The children were in the general classroom and received additional services from a teacher of children who are deaf or hard of hearing. The teachers reported that the children who were deaf or hard of hearing performed academically within the range of hearing children in the classroom and that they had positive interactions with hearing peers, both in the classroom and on the playground. As mentioned previously, some classroom teachers learned sufficient sign to interact with the children who were deaf. However, as the teachers of children who are deaf or hard of hearing were in the classrooms for only a short period of time, classroom teachers mentioned that the person whom they most depended on was the interpreter/aide. The major difficulties reported by the teachers centered around the special educators' caseload and their visitor status in the classroom, the teachers' different perceptions about classroom adaptations, and the need for pull-out services. The special educators found it difficult to adapt materials and instructions for the many different grade levels, teachers, and children on their caseload. One classroom teacher expressed concern that because the special educator visited the classroom for short periods of time, she had an incomplete picture of classroom instruction and, con-sequently, made adaptations and suggestions that were inappropriate. The special educators thought that pull-out time was necessary for the children because they needed concentrated work in several areas, particularly literacy. The classroom teachers, in contrast, thought that it was disruptive to have children go in and out of the classroom.

Co-enrollment (or Cluster Model)

In the co-enrollment model, several children who are deaf or hard of hearing along with hearing peers are team taught by the general classroom teacher and a teacher who specializes in education of children who are deaf or hard of hearing (see Chapter 1). Ideally, the teachers share decision making about instruction, and each teacher takes responsibility for instruction of all of the children both hearing and deaf or hard of hearing (Luckner, 1999). The co-enrolled classroom has several advantages over the co-taught classroom: The deaf or hard of hearing children have both deaf or hard of hearing and hearing peers available for social interaction, the constant presence of a teacher of children who are deaf or hard of hearing allows for consistent attention to the children's need for communication access, the presence of signing adults and peers in the classroom can be a major incentive to the hearing children and the general classroom teacher to learn to sign, and the teacher of children who are deaf or hard of hearing can provide access to Deaf adults and the Deaf community. The co-enrollment model has the potential to solve some of the difficulties that are inherent in the co-teaching model, as the special education teacher is a full-time member of the team, and not a visitor. He or she does not have to deal with caseloads, with making adaptations for different teachers, or with difficulties caused by visitor status. The special educator can provide intensive instruction integrated into the curriculum rather than through pull-out services. Positive results have been reported from several investigations of co-enrolled classrooms. A group of case studies (Jimenez & Antia, 1999; Luckner, 1999; Winter & Van Reusen, 1997) provided information on perceptions of individuals who were involved in co-enrollment classrooms, whereas another group of studies (Kluwin, 1997; Kluwin & Gonsher, 1994; Kreimeyer et al., 2000) reported preliminary outcome data for children in co-enrolled classrooms.

Winter and Van Reusen (1997) examined a team-taught, co-enrolled kindergarten that included three teachers (two kindergarten teachers and one special educator), an ASL interpreter, 40 children who were hearing, and 7 children who were deaf or hard of hearing. The hearing children received instruction in sign language, and all communication was conducted in sign and speech simultaneously. The authors found that the kindergarten teachers were able to make visual adaptations for the children who were deaf or hard of hearing, to modify instruction by providing multiple examples and simplified vocabulary, and to use physical cues to get children's attention.

Jimenez and Antia (1999) and Luckner (1999) also reported on co-enrollment programs in elementary and middle school classrooms. Luckner interviewed teachers, parents, children, and administrators who were involved in two multigrade co-enrolled classrooms (grades 1–2 and grades 2–4) and observed extensively in these classrooms for a period of 1 year. Jimenez and Antia interviewed five teachers who had teamed in co-enrolled elementary or middle school classrooms for several years. These researchers reported remarkably similar results. All of the teachers, in both studies, reported favorable opinions of co-enrollment. They stated that the students, deaf or hard of hearing and

hearing, were exposed to age-appropriate curriculum and were held to a similar standard of performance and responsibility. Both teachers on each team were equally responsible for instructional planning and curriculum delivery for all children. By observation and report, it was noted that teachers and hearing peers learned to sign, some fluently. Luckner also reported that true friendships developed across children of different hearing status. Jimenez and Antia found that although the special education teachers took more responsibility for the IEPs, both team teachers jointly developed the goals and attended IEP meetings. In both studies, teachers reported that a high level of commitment was needed from them and their administrators to make the model work and that finding sufficient time to plan was a major difficulty.

There are also a few reports on the social and academic outcomes of co-enrollment for school-age students who are deaf or hard of hearing (Kluwin, 1997; Kluwin & Gonsher, 1994; Kreimeyer et al., 2000). Kluwin found no differences between children who were hearing or deaf or hard of hearing in self-concept, popularity, or happiness in a co-enrollment program for students in grades 4–8. Kreimeyer and colleagues reported on the social and academic outcomes of a co-enrolled multigrade classroom that included children in grades 2–4. In the social realm, they found that during the course of the school year, children who were deaf or hard of hearing and hearing increased their frequency of interaction with each other in the classroom and in the cafeteria. Looking at academic outcomes, they found that students who were deaf or hard of hearing in the co-enrolled classroom scored above the national norms for students with similar hearing status in the area of reading comprehension. The Kluwin and Gonsher (1994) study, reported previously in this chapter, is the only study to report outcome data for young children in a co-enrolled environment. These authors reported positive results for friendship, social acceptance, and hearing children's sign language learning.

Although the co-enrollment model seems to be the most promising to promote inclusion, there is comparatively little research on the effectiveness of any of these models for preschool-age children. Although the data from school-age children and classrooms are of interest, the needs of preschool-age children and the structure of preschool classrooms are distinct and deserving of separate study. There is a need for research in preschool classrooms that systematically describes both process and outcomes for each model. Perceptions of parents and administrators regarding the effectiveness of these models may then need to be explored. Cost is often seen as a barrier when setting up co-teaching or co-enrollment models; therefore, research on comparative costs and benefits may need to be completed. This research should be combined with the data on outcomes and evaluated with a view toward balancing what is appropriate for each child with what is reasonable for each agency.

Given the effort and time needed to be expended by teachers, it will be crucial to determine whether these models can continue to operate after the first few years and the kind of parental and administrative support that they need to become permanent. Because many co-enrollment classrooms seem to be informally developed by teams of teachers, they may not be institutionalized or receive any institutional support.

AGENDA FOR CHANGE

Young children who are deaf or hard of hearing face challenges that affect interactions with family members, communication and programming choices, and delivery of specialized services. This chapter has addressed some of the major barriers that a hearing loss of any degree poses to enrollment in inclusive preschool environments. There are several practices that may help overcome these barriers in the areas of low incidence; language and communication; social integration; and the attitudes of parents, professionals, and the Deaf community.

Low Incidence

Just under 6,000 preschool-age children in the United States are deaf or hard of hearing (45 states reporting data), making it unlikely that most preschool programs will be faced with the task of making accommodations for a child with a hearing loss. It is difficult and costly to provide a quality, inclusive preschool experience that also meets the unique communication and social needs of children who are deaf or hard of hearing. School districts in rural areas are particularly challenged to provide access to other deaf children and adults and to professionals who are knowledgeable about deafness and competent in sign language. School administrators must determine how to balance costly services with the legal and ethical responsibility of providing quality programming. Parents must also make decisions concerning preferred communication mode and whether to relocate to a place where a variety of program options and services are available.

The problem of low incidence can be alleviated by cooperative agreements between school districts and agencies for pooling personnel resources to offer services that would not be feasible for a single district. In some states, cooperative agreements have already been developed between the state school for the deaf and individual districts. In such a model, the state school for the deaf contracts with districts to provide educational and related services to children within the districts; employs the teachers, audiologists, interpreters, and other staff; offers consultations to the school staff; monitors quality of services; and provides needed in-service training. Such cooperative agreements can provide several benefits:

1. *Ensure enrollment and personnel for establishing inclusive programming:* When children can be grouped across school districts, it is more likely that there will be the staff and numbers of children within a reasonable geographic area to develop good co-teaching and co-enrollment programs in a few preschool environments.

2. *Provide appropriate professional resources:* State schools for the deaf have the resources to assemble a skilled team of professional staff and administrators, which is often an impossible task for individual school districts. By centralizing the hiring, statewide programs can provide services to districts that cannot locate even one appropriately trained professional within the community.

3. *Alleviate professional isolation:* Teachers who are employed under cooperative agreements have the opportunity for professional exchange and support. Many teachers hesitate to work for districts or reside in communities in which they are the sole professional responsible for providing all services necessary for children who are deaf or hard of hearing.

For cooperative agreements between districts and state schools for the deaf to be successful, it is imperative that the professional staff who are hired to provide services to districts be committed to developing inclusion programs that are well constructed and carried out. Merely transferring staff from self-contained programs at schools for the deaf may be inappropriate, as historically, staff at state

schools for the deaf are familiar with (and often prefer) the segregated school model. It is necessary to provide a philosophical orientation to inclusion and some practical experience in inclusive environments to staff who have worked only in self-contained environments.

Communication and Language

This chapter has stressed that the communication and language barrier is the overriding issue for children who are deaf or hard of hearing. For most children with special educational needs, the social and communication benefits provided by inclusive programming seem clear. This is not the case for children without access to the spoken language of the classroom. Given what is known about the importance of frequent and enriched language experiences during critical periods of acquisition, it is unlikely that children who are deaf or hard of hearing will acquire adequate communication and language skills in an inclusive classroom unless intensive efforts are made to ensure access.

Another important point to consider is that the needs of children who are deaf are different from those of children who are hard of hearing. Professionals speak in general terms about those with hearing loss, when in reality individuals with differing levels of hearing have different needs regarding access to spoken and/or signed language. Children who are deaf face greater challenges for language acquisition than do those who are hard of hearing. Although children who are hard of hearing may benefit greatly from amplification, preferential seating, and other accommodations, they need access to the Deaf community and signing because, like children who are deaf, they grow up to be part of this community.

Co-enrollment, or cluster programs, is a promising model to solve issues of communication access. Initial reports of these programs suggest that the presence of several signing children and adults promotes the learning of sign language, allowing children who are deaf to have access to communication and to interact with peers and teachers without relying only on interpreters. These programs cannot succeed without administrative support, however. When a program is served by a preschool teacher who is just learning to sign and is also being supported by a teacher of the deaf, a great deal of time is required for planning and implementing accommodations. Administrators need to be aware of these needs and schedule time for this into the teachers' day. To be successful, any inclusive co-teaching program will take more resources than a self-contained program. Teachers of children who are deaf or hard of hearing who co-teach with several teachers in different preschools will need small case loads, necessitating the hiring of more teachers. Hearing teachers who are expected to learn sign language will need compensatory time or a reward system to motivate and support this training.

Parents who are deaf and other individuals in the Deaf community should be viewed as valuable resources in the formulation and implementation of inclusive programs. Young children who are deaf or hard of hearing need role models and access to competent signers. The children also need models of deaf and hearing adults working together and communicating successfully. It is the authors' opinion that all children who are deaf or hard of hearing, regardless of their preferred mode of communication, need access to the Deaf community because they will eventually be a part of this community. Inclusive programs should make extraordinary efforts to employ teachers and paraprofessionals who are deaf or hard of hearing and to reach out to their local Deaf communities

and interest them in assisting with facilitation of an inclusive program.

Social Integration

The term *social integration* may have different meanings for each professional, but it usually implies a social connectedness between and among participating children (Guralnick, 1999). Guralnick suggested that it is essential for each program to formulate expectations for realistic, successful social outcomes for that particular program and group of children. Research in promoting social integration between deaf or hard of hearing and hearing children has provided a picture that is hopeful concerning successful outcomes and the circumstances under which good social integration can occur. These include co-enrollment models, facilitation of interpersonal interactions by staff members, and sign language learning by peers. Although the majority of young children who are deaf or hard of hearing already attend public schools, most programs within those facilities are separate from those of hearing children and are based on the older mainstreamed "visitor" model. Given the right support, inclusive programs are superior to visitor programs for fostering social integration that results in positive social connections.

Within inclusive programs, special attention should be paid to promoting positive peer interaction. Many peer interaction intervention programs seem to have reasonably positive results, including those that teach children entry to social groups, social play skills, or specific social skills.

Attitudes of Parents, Professionals, and the Deaf Community

Professionals and advocates for the deaf often want children exposed to early socialization within the Deaf culture and argue that language and communication needs cannot be adequately met by untrained personnel and can only be addressed within a self-contained model of service delivery. Advocates for self-contained programming believe that environments that are labeled as *inclusive* are actually *exclusive*; that LRE depends on access to adults and peers who can communicate in the same language mode. But the fact remains that the majority of children who are deaf or hard of hearing attend public school programs and are being socialized within the dual framework of hearing and Deaf cultures. It is also the case that there simply is not enough information to know what outcomes are produced when children who are deaf or hard of hearing are educated in inclusive programs and provided with needed supports to progress socially, linguistically, and academically. It is clear that inclusion programs that are *presumed* to fail will fail. Those who are committed to providing quality inclusive preschool opportunities must address parents', professionals', and communities' attitudes toward inclusion.

Parents need to be informed and educated about *all* of their choices as early as possible. Professionals who work in homes with newborns, infants, and toddlers, regardless of their disciplinary background (e.g., special education, speech-language pathology, audiology), should be well educated about all of the available options and should be able to present these to parents in a relatively unbiased manner. Home-based teachers, early interventionists, therapists, and other service providers, as well as those who are preparing to be preschool teachers of children who are deaf or hard of hearing, should be given opportunities to participate in successful co-enrollment and co-teaching programs as well as in self-contained programs to gain a clear understanding of these models. When they do so, they will be better able to

explain the available service options to parents.

Professionals are likely to retain their current attitudes unless there is a major educational effort made to 1) create an awareness of the components of good inclusion programs, 2) demonstrate the advantages that these programs provide for the acquisition of social relationships within and outside the Deaf community, and 3) provide opportunities to develop skills to implement developmentally appropriate practices within inclusive environments. Preservice teachers also need to learn about good inclusive practices for young children and understand that this age group is unique in its need for learning within social, communication, and play contexts. They must become aware that many practices that prevail in elementary school environments cannot be transferred to preschool environments. Programs that prepare teachers of the deaf and hard of hearing also need to emphasize the development of collaboration skills. Students who are preparing to teach young children who are deaf or hard of hearing need to view themselves as working partners of preschool teachers without this specialized training. They should have ample experiences in general preschool programs to foster understanding of collaboration and how to help community teachers make reasonable accommodations for a child who is deaf or hard of hearing.

The negative attitudes of individuals in the Deaf community toward inclusion may change as programs begin to proliferate, research begins to demonstrate positive social outcomes, and it becomes clear that educational inclusion in the hearing community does not necessitate exclusion from the Deaf community and Deaf culture. The involvement of deaf adults and the appreciation and understanding of sign language and Deaf culture in inclusion programs will ensure that children can be included in both the hearing and the Deaf communities. At the same time, the Deaf community should be encouraged to welcome families of children who are deaf or hard of hearing whether they choose to educate them in inclusive or segregated programs.

CONCLUSION

There is a great need for a well-conducted research agenda concerning the outcomes of promising models, particularly co-teaching and co-enrollment. The arguments concerning the value of inclusive programs at the preschool level will continue to rage until there are more empirical studies to provide solid evidence to support the cost, time, and energies needed to devise such programs. A strong, carefully planned research agenda is needed to examine the many facets of inclusive programming. Those who are convinced of the ultimate value of inclusive programming have a high stake in ensuring that these programs continue and that careful, unbiased investigation of their outcomes is conducted.

Instituting inclusive programs is an expensive and complex task and may not be the right choice for every child, given the developmental challenges presented by hearing loss. The decision may rest on the child's needs, the desires of the family, and the ethical question concerning the balance of these with the expense of tailoring an environment to provide needed access to language and communication. Once quality access *is* provided, the other problems may solve themselves. The authors believe that there are apparent social, emotional, communication, and cognitive benefits derived from educating deaf or hard or hearing and hearing children together in one classroom. These benefits pose a powerful argument for making the effort to formulate pro-

grams, one by one, to make a difference for many young children who are deaf or hard of hearing, despite all of the barriers. The nature of childhood hearing loss presents a formidable challenge to inclusion, and although the barriers may seem insurmountable, they are not impossible to overcome.

REFERENCES

Afzali-Nomani, E. (1995). Educational conditions related to successful full inclusion programs involving deaf/hard of hearing children. *American Annals of the Deaf, 140,* 396–401.

Aldridge, M., Timmins, K., & Wood, J. (1995). Professional attitudes toward provision of hearing-impaired children. *Journal of the British Association of Teachers of the Deaf, 19*(5), 120–134.

Alexander, L. (1992). *Deaf students' education services: Policy guidance* (FR doc. 92026319). Washington, DC: U.S. Department of Education, Office for Civil Rights.

Antia, S.D. (1985). Social integration of hearing-impaired children: Fact or fiction. *The Volta Review, 87,* 279–289.

Antia, S.D. (1998). School and classroom characteristics that facilitate the social integration of deaf and hard of hearing children. In A. Weisel (Ed.), *Issues unresolved: New perspectives on language and deaf education* (pp. 148–160). Washington, DC: Gallaudet University Press.

Antia, S.D. (1999). The roles of special educators and classroom teachers in an inclusive school. *Journal of Deaf Studies and Deaf Education, 4*(3), 203–214.

Antia, S.D., & Ditillo, D.A. (1998). A comparison of the peer social behavior of children who are deaf/hard of hearing and hearing. *Journal of Children's Communication Development, 19,* 1–10.

Antia, S.D., & Kreimeyer, K. (1996). Social interaction and acceptance of deaf/hard of hearing children and their peers: A comparison of social skills and familiarity-based intervention. *The Volta Review, 98,* 157–180.

Antia, S.D., Kreimeyer, K., & Eldredge, N. (1994). Promoting social interaction between young children with hearing impairments and their peers. *Exceptional Children, 60,* 262–275.

Antia, S.D., Kreimeyer, K.H., & Williams, L. (1998, April). *The role of the interpreter in inclusive classrooms.* Paper presented to the American Education and Research Association, San Diego.

Brown, A.S., & Yoshinaga-Itano, C. (1994). F.A.M.I.L.Y. Assessment: A multidisciplinary evaluation tool. In J. Roush & N. Matkin (Eds.), *Infants and toddlers with hearing loss* (pp. 133–162). Timonium, MD: York Press.

Brown, M.P., Prescott, S.J., Rickards, F.W., & Paterson, M.M. (1994). Communicating about pretend play: A comparison of the utterances of 4-year-old normally hearing and deaf or hard of hearing children in an integrated kindergarten. *The Volta Review, 96,* 5–17.

Bunch, G. (1994). An interpretation of full inclusion. *American Annals of the Deaf, 139,* 150–152.

Cappelli, M., Daniels, T., Durieux-Smith, A., McGrath, P.J., & Neuss, D. (1995). Social development of children with hearing impairments who are integrated into general education classrooms. *The Volta Review, 97,* 197–208.

Chorost, S. (1988). The hearing-impaired child in the mainstream: A survey of the attitudes of regular classroom teachers. *The Volta Review, 90,* 7–12.

Clark, T., & Watkins, S. (1985). *The SKI*HI Model—Programming for hearing-impaired infants through home intervention: Home visit curriculum* (4th ed.). Logan, UT: HOPE.

Cohen, O. (1994, April). "Inclusion" should not include deaf students [4 pages]. *Education Week* [On-line serial]. Available: http://www.edweek. org/ew/1994/30cohen.h13.

Commission on Education of the Deaf. (1988). *Toward equality: Education of the deaf.* Washington, DC: U.S. Government Printing Office.

Corsaro, W.A. (1985). *Friendship and peer culture in the early years.* Stamford, CT: Ablex Publishing Corp.

Corson, H.J., & Stuckless, E.R. (1994). Special programs, full inclusion and choices for students who are deaf. *American Annals of the Deaf, 139,* 148–149.

Craig, H.B. (1992). Parent–infant education in schools for deaf children before and after PL 99-457. *American Annals of the Deaf, 137,* 69–78.

DeConde-Johnson, C. (1998). *Amplification in inclusive classrooms.* Unpublished manuscript.

Education of the Handicapped Act Amendments of 1986, PL 99-457, 20 U.S.C. §§ 1400 *et seq.*

Elfenbein, J., Bentler, R., Davis, J., & Niebuhr, D. (1988). Status of school children's hearing aids relative to monitoring practices. *Ear and Hearing, 9,* 212–215.

Esposito, B.G., & Koorland, M.A. (1989). Play behavior of hearing-impaired children: Integrated and segregated settings. *Exceptional Children, 55,* 412–419.

Finitzo-Heiber, T., & Tillman, T. (1978). Room acoustics effects on monosyllabic word discrimination ability for normal and hearing-impaired children. *Journal of Speech and Hearing Research, 21,* 440–458.

Gallagher, P.A. (1997). Teachers and inclusion: Perspectives on changing roles. *Topics in Early Childhood Special Education, 17*(3), 363–386.

Greenberg, M.T., & Kusche, C.A. (1993). *Promoting social and emotional development in deaf children: The Paths Project.* Seattle: University of Washington Press.

Guralnick, M.J. (1994). Mothers' perceptions of the benefits and drawbacks of early childhood mainstreaming. *Journal of Early Intervention, 18,* 168–183.

Guralnick, M.J. (1999). The nature and meaning of social integration for young children with mild developmental delays in inclusive settings. *Journal of Early Intervention, 22,* 70–86.

Harrison, M., Dannhardt, M., & Roush, J. (1996). Families' perceptions of early intervention services for children with hearing loss. *Language, Speech and Hearing Services in Schools, 27,* 203–214.

Hart, B., & Risley, T.R. (1995). *Meaningful differences in the everyday experience of young American children.* Baltimore: Paul H. Brookes Publishing Co.

Holden-Pitt, L., & Diaz, A. (1998). Thirty years of the Annual Survey of Deaf and Hard of Hearing Children and Youth. A glance over the decades. *American Annals of the Deaf, 142,* 72–76.

Hulsing, M.M., Luetke-Stahlman, B., Loeb, D.F., Nelson, P., & Wegner, J. (1995). Analysis of successful initiations of three children with hearing loss mainstreamed in kindergarten classrooms. *Language, Speech and Hearing Services in Schools, 26,* 45–52.

Humphrey, J.H., & Alcorn, B.J. (1994). *So you want to be an interpreter? An introduction to sign language interpreting.* Amarillo, TX: H&H Publishers.

Individuals with Disabilities Education Act Amendments of 1997, PL 105-17, 20 U.S.C. §§ 1400 *et seq.*

Jensema, C.J. (1977). *Parental income: Its relation to other characteristics of hearing-impaired students.* Washington, DC: Gallaudet College, Office of Demographic Studies.

Jimenez, C., & Antia, S.D. (1999). Team teaching in an integrated classroom: Perceptions of deaf and hearing teachers. *Journal of Deaf Studies and Deaf Education, 4,* 215–224.

Kluwin, T.N. (1997, February). *Co-teaching deaf and hearing students: Research on social integration.* Paper presented at the annual meeting of The Association of College Educators–Deaf and Hard of Hearing, Lexington, KY.

Kluwin, T.N., & Gonsher, W. (1994). A single school study of social integration of children with and without hearing losses in a team taught kindergarten. *ACEHI/ACEDA, 20,* 71–86.

Kreimeyer, K.H., Crooke, P., Drye, C., Egbert, V., & Klein, B. (2000). Academic and social benefits of a co-enrollment model of inclusive education for deaf and hard of hearing children. *Journal of Deaf Studies and Deaf Education, 5,* 174–186.

Lampropoulou, V., & Padeliadu, S. (1997). Teachers of the deaf as compared with other groups of teachers: Attitudes toward people with disabilities and inclusion. *American Annals of the Deaf, 142,* 26–33.

Lederberg, A., Ryan, H.B., & Robbins, B. (1986). Peer interaction in young deaf children: The effect of partner hearing status and familiarity. *Developmental Psychology, 22,* 691–700.

Levine, L.M., & Antia, S.D. (1997). The effect of partner hearing status on social and cognitive play. *Journal of Early Intervention, 21,* 21–35.

Luckner, J. (1999). An examination of two co-teaching classrooms. *American Annals of the Deaf, 144,* 24–34.

Luterman, D.M. (1999). *The young deaf child.* Timonium, MD: York Press.

Marchant, C. (1995). Teachers' views of integrated preschools. *Journal of Early Intervention, 19,* 61–73.

Marschark, M. (1993). *Psychological development of deaf children.* New York: Oxford University Press.

Marschark, M. (1997). *Raising and educating a deaf child: A comprehensive guide to the choices, controversies, and decisions faced by parents and educators.* New York: Oxford University Press.

Mather, S. (1989). Visually oriented teaching strategies with deaf preschool children. In C. Lucas (Ed.), *The sociolinguistics of the Deaf community* (pp. 165–190). New York: Harcourt.

McCartney, B.D. (1994). Inclusion as a practical matter. *American Annals of the Deaf, 139,* 161–162.

Meadow, K.P., Greenberg, E.T., Erting, C., & Carmichael, H. (1981). Interactions of deaf mothers and deaf preschool children: Comparisons with three other groups of deaf and hearing dyads. *American Annals of the Deaf, 126,* 454–468.

Meadow-Orlans, K.P. (1990). The impact of childhood hearing loss on the family. In D.F. Moores & K.P. Meadow-Orlans (Eds.), *Educational and developmental aspects of deafness* (pp. 321–338). Washington, DC: Gallaudet University Press.

Meadow-Orlans, K.P., Mertens, D.M., Sass-Lehrer, M., & Scott-Olson, K. (1997). Support services for parents and their children who are deaf or hard of hearing. *American Annals of the Deaf, 142,* 278–293.

Meadow-Orlans, K.P., & Sass-Lehrer, M. (1995). Support services for families with children who are deaf: Challenges for professionals. *Topics in Early Childhood Special Education, 15,* 314–334.

Meadow-Orlans, K.P., Sass-Lehrer, M., & Mertens, D.M. (1998). Children who are hard of hearing: Are they forgotten? *Perspectives, 16,* 6–24.

Messenheimer-Young, T., & Kretschmer, R.R. (1994). "Can I play?" A hearing-impaired preschooler's requests to access maintained social interaction. *The Volta Review, 96,* 5–18.

Minnett, A., Clark, K., & Wilson, G. (1994). Play behavior and communication between deaf and hard of hearing children and their hearing peers in an integrated preschool. *American Annals of the Deaf, 139*(4), 420–429.

Moores, D.K. (1993). Total inclusion/zero reject models in general education: Implications for deaf children. *American Annals of the Deaf, 138,* 251.

Moores, D.K. (1995). Inclusion and segregation: Separate and unequal. *American Annals of the Deaf, 140,* 309.

Moores, D.K. (1996). Belief and knowledge. *American Annals of the Deaf, 141,* 331.

Polowe-Aldersley, S. (1994). Human resources and full inclusion in the education of students who are deaf. *American Annals of the Deaf, 139,* 162–163.

Potts, P., & Greenwood, J. (1983). Hearing aid monitoring: Are looking and listening enough? *Language, Speech and Hearing Services in Schools, 14,* 157–163.

Ries, P.W. (1994). Prevalence and characteristics of persons with hearing trouble: United States, 1990–91. *National Center for Health Statistics, Vital Health Statistics Series No. 10*(188).

Ross, M. (1990). *Hearing-impaired children in the mainstream.* Timonium, MD: York Press.

Ross, M., Brackett, D., & Maxon, A. (1991). *Assessment and management of mainstreamed hearing-impaired children.* Austin, TX: PRO-ED.

Sass-Lehrer, M. (1998, December). *Components of appropriate and inappropriate practices for inclusion of deaf and hard of hearing youngsters.* Material distributed at the International DEC Conference, Chicago, IL.

Seal, B.C. (1998). *Best practices in educational interpreting.* Needham Heights, MA: Allyn & Bacon.

Shaw, J., & Jamieson, J. (1997). Patterns of classroom discourse in an integrated, interpreted elementary school setting. *American Annals of the Deaf, 142,* 40–47.

Siegel, P. (1995). What they didn't know may have helped us: How the Supreme Court misinterpreted the role of sign language interpreters. *American Annals of the Deaf, 140,* 386–395.

Spencer, P., Koester, L.S., & Meadow-Orlans, K.P. (1994). Communicative interactions of deaf and hearing children in a day care center. An exploratory study. *American Annals of the Deaf,* *139,* 512–518.

Spencer, P.E., & Lederberg, A.R. (1997). Different modes, different models: Communication and language of young deaf children and their mothers. In L.B. Adamson & M.A. Romski (Eds.), *Communication and language acquisition: Discoveries from atypical development* (pp. 203–230). Baltimore: Paul H. Brookes Publishing Co.

Stewart, D.A., & Kluwin, T.N. (1996). The gap between guidelines, practice, and knowledge in interpreting services for deaf students. *Journal of Deaf Studies and Deaf Education, 1,* 29–39.

Stinson, M.S., & Antia, S.D. (1999). Considerations in education of deaf and hard of hearing students in inclusive settings. *Journal of Deaf Studies and Deaf Education, 4,* 163–175.

Stinson, M., & Lang, H.G. (1994). Full inclusion: A path for integration or isolation? *American Annals of the Deaf, 139,* 156–157.

U.S. Department of Education, Office of Special Education and Rehabilitative Services. (1998). *Twentieth annual report to Congress on the implementation of the Individuals with Disabilities Education Act, Section 618.* Washington, DC: Author.

Vandell, D., & George, L. (1981). Social interaction in hearing and deaf preschoolers: Successes and failures in initiations. *Child Development, 52,* 627–635.

Vernon, M. (1988). Mainstreaming and the deaf community. *American Annals of the Deaf, 133,* 313.

Watkins, S., Pittman, P., & Walden, B. (1998). The deaf mentor experimental project for young children who are deaf and their families. *American Annals of the Deaf, 143,* 29–34.

Winter, S.M., & Van Reusen, A.K. (1997). Inclusion and kindergartners who are deaf or hard of hearing: Comparing teaching strategies with recommended guidelines. *Journal of Research in Early Childhood Education, 11,* 114–134.

Yoshinaga-Itano, C., Sedey, A.L., Coulter, D.K., & Mehl, A.L. (1998). Language of early and late identified children with hearing loss. *Pediatrics, 102,* 1161–1172.

Zink, C. (1972). Hearing aids children wear: A longitudinal study of performance. *The Volta Review, 74,* 41–51.

17

ALLEN C. CROCKER

STEPHANIE M. PORTER

Inclusion of Young Children with Complex Health Care Needs

Young children with complex and/or serious health care needs have many challenges. These young children typically have important expression of disability syndromes, complications or obligations of various therapies, or onerous acquired chronic illnesses. Good, modern data exist for one group of children with complex health care needs—those with ongoing conditions who are assisted by medical technology. Included here are boys and girls with special equipment or supports. Community care needs for these children received increasing attention in the early to mid-1980s, much expedited by the Surgeon General's Workshop in 1982 ("Report of the Surgeon General's Workshop," 1982). The urgency was enhanced by the success of intensive care nursery programs for preterm babies, improved capacity for surgical intervention in the care of children with complicated congenital anomalies, and the growing energy of child development programs and concerns for children's rights. The majority of this chapter is devoted to the personal and educational experiences in the community of the children who are assisted by medical technology.

A total state census of children who were dependent on 1 or more of 12 specific supports (Palfrey et al., 1991; Palfrey et al., 1994) was undertaken in Massachusetts in 1987 and again in 1990. The supports, listed in Table 17.1, involve assistance to the airway, oxygen administration, use of a portable ventilator, gastrointestinal tube feedings, urostomy or colostomy care, clean intermittent catheterization, intravenous medications or feedings (with pumps), and renal dialysis. The results of the census were gleaned from reports from hospitals, nursing homes, visiting nurse associations, public and private schools, special education collaboratives, state schools, and early intervention programs regarding the special child supports in use in a given reference month.

Much was learned about who these children are. Noting the range for prevalence within the group for the 2 years surveyed, 42%–46% of all ages had syn-

This project was supported in part by Health Resources and Services Administration, the U.S. Department of Health and Human Services, Grant No. MCJ-259150 from the Maternal and Child Health Bureau, and Grant No. 90DD0357 from the Administration for Children and Families.

Table 17.1. Census results for Massachusetts children with medical technology assistance, 1990s

Technology	Adjusted estimate
Overall	2237
Tracheostomy	219
Suctioning	434
Respirator	70
Oxygen	405
Nasogastric tube	121
Gastrostomy tube	972
Ileo-colostomy	118
Jejunostomy tube	67
Urostomy	42
Catheterization	526
Intravenous line	299
Dialysis	48

From Palfrey, J.S., Haynie, M., Porter, S., Fenton, T., Cooperman-Vincent, P., Shaw, D., Johnson, B., Bierle, T., & Walker, D.K. (1994). Prevalence of medical technology assistance among children in Massachusetts in 1987 and 1990. *Public Health Reports, 109*, 228.

dromes of congenital anomalies (e.g., cerebral dysgenesis, neural tube defects, gastrointestinal malformations); 35%–41% actually had acquired conditions (e.g., malignancies, immunodeficiency, renal failure, and heart disease, plus some with cerebral palsy and seizure disorders). Approximately 10%–12% had difficulties from preterm birth, most with bronchopulmonary dysplasia. Smaller numbers had hereditary or genetic conditions (e.g., trisomy 18, muscular dystrophy, mucopolysaccharidosis [7%–8%]) or injuries (e.g., head, spinal cord, drowning, burns [4%–7%]). Of the children identified in 1990, 41% were in the first 5 years of life.

Overall, the developmental level of the children had a bimodal distribution; a little more than half had normal intelligence, and 25% were in the range of severe or profound mental retardation. The developmental status showed much variation for those with congenital anomalies, was near normal in those with urethral catheterization (principally children with myelomeningocele), and

mostly significantly limited in those who had major injury. Levels were not available for many of the younger children.

The results of the Massachusetts survey yielded a prevalence figure of 0.16% for children assisted by medical technology. This finding, roughly 1–2 per 1,000 children, is a little higher than expected. Developmental disabilities are generally regarded to be at approximately 20 per 1,000, significant congenital anomalies present in the newborn infant at approximately 20 per 1,000 (Hudgins & Cassidy, 1999), very low birth weight (VLBW) infants (birth weight below 1,500 grams) at 12 per 1,000 (Crocker, 1992), and important inborn errors of metabolism identified in early life at approximately 0.4 per 1,000 (Applegarth, Toone, & Lowry, 2000). Comparable chronic illness figures are not available.

THE PERSONAL AND FAMILY IMPACT OF SERIOUS DISABILITY OR CHRONIC ILLNESS

Children who have complex health care needs are assuredly in a personal circumstance of "specialness" or "differentness." There are consequences to that state, with multiple impacts (see Crocker, 1997, 1998; Murphy & Crocker, 1987), including effects on phenotype, function, and vitality. The requirements for parental accommodation are often very compelling. A familiar list of seven limitations in life activity is included in the definition of *developmental disabilities* (first given in the Rehabilitation, Comprehensive Services and Developmental Disabilities Amendments of 1978, PL 95-602; see Crocker, 1989), including those in self-care, language, learning, and mobility. For children who depend on medical technology, an eighth item must be added: *loss of autonomy per the necessity to continue with specific therapeutic support.*

This group of children often has many other health and functional concerns. Some of these constitute *comorbidity:* conditions other than the primary health concern that arise from the same target organ, such as seizures or cerebral palsy accompanying mental retardation. In other regards, the further problems are add-ons from the full expression of the disorder and its complications or contingencies. As a result, many children with complex health care needs also have major movement difficulties, behavioral aberrations, threats to survival, and a family pressed by special challenges. Children with these multiple concerns present in all age groups (Nelson & Crocker, 1999).

There are diverse indications for assistance by medical technology. The same support mode may be applicable to the care needs of very different children. The chief backgrounds for these interventions are listed next (Porter, Haynie, Bierle, Caldwell, & Palfrey, 1997). *Gastrostomy (and nasogastric) tube feedings* are given when there is an obstruction in the esophagus, swallowing is impaired, or maintaining nutritional requirements is difficult. *Jejunostomy tubes* are used for blockage of the esophagus or stomach, serious risk for reflux and aspiration, nutritional failure, or short bowel syndrome. An in-dwelling *central venous catheter* is designed to allow long-term delivery of intravenous food or medication (e.g., antibiotics, chemotherapy). *Peritoneal dialysis or hemodialysis* serves to remedy effects of chronic renal failure (actual dialysis may or may not take place in the school environment, but the tubing is in place). *Clean intermittent catheterization* is used for children with reduced nerve function to the bladder, generally from myelodysplasia or spinal cord injuries. A *colostomy* allows emptying of the bowel when there is obstruction, inflammation, injury, or abnormal motility; an *ileosotomy* is used when the colon has been removed or is unable to function. *Urostomies* may be used when the bladder has been removed or bypassed.

Various kinds of assistance are available for respiratory concerns. *Supplemental oxygen,* given by mask, nasal cannula, or tracheostomy collar, helps children with oxygen deficiency, such as those with bronchopulmonary dysplasia, cystic fibrosis, or serious heart disease. A *tracheostomy* allows passage of air or oxygen when the upper airway is blocked, secretions must be cleared, or breathing needs help in neurological or muscular disorders. A *manual resuscitation bag* is used for temporary assistance in breathing. *Nose and mouth suctioning* can help relieve obstructing secretions. Medication for the airway and lungs can be delivered by *nebulizer treatments. Mechanical ventilators* provide lifesaving aid in breathing for children with muscle weakness, neurological injury, or severe pulmonary disease.

Transporting and preventing infections are two other special needs that children with complex health care needs have that bear on the educational and child care environment. The laws and regulations regarding child transportation are particularly strategic here, including restraint systems, positioning devices, and accommodation for wheelchair transport: Personnel require additional training (including health care procedures and resuscitation); there are equipment needs; and there often must be a power source, back-up arrangements, and perhaps even oxygen. Precautions regarding promulgation of localized infections (e.g., at catheter sites) or more general ones (e.g., pneumonia) are of high importance.

THE CONCEPT OF BARRIERS IN EDUCATIONAL INCLUSION

Inasmuch as the world of children with complex health care needs has many remarkable features, it is appropriate to give regard to the conceptual base for inclusion of these children in educational efforts. By current provisions, the fact of a child's exceptionality, per se, is assuredly not an issue. The Individuals with Disabilities Education Act (IDEA) of 1990 (PL 101-476) and its amendments (PL 102-119 and PL 105-17) reach to *all* children with disabilities; this is reinforced by Section 504 of the Rehabilitation Act of 1973 (PL 93-112) and the Americans with Disabilities Act (ADA) of 1990 (PL 101-336). Furthermore, the capacity to receive "school health services" establishes that key supports can be planned, as these will assist a child in benefiting from teaching. Certain key legal precedents have given substantial security to these rights: *Timothy W. v. Rochester, NH School District* noted that the "most severely handicapped" children are to be given priority, *Irving Independent School District v. Tatro* affirmed that activities such as catheterization are indeed "related services," and *Tanya v. Cincinnati Board of Education* clarified that "related services can stand alone for those students who need only those services to succeed" (Janz et al., 1997). In 1999, the Supreme Court ruled that complex nursing service (ventilator care) is a related service in *Cedar Rapids Community School District v. Garret F.* (American Academy of Pediatrics, 2000).

Certain potential barriers to best learning could be hypothesized for children with complex health care needs, although it is apparent that these elements are irregular in incidence and relevance, and can be accommodated: possible frequent absences, side effects of medications, pain, fatigue, attention problems, short- or long-term emotional or physical effects of undergoing medical treatments, reduced class time because of therapies, and others (Caldwell et al., 1997). Educational planning must proceed with thorough knowl-edge of the student's health care and learning needs.

Converse to the supposition of barriers, there are numerous promotional elements that will facilitate educational inclusion (Caldwell et al., 1997; Drazin, 1996). In some regards, these constitute a system or movement:

1. *School environment and feelings*
   A gentle and creative atmosphere
   Ramps, elevators, and other access
   Favorable policies and procedures in the local district
   Compassionate interpretation of regulations, availability of resources, and faith in the child's adaptation
   Flexible, immediate home or hospital instruction services based on child's condition
2. *Teachers, administrators, nurses, other staff*
   Good staff interaction with child and with each other
   Guidance leading to peer understanding
   Sufficient nursing resources
   Adequate support personnel
   Access to health care during field trips
   Good support to head teacher
   Meaningful collaboration among school, child care, and Head Start

PARTICIPATION IN BIRTH-TO-THREE, CHILD CARE, HEAD START, PRESCHOOL, AND SCHOOL PROGRAMS

The story of the incorporation of young children with complex and/or serious health care needs into the world of education is one of exploration, learning, and conviction. All of this is considered in the following sections.

Early Intervention for Children from Birth to Three

Because children with complex health care needs, including many who use assistive medical technology, qualify as having an "established disability," it is reasonable to assume that their engagement with early intervention would be prompt and substantial. It is, but commonly with special features of transfer and of concurrent support. Many of the youngest children are referred after an extended stay in the newborn intensive care unit or from critical surgical habilitation for serious congenital anomalies. Developmental support services (particularly physical therapy) may have been begun in the hospital environment, with recommendations formulated for continuing guidance (Vohr, Cashore, & Bigsby, 1999). Frequently some home-based services, by nursing or related professionals, are in place in the early weeks or months. In many regards, these infants with their diverse needs are received into community care. The leadership of the local early intervention program can be crucial. There are also the investments of the primary medical care provider (and perhaps also the managed care facility), the medical specialists (e.g., neurologists, orthopedists, cardiologists, pulmonary specialists, gastroenterologists), respite care, additional rehabilitation resources, health department allies, child welfare or medical financing assistance, housing or social services help, and sometimes involvement of legal or mental health counseling.

Birth-to-3 programs, with the design of the individualized family service plan (IFSP), create a service coordinator and, in the plan, are obliged to have accounting of the family's predominant concerns, priorities, and resources. The service coordinator is a wonderful asset, but in a practical sense, it is difficult to provide regularly for this type of management. It is some measure of an early intervention program's commitment to note the effectiveness of the service coordination. The primary home visitor will take some initiative in guiding the family in obtaining needed services; strictly speaking, the coordination is unreimbursible activity and impinges on program budgeting. Nurses, either from early intervention or from other community agencies, have a strategic role as the family establishes a sustaining environment.

Information from the Massachusetts Department of Public Health (lead agency for Part C) provides heartening data about the current incorporation of children assisted by medical technology into the early intervention system (K. Welford, personal communication, February 2000). In fiscal year 1999, there were 880 such children in various community-based early intervention programs in Massachusetts (where there is a total child enrollment of 18,300), including those with tracheostomies, ventilators, feeding tubes of all sorts, catheterization, and dialysis. It is believed that their referral was actually assisted to some extent by their visible medical and developmental needs. They are full participants in the various components of the program activities.

While the health-related elements of the young child's care are being stabilized, developmental teaching is encouraged. Ahmann and Lipsi (1991) presented a representative prospectus for design of an early intervention program for infants and young children who may require tube feedings, assisted respiration, suction, and other movement-restricting equipment. This is described in relation to care at home, but it would be helpful for other environments as well (e.g., child care). Table 17.2 recounts these principles. The authors wisely urge that the family (and other caregivers) be partners in all aspects of planning and assessment. The discussion of the significant interaction of health support and developmental programming would be assisted by the type of curriculum being promoted in Utah for early intervention staff, in which health principles and health services are taught more extensively than has been usual (Godfrey, Haake, & Saunders, 1998). It is also recommended there that a registered nurse be on the staff of each Part C program.

An interesting specialized program consultation model for a particular group of highly involved children has been created by the Perkins School for the Blind in Watertown, Massachusetts. These are children with very low vision or blindness, and many have multiple disabilities (and needs including medical technology).

Approximately 400 children in Massachusetts from birth to 3 years of age receive biweekly home or community program visits from Perkins staff, using (especially) low vision educators and/or social workers (A. Ross, personal communication, July 1999). This serves as a supplement to local early intervention programs. Parent education and counseling are accomplished in the home or in child care centers. Several dozen children are involved as well in weekly sessions at Perkins School for more intense work in an adapted environment. This also involves activities for sisters and brothers of the children with complex health care needs and teaching for child care centers and community workers. This is a very supportive and effective program with strong family appreciation.

A more broadly based endeavor for instruction and support to programs that

Table 17.2.   Developmental issues to be considered in the home care of an infant or toddler with high technology support

Developmental stage	Developmental issues	Interventions
Infant (birth–1 year)	Sensory experience	Encourage tactile and verbal interactions
		Provide visual and auditory stimulation as tolerated
	Motor experience	Vary positioning to encourage freedom of movement
	Development of trust	Support parents in efforts to consistently meet infant's needs
		Encourage close relationship with one caregiver
	Oral-motor experience	Encourage nonnutritive sucking if necessary and tolerated
Toddler (1–3)	Development of autonomy Freedom of mobility	Arrange equipment to facilitate mobility (e.g., long oxygen tubing)
		When mobility must be restricted, provide suitable alternate activities (e.g., reading a story, playing with blocks)
	Opportunity to explore	Provide safe environment (e.g., cover electric outlets, secure knobs and dials on equipment)
	Oppositional behavior	Allow as much control as possible (e.g., child can hold saline during suctioning)
		Do not offer choice when there is none
	Development of language	Provide simple explanation
		Repetition is necessary
		Assist tracheostomized ventilator-dependent child with alternate expressive modality

From Ahmann, E., & Lipsi, K.A. (1991). Early intervention for technology-dependent infants and young children. *Infants and Young Children, 3,* 69; reprinted by permission.

serve young children with complex health care needs is being planned by the Division for Special Health Needs of the Massachusetts Department of Public Health. This will be an "Early Intervention Regional Consultation Program," constituted of teams who have expertise in special medical needs, feeding, adaptive equipment, and assistive technology. Based in six centers around the state, the teams will consult to individual families, the staff of early intervention programs, and the staff of other community environments for children. There will be identification of resources, regional workshops, parent-to-parent networks, equipment exchange, referral, and evaluations. This timely assistance is designed to potentiate the inclusion of children with complex care requirements in safe, healthy environments.

Child Care Programs

Child care programs are undergoing a gentle philosophic revolution regarding the inclusion of children with special health care needs, but for youngsters with complex health requirements, the progress is modest. Crowley (1990) surveyed 49 child care centers in New Haven, Connecticut, and found that 65% enrolled some children with "handicaps or chronic illness" of all types but the numbers were small. Eight cared for children with colostomies, four cared for children with tracheostomies, and one had a child who required a ventilator. Inadequate physical environment, lack of staff training, and lack of support services were listed as concerns. Markos-Capps and Godfrey (1999) contacted the licensed child care centers of Salt Lake City, Utah. Of 86, 5 could administer oxygen and 2 had suctioning devices, but no children with tube feedings or catheterization were being served at that time. To assist growth in this area, workshops and in-service instruction were sought by most directors, as well as more funding for the additional activities. Craig and Haggart (1994) pointed out the importance of establishing collaborative teams of early intervention and child care providers if accessibility to child care is to be ensured for children with significant special needs.

The majority of child care center staff have little or no experience with children who have complex medical requirements, and the presence of open outreach for staff training creates a strong market for effective curricula. Bruder (1998) applied a "Training for Inclusion" model in Connecticut, using regional teaching teams. Ann G. Haggart Associates (1993) developed a series of modules called *Including All Children: Caregiving for Infants and Toddlers with Disabilities*. The volume on health, for example, attempts to demystify many special care issues. The *Guidelines for Out-of-Home Child Care Programs* (National Center for Education in Maternal and Child Health, 1992) has certain standards that are relevant to children with special health care needs, including a requirement for outcome objectives for child health, contacts with sources of medical care, and attention to apparatus and prostheses.

Child care is important for young families. Ten million children younger than 5 years in the United States require such care while their parents work (Caldwell, 1999). Clearly, the children among them with serious health care needs must also be safely accommodated, something that is often not feasible (Thyen, Kuhlthau, & Perrin, 1999). Two models, both with segregated environments, have had valuable effects in local circumstances but cannot be generalized because they have unique support. One is the so-called "developmental day care" model, or "developmental day program." These centers meet care requirements for a very challenging group of children. Four excellent programs in Massachusetts provide child care and much therapy for 70 or more infants, toddlers, and young children with severe syndromes, many with medical technology dependence. They do so with 1:1 or 1:2 staff-to-child ratios and hours that meet specific family schedules. There is obvious conflict with the modern reach toward both inclusion and natural environments. Until the 1990s, many of these children would have been placed in residential programs (e.g., pediatric nursing homes); even now, the capacity for their integration in usual child care centers has some limitations. The other design is the occasional "medical day care" program, operated by a children's hospital or a nursing group, staffed primarily by nurses (but with child development professionals as well). These usually receive children transferred from direct hospital care, many after surgical procedures or major illness, often with medical technology dependence. Enrollments are for a few weeks to a few months, usually to achieve certain direct health care goals, but with significant attention to developmental learning experiences. Most commonly, there is full-day attendance. In some regards, these centers provide an alternative to home nursing care.

Head Start

Although Head Start has required admission of children with special needs since 1972, the achievement of substantial inclusion has been difficult (see Chapter 12). The principal sources of referral are the local school districts. There the perception has been that Head Start is designed for disadvantaged children with most need for general support. Consequently, among children with disabilities and chronic illness, only those with mild involvement are referred. For example, 1998 figures show 28,500 children enrolled in Head Start from the six New England states, with a requisite percent-

age having some disability (actually, 15.1%, or 4,300 children). Among them, only five children were identified as having mental retardation. Characteristically, children with more serious disability or health care needs go on to attend preschool classes rather than Head Start, and there one finds more personnel dedicated to teaching such youngsters.

An extraordinary system for enhancement of health and community development programs for young children is the HealthyCHILD model from the University Affiliated Program at the University of Pittsburgh.[1] HealthyCHILD is a school-linked developmental health care collaboration among hospital-university-community partners: the Pittsburgh Public Schools, MOSAIC Early Intervention Program, Children's Hospital of Pittsburgh, the UCLID Center at the University, primary care physicians, and Head Start and other early childhood education programs in the Pittsburgh region. It was funded from 1994 to 1998 by the U.S. Department of Education and the Jewish Healthcare Foundation of Pittsburgh and is now supported through foundation grants and interagency contracts.

The primary mission of Healthy-CHILD has been to design, deliver, and research the quality, outcomes, efficiency, and effectiveness of a transagency model for school-based developmental health care consultation and support in inclusive early childhood classrooms for infants and young children with chronic medical conditions, neurodevelopmental delays or disabilities, and behavioral health problems and for their parents, teachers, and other professionals who work to help them (Bagnato, 1999). A significant number of the children require medical technology assistance, including some who are now enrolled in the Pittsburgh Head Start program. Of the 4,000 children matriculated in the

---

[1]Thanks to Dr. Stephen J. Bagnato for information on the HealthyCHILD model.

Allegheny Intermediate Unit of Head Start, several dozen are involved with medical technology, including 12 with ventilators and 12 with clean intermittent catheterization. The primary operational dimension is a mobile health care team composed of a parent and professionals from partner agencies that provide a wide array of services in situ in early childhood intervention classroom environments. This Developmental Healthcare Resource Team is a "metateam" of professionals from cooperating agencies who work in a collaborative manner beyond the administrative boundaries and structures of their own separate agencies. Each professional has transdisciplinary training and experience in health care, human services, developmental disabilities, and early childhood intervention.

Preschool and School-Age Programs, Including Project School Care

Arrangements for enrollment in preschool and school for children who are assisted by medical technology has more established systems than exist for children in earlier stages of development. The aggregate program for school children is discussed, although there is an obvious identification here most specifically with the years before kindergarten. Consideration of a model program is presented next.

The census efforts of 1987 and 1990 of children who were dependent on 1 or more of 12 specific medical supports mentioned in the first section proved to be a defining experience. In the New England area, it underlined the services needed and brought together medical and educational professionals and advocates. Project School Care at the Children's Hospital in Boston was formed in 1987 and quickly became a focal point for assurance of school-based education for children with complex medical needs. A large and diverse advisory committee guided the project's resolves, and work

was begun to assemble principles of care for children with special technology needs in education programs. Soon after this, consultation by a nurse and pediatrician team provided assistance for individual school districts to allow careful planing and training for the accommodation and safety of specific children. Sometimes this involved working with birth-to-3 programs for transfer of children to preschool, but more commonly it engaged the school district directly.

A system was established for referral, building of a local team, assessment, production of a health care plan, personnel training, enrollment of the child, and later follow-up and evaluation (Palfrey et al., 1992). An Individualized Health Care Plan was modeled after an individualized education program (IEP) but contained important additional information on medications, nutrition, and equipment needs (its columns included Health Need/Nursing Diagnosis, Goals, and Action/Intervention). There was also establishment of an Emergency Plan that listed "if you see this. . .do this," plus a compendium of emergency resources. From the beginning, the children referred for consultation had medical assistance needs reflecting all of the kinds of serious supports presented in Table 17.1. For a considerable number of these children, previous education had been only in the home or a hospital, and collaborative efforts such as Project School Care secured for them programs that were with peers and in a neighborhood educational setting.

The legacy of Project School Care has been extensive. The health consultations and plans entered the educational scene while preserving the developmental and instructional missions. Many different people's roles were honored and reinforced in the ultimate problem solving. Nursing contributions are appropriately central. Here and elsewhere, the principles of the various state Nurse

Practice Acts influenced the behavioral elements. Many nursing organizations have reflected on the challenge of admission of medically dependent children into school and offered guidelines to their members, including the National Association of School Nurses, the National Association of State School Nurse Consultants, the National Council of State Boards of Nursing, and most state Boards of Registration in Nursing. Nursing leaders spoke of the new national requirement for enrollment of all children (IDEA, Section 504, ADA), a broadened role of nurses in educational planning, health care responsibility within school systems by dedicated nurses and physicians, use of an Individualized Health Care Plan as the vehicle of management, and the extraordinarily thoughtful process that must be involved in delegation of nursing activities to other personnel.

Other capacities are drawn upon to achieve special child goals. For teachers, the challenges are obviously particularly cogent, including questions about

- The student's technology needs
- The type of assistance and supports that the teacher will receive
- The student's educational needs
- The impact of the student's special needs on classmates
- Who will provide health care procedures in school (Caldwell et al., 1997)

Program administrators have additional involvement, such as risk management concerns, securing resources and funding, arrangements for transportation, electric and other utility needs, storage for back-up supplies and equipment, and building and playground accessibility (Caldwell et al., 1997). The families' stakes are far reaching.

Projects of this sort have served to unburden the frontier between children with complex medical care needs and the developmental imperative. The Project School Care guidelines for care, titled *Children and Youth Assisted by Medical Technology in Educational Settings,* was first distributed as a notebook (Haynie, Porter, & Palfrey, 1989) and has been reissued in a richly reinforced version (Porter et al., 1997). Project School Care has formed a number of partnership programs elsewhere in the United States, including Virginia, New York, North Carolina, and California. In Massachusetts, the consultation capacity is now called MASSTART (Massachusetts Technology Assistance Resource Team) and is funded by the state Department of Public Health. It consists of a network of five regional vendors for children assisted by medical technology who are planning to enroll in a primary or secondary school. MASSTART offers organizing, liaison work, training, information, and referral (approximately 100 children are helped each year in the state at large and approximately another 100 in Boston). Obviously, the activities of HealthyCHILD in Pittsburgh have similar assistive functions. The most notable aspect about this work is the accompanying empowerment (and the "can-do" feeling) that has occurred in an area that had seemed so difficult, as this involves children, families, teachers, nurses, and administrators; all have gained.

An early article by Mulligan-Ault, Guess, Struth, and Thompson (1988) looked at the experience of special education teachers who were receiving children of various ages with notable medical care requirements in their classes in Kansas. The resolution adopted by that group was an involvement by the teachers on relatively less stringent care procedures (postural drainage, use of oxygen, gastrostomy feeding, etc.), but nurse responsibility was identified for catheterization, changing tracheostomy tubes, and machine suctioning. Lowman (1993) reported on preschool-age children in Virginia and a hierarchy of tasks, having gastrostomy tube feeding and medication administration accomplished by the education staff. Fauvre (1988) pointed out the unusual nature of some "new" chronic illnesses in young children being enrolled in school: children who are surviving serious involvement with cancer or extensive surgical revision of congenital anomalies. She reflected on the dynamics between family and school staff that are essential for a successful program.

AGENDA FOR CHANGE

A review of participation in this field gives a feeling of work in progress. Regard for the early education rights of children with special health care needs is broadly held. Specifically, though, young people who have complex health care needs—with special reference to children who are assisted by medical technology—are more recently established and require dedicated training and commitment. However, numerous documentations of enlightened programming cause modern planners to feel that we are assuredly partway there. Preschool success is conspicuous, and birth-to-3 programs are doing better than we know. Child care is a sleeping giant. Head Start wants to do it but needs a great deal of help.

As noted in this chapter, the infrastructure is largely in place; continuation requires leadership, advocacy, and sound professional planning. Appropriate educational opportunities for children who have developmental risk or need are a simple outgrowth of the right to treatment. Furthermore, for young children with special health care needs (including disabilities), services and supports are qualitatively similar but require additional professional commitment, understanding, and skill. Beyond that, the extension of this deliberation indicates that earnest education and support pro-

grams for children with complex health care needs, including those assisted by medical technology, are ultimately of the same nature (same issues, same rights) but require yet additional provision of attentive arrangements and resources.

Eight components emerge as areas of potential enhancement relevant to progress for the educational rights of these children. In many ways, the elements are interdependent:

1. *Identification and referral*—Children with complex health care needs are obviously known, but they need referral to appropriate systems. Their considered referral will be aided by interdisciplinary and interagency training and information. Child Find activities should be encouraged to seek them out, hospital services need to share control, and educators should have increased awareness.

2. *Early child program collaboration*—The present fragmentation of young child support programs is in danger of losing our children with complex health care needs. Shared responsibility for coverage can be inhibited when it is among diverse sections of the service world. These children are almost never listed in demographics, state reports, or program goals. The new trend to join services is encouraging indeed (e.g., the planned new state agency in Massachusetts, the Department of Children, Families, and Learning).

3. *A mindset for inclusion*—Inclusion of children with complex health care needs should be a fully acknowledged anticipated program outcome. Good studies, reports, education, and dissemination should secure the planned enrollment of the children in creative programs. It should not be viewed as an exception; it should be viewed as the norm.

4. *Coordination for children and families*—
Intelligent and coordinated support
for families who are negotiating the
system is the only meaningful way to
ensure that quality is monitored. It is
so simple, yet it continually fails to
receive appropriate priority. The cost
of coordination activities should be
realistically supported in the budget
for birth-to-3 programs (including
compliance with IFSP regulations).
Consultation, therapy, and training
should be brought into programs by
coordinated planning. Families
deserve to be intelligently guided.
Perrin and Bloom (1994) pointed
out that this work is best conceptualized as *care coordination* rather than as
case management.

5. *Other personnel preparation*—The sense
of uncertainty of administrators and
care providers about children who
are assisted by medical technology
should be addressed. As mentioned,
some curricula already exist; their
implementation is incomplete.

6. *Nursing alliance*—The other most
essential item to successful programs,
in addition to coordination for families, is well-founded nursing collaboration. This is exemplified in the
Project School Care design. As Klein-
Walker indicated, "Ideally all schools
should have a full-time, well-trained
school nurse" (1994, p. 751) who
would bring support and expertise to
the programs for children with special health care needs within the
school and between the school and
the child's health care providers in
the community. The nursing professional groups are already in a
thoughtful planning position. Educational and pediatric interactions can
be increased.

7. *Pediatric perspectives*—Project School
Care was an expansive pediatric

proving ground for more inspired
relations with children in school.
The current thrust of professionalism in neurodevelopmental and
developmental-behavioral pediatrics
can support these important commu-
nity-related behaviors. A declara-
tion by the American Academy of
Pediatrics, Committee on Children
with Disabilities (2000), underlines
broader roles for pediatrics in supporting educational implementation.
It should become more deeply established in pediatric graduate training.

8. *Important parents*—Parents are the
ultimate experts in the central areas:
characteristics of the children, reality
in planning goals, and hopes based
on love. Educational, nursing, and
pediatric programmers have much to
learn about family feelings and collaboration. More analysis and reporting are needed.

CONCLUSION

Included within the special cohort of children with complex health care needs are
many who are very needy, who are emerging from challenged or compromised
personal positions, and who have had
only in these modern times a promising
prospect for larger fulfillment. Planning
for their best education and support is
exciting indeed, especially when they participate fully with their peers in all aspects
of community life.

REFERENCES

Ahmann, E., & Lipsi, K.A. (1991). Early intervention for technology-dependent infants and young
children. *Infants and Young Children, 3,* 67–77.
American Academy of Pediatrics/Committee on
Children with Disabilities. (2000). Provision of
educationally-related services for children and
adolescents with chronic diseases and disabling
conditions. *Pediatrics, 105,* 448–451.

Americans with Disabilities Act (ADA) of 1990, PL 101-336, 42 U.S.C. §§ 12101 *et seq.*

Ann G. Haggart Associates. (1993). *Including all children: Caregiving for infants and toddlers with disabilities.* Hampton NH: Author.

Applegarth, D.A., Toone, J.R., & Lowry, R.B. (2000). Incidence of inborn errors of metabolism in British Columbia, 1969–1996 [Abstract]. *Pediatrics, 105,* 109.

Bagnato, S.J. (1999). *Efficacy of collaborative developmental healthcare support in inclusive early childhood programs. Final research report of HealthyCHILD (H023D40013) (1994–1998).* Washington DC: U.S. Department of Education, Office of Special Education and Rehabilitative Services.

Bruder, M.B. (1998). A collaborative model to increase the capacity of childcare providers to include young children with disabilities. *Journal of Early Intervention, 21,* 177–186.

Caldwell, B.M. (1999). Child care. In M.D. Levine, W.B. Carey, & A.C. Crocker (Eds.), *Developmental-behavioral pediatrics* (3rd ed., pp. 201–208). Philadelphia: W.B. Saunders Company.

Caldwell, T.H., Sirvis, B.P., Still, J., Still, M., Schwab, N., Jones, J., Anderson, B., Blanchard, R., & Appel, S. (1997). Students who require medical technology in school. In S. Porter, M. Haynie, T. Bierle, T.H. Caldwell, & J.S. Palfrey (Eds.), *Children and youth assisted by medical technology in educational settings: Guidelines for care* (2nd ed., pp. 3–18). Baltimore: Paul H. Brookes Publishing Co.

Craig, S.E., & Haggart, A.G. (1994). Including all children: The ADA's challenge to early intervention. *Infants and Young Children, 7,* 15–19.

Crocker, A.C. (1989). The spectrum of medical care for developmental disabilities. In I.L. Rubin & A.C. Crocker (Eds.), *Developmental disabilities: Delivery of medical care for children and adults* (pp. 10–22). Philadelphia: Lea & Febiger.

Crocker, A.C. (1992). Data collection for the evaluation of mental retardation prevention activities: The Fateful Forty-Three. *Mental Retardation, 30,* 303–317.

Crocker, A.C. (1997). The impact of disabling conditions. In H.M. Wallace, R.F. Biehl, J.C. MacQuenn, & J.A. Blackman (Eds.), *Mosby's resource guide to children with disabilities and chronic illness* (pp. 22–29). St. Louis, MO: Mosby.

Crocker, A.C. (1998). Exceptionality. *Journal of Developmental & Behavioral Pediatrics, 19,* 300–305.

Crowley, A.A. (1990). Integrating handicapped and chronically ill children into day care centers. *Pediatric Nursing, 16,* 39–44.

Drazin, D.M. (1996). Your child's education. In H. Charkins (Ed.), *Children with facial difference* (pp. 207–230). Bethesda, MD: Woodbine House.

Fauvre, M. (1988). Including young children with "new" chronic illnesses in an early childhood education setting. *Young Children, 43,* 71–77.

Godfrey, A.B., Haake, J., & Saunders, D. (1998). A curriculum preparing staff to integrate health services into early intervention programs. *Infants and Young Children, 10,* 56–70.

Haynie, M., Porter, S., & Palfrey, J.S. (1989). *Children assisted by medical technology in educational settings: Guidelines for care.* Boston: Children's Hospital.

Hudgins, L., & Cassidy, S.B. (1999). Congenital anomalies. In M.D. Levine, W.B. Carey, & A.C. Crocker (Eds.), *Developmental-behavioral pediatrics* (3rd ed., pp. 249–262). Philadelphia: W.B. Saunders Company.

Janz, J.R., Beyer, H.A., Schwab, N., Anderson, B., Caldwell, T.H., & Harrison, J. (1997). Legal issues in the education of students with special health care needs. In S. Porter, M. Haynie, T. Bierle, T.H. Caldwell, & J.S. Palfrey (Eds.), *Children and youth assisted by medical technology in educational settings: Guidelines for care* (2nd ed., pp. 19–39). Baltimore: Paul H. Brookes Publishing Co.

Individuals with Disabilities Education Act Amendments of 1991, PL 102-119, 20 U.S.C. §§ 1400 *et seq.*

Individuals with Disabilities Education Act Amendments of 1997, PL 105-17, 20 U.S.C. §§ 1400 *et seq.*

Individuals with Disabilities Education Act (IDEA) of 1990, PL 101-476, 20 U.S.C. §§ 1400 *et seq.*

Klein-Walker, D. (1994). Children with special health care needs in the schools. In H.M. Wallace, R.P. Nelson, & P.J. Sweeney (Eds.), *Maternal and child health practices* (4th ed., pp. 748–753). Oakland, CA: Third Party Publishing.

Lowman, D.K. (1993). Preschoolers with complex health-care needs: A survey of early childhood special education teachers in Virginia. *Topics in Early Childhood Special Education, 13,* 445–460.

Markos-Capps, G., & Godfrey, A.B. (1999). Availability of day care services for preschool children with special health care needs. *Infants and Young Children, 11,* 62–78.

Mulligan-Ault, M., Guess, D., Struth, L., & Thompson, B. (1988). The implementation of health-related procedures in classrooms for students with severe multiple impairments. *Journal of The Association for Persons with Severe Handicaps, 13,* 100–109.

Murphy, A., & Crocker, A.C. (1987). Impact of handicapping conditions on the child and family.

In H.M. Wallace, R.F. Biehl, A.C. Oglesby, & L.T. Taft (Eds.), *Handicapped children and youth: A comprehensive community and clinical approach* (pp. 26–41). New York: Human Sciences Press.

National Center for Education in Maternal and Child Health. (1992). *Guidelines for out-of-home child care programs.* Arlington, VA: Author.

Nelson, R.P., & Crocker, A.C. (1999). The child with multiple disabilities. In M.D. Levine, W.B. Carey, & A.C. Crocker (Eds.), *Developmental-behavioral pediatrics* (3rd ed., pp. 607–614). Philadelphia: W.B. Saunders Company.

Palfrey, J.S., Haynie, M., Porter, S., Bierle, T., Cooperman, P., & Lowcock, J. (1992). Project School Care: Integrating children assisted by medical technology into educational settings. *Journal of School Health, 62,* 50–54.

Palfrey, J.S., Haynie, M., Porter, S., Fenton, T., Cooperman-Vincent, P., Shaw, D., Johnson, B., Bierle, T., & Walker, D.K. (1994). Prevalence of medical technology assistance among children in Massachusetts in 1987 and 1990. *Public Health Reports, 109,* 226–233.

Palfrey, J.S., Walker, D.K., Haynie, M., Singer, J.D., Porter, S., Bushey, B., & Cooperman, P. (1991). Technology's children: Report of a statewide census of children dependent on medical supports. *Pediatrics, 87,* 611–618.

Perrin, J.M., & Bloom, S.R. (1994). Case management and care coordination for families with children with special health needs. In H.M. Wallace, R.P. Nelson, & P.J. Sweeney (Eds.), *Maternal and child health practices* (4th ed., pp. 711–718). Oakland, CA: Third Party Publishing.

Porter, S., Haynie, M., Bierle, T., Caldwell, T.H., & Palfrey, J.S. (Eds.). (1997). *Children and youth assisted by medical technology in educational settings: Guidelines for care* (2nd ed.). Baltimore: Paul H. Brookes Publishing Co.

Rehabilitation Act of 1973, PL 93-112, 29 U.S.C. §§ 701 *et seq.*

Report of the Surgeon General's workshop on children with handicaps and their families (DHHS Publication No. PH3-83-50194). (1982). Washington, DC: U.S. Government Printing Office.

Thyen, U., Kuhlthau, K., & Perrin, J.M. (1999). Employment, child care, and mental health of mothers caring for children assisted by technology. *Pediatrics, 103,* 1235–1242.

Vohr, B.R., Cashore, W.J., & Bigsby, R. (1999). Stresses and interventions in the neonatal intensive care unit. In M.D. Levine, W.B. Carey & A.C. Crocker (Eds.), *Developmental-behavioral pediatrics* (3rd ed., pp. 263–273). Philadelphia: W.B. Saunders Company.

18

MARCI J. HANSON

CRAIG ZERCHER

The Impact of Cultural and Linguistic Diversity in Inclusive Preschool Environments

Miss Marie worries that Nalani never speaks up. During circle time, Nalani sits with her eyes down when Miss Marie asks the children questions. This teacher believes that she should meet with Nalani's parents to discuss the child's withdrawal.

Ling-Ling bounds around the classroom and is a favorite of his teacher. He is often given the opportunity to sit on her lap during storytime. Though he seems to be well liked by the other children, he is almost always on the periphery of their groups, riding tricycles alone or playing with cars by himself. The teacher notes that he rarely initiates interaction.

Van often wanders over to the group of children in the playhouse or sandbox. Though he seldom makes an attempt to talk, on one occasion in the free-play area, he shouts, "Get out!" (a phrase he has often heard other children use) as another boy approaches. He seems perplexed when his would-be playmate shrugs and walks away.

Jamar is always in the thick of things on the playground. He is at the top of the slide, crawling to the most hidden spot in the tire structure, and racing at the front of the pack on his tricycle. He displays his emotions with great intensity whether enraged, joyful, or distraught. His high activity level and gusto are a source of pride to his mother, who is pleased that he is "all boy!"

Juanita likes to play in the playhouse. She attempts to join two other girls who are "cooking dinner." The other girls make fun of the way she rolls the play-dough and exclude her from their dialogue because they cannot understand what she is saying.

These children attend inclusive preschools in the United States. They all have disabilities. They all come from non–Anglo-European cultures. They all grew up with a language other than Standard American English. In each case, their interaction styles have alarmed their

The authors acknowledge the contributions of the other investigators and associates of the Early Childhood Research Institute on Inclusion (ECRII) (U.S. Department of Education Grant No. H024K4004) through which some of the research reviewed was conducted.

413

teachers. The explanations for their behavior, however, are not readily apparent. Certainly, these children have disabilities that affect their behavior and interaction and communication skills. Each child's family also comes from a cultural and linguistic group that is different from the dominant or mainstream culture in the United States.

Americans are privileged to live in a wonderfully diverse country. This diversity is apparent in the country's history and will undoubtedly shape the future. This ever-increasingly diverse mix of children and families receiving services in the education, health, and social services systems presents new challenges for practitioners. It demands that professionals seek new information, develop new skills, review their goals and priorities, and adapt their methods and models to more appropriately support the full range of children and families served.

This chapter examines the influence of diverse cultural and linguistic perspectives on inclusive preschool services. The influence of culture and language is discussed in light of changing demographics in the United States. The implication of cultural and linguistic diversity on children's social competence and interaction in their peer culture is explored, and the impact of cultural/linguistic diversity on family perspectives and participation in preschool is analyzed. Teachers' attitudes, goals, and perspectives, as well as the administrative structures and organizational procedures and philosophies, are examined with respect to the influence of cultural and linguistic diversity.

THE INFLUENCE OF CULTURE AND LANGUAGE

Culture has been defined in a variety of ways by anthropologists throughout the years. However, several common themes predominate (see discussions in Garcia & McLaughlin, 1995, and Okun, Fried, & Okun, 1999). *Culture* typically refers to the tendencies or shared perspectives of a group of individuals and includes all facets of life, such as values, beliefs, behavior, and ideas. Though all members of a group may not share the same ideas or behavior, their cultural orientation provides a common framework for their lifestyles. Culture generally is viewed as something that is learned and passed on through the generations. The transmission of cultural values also is seen as highly social in nature.

The influence of one's language system on one's life also is of great significance. As described by Okun and colleagues, "Language shapes experience, and experience shapes language. It predetermines modes of observation and interpretation, shaping interpretation of experiences, recreating experiences, and empowering members to imagine and create new experiences" (1999, p. 9). Thus, the meanings that are attributed to an individual's speech, gesture, or behavior must be considered in light of his or her linguistic and cultural heritage and orientation.

Early childhood educators encounter children as they are involved in learning their family's culture and language. They come to the educational environments with their family's cultural and linguistic heritage, their earliest experiences, and their families' notions about preschool experience and disability. The expectations and assumptions that early childhood educators make about these children's behavior, as well as the roles that they play and the attitudes that they hold, are influenced by their own cultural perspectives and knowledge of the children's and families' backgrounds. Children's and families' behaviors and routines regarding eye contact, touching, smiling, personal space, and time all are governed by their cultural perspectives, just as early childhood educators are as teachers. As service providers, too, early childhood educators' notions about children's schedules, diets, behavioral expectations, discipline, academics, and play likewise are influenced by their cultural backgrounds. Early childhood educators' philosophies regarding the classroom routines and environment, the involvement of families, goals for children in preschool, and decision-making procedures all are governed by the cultural perspective to which they adhere. Families' choices about whether to send their young children to a group environment, their goals and expectations for their children in preschool, the meaning of their children's disabilities, and their notions about learning and child rearing all are framed by their cultural perspectives. Thus, many of the actions and communications, both subtle and overt, that occur in the preschool environment are highly influenced by cultural mores and values.

Although culture may frame behavior and ways of thinking, it is not a static phenomenon. Individuals are constantly working and reworking their perspectives based on experience. Clearly, many factors influence an individual's behavior, such as socioeconomic class, living experiences, education levels, and immigration experiences, to name a few (Lynch & Hanson, 1998). Families' and service providers' degree of acculturation to the dominant culture of the school environment also affects their styles and modes of responding.

Demographic Shifts

In some parts of the United States, the term *minority* is a misnomer because there is no cultural majority. This phenomenon is reflected in the school population as well. For instance, by 1989, more than half of the children enrolled in California's public schools were children of color; since that time, no single cultural or racial group has represented more than 50% of the population.

With respect to the population of the United States, census data from November 1998 indicated a total population of 270,933,000 (U.S. Census Bureau, 1999). Of this number, approximately 72% were Caucasian (non-Hispanic); 12% were African American (non-Hispanic); 11% were Hispanic; 4% were Asian or Pacific Islander (non-Hispanic); and 1% were American Indian, Eskimo, Aleut (non-Hispanic), or other. Greater diversity was evident in some states. For example, in California, census data showed that approximately 51% of the people were Caucasian; 29% were Hispanic; 12% were Asian or Pacific Islander; 7% were African American; and 1% were American Indian, Eskimo, Aleut, or other (U.S. Census Bureau, 1997).

Demographic shifts are evident as well with respect to the population of children (Federal Interagency Forum on Child and Family Statistics, 1998). In 1997, approximately 66% of children were Caucasian (non-Hispanic), 15% were African American (non-Hispanic), 15% were Hispanic, 4% were Asian and Pacific Islander, and 1% were American Indian or Alaskan Native. Since the early 1980s, the number of Caucasian, non-Hispanic children has decreased, whereas the number of Hispanic children has increased significantly. The percentage of Asian children also has increased, whereas the percentages of African American and American Indian children have remained relatively stable. In their projections for the future, the Children's Defense Fund estimated that by the year 2030, as compared with 1985, there will be "5.5 million more Hispanic children; 2.6 million more African-American children; 1.5 million more children of other races; and 6.32 million fewer white, non-Hispanic children" (1989, p. 166).

Many young children ages 3–4 years participate in some type of school program. Census data indicated that by 1996,

48.3% of preschool-age children were enrolled in school. Of the children enrolled in preschool, 47.9% were Caucasian, 49.9% were African American, and 38.1% were Hispanic (U.S. Census Bureau, 1998). Thus, many young children in the United States now attend a preschool program and many of them are children of color and are nonnative non-English speakers.

It is evident from these data that the population of preschool-age children enrolled in schools represents great cultural and linguistic diversity. Thus, these preschool experiences must be tailored to the diverse needs of these young children and their families.

Social Competence

The development of social competence is a central goal during preschool and has been a primary focus of the movement to include young children with disabilities in educational experiences with their typically developing peers (Guralnick, 1999). Indeed, social competence has been a major focus of the research and practice in preschool inclusion (Guralnick, 1990, 1992, 1994, 1999; Odom & Brown, 1993; Odom & Diamond, 1998; Odom, McConnell, & McEvoy, 1992). This research, which examines intervention and program effects regarding social development and social competence, is considered elsewhere in this book (see Chapter 21). However, implications generated by this area of inquiry for work in culturally and linguistically diverse preschool educational environments are noted in this discussion.

Interaction patterns between preschool-age children with disabilities and their typically developing peers have been documented and analyzed in a number of research investigations (reviewed in Guralnick, 1999 [see also Chapter 1]; Diamond, 1994, and Odom & Diamond, 1998). Though successful interactions

between children in these groups have been observed in a variety of environments, common findings that have emerged from this literature are that children with disabilities are less likely than typically developing children to be selected as playmates and that the degree of severity of the child's disability may increase social separation. Furthermore, for children with disabilities, the development of friendships has been discovered to be more problematic (Guralnick, Gottman, & Hammond, 1996; Guralnick & Groom, 1988; Guralnick & Neville, 1997). However, parents' reports indicate that children with disabilities do form friendships (Guralnick, Connor, & Hammond, 1995). Research from the Early Childhood Research Institute on Inclusion indicates that the source of friendships and interaction possibilities may come primarily from the family and community through family networks, activities, and neighborhoods (Beckman et al., 1998).

The literature on child development shows ample evidence of preschool-age children's ability to perceive differences among peers in terms of characteristics such as gender and race (Maccoby, 1988; Ramsey & Myers, 1990). Children's differences in their social interaction selections and patterns may be attributable to attitudes that they are developing about differences (Thurman & Lewis, 1979). From the body of research on social integration and interaction patterns between children with and without disabilities, it seems that preschool-age children are able to differentiate their peers' interactional and behavioral capabilities. These considerations may affect interaction and friendship patterns, and children may have a tendency to prefer playmates "like" themselves (see Chapter 7).

The research is less informative on the role that cultural and language differences play with respect to children's interaction in inclusive environments.

However, it is likely that the influence of culture and language variables on children's and families' experiences in preschool environments is substantial.

Notions of social competence are socially constructed. As such, they are defined by society and are strongly linked to cultural expectations and mores. How social competence is defined, ranging from children's style of interaction to teachers' roles in classrooms, assumes shared consensus about attributes and behavior. Because social competence by its very nature is framed by the cultural, linguistic, and racial perspective of the child and family, that perspective may be synchronous with that of the dominant culture of the school, classroom, or teacher (as well as of other children and family participants) or it may vary in important ways. Some of these ways are evident, whereas others are subtle and not easy to discern or define.

Role of Language

Theories and research related to the development of language and the role of language in the developmental process have filled numerous volumes. Vygotsky's (Berk & Winsler, 1995; Vygotsky, 1978, 1986) theoretical perspective has held particular meaning for educators. According to this perspective, language skills develop through social interactions and are then internalized. Wertsch described Vygotsky's theoretical framework as having three core themes:

> 1) a reliance on a genetic or developmental method, 2) the claim that higher mental processes in the individual have their origin in social processes, and 3) the claim that mental processes can be understood only if we understand the tools and signs that mediate them. (1985, pp. 14–15)

Young children's participation in interactions with family members and others who support or mediate their development have shed important insights on how children learn language and learn to think (Fivish, 1992; Miller, Potts, Fung, Hoogstra, & Mintz, 1990; Snow & Ferguson, 1977). The work of Miller and colleagues (Miller, Wiley, Fung, & Liang, 1997; Wiley, Rose, Burger, & Miller, 1998), in particular, highlights how personal event narratives become an important medium for child socialization in their cultural ways.

Although teacher–child and peer–peer interactions may be less well understood in this socialization process, these interactions can play an important role in the development of children's social and cognitive competence. For children whose full participation in the social environment is limited because of disability, cultural and linguistic characteristics, or both, their abilities to interact and to glean meaningful information may be limited or modified.

Many children who attend preschool programs are raised in bicultural environments or in environments that differ from the school environment. For many of these children, English, the predominant language in most preschool programs, is a second language. It was estimated that in 2000 there were 5.2 million preschoolers in the United States whose families speak a language other than English at home (Kagan & Garcia, 1991). For many of these children, they not only must learn their first or primary language, but they also must learn a second language, such as English. As Tabors (1997) described, learning a second language can put children in a "double bind" in that these children must be accepted socially to learn the new language, but they must often speak the new language to be socially accepted. Thus, communicative competence and social competence are integrally related.

The interrelationship between bilingual language development and children's cognitive development is receiving increased research attention as well

(Diaz, Padilla, & Weathersby, 1991). Researchers and practitioners, thus, are focusing efforts on defining the influence of cultural and social variables on language acquisition (Gutierrez & Garcia, 1989; Hakuta & Garcia, 1989) and on identifying the most appropriate ways to support the development of young children from diverse cultural and linguistic backgrounds (Wong Fillmore, 1991).

Children who are deaf or hard of hearing are another example of a group of children whose language is different from the mainstream society's (see Chapter 16). Evidence from research studies on children's play and interaction patterns shows that both children with and without hearing impairments tend to interact with children of the same hearing status as they are (Antia, Kreimeyer, & Eldredge, 1994; Levine & Antia, 1997; Minnett, Clark, & Wilson, 1994). This relationship between social integration and having a shared communication system has been explored in the research literature (Luetke-Stahlman, 1994). In addition to the obvious challenges of supporting children's peer interactions and communication, special supports for the families of children who are deaf or hard of hearing may be warranted (Meadow-Orlans & Sass-Lehrer, 1995).

Thus, children's language and communication patterns both shape the kind of experience that they may have in preschool and are being shaped by the preschool experience. Children's communication skills may allow them to be actively engaged in the preschool environment or may serve to segregate or preclude their active participation and involvement.

THE CHALLENGE OF CULTURAL AND LINGUISTIC DIVERSITY

Children and their families bring their experience, their heritage, their personalities, their skills, and their values and beliefs to the preschool environment.

The preschool environment may be in line with these perspectives and may offer support for their development, or the goals and practices of that preschool environment may be at odds with the characteristics that the children and their families bring. If the preschool goals and values for children's learning, social and behavioral expectations, and demands for interactional and communication abilities differ from those that the children and their families possess, then potential differences may arise. Service providers increasingly are challenged to adapt and adjust services for children and families whose backgrounds and language may be different from those of families served in the past.

Family Perspectives

Preschool children experience their primary and most crucial learning opportunities in the context of their families. Families' characteristics and backgrounds also play a tremendous role in children's school experiences. Values, beliefs, and expectations for children's development and the experiences that families encounter when interacting with service systems are strongly influenced by cultural and linguistic variables (Harry, 1992b; Lynch & Hanson, 1998). Families' cultural, ethnic, and linguistic heritage and orientation influence their views of child rearing, disability and its cause, change and intervention, health and healing, family and family roles, and communication and language patterns (Hanson, Lynch, & Wayman, 1990). Differences in families' experiences of having a child with disabilities and interacting with service delivery systems have been noted for different cultural or ethnic groups with respect to access to information, choices and decision making, interaction patterns with professionals, and goal setting (Bailey, Skinner, Rodriguez, Gut, & Correa, 1999; Lynch & Stein, 1987; Mary, 1990; Smith & Ryan,

1987). The need for service delivery systems to provide services in a respectful, appropriate, and culturally competent manner has been highlighted as a major service goal and concern (Bowman & Stott, 1994; Chan, 1990; DeGangi, Wietlisbach, Poisson, Stein, & Royeen, 1994; Hanson & Lynch, 1992; Harry, 1992a, 1992b; Lynch & Hanson, 1998; McGonigel, Kaufman, & Johnson, 1991; Randall-David, 1989).

Although attention to issues of cultural diversity has increased in service delivery systems, the research literature remains limited in this area. This limitation is surprising in light of the multicultural priority in early childhood education, early childhood special education, and Head Start. Several studies, however, have examined the influence of cultural and language family variables on the preschool inclusion process. Hanson and colleagues (1998) investigated how preschool programs and community sites adapted to the diverse needs of children and families and acknowledged cultural backgrounds and preferences of children and their families in inclusive preschools. A qualitative research methodology was used to identify key themes related to inclusion in preschool environments. With the use of an ecological systems framework, themes were identified with respect to children's peer interactions regarding belonging and membership within their peer culture, teachers' practices and philosophies that influenced support for diversity in the classroom culture, and families' perspectives on the meaning of disabilities and their relationships with personnel and other children and families within the preschool environments. The larger context of community and school climate also was analyzed in terms of how the school defined its goals and priorities for inclusive services with respect to diversity.

Families observed in this study reflected a wide range of socioeconomic, cultural, ethnic, and language backgrounds. Families of children both with and without disabilities who participated in inclusive preschools across a number of different environments (public school, Head Start, child care) were observed and interviewed. One key finding was that parents of children both with and without disabilities shared many common goals for their children, such as wanting their children to have friends, be good citizens, do well in school, and be accepted and treated with respect. A second finding concerned the type of preschool placement; although most families wanted their children to be treated as typically as possible, the goal of placing their children in inclusion programs was just one among many concerns that families had. Typically, other family issues related to economics and health, for instance, were placed at a greater priority. Families (of children both with and without disabilities), however, strongly expressed the desire that their children learn about and respect differences among people and have friends.

The impact of cultural and linguistic differences was noted in this research, though, in the ways in which parents described and explained their children's disabilities. Language differences were frequently cited as a source of potential difficulty. Often, children did not receive services in their primary language and did not share the same language as the majority of the other children served.

Cultural and language differences also seemed to influence families' abilities to "work" the system and to get the information and/or placements that they desired. Families who were English speaking, more well educated, and "savvy," had greater access to information and supports than did other families. In addition, the preschool environments varied in their abilities to accommodate and support differences in families' languages, values, religious practices, and service expectations. In general, schools and classrooms in which diversity was emphasized and valued seemed better able to address the needs expressed by families, although clashes and difficulties sometimes were present even in subtle ways (e.g., staff members' failure to learn correct pronunciation of child's name).

Linkages between cultural and language diversity and disability also were investigated by Hanson, Gutierrez, Morgan, Brennan, and Zercher (1997). The impact of language differences between home and school with respect to children's and families' experiences in inclusive preschool environments was documented. Qualitative data revealed the lack of individualized education program (IEP) goals related to language for second-language learners, the influence of language differences on children's friendships and social relationships, and the complex interactions between disabling conditions and language differences. The influence of language differences on communication systems between home and school was noted, as were influences on parent-to-parent communication and relationships. Families expressed concerns regarding their children's language learning, as well as their opportunities and abilities to interact with other children. This concern was mirrored in the parents' interaction opportunities as well. For example, one mother, who was an English-speaking single parent, expressed concern that she was unable to communicate with most of the other mothers who were Spanish speaking. She noted that most of the other mothers were married and did not work outside the home, which made it difficult for her to form relationships with them. Thus, cultural and language differences influenced the interactions of both children and their families with others in the preschool program.

Family and Classroom Cultures

At the classroom level, researchers and practitioners have long recognized the need for early childhood education programs to address the needs of children and their families from diverse cultural and linguistic backgrounds (Barrera, 1993; Bredekamp & Copple, 1997; Garcia & McLaughlin, 1995; Garcia & Malkin, 1993; Salend, 1997). In the ecological systems model (Bronfenbrenner, 1979), the values, beliefs, and lifestyles of particular ethnic, religious, and socioeconomic groups indeed are thought to provide a "blueprint" for the organization of the immediate environments in which children participate. Cultural perspectives and practices form a macrosystem that shapes and informs classroom microsystems. Documentation of the linkages between these system levels has only begun and constitutes an important area for future research regarding preschool inclusion (Odom & Diamond, 1998). In their own work, the authors have found that these linkages are more easily apprehended when macrosystems and microsystems are defined in similar ways—that is, when the classroom itself is viewed as a kind of local culture with its own set of values, beliefs, and practices. This conceptualization facilitates direct comparisons between the classroom culture and the larger cultural context.

Two important elements of the larger cultural context that are relevant for the development of inclusive classroom cultures are the influence of the professional cultures of special education and early childhood education and also families' identification with the culture of a particular group (Odom et al., 1996). The second set of influences is the focus here. In the authors' work, one underlying value shared between the classroom cultures and parents from a variety of cultural backgrounds was that children with and without disabilities should be educated together. A teacher put it this way: "Everyone needs to be exposed to everyone; it's that simple. There should be no questions about it. . .If they are included all of the way, it just makes a better world" (Hanson et al., 1998, p. 195). A number of parents echoed this general support for diversity. One parent said, "I think it is wonderful, actually. Children should know at an early age that there are people out there who have special needs" (Hanson et al., 1998, p. 199). Another parent related her family's support for classroom diversity this way:

> In my little town where I am in Mexico, if somebody's different, that's okay. It's just like they are in the town. Everybody's different, you don't think about it. Just like I only went to third grade, but we had one little boy in my class, he couldn't read. He couldn't really verbalize. But when it was his turn to read he would stand up and make sounds. We all listened to him just like he could read. We knew that was his way. (Told to the educational coordinator by a parent in an inclusive preschool classroom)

This set of shared values seemed to form a bond between home and classroom cultures and led to classroom practices, such as individualization and curricular modifications, that facilitated inclusion.

A related aspect of the classroom culture of inclusive programs was a demonstrated respect for racial, ethnic, linguistic, and socioeconomic diversity. The authors have found that when the unique needs of every child and family were considered and appropriate services were provided, each child and family was seen as having special needs. Curricular materials and activities were enriched by drawing on the background cultures of the parents and program staff. Artifacts, songs, stories, foods, and crafts were brought into the classroom as the direct result of parents' and staff members' sharing their home cultures.

The significance of this situation for inclusion is that the classroom culture is such that similarities and differences between people are represented, discussed, normalized, and accepted. Children may learn about a special food that one child and family prepares at home as part of a cooking activity and then help a peer with cerebral palsy try a new walker at recess. The teacher may translate between English and Spanish to help two playmates settle a dispute and a few minutes later help a child interpret the communicative efforts of a classmate with autism. In these classrooms, disability becomes just one of the many ways that people may differ from one another while sharing many basic similarities.

At the same time, there may be tensions between home and classroom cultures. Parents may see preschool as a way of preparing for future success and may not share the high estimation of play and child choice that is often part of the classroom culture, or they may see the group environment as a place for the development of personality and may be unhappy with classroom cultures that are "too strict" (Hanson et al., 1998). Some parents also may question the inclusion of children with disabilities out of concern that their child may not receive enough attention or may acquire some negative behaviors. Bilingual instruction may be another point of contention. The goals that parents have for their children, of course, are culturally based. The result of this tension is that the classroom culture may be in periodic flux and different values and beliefs may come to the fore at different times. The interaction of home and classroom cultures may shift also as the makeup of the community and the school population changes from year to year. Extremely important in this regard may be the movement of bilingual and bicultural staff members—teachers, para-professionals, and related services personnel—into and out of inclusive programs.

It can be said, then, that classroom cultures that support the inclusion of young children are those that 1) reflect an underlying cultural belief that it is right and natural for children with and without disabilities to be educated together, 2) value and accommodate diversity of all types: racial, ethnic, linguistic, economic, and ability, and 3) are sensitive to the perspectives and wishes of the families and communities that they serve.

Peer Culture

Related to the classroom culture but standing somewhat apart from it is the distinct culture created by the children themselves. Although Piaget (1932) recognized early that child–child relationships constituted a different interaction order that contributed in a unique way to individual development, the first mention of a children's culture was by Opie and Opie, who described "a thriving unselfconscious culture (the word culture is used here deliberately) which is. . . unnoticed by the sophisticated world" (1959, p. 74), a self-contained community marked by its own customs, lore, and language. Denzin (1977) also pointed out that children create a social world of their own that transcends the individuals who create it, that generates strategies for conducting interaction, and into which children socialize one another. He offered several dimensions that establish the differences between adult and child worlds: linguistic uniqueness, candor, play, shifting group alliances, deference, demeanor, tact, and taste. Corsaro (1985) noted three major features of the peer cultures of preschool-age children: a sense of collective identity, continual construction and renewal by children, and particular processes (interpretive proce-

dures, fantasy play, and discourse forms) and content (valued behavioral routines and childhood beliefs, values, and concerns).

Consideration of the meaning and importance of peer culture allows for a reconceptualization of social competence. Social competence may be viewed as mastery of the various elements of the local peer culture—the humor, play themes, beliefs, concerns, and interactive routines that are unique to children. Children who experience delays in the development of social skills, language, and play are at a distinct disadvantage in acquiring and using behaviors that will allow them to participate most fully in the peer culture. This disadvantage may be multiplied when the child's cultural and linguistic background differs from that of the majority of the other children in the classroom.

The majority of the activities that compose the peer culture, such as establishing play themes and roles, engaging in arguments, and word play and humor (Corsaro, 1985), require a common language and shared experience. One can imagine the difficulties experienced by a child with cognitive and language delays in entering into this new, complex, and subtle social world. Although there is some evidence that taking the initiative and engaging in interaction at a purely behavioral level may lead to social acceptance despite linguistic differences (Hanson et al., 1997), the tendency to initiate interactions may be reduced in children with disabilities. Efforts to overcome language differences by providing a one-to-one adult aide or interpreter may actually serve to isolate the child further from the peer culture by disrupting child–child interactions or creating mostly adult–child interactions (Hanson et al., 1997) unless the adult is well trained in social support techniques.

Issues of belonging and membership in the peer culture are critical to the inclusion of children with disabilities in early childhood programs. To be fully included in the peer culture means to be included in the collective identity of that group—to see oneself and be seen by others as a member of the group—and to participate in the web of social relationships that the group provides (Corsaro, 1985). Children with disabilities demonstrate through a variety of means a desire to be with, like, and accepted by peers (Wolfberg et al., 1999). Having a one-to-one paraprofessional, arriving at the preschool in a yellow school bus, and having differences in physical appearance and behavior may put children with disabilities at risk for exclusion as members of the peer culture. Children with disabilities do seem to experience some degree of exclusion from the peer culture in inclusive classrooms (Wolfberg et al., 1999).

If, as noted previously, children exhibit a preference for playing with children who are like themselves, then racial, ethnic, and linguistic differences between the child with a disability and the other children in the environment may further increase this risk. Teachers may help to overcome these risks by acting as cultural interpreters and guides for the children with disabilities and by helping children to discover common interests and abilities (Wolfberg et al., 1999). This may require, however, that the teacher be bilingual/bicultural, as well as conversant in the peer culture of the classroom, to promote the membership of children with disabilities in the social life of the group.

An important question regarding inclusion and peer culture is the extent to which the adults can influence the codes and conventions of the peer culture to foster acceptance of differences and increase interactions between children with and without disabilities. Two opposing tendencies are at work. On the one hand, much of what makes up the peer culture is originally presented to children by adults (Corsaro, 1985). On the other hand, this "raw material" is reworked by the children and assimilated within the existing peer culture. A defining element of peer culture is that children see themselves as different from adults and emerging out of—and simultaneously re-creating—their sense of their own uniqueness, and they will often actively resist adult demands and the expectations of adults. Things are done in secret and in violation of adult rules. The teacher may succeed in creating a classroom culture in which diversity is valued and accepted, but the children may covertly, yet actively, resist these standards when they are away from adults.

In summary, the influence of cultural and linguistic diversity in the preschool environment has been examined in light of family perspectives, teacher and family linkages, and the children's own peer culture. The influence of culture and language can be witnessed at all levels, and culture and language interact with issues of disability as children and their families are included in preschool services.

RECOMMENDATIONS FOR PRACTICE

Few research studies have examined the effects of cultural and language diversity on children's interactions and experiences in inclusive preschool environments. With the exception of the investigations previously reviewed, the experience for families remains relatively undocumented as well. Clearly, greater research attention to these issues would inform the fields of early childhood education and early childhood special education.

A number of publications, however, have highlighted the importance of addressing cultural and linguistic diversity in service environments for young children and their families (Bredekamp & Copple, 1997; Garcia & McLaughlin, 1995; Hanson et al., 1990; Kagan & Garcia, 1991; Lynch & Hanson, 1993, 1998; Wayman, Lynch, & Hanson, 1991). In the discussion that follows, recommendations to the field of practice are identified for strengthening services to young children with disabilities and their families, who are representative of the diverse cultural and linguistic population.

Importance of Cultural and Linguistic Diversity in Preschool Environments

First and foremost, the issue of cultural and linguistic diversity must be brought to the forefront. Although numerous early childhood curricula focus on issues of anti-bias and multicultural approaches, few preschools are able to address the full spectrum of children who come through their doors. Personnel who speak the same languages as the children and families served may be lacking. Program personnel may not be aware of the needs or the perspectives of families that come from nondominant cultural lifestyles. These service weaknesses may be exacerbated for children with disabilities, who may require specialists who not only are trained in their specialty areas, such as speech-language therapy and physical or occupational therapy, but also are able to speak the native language of the child and family and are knowledgeable about the child's and family's cultural lifestyles.

Substantial differences may be apparent between the cultural and behavioral expectations in the classroom and those of the family. How children are taught to speak, to respond, when and how to interact, and in what behaviors to engage under different social situations are only a few of the differences that may arise. Some children may come from environments in which active engagement and speaking out are valued; others

may be expected to remain quiet until asked to speak. Some children may be encouraged to work together with others; other children may be encouraged to act independently. Some children may experience a great deal of adult–child attention and elaboration; for others, adults may foster early independence. The possibilities go on and on. These experiences shape the child's behavior and language and interact with other factors such as disability to determine the resources and characteristics that the child brings to the preschool environment. The child's and family's culture and language do have a strong impact on their interactions and needs for service delivery. This impact must be addressed by service providers.

Coordination and Collaboration Among Fields and Service Systems

The fields of early childhood education, early childhood special education, and bilingual education are increasingly overlapping in the professional literature and through professional exchanges such as conferences. However, disciplinary barriers continue. Although each field, as well as the disciplines represented within that field, holds many interests and values in common with other fields in terms of supporting the development of young children, different parts of the picture may be represented by each. Efforts to coordinate programs and collaborate more fully could enhance opportunities to address the diverse needs of children. For example, coordinated services should be reflected in IEP goals and practices for children with disabilities who come from nondominant cultures and language backgrounds. Goals and strategies directed toward enhancing these children's abilities to interact with and benefit from their preschool experiences require a collaborative approach.

Second-language learning is receiving increased attention as well, and many capable researchers and practitioners are addressing these issues. For instance, Barrera (1993) and Tabors (1997) offered reviews of major approaches to second-language learning and also presented suggestions for teachers in supporting children's language development and organizing classroom environments. These resources need to be widely disseminated to professionals who cross these fields, and professional discussions of these areas must be initiated.

Personnel Training and Professional Development

The need for culturally respectful and culturally sensitive services for young children and their families has been well established (Anderson & Fenichel, 1989; Barrera & Kramer, 1997; Lynch & Hanson, 1998). A number of resources are available to professionals to enhance their development of cultural awareness and cultural competence (Green, 1995; Lynch & Hanson, 1998; Okun et al., 1999). These strategies for developing cross-cultural competence provide professionals with the knowledge and skills necessary to bridge effectively the needs of children and families between the home and service environment.

Lynch and Hanson defined *cross-cultural competence* as "the ability to think, feel, and act in ways that acknowledge, respect, and build upon ethnic, [socio]cultural, and linguistic diversity" (1993, p. 50). The development of self-awareness and the acquisition of culture-specific information and understanding are seen as essential steps in this process (Lynch & Hanson, 1998). Service providers have their own cultural heritage, and it is through exploring their own values, beliefs, and life practices that they begin the journey of understanding how these perspectives have an impact on their work. In addition to becoming aware of their own cultural understandings, service providers also must become acquainted with the values, beliefs, and

practices of the children and families with whom they work. Thus, learning about other cultures through books, film, travel, and the arts, as well as talking with individuals from other cultures, can be important tools for gaining this awareness and information. Individuals who cross cultures can be crucial cultural guides or interpreters in the quest to understand the cultures of others. Working directly with interpreters and translators also is an essential role in service delivery. Lynch and Hanson (1998) provided suggestions for working more effectively with these service supports.

The provision of effective and respectful early childhood services requires an attitude of openness and respect for the many values, beliefs, and behaviors that children and their families present. The opportunities to learn new possibilities for behavior and new ways to view the world are endless and offer myriad growth and learning experiences for early childhood educators.

Making Family-Centered Services Culturally Sensitive Services

The field of early intervention has promoted a family-centered approach to service delivery. Although "family-centered" carries different definitions in different service environments, few services make the link to culture. To be truly child and family centered, services must also be culturally sensitive.

Educational philosophies and organizational structures may be at odds with the perspectives of families. Some families, because of their own experiences or the historical experiences of their cultural or ethnic group, may prefer models (e.g., compensatory, academic orientation) that differ from the philosophies (e.g., child centered, play focused) that are found in many preschool environments. Educators must be prepared to identify and respect these family preferences while recognizing the differences among the many children and families enrolled in the program.

Teacher Support for Children's Interactions

With regard to peer interactions and the development of social competence, the starting point for teachers, paraprofessionals, and related services personnel is to recognize the existence and importance of the social world created and occupied by the children in their classrooms. With this awareness, teachers can begin to identify the norms and content of this social world and use this knowledge to support the participation of children who are experiencing difficulty with mastering the requisite knowledge and behaviors on their own. This support may include interpreting communicative behavior, finding roles that children with disabilities can fill within the most popular play themes, and suggesting to parents ways that the child may be exposed to features of popular culture that are "required knowledge" in the peer culture of the classroom. If the children have different linguistic and cultural backgrounds, then the necessity of serving as an interpreter and guide may be increased. At the same time, however, adults need to be sensitive to issues of collective identity by facilitating interactions and then pulling back so that the child with a disability can participate in child-only groups as much as possible. Thus, teachers can provide valuable support and scaffolds to children's interactions with their peers, even when children differ markedly from one another in their communicative and interactional backgrounds and abilities.

Research Needs

Though program practices reflect increased acknowledgment of the issues posed by cultural and linguistic diversity, few research efforts have focused on these issues. Given the socialization and communication development that occurs in the early years, greater attention to this area is warranted.

AGENDA FOR CHANGE

The population of the United States throughout its history has been radically modified through immigration. The United States has one of the most diverse populations of any country in the world. Although this diversity often has not been recognized in the design of education services, cultural and linguistic diversity are apparent in every facet of American life. The tremendous diversity of the population of children served in the United States mandates attention to the provision of services in a more culturally sensitive manner. In addition to the recommendations for practice previously discussed, a number of policy steps are warranted.

Training in cross-cultural competence: Training for teachers, therapists, and other service providers should include an examination of cultural perspectives, starting from an awareness of the service provider's own biases and perspectives to an appreciation of the range of lifestyles and perspectives of others. Though one will never be able to walk in another's shoes, knowledge of other perspectives is essential for more respectful and flexible services. It is not enough for programs to have materials, days, or events devoted to particular cultural orientations (e.g., celebrations of Chanukah, Christmas, and Cinco de Mayo; sampling foods from other lands). Although the introduction of diverse cultural materials and events may broaden the knowledge of children, families, and staff members and lead to great enjoyment, it does not ensure that a range of lifestyles, values, beliefs and practices are respected, allowed, or practiced in the program. Service providers must learn the different styles of communication, the meaning of different words and gestures, and the different values and belief systems for the children and families they serve.

Recruitment of personnel from a broad range of cultural and ethnic groups: Given that the population of service providers generally does not match the population of children and families that they are required to serve with respect to culture and ethnicity, recruiting from groups that typically have been underrepresented in professional populations is essential. This challenge is issued not only for teacher and other professional training programs but also for administrators of school and child care services. Such efforts must be directed toward recruitment in related-services professions (e.g., speech-language therapy) as well as in the teaching profession.

Linked services: Typically, agencies and systems that are designed or mandated to serve young children, children with special needs, and children from non–English-speaking backgrounds are distinct units. As such, often little coordination or blending of services occurs. As these agencies and systems begin to design programs jointly and more collaboratively, it is likely that the needs of children with disabilities and their families, who also may be children of color or non–English speaking, will be more fully included in program design. Blended services and policies must be reflected not only at the policy level but also through the provision of integrated services at specific sites.

Respecting the range of organizational and theoretical perspectives in early childhood education: Given that families have different goals for their young children on the basis of their heritage, their values and beliefs, and their family experiences, a range of organizational and theoretical perspectives are needed to ensure that families are able to participate in their services of choice. Some families prefer very open, nonstructured services for their young children. For others, a more academic or compensatory program model may be desired. Given the diverse needs of children and their families and the many experiences through which children learn, a "one size fits all" model or perspective does not seem warranted for early childhood services.

Support for non–English-speaking children and families: Communication is fundamental to belonging and participating in any organization, group, or service. Full participation in programs can be compromised for children and families who do not speak English. The use of interpreters who are versed not only in the language of the child and family but also in the family's cultural lifestyle is essential. The use of interpreter services is complex and requires careful consideration; many guidelines for the use of interpreters are available (see, e.g., Lynch & Hanson, 1998). As increasing numbers of staff members from previously underrepresented groups are recruited and trained to provide services, the abilities of programs to encompass a wider range of children and their families in their services will be strengthened. Children and families who identify with cultural ways that may differ from the traditional or dominant mainstream culture are not a special population. All children and their families deserve to have their individual preferences and needs addressed in programs that are designed to serve young children.

Need to improve special education components of early childhood education services: Children with special needs who are enrolled in inclusive early education services through Head Start and community preschool and child care placements often do not adequately have their special service needs addressed. It is essential that culturally sensitive instruments and procedures for determining and measuring difficulties (including language difficulties) be applied in screening, assessing, and qualifying non-native and non–English-speaking children with disabilities for services. Furthermore, although IEPs may exist for these children, these special services may not be integrated into the general curriculum or, in some cases, provided at all. In their research, the authors have found that families often are faced with having to choose segregated special services or inclusion with few or no special supports. As services in the fields of special education and early childhood education become more collaborative and integrated, these issues may be rectified. The development and dissemination of training and program models that educate young children with disabilities who also come from non–English-speaking and/or nondominant cultures are essential.

CONCLUSION

As the United States continues to become increasingly diverse, attention to issues of cultural and linguistic diversity assumes even greater importance. Early childhood educators work closely with young children and their families at a particularly crucial period in their lives, when families are just beginning their journeys through the education service system. They are faced with defining goals and expectations for their children and locating and selecting the services that best fit their needs. During this period, children also are undergoing crucial development. They are developing a sense of self, increasing their skills and ability to interact and communicate with others, and gaining a knowledge of the social parameters for their behavior. Their cultural and linguistic heritage and context play a

tremendous role in this developmental process. Services can either enhance this process for children and their families or interfere with it.

The cultural and linguistic diversity of children and their families presents new challenges for the development and implementation of child and family services. New opportunities allow service providers to reflect on their own perspectives and learn a broader set of options for their own behavior and understanding.

Cultural and language differences, like disabilities, can influence and even hamper children's learning and interactions. These differences, too, can affect families' abilities to participate in the services, be heard, communicate with program staff members, and even interact with other families. However, for children and families participating in early childhood experiences in which differences are acknowledged and celebrated, supportive and nurturing experiences can be found.

REFERENCES

Anderson, P.P., & Fenichel, E.S. (1989). *Serving culturally diverse families of infants and toddlers with disabilities.* Washington, DC: National Center for Clinical Infant Programs.

Antia, S.D., Kreimeyer, K.H., & Eldredge, N. (1994). Promoting social interaction between young children with hearing impairments and their peers. *Exceptional Children, 60,* 262–275.

Bailey, D.B., Skinner, D., Rodriguez, P., Gut, D., & Correa, V. (1999). Awareness, use, and satisfaction with services for Latino parents of young children with disabilities. *Exceptional Children, 65,* 367–381.

Barrera, I. (1993). Effective and appropriate instruction for all children: The challenge of cultural/linguistic diversity and young children with special needs. *Topics in Early Childhood Special Education, 13,* 461–487.

Barrera, I., & Kramer, L. (1997). From monologues to skilled dialogues: Teaching the process of crafting culturally competent early childhood environments. In P.J. Winton, J.A. McCollum, & C. Catlett (Eds.), *Reforming personnel preparation in early intervention: Issues, models, and practical strategies* (pp. 217–251). Baltimore: Paul H. Brookes Publishing Co.

Beckman, P.J., Barnwell, D., Horn, E., Hanson, M.J., Gutierrez, S., & Lieber, J. (1998). Communities, families, and inclusion. *Early Childhood Research Quarterly, 13,* 125–150.

Berk, L.E., & Winsler, A. (1995). *Scaffolding children's learning: Vygotsky and early childhood education.* Washington, DC: National Association for the Education of Young Children.

Bowman, B.L., & Stott, F.M. (1994). Understanding development in a cultural context. In B.L. Mallory & R. New (Eds.), *Diversity and developmentally appropriate practice* (pp. 119–134). New York: Teachers College Press.

Bredekamp, S., & Copple, C. (1997). *Developmentally appropriate practice in early childhood programs* (Rev. ed.). Washington, DC: National Association for the Education of Young Children.

Bronfenbrenner, U. (1979). *The ecology of human development.* Cambridge, MA: Harvard University Press.

Chan, S. (1990). Early intervention with culturally diverse families of infants and toddlers with disabilities. *Infants and Young Children, 3,* 78–87.

Children's Defense Fund. (1989). *A vision of America's future.* Washington, DC: Author.

Corsaro, W.A. (1985). *Friendship and peer culture in the early years.* Stamford, CT: Ablex.

DeGangi, G.A., Wietlisbach, S., Poisson, S., Stein, E., & Royeen, C. (1994). The impact of culture and socioeconomic status on family–professional collaboration: Challenges and solutions. *Topics in Early Childhood Special Education, 14,* 503–520.

Denzin, N. (1977). *Childhood socialization.* San Francisco: Jossey-Bass.

Diamond, K.E. (1994). Evaluating preschool children's sensitivity to developmental differences in their peers. *Topics in Early Childhood Special Education, 14,* 49–63.

Diaz, R.M., Padilla, K.M., & Weathersby, E.K. (1991). The effects of bilingualism on preschoolers' private speech. *Early Childhood Research Quarterly, 6,* 377–393.

Federal Interagency Forum on Child and Family Statistics. (1998). *America's children: Key national indicators of well-being.* Washington, DC: U.S. Government Printing Office.

Fivish, R. (1992). The social construction of personal narratives. *Merrill-Palmer Quarterly, 37,* 59–82.

Garcia, E.E., & McLaughlin, B. (with Spodek, B. & Saracho, O.N.). (Eds.). (1995). *Meeting the challenge of linguistic and cultural diversity in early childhood education.* Yearbook in early childhood education (Vol. 6). New York: Teachers College Press.

Garcia, S.B., & Malkin, D.H. (1993). Toward defining programs and services for culturally and linguistically diverse learners in special education. *Teaching Exceptional Children, 26,* 52–58.

Green, J.W. (1995). *Cultural awareness in the human services: A multi-ethnic approach* (2nd ed.). Needham Heights, MA: Allyn & Bacon.

Guralnick, M.J. (1990). Social competence and early intervention. *Journal of Early Intervention, 14,* 3–14.

Guralnick, M.J. (1992). A hierarchical model for understanding children's peer-related social competence. In S.L. Odom, S.R. McConnell, & M.A. McEvoy (Eds.), *Social competence of young children with disabilities: Issues and strategies for intervention* (pp. 37–64). Baltimore: Paul H. Brookes Publishing Co.

Guralnick, M.J. (1994). Social competence with peers: Outcome and process in early childhood special education. In P.L. Safford (Ed.), *Yearbook in early childhood education: Early childhood special education* (Vol. 5, pp. 45–71). New York: Teachers College Press.

Guralnick, M.J. (1999). The nature and meaning of social integration for young children with mild developmental delays in inclusive settings. *Journal of Early Intervention, 22,* 70–86.

Guralnick, M.J., Connor, R., & Hammond, M. (1995). Parent perspectives of peer relations and friendships in integrated and specialized programs. *American Journal on Mental Retardation, 99,* 457–476.

Guralnick, M.J., Gottman, J.M., & Hammond, M.A. (1996). Effects of social setting on the friendship formation of young children differing in developmental status. *Journal of Applied Developmental Psychology, 17,* 625–651.

Guralnick, M.J., & Groom, J.M. (1988). Friendships of preschool children in mainstreamed playgroups. *Developmental Psychology, 24,* 595–604.

Guralnick, M.J., & Neville, B. (1997). Designing early intervention programs to promote children's social competence. In M.J. Guralnick (Ed.), *The effectiveness of early intervention* (pp. 579–610). Baltimore: Paul H. Brookes Publishing Co.

Gutierrez, K., & Garcia, E. (1989). Academic literacy in linguistic minority children: The connections between language, cognition and culture. *Early Child Development and Care, 51,* 109–126.

Hakuta, K., & Garcia, G. (1989). Bilingualism and education. *American Psychologist, 44,* 374–379.

Hanson, M.J., Gutierrez, S., Morgan, M., Brennan, E.L., & Zercher, C. (1997). Language, culture, and disability: Interacting influences on preschool inclusion. *Topics in Early Childhood Special Education, 17,* 307–336.

Hanson, M.J., & Lynch, E.W. (1992). Family diversity: Implications for policy and practice. *Topics in Early Childhood Special Education, 12,* 283–306.

Hanson, M.J., Lynch, E.W., & Wayman, K.I. (1990). Honoring the cultural diversity of families when gathering data. *Topics in Early Childhood Special Education, 10,* 112–131.

Hanson, M.J., Wolfberg, P., Zercher, C., Morgan, M., Gutierrez, S., Barnwell, D., & Beckman, P. (1998). The culture of inclusion: Recognizing diversity at multiple levels. *Early Childhood Research Quarterly, 13,* 185–209.

Harry, B. (1992a). *Cultural diversity, families, and the special education system: Communication and empowerment.* New York: Teachers College Press.

Harry, B. (1992b). Developing cultural awareness: The first step in values clarification for early interventionists. *Topics in Early Childhood Special Education, 12,* 333–350.

Kagan, S., & Garcia, E. (1991). Education of culturally and linguistically diverse preschoolers: Moving the agenda. *Early Childhood Research Quarterly, 6,* 427–443.

Levine, L.M., & Antia, S.D. (1997). The effect of partner hearing status on social and cognitive play. *Journal of Early Intervention, 21,* 21–35.

Luetke-Stahlman, B. (1994). Procedures for socially integrating preschoolers who are hearing, deaf, and hard-of-hearing. *Topics in Early Childhood Special Education, 14,* 472–487.

Lynch, E.W., & Hanson, M.J. (1993). Changing demographics: Implications for training in early intervention. *Infants and Young Children, 6,* 50–55.

Lynch, E.W., & Hanson, M.J. (1998). *Developing cross-cultural competence: A guide for working with children and their families* (2nd ed.). Baltimore: Paul H. Brookes Publishing Co.

Lynch, E.W., & Stein, R.C. (1987). Parent participation by ethnicity: A comparison of Hispanic, black, and Anglo families. *Exceptional Children, 54,* 105–111.

Maccoby, E.E. (1988). Gender as a social category. *Developmental Psychology, 55,* 755–765.

Mary, N.L. (1990). Reactions of black, Hispanic and white mothers to having a child with handicaps. *Mental Retardation, 28,* 1–5.

McGonigel, M., Kaufman, R.K., & Johnson, B.H. (1991). *Guidelines and recommended practices for the individualized family service plan* (2nd ed.). Alexandria, VA: Association for the Care of Children's Health.

Meadow-Orlans, K.P., & Sass-Lehrer, M. (1995). Support services for families with children who are deaf: Challenges for professionals. *Topics in Early Childhood Special Education, 15,* 314–334.

Miller, P., Potts, R., Fung, H., Hoogstra, L., & Mintz, J. (1990). Narrative practices and the social construction of self in childhood. *American Ethnologist, 17,* 292–311.

Miller, P., Wiley, A., Fung, H., & Liang, C. (1997). Personal storytelling as a medium of socialization in Chinese and American families. *Child Development, 68,* 557–568.

Minnett, A., Clark, K., & Wilson, G. (1994). Play behavior and communication between deaf and hard of hearing children and their hearing peers in an integrated preschool. *American Annals of the Deaf, 139*(4), 420–429.

Odom, S.L., & Brown, W.H. (1993). Social interaction skills interventions for young children with disabilities in integrated settings. In C.A. Peck, S.L. Odom, & D.D. Bricker (Eds.), *Integrating young children with disabilities into community programs: Ecological perspectives on research and implementation* (pp. 39–64). Baltimore: Paul H. Brookes Publishing Co.

Odom, S.L., & Diamond, K.E. (1998). Inclusion of young children with special needs in early childhood education: The research base. *Early Childhood Research Quarterly, 13,* 3–25.

Odom, S.L., McConnell, S.R., & McEvoy, M.A. (1992). *Social competence of young children with disabilities: Issues and strategies for intervention.* Baltimore: Paul H. Brookes Publishing Co.

Odom, S.L., Peck, C.A., Hanson, M.J., Beckman, P.J., Kaiser, A.P., Lieber, J., Brown, W.H., Horn, E.M., & Schwartz, I.S. (1996). Inclusion at the preschool level: An ecological systems analysis. *Social Policy Report: Society of Research in Child Development, 10,* 18–30.

Okun, B.F., Fried, J., & Okun, M.L. (1999). *Understanding diversity: A learning-as-practice primer.* Pacific Grove, CA: Brooks/Cole Publishing.

Opie, I., & Opie, P. (1959). *The lore and language of school children.* New York: Oxford University Press.

Piaget, J. (1932). *The language and thought of the child.* London: Routledge & Kegan Paul.

Ramsey, P.G., & Myers, L.C. (1990). Salience of race in young children's cognitive, affective, and behavioral responses to social environments. *Journal of Applied Developmental Psychology, 11,* 49–67.

Randall-David, E. (1989). *Strategies for working with culturally diverse communities and clients.* Alexandria, VA: Association for the Care of Children's Health.

Salend, S.J. (1997). What about our schools, our languages. *Teaching Exceptional Children, 29,* 38–41.

Smith, M.J., & Ryan, A.S. (1987). Chinese-American families of children with developmental disabilities: An exploratory study of reactions to service providers. *Mental Retardation, 25,* 345–350.

Snow, C., & Ferguson, C. (1977). *Talking to children: Language input and acquisition.* New York: Cambridge University Press.

Tabors, P.O. (1997). *One child, two languages: A guide for preschool educators of children learning English as a second language.* Baltimore: Paul H. Brookes Publishing Co.

Thurman, S.K., & Lewis, M. (1979). Children's response to differences: Some possible implications for mainstreaming. *Exceptional Children, 45,* 468–470.

U.S. Census Bureau. (1997). *Estimates of the population of states by race and Hispanic origin: July 1, 1997* [On-line]. Available: http://www.census. gov

U.S. Census Bureau. (1998). *School enrollment of the population.* Internet release date: August 14, 1998 [On-line]. Available: http://www.census. gov

U.S. Census Bureau. (1999). [On-line] Available: http://www.census.gov/population/estimates/nation/intfile3-1.txt

Vygotsky, L. (1978). *Mind in society.* Cambridge, MA: Harvard University Press.

Vygotsky, L. (1986). *Thought and language.* Cambridge, MA: Harvard University Press.

Wayman, K.I., Lynch, E.W., & Hanson, M.J. (1991). Home-based early childhood services: Cultural sensitivity in a family systems approach. *Topics in Early Childhood Special Education, 10,* 56–75.

Wertsch, J.V. (1985). *Vygotsky and the social formation of mind.* Cambridge, MA: Harvard University Press.

Wiley, A., Rose, A., Burger, L., & Miller, P. (1998). Constructing autonomous selves through narrative practices: A comparative study of working-class and middle-class families. *Child Development, 69,* 833–847.

Wolfberg, P.J., Zercher, C., Lieber, J., Capell, K., Matias, S.G., Hanson, M.J., & Odom, S.L. (1999). "Can I play with you?" Peer culture in inclusive preschool programs. *Journal of The Association for Persons with Severe Handicaps, 24*(2), 69–84.

Wong Fillmore, L. (1991). When learning a second language means losing the first. *Early Childhood Research Quarterly, 6,* 323–346.

19

DIANE PAUL-BROWN

CAROL J. CAPERTON

Inclusive Practices for Preschool-Age Children with Specific Language Impairment

Children with specific language impairment (SLI) have a significant limitation in language abilities in the absence of other intellectual, socioemotional, or auditory impairments (Leonard, 1998; Stark & Tallal, 1981; Watkins & Rice, 1994). Similar to other groups of children with developmental delays, a number of converging legislative, societal, and professional trends have had a strong influence on the intervention setting for preschool-age children with SLI. In particular, the press for full participation of all children in early childhood education activities; the recognition that natural contexts provide opportunities for fostering communication; and the emergence of a functional, social perspective of language have created the basis for young children with SLI to receive services in classroom settings with children who have typically developing communication skills (i.e., inclusive settings).

The concept of inclusion is one of the most prominent forces influencing contemporary services for preschool-age children with SLI. The landmark civil rights legislation, the Education for All Handicapped Children Act of 1975 (PL 94-142), and subsequent legislation (Education of the Handicapped Act Amendments of 1986 [PL 99-457]) that extended services from birth to 21 years of age provided the mandate for services and supports needed by young children with disabilities, including those with communication disabilities. The "least restrictive environment" (LRE) stipulation in this federal law (the law is now known as the Individuals with Disabilities Education Act [IDEA] of 1990 [PL 101-476] and includes its amendments of 1991 [PL 102-119] and 1997 [PL 105-17]) has required reconsideration of the intervention setting for providing speech and language services for young children with SLI. The legislation conveys a clear preference for providing services for children with disabilities in settings that include typically developing children.

The authors gratefully acknowledge Carolyn Stancliff and Charles C. Diggs for their assistance with the preparation of this chapter.

433

Recognizing the need to assist speech-language pathologists who are in a position to influence placement decisions for preschool-age children with communication disorders, the American Speech-Language-Hearing Association (ASHA) developed a position statement on inclusive practices (ASHA, 1996). ASHA defines inclusive practices as "intervention services that are based on the unique and specific needs of the individual, provided in a setting that is least restrictive" (1996, p. 36). ASHA's position is that "an array of speech, language, and hearing services should be available in educational settings to support children and youths with communication disorders" (ASHA, 1996, p. 35). This position places greater emphasis on the availability of a continuum of service settings rather than expressing a definite preference for inclusive settings. Nevertheless, ASHA clearly recognizes the potential value of inclusive practices for children with communication disorders, depending on the individual needs of each child.

The defining features of inclusive practices for young children with communication disorders delineated by ASHA and others include the following (ASHA, 1996; Ferguson, 1991; McCormick, 1997; Nelson, 1989; Paul-Brown, 1999; Rice & Wilcox, 1995; Westby, Watson, & Murphy, 1994; Wilcox & Shannon, 1996):

1. Encouraging peer interactions with *typical language models*
2. Providing services in the *natural educational environment*
3. Integrating speech and language intervention within the *classroom curriculum and activities*
4. *Collaborating* with speech-language pathologists, teachers, parents, and others to achieve communication goals

5. Bringing speech and language *services to the child* rather than taking the child to a separate treatment room

COMMUNICATION DISORDERS IN PRESCHOOL-AGE CHILDREN

It is estimated that 8%–12% of preschool-age children have some form of language impairment (National Institute on Deafness and Other Communication Disorders, 1995). This figure encompasses all communication disorders including those that co-occur or are secondary to other disorders such as hearing loss, developmental (cognitive) delay, or autistic spectrum disorders. This chapter focuses primarily on preschool-age children with SLI who are developing typically in all domains except language structure, content, and/or function. Approximately 5% of preschool-age children are identified as having SLI, and boys are nearly twice as likely to be affected as girls (National Institute on Deafness and Other Communication Disorders, 1995).

Preschool-age children with SLI are a heterogeneous group (Leonard, 1998; Watkins & Rice, 1994). However, some language comprehension and production deficits are characteristic of young children with SLI and encompass the full spectrum of communication disorders: structure (i.e., phonological, morphosyntactic), content (i.e., semantic), and function (i.e., pragmatic). Most children with SLI are late in first-word acquisition and first-word combinations and have production problems that typically exceed comprehension difficulties (Trauner, Wulfeck, Tallal, & Hesselink, 1995), and preschool-age children with SLI often have a more limited variety of verbs compared with that of same-age peers and peers matched on mean length of utterance (MLU) (Watkins, Rice, & Moltz, 1993). These young children also typically omit major syntactic categories (e.g., nouns, verbs, embedded phrases), show lower use of grammatical morphemes than children in MLU control groups (Leonard, 1998), and demonstrate phonological skills below age expectations (Shriberg & Kwiatkowski, 1994).

Conversational skills are also compromised in children with SLI, particularly when more than one other child is involved (Leonard, 1998). Preschool- and school-age children with SLI have difficulty joining established conversations with typically developing peers (Corsaro, 1979, 1981; Craig & Washington, 1993). Although young children with SLI are just as likely as their age-matched peers to initiate conversations with peers more than with adults, this similarity is limited to dyadic interactions (Fey & Leonard, 1984). In interactions with more than one partner, children with SLI are more likely than typically developing peers to initiate interactions with adults than with peers in preschool classrooms (Rice, Sell, & Hadley, 1991). Children with SLI also seem to have difficulties resolving conflicts verbally, resorting to physical aggression or withdrawal more often (Baker, Cantwell, & Mattison, 1980).

All of these characteristics of children with SLI culminate in an inability to communicate effectively. Given the range and magnitude of these difficulties, it is no surprise that young children who experience such communication problems engage in fewer peer interactions and could become socially isolated (see Craig, 1993; Guralnick, Connor, Hammond, Gottman, & Kinnish, 1996; Hadley & Rice, 1991; Rice, 1993; Rice et al., 1991). The availability and value of peer language models in inclusive settings could mitigate the potential for social separation of young children with SLI.

POTENTIAL VALUE OF PEER LANGUAGE MODELS

Inclusive settings afford opportunities for natural, meaningful language use with peers with typical speech and language development. Peer modeling and support have the potential to enhance the communication of young children with SLI. A number of studies have demonstrated that typically developing young children can adjust their language complexity and functions during interactions with communication partners at different chronological (and, therefore, developmental) ages (Garvey & BenDebba, 1974; Masur, 1978; Sachs & Devin, 1976; Shatz & Gelman, 1973; see also Goldstein & Kaczmarek, 1992, for a review). Typically developing young children also can modify aspects of language structure (e.g., MLU, syntactic complexity), content (e.g., word choice), and use (e.g., directives, information statements) to accommodate the developmental level of a companion with varying degrees of developmental delay (Guralnick & Paul-Brown, 1977, 1980, 1984, 1986, 1989; Guralnick et al., 1998). This research demonstrates the adaptability of the language of typically developing preschool-age children and suggests that these children are capable of serving as appropriate language models in inclusive settings.

The social-communication patterns of children with mild developmental delays provide further support to the value of typically developing children as communication partners. Preschool-age children with mild developmental delays also are capable of adjusting their language patterns according to the developmental level of their listener. In particular, they demonstrate increased syntactic complexity during interactions with typically developing peers and those with mild delays compared with exchanges with children who have moderate or severe delays (Guralnick & Paul-Brown, 1986). Patterns of adjustment in communication function, style, and affective quality are even more finely tuned than are modifications in language structure. Although language structure does not vary during interactions with partners who have mild or no delays, children with mild delays use more information statements, make more solicitations for joint actions, have fewer strong directives, and have fewer disagreements during exchanges with typically developing peers than with other peers with mild delays (Guralnick & Paul-Brown, 1989).

Children with SLI also can modify their communication patterns according to the chronological age of their partner in a manner similar to that of same-age, linguistically advanced peers. Exchanges with same-age children can elicit more complex language in children with SLI than can a pairing with younger children with similar language levels (Fey, Leonard, & Wilcox, 1981). This pattern is not consistent, however, perhaps because of the heterogeneity of these children and their inherent difficulty with the structural features of language. Nevertheless, children with SLI can make listener-based modifications in communication function and style (e.g., acknowledgments, contingent queries; Fey & Leonard, 1984). Therefore, the potential for children with SLI to develop and refine their communication interaction patterns may be enhanced when same-age typically developing children are available.

Structured interactions between typically developing preschool-age children and peers with SLI or developmental disabilities provide another source of evidence for the potential communication benefits of such pairings. In structured dyadic play sessions, typically developing young children were found to elicit more elaborate play scripts (e.g., longer, more diverse word use) from partners with

SLI compared with SLI–SLI dyads (Robertson & Ellis Weismer, 1997). In addition, peer-mediated communication training has been used with typically developing preschool-age children during interactions in classrooms with children with moderate developmental disabilities (Goldstein, English, Shafer, & Kaczmarek, 1997). After such training, both groups of children show improvements in social-communication interactions, primarily in the variety and frequency of their communication acts (e.g., verbal requests, comments).

In sum, typically developing young children can modify their language use according to the age and developmental or linguistic level of their communication partner. These language adjustments seem to elicit more varied, collaborative, informative, positive, and complex interactions from preschool-age children with mild developmental delays and SLI compared with interactions with children with disabilities. Thus, typically developing peers have the potential to create a communication environment that is conducive to language learning in inclusive classroom settings. Communication interactions between typically developing peers and those with SLI may not occur spontaneously, however, even in inclusive classrooms. It may be necessary to structure and prompt such interactions to help peers be effective language models in inclusive settings and create opportunities for preschool-age children with SLI to test their developing communication skills (e.g., Guralnick, 1976; Rice et al., 1991; Weiss & Nakamura, 1992).

EXTENT OF INCLUSIVE PRACTICES

Despite the potential communication benefits of peer models in inclusive classroom settings, other advantages of inclusive practices, and legal considerations, the fact remains that although service changes have occurred, inclusive settings are not the norm for preschool-age children with SLI. To determine the extent of inclusive practices for preschool-age children with SLI, the authors contacted, via e-mail, speech and language consultants in state education agencies and speech-language pathologists who compose an ASHA network of state education contacts. They received detailed descriptions from 18 states about setting options and placement criteria. They also contacted federal employees who are responsible for monitoring compliance with IDEA across the United States for preschool-age children. These reports suggest that there is tremendous variability in setting options and service delivery models within and across states with no obvious criteria to guide placement decisions.

A prominent service option seems to be a clinic rather than a classroom model. Preliminary data from a national survey of school-based speech-language pathologists who work with preschool-age children reinforce these findings (ASHA, 2000b). With a clinic model, young children typically receive direct one-to-one or small-group speech and language services for 1–2 hours per week with no classroom activities. In addition to the clinic option, speech-language pathologists report that inclusive and specialized classroom settings are available, but more restrictive specialized classrooms (in which all children have some form of disability) or specialized language classrooms (in which all children have a primary communication disorder) are more common than inclusive classrooms. Some states fund speech and language services for children who are enrolled in private preschool and child care programs, but tuition often is the responsibility of the family.

Basing placements on individualized communication needs is a primary consideration. Most programs offer only a limited number of placement options, however, so placement decisions seem to be based more on availability than individual needs. With a few notable exceptions, the overarching practice seems to be, "settings and services are individualized as long as a child needs what we have." Many programs are beginning to consider broadening the placement options and expanding the availability of inclusive settings to be more consistent with IDEA regulations. Lack of publicly funded preschool classrooms for typically developing children is the largest barrier to the availability of inclusive classrooms for young children with SLI.

Different models of inclusion may be used for preschool-age children with SLI (see Chapter 1), although no systematic data on their application are available. Informal reports at the state level suggest that two models that are used with this population are the *full inclusion model* (i.e., the primary educational setting for young children with SLI is a classroom in which the majority of children have no disabilities) and the *reverse inclusion model* (i.e., the primary educational setting is a classroom in which a few children without disabilities are included with children who have SLI).

Although, as noted, inclusion is not widely practiced for children with SLI, when it occurs, the full inclusion model is the most prevalent, often involving Head Start and community child care programs. The reverse inclusion model, although used infrequently or not at all in most school districts, typically is used in the few university-based speech and language clinics that have inclusive preschool programs. Some graduate clinics promote an inclusive philosophy and encourage enrollment by children without disabilities; nevertheless, even some of these well-intentioned programs have been unsuccessful in recruiting typically developing children (e.g., C.L. Ackerson, personal communication, June 1999; N. Bernstein Ratner, personal communication, April 1998).

PURPOSE OF CHAPTER

Any shift to more inclusive settings constitutes a major challenge in the field of speech-language pathology. In fact, many barriers, which are discussed later in this chapter, need to be addressed from a systems, programmatic, and research perspective before a vision of inclusive practices for preschool-age children with SLI can be realized fully.

Accordingly, this chapter examines concepts and evidence related to the impact of inclusive classroom settings on the speech and language performance of preschool-age children (3–5 years old) with SLI. Special emphasis is placed on understanding the connection between inclusion and changing models of the delivery of speech and language services. In addition, program characteristics are proposed that may be essential to the success of inclusive preschools for these children. After these discussions, barriers to the provision of speech and language services within inclusive settings are addressed, information and training gaps in relation to inclusive practices are identified, and critical research needs are discussed. Finally, an agenda for change is proposed to provide the most appropriate, effective services for children with SLI within the context of early childhood inclusion.

SERVICE DELIVERY MODELS FOR SPEECH-LANGUAGE PATHOLOGY

Communication services can take many forms in inclusive settings, ranging from traditional pull-out services in which treatment is provided in a separate room to more indirect collaborative approaches (see ASHA, 1993, 1999; Holzhauser-Peters & Husemann, 1988; Meyer, 1997). Described are the components and possible rationale for the three main service delivery models used in

school speech-language pathology practice. After the description of the models, the conceptual and empirical bases for using a particular model or models in inclusive classroom settings are addressed.

Pull-Out Model

Traditionally, the predominant, if not exclusive, model of service delivery for preschool-age children with communication disorders, irrespective of setting, has been a "pull-out" model in which a speech-language pathologist provides direct treatment in a separate therapy room with an individual or small group (ASHA, 1993, 1999). The components of a pull-out model include the following:

Role: The speech-language pathologist serves in a direct role.

Context: A separate treatment room is the primary context for speech and language intervention. The communication partners typically are adults; partners may also be peers with speech and language disabilities when small groups are used.

Goals: Communication goals typically are separate from the classroom curriculum but may be integrated.

Collaboration: Collaboration is not a characteristic of this model, but it may occur among the speech-language pathologist, teacher, parents, and others.

The pull-out model evolved from a clinic model of service delivery that was the prevailing context for providing speech and language services in the early years of the field (Miller, 1989). A survey of school-based speech-language pathology services demonstrates that a traditional pull-out model continues to be the most used service delivery model for preschool- and school-age children with communication disorders (ASHA, 1995).

Typically, communication intervention using this model has focused on discrete language units such as articulation, grammar, and vocabulary taught in an isolated context rather than on the establishment of more functional communication goals within a social, interactive context (see Cirrin & Penner, 1995). Yet, the content of the classroom curriculum may also provide the focus of intervention activities within a pull-out model (Nelson, 1998). Speech-language pathologists confer with classroom teachers when they use a pull-out model, although they do so less often than with classroom-based models (see the next section) (ASHA, 1995).

Reasons offered for a pull-out model are usefulness for 1) teaching certain skills that require repetitive drills, 2) teaching a new behavior, 3) working with children who are easily distracted, and 4) working with children who have more severe disabilities (see Nelson, 1990; Wilcox & Shannon, 1996). Some children may also prefer to receive special services out of the view of peers. Another reason for the prevalence of the pull-out model is the opportunity afforded to the speech-language pathologist to control communication variables by limiting auditory and visual distractions and structuring conversational exchanges (Nelson, 1998).

Problems that are inherent to a pull-out model are the isolation of the child, the difficulty with generalization to natural settings, and the lack of meaningful social-communication interactions—what Nelson referred to as the "context stripping" (Nelson, 1998, p. 166) that tends to accompany communication in pull-out rooms. Although these reasons and concerns represent prevalent views about the pull-out model, only a few studies have tested these assumptions.

Classroom-Based Model

With a classroom-based model, the speech-language pathologist provides service directly in the classroom in coordination with the classroom teacher. Classroom-based service delivery models in inclusive settings have the following main features (see Cirrin & Penner, 1995; Nelson, 1998; Paul-Brown, 1988, 1992; Simon, 1987b):

Role: The speech-language pathologist serves in a direct role.

Context: The classroom is the primary context for speech and language intervention. The communication partners are adults and peers with and without disabilities.

Goals: Communication goals are integrated within the general classroom curriculum.

Collaboration: The teacher, speech-language pathologist, parents, and others work together to select goals and determine appropriate intervention strategies.

There are several ways that speech-language pathologists and teachers can work together to provide classroom-based communication services. The three most commonly used forms of interaction include 1) one teaches, one "drifts" (the teacher or the speech-language pathologist assists students as needed while the other provides instruction), 2) team teaching (the speech-language pathologist and the teacher share responsibilities for all teaching tasks), and 3) one teaches, one observes (the speech-language pathologist or the teacher collects observational classroom data while the other teaches the class) (Elksnin & Capilouto, 1994).

Cirrin and Penner (1995) suggested that possible advantages of a classroom-based model of service delivery include 1) the targeting of language goals that are more relevant to classroom needs, 2) better generalization of new skills, 3) the opportunity for professionals other than the speech-language pathologist to work with a student, thereby increasing the frequency of intervention, 4) alleviation of problems incurred by pulling the student out of the classroom, and 5) provision of services to students who are at risk but not identified or receiving services for a communication disorder. Classroom-based models within inclusive settings also provide opportunities to foster communication interactions with typically developing peers, who can model appropriate language forms and functions.

Collaborative Consultation Model

Collaborative consultation models in speech-language pathology involve problem solving and mutual goal setting from multiple perspectives that are relevant to a child's communication needs (Idol, Paolucci-Whitcomb, & Nevin, 1986). Typically, the teacher is responsible for direct implementation, and the speech-language pathologist plays a more indirect role, offering information and guidance. The speech-language pathologist assists with decision points and changes in treatment plans. Collaborative consultation models in inclusive settings have the following characteristics:

Role: The speech-language pathologist serves in an indirect role.
Context: The classroom is the primary context for speech and language intervention. The communication partners are adults and peers with and without disabilities.
Goals: Communication goals are integrated within the general classroom curriculum.
Collaboration: The teacher, speech-language pathologist, parents, and others work together to select goals and determine appropriate intervention strategies.

The responsibility, accountability, and resources all are shared in this model (Brandel, 1992; Coufal, 1993; Damico, 1987; Ferguson, 1992; Frassinelli, Superior, & Meyers, 1983; Magnotta, 1991; Marvin, 1987, 1990; Montgomery, 1992; Russell & Kaderavek, 1993; Secord, 1990;

Silliman & Wilkinson, 1991; Simon, 1987a, 1987b; Simon & Myrold-Gunyuz, 1990).

In the evaluation of the effectiveness of consultation models, the fidelity of intervention is an especially important consideration. Specifically, this refers to the "quality, intensity, and consistency with which an intervention is implemented" (Cirrin & Penner, 1995, p. 347). With an indirect approach, the speech-language pathologist needs to make certain that teachers are implementing in the classroom communication strategies that support communication goals and that the strategies are used consistently and frequently.

Compatibility of Service Delivery Models with Inclusive Practices

Any one of these service delivery models may be used singly or in combination in inclusive classroom settings for preschool-age children with SLI. However, a certain model or models may be more consistent conceptually with inclusive practices or may lead to more favorable speech and language outcomes for children in inclusive classrooms. As shown in Table 19.1, classroom-based and collaborative service delivery models seem to be more compatible with the defining features of inclusive practices discussed previously. Consistent with inclusive settings, both practice models provide increased opportunities for children with SLI to have interactions with peers who can serve as appropriate language models. Furthermore, the models provide services in the natural environment, involve collaboration to foster communication goals that are consistent with curricular goals, and bring services to the child in the typical educational setting. Although a pull-out model is not as compatible with inclusive practices, pull-out services still may be appropriate at certain times for children in inclusive settings,

Table 19.1. Compatibility of service delivery models with features of inclusive practices for preschool-age children with specific language impairment

Features of inclusive practices	Service delivery model		
	Pull-out	Classroom-based	Collaborative consultation
Provides opportunities for peer language models	No	Yes	Yes
Provides services in natural educational setting	No	Yes	Yes
Integrates speech and language intervention within the classroom curriculum and activities	Possible	Yes	Yes
Collaboration occurs among speech-language pathologists, teachers, parents, and others to achieve communication goals	Possible	Yes	Yes
Brings speech and language services to the child rather than taking the child to a separate treatment room	No	Yes	Yes

either exclusively or in combination with other practice models.

The authors reviewed studies that compared speech and language outcomes using different service delivery models to determine whether there is an empirical basis as well as a conceptual basis for using particular service delivery models in inclusive settings. Despite the movement toward alternative service delivery models, only a few studies have compared their use and only one study focused on service models specifically within an inclusive classroom. In a study that evaluated different service delivery models with children in an inclusive classroom, Valdez and Montgomery (1997) compared a traditional pull-out model and an in-class model of language intervention with 40 Head Start students with primary language disorders (ages 3–5 years). Both groups of children who were receiving services from the speech-language pathologist, regardless of service delivery model, showed improvement for the total language score from pretest to posttest on a standardized language measure; there were no significant clinical differences with this measure between the two groups. It is possible that differences exist; however, such a global dependent variable is not sensitive to the strengths identified for in-class models

(e.g., conversational interactions with peers, generalization, language goals consistent with classroom goals).

In another study focused on service delivery models, irrespective of setting, Wilcox, Kouri, and Caswell (1991) compared classroom-based language intervention with an individual pull-out approach for preschool-age children (ages 20–47 months) with SLI. The intervention goal was to increase children's spontaneous and productive use of individually identified target words. There were no significant differences between the two intervention conditions in the use of target words in the classroom. Children in both groups were more likely to use their target words productively at home than in either intervention condition in school. However, the children who received the classroom-based intervention had a significantly higher use of target words in their homes. A similar study with older children with speech and language problems (kindergarten through third grade) demonstrated an advantage in vocabulary acquisition with a collaborative model compared with a classroom-based or exclusively pull-out approach (Throneburg, Calvert, Sturm, Paramboukas, & Paul, 2000). However, the children in the collaborative and classroom-based conditions also received pull-out services; the combination of the two models may have been the contributing factor to the relative success of one approach over another.

The effects of in-class and pull-out models on the nature of conversations that occur in the two conditions were compared in a study by Roberts, Prizant, and McWilliam (1995), although the type of classroom setting was not specified. Investigators compared conversational turn taking between young children (ages 1–5 years) and speech-language pathologists, with children randomly assigned to either a pull-out or in-class condition. Analyses of turn taking and the function of the turn revealed that speech-language pathologists took significantly more turns in the pull-out sessions but did not differ in the types of responses that they made to the children (e.g., information sharing, behavior requests, acknowledgments). The children in the pull-out sessions had a significantly higher rate of compliance to requests, whereas children in the classroom condition had a significantly higher rate of no responses to requests. However, neither service delivery model affected the number of turns or percentage of responses by the children.

In sum, although only a few empirical studies contrast speech-language pathology service delivery models, they generally are consistent in their findings (cf. McWilliam, 1996a). In terms of language outcomes, preschool-age children showed the same improvement in target word use and in overall language score with either a pull-out or a classroom-based model. With regard to the nature of conversational exchange, clinicians used the same type of response in both conditions, and children used the same number of turns. Two differences obtained were the higher number of turns by speech-language pathologists and the higher rate of compliance to requests by children receiving pull-out

services; fewer distractions may account for the increased responsiveness. A unique advantage to the classroom-based model was the greater degree of generalization of target words at home after classroom-based service. Thus, even though data are limited, the available evidence demonstrates that language performance improves with the use of both service models; furthermore, an apparent advantage is seen with a classroom-based model in terms of generalization to the home setting. Additional research with more diverse language measures may reveal other differences based on service delivery model.

FACTORS THAT INFLUENCE INCLUSIVE SETTINGS AND COMPATIBLE SERVICE DELIVERY MODELS

Although the data demonstrating the potential benefits of different service delivery models in inclusive classrooms are sparse, other factors provide support for the value of inclusive classrooms in conjunction with compatible service delivery models for preschool-age children with SLI. Influences that lead to strong consideration of inclusive settings and compatible service delivery models include legislative and societal expectations, theoretical perspectives about language acquisition, expanding views about language use, and research findings.

Legislative and Societal Expectations

In addition to influencing the setting in which services are provided through the LRE provisions and the clear preference for inclusive settings, the IDEA legislation and regulations have influenced the selection of service delivery model. IDEA requires that a child's individualized education program (IEP) address how the child's disability affects his or her participation in popular program activities. This legal mandate and societal pressures for inclusion have provided the impetus for using more classroom-based and consultative service delivery models in the field of speech-language pathology; parallel movements have been noted in other fields as well (see McWilliam, 1996b).

Preparation of the IEP means that speech-language pathologists, teachers, parents, and others need to collaborate to ensure that the most appropriate goals are selected, monitored, revised, and achieved on the basis of the specific needs of the child. The emergence of more classroom-based and consultative models fosters more collaboration in the development and implementation of individualized language intervention programs. Indeed, "One of the most dominant trends cutting across *all* special services disciplines is 'working together'" (Friend & Cook, 1990, p. 67, emphasis in original). Thus, public policy and public pressure have created a context for inclusive classrooms, service models that are more consistent with inclusive practices, and service provider roles that are more team based and collaborative.

Influence of Language Acquisition Theories

The theoretical framework for understanding language development influences the intervention setting, the focus of treatment, and the type of service model used (see Chapman, 1991; Fey, 1986; Nelson, 1998; van Kleeck & Richardson, 1988). For example, the traditional service delivery model is consistent with a behavioral view of language. From this perspective, children learn language because of selective reinforcement of discrete verbal behavior. The consequent focus for treatment is on target phonological, semantic, and syntactic structures. A pull-out model, in which the speech-language pathologist can isolate and provide repetitive trials and reinforce correct target behaviors, is a compatible

means of service delivery from this perspective.

More contemporary language acquisition theories are grounded in contextualism and view language from a social-interactive perspective (see Chapman, 1991; Fey, 1986; Nelson, 1998; van Kleeck & Richardson, 1988). The goals of language intervention from this perspective relate more to the social purposes of speaking or the function of the communication act rather than the linguistic structure alone. Contextual variables—where and with whom communication occurs—are critical dimensions of language treatment from this perspective. A social-interactive perspective of language leads to more context-based language intervention practices in the classroom; more collaboration and consultation occurs between teachers and speech-language pathologists, and treatment goals are focused on socially appropriate and useful communication. The pull-out model, in which language essentially is decontextualized, is inconsistent with treatment goals from a social-interactive view of language. The evolution of service delivery models from exclusively pull-out to within-class models is directly related to the emerging functional, interactive view of language (see Blosser & Kratcoski, 1997; Losardo, 1996). This language perspective is also compatible with the more social-interactive goals of inclusion.

Expanding View of Language

Another factor that motivates speech-language pathologists to use more classroom-based, collaborative practice models within inclusive settings is a broadened view of language from an exclusively structural to a more functional perspective. As the contextual aspects of language development have been illuminated, treatment models have correspondingly changed. In the 1970s, Bloom and Lahey (1978) first introduced the form–content–use dimensions of language, expanding the more limited structural view of language to include the intersection of linguistic structure (i.e., language form), word meanings (i.e., language content), and the social purposes of language (i.e., language use). With this contemporary view of language, specialists have expanded assessment and intervention practices beyond structural aspects of language alone. When language goals focus on the meanings and purposes of language, the most compatible context for intervention is the natural setting in which language is used, ideally an inclusive preschool classroom.

Also in the 1970s, the attention to pragmatics—the use of language in its social context (Bates, 1976)—served as another catalyst to the provision of language treatment in more natural settings. Even with traditional service delivery models, speech-language pathologists recognized the need to establish goals for generalization of new language skills in different, more natural settings outside of the treatment room. With alternative models that provide more context-based services in inclusive classrooms, generalization is not considered a second line of skill development but the primary impetus for all treatment. Thus, classroom-based and collaborative models in inclusive settings are the most sensible intervention approaches when a child's goal is to achieve socially appropriate and useful communication with peers. In contrast to a pull-out model, such models offer services for children that foster generalization from the start, provide more opportunities for conversational interactions with peers, are more conducive to fostering functional language in natural contexts, and are more compatible with the features of inclusive practices.

Research on Speech and Language Outcomes

In addition to the legislative, social, and professional rationales for placing preschool-age children with SLI in inclusive settings, the authors reviewed the literature to determine whether there is empirical support for such placements. Unfortunately, no data compare speech or language outcomes of preschool-age children with SLI as a function of setting. Studies that compared language outcomes in inclusive or specialized settings have not focused specifically on preschool-age children with SLI. Rather, children with communication difficulties secondary to other developmental disabilities have been included in heterogeneous groupings, and it has not been possible to extract results for particular subgroups. Results for heterogeneous preschool-age populations do not favor one setting over the other. Gains in language development are made in both inclusive and specialized settings for children with a range of developmental disabilities (Mills, Cole, Jenkins, & Dale, 1998; see Buysse & Bailey, 1993, for review).

Although comparative language analyses between settings have not been conducted for children with SLI, limited data are available on treatment outcomes in inclusive preschool programs. For example, speech and language outcomes have been reported for one model demonstration inclusive preschool program, the Language Acquisition Preschool (LAP; Rice & Wilcox, 1995). The LAP includes an equal number of children with speech and/or language impairments, children with typically developing language skills, and children who are learning English as a second language. The program follows a classroom-based service model with a language-focused curriculum (Bunce, 1995). Standardized tests and observational tools demonstrated that children with SLI in the program made progress in their language skills, moving from below average to average on most language measures. Children with typically developing language skills moved from average to slightly above average on the same measures (Rice & Hadley, 1995). Children with speech impairments showed growth in articulation skills, with an average decrease of 42% in mean number of speech errors (Wilcox & Morris, 1995).

A number of factors affected the general growth of speech and language skills, including the students' length of enrollment in the LAP and the nature and severity of the impairment. In general, children who were enrolled longer made greater gains. Children who were enrolled for one year improved in single-word production and general language comprehension, whereas children who were enrolled for a second year improved in language production. Children with speech production errors were less likely to have continued problems than were children with primary language problems, and children with only language production problems had better outcomes than did children with both receptive and expressive problems.

Thus, at least one sophisticated model program, which serves as a site for clinical preparation of speech-language pathologists as well as a local public school option, demonstrates that preschool-age children with SLI can be expected to do reasonably well in an inclusive classroom setting with a full inclusion model. The Valdez and Montgomery (1997) study previously discussed also provides empirical support for improved language outcomes in inclusive settings for young children with SLI.

Summary: Options for Speech-Language Pathology Services

In accord with provisions in IDEA, an IEP team, including the child's parent, teacher, speech-language pathologist, and others, makes decisions about placement options and service delivery models on the basis of the individual needs of each child. In addition to other IEP func-

tions such as specifying goals and objectives, an IEP team has three sequential decisions to make regarding communication services for young children with SLI: 1) Should the child receive services in a classroom or clinic setting (i.e., direct, one-to-one, or small-group focusing on individual children with communication disorders)? 2) If a classroom placement is recommended, should the child be placed in an inclusive or a specialized program or some combination? 3) Which service delivery model or models should be used in a classroom setting?

One of the first decisions that the IEP team makes for a young child with SLI is the context in which services should be provided, with consideration given to the LRE mandate in IDEA. Specifically, the team needs to decide whether to place a child in a preschool classroom or to provide speech and language services using a more restrictive one-to-one or small-group clinic model, with no classroom activities. The framework for services under federal law and contemporary language development perspectives indicates that communication services should be tied to the social context, with an opportunity for interaction with peers in the environment in which natural communication occurs. This seems to provide prima facie support for classroom placement for young children with SLI unless there is a strong rationale for doing otherwise.

Despite the legal and communication framework for classroom placement, the clinic model remains a prominent feature of SLI services for preschool-age children (ASHA, 2000b). Are there circumstances under which it would be in the best interest of the child (and therefore compatible with the LRE provisions) to use a clinic model without classroom activities? Unfortunately, the authors are not aware of any studies that compare a young child's speech and language performance on the basis of a classroom or a clinic model. Nevertheless, there may be a subgroup of children with SLI who could benefit from a one-to-one or small-group approach either part or all of the time. Indications for such services may include factors such as sensitivity to noise or other distractions, need for massed learning trials (e.g., drill and repeated practice for articulation training), need to learn a new skill in a highly responsive and nondistracting setting, or severe language or behavior problems that would preclude a child from benefiting from classroom interactions. Even with such indications, however, the advantages of classroom placement are compelling: availability of peers as communication partners and appropriate language models (particularly in an inclusive classroom), use of language in its natural social context, opportunity to practice new skills in the classroom setting, and increased likelihood of generalization with more people in diverse situations. Moreover, a pull-out model, combined with classroom activities, provides the same value as an exclusive clinic model with the added classroom benefits. Considering multiple factors—legal, social, communication perspectives, and research—it seems that the preferable setting and service model for young children with SLI is an inclusive program with a classroom-based or collaborative service delivery model with pull-out services as needed. The next section discusses certain program features that may be crucial to the effectiveness of such inclusive programs.

ESSENTIAL CHARACTERISTICS OF PROGRAMS

The basis for inclusion for preschool-age children with SLI has been discussed, as have inclusion models, the extent of inclusive practices, and the relation of inclusion to changing models of speech-language pathology service delivery.

Drawing on this information, clinicians need to decide how best to provide services for these children in inclusive settings. Emerging from the general literature on classroom settings and service delivery models is a set of critical features that may well be fundamental to the success of inclusive programs that serve young children with SLI. These five characteristics, summarized in Table 19.2 and discussed next, can be viewed as quality indicators for inclusive programs that serve these children. These program characteristics are proposed to clarify issues related to inclusive practices and to help clinicians make informed decisions regarding classroom placement and service delivery models within the context of early childhood inclusion.

Program Philosophy

It is essential that administrators, service providers, and others operate from a common philosophical perspective. Current legislation, societal pressures, and professional policies all lead to a philosophy that embraces the need for individualized programming on the basis of education curriculum objectives, specific communication needs, and preference for inclusive settings for preschool-age children with SLI as appropriate.

Service Delivery Model

All service providers—administrators, speech-language pathologists, other specialists, and teachers—need to be familiar with the variety of service delivery models that are available and the ways in which each can be used to meet best the communication needs of young children in inclusive settings. The key is that service delivery models are dynamic (cf. ASHA, 1993, 1999) and that models or combinations of models may vary over time. Service delivery models should be selected on the basis of individual communication needs and compatibility with inclusive practices. A number of fac-

Table 19.2. Essential characteristics of programs for children with specific language impairment within the context of early childhood inclusion

Follows common program philosophy

   Individualized programming based on specific communication needs

   Preference for inclusive practices

Decides on service delivery model or models on the basis of individual communication needs and changes over time

   Draws from social-interactive language theory

   Views language within its social context

   Provides opportunities for language interactions in natural environments

   Bases decisions on relevant research

Forms collaborative partnerships for selecting and achieving communication goals

Provides in-service education on an ongoing basis to administrators, teachers, and related service providers

   Encourages mentoring relationships for education and follow-up

Conducts program evaluation and fosters research on treatment outcomes and effectiveness with respect to setting and service delivery variables

tors can assist with service delivery decisions:

- A social-interactive theory of language acquisition and a perspective of language within a social context lead to language intervention in natural environments, with typically developing peers who can serve as appropriate language models.
- Service providers need to consider that classroom-based and collaborative consultation service models are compatible with inclusive practices and offer services in a child's natural, interactive environment. Such models, which are integrated in the classroom, may also counterbalance the tendency toward social separation for preschool-age children with SLI.
- Studies that compare service delivery models demonstrate similar language outcomes with pull-out and in-class models; however, greater generalization to home settings is seen after a classroom-based model.
- A pull-out model offers a less distracting, more responsive environment

and may be beneficial for some children at certain times even in an inclusive program.

Collaborative Partnerships

The prevailing view in clinics and education settings is that collaboration and team approaches are appropriate and preferred practice (see Friend & Cook, 1990). In schools, the IEP process institutionalizes collaborative partnerships for selecting and achieving goals. In relation to young children with SLI, teachers, speech-language pathologists, and parents are expected to work together to determine relevant communication goals. Particular service delivery models, such as classroom-based and collaborative consultation, necessitate collaborative relationships among service providers.

In-Service Education

In-service education is one way to provide current information about inclusive practices and compatible service delivery models to administrators, teachers, and related service providers on an ongoing basis. Suggested topics include the following:

- Nature of communication disorders (i.e., phonology, semantics, syntax, pragmatics)
- Impact of communication disorders (e.g., behavior, social interactions, learning, literacy)
- Value of inclusive settings and peers as language models
- Types and potential benefits of various service delivery models in inclusive settings
- Ways to coordinate and collaborate with parents and professionals
- Types of intervention techniques (e.g., modeling, recasting, use of questions, following child's lead, nondirective)
- Awareness of cultural and linguistic differences

Such in-service education programs may be particularly important because graduate programs for speech-language pathologists have only begun to provide coursework and some clinical practicum opportunities in inclusive preschool settings or with classroom-based and collaborative consultation service delivery models (ASHA, 2000a, 2000b). Speech-language pathologists with more background and experience with inclusive practices, typically the more recent graduates, could assist with in-service programs and follow-up by serving as mentors for other professionals (see Elksnin & Capilouto, 1994).

Program Evaluation and Research

Evaluation is a crucial component of any quality program. Programs need to evaluate the overall efficiency and effectiveness of service provision, including treatment outcomes, service delivery models used, professional attitudes and performance, nature and success of collaborative efforts, quality and frequency of staff education, and extent of parent involvement. Programs could also develop a means for evaluating how well they incorporate these five essential components in inclusive classrooms. Furthermore, research related to inclusive settings and changing service delivery models for young children with SLI is scarce. Therefore, programs that initiate, participate in, or encourage research on these issues could make an invaluable contribution to the knowledge base in this area.

AGENDA FOR CHANGE

Multiple reasons for encouraging placement in inclusive classroom settings have been identified, and program features that seem essential for inclusive classrooms for preschool-age children with SLI have been proposed. Nevertheless, a number of barriers have prevented widespread acceptance and implementation of inclusive practices with these children. Barriers encompass systemwide issues (e.g., resistance to change, limited professional education and experience), program development issues (e.g., lack of administrative support, inadequate time for collaboration, family attitudes and preferences), and a paucity of research. The remaining section of this chapter addresses these barriers and proposes an agenda for change to promote inclusive practices where appropriate. Table 19.3 provides a summary of the suggested systems and programmatic strategies and the proposed research agenda. Although the greatest barrier to inclusive classrooms for preschool-age children may well be the lack of public funding for typically developing preschool-age children with no risk factors, the focus is on systemic and programmatic barriers that realistically could be addressed within this educational context.

Table 19.3.   Suggestions for encouraging placement of preschool-age children with SLI in inclusive classrooms

Systemwide strategies

Lead the change effort:

Provide leadership to ease resistance and enlist support in change efforts related to intervention settings and service delivery models consistent with inclusive practices.

Enhance professional education and experience:

Provide educational and clinical opportunities in inclusive preschool programs and with classroom-based and collaborative consultation practice models.

Develop competency guidelines and training in collaboration.

Establish mentoring partnerships to foster collaboration.

Develop partnerships with community programs:

Coordinate with program staff on communication goals.

Expand participation on individualized education program (IEP) teams.

Provide education to program staff.

Hire personnel from school to work in a community program.

Develop partnerships with professional organizations:

Update accreditation standards to encourage inclusive practices.

Disseminate information through national and statewide communication networks.

Use national outcome measurement systems to assist with clinical planning.

Update professional policies regarding inclusive practices, caseload size, and service delivery models.

Establish funding mechanisms for model programs and research.

Program development

Gain administrative support:

Develop and implement a plan to gain administrative support for the use of inclusive settings and compatible practice models.

Provide time for collaboration:

Establish a mechanism for collaborative partnerships.

Service as a resource to families:

Convey information on the value of inclusive practices, alternative service models, and the role of typically developing children.

Research needs

Design and conduct studies to address pressing research questions:

What are the conditions that maximize the communication benefits of inclusive settings for preschool-age children with SLI?

Which service delivery model or combination of models result in the most favorable speech and language outcomes and educational outcomes for children in inclusive settings?

What is the impact of preservice/in-service education programs on the implementation of inclusive settings and compatible service delivery models?

Systems Change

At least two large-scale systems issues need to be addressed to implement successfully preschool inclusion programs with appropriate service delivery models for young children with SLI: adopting a framework for leading successful change efforts and enhancing professional education and experience. Partnering with community programs and professional organizations is discussed as another way to support systems change efforts.

Leading Change Efforts   One of the main barriers to large-scale consideration and use of inclusive settings and alternative service models is simply a natural resistance to change (see Gutkin, 1990; Montgomery, 1990). Anything new and different can affect comfort levels and feelings of competence and can precipitate defensive statements such as, "It's what I've always done," "It's what I know best," "I'm getting pressure from parents and administrators," "Teachers think I'm intruding in their classrooms," and "There's no time." Settings and practice models should be selected on the basis of a child's specific communication needs rather than on availability, convenience, lack of information, or personal comfort. A plan for leading change can be developed to break through resistance and effect broad systems change (see Kotter, 1995).

Speech-language pathologists can serve in leadership roles and create the context for changes that are consistent with inclusive practices. Through educational forums and informal exchanges, they can motivate others by conveying information about the nature, impact, and persistence of communication disorders and the value of inclusive settings and compatible practice models. Speech-language pathologists could form collaborative alliances with teachers, parents, and others who could serve as a guiding team and encourage and assist others. Strong leadership from the speech-language pathologist and the guiding team is critical to monitor progress, reinvigorate people with new ideas and strategies, and make necessary policy and practice changes.

Professional Education and Experience   Another potential barrier to systemwide adoption of inclusive practices, besides general resistance to change, relates to professional education and experience. There is a lag between academic education models and actual practice in community clinics (R.V. Watkins, personal communication, December 1998). As preliminary data from an ASHA (2000a) survey of academic programs demonstrate, graduate programs provide coursework on inclusive practices and on the array of possible service delivery models. In addition, some students have clinical practice opportunities in inclusive preschools or with alternative service delivery models. However, such practicum experiences are not consistently available within or across graduate programs in speech-language pathology. Moreover, only recent graduates have had any coursework or practica in inclusion or alternative service delivery models (ASHA, 2000b).

Speech-language pathologists may not have the skills or comfort level to provide services in an inclusive preschool classroom, particularly when professional preparation was limited to specialized settings and direct one-to-one practice models. Management of behavior often is easier in a one-to-one situation; working in inclusive classrooms requires more group and behavior management skills and the need to structure and monitor interactions between children with communication disorders and typically developing peers.

Many speech-language pathologists believe that they need to be directly involved in service provision and may be hesitant to try classroom-based or indirect models. They may believe that they have enough direct contact with children only when using a pull-out model even with an inclusive setting. In fact, speech-language pathologists and teachers have difficulty releasing their individual roles with children, even though they understand the value of working as a team (McWilliam, 1996c). Furthermore, teachers may perceive that they are losing control, do not have as much direct contact in the classroom, and have their workload increased when speech-language pathologists work directly in the classroom (see McWilliam, 1996c). In a survey by Beck and Dennis (1997) on teacher and speech-language pathologist perceptions of classroom-based speech and language interventions, 33% of the speech-language pathologists believed that the teachers did not support or had no interest in using classroom-based service delivery in their classrooms.

Clearly, there is a need at the preservice level for more consistent clinical practicum opportunities in inclusive preschool programs with classroom-based and collaborative consultation service delivery models. Developing competencies needed for successful collaboration between speech-language pathologists and teachers is an important goal. An array of resources is available to focus educational efforts on professional competencies in collaboration (e.g., Coufal, 1993; Gerber, 1987; Hadley & Schuele, 1998).

Practicing speech-language pathologists could make the shift to more inclusive practices through self-study, in-service programs, on-the-job experience, or mentoring opportunities. Education efforts should be ongoing through repeated discussions and presentations (e.g., Moore-Brown, 1991). ASHA maintains a list of speech-language pathology programs for referral, and the list, which includes self-selected areas of clinical expertise, could be broadened to include specification of intervention settings and

service delivery models used. ASHA could then establish a network of speech-language pathologists who have experience working in inclusive preschool settings and using classroom and consultative models and identify those who are willing to mentor others.

Partnerships with Community Programs Addressing resistance to change and enhancing professional education and experience are two systems changes that could lead to more extensive acceptance and implementation of inclusive practices. Nevertheless, even if such changes occur, another barrier that has been discussed still needs to be confronted: the lack of availability of typically developing children at the preschool level. Establishing partnerships with community programs may be a way to support inclusion of young children with SLI. Some states report that they do not offer inclusive preschool programs as an option because funding is not available to support the involvement of typically developing children. However, lack of programs for typically developing children is not a defensible reason for failing to provide inclusive options for children with SLI.

A creative and cost-effective solution for addressing this barrier may be for public schools to collaborate with private community nursery school, child care, and Head Start programs and provide speech and language services to children with SLI who are in such programs. Such partnerships could take a variety of different forms, including coordination between the school and programs in terms of communication goals, participation by the private staff members on the IEP team, and provision of staff education on effective communication strategies by the speech-language pathologist.

One barrier to effective implementation of such a collaborative effort may be that staff in private programs, who are not employees of the school system, may not be willing or able to implement communication intervention plans. One alternative to this situation could be for the school system to hire personnel to work in the private program on a short- or long-term basis. Within the community programs, personnel could provide speech and language services and educate the staff to work effectively with children with SLI. An added benefit may be enhanced communication skills for children without disabilities.

Such a collaborative approach between the public and private sectors opens options that can maximize inclusion for children with SLI. Using existing community programs as potential inclusive settings is one way to address directly the lack of typically developing preschool-age children in public schools. It is also important to note that states are demonstrating increasing interest in expanding preschool opportunities for all children. Most state-supported preschool programs are limited to children whose families have demonstrated financial need, in addition to the programs for children with disabilities. Some states, however, such as Georgia, Oklahoma, and New York, are starting to offer more extensive preschool programs (Salmon & Grimsley, 2000).

Leadership by Professional Organizations   Professional associations can assist with systems change efforts related to inclusion in a variety of ways, including developing standards, organizing networks, collecting outcome data, writing and promoting relevant policies, and establishing funding mechanisms.

Standards for Accreditation   Professional organizations can develop and update standards that guide practitioners on issues related to classroom composition, service delivery models, program development and evaluation, and the conduct of research relating to preschool-age children with communication disorders. ASHA, as the national accreditation and certification agency for speech-language pathology and audiology, develops and implements certification standards for these professionals (Council on Professional Standards in Speech-Language Pathology and Audiology, 1993a, 1993b) and has standards for accreditation of graduate education programs in speech-language pathology and audiology (Council on Academic Accreditation in Audiology and Speech-Language Pathology, 1997). ASHA also has professional standards for accrediting clinical programs in these fields (Council on Professional Standards in Speech-Language Pathology and Audiology, 1992). The trend is for standards to be more general, less prescriptive, and focused on competencies and outcomes. Accordingly, the ASHA education standards do not require specific courses or course content, and the clinical standards do not specify the type of setting or service model to be used. Nevertheless, it is possible that the education standards could be revised to require students to have coursework and practicum experience involving a range of intervention settings and service delivery models. An expected outcome could be familiarity and experience with classroom-based and collaborative service delivery models in inclusive classrooms for children of different ages.

Similarly, the clinical standards for professional services programs could include a section that addresses intervention settings and service delivery models. The current clinical standards require that services be based on current research, be appropriate to the needs of individuals with communication disorders, and be effective. The application of standards that require current, appropriate, and effective practices could also be evaluated with respect to the types of settings and service delivery models selected for the individuals served. ASHA has established mechanisms for changing and updating standards that could be used to make such modifications in education, certification, and clinical standards.

Professional Communication Networks Networks of speech-language pathologists organized at the national and state levels could serve in a leadership role to provide information about inclusive settings and optimal practice models for preschool-age children with communication disorders. ASHA has special interest divisions that provide opportunities for division affiliates to exchange information with colleagues, speech-language pathology students, and consumers who share common needs and interests. The division on language learning and education and the newly established division on school-based issues could offer communication forums (e.g., study groups, newsletters, electronic networks) related to inclusive practices. ASHA also could foster new or broaden existing liaisons with national education groups (e.g., National Education Association, American Federation of Teachers, National Association of State Directors of Special Education) as another means to generate national attention and planning related to inclusive practices for preschool-age children with SLI.

To encourage and support the increasing focus on inclusive practices for preschool-age children with SLI, ASHA could identify a number of preschools that are committed to serving as model inclusive programs. ASHA could be directly involved in initial on-site staff education efforts with continued web-based and other distance learning opportunities. In addition, ASHA could develop and host conferences to showcase these exemplary programs; generate excitement about changing practices; and provide a time for practitioners to come together for support, to share problems and solutions, and to keep the momentum going. Such conferences also could include research strands and national education programs that are focused on inclusive practices.

ASHA has established a network of state association school contacts. The mission of the State Education Advocacy Leaders (SEALs) network is to enhance and perpetuate the advocacy, leadership, and clinical management skills of school-based ASHA members at the state level and to influence administrative and public policy decisions that have an impact on the delivery of speech-language pathology and audiology in school settings. There are 50 states plus the District of Columbia represented with a designated SEAL. Each state's leader has been identified as an advocate to implement the IDEA in his or her state plan. The SEALs could be encouraged to focus attention, resources, and support on inclusive settings and appropriate service delivery models as part of their state plans.

National Outcome Measurement and Reporting Aggregated national outcome data are used to assist clinicians and administrators in caseload planning and management, meeting IDEA regulations, and demonstrating the effectiveness and value of communication services. ASHA has established a National Outcomes Measurement System (NOMS) for speech-language pathologists and audiologists who work with preschool- or school-age children and adults.

The prekindergarten component of the NOMS was initiated in March 1999. This component focuses on children (age 3 years to entrance into kindergarten) who are receiving speech and language services in either a school or a health care setting. Functional Communication Measures, seven-point scales used to measure change in a child's functional communication skills over the course of treatment, were developed for these children in the areas of articulation/intelligibility, cognitive orientation, pragmatics, spoken language comprehension and production, and swallowing.

ASHA plans to issue two different national data reports—one for health care and one for schools. As of October 2000, 139 health care facilities and 43 school systems signed up to participate in prekindergarten NOMS. Data on intervention setting and predominant service delivery model(s) are being collected at admission and discharge, respectively.

Such outcome data will be invaluable to speech-language pathologists who seek information to assist with decisions related to optimal intervention setting and practice models for preschool-age children with specific communication needs. In future years, data could also be collected on the timing of various practice models when more than one model is used and on the application of different models across settings.

Policy Development and Dissemination   Through ongoing policy development, review, and revision, national professional organizations can influence and guide practitioners in areas that are relevant to the provision of communication services in inclusive settings. Policy documents also can be used for leverage when there are discrepancies in philosophy or practice between administrators and clinicians. For example, if an administrator expects a clinician to use exclusively a pull-out model to provide services, then a clinician can show the administrator relevant sections of ASHA's guidelines relative to inclusive practices (ASHA, 1996), caseload size (ASHA, 1993), and service delivery models (ASHA, 1993) and discuss a professional's ethical responsibility to "hold paramount the welfare of persons they serve professionally" (ASHA, 1994, p. 1). Dissemination efforts through professional publications, products, and networks can focus on getting information to decision makers concerning intervention settings and

service delivery models. National professional organizations also are in a position to disseminate information about current research as a mechanism to encourage the use of the most up-to-date, evidence-based information and recommended practice models to inform practice decisions.

Funding Mechanisms   Two clear financial needs relative to achieving goals for inclusion are incentives to establish model programs and funding for typically developing children to participate in inclusive preschool programs. Professional foundations (e.g., American Speech-Language-Hearing Foundation) could offer grants to assist with funding of model demonstration programs, research, and dissemination efforts. The federally funded Association of Service Providers Implementing IDEA Reforms in Education (ASPIIRE) partnership grant among the Council for Exceptional Children, ASHA, and other organizations could be a means of funding collaborative initiatives over the next few years. Other professional organizations such as those representing teachers and related services providers could develop similar standard setting, networking, outcome measurement, policy development, and funding initiatives to support inclusive practices in schools and facilitate systems change efforts.

Program Development

Even with these leaders driving systems change, development of the essential characteristics for effective inclusive programs for preschool-age children with SLI described previously (see Table 19.2) will face certain obstacles. Following is a consideration of the potential barriers to instituting such program features and recommendations for addressing each one.

Need for Administrative Support   To work within a common philosophy that is consistent with goals for inclusion and the use of compatible practice models, it is crucial to have administrative support and leadership (see Montgomery, 1990). Necessary resource allocation (e.g., funding to permit participation of typically developing children in a preschool program; funding for a child with SLI to participate in a private community child care or nursery; time for collaboration and staff education) is dependent on the administrator's understanding the value of inclusive practices and compatible models and the potential benefits for young children with communication disorders. A collaborative guiding team can develop a plan to gain administrative support for the program. Necessary components of such a plan include 1) providing clear information about goals and the rationale for the settings and service models proposed and 2) offering regular and frequent communication about child outcomes and program advances on the basis of regular program evaluation (cf. Blosser, 1990). Goodin and Mehollin (1990) also suggested elements of an administrative plan of action: 1) seek grant funds for pilot programs; 2) establish a district-level task force or teaming project with other programs that use alternative service models; 3) develop a plan for documenting program outcomes, including methods of instituting program changes, data collection, and program evaluation; and 4) address key issues, such as transitions from traditional to alternative models, flexibility in service delivery formats, caseload size, guidelines and procedures for referral, data collection, assessment, intervention, and placement.

A systematic plan for gaining and maintaining support from administrators that includes mechanisms for increasing understanding about program rationale, goals, and outcomes can create an environment in which critical program components (embracing a common philosophy supporting inclusion, selecting appropriate service delivery models, fostering collaborative partnerships, providing in-service training, and conducting ongoing program evaluation) can be realized and sustained.

Time for Collaboration Speech-language pathologists and teachers need time to coordinate communication goals and objectives in conjunction with the classroom curriculum of an inclusive program (Holzhauser-Peters & Husemann, 1989). They also need time to discuss student progress and modifications in intervention plans. Speech-language pathologists, teachers, and administrators rate the lack of time for planning as a major obstacle to inclusion and successful classroom-based language interventions (Beck & Dennis, 1997; Evans, Holland, & Nichol, 1996; McWilliam, 1996a).

Time for collaborative endeavors is a programmatic issue that requires administrative support to foster inclusive practices and appropriate service delivery modes (cf. National Joint Committee on Learning Disabilities, 1991). A study of the effects of a collaborative consultation model for kindergarten and first-grade students showed significantly improved outcomes not only on the increase in students' language skills but also for the teachers and speech-language pathologists involved in the study (Farber & Klein, 1999). The teachers and speech-language pathologists reported feeling energized by the collaboration and sharing the workload and resources. Both groups developed appreciation of the skills and expertise of the other group. All of the teachers involved in this program volunteered to participate again the following year. The authors reported that the key to the positive outcome was a 2-day meeting, before beginning the school year, to establish schedules, review the curriculum, and plan lessons.

A number of recommendations have been made at both systemwide and schoolwide levels to facilitate time and collaboration including requiring in-service training for all school staff, adjusting staff schedules, and creating instructional conditions for planning (Evans et al., 1996; National Joint Committee on Learning Disabilities, 1991). Certainly, the ability of all professionals to work together with a focus on common goals for young children with communication disorders can influence the success of inclusive programs. Hoskins considered the ability to "establish mutual concerns, develop a partnership, and plan together" (1990, p. 33) to be the three fundamental principles for building collaborative relationships. Despite the obstacles, efforts to make time for collaboration are crucial for success, because, as Gutkin pointed out, "Ultimately, nothing is as time-consuming as ineffective services" (1990, p. 63).

Family Attitudes and Preferences
Family concerns about the value of inclusion can have an impact on the availability or composition of inclusive programs. For example, such concerns may prevent parents of typically developing children from enrolling their children in an inclusive preschool. Their decision may be based on many factors, especially a fear that their child will be held back by the slower progress of the students with communication disorders. Yet, evidence indicates that typically developing children are not slowed in their academic progress by the presence of children with communication disorders (see Staub & Peck, 1995, for review). In fact, Rice and Wilcox (1995) found that typically developing children actually improved to above average scores in many educational measures when they were enrolled in an inclusive preschool classroom (cf. Harris, Handleman, Kristoff, Bass, & Gordon, 1990). This information should be shared with parents who are considering an inclusive classroom for their typically developing child. Speech-language pathologists also can provide evidence to

parents of typically developing children demonstrating that their children may reap additional benefits related to compassion, acceptance of disability, and appreciation of individual differences (see Voorhees, Landon, & Harvey, 1997, for summary).

From the perspective of parents of children with communication disorders, speech-language pathologists, teachers, and others need to convey information to those parents about the advantages of inclusive practices, the value of typically developing preschool-age children serving as speech and language models, and the benefits of classroom-based and collaborative consultation service delivery models (see Sergeant, 1995). The value of inclusive practices and alternative models may be more salient if parents have the opportunity to understand the communication objectives in classroom settings. Also, parents should know that decisions about classroom placement and service model are based on a child's individual communication needs.

Families of children with communication disorders also may have negative perceptions about nondirect service delivery models and may believe that direct service is always preferable (e.g., McWilliam, 1996c). Parents who hold such beliefs may not want to give up the individual attention that their children receive with direct service. McWilliam (1996a) conducted a study to compare family perspectives about pull-out and classroom-based services from the beginning to the end of the school year. He found that most family preferences stayed the same after a year. O'Brien and O'Leary (1988) described the efforts of one school system to provide speech and language services for children with disabilities in the general classroom. They reported a reluctance on the part of parents to relinquish the individual services that their children were receiving. Parents can be reassured that the provision of communication services in inclusive classrooms does not preclude the use of direct, one-to-one intervention. Indeed, even with a vision that supports inclusion, decisions regarding intervention setting and service delivery models in early childhood education should be based on the child's individual needs with consideration given to the preferences and expectations of parents.

Research Issues

The weak empirical base regarding communication outcomes of preschool-age children with SLI in inclusive settings demonstrates a pressing need for research to guide placement decisions and selection of service delivery models. Three key research questions address this need.

What are the conditions that maximize the communication benefits of inclusive settings for preschool-age children with SLI? It is necessary to evaluate how well children with SLI do in certain programs. Are there speech-language or program characteristics that predict which children will thrive in an inclusive setting? Are there any circumstances under which a preschool-age child with SLI might benefit from placement for part or all of the school day in a specialized language program, with a reverse inclusion model, or with individual or small-group clinic services? Large-scale evaluation studies are needed to investigate these complex issues to be able to identify consistent patterns.

Which service delivery model or combination of models results in the most favorable speech and language as well as educational outcomes for children in inclusive settings? Literature comparing service delivery models for preschool-age children with SLI is sparse, and the few existing studies have addressed only a small set of outcome measures. The range of structural

and functional outcomes for various practice models within inclusive settings must be determined. There may be compelling reasons for selecting certain models for particular children at different stages of development, including models that are not intrinsically compatible with inclusive settings. For instance, it has been suggested that a pull-out model may be more appropriate for children with severe disabilities, for those who are highly distractible, and for those who are learning a new skill. However, these assumptions are not empirically based; it is not known whether such models work best when used as the sole means of intervention or when used in combination with another manner of delivering service (e.g., pull-out and collaborative consultation); it also is not known how long one model or models should be maintained before another is introduced. Moreover, outcomes may differ depending on the speech and/or language profile of the children. For example, no data are available concerning the relative benefit of a certain service delivery model or models for children with speech problems compared with children with receptive and expressive language problems. Longitudinal designs may be useful for determining the persistence of communication effects and the reduced educational performance of children as a function of the service delivery model or models used in inclusive preschool classrooms.

What is the impact of preservice and inservice education programs on the implementation of inclusive settings and compatible service delivery models? With the need for clinicians who work in schools to be responsive to the concepts and requirements of IDEA regulations, preservice and in-service education programs may increase their emphasis on the use of inclusive settings, consistent service delivery models, and natural language interactions as the context for speech and language intervention. The impact of such education programs in actual practice is not known. It would be beneficial to know whether and how speech-language pathologists and other practitioners with such training translate these precepts into practice. ASHA could conduct a follow-up survey of academic programs to determine the philosophy, coursework, and clinical practicum opportunities related to inclusion and compare those results with the practice patterns of school clinicians.

CONCLUSION

Many critical issues related to inclusion now confront young children with SLI and their families and the service system. There is a federal mandate and a societal recognition of the value of inclusion for children with disabilities. There is evidence that typically developing children have the potential to serve as appropriate language models during interactions with children with specific communication needs. Contemporary service delivery models that are more classroom based and collaborative are compatible with and support the goals of inclusion. Although empirical studies comparing classroom settings for preschool-age children with SLI are lacking, it is known that these children show improvements in speech and language skills in inclusive classrooms. Moreover, there is no evidence to demonstrate that specialized settings offer any advantage for these children.

Despite this awareness and encouragement for inclusion, many preschool-age children with SLI are not receiving services in this setting. Specialized language classrooms, heterogeneous disability groups, and itinerant, one-to-one, decontextualized services are still prevalent. The challenge is to determine how best to address the barriers that have limited the prospects of inclusion for these young children. Fortunately, the barriers

that prevent these children from moving toward more inclusive settings are not insurmountable.

Toward that goal, this chapter has outlined program features that seem to be essential for successful inclusive preschools and has offered strategies to create the context for programs to embrace the vision of inclusion. In addition, the systemwide strategies (e.g., providing leadership to ease resistance to change, enhancing professional education and experience, collaborating with community preschool programs, tapping the resources of professional associations) and program development goals (e.g., gaining administrative support, providing time for collaboration, serving as a family resource) that are proposed in this chapter could serve as a national model and provide direction for addressing the barriers that are preventing more widespread understanding and use of inclusive practices for preschool-age children with SLI. Research focused on determining the conditions, models, and educational practices that lead to optimal communication outcomes could also provide a stronger basis to guide decisions about classroom settings and practice models.

The proposed agenda for change focuses exclusively on preschool-age children with SLI, although some suggestions may be applicable to children with other needs. Additional systems changes, program development issues, and research designs need to be considered for different groups of children, such as young children with communication disorders secondary to other conditions (e.g., Down syndrome, autism, fragile X syndrome, hearing loss).

The value of peer language models in inclusive settings and more context-based functional language intervention in natural environments needs to be realized and implemented, even in the absence of publicly funded preschool programs for typically developing children.

Many opportunities for inclusion exist. Strong leadership, dedicated educational and professional opportunities, and targeted research initiatives that are geared toward optimizing inclusive practices will provide the catalyst for necessary changes. Young children with communication disorders are entitled to individualized help in an environment that maximizes their communication development, provides educational benefits, and recognizes their right to be fully included.

REFERENCES

American Speech-Language-Hearing Association. (1993). Guidelines for caseload size and speech-language service delivery in the schools. *Asha, 35*(Suppl. 10), 33–39.

American Speech-Language-Hearing Association. (1994, March). Code of ethics. *Asha, 16*(Suppl. 13), 1–2.

American Speech-Language-Hearing Association. (1995). *Survey of speech-language pathology services in school-based settings: Final report.* Rockville, MD: Author.

American Speech-Language-Hearing Association. (1996). Inclusive practices for children and youth with communication disorders: Position statement and technical paper. *Asha, 38*(Suppl. 16), 35–44.

American Speech-Language-Hearing Association. (1999). *Guidelines for the roles and responsibilities of the school-based speech-language pathologist.* Rockville, MD: Author.

American Speech-Language-Hearing Association. (2000a). *Topical survey of academic programs in communication sciences and disorders.* Rockville, MD: Author.

American Speech-Language-Hearing Association. (2000b). *Topical survey of school-based speech-language pathologists working with preschool children (3–5 years).* Rockville, MD: Author.

Baker, L., Cantwell, D., & Mattison, R. (1980). Behavior problems in children with pure speech disorders and in children with combined speech and language disorders. *Journal of Abnormal Child Psychology, 8,* 245–256.

Bates, E. (1976). *Language and context: Studies in the acquisition of pragmatics.* San Diego: Academic Press.

Beck, A.R., & Dennis, M. (1997). Speech-language pathologists' and teachers' perceptions of classroom-based interventions. *Language, Speech, and Hearing Services in Schools, 28,* 146–153.

Bloom, L., & Lahey, M. (1978). *Language development and language disorders.* New York: John Wiley & Sons.

Blosser, J.L. (1990). A strategic planning process for service delivery changes. In W.A. Secord (Ed.), *Best practices in school speech-language pathology: Collaborative programs in the schools. Concepts, models, and procedures* (pp. 81–88). San Antonio, TX: The Psychological Corporation.

Blosser, J.L., & Kratcoski, A. (1997). PACs: A framework for determining appropriate service delivery options. *Language, Speech, and Hearing Services in Schools, 28,* 99–107.

Brandel, D. (1992). Collaboration: Full steam ahead with no prior experience! *Language, Speech, and Hearing Services in Schools, 23,* 369–370.

Bunce, B.H. (1995). *Building a language-focused curriculum for the preschool classroom: Volume II. A planning guide.* Baltimore: Paul H. Brookes Publishing Co.

Buysse, V., & Bailey, D.B. (1993). Behavioral and developmental outcomes in young children with disabilities in integrated and segregated settings: A review of comparative studies. *The Journal of Special Education, 26,* 434–461.

Chapman, R.S. (1991). Models of language disorders. In J.F. Miller (Ed.), *Research on child language disorders: A decade of progress* (pp. 287–297). Austin, TX: PRO-ED.

Cirrin, F.M., & Penner, S.G. (1995). Classroom-based and consultative service delivery models for language intervention. In S.F. Warren & J. Reichle (Series Eds.) & M.E. Fey, J. Windsor, & S.F. Warren (Vol. Eds.), *Communication and language intervention series: Vol. 5. Language intervention: Preschool through the elementary years* (pp. 333–362). Baltimore: Paul H. Brookes Publishing Co.

Corsaro, W.A. (1979). We're friends, right? Children's use of access rituals in a nursery school. *Language and Society, 8,* 315–336.

Corsaro, W.A. (1981). Friendship in the nursery school: Social organization in a peer environment. In S. Asher & J. Gottman (Eds.), *The development of children's friendships* (pp. 207–241). New York: Cambridge University Press.

Coufal, K.L. (1993). Collaborative consultation for speech-language pathologists. *Topics in Language Disorders, 14,* 1–14.

Council on Academic Accreditation in Audiology and Speech-Language Pathology. (1997). Standards for accreditation of graduate education programs in speech-language pathology and audiology. *Asha Leader, 2,* 7–8.

Council on Professional Standards in Speech-Language Pathology and Audiology. (1992, September). Standards for professional service programs in audiology and speech-language pathology. *Asha, 34,* 63–70.

Council on Professional Standards in Speech-Language Pathology and Audiology. (1993a). *Standards and implementation procedures for the certificate of clinical competence in audiology.* Rockville, MD: American Speech-Language-Hearing Association.

Council on Professional Standards in Speech-Language Pathology and Audiology. (1993b). *Standards and implementation procedures for the certificate of clinical competence in speech-language pathology.* Rockville, MD: American Speech-Language-Hearing Association.

Craig, H.K. (1993). Social skills of children with specific language impairment: Peer relationships. *Language, Speech, and Hearing Services in Schools, 24,* 206–215.

Craig, H.K., & Washington, J.A. (1993). Access behaviors of children with specific language impairment. *Journal of Speech and Hearing Research, 36,* 322–337.

Damico, J.S. (1987). Addressing language concerns in the schools: The SLP as consultant. *Journal of Childhood Communication Disorders, 11,* 17–42.

Education for All Handicapped Children Act of 1975, PL 94-142, 20 U.S.C. §§ 1400 *et seq.*

Education of the Handicapped Act Amendments of 1986, PL 99-457, 20 U.S.C. §§ 1400 *et seq.*

Elksnin, L.K., & Capilouto, G.J. (1994). Speech-language pathologists' perceptions of integrated service delivery in school settings. *Language, Speech, and Hearing Services in Schools, 25,* 258–267.

Evans, M., Holland, B., & Nichol, P. (1996). Implementing a balanced inclusion program. *Principal, 75,* 33–35.

Farber, J.G., & Klein, E.R. (1999). Classroom-based assessment of a collaborative intervention program with kindergarten and first-grade students. *Language, Speech, and Hearing Services in Schools, 30,* 83–91.

Ferguson, M.L. (1991). Collaborative/consultative service delivery: An introduction. *Language, Speech, and Hearing Services in Schools, 22,* 147.

Ferguson, M.L. (1992). Implementing collaborative consultation: The transition to collaborative teaching. *Language, Speech, and Hearing Services in Schools, 23,* 371–372.

Fey, M.E. (1986). *Language intervention with young children.* San Diego: College Hill Press.

Fey, M., & Leonard, L. (1984). Partner age as a variable in the conversational performance of specifically language-impaired children and normal-language children. *Journal of Speech and Hearing Research, 27,* 413–423.

Fey, M.E., Leonard, L.B., & Wilcox, K.A. (1981). Speech style modifications of language-impaired children. *Journal of Speech and Hearing Disorders, 46,* 91–96.

Frassinelli, L., Superior, K., & Meyers, J. (1983). A consultation model for speech and language intervention. *Asha, 25,* 25–30.

Friend, M., & Cook, L. (1990). Assessing the climate for collaboration. In W.A. Secord (Ed.), *Best practices in school speech-language pathology: Collaborative programs in the schools. Concepts, models, and procedures* (pp. 67–73). San Antonio, TX: The Psychological Corporation.

Garvey, C., & BenDebba, M. (1974). Effects of age, sex, and partner on children's dyadic speech. *Child Development, 45,* 1159–1161.

Gerber, A. (1987). Collaboration between SLPs and educators: A continuing education process. *Journal of Childhood Communication Disorders, 11,* 107–122.

Goldstein, H., English, K., Shafer, K., & Kaczmarek, L. (1997). Interaction among preschoolers with and without disabilities: Effects of across-the-day peer interaction. *Journal of Speech, Language, and Hearing Research, 40,* 33–48.

Goldstein, H., & Kaczmarek, L. (1992). Promoting communicative interaction among children in integrated intervention settings. In S.F. Warren & J. Reichle (Series Eds.) & S.F Warren & J. Reichle (Vol. Eds.), *Communication and language intervention series: Vol. 1. Causes and effects in communication and language intervention* (pp. 81–111). Baltimore: Paul H. Brookes Publishing Co.

Goodin, G., & Mehollin, K. (1990). Developing a collaborative speech-language intervention program in the schools. In W.A. Secord (Ed.), *Best practices in school speech-language pathology: Collaborative programs in the schools. Concepts, models, and procedures* (pp. 89–100). San Antonio, TX: The Psychological Corporation.

Guralnick, M.J. (1976). The value of integrating handicapped and nonhandicapped preschool children. *American Journal of Orthopsychiatry, 46,* 236–245.

Guralnick, M.J., Connor, R.T., Hammond, M.A., Gottman, J.M., & Kinnish, K. (1996). The peer relations of preschool children with communication disorders. *Child Development, 67,* 471–489.

Guralnick, M.J., & Paul-Brown, D. (1977). The nature of verbal interactions among handicapped and nonhandicapped preschool children. *Child Development, 48,* 254–260.

Guralnick, M.J., & Paul-Brown, D. (1980). Functional discourse analyses of nonhandicapped preschool children's speech to handicapped children. *American Journal of Mental Deficiency, 84,* 444–454.

Guralnick, M.J., & Paul-Brown, D. (1984). Communicative adjustments during behavior-request episodes among children at different developmental levels. *Child Development, 55,* 911–919.

Guralnick, M.J., & Paul-Brown, D. (1986). Communicative interactions of mildly delayed and normally developing preschool children: Effects of listener's developmental level. *Journal of Speech and Hearing Research, 29,* 2–10.

Guralnick, M.J., & Paul-Brown, D. (1989). Peer-related communicative competence of preschool children: Developmental and adaptive characteristics. *Journal of Speech and Hearing Research, 32,* 930–943.

Guralnick, M.J., Paul-Brown, D., Groom, J.M., Booth, C.L., Hammond, M.A., Tupper, D.B., & Gelenter, A. (1998). Conflict resolution patterns of preschool children with and without developmental delays in heterogeneous playgroups. *Early Education & Development, 9,* 49–77.

Gutkin, T.B. (1990). Consultative speech-language services in the schools: A view through the looking glass of school psychology. In W.A. Secord (Ed.), *Best practices in school speech-language pathology: Collaborative programs in the schools. Concepts, models, and procedures* (pp. 57–66). San Antonio, TX: The Psychological Corporation.

Hadley, P.A., & Rice, M.L. (1991). Conversational responsiveness of speech- and language-impaired preschoolers. *Journal of Speech and Hearing Research, 34,* 1308–1317.

Hadley, P.A., & Schuele, C.M. (1998). Facilitating peer interaction: Socially relevant objectives for preschool language intervention. *American Journal of Speech-Language Pathology, 7,* 25–36.

Harris, S.L., Handleman, J.S., Kristoff, B., Bass, L., & Gordon, R. (1990). Changes in language development among autistic and peer children in segregated and integrated preschool settings. *Journal of Autism and Developmental Disorders, 20,* 23–31.

Holzhauser-Peters, L., & Husemann, D.A. (1988, Fall). Alternative service delivery models for more efficient and effective treatment programs. *Clinical Connection, 3,* 16–18.

Holzhauser-Peters, L., & Husemann, D.A. (1989, Summer). Alternate service delivery models: Practical implementation. *Clinical Connection, 4,* 18–21.

Hoskins, B. (1990). Collaborative consultation: Designing the role of the speech-language pathologist in a new educational center. In W.A. Secord (Ed.), *Best practices in school speech-language pathology: Collaborative programs in the schools. Concepts, models, and procedures* (pp. 29–36). San Antonio, TX: The Psychological Corporation.

Idol, L., Paolucci-Whitcomb, P., & Nevin, A. (1986). *Collaborative consultation.* Gaithersburg, MD: Aspen Publishers.

Individuals with Disabilities Education Act Amendments of 1991, PL 102-119, 20 U.S.C. §§ 1400 *et seq.*

Individuals with Disabilities Education Act Amendments of 1997, PL 105-17, 20 U.S.C. §§ 1400 *et seq.*

Individuals with Disabilities Education Act (IDEA) of 1990, 101-476, 20 U.S.C. §§ 1400 *et seq.*

Kotter, J.P. (1995, March–April). Leading change: Why transformation efforts fail. *Harvard Business Review,* 59–67.

Leonard, L.B. (1998). *Children with specific language impairment.* Cambridge, MA: The MIT Press.

Losardo, A. (1996). Preparing communication specialists. In D. Bricker & A. Widerstrom (Eds.), *Preparing personnel to work with infants and young children and their families: A team approach* (pp. 91–113). Baltimore: Paul H. Brookes Publishing Co.

Magnotta, O.H. (1991). Looking beyond tradition. *Language, Speech, and Hearing Services in Schools, 22,* 105–151.

Marvin, C.A. (1987). Consultation services: Changing roles for SLP's. *Journal of Childhood Communication Disorders, 11,* 1–16.

Marvin, C.A. (1990). Problems in school-based speech-language consultation and collaboration services: Defining the terms and improving the process. In W.A. Secord (Ed.), *Best practices in school speech-language pathology: Collaborative programs in the schools. Concepts, models, and procedures* (pp. 37–47). San Antonio, TX: The Psychological Corporation.

Masur, E.F. (1978). Preschool boys' speech modifications: The effect of listeners' linguistic levels and conversational responsiveness. *Child Development, 49,* 924–927.

McCormick, L. (1997). Language intervention in the inclusive preschool. In L. McCormick, D.F. Loeb, & R.L. Schiefelbusch (Eds.), *Supporting children with communication difficulties in inclusive settings: School-based language intervention* (pp. 335–368). Needham Heights, MA: Allyn & Bacon.

McWilliam, R.A. (1996a). A program of research on integrated versus isolated treatment in early intervention. In R.A. McWilliam (Ed.), *Rethinking pull-out services in early intervention: A professional resource* (pp. 71–102). Baltimore: Paul H. Brookes Publishing Co.

McWilliam, R.A. (Ed.). (1996b). *Rethinking pull-out services in early intervention: A professional resource.* Baltimore: Paul H. Brookes Publishing Co.

McWilliam, R.A. (1996c). Service delivery issues in center-based early intervention. In R.A. McWilliam (Ed.), *Rethinking pull-out services in early intervention: A professional resource* (pp. 3–25). Baltimore: Paul H. Brookes Publishing Co.

Meyer, J. (1997). Models of service delivery. In K.G. Butler (Ed.), *Speech, language, and hearing programs in schools: A guide for students and practitioners* (pp. 241–285). Gaithersburg, MD: Aspen Publishers.

Miller, L. (1989). Classroom-based language intervention. *Language, Speech, and Hearing Services in Schools, 20,* 153–169.

Mills, P.E., Cole, K.N., Jenkins, J.R., & Dale, P.S. (1998). Effects of differing levels of inclusion on preschoolers with disabilities. *Exceptional Children, 65,* 79–90.

Montgomery, J.K. (1990). Building administrative support for collaboration. In W.A. Secord (Ed.), *Best practices in school speech-language pathology: Collaborative programs in the schools. Concepts, models, and procedures* (pp. 75–80). San Antonio, TX: The Psychological Corporation.

Montgomery, J.K. (1992). Implementing collaborative consultation: Perspectives from the field: Language, speech, and hearing services in schools. *Language, Speech, and Hearing Services in Schools, 23,* 363–364.

Moore-Brown, B.J. (1991). Moving in the direction of change: Thoughts for administrators and speech-language pathologists. *Language, Speech, and Hearing Services in Schools, 22,* 148–149.

National Institute on Deafness and Other Communication Disorders. (1995). *National strategic research plan for language and language impairments, balance and balance disorders, and voice and voice disorders* (NIH Publication No. 97-3217). Bethesda, MD: Author.

National Joint Committee on Learning Disabilities. (1991). Providing appropriate education for students with learning disabilities in regular education classrooms. *Asha, 33*(Suppl. 5), 15–17.

Nelson, N.W. (1989). Curriculum-based language assessment and intervention. *Language, Speech, and Hearing Services in Schools, 20,* 170–184.

Nelson, N.W. (1990). Only relevant practices can be best. In W.A. Secord (Ed.), *Best practices in school speech-language pathology: Collaborative programs in the schools. Concepts, models, and procedures* (pp. 15–28). San Antonio, TX: The Psychological Corporation.

Nelson, N.W. (1998). *Childhood language disorders in context: Infancy through adolescence* (2nd ed.). Needham Heights, MA: Allyn & Bacon.

O'Brien, M.A., & O'Leary, T.S. (1988). Evolving to the classroom model: Speech-language service for the mentally retarded. *Seminars in Speech and Language, 9,* 355–366.

Paul-Brown, D. (1988). A classroom-based model of language intervention for preschool language-impaired children: Principles and procedures. *Annals of Dyslexia, 38,* 193–207.

Paul-Brown, D. (1992). Preschool language intervention in the classroom: Rationale and organizational structure. In S.A. Vogel (Ed.), *Educational alternatives for students with learning disabilities* (pp. 3–42). New York: Springer-Verlag New York.

Paul-Brown, D. (1999). Inclusive practices and service delivery models for preschool children with speech and language disorders. *Asha, 41,* 53–54.

Rice, M.L. (1993). "Don't talk to him; He's weird": A social consequences account of language and social interactions. In S.F. Warren & J. Reichle (Series Eds.) & A.P. Kaiser & D.B. Gray (Vol. Eds.), *Communication and language intervention series: Vol. 2. Enhancing children's communication: Research foundations for intervention* (pp. 139–158). Baltimore: Paul H. Brookes Publishing Co.

Rice, M.L., & Hadley, P.A. (1995). Language outcomes of the language-focused curriculum. In M.L. Rice & K.A. Wilcox (Eds.), *Building a language-focused curriculum for the preschool classroom: Vol. I. A foundation for lifelong communication* (pp. 155–169). Baltimore: Paul H. Brookes Publishing Co.

Rice, M.L., Sell, M.A., & Hadley, P.A. (1991). Social interactions of speech- and language-impaired children. *Journal of Speech and Hearing Research, 34,* 1299–1307.

Rice, M.L., & Wilcox, K.A. (Eds.) (1995). *Building a language-focused curriculum for the preschool classroom: Volume I. A foundation for lifelong communication.* Baltimore: Paul H. Brookes Publishing Co.

Roberts, J.E., Prizant, B., & McWilliam, R.A. (1995). Out-of-class versus in-class service delivery in language intervention: Effects on communication interactions with young children. *American Journal of Speech-Language Pathology, 4,* 87–93.

Robertson, S.B., & Ellis Weismer, S. (1997). The influence of peer models on the play scripts of children with specific language impairments. *Journal of Speech, Language, and Hearing Research, 40,* 49–61.

Russell, S.C., & Kaderavek, J.N. (1993). Alternative models for collaboration. *Language, Speech, and Hearing Services in Schools, 24,* 76–78.

Sachs, J., & Devin, J. (1976). Young children's use of age-appropriate speech styles. *Journal of Child Language, 3,* 81–98.

Salmon, J.A., & Grimsley, K.D. (2000, March 13). States expect early education benefits. *The Washington Post,* A05.

Secord, W.A. (Ed.). (1990). *Best practices in school speech-language pathology: Collaborative programs in the schools. Concepts, models, and procedures.* San Antonio, TX: The Psychological Corporation.

Sergeant, J.F. (1995). Collaborating with families. In M.L. Rice & K.A. Wilcox (Eds.), *Building a language-focused curriculum for the preschool classroom: Vol. 1. A foundation for lifelong communication* (pp. 127–154). Baltimore: Paul H. Brookes Publishing Co.

Shatz, M., & Gelman, R. (1973). The development of communication skills: Modification in the speech of young children as a function of the listener. *Monographs of the Society for Research in Child Development, 38*(5, Serial No. 152).

Shriberg, L., & Kwiatkowski, J. (1994). Developmental phonological disorders I: A clinical profile. *Journal of Speech and Hearing Research, 37,* 1100–1126.

Silliman, E., & Wilkinson, L. (1991). *Communication for learning: Classroom observation and collaboration.* Gaithersburg, MD: Aspen Publishers.

Simon, C.S. (Ed.). (1987a). Making the collaborative consultation model work: The speech-language pathologist as consultant and teacher in mainstream education [Special issue]. *Journal of Childhood Communication Disorders, 11*(1).

Simon, C.S. (1987b). Out of the broom closet and into the classroom: The emerging SLP. *Journal of Childhood Communication Disorders, 11,* 41–66.

Simon, C.S., & Myrold-Gunyuz, P. (1990). *Into the classroom: The SLP in the collaborative role.* San Antonio, TX: Communication Skill Builders.

Stark, R., & Tallal, P. (1981). Selection of children with specific language deficits. *Journal of Speech and Hearing Disorders, 46,* 114–122.

Staub, D., & Peck, C.A. (1995, Winter). What are the outcomes for nondisabled students? *Educational Leadership, 52,* 6–40.

Throneburg, R.N., Calvert, L.K., Sturm, J.J., Paramboukas, A.A., & Paul, P.J. (2000). A comparison of service delivery models: Effects on curricular vocabulary skills in the school setting. *American Journal of Speech-Language Pathology, 9,* 10–20.

Trauner, D., Wulfeck, B., Tallal, P., & Hesselink, J. (1995). *Neurological and MRI profiles of language impaired children* (Technical Report CUD-9513). San Diego: University of California at San Diego, Center for Research in Language.

Valdez, F.M., & Montgomery, J.K. (1997). Outcomes for two treatment approaches for children with communication disorders in Head Start. *Journal of Children's Communication Development, 18,* 65–71.

van Kleeck, A., & Richardson, A. (1988). Language delay in children. In N. Ladd, L. McReynolds, J. Northern, & D. Yoder (Eds.), *Handbook of speech-language pathology and audiology* (pp. 655–684). Hamilton, Canada: B.C. Decker.

Voorhees, M.D., Landon, R., & Harvey, J. (1997). Early childhood education. In L.A. Power-deFur & F.P. Orelove (Eds.), *Inclusive education: Practical implementation of the least restrictive environment* (pp. 131–152). Gaithersburg, MD: Aspen Publishers.

Watkins, R.V., & Rice, M.L. (Vol. Eds.). (1994). *Specific language impairments in children.* In S.F. Warren & J. Reichle (Series Eds.), *Vol. 4. Communication and language intervention series.* Baltimore: Paul H. Brookes Publishing Co.

Watkins, R.V., Rice, M.L., & Moltz, C.C. (1993). Verb use by language-impaired and normally developing children. *First Language, 13,* 133–143.

Weiss, A.L., & Nakamura, M. (1992). Children with normal language skills in preschool classrooms for children with language impairments: Differences in modeling styles. *Language, Speech, and Hearing Services in Schools, 23,* 64–70.

Westby, C., Watson, S., & Murphy, M. (1994). The vision of full inclusion: Don't exclude kids by including them. *Journal of Childhood Communication Disorders, 16,* 13–22.

Wilcox, K.A., & Morris, S.R. (1995). Speech intervention in a language-focused curriculum. In M.L. Rice & K.A. Wilcox (Eds.), *Building a language-focused curriculum for the preschool classroom: Vol. 1. A foundation for lifelong communication* (pp. 73–89). Baltimore: Paul H. Brookes Publishing Co.

Wilcox, M.J., Kouri, T.A., & Caswell, S.B. (1991). Early language intervention: A comparison of classroom and individual treatment. *American Journal of Speech-Language Pathology, 1,* 49–62.

Wilcox, M.J., & Shannon, M.S. (1996). Integrated early intervention practices in speech-language pathology. In R.A. McWilliam (Ed.), *Rethinking pull-out services in early intervention: A professional resource* (pp. 217–242). Baltimore: Paul H. Brookes Publishing Co.

20

MARY ANN ROMSKI

ROSE A. SEVCIK

SUSAN FORREST

Assistive Technology and Augmentative and Alternative Communication in Inclusive Early Childhood Programs

Max is a 28-month-old boy with a diagnosis of partial trisomy 13 syndrome. He has a hearing loss and a seizure disorder and faces cognitive, mobility, and both receptive and expressive communication development challenges. At a very young age, it was clear to Max's mother that assistive technology (AT) devices and services were needed to facilitate his development as well as his inclusion in education and society in general.

Mrs. S., the mother of a 19-year-old son named Joe, is pleased with the communication gains he has made with his first augmentative and alternative communication (AAC) device. Joe can communicate basic wants and needs to partners in a variety of environments. Mrs. S. wonders, however, what other far-reaching gains Joe would have made if he had access to an AAC device and intervention during his early childhood years.

Both of these parents' views support the use of AT during early childhood from two different stages in development. One parent is looking ahead to an optimistic future because of AT whereas the other parent is looking back wondering what broader more encompassing effects AT could have had for her son if he had access to it during his first 3 years of life.

This chapter examines the role that AT can play in inclusive classrooms and communities during early childhood. To accomplish this, the authors highlight the use of one type of AT, AAC devices and intervention services. AAC devices are those that permit children who are not speaking to develop independent communication skills that can be used to interact with parents, siblings, and extended family; to play and develop friendships with peers; and to develop

The preparation of this chapter was in part supported by Grant No. NICHD-06016 and a Research Program Enhancement Grant from Georgia State University, Atlanta.

some control over their environments (see Beukelman & Mirenda, 1998, for an overview). The authors chose to highlight AAC for two reasons: 1) having access to communication is the area in which AT may have the most important effect on participation in inclusive environments for young children with a wide range of disabilities and 2) the research and practice literature in AAC is one of the most well-developed areas of AT.

This chapter is divided into three sections. First, a brief introduction to AT, including definitions, terminology, and federal legislation that serves as the foundation for AT use during early childhood, is presented. Next, a profile is presented of the young children who may use AAC devices and services as well as considerations of the extant literature on research and recommended practices for AAC with respect to young children. Finally, presented are challenges that must be considered if AAC and AT are to be used to facilitate early childhood education in inclusive environments.

ASSISTIVE TECHNOLOGY

An AT device is any item, piece of equipment, or product system, whether acquired commercially, modified, or customized, that is used to increase, maintain, or improve functional capabilities of individuals with disabilities. Included are devices that facilitate mobility, play, feeding, environmental control and access, classroom participation, communication, and literacy (Church & Glennen, 1992). During early childhood, children may use one or more of these devices, depending on their individual needs, to facilitate their inclusion.

Federal Legislation and Assistive Technology

The Technology-Related Assistance for Individuals with Disabilities Act of 1988

(PL 100-407) highlighted, for the first time, the role AT devices and services can play in ensuring that all children and adults with disabilities are able to participate fully in society. Under this act, funding was provided to states through the National Institute on Disability and Rehabilitation Research (NIDRR) for the development of consumer-driven AT programs whose goal was the comprehensive incorporation of AT devices and services into extant public and private service delivery systems (e.g., early intervention, education, rehabilitation). This act was replaced by the Assistive Technology Act of 1998 (PL 105-394), which continued the tenets set out in the earlier legislation and focused attention on advocacy issues. In 1990, landmark legislation, the Americans with Disabilities Act (PL 101-336), guaranteed the basic civil rights of people with disabilities and addressed the use of supports and accommodations (including AT/AAC devices and services) to counter the employment and educational access challenges they have traditionally experienced. The 1997 Amendments to the Individuals with Disabilities Education Act (IDEA; PL 105-17) state that on a case-by-case basis, school-purchased AAC devices can be used at home and in other environments if the individualized education program (IEP) team determines that it is necessary for the child to receive a free appropriate public education.

The cumulative impact of these fundamental pieces of federal legislation is that children with disabilities now have a guaranteed legal right to be provided with the supports needed to participate in inclusive environments. Communication skills are essential for the successful implementation of any and all of this legislation. Without the ability to communicate, education, inclusion, self-determination, and, later, employment, clearly are compromised. These laws have placed demands on interventionists to develop approaches to both assess and intervene with children who previously had been excluded from AT and AAC services. Unfortunately, in many cases, these children had been considered "too disabled" or "too young" to benefit from AT and AAC.

CHILDREN WHO MAY USE AAC DEVICES AND SERVICES

Children who encounter difficulty using speech as their primary means of communication are usually either born with some type of congenital disability that hinders their development of speech or experience an injury or illness early in life that substantially limits their existing speech and language abilities. Congenital disabilities that impede the development of speech and language may include autism, cerebral palsy, dual sensory impairments, various genetic syndromes, mental retardation, multiple disabilities (including hearing impairment), and even a stroke at or near birth. During the early childhood period of development, a child may acquire an inability to communicate via speech through a traumatic brain injury caused by some type of accident, stroke, or, in a rare instance, severe psychological trauma. Sickle cell anemia, for example, can cause debilitating strokes that, when severe, may hinder a child's ability to speak. It is also important to note that all of the disabilities described previously can result in a broad range of communication outcomes from functional speech and language skills to not speaking at all. There are certainly individual differences in communication patterns. Not every child with one of these disabilities is, or will be, nonspeaking throughout his or her life, but many may use AAC at some point during their development.

Augmentative and Alternative Communication Terminology

AAC is an area of clinical practice that attempts to compensate (either temporarily or permanently) for the impairment and disability patterns of individuals with severe expressive communication disorders, including speech-language and writing (ASHA, 1989). Any intervention that uses AAC should incorporate the individual's full communication abilities. These abilities may include any existing speech or vocalizations, gestures, manual signs, communication boards, and speech-output communication devices (ASHA, 1991). In this instance, then, AAC is truly multimodal, permitting a child to use every mode possible to communicate messages and ideas. AAC abilities may change over time, although sometimes very slowly, and thus, the AAC system selected for today may need to be modified for tomorrow (Beukelman & Mirenda, 1998). An AAC system is an integrated group of four components used by an individual to enhance communication (ASHA, 1991). The following are the four components: symbols, aids, techniques, and strategies.

Symbols refer to the methods used for "visual, auditory, and/or tactile representation of conventional concepts" (ASHA, 1991, p. 10). Symbols can be referred to as aided or unaided. Unaided symbols include gestures, manual sign sets, and spoken words because their use does not rely on an external medium. Aided symbols include visual-graphic representations, such as objects, pictures, photographs, line drawings, written words, and braille.

An *aid* is "a physical object or device used to transmit or receive messages (e.g., communication book, communication board, chart, mechanical or electronic device, computer)" (ASHA, 1991, p. 10).

Techniques are the methods by which an individual transmits messages. Techniques can be divided into two broad categories: direct selection and scanning. Direct selection allows the child to communicate specific messages from a large set of options. Direct selection techniques include pointing, signing, natural gesturing, or touching. Some children use head pointers, head sticks, or eye gaze (or eye pointing) to directly select symbols. Scanning is a technique in which the message elements are presented to the child in a sequence. The child specifies his or her choice by responding "yes" or "no" to the person or the device presenting the elements. Scanning techniques include linear scanning, row-column scanning, and encoding (ASHA, 1991). Encoding is a technique in which the child uses a code to convey messages (e.g., Morse code).

Strategies are specific ways in which the AAC aids, symbols, and techniques are used to develop and/or enhance communication. A strategy includes the intervention plan for facilitating an individual's performance (ASHA, 1991).

Role of Assistive Technology and Augmentative and Alternative Communication in Inclusion

For many years, AAC was considered a last resort for communication once every other intervention had failed. During that time, AAC was never considered for young children. Current perspectives suggest that the functions AAC can play in language and communication development vary, depending on the child's chronological age, degree of disability, and specific environmental needs. In addition to providing a means by which children can convey information, AAC can augment existing speech and vocalizations to improve message intelligibility, provide an input mode as well as an output mode for communication for children with limited speech comprehension

skills, and serve as a language teaching tool (Beukelman & Mirenda, 1998). AAC can also replace or mitigate a child's challenging behaviors, such as screaming or hitting, with a conventional means of communication (Donnellan, Mirenda, Mesaros, & Fassbender, 1984; Doss & Reichle, 1991). Johnny, for example, is a preschool-age child with severely dysarthric speech due to cerebral palsy. His speech is intelligible only to familiar communicative partners, such as his family and teachers. When he goes to a fast-food restaurant and orders lunch, the server cannot understand his speech. An AAC device augments Johnny's existing speech in inclusive situations in which it is difficult for him to be understood. AAC serves a very different role for Annie, a 3-year-old who has severe spastic cerebral palsy, almost age-appropriate speech comprehension skills, and a few undifferentiated vocalizations. For Annie, AAC serves as an output mode for communication as well as a teaching strategy for further language development. Max, to whom you were introduced at the beginning of this chapter, uses AAC to take in linguistic information as well as for beginning expressive communication. These diverse roles all have the effect of improving a child's communication skills, which, in turn, permits greater independence and participation in daily activities across a range of inclusive environments. It also can significantly alter unfamiliar persons' perceptions of the child's capabilities and, thus, facilitate inclusion at school and in the community (Romski & Sevcik, 1996).

Research Knowledge Base and Early Childhood

Since the 1970s, it has been recognized that augmentation might be an effective aspect of language intervention for school-age children with disabilities who do not speak. AAC permits them to compensate for their lack of speech and augment their existing communication skills (Beukelman & Mirenda, 1998; Reichle, York, & Sigafoos, 1991). For very young children, a significant delay in communication development affects all aspects of development; however, AAC interventions have only begun to be considered for them since the late 1980s.

Traditional communication intervention research and practice for young children has focused on developing spoken language skills (Fey, 1986) and/or teaching prelinguistic skills (e.g., Warren, Yoder, Gazdag, Kim, & Jones, 1993; Yoder & Warren, 1993). Developing functional, intelligible speech production skills is the ultimate goal for any young child who is encountering great difficulty learning to speak. Traditional approaches that focus on speech, however, can frustrate the child and his or her family (sometimes resulting in challenging behaviors) because they do not provide a way to communicate while the child is slowly (and sometimes unsuccessfully) learning to talk. Teaching prelinguistic skills focuses on establishing a strong intentional communicative foundation on which to build linguistic skills. Even with such a prelinguistic base, often the child with a severe communication disability does not smoothly make the transition from intentional communication to spoken language skills, which sometimes results in frustrations for the entire family and behavior difficulties for the child. If these children had a more conventional mode by which to take in linguistic information and then intentionally communicate early in childhood, perhaps their overall communicative interaction skills and adaptive behavior skills might not lag as far behind other children without such experience. Schiefelbusch (1984, 1985) and others have speculated that if young children at significant risk for speech and language (receptive and expressive) difficulties received augmented language experience early in the course of their development, their communication skills may follow a more typical developmental route. With the aid of an AAC system, comprehension and production skills may emerge earlier than they would through other therapeutic approaches that focus on speech alone. A number of research and practice concerns must be considered when AAC is to be employed with young children during the earliest stages of development. They include symbols, instructional approaches, perceptions and responses of typically developing children, and, perhaps the most critical concern, facilitating and not inhibiting speech.

Symbols   One issue that has dominated the clinical and research literature on AAC has been the extent to which features of the medium by which language is represented, symbols, may affect its learning and use (Sevcik, Romski, & Wilkinson, 1991). AAC symbols have been classified as unaided—including manual signs and gestures—or aided—including visual-graphic symbols that range from objects, pictures, and photographs to highly abstract or arbitrary ones (e.g., Blissymbols, English orthography; Lloyd & Fuller, 1986). The level of arbitrariness of different symbols (i.e., the degree to which a symbol does or does not physically resemble its referent or meaning) has consistently been judged to be an important factor in the choice of a symbol set for young children (see, e.g., Musselwhite & St. Louis, 1982; Sevcik et al., 1991, for additional discussions of terms). This judgment is based on the belief that the more a symbol looks like what it represents, the more likely it is to be learned by young children. This issue has been a complex and, at times, controversial one.

The majority of research on this topic, to date, has focused on how typically developing preschool children and adults with intact cognitive skills perceive symbols and/or learn the association between symbols and spoken words. The findings from this work have indicated that for young children with intact cognitive skills, symbol learning is affected by the level of symbol arbitrariness (e.g., concrete, abstract) and the physical configuration (e.g., complexity, shape) of symbols (e.g., Ecklund & Reichle, 1987; Mizuko, 1987; Musselwhite & Ruscello, 1984).

Some researchers, however, have questioned whether these findings may be extended to children with cognitive disabilities who are not speaking (see Sevcik et al., 1991, for a review). Very little symbol research has actually been conducted in which individuals with developmental disabilities who were not speaking serve as participants. Of the studies that have been conducted, the focus of investigation has been on the representational abilities of the participants or on the ability of the participants to learn symbol meanings.

There is one group of studies that has examined the representational abilities of children with severe mental retardation. Findings from these studies suggest that a number of factors related to the representational medium may influence how symbols are learned by individuals with developmental disabilities. These factors may include intrinsic factors, such as the child's speech comprehension abilities (Franklin, Mirenda, & Phillips, 1996; Mirenda & Locke, 1989; Sevcik & Romski, 1986), and extrinsic factors, such as the degree of arbitrariness of the symbols used (Dixon, 1981; Hurlbut, Iwata, & Green, 1982; Sevcik & Romski, 1986).

Instructional Approaches   The majority of research in AAC has centered on developing instructional approaches that are designed to replace or augment the existing receptive and expressive communication skills of children with disabilities (see Beukelman & Mirenda, 1998; Romski & Sevcik, 1997, for re-

views). Because spoken language has not been a successful avenue for communicative development, specialized instruction via manual signs or visual-graphic symbols is required to acquire language. Four issues have been the focus of study with respect to instruction: approaches for teaching communicative functions, such as requesting, negating, and commenting via manual signs or visual-graphic symbols; the locale and format of instruction; the integration of technology into instruction; and the role of speech comprehension.

Approaches for Teaching Communicative Functions   Strategies that vary in the amount of direct instruction and structure they require have been developed to teach initial communicative functions to children with severe disabilities. Two approaches to facilitate requesting, the earliest communicative function to develop (Bruner, 1983), have been investigated. Reichle and his colleagues (Reichle et al., 1991) have espoused the use of a generalized requesting procedure. This approach begins with a single consistent symbol, such as "want," and is used in multiple situations to initiate requesting. Once a request is initiated, the child is given a choice of items (e.g., a cookie or a drink). After the child learns to make these generalized requests, differentiated requests for specific referents, such as "want cookie" versus "want drink," are incorporated into the child's communicative repertoire. A second approach is to begin with requests that specify each item requested using signs or symbols (Romski, Sevcik, & Pate, 1988). Using this approach, children must establish a series of conditional discriminations between the item requested and the sign or symbol used to execute the request.

Another early developing communicative function is rejecting, that is, the ability to refuse an undesired item or to cease an activity (e.g., "no"). Reichle and colleagues (1991) developed an instructional strategy for teaching this communicative function as well.

These approaches have been used to establish initial symbol and communicative repertoires in structured environments. What is still needed, however, are studies to compare the efficacy of the approaches to facilitate generalization to other contexts and with other communicative partners. In turn, studies that examine these skills as the foundation for the development of more sophisticated communication and language skills, such as combinatorial symbol use, are essential.

Locale and Format of Instruction Another dimension of instruction has been the location in which intervention occurred and the format in which it was implemented. Prevailing research and practice recommend that instruction take place in everyday environments, such as the home, school, and community. Furthermore, the literature strongly supports the use of naturalistic communicative exchanges as formats for instruction within these environments (e.g., Beukelman & Mirenda, 1998; Calculator & Jorgensen, 1991).

Although the majority of studies in the literature have been short-term investigations, Romski and Sevcik (1996) studied the communication abilities of 13 school-age youth with moderate or severe mental retardation over a 2-year period. They introduced the System for Augmenting Language (SAL) to these youths who had, at the beginning of the study, fewer than 10 spoken word approximations at home and school. The SAL included five components: 1) a speech-output communication device, 2) an appropriate arbitrary symbol vocabulary, 3) naturalistic communicative experiences during which the youth were encouraged, but not required, to communicate, 4) partners (teachers, parents, and siblings) who were taught how to use the device and how to provide both a

symbol model and input via speech + symbols to the youth, and 5) investigators who provided a resource and feedback mechanism to monitor progress across the study. During naturalistic communicative experiences at home and school, the youth had opportunities to employ a range of communicative functions from greeting, requesting, and attention directing to answering and questioning.

Romski and Sevcik (1996) found that the 13 youth integrated their use of the SAL within their extant vocalizations and gestures, resulting in a rich multimodal form of communication that they used to successfully and effectively communicate with adults (Romski, Sevcik, Robinson, & Bakeman, 1994) and peers (Romski, Sevcik, & Wilkinson, 1994). These youth developed a vocabulary that integrated referential and social-regulative symbols (Adamson, Romski, Deffebach, & Sevcik, 1992). Some of these youth also then developed combinatorial symbol skills (Wilkinson, Romski, & Sevcik, 1994) as well as intelligible spoken words and rudimentary reading skills (Romski & Sevcik, 1996). Perhaps, most important, the SAL facilitated their abilities to learn, play, work, and be included in society (Romski & Sevcik, 1996).

These findings support the use of naturalistic instructional strategies in everyday environments. They illustrate that children with mental retardation do not necessarily require repeated drill and practice to acquire language through augmented means. They also suggest that AAC naturalistic instruction can be used effectively for young children in inclusive environments.

To explore the influence of the child's chronological age at the beginning of SAL intervention, Romski, Sevcik, and Adamson (1997) introduced the SAL to a 4-year-old boy with a history of significant generalized developmental delays (score of 39 on the Vineland Adaptive Behavior Scales [VABS; Sparrow, Balla, &

Cicchetti, 1984]) and a seizure disorder diagnosed at age 8 months. He evidenced limited speech comprehension, no spoken words, and only a few intentional, but unintelligible, vocalizations and gestures. When the SAL was introduced, there was an immediate positive shift in the frequency of his communication attempts, all of which involved using the device. The outcome of this work suggested that the SAL could be readily incorporated into the daily activities of a young child and his family. Romski, Sevcik, and Adamson (1999) then examined the communication development of 10 toddlers with established disabilities after 12 months of SAL intervention. Although the toddlers evidenced no increase in their spoken language production skills, they developed expressive symbol vocabularies that averaged 29 symbols (range from 12 to 72 symbols).

Use of Technology   With the exception of a few early studies (Locke & Mirenda, 1988; Romski et al., 1988; Romski, White, Millen, & Rumbaugh, 1984), manual signs and cardboard communication boards were the AAC systems of choice for people with severe cognitive disabilities but no severe physical impairments. The prevailing belief had been that people with limited intellectual ability could not benefit from the use of more sophisticated technologies, such as computer-linked communication systems. Romski and Sevcik (1996), however, have argued that the use of a speech-output communication device was a critical component of the successful use of the SAL by their participants. They contended that the speech output provided a link to the natural auditory world for the participants. They, however, did not provide a direct comparison of SAL acquisition (speech + symbols) with learning symbols alone. Schlosser, Belfiore, Nigam, and Blischak (1995) compared the acquisition of visual-graphic symbols coupled with speech output with the

acquisition of visual-graphic symbols alone by three adults with severe mental retardation. They found that the speech output + visual-graphic symbols resulted in more efficient learning with fewer errors than the visual-graphic symbols alone. These results support the argument that speech output plays a critical role in initial augmented language learning. Advances in technology have afforded new opportunities for both facilitating language learning in naturalistic environments and exploring additional dimensions of instruction. Another important outcome of using speech output may be the effect it has on others' perception of the child's competence (Romski & Sevcik, 1996).

The Role of Speech Comprehension
Although a focus on language expression in AAC is essential and permits children to have an immediate and visible communicative effect on their environment, it does not exist in isolation (Romski & Sevcik, 1993; Sevcik & Romski, 1997). Communication skills also demand that children assume the role of listener, or message receiver. To flexibly assume this role, children must comprehend the information that is being conveyed to them by their communicative partners. A young typically developing child first hears language during rich social-communicative interactions that include reoccurring familiar situations or events (Bruner, 1983; Nelson, 1985). Prior to actually producing words, the social and environmental interactional contexts converge with the available linguistic information to produce understandings (Huttenlocher, 1974). By the time the typical child is between 12 and 15 months of age, he or she understands, on average, about 50 words (Benedict, 1979). As this child moves through his or her second year of life, he or she quickly begins to understand relational commands, such as "Give mommy the truck," and can carry them out. Given the typical devel-

opmental path, children who evidence a significant delay fall behind almost immediately. A shift in focus to comprehension may permit the child to observe and to actively engage in the communicative process prior to actually taking on the role of speaker. Like very young typical developing children, young children with disabilities should have the opportunity to be exposed to a mode for language production before they are asked to use it. Such exposure permits the young language learner to focus his or her attention on word forms and their referents in the environment. It also permits the caregiver to create new learning opportunities by capitalizing on well-established routines. The ability to comprehend spoken words permits the child to bootstrap his or her way into the world of productive language in an alternate mode. When children do not have such a foundation, their productive language learning is slow and constrained, even in an alternative mode (Romski & Sevcik, 1993; Sevcik & Romski, 1997).

Not all young children with disabilities come to AAC intervention comprehending speech. Sevcik and Romski (1997) described two distinct paths to symbol acquisition for the youth with moderate and severe mental retardation that they have studied. The extant spoken language comprehension skills some of these youth brought to the language-learning task allowed them to rapidly acquire and use symbols for communication. Their performance was in sharp contrast to youth who did not evidence such speech comprehension skills.

Similarly, Peterson, Bondy, Vincent, and Finnegan (1995) reported that two school-age boys with autism and no speech responded better to communicative input that included pictures and gestures than to speech input alone. Sevcik, Romski, Watkins, and Deffebach (1995) reported that parents and teachers spontaneously increased the amount of aug-

mented input (speech + symbol) they employed when communicating with youth who had very little speech comprehension than with those youth who understood speech. Receptive skills serve as the foundation not only for productive symbol learning but as a vehicle for language instruction.

For very young children with disabilities, the field has not yet addressed how to inculcate both understanding and expression in augmented language intervention efforts. In practice, the focus of early augmented language intervention is on physical access to a device and production of messages (Beukelman & Mirenda, 1998). When children do not quickly begin to produce messages using this production focus, they can become frustrated and, often times, are viewed as unable to learn to communicate.

Romski, Sevcik, Adamson, Browning, and colleagues (1999) completed a pilot study of a 34-month-old boy with a diagnosis of partial trisomy 13 syndrome, cerebral palsy, and significant developmental delay. The child had an adaptive behavior composite score of 55 on the VABS (age equivalent = 1 year, 3 months). The child was the oldest of three children (his two siblings were 18 months and 6 months old) from a two-parent, middle class family of Hispanic background. He and his mother participated in the 12-week intervention protocol designed to focus on augmented communication input. Receptively, he had speech comprehension skills at about 15 months. Expressively, he had some undifferentiated vocalizations and a laugh that he did not use communicatively. He did not comprehend the meanings for any of the symbols to be taught (e.g., "more," "all done," "book," "snack," "drink," "bubbles," "jack-in-the-box"). The intervention increased his symbol and speech comprehension skills for the target vocabulary from 0 to 8 words across a 12-week period. After 6 weeks, there was also a steady increase in his spontaneous use of symbols to communicate messages. There was no comparable change in spoken-language production skills, however, over the course of the intervention. His mother spontaneously reported that she appreciated the intervention because it did not place demands on her to make her son use the device. This input strategy permitted the parent to be successful regardless of the child's response. That is, the child did not have to perform a specific action in order for the parent to think he or she was implementing the intervention strategy.

Perceptions and Responses of Typically Developing Children to AAC

How do typically developing children respond to the use of AAC devices by their peers with disabilities? Unfortunately, there are very few empirical studies to guide us on this topic. With respect to older school-age children, Blockberger, Armstrong, O'Connor, and Freeman (1993) examined the attitudes of fourth-grade children toward a nonspeaking peer who was using three different types of communication techniques. They found that gender, reading abilities, and experience with children with disabilities influenced the likelihood of a positive attitude toward the child who used an AAC device. Romski and Sevcik (1996) also reported that the use of the SAL enhanced not only communications but also judgments of overall competence by familiar and unfamiliar observers.

Young children today have experience with computers from infancy. Toys and picture books are often computer-based and include both digital and synthetic voice output. Toddlers can manipulate computer software programs via touch screens and large track balls. Such experiences should make young typically developing children familiar and, it is hoped, comfortable with an AAC voice and the computer that generates it. In the completed pilot study by Romski,

Sevcik, Adamson, Browning, and colleagues (1999), the toddler's 18-month-old, typically developing brother interacted positively with the child and the AAC device. Certainly, this is an important area of study in need of substantial research.

Facilitating Speech

The fear of many parents, and some practitioners, is that AAC will become the child's primary communication mode and will take away the child's motivation to speak. The empirical data, to date, do not support this fear. In fact, they suggest just the opposite (Romski & Sevcik, 1996). With respect to very young children, Sedey, Rosin, and Miller (1991), for example, reported that manual signs had been taught to 80% of the 46 young children with Down syndrome (mean chronological age = 3 years, 11 months) that they surveyed. The families of these children reported that they discontinued the use of the manual signs when the child began talking or when the child's speech became easier to understand. Miller, Sedey, Miolo, Rosin, and Murray-Branch (1991) also reported that when sign vocabularies were included, the initial vocabularies of a group of children with Down syndrome were not significantly different from those of typically developing children who were at the same developmental age. Adamson and Dunbar (1991) described the communication development of a 2-year-old girl with a long-term hospitalization and a tracheostomy. This girl used manual signs to communicate during this long-term hospitalization. When the tracheostomy tube was removed, she immediately attempted to speak and quickly used speech as her primary means of communication. Romski and colleagues (1997) evaluated the effects of AAC on the language and communication development of toddlers with established developmental disabilities who were not speaking at the onset of the study. Though families of these very young children were much more receptive to using AAC than the investigators initially thought they would be, they were quick to focus exclusively on speech when their child produced his or her first word approximation. In summary, for very young children, the use of AAC does not appear to hinder speech development. In fact, although more research is needed, it appears to enhance the development of spoken communication.

AGENDA FOR CHANGE: PROMOTING ASSISTIVE TECHNOLOGY USE IN INCLUSIVE ENVIRONMENTS

Overall, then, the literature about AAC use suggests that what is known serves as a strong foundation on which to extend the use of AAC to younger children in inclusive environments. As we continue to promote the use of AAC and other forms of AT with young children in inclusive programs, a range of challenges confront us. These challenges include issues in three main areas: professional issues, child and family issues, and issues related to the technology itself.

Professional Issues

There are a number of professional challenges that affect the use of AT in inclusive environments. One of the most challenging and frustrating issues is a lingering one—professional attitudes, philosophies, and beliefs about the use of AT, particularly AAC, during the early childhood years. Although the research literature and recommended practices data support the notions that very young children can use and benefit from AT (Pierce, 1999; Romski & Sevcik, 1996), some professionals still believe that AAC is a last resort to be tried only after all else has failed and the child is still not talking. This belief can and does hinder the use of AT with very young children. For example, Max, the child introduced at the beginning of the chapter, was successfully using an AAC device for receptive communication and beginning to use it for his own communication. When he turned 3 years old and was to begin a preschool program in the local public school, the school's evaluation team determined that he did not have the cognitive skills necessary to use an AAC device. Thus, they determined that his IEP would not include AT devices and services until he had developed prerequisite skills. This circular argument is not supported by the empirical literature. How will a child ever be able to use an AAC device if he or she does not have the opportunity to gain experience with it? Changing philosophy and attitude is a difficult task and must be accomplished via preservice and in-service education that includes knowledge and skills about AT. In addition, in-service educational programs must target teachers and practitioners who need to update their knowledge and skills. The National Joint Committee on the Communication Needs of Persons with Severe Disabilities (1992) has specified guidelines for competencies necessary for communication. There are still far too few educational training programs that address this philosophical issue. If the field is to move forward in providing AT services to young children, then the field must produce competent professionals who are knowledgeable about AAC and other AT assessment and intervention strategies.

Family and Child Issues

There are a number of important issues related to the family and the child. When AT intervention is started during the school year, there is a natural structure in place in the school routine on which to overlay initial communication experiences in the environment. In the intervention process, then, the parent is a partner with the speech-language pathologist and the teacher. When AAC intervention is started early in life, at least two additional issues need to be considered (Berry, 1987). First, families are still coming to terms with their young child's disability (Wright, Granger, & Sameroff, 1984) and often seek a variety of interventions (e.g., speech-language pathology, occupational therapy, physical therapy) to minimize or overcome their child's limitations. Second, there appears to be fewer structured routines outside the home in which to place AAC intervention during the young child's day than the school child's day. Thus, the toddler's family must assume a primary role in the intervention process in addition to their other parenting responsibilities (Crutcher, 1993). Fulfilling this primary interventionist role may require different external supports and organization than is the case when a child is school age. Kaiser (1993) reported that parent-implemented language intervention is a complex phenomenon that requires a multicomponent intervention approach. Romski and colleagues' (1997) preliminary findings about initial choice suggest that engaging in early augmented language intervention may be a more complex decision than professionals initially anticipate. Parent perception about communication and parental stress may play a role in augmented language intervention. In general, today's parents may not be afraid of using technology because of extensive parent education about the importance of getting communication started and the increased computerization of daily life. Understanding how to arrange early augmented language intervention to capitalize on the family's roles has not been examined as of this writing. In addition, sometimes parental knowledge about AT exceeds professional knowledge and experience. Such discrepancies can serve to create challenges for teams in determining and providing services.

One of the difficulties families face is that they want their young children to produce communications (preferably speech, but symbols are acceptable). Their expectations for production lead to competition between a focus on providing input and a focus on having the child produce symbols, even if the productions are imitative in nature. Thus, interventions that do not confuse the parents or children, but instead permit them to focus their energies on a specific goal, are needed.

For young children who have significant communication disabilities, there are also limited tools available that can provide an adequate assessment of the child's strengths and weaknesses. The more challenging the child's disabilities, the more difficult it appears to implement AT devices and services at a young age. Although it is often clear that the child needs AT support, it is also incorrectly thought that he or she must have skills in place to implement AT. At the beginning of the 21st century, there are many choices of AAC devices, from simple inexpensive technology (e.g., single switches) to complex systems that permit access to communication. These simple devices require little skill and can provide a point at which the young child can be introduced to AT.

Assistive Technology Devices and Service Issues

AT devices are tools that must be employed in coordination with assessment and intervention approaches. One striking characteristic of the AT field today is the rapid development of new technologies. Changes in the types of devices that are available occur so frequently that it may be difficult for the family and practitioners to keep abreast of every device available. Additions to the AAC device market in the late 1990s are able to provide a range of capabilities within one device that may enable a child to use one piece of equipment for a longer period of time during development.

Funding devices during early childhood is another concern. There is a range of funding sources available for the purchase of individual AAC devices. These include, but are not limited to, local or state education and/or rehabilitation agencies; private medical insurance; public health assistance; and charitable agencies, foundations, and corporations. The process, however, for obtaining devices may not be consumer friendly. AAC services are also expensive because they require costly equipment and a large amount of personnel time. Local education agencies must be creative in how they fund AAC services. For example, speech-language pathology services may combine resources with special education services to fund equipment. In addition, informal agreements can be developed with school principals to ensure that the speech-language pathologist can adjust his or her schedule to provide services during appropriate times during the inclusive school day (e.g., in the lunchroom, on the playground).

CONCLUSION

Much research remains to be completed to understand the language development of young children with disabilities who use AAC and other forms of AT. Research must continue to examine the contributions and interactions of a range of factors to communication and language development, including speech comprehension, instructional conditions, the symbol set available to the child, the environments of use, and the partners with whom the child communicates. Augmentative communication and other forms of AT offer great promise for facilitating inclusion during early childhood.

Research and recommended practices are continuing to develop, and the future is promising for young children with AT needs.

REFERENCES

Adamson, L.B., & Dunbar, B. (1991). Communication development of young children with tracheostomies. *Augmentative and Alternative Communication, 7,* 275–283.

Adamson, L.B., Romski, M.A., Deffebach, K.P., & Sevcik, R.A. (1992). Symbol vocabulary and the focus of conversations: Augmenting language development for youth with mental retardation. *Journal of Speech and Hearing Research, 35,* 1333–1344.

American Speech-Language-Hearing Association (ASHA). (1989). Competencies for speech-language pathologists providing services in augmentative communication. *Asha, 31,* 107–110.

American Speech-Language-Hearing Association (ASHA). (1991). Report: Augmentative and alternative communication. *Asha, 33*(Suppl. 5), 9–12.

Americans with Disabilities Act (ADA) of 1990, PL 101-336, 42 U.S.C. §§ 12101 *et seq.*

Assistive Technology Act of 1998, PL 105-394, 29 U.S.C. §§ 3001 *et seq.*

Benedict, H. (1979). Early lexical development: Comprehension and production. *Journal of Child Language, 6,* 183–200.

Berry, J. (1987). Strategies for involving parents in programs for young children using augmentative and alternative communication. *Augmentative and Alternative Communication, 3,* 90–93.

Beukelman, D.R., & Mirenda, P. (1998). *Augmentative and alternative communication: Management of severe communication disorders in children and adults* (2nd ed.). Baltimore: Paul H. Brookes Publishing Co.

Blockberger, S., Armstrong, R., O'Connor, A., & Freeman, R. (1993). Children's attitudes toward a nonspeaking child using various augmentative and alternative communication techniques. *Augmentative and Alternative Communication, 9,* 243–250.

Bruner, J. (1983). *Child's talk.* New York: W.W. Norton and Company.

Calculator, S., & Jorgensen, C. (1991). Integrating AAC instruction into regular education settings: Expounding on best practices. *Augmentative and Alternative Communication, 7,* 204–212.

Church, G., & Glennen, S. (1992). *The handbook of assistive technology.* San Diego: Singular Publishing Group.

Crutcher, D.M. (1993). Parent perspectives: Best practice and recommendations for research. In S.F. Warren & J. Reichle (Series Eds.) & A.P. Kaiser & D.B. Gray (Vol. Eds.), *Communication and language intervention series: Vol. 2. Enhancing children's communication: Research foundations for intervention* (pp. 365–373). Baltimore: Paul H. Brookes Publishing Co.

Dixon, L. (1981). A functional analysis of photo-object matching skills of severely retarded adolescents. *Journal of Applied Behavior Analysis, 14,* 465–478.

Donnellan, A., Mirenda, P., Mesaros, R., & Fassbender, L. (1984). Analyzing the communicative functions of aberrant behavior. *Journal of The Association for Persons with Severe Handicaps, 9,* 141–150.

Doss, L.S., & Reichle, J. (1991). Replacing excess behavior with an initial communicative repertoire. In J. Reichle, J. York, & J. Sigafoos (Eds.), *Implementing augmentative and alternative communication: Strategies for learners with severe disabilities* (pp. 215–237). Baltimore: Paul H. Brookes Publishing Co.

Ecklund, S., & Reichle, J. (1987). A comparison of normal children's ability to recall symbols from two logographic systems. *Language, Speech, and Hearing Services in Schools, 18,* 34–40.

Fey, M. (1986). *Language intervention with young children.* San Diego: College-Hill Press.

Franklin, K., Mirenda, P., & Phillips, G. (1996). Comparison of five symbol assessment protocols with nondisabled preschoolers and learners with severe intellectual disabilities. *Augmentative and Alternative Communication, 12,* 63–77.

Hurlbut, B., Iwata, B., & Green, J. (1982). Nonvocal language acquisition in adolescents with severe physical disabilities: Blissymbol versus iconic stimulus formats. *Journal of Applied Behavior Analysis, 15,* 241–258.

Huttenlocher, J. (1974). The origins of language comprehension. In R.L. Solso (Ed.), *Theories of cognitive psychology* (pp. 331–368). Mahwah, NJ: Lawrence Erlbaum Associates.

Individuals with Disabilities Education Act Amendments of 1997, PL 105-17, 20 U.S.C. §§ 1400 *et seq.*

Kaiser, A.P. (1993). Parent-implemented language intervention: An environmental system perspective. In S.F. Warren & J. Reichle (Series Eds.) & A.P. Kaiser & D.B. Gray (Vol. Eds.), *Communication and language intervention series: Vol. 2. Enhancing children's communication: Research foundations for intervention* (pp. 63–84). Baltimore: Paul H. Brookes Publishing Co.

Lloyd, L.L., & Fuller, D. (1986): Towards an augmentative and alternative communication system taxonomy: A proposed superordinate classification. *Augmentative and Alternative Communication, 2,* 165–171.

Locke, P., & Mirenda, P. (1988). A computer supported communication approach for a nonspeaking child with severe visual and cognitive impairments. *Augmentative and Alternative Communication, 4,* 15–22.

Miller, J., Sedey, A., Miolo, G., Rosin, M., & Murray-Branch, D. (1991, November). *Spoken and sign vocabulary acquisition in children with Down syndrome.* Poster presented at the annual meeting of the American Speech-Language-Hearing Association, Atlanta, GA.

Mirenda, P., & Locke, P. (1989). A comparison of symbol transparency in nonspeaking persons with intellectual disabilities. *Journal of Speech and Hearing Disorders, 54,* 131–140.

Mizuko, M. (1987). Transparency and ease of learning of symbols represented by Blissymbols, PCS, and Picsyms. *Augmentative and Alternative Communication, 3,* 129–136.

Musselwhite, C., & Ruscello, D. (1984). Transparency of three communication symbol systems. *Journal of Speech and Hearing Research, 27,* 436–443.

Musselwhite, C., & St. Louis, K. (1982). *Communication programming for the severely handicapped.* San Diego: College-Hill Press.

National Joint Committee on the Communication Needs of Persons with Severe Disabilities. (1992, March). Guidelines for meeting the communication needs of persons with severe disabilities. *Asha, 34*(Supp. 7), 1–8.

Nelson, K. (1985). *Making sense: The acquisition of shared meaning.* San Diego: Academic Press.

Peterson, S., Bondy, A., Vincent, Y., & Finnegan, C. (1995). Effects of altering communicative input for students with autism and no speech: Two case studies. *Augmentative and Alternative Communication, 11,* 93–100.

Pierce, P. (1999). *Baby power: A guide for families for using assistive technology with their infants and toddlers.* Chapel Hill: The University of North Carolina Press, The Center for Literacy and Disabilities Studies.

Reichle, J., York, J., & Sigafoos, J. (1991). *Implementing augmentative and alternative communication: Strategies for learners with severe disabilities.* Baltimore: Paul H. Brookes Publishing Co.

Romski, M.A., & Sevcik, R.A. (1993). Language comprehension: Considerations for augmentative and alternative communication. *Augmentative and Alternative Communication, 9,* 281–285.

Romski, M.A., & Sevcik, R.A. (1996). *Breaking the speech barrier: Language development through aug-*

mented means. Baltimore: Paul H. Brookes Publishing Co.

Romski, M.A., & Sevcik, R.A. (1997). Augmentative and alternative communication for children with developmental disabilities. *Mental Retardation and Developmental Disabilities Research Reviews, 3,* 363–368.

Romski, M.A., Sevcik, R.A., & Adamson, L.B. (1997, March). Toddlers with developmental disabilities who are not speaking: Family stress, home environment, and language intervention. In N. Brady (Chair), *Communication Disorders and Families.* Symposium conducted at the 30th annual Gatlinburg Conference on Research and Theory in Mental Retardation and Developmental Disabilities, Riverside, CA.

Romski, M.A., Sevcik, R.A., & Adamson, L.B. (1999, March). *Toddlers with developmental disabilities who are not speaking: Vocabulary growth and augmented language intervention.* Paper presented at the 32nd annual Gatlinburg Conference on Research and Theory in Mental Retardation and Developmental Disabilities, Charleston, SC.

Romski, M.A., Sevcik, R.A., Adamson, L.B., Browning, J., Williams, S., & Colbert, N. (1999, November). *Augmented communication input intervention for toddlers: A pilot study.* Poster presented at the annual meeting of the American Speech-Language-Hearing Association, San Francisco.

Romski, M.A., Sevcik, R.A., & Pate, J.L. (1988). The establishment of symbolic communication in persons with mental retardation. *Journal of Speech and Hearing Disorders, 53,* 94–107.

Romski, M.A., Sevcik, R.A., Robinson, B.F., & Bakeman, R. (1994). Adult-directed communications of youth with mental retardation using the System for Augmenting Language. *Journal of Speech and Hearing Research, 37,* 617–628.

Romski, M.A., Sevcik, R.A., & Wilkinson, K.M. (1994). Peer-directed communicative interactions of augmented language learners with mental retardation. *American Journal on Mental Retardation, 98,* 527–538.

Romski, M.A., White, R., Millen, C.E., & Rumbaugh, D.M. (1984). Effects of computer-keyboard teaching on the symbolic communication of severely retarded persons: Five case studies. *The Psychological Record, 34,* 39–54.

Schiefelbusch, R.L. (1984). Speech, language and communication disorders of the multiply handicapped. *Folia Phoniatrica, 36,* 8–23.

Schiefelbusch, R.L. (1985). *Risk conditions for the development of speech and language.* Unpublished manuscript. Lawrence: University of Kansas.

Schlosser, R., Belfiore, P., Nigam, R., & Blischak, D. (1995). The effects of speech output technology in the learning of graphic symbols. *Journal of Applied Behavior Analysis, 28,* 537–549.

Sedey, A., Rosin, M., & Miller, J. (1991, November). *The use of signs among children with Down syndrome.* Poster presented at the annual meeting of the American Speech-Language-Hearing Association, Atlanta, GA.

Sevcik, R.A., & Romski, M.A. (1986). Representational matching skills of persons with severe retardation. *Augmentative and Alternative Communication, 2,* 160–164.

Sevcik, R.A., & Romski, M.A. (1997). Comprehension and language acquisition: Evidence from youth with severe cognitive disabilities. In L.B. Adamson & M.A. Romski (Eds.), *Communication and language acquisition: Discoveries from atypical development* (pp. 187–202). Baltimore: Paul H. Brookes Publishing Co.

Sevcik, R.A., Romski, M.A., Watkins, R., & Deffebach, K.P. (1995). Adult partner-augmented communication input to youth with mental retardation using the System for Augmenting Language (SAL). *Journal of Speech and Hearing Research, 38,* 902–912.

Sevcik, R.A., Romski, M.A., & Wilkinson, K. (1991). Roles of graphic symbols in the language acquisition process for persons with severe cognitive disabilities. *Augmentative and Alternative Communication, 7,* 161–170.

Sparrow, S., Balla, D., & Cicchetti, D. (1984). *Vineland Adaptive Behavior Scales.* Circle Pines, MN: American Guidance Service.

Technology-Related Assistance for Individuals with Disabilities Act of 1988, PL 100-407, 29 U.S.C. §§ 2201 *et seq.*

Warren, S., Yoder, P., Gazdag, G., Kim, K., & Jones, H. (1993). Facilitating prelinguistic communication skills in young children with developmental delay. *Journal of Speech and Hearing Research, 36,* 83–97.

Wilkinson, K.M., Romski, M.A., & Sevcik, R.A. (1994). Emergence of visual-graphic symbol combinations by youth with moderate or severe mental retardation. *Journal of Speech and Hearing Research, 37,* 883–895.

Wright, J., Granger, R., & Sameroff, A. (1984). Parental acceptance and developmental handicap. In J. Blancher (Ed.), *Severely handicapped young children and their families: Research in review* (pp. 51–90). San Diego: Academic Press.

Yoder, P.J., & Warren, S.F. (1993). Can developmentally delayed children's language development be enhanced through prelinguistic intervention? In S.F. Warren & J. Reichle (Series Eds.) & A.P. Kaiser & D.B. Gray (Vol. Eds.), *Communication and language intervention series: Vol. 2. Enhancing children's communication: Research foundations for intervention* (pp. 35–61). Baltimore: Paul H. Brookes Publishing Co.

21

M I C H A E L   J.   G U R A L N I C K

Social Competence with Peers and Early Childhood Inclusion

Need for Alternative Approaches

Children's efforts to establish relationships with their peers and to develop friendships are apparent even at very young ages. Whatever the source of this social motivation, it encourages children to embark on an enjoyable yet perilous journey. The enjoyment, of course, stems from the camaraderie, inventiveness, and excitement so evident in peer relationships. The emotional support and shared confidences provided by those selected as friends constitute other important enjoyable aspects of interactions with peers. The perilous nature of this journey, however, is reflected in the numerous difficulties children encounter during interactions with peers. Having social bids ignored, rejected, or even mocked are frequent occurrences. Conflicts of all types abound, which serve as constant reminders that establishing and maintaining peer relationships and friendships pose significant challenges. Yet, children seem to have a prescience that peers will occupy critical social roles in their lives as development proceeds and, therefore, press to solve these ongoing social interaction problems during their early childhood years.

DEVELOPING PEER RELATIONSHIPS

The developmental sequences that mark this journey have been well described for toddlers and preschoolers (Howes, 1988; Howes & Matheson, 1992; Mueller & Lucas, 1975; Parten, 1932). During the early toddler period, independent parallel play gives way to parallel play in which children become more aware of each other's presence. Simple social play also begins to emerge during this time as children give and receive toys and materials, take turns, and seem to establish firm relationships. Indeed, most toddlers elaborate further on this process and establish play that is both complementary to their peers and reciprocal as indicated by role reversal and social games. As children reach preschool age, cooperative social play or group play, particularly in pretend play form, becomes a prominent feature of their interactions. Even later,

481

but well within the preschool period, children plan and talk about their roles in pretend play, proposing and arranging scripts. Stable friendships, too, emerge during the toddler years and become more frequent and flexible across the early childhood years (Howes, 1988, 1996).

These changes represent at least two interrelated developmental patterns. First, children gradually become more interested in their peers (i.e., they figure out how to shift from solitary to more interactive forms of play, including group play; Rubin & Coplan, 1992). Second, play becomes structurally more complex, taking on sophisticated meanings and integrating and organizing play materials and social exchanges (Howes, 1980). These latter changes clearly reflect corresponding advances in cognitive, linguistic, motor, and affective development as well as the variety of derivative social information processes and emotional regulation processes that comprise the fundamental framework for peer relationships and friendship formation (Brownell, 1986; Guralnick, 1999b).

Peer-Related Social Competence

From a larger perspective, these developmental changes may be said to be characteristic of an emerging *social competence*—more specifically, peer-related social competence (Guralnick, 1992, 1994). The construct of peer-related social competence has been difficult to establish both conceptually and empirically. Nevertheless, substantial interrelationships among numerous and diverse measures of peer relationships and friendships (e.g., aspects of social participation, peer sociometric ratings, negative interactions, conflicts) have been found, suggesting a common underlying structure (see Guralnick & Neville, 1997; LaFreniere & Sroufe, 1985). Moreover, the emergence of more advanced developmental sequences of peer interactions described previ-

ously is associated with subsequent measures designed to assess aspects of peer-related social competence (Howes & Matheson, 1992). Taken together, this suggests the potential value of a more general construct referred to as peer-related social competence with a wide range of measures serving as indicators of this broader construct (Guralnick, 1999b).

Peer-related social competence can be defined as the "*ability of young children to successfully and appropriately carry out their interpersonal goals*" (Guralnick, 1990b, p. 14, emphasis in original). The interpersonal goals of young children engaged in social play with peers usually take the form of specific *social tasks*, particularly gaining entry into play, resolving conflicts, and maintaining play. The particular peer interaction patterns and contexts for these social tasks vary with the developmental period, but these tasks nevertheless represent the essence of peer-related social competence across the early childhood years.

Peer Interaction Patterns of Children with Disabilities

Fortunately, the vast majority of typically developing children are able to negotiate the peer-interaction journey successfully, functioning in a socially competent manner to establish peer relationships and to develop friendships (Asher, 1990). This is not true, however, for children with developmental disabilities. For example, for the most well-studied group (i.e., children with mild [cognitive] developmental delays), comparisons between typically developing chronological age-mates during unstructured activities (e.g., free play) have revealed substantial differences between these two groups of children (see Guralnick, 1999b). For patterns related to social tasks, children with delays exhibit less play that is maintained (and more solitary play), display more negativity, especially during conflicts, and have less success in peer group entry and in having peers respond appropriately to their social bids (Guralnick, Connor, Hammond, Gottman, & Kinnish, 1996a; Guralnick & Groom, 1987a, 1987b; Guralnick & Paul-Brown, 1989; Guralnick et al., 1998; Kopp, Baker, & Brown, 1992; Wilson, 1999). Children with delays also infrequently form reciprocal friendships (Buysse, 1993; Guralnick, Gottman, & Hammond, 1996; Guralnick & Groom, 1988). It is important to note that the majority of these differences for children with primarily mild developmental delays in comparison with typically developing chronological age-mates remain even after controlling for children's developmental level (see Guralnick, 1999c).

These findings suggest that young children with developmental delays exhibit an unusual pattern of peer-related social competence difficulties—a pattern that, left unaltered, is likely to lead to later adjustment difficulties (Parker & Asher, 1987) and social isolation (Taylor, Asher, & Williams, 1987; Williams & Asher, 1992). Although less well documented, similar difficulties are evident for young children with communication disorders (Craig & Washington, 1993; Gertner, Rice, & Hadley, 1994; Guralnick, Connor, Hammond, Gottman, & Kinnish, 1996b; Hadley & Rice, 1991; Rice, Sell, & Hadley, 1991), difficulties that also persist beyond the early childhood period (Fujiki, Brinton, & Todd, 1996; Stevens & Bliss, 1995). Similar problems for children with a range of sensory, motor, and other disabilities have also been identified (see Guralnick, 1990a).

Implications for Early Childhood Inclusion

These pervasive and significant peer-related social competence problems exhibited by young children with disabilities have important implications for early childhood inclusion. This connection is perhaps most apparent in relation to social integration, which is discussed in Chapter 1. Although many factors contribute to the extent to which children with disabilities are socially integrated with their typically developing peers (e.g., attitudes transmitted by families, home and community experiences, experiences in inclusive preschools), the level of peer-related social competence that the child with a disability has makes a strong, independent contribution as well (Guralnick, 1999c). Consequently, improvements in social competence are likely to enhance the level of social integration in inclusive early childhood programs and in the child's community. Moreover, improved social competence is likely to yield benefits for other, more fundamental developmental domains, including cognitive and communicative development as well as various forms of prosocial behavior (Bates, 1975; Garvey, 1986; Hartup, 1983; Howes, 1988; Rubin & Lollis, 1988).

Purpose of This Chapter

Given the central importance of peer-related social competence to young children's development and to their quality of life, it comes as no surprise that researchers have devoted considerable energy to developing and evaluating the effectiveness of specific interventions. For children with disabilities in particular, an extraordinary number of creative, often ingenious, methods have been developed to promote their peer-related social competence. Thoughtful summaries of this large and diverse literature can be found elsewhere (Chandler, Lubeck, & Fowler, 1992; Grubbs & Niemeyer, 1999; McEvoy, Odom, & McConnell, 1992; Odom & Brown, 1993). Nevertheless, as these authors point out, despite the fact that much has been accomplished, interventions have for the most part been unsuccessful in developing social skills with peers that generalize to new situations and are sustained over time. This problem is not unique to children with disabilities or even young children, as similar concerns have been raised about interventions for otherwise typically developing children experiencing peer-interaction problems (La Greca, 1993; Schneider, 1992). After 25 years of interventions, it is more than reasonable to ask why those in the early intervention field have not been able to achieve better outcomes. Are there critical factors that govern social behavior in general and peer-related social competence in particular that researchers are not aware of or do not fully appreciate? Have professionals in the field underestimated the possibility that the influences that matter are primarily intrinsic to the child and, therefore, not as amenable to experientially based interventions as first thought? What makes this important problem so intractable?

This chapter addresses these and related questions. First identified are factors that may have contributed to the field's inability to achieve effective (generalizable and sustainable) interventions to improve children's peer-related social competence. Then, issues regarding the comprehensiveness of interventions are examined as well as the application of a developmental framework, the individualization of interventions, and the commitment of practitioners to invest in this area of development through long-term interventions and by according peer-related social competence concerns a higher priority than currently exists. In anticipation of this discussion, the available evidence suggests that none of these factors has been adequately considered in the design of interventions to promote children's competence with peers. Consequently, as each factor is discussed, suggestions are made with respect to how these concerns could be addressed in the design of subsequent interventions. Taken together, serious consideration of these issues will require a fundamental reconceptualization of the field's approach to promoting children's competence with peers. In the final section, the future development of alternative approaches is discussed, focusing on increasing the awareness of the problem, establishing an agenda for research, refining professional training programs, and promoting systems change.

FACTORS THAT CONTRIBUTE TO EFFECTIVE INTERVENTIONS

As noted previously, there may be factors, both intrinsic and extrinsic, that govern peer-related social competence but that simply have not been identified and, therefore, can account for failures to achieve effective peer-related social competence interventions. Yet, a rationale can be developed suggesting that many relevant factors are indeed known and are highly likely to influence the level of children's peer-related social competence but have simply not been incorporated into existing intervention programs. Admittedly, what follows is highly speculative. These speculations, however, can be transformed into intervention programs in which effectiveness can be carefully tested.

Comprehensiveness

Virtually all efforts to promote the peer-related social competence of young children with disabilities within a research framework have occurred in classroom-type environments. Teachers, often aided by consultants or the experimenters themselves, have been the primary organizers and implementers of the intervention. Three general approaches of intervention can be identified.

First, the ecology of the classroom is altered. Specifically, physical or structural barriers to social interactions with peers are removed, toys and materials are carefully selected to encourage social play, and, whenever possible, teachers plan activities that enhance the "social focus" of their program. Affection training is one example of the latter approach (Twardosz, Nordquist, Simon, & Botkin, 1983). The ecology can also be altered by redesigning the early childhood program to include typically developing children if that has not already occurred.

Second, teachers (or experimenters) attempt to directly facilitate a particular child's social play by organizing play with other children, setting the conditions to maximize peer play, and, even actively participating themselves, drawing children into productive social exchanges with one another. The degree of participation or involvement of the adults will vary with the child or circumstances, and a principle of "do the least necessary" to encourage productive play is usually in place to guide the interventions. Occasionally, but quite infrequently, teachers adopt a formal curriculum designed to enhance children's social skills.

Third, interventionists can enlist the aid of peers, generally typically developing children, to encourage children with disabilities to interact—often through a scripted set of activities.

Taken together, all of these approaches can be effective, at least in the short-term, but, as mentioned previously, have not yet achieved on a regular basis the types of generalized and sustained social behaviors associated with improvements in peer-related social competence. Altering the ecology by increasing the number of typically developing children is a case in point. There is no doubt that the level of social interaction with peers of children with disabilities increases when in the presence of typically developing children. This increase in social interaction level, however, does not translate to improvements on indices of peer-related social competence (Guralnick, Connor, et al., 1996a). Parents recognize the more limited, but nevertheless im-

portant, contribution of placing their child with a disability in an inclusive program (Guralnick, Connor, & Hammond, 1995). Moreover, evidence suggests that inconsistent and even counterintuitive findings may result when these various approaches are implemented (Odom et al., 1999).

Perhaps what is needed is simply to extend the number of environments or to vary the activities and participants even further to at least achieve some degree of generalization. Combining some or all of the three approaches throughout the day will certainly enhance the *comprehensiveness* of the interventions. Not only will interactions devoted to fostering peer interactions occur more frequently (a typical by-product of expanding the comprehensiveness of programs), but interventions will involve children in different environments with different children. Indeed, evidence is available to suggest that extending programs to various contexts does increase the likelihood of generalization (Goldstein, English, Shafer, & Kaczmarek, 1997). In fact, extending the principle even further by conducting the intervention when children are in different programs and at different times of the day (e.g., when children attend both preschool and child care) should also be beneficial. Problems in coordination across two different programs and difficulties enlisting the assistance of child care staff are likely to be encountered (Donegan, Ostrosky, & Fowler, 1996), but solutions to these problems to enhance comprehensiveness may be necessary to promote peer-related social competence.

Family Involvement More dramatic changes in the comprehensiveness of an intervention program, however, may be needed to yield the desired levels of effectiveness. As important and as appropriate as early childhood programs may be to foster peer-related social competence, comprehensiveness can be extended only so far in those environments. Involving *families* in the process may be an essential ingredient in maximizing comprehensiveness and ultimately the success of peer-related social competence interventions. Indeed, since the mid-1990s, linkages between the family system and the peer system have been apparent for both typically developing children and children with disabilities (Guralnick & Neville, 1997).

Specifically, it now seems that families of typically developing children have much to contribute to the emerging peer-related social competence of their children (see Parke & Ladd, 1992). For example, focusing on preschool-age children, parents are often quite active in helping to establish the peer social networks of their children as well as arranging play dates and monitoring and facilitating play at home. Parental activity in these roles is associated with larger peer social networks and increased social competence with peers for their children (Finnie & Russell, 1988; Ladd & Golter, 1988; Ladd & Hart, 1992). Similarly, certain forms of parent–child interactions and parental styles reveal positive associations with peer-related social competence (Cohn, Patterson, & Christopoulos, 1991). In particular, positive parental affective styles, strategies that teach children to regulate their emotions, feedback regarding the rules of social discourse, especially negotiation strategies, and experiences that foster children's abilities to encode and decode emotional cues all contribute to the development of children's peer-related social competence (Harrist, Pettit, Dodge, & Bates, 1994; Isley, O'Neil, Clatfelter, & Parke, 1999; LaFreniere & Dumas, 1992; Mize & Pettit, 1997; Parke, Cassidy, Burks, Carson, & Boyum, 1992; Putallaz, 1987). Finally, parental beliefs and attitudes with respect to the perceived importance and modifiability of their child's peer-related social competence and the role of experience with peers provide a cognitive framework

for parents to guide family–child interaction patterns associated with their children's competence with peers (Mize, Pettit, & Brown, 1995).

These same family–child interaction patterns are likely to be relevant for children with disabilities. Yet, it turns out that the family–peer linkages involving children with disabilities can be problematic in the context of promoting peer-related social competence (see Guralnick & Neville, 1997). For example, for a variety of reasons, some groups of children with disabilities have more restrictive peer social networks (Guralnick, 1997); parent–child interaction patterns do not always provide sufficient opportunities for the children to develop emotional regulation skills, to develop reciprocity, or to participate in play activities or daily events that might provide the substance for play themes with peers (Beeghly & Cicchetti, 1997; Crowell & Feldman, 1988; Stoneman, 1997); and many parents have attitudes about factors governing peer-related social competence that are inconsistent with taking an active role in promoting its development (Booth, 1999).

Therefore, risk factors exist that suggest that many families of children with disabilities can benefit from a more comprehensive intervention program that seeks to expand peer social networks, promote parent–child experiences that are relevant to peer-related social competence, and alter attitudes that may operate to minimize their child's involvement with peers. Beyond the justification of family–peer linkages, however, there are other reasons why involving families in a peer-related social competence intervention program would be valuable. Specifically, the home environment or community environment markedly extend opportunities for peer interactions. After school, weekends, and vacations are all ideal times for play with peers. Especially when occurring in the home, the environment is highly supportive of peer play as children usually participate with one peer or a small number of familiar peers in a comfortable and familiar environment. These are ideal conditions for parents to systematically expand their child's peer social network through a program of parental arranging, monitoring, and facilitating their child's play. In many respects, adding a family component, especially with respect to peer-related social network issues, serves as a means of promoting inclusion in the general community. This occurs through activities supporting participation in natural playgroups and encouraging participation in peer groups associated with community recreational, social, or religious groups. Moreover, extending intervention programs to involve families not only increases the program's comprehensiveness but adds to the intensity of the intervention as well. As discussed in a subsequent section, increasing the intensity of interventions relying on the various modifications of the classroom ecology and related activities is limited by issues of time, resources, and competing interests from other aspects of the overall classroom program.

New Roles for Educators   Comprehensiveness can be increased within the early childhood classroom environment, and more effective outcomes are likely to result. The comprehensiveness of an intervention program can be dramatically enhanced by families' involvement. To do so requires teaching or resource personnel to adopt new roles, assuming that the early childhood program would be the focal point for this expanded intervention.

Clearly, additional and substantial demands will be placed on professionals' knowledge, time, and resources should more comprehensive programs be implemented. Assessing peer social networks of children in the community, gaining a sense for parent–child interactions rele-

vant to peer competence, and evaluating attitudes and beliefs regarding the importance and malleability of the child's peer-related social competence are challenging tasks. Designing corresponding interventions will require considerable effort and technical support. For preschool teachers in particular, it means adopting a consultant role in what is clearly a family-centered process. For families, however, it may mean involvement at a level many may not feel entirely comfortable with or, because of other commitments or family stresses, simply cannot participate in a meaningful way. Irrespective of these issues, expanding comprehensiveness in peer-related social competence interventions to include the family clearly requires substantial accommodations and change in many facets of the early intervention system.

Developmental Approach

The importance of conducting assessments and interventions within a developmental framework is a generally accepted principle in the field of early childhood education. Even for practitioners of early childhood special education, developmental models are highly valued, although other approaches, particularly behavioral ones, are usually integrated within intervention programs (see Bowe, 1995). Nevertheless, although many will certainly debate this point, existing research and related programs designed to improve the peer-related social competence of children with disabilities rarely consider the developmental context when selecting the objectives of the intervention or its broader implications for social behavior with peers. There are two aspects to this issue: 1) objectives of the intervention are not often referenced to expected developmental sequences based on the child's developmental profile, and 2) the social behaviors targeted tend to be poorly integrated, without a pattern or context, suggesting that these social behaviors are really means to achieve important interpersonal goals.

With respect to the first issue, as discussed previously, the developmental sequences characterizing children's relationships with their peers have been carefully documented. These sequential patterns can and should serve as frameworks for peer-related social competence intervention programs. Observations of the child's typical and highest levels of social play with peers can provide reasonable expectations when setting goals for intervention. Correlating a child's current level of peer interactions with other aspects of development, especially cognition and language, provides an additional perspective with respect to expectations within a larger developmental context. Observations of the child's highest level of peer play can be especially informative with respect to identifying environmental circumstances that maximize peer interactions (e.g., dyadic environments, familiar materials). Moreover, the shifting patterns of play children exhibit at any one time across levels can be informative as well. For example, even when attempting to encourage children to maintain the developmental sequence of simple social play (Howes & Matheson, 1992), an understanding of the developmental dynamics can be valuable, such as the strategic use of parallel play as a means of subsequently engaging in more social forms of play. These patterns have been well documented both for typically developing children (Bakeman & Brownlee, 1980) and for children with disabilities (Guralnick & Hammond, 1999).

With respect to the second issue, contemporary developmental approaches to peer-related social competence discussed previously conceptualize social behaviors as *social strategies* enlisted to serve specific interpersonal goals. It is the elaboration of these strategies to accomplish developmentally reasonable goals (i.e., social tasks) that provides the structure often absent when seemingly goal-free social behaviors are targeted for intervention. Consequently, an awareness of the strategies that young children use to accomplish interpersonal goals attached to reasonable developmental expectations may need to be an essential feature of an effective intervention program designed to promote peer-related social competence.

Interpersonal goals themselves can take many forms, but gaining entry to a playgroup (peer group entry), resolving conflicts, and maintaining play have been the most extensively studied. The following interpersonal goals all have been thoroughly investigated: peer group entry strategies, such as establishing a frame of reference or appropriately varying intrusiveness (e.g., Black & Hazen, 1990; Hazen & Black, 1989; Putallaz & Wasserman, 1989; Ramsey & Lasquade, 1996); conflict resolution strategies, such as the use of conciliatory-type strategies (e.g., Eisenberg & Garvey, 1981; Hartup, Laursen, Stewart, & Eastonson, 1988); and maintaining play strategies, such as appropriate ways to disengage when play escalates (Gottman, 1983; Howes, 1988). It is the case, however, that the developmental sequences or patterns of these strategies within social tasks are not yet fully known. Nevertheless, even with current knowledge, it may be that organizing interventions within a framework of social tasks will carry more meaning for the child, with the strategies serving as tools in other contexts when similar interpersonal goals are sought.

By helping to make social tasks more salient to young children and encouraging the use of strategies relevant to the appropriate developmental context, the expectation is that a structure will emerge to assist children in organizing the complex and dynamic social patterns they face. Whether such interventions are workable and can accomplish what is intended is, of course, a question of research and practice. There seems to be sufficient justification to warrant consideration of the *developmental/social task/social strategy conceptualization*. A clinical assessment tool, the Assessment of Peer Relations (Guralnick, 1999a), has been developed that incorporates the major elements of this approach, but much more work is needed to determine its value in designing interventions and producing desired outcomes.

Individualizing Interventions: The Role of Strategies and Processes

One of the most fundamental concepts in the field of early intervention is *individualizing*. This occurs at many levels, including assessment, program placement, and plans for specific interventions. This concept has been codified in the individualized family service plan (IFSP) and the individualized education program (IEP). Unfortunately, there are surprisingly few interventions in the area of peer-related social competence that have developed the level of individualizing that may be necessary to yield effective outcomes. Adjusting intervention objectives to be consistent with developmental expectations is one important way to individualize, but, as noted previously, few reports in the disability literature have explicitly referenced this framework.

Many forms of intervention do not require a high level of individualization. For example, virtually all of the ecologically based interventions (e.g., altering toys or including typically developing children) and many of those orchestrated by the teacher (e.g., affection training) do not require a high level of individualization. It is important to note that adaptations to specific children are generally made even for these interventions, but systematic planning through tailoring interventions to individual children is the exception and is usually unnecessary. To effectively foster competence with peers, however, these interventions should be seen as only prerequisites for more highly individualized programs.

Social Strategies   As a starting point, the social strategies that children use within social tasks should be carefully assessed. Combining these observations with the child's developmental profile provides the basis for selecting strategies to be encouraged within a social task. Through an analysis of developmental expectations, corresponding strategies, and social tasks, a foundation can be established for developing highly individualized intervention programs.

Intervention techniques to promote children's use of these strategies are certainly available. They include script training, modeling, coaching, and more directive teacher- and peer-mediated approaches (see Goldstein & Gallagher, 1992; Grubbs & Niemeyer, 1999; McEvoy et al., 1992). Another level of individualization, however, may be needed. In particular, it is important to ask *why* a particular child is not demonstrating an expected level of peer interactions or, more appropriately, why the specific social strategies that would reasonably be expected to occur based on that child's developmental profile are not evident. It may well be that similar patterns of strategies exhibited by different children occur for entirely different reasons.

The "why" question is rarely asked in peer-related social competence interventions. In many respects, the why question is an attempt to understand at a deeper level the unusual difficulties in peer relations and friendships experienced by young children with disabilities described at the beginning of this chapter. It leads the field to examine or at least speculate about the *processes* that may underlie and govern the strategies selected by children in the context of a social task. In fact, consideration of these processes and individualizing interventions accordingly may well be a key to generating effective interventions.

The Role of Processes New conceptualizations designed to identify and understand probable processes relevant to peer-related social competence emerged in the 1990s. These processes were of two general types: 1) social information and 2) emotional regulation. Social information processes include sequences of underlying *social-cognitive* events that relate to how young children encode and interpret social information during a social task; how they generate specific social strategies; how they evaluate the effectiveness of particular strategies if chosen in the given context; and, eventually, how to enact a specific strategy (see Dodge, Pettit, McClaskey, & Brown, 1986; Rubin & Coplan, 1992). In addition, for peer-related social competence to develop appropriately, a longer-term perspective is essential as children must monitor and sustain their attention across numerous exchanges in order to generate strategies consistent with the social task (i.e., interpersonal goal; see Asher, 1983). This type of social information process is an organizational one and represents what is best referred to as a *higher-order process* or perhaps an executive function (see Pennington & Welsh, 1995).

Social information processes (social-cognitive and higher-order) depend on a different process that has been referred to as *shared understanding*. This shared understanding process forms among children with regard to the social roles they may assume during play and to the social rules that govern their behaviors in the larger context (i.e., sharing rules in the early childhood classroom). Particularly for social roles, shared understanding constitutes a set of "scripts" or event structures that help children organize the sequence of events during peer interactions, especially pretend play (Furman & Walden, 1990; Nelson, 1986; Nelson & Seidman, 1984). When a shared understanding exists among peers, decisions related to social information processes are likely to lead to more effective and appropriate social strategies. As such, shared understanding constitutes what might best be referred to as a *foundation process*.

Even if social-cognitive and higher-order processes as well as shared understanding are operating well, however, the entire sequence of events that underlie strategy selection for a given social task can be disrupted by emotional regulation difficulties, also considered a foundation process. This is perhaps the most salient of processes, as many children manifest difficulties in emotional reactions (e.g., anxiety, impulsiveness) such that they override or substantially interfere with the operation of the other social information-based processes and allow both ineffective and inappropriate strategies to prevail (Dodge, 1991).

A model incorporating these four processes (the foundation processes of shared understanding and emotional regulation, social-cognitive processes, and higher-order processes) has been developed that is applicable to young children with developmental delays (Guralnick, 1992, 1999b). Of note, an impressive array of research has demonstrated how these four processes can be adversely affected by both child characteristics and family influences (see Guralnick & Neville, 1997). Disruptions in one or more of these processes would be expected to lead to strategy selection that is nonoptimal. Judgments of poor social competence with peers by others (e.g., parents, adults, playmates) would follow.

For children with developmental delays, child characteristics that can actually affect these processes can be seen in the cognitive problems associated with their delayed development, such as those related to attention, working memory, scripts, and executive functions (Bray, Fletcher, & Turner, 1997; Kopp, 1990; Tomporowski & Tinsley, 1997). Clearly, these child characteristics can all contribute to difficulties in the peer context of social problem solving (social tasks). Indeed, the dynamics of the social task create unusual demands on these four processes. Similarly, as noted previously, families can substantially influence children's peer-related social competence. The development of peer social networks, styles of parent–child interactions, and parent attitudes toward their child's social development with peers were discussed. Evidence now suggests that the mechanisms producing these family effects on a child's peer-related social competence operate through these four processes. Although the evidence is stronger for typically developing children, considerable support for similar mechanisms operating for children with disabilities has emerged (Guralnick, 1999b; Guralnick & Neville, 1997).

Guiding Individualization   The argument presented here is that awareness of how these processes operate for individual children can serve as a further guide for individualizing interventions to promote peer-related social competence. How then can processes not obviously accessible to observation be examined? More important, if this information were available, how could it be used to guide the design of interventions?

Even assuming that this process model has validity, a primary problem is that these processes occur extremely rapidly in the context of a social task. Moreover, most children are not aware of these events or able to articulate what has occurred even when asked to reflect on how they came to choose specific social strategies. Researchers have developed ways of assessing the status of these processes under experimental conditions, and these studies have provided important information (Dodge et al., 1986; Leffert & Siperstein, 1996). These techniques, however, are not easily adapted for clinical situations or to very

young children, thereby requiring a more speculative approach.

Foundation processes are clearly more amenable to clinical assessment, as measures of observable behaviors regarding emotional regulation and shared understanding processes can serve as meaningful indicators of these processes (see Guralnick, 1999b). Speculation is likely to be needed here as well, however. For the social information processes, there is even a greater reliance on generating hypotheses. Nevertheless, an assessment tool exists that enables clinicians to generate reasonable hypotheses concerning the role that specific processes might play in determining a pattern of social strategies (Guralnick, 1999a). Does the child have a concept of the social task? Is impulsive responding short-circuiting social-cognitive processes although all other processes seem capable of yielding appropriate and effective strategies? Are poorly developed scripts for pretend play sequences responsible for the absence of appropriate social strategies during the dramatic play sequence and, thereby, minimizing the child's ability to maintain play? Is the child failing to identify the peers' toy play accurately and, thereby, choosing intrusive (inappropriate) strategies during peer group entry attempts? Once tentative answers (hypotheses) to these and numerous other questions emerge from the assessment process, they can be included in a more systematic and individualized intervention program; that is, a process level of individualization is added to individualization focusing on establishing developmental expectations and the profile of social strategies exhibited during social tasks.

Reflections on the why questions, in particular, and the speculations generated by observations of the status of the underlying processes can provide entirely new ways of thinking about intervention design. It encourages educators and clinicians to consider the various factors influencing peer-related social competence. By their very nature, these considerations invite a collaborative activity, as different specialists have much to contribute. In some respects, the value of this information to individualizing interventions is straightforward and builds on existing work. This is most apparent for the foundation process of shared understanding, as social rules and social scripts can be taught in a relatively direct manner and their application readily incorporated into social play activities. Goldstein and his colleagues reported success in teaching children to use scripts in pretend play sequences (Goldstein & Cisar, 1992; Goldstein & Gallagher, 1992). Similarly, considerable research relevant to emotional regulation processes has been carried out and can be adapted to social play and social task situations in early childhood environments (see Barkley, 1990). Other processes, however, are far more difficult to address. Attempting to "strengthen" processes independently, such as teaching children to generate a series of positive alternative strategies or to practice attending (encoding) to relevant information in social play tasks, is too artificial and not linked to the flow of events. Moreover, interventionists may simply not have the knowledge or technology to alter processes. In these instances, individualization would take the form of *adapting or accommodating* to the processes of concern, emphasizing those processes exhibiting relative strengths and providing techniques for the children to enable them to engage in productive exchanges despite these process-based difficulties. A number of "enhancement" tools are being developed within this framework (Guralnick, Connor, & Neville, in preparation), but these efforts have yet to be properly evaluated.

Long-Term Investment and Continuity

Most interventions designed to improve peer-related social competence have been short-term, typically lasting only a few weeks at most. Examples of longer-term efforts can be found, but usually these are in the form of general intervention curricula extending for the school year with little or no individualization. As noted previously, even though short-term, these interventions have made important contributions to practice. In view of early 21st-century thinking about the nature, dynamics, and complexity of peer-related social competence, however, it may not be reasonable to expect short-term efforts to have a generalizable and sustained impact.

By adopting a longer-term perspective, interventionists are able to establish more ambitious and integrated goals compatible with the nature of peer competence. Usually multiple interventions, implemented both concurrently and sequentially, are needed (e.g., when addressing both emotional regulation and shared understanding concerns). Hypotheses need to be tested, numerous steps must be taken in fostering children's abilities to solve social problems within social tasks, and considerable time is required to integrate activities into the general class program. Adding a family dimension demands even more time for the comprehensive intervention to be placed into action. Conducting family assessments—including the child's peer social network, designing interventions with the family, and coordinating with the early childhood program component—requires substantial and long-term commitments on the part of all involved. Moreover, children's progress in peer interactions can be easily disrupted in the absence of a supportive peer environment with familiar peers (Guralnick & Weinhouse, 1984). Consequently, continuity over time may well be essential. An intervention period spanning 2 or more years should not be considered unusual even for what seem to be relatively modest goals. The end product, however, is more likely to be an enduring and developmentally meaningful set of social skills that will provide a basis for further development of peer competence.

This long-term perspective is a departure from typical practice, as relatively few intervention programs are carried over from year to year. After even 1 year of intensive intervention, preschoolers find themselves with new teachers with differing approaches to intervention, new classmates, and perhaps changing program priorities. In many respects, maintaining continuity is a systems problem, as methods to ensure proper communication across time and to maintain needed resources must be devised.

Preventive Interventions for Infants and Toddlers

Most interventions in the peer-related social competence area have focused on preschool-age children, because that is both the age at which the problems become most apparent and reasonable developmental expectations can be established. Yet, many of the foundations for children's peer-related social competence are established during the infant and toddler periods. The forms that the interventions might take during these earlier years would, of course, differ, primarily emphasizing family influences. Development of these "preventive interventions," however, may well be successful in minimizing difficulties observed when children reach preschool age. It is certainly the case that, for a variety of reasons, many children with disabilities are not identified during the infant and toddler years and, therefore, do not participate in infant-toddler early intervention programs. As identification continues to improve, however, particularly for children with milder disabilities, greater opportunities exist for preventive interventions with respect to peer-related social competence. Consequently, it becomes increasingly important to

attempt to *integrate* peer-related social competence issues into the larger context of early intervention programs.

For families of children with disabilities, comprehensive early intervention programs are designed first to identify stressors affecting family interaction patterns and then develop strategies to address these stressors (Guralnick, 1998). Through a coordinated program of resource and social supports as well as information and services, stressors can be successfully minimized and child development can be maximized. Although there are many components of comprehensive early intervention programs, one universal aspect is to maximize parent–child transactions and to help families provide the most supportive home and community environments possible. Promoting early parent–child relationships, especially fostering secure attachments, is of considerable relevance to a child's subsequent competence with peers (Cohn et al., 1991; Guralnick & Neville, 1997). Similarly, interventions intended to mitigate stressors that can result in social isolation of the family and threaten the development of a child's peer social network are generally included as part of an early intervention program. The key point here is that many of the components of comprehensive early intervention programs for infants and toddlers are of considerable relevance to peer-related social competence and, in many ways, constitute preventive interventions that can help minimize difficulties when children make the transition to preschool programs.

To maximize these preventive intervention programs with respect to peer-related social competence, it is necessary to become sensitive to the relevant risk factors or stressors (see Patterson, Vaden, & Kupersmidt, 1991), assess them regularly, and monitor the course of interventions. The IFSP process can be valuable here. A special emphasis on ensuring smooth transitions from year to year is needed as well. This is particularly the case when children make the transition from the infant-toddler to the preschool program. In fact, as part of this transition, the continuity of the family aspects of the program should be maintained by communicating issues relevant to family patterns of interaction and their child's emerging peer-related social competence. Although a more extensive program involving families is envisioned as part of a more comprehensive effort at the preschool level (see the previous discussion), an effective transition constitutes an important first step and increases the likelihood that interventions considering family influences will be maintained across the early childhood years.

Priority and Commitment

Evaluations of the extent to which peer-related social competence intervention strategies for children with disabilities are actually implemented in early childhood programs have suggested that peer-related social development is given a low priority. For example, direct observations of teacher behavior in inclusive preschool classrooms have revealed that teachers hardly supported play with peers (less than 2% of the time). Although the teachers did indicate an awareness of the peer interaction problems of children with disabilities, children with and without disabilities nevertheless were treated similarly (File, 1994). The lack of priority, and perhaps commitment, to promoting peer-related social competence was also apparent in an analysis of the content of IEPs generated by early childhood special education teachers (McConnell, McEvoy, & Odom, 1992; Michnowicz, McConnell, Peterson, & Odom, 1995). Overall, social goals and objectives in the IEP were few in number and generally of poor quality. Nearly 50% of the children had no social goals or objectives whatsoever, and the majority of those that were developed

were not written clearly or explicitly, thereby making outcome evaluations difficult to accomplish. Although the IEP framework may not be the appropriate vehicle for capturing the complexity of peer-related social competence interventions (McCollum, 1995), these findings nevertheless indicate the absence of a systematic and meaningful effort to promote the peer-related social competence of children with disabilities. In fact, the lack of priority for peer issues extends far beyond the early childhood years. A study of the relationship between IEPs and peer interaction programs for school-age children concluded the following: "This research found that general and special education teachers did not provide and did not seem to understand the need for systematic, individualized, and extensive instruction targeted to the peer interaction needs for students with disabilities" (Gelzheiser, McLane, Meyers, & Pruzek, 1998, p. 63).

In some ways, these are curious findings. Most teachers in early childhood special education (nearly 75%) recognize the need for a peer intervention program (Odom, McConnell, & Chandler, 1993). The intervention strategies that research has demonstrated to be of at least short-term value (e.g., environmental manipulations, peer-mediated interventions) are judged to be acceptable (it fits with their teaching philosophy) and feasible (it can be implemented given existing resources). Despite this, as suggested by other work, use of those strategies is low (Odom et al., 1993). This is an especially troubling issue because intensity has proved to be perhaps the most important element of successful programs in the general field of early intervention (Guralnick, 1998), and there is no reason to expect intensity to play a lesser role in peer-related social competence interventions.

Given this perspective, it is difficult to understand why peer-related social competence interventions are accorded such a low priority. Perhaps teachers do not have confidence that these interventions matter and are, therefore, unwilling to press to reallocate their time and activities. Even without knowledge of the research literature questioning the ability for generalization and of sustaining gains, teachers may intuit that these tactics are not entirely adequate. Alternatively, teachers simply may not have the knowledge and skills to carry out an effective intervention, even when problems are recognized.

It is important to note that some groups of teachers have expressed a need for more curricula and materials relevant to this area (Odom et al., 1993), but still little of what exists is actually implemented. In view of the lack of information about methods to facilitate social skills found at the preservice level, a corresponding in-service training program would be essential (McConnell et al., 1992). Even with the creation of additional relevant materials, however, a higher priority for peer-related social competence intervention programs cannot be expected to occur in inclusive programs that are part of the early childhood community serving primarily typically developing children. The fact that the strategies advocated by early childhood special education teachers have been developed primarily within a behaviorally based special education tradition creates numerous problems for teachers trained in the more general early childhood tradition, especially those associated with developmentally appropriate practices (Bredekamp & Copple, 1997). Indeed, general education teachers in inclusive early childhood programs do tend to believe that the development of children's social skills has a strong intrinsic component (File, 1994). It may be that peer competence interventions that adopt a developmental framework will be more compatible with general early childhood

theory and practice (Guralnick, 1993). Whatever the case may be, it is clear that early childhood programs devote little systematic effort to address the complex peer-related social competence difficulties of children with developmental disabilities.

AGENDA FOR CHANGE

It is evident from the nature of these barriers to the development of effective peer-related social competence programs that needed changes will require a long-term investment. Recognition of this fact is somewhat distressing given the importance of peer-related social competence to children's lives and the urgency of the problem. As noted previously, this is an especially important area because peer-related social competence is one key to social integration in both early childhood programs and in the community, and social competence fosters other important domains of child development as well. In addition, a reasonable level of peer-related social competence is essential for children to be able to achieve the interpersonal goals they themselves select. As a consequence, peer-related social competence is clearly aligned with issues of personal independence and, particularly for individuals with disabilities, personal choice. The ability to achieve successfully and appropriately interpersonal goals involving one's peers is empowering in perhaps the most meaningful sense of the term. In addition, the urgency of the problem is related to both its magnitude and scope as well as to the fact that it is extraordinarily difficult to alter the trajectory of peer-related social competence once it becomes established during the early years (Guralnick, 1999b).

How then do interventionists go about creating the conditions that will produce change? After all, the barriers that have been identified in this chapter are formidable. Addressing any one of the barriers identified previously (i.e., the lack of comprehensiveness, the absence of a developmental perspective, the failure to properly individualize and consider underlying processes, the difficulties in establishing long-term interventions, the low priority generally accorded interventions to improve peer-related social competence) would seem demanding enough. Taken together, however, the combined force of these issues suggests the need for fundamental changes. Four possible approaches for creating such fundamental change are discussed next.

Increasing Awareness

As an initial step, it is essential that awareness of the importance and urgency of the problem of peer-related social competence is increased together with a recognition of the barriers. If done well, it will make clear to professionals in the field that any significant change will indeed require consideration of an entirely new set of approaches. Fortunately, in part because of inclusion, issues of peer relationships and friendships of children with disabilities have become more salient. Moreover, extensive participation of *all* children in child care has contributed to a greater awareness of the dynamics and importance of early social relationships. Not only has social development, particularly peer-related social development, become a more central topic for professionals, interest by the general public has increased as well partly as a result of publications that have captured national attention (Goleman, 1995; Harris, 1998).

As a consequence, this process has already begun. To further accelerate changes in the disability field, however, it is important that parents of children with disabilities press the issue. Evidence suggests that competence with peers is given a high priority by these parents (Booth, 1999; Guralnick et al., 1995), but it is nec-essary to communicate those priorities to staff in children's early intervention and early childhood programs. Both the IFSP and IEP processes could serve as catalysts for promoting sensible goals addressing peer-related social competence issues. Experts in the field could be of considerable value in this regard by developing information and disseminating it to parent groups that will assist the parents in making their point as their children's early intervention programs develop.

Research and Development

The research and development program that lies ahead is perhaps the most daunting task of all. Most of the suggestions for change discussed in this chapter, as conceptually sound and consistent with our knowledge base as they may be, are nevertheless hypotheses that must be formally tested. This will first require a translation of these ideas into intervention programs with the development of all the supporting materials necessary to accompany these programs (e.g., assessments, linked interventions, evaluation strategies). The design of feasible and acceptable service delivery mechanisms, especially given the differing perspectives of teachers from different training backgrounds found in inclusive programs, is particularly important. Any successful process will require close coordination among researchers, parents, educators, resource personnel, and administrators. Ensuring that high-quality interventions compatible with inclusive program models (see Chapter 1) and family lifestyles can be implemented is of course paramount, as is developing strategies that will yield an intervention intensity adequate to maximize effectiveness. A long-term process of model development and evaluation; small-scale studies, including evaluations of newly developed materials; and, finally, iterations and refinements of smaller and eventually larger scale randomized prospective controlled clinical trials will be required to empirically test the effectiveness of newly developed programs and to further understand the mechanisms through which such interventions operate. If the history of research in the field of early intervention designed to promote children's cognitive and other aspects of development is an indication of the demands ahead, then this task will constitute a major challenge.

Professional Training

At the same time, it is essential to build an infrastructure composed of individuals knowledgeable in the area of peer-related social competence. Teacher training programs for both early childhood special educators and general early childhood educators must be modified to include information relevant to these changing perspectives and incorporate methods that will allow teachers to put these ideas into practice. A dialogue needs to be established as well between the general early childhood community and the disability community to address precisely how issues of promoting children's peer-related social competence will be addressed. For the most part, the existing dialogue has been at a more academic level but must now consider each domain specifically and develop both generally agreed-upon guidelines and methods. A close association with the research and development efforts will be necessary for this process to succeed. In addition, more and more early childhood special educators are assuming consultant roles in inclusive programs. This group seems to be in an ideal position to develop a special expertise in peer-related social competence. Although focusing on children with disabilities, much of their expertise will certainly be relevant to otherwise typically developing children who have peer interaction difficulties. A *consultant specialist model* has been proposed elsewhere (Guralnick, 2000) in which highly trained interdisciplinary specialists provide support to educators in inclusive environments. It is intended that this group function as a bridge between researchers and practitioners. Consultations regarding specific children could serve as a mechanism for in-service training, and these consultant specialists would also be responsible for organizing more formal continuing education programs as new information becomes available. These same consultant specialists could support the primarily family-based interventions occurring in the birth-to-3 programs in an effort to help prevent peer interaction problems from developing.

Systems Change

Finally, change will require support of a more systemic nature. A commitment by state and local education agencies to address the problems of peer-related social competence and to work closely with community preschool and child care programs is essential. New issues with respect to increasing the coordination of interventions across different environments and over time, expanding the roles of teaching staff at the preschool level, and identifying mechanisms to incorporate some form of consultation regarding peer-related social competence need to be resolved. Similarly, the IEP format may need to be altered to ensure that peer-related social competence goals and objectives can be meaningfully presented. For changes at this level to occur, parents and professionals must be persistent in pressing for more and better interventions for peer competence and take every opportunity at every conference and meeting to raise the level of awareness of this issue.

CONCLUSION

The need for a reconceptualization of existing approaches to promote the peer competence of young children with disabilities implies the need for radical change. Realistically, however, given the intrinsic constraints associated with research and program development, disseminating existing and new information, modifying professional training, and creating even relatively small changes in well-established systems, dramatic changes are unlikely to result. Through a recognition of and commitment to alternative approaches, however, gradual and significant progress will certainly follow from systematic advances in the field's knowledge; from new models of professional training; and from the daily interactions of parents, teachers, and children struggling with one of the most important issues in early childhood development and early childhood inclusion.

REFERENCES

Asher, S.R. (1983). Social competence and peer status: Recent advances and future directions. *Child Development, 54,* 1427–1434.

Asher, S.R. (1990). Recent advances in the study of peer rejection. In S.R. Asher & J.D. Coie (Eds.), *Peer rejection in childhood* (pp. 3–14). New York: Cambridge University Press.

Bakeman, R., & Brownlee, J.R. (1980). The strategic use of parallel play: A sequential analysis. *Child Development, 51,* 873–878.

Barkley, R.A. (1990). *Attention-deficit hyperactivity disorder: A handbook for diagnosis and treatment.* New York: Guilford Press.

Bates, E. (1975). Peer relations and the acquisition of language. In M. Lewis & L.A. Rosenblum (Eds.), *Friendship and peer relations* (pp. 259–292). New York: John Wiley & Sons.

Beeghly, M., & Cicchetti, D. (1997). Talking about self and other: Emergence of an internal state lexicon in young children with Down syndrome. *Development and Psychopathology, 9,* 729–748.

Black, B., & Hazen, N.L. (1990). Social status and patterns of communication in acquainted and unacquainted preschool children. *Developmental Psychology, 26,* 379–387.

Booth, C.L. (1999). Beliefs about social skills among mothers of preschoolers with special needs. *Early Education and Development, 10,* 455–474.

Bowe, F.G. (1995). Population estimates: Birth-to-5 children with disabilities. *The Journal of Special Education, 20,* 461–471.

Bray, N.W., Fletcher, K.L., & Turner, L.A. (1997). Cognitive competencies and strategy use in individuals with mental retardation. In W.E. MacLean, Jr. (Ed.), *Ellis' handbook of mental deficiency, psychological theory and research* (3rd ed., pp. 197–217). Mahwah, NJ: Lawrence Erlbaum Associates.

Bredekamp, S., & Copple, C. (Eds.). (1997). *Developmentally appropriate practice in early childhood programs* (Rev. ed.). Washington, DC: National Association for the Education of Young Children.

Brownell, C.A. (1986). Convergent developments: Cognitive-developmental correlates of growth in infant/toddler peer skills. *Child Development, 57,* 275–286.

Buysse, V. (1993). Friendships of preschoolers with disabilities in community-based child care settings. *Journal of Early Intervention, 17,* 380–395.

Chandler, L.K., Lubeck, R.C., & Fowler, S.A. (1992). Generalization and maintenance of preschool children's social skills: A critical review and analysis. *Journal of Applied Behavior Analysis, 25,* 415–428.

Cohn, D.A., Patterson, C.J., & Christopoulos, C. (1991). The family and children's peer relations. *Journal of Social and Personal Relationships, 8,* 315–346.

Craig, H.K., & Washington, J.A. (1993). Access behaviors of children with specific language impairment. *Journal of Speech and Hearing Research, 36,* 322–337.

Crowell, J.A., & Feldman, S.S. (1988). Mothers' internal models of relationships and children's behavioral and developmental status: A study of mother–child interaction. *Child Development, 59,* 1273–1285.

Dodge, K.A. (1991). Emotion and social information processing. In J. Garber & K.A. Dodge (Eds.), *The development of emotion regulation and dysregulation* (pp. 159–181). New York: Cambridge University Press.

Dodge, K.A., Pettit, G.S., McClaskey, C.L., & Brown, M.M. (1986). Social competence in children. *Monographs of the Society for Research in Child Development, 51*(2, Serial No. 213).

Donegan, M.M., Ostrosky, M.M., & Fowler, S.A. (1996). Children enrolled in multiple programs: Characteristics, supports, and barriers to teacher communication. *Journal of Early Intervention, 20,* 95–106.

Eisenberg, A.R., & Garvey, C. (1981). Children's use of verbal strategies in resolving conflicts. *Discourse Processes, 4,* 149–170.

File, N. (1994). Children's play, teacher–child interactions, and teacher beliefs in integrated early childhood programs. *Early Childhood Research Quarterly, 9,* 223–240.

Finnie, V., & Russell, A. (1988). Preschool children's social status and their mothers' behavior and knowledge in the supervisory role. *Developmental Psychology, 24,* 789–801.

Fujiki, M., Brinton, B., & Todd, C.M. (1996). Social skills of children with specific language impairment. *Language, Speech, and Hearing Services in Schools, 27,* 195–202.

Furman, L.N., & Walden, T.A. (1990). Effect of script knowledge on preschool children's communicative interactions. *Developmental Psychology, 26,* 227–233.

Garvey, C. (1986). Peer relations and the growth of communication. In E.C. Mueller & C.R. Cooper (Eds.), *Process and outcome in peer relationships* (pp. 329–345). San Diego: Academic Press.

Gelzheiser, L.M., McLane, M., Meyers, J., & Pruzek, R.M. (1998). IEP-specified peer interaction needs: Accurate but ignored. *Exceptional Children, 65,* 61–65.

Gertner, B.L., Rice, M.L., & Hadley, P.A. (1994). Influence of communicative competence of peer preferences in a preschool classroom. *Journal of Speech and Hearing Research, 37,* 913–923.

Goldstein, H., & Cisar, C.L. (1992). Promoting interaction during sociodramatic play: Teaching scripts to typical preschoolers and classmates with disabilities. *Journal of Applied Behavior Analysis, 25,* 265–280.

Goldstein, H., English, K., Shafer, K., & Kaczmarek, L. (1997). Interaction among preschoolers with and without disabilities: Effects of across-the-day peer intervention. *Journal of Speech, Language, & Hearing Research, 40,* 33–48.

Goldstein, H., & Gallagher, T.M. (1992). Strategies for promoting the social-communicative competence of young children with specific language impairment. In S.L. Odom, S.R. McConnell, & M.A. McEvoy (Eds.), *Social competence of young children with disabilities: Issues and strategies for intervention* (pp. 189–213). Baltimore: Paul H. Brookes Publishing Co.

Goleman, D. (1995). *Emotional intelligence.* New York: Bantam Books.

Gottman, J.M. (1983). How children become friends. *Monographs of the Society for Research in Child Development, 48*(3, Serial No. 201).

Grubbs, P.R., & Niemeyer, J.A. (1999). Promoting reciprocal social interactions in inclusive classrooms for young children. *Infants and Young Children, 11,* 9–18.

Guralnick, M.J. (1990a). Peer interactions and the development of handicapped children's social and communicative competence. In H. Foot, M. Morgan, & R. Shute (Eds.), *Children helping children* (pp. 275–305). Sussex, England: John Wiley & Sons.

Guralnick, M.J. (1990b). Social competence and early intervention. *Journal of Early Intervention, 14,* 3–14.

Guralnick, M.J. (1992). A hierarchical model for understanding children's peer-related social competence. In S.L. Odom, S.R. McConnell, & M.A. McEvoy (Eds.), *Social competence of young children with disabilities: Issues and strategies for intervention* (pp. 37–64). Baltimore: Paul H. Brookes Publishing Co.

Guralnick, M.J. (1993). Developmentally appropriate practice in the assessment and intervention of children's peer relations. *Topics in Early Childhood Special Education, 13*(3), 344–371.

Guralnick, M.J. (1994). Social competence with peers: Outcome and process in early childhood special education. In P.L. Safford (Ed.), *Yearbook in early childhood education: Early childhood special education* (Vol. 5, pp. 45–71). New York: Teachers College Press.

Guralnick, M.J. (1997). The peer social networks of young boys with developmental delays. *American Journal on Mental Retardation, 101,* 595–612.

Guralnick, M.J. (1998). The effectiveness of early intervention for vulnerable children: A developmental perspective. *American Journal on Mental Retardation, 102,* 319–345.

Guralnick, M.J. (1999a). *The assessment of peer relations.* Seattle: University of Washington Press, Center on Human Development and Disability.

Guralnick, M.J. (1999b). Family and child influences on the peer related social competence of young children with developmental delays. *Mental Retardation and Developmental Disabilities Research Reviews, 5,* 21–29.

Guralnick, M.J. (1999c). The nature and meaning of social integration for young children with mild developmental delays in inclusive settings. *Journal of Early Intervention, 22,* 70–86.

Guralnick, M.J. (2000). Early childhood intervention: Evolution of a system. In M. Wehmeyer & J. Patton (Eds.), *Mental retardation in the 21st century* (pp. 37–58). Austin, TX: PRO-ED.

Guralnick, M.J., Connor, R., & Hammond, M. (1995). Parent perspectives of peer relations and friendships in integrated and specialized programs. *American Journal on Mental Retardation, 99,* 457–476.

Guralnick, M.J., Connor, R., Hammond, M., Gottman, J.M., & Kinnish, K. (1996a). Immediate effects of mainstreamed settings on the social interactions and social integration of preschool children. *American Journal on Mental Retardation, 100,* 359–377.

Guralnick, M.J., Connor, R., Hammond, M., Gottman, J.M., & Kinnish, K. (1996b). The peer relations of preschool children with communication disorders. *Child Development, 67,* 471–489.

Guralnick, M.J., Connor, R.A., & Neville, B. (in preparation). *Strategies to improve children's peer-related social competence.*

Guralnick, M.J., Gottman, J.M., & Hammond, M.A. (1996). Effects of social setting on the friendship formation of young children differing in developmental status. *Journal of Applied Developmental Psychology, 17,* 625–651.

Guralnick, M.J., & Groom, J.M. (1987a). Dyadic peer interactions of mildly delayed and nonhandicapped preschool children. *American Journal of Mental Deficiency, 92,* 178–193.

Guralnick, M.J., & Groom, J.M. (1987b). The peer relations of mildly delayed and nonhandicapped preschool children in mainstreamed playgroups. *Child Development, 58,* 1556–1572.

Guralnick, M.J., & Groom, J.M. (1988). Peer interactions in mainstreamed and specialized classrooms: A comparative analysis. *Exceptional Children, 54,* 415–425.

Guralnick, M.J., & Hammond, M.A. (1999). Sequential analysis of the social play of young children with mild developmental delays. *Journal of Early Intervention, 22,* 243–256.

Guralnick, M.J., & Neville, B. (1997). Designing early intervention programs to promote children's social competence. In M.J. Guralnick (Ed.), *The effectiveness of early intervention* (pp. 579–610). Baltimore: Paul H. Brookes Publishing Co.

Guralnick, M.J., & Paul-Brown, D. (1989). Peer-related communicative competence of preschool children: Developmental and adaptive characteristics. *Journal of Speech and Hearing Research, 32,* 930–943.

Guralnick, M.J., Paul-Brown, D., Groom, J.M., Booth, C.L., Hammond, M.A., Tupper, D.B., & Gelenter, A. (1998). Conflict resolution patterns of preschool children with and without developmental delays in heterogeneous playgroups. *Early Education and Development, 9,* 49–77.

Guralnick, M.J., & Weinhouse, E.M. (1984). Peer-related social interactions of developmentally delayed young children: Development and characteristics. *Developmental Psychology, 20,* 815–827.

Hadley, P.A., & Rice, M.L. (1991). Conversational responsiveness of speech- and language-impaired preschoolers. *Journal of Speech and Hearing Research, 34,* 1308–1317.

Harris, J.R. (1998). *The nurture assumption: Why children turn out the way they do.* New York: The Free Press.

Harrist, A.W., Pettit, G.S., Dodge, K.A., & Bates, J.E. (1994). Dyadic synchrony in mother–child interaction: Relations with children's subsequent kindergarten adjustment. *Family Relations, 43,* 417–424.

Hartup, W.W. (1983). Peer relations. In E.M. Hetherington (Ed.) & P.H. Mussen (Series Ed.), *Handbook of child psychology: Vol. 4. Socialization, personality, and social development* (pp. 103–196). New York: John Wiley & Sons.

Hartup, W.W., Laursen, B., Stewart, M.I., & Eastonson, A. (1988). Conflict and the friendship relations of young children. *Child Development, 59,* 1590–1600.

Hazen, N.L., & Black, B. (1989). Preschool peer communication skills: The role of social status and interaction context. *Child Development, 60,* 867–876.

Howes, C. (1980). Peer play scale as an index of complexity of peer interaction. *Developmental Psychology, 16,* 371–372.

Howes, C. (1988). Peer interaction of young children. *Monographs of the Society for Research in Child Development, 53*(1, Serial No. 217).

Howes, C. (1996). The earliest friendships. In W.M. Bukowski, A.F. Newcomb, & W.W. Hartup (Eds.), *The company they keep: Friendship in childhood and adolescence* (pp. 66–86). New York: Cambridge University Press.

Howes, C., & Matheson, C. (1992). Sequences in the development of competent play with peers: Social and social pretend play. *Developmental Psychology, 28,* 961–974.

Isley, S.L., O'Neil, R., Clatfelter, D., & Parke, R.D. (1999). Parent and child expressed affect and children's social competence: Modeling direct and indirect pathways. *Developmental Psychology, 35,* 547–560.

Kopp, C.B. (1990). The growth of self-monitoring among young children with Down syndrome. In D. Cicchetti & M. Beeghly (Eds.), *Children with Down syndrome: A developmental perspective* (pp. 231–251). New York: Cambridge University Press.

Kopp, C.B., Baker, B.I., & Brown, K.W. (1992). Social skills and their correlates: Preschoolers with developmental delays. *American Journal on Mental Retardation, 96,* 357–366.

Ladd, G.W., & Golter, B.S. (1988). Parents' management of preschooler's peer relations: Is it related to children's social competence? *Developmental Psychology, 14,* 109–117.

Ladd, G.W., & Hart, C.H. (1992). Creating informal play opportunities: Are parents' and preschoolers' initiations related to children's competence with peers? *Developmental Psychology, 28,* 1179–1187.

LaFreniere, P.J., & Dumas, J.E. (1992). A transactional analysis of early childhood anxiety and social withdrawal. *Development and Psychopathology, 4,* 385–402.

LaFreniere, P.J., & Sroufe, L.A. (1985). Profiles of peer competence in the preschool: Interrelations between measures, influence of social ecology, and relation to attachment history. *Developmental Psychology, 21,* 56–69.

La Greca, A.M. (1993). Social skills training with children: Where do we go from here? *Journal of Clinical Child Psychology, 22,* 288–298.

Leffert, J.S., & Siperstein, G.N. (1996). Assessment of social-cognitive processes in children with mental retardation. *American Journal on Mental Retardation, 100,* 441–455.

McCollum, J. (1995). Social competence and IEP objectives: Where's the match? *Journal of Early Intervention, 19,* 283–285.

McConnell, S.R., McEvoy, M.A., & Odom, S.L. (1992). Implementation of social competence interventions in early childhood special education classes: Current practices and future directions. In S.L. Odom, S.R. McConnell, & M.A. McEvoy (Eds.), *Social competence of young children with disabilities: Issues and strategies for intervention* (pp. 277–306). Baltimore: Paul H. Brookes Publishing Co.

McEvoy, M.A., Odom, S.L., & McConnell, S.R. (1992). Peer social competence intervention for young children with disabilities. In S.L. Odom, S.R. McConnell, & M.A. McEvoy (Eds.), *Social competence of young children with disabilities: Issues and strategies for intervention* (pp. 113–133). Baltimore: Paul H. Brookes Publishing Co.

Michnowicz, L.L., McConnell, S.R., Peterson, C.A., & Odom, S.L. (1995). Social goals and objectives of preschool IEPs: A content analysis. *Journal of Early Intervention, 19,* 273–282.

Mize, J., & Pettit, G.S. (1997). Mothers' social coaching, mother–child relationship style, and children's peer competence: Is the medium the message? *Child Development, 68,* 312–332.

Mize, J., Pettit, G.S., & Brown, E.G. (1995). Mothers' supervision of their children's peer play: Relations with beliefs, perceptions, and knowledge. *Developmental Psychology, 31,* 311–321.

Mueller, E., & Lucas, T. (1975). A developmental analysis of peer interaction among toddlers. In M. Lewis & L.A. Rosenblum (Eds.), *The origins of behavior: Vol. 4. Friendship and peer relations* (pp. 223–257). New York: John Wiley & Sons.

Nelson, K. (Ed.). (1986). *Event knowledge: Structure and function in development.* Mahwah, NJ: Lawrence Erlbaum Associates.

Nelson, K., & Seidman, S. (1984). Playing with scripts. In I. Bretherton (Ed.), *Symbolic play: The development of social understanding* (pp. 45–71). San Diego: Academic Press.

Odom, S.L., & Brown, W.H. (1993). Social interaction skills interventions for young children with disabilities in integrated settings. In C.A. Peck, S.L. Odom, & D.D. Bricker (Eds.), *Integrating young children with disabilities into community programs: Ecological perspectives on research and implementation* (pp. 39–64). Baltimore: Paul H. Brookes Publishing Co.

Odom, S.L., McConnell, S.R., & Chandler, L.K. (1993). Acceptability and feasibility of classroom-based social interaction interventions for young children with disabilities. *Exceptional Children, 60,* 226–236.

Odom, S.L., McConnell, S.R., McEvoy, M.A., Peterson, C., Ostrosky, M., Chandler, L.K., Spicuzza, R.J., Skellenger, A., Creighton, M., & Favazza, P.C. (1999). Relative effects of interventions supporting the social competence of young children with disabilities. *Topics in Early Childhood Special Education, 19,* 75–91.

Parke, R.D., Cassidy, J., Burks, V.M., Carson, J.L., & Boyum, L. (1992). Familial contributions to peer competence among young children: The role of interactive and affective processes. In R.D. Parke & G.W. Ladd (Eds.), *Family–peer relationships: Modes of linkage* (pp. 107–134). Mahwah, NJ: Lawrence Erlbaum Associates.

Parke, R.D., & Ladd, G.W. (Eds.). (1992). *Family–peer relationships: Modes of linkage.* Mahwah, NJ: Lawrence Erlbaum Associates.

Parker, J.G., & Asher, S.R. (1987). Peer relations and later personal adjustment: Are low-accepted children at risk? *Psychological Bulletin, 102,* 357–389.

Parten, M.B. (1932). Social participation among preschool children. *Journal of Abnormal Social Psychology, 27,* 243–269.

Patterson, C.J., Vaden, N.A., & Kupersmidt, J.B. (1991). Family background, recent life events and peer rejection during childhood. *Journal of Social and Personal Relationships, 8,* 347–361.

Pennington, B.F., & Welsh, M. (1995). Neuropsychology and developmental psychopathology. In D. Cicchetti & D. Cohen (Eds.), *Handbook of developmental psychopathology* (pp. 254–290). New York: Cambridge University Press.

Putallaz, M. (1987). Maternal behavior and children's sociometric status. *Child Development, 58,* 324–340.

Putallaz, M., & Wasserman, A. (1989). Children's naturalistic entry behavior and sociometric status: A developmental perspective. *Developmental Psychology, 25,* 297–305.

Ramsey, P.G., & Lasquade, C. (1996). Preschool children's entry attempts. *Journal of Applied Developmental Psychology, 17,* 135–150.

Rice, M.L., Sell, M.A., & Hadley, P.A. (1991). Social interactions of speech- and language-impaired children. *Journal of Speech and Hearing Research, 34,* 1299–1307.

Rubin, K.H., & Coplan, R.J. (1992). Peer relationships in childhood. In M.H. Bornstein & M.E. Lamb (Eds.), *Developmental psychology: An advanced textbook* (3rd ed., pp. 519–578). Mahwah, NJ: Lawrence Erlbaum Associates.

Rubin, K.H., & Lollis, S.P. (1988). Origins and consequences of social withdrawal. In J. Belsky & T. Nezworski (Eds.), *Clinical implications of attachment* (pp. 219–252). Mahwah, NJ: Lawrence Erlbaum Associates.

Schneider, B.H. (1992). Didactic methods for enhancing children's peer relations: A quantitative review. *Clinical Psychology Review, 12,* 363–382.

Stevens, L.J., & Bliss, L.S. (1995). Conflict resolution abilities of children with specific language impairment and children with normal language. *Journal of Speech and Hearing Research, 38,* 599–611.

Stoneman, Z. (1997). Mental retardation and family adaptation. In W.E. MacLean, Jr., (Ed.), *Ellis' handbook of mental deficiency, psychological theory and research* (3rd ed., pp. 405–437). Mahwah, NJ: Lawrence Erlbaum Associates.

Taylor, A.R., Asher, S.R., & Williams, G.A. (1987). The social adaptation of mainstreamed mildly retarded children. *Child Development, 58,* 1321–1334.

Tomporowski, P.D., & Tinsley, V. (1997). Attention in mentally retarded persons. In W.E. MacLean, Jr. (Ed.), *Ellis' handbook of mental deficiency, psychological theory and research* (3rd ed., pp. 219–244). Mahwah, NJ: Lawrence Erlbaum Associates.

Twardosz, S., Nordquist, V.M., Simon, R., & Botkin, D. (1983). The effect of group affection activities on the interaction of socially isolate children. *Analysis and Intervention in Developmental Disabilities, 3,* 311–338.

Williams, G.A., & Asher, S.R. (1992). Assessment of loneliness at school among children with mild mental retardation. *American Journal on Mental Retardation, 96,* 373–385.

Wilson, B. (1999). Entry behavior and emotion regulation abilities of developmentally delayed boys. *Developmental Psychology, 35,* 214–222.

22

R.A. McWILLIAM

MARK WOLERY

SAMUEL L. ODOM

Instructional Perspectives in Inclusive Preschool Classrooms

The success of inclusion for young children with disabilities depends, to a large extent, on the quality and perhaps even the quantity of individualized instruction. How do educators need to modify their teaching to make inclusion work? What changes to the staffing are needed to ensure that children receive individualized instruction? What changes to the state of teaching does research indicate are needed. This chapter discusses issues of instruction and inclusion, the current status, and what changes are needed.

When children with disabilities are placed in inclusive preschool classrooms, individuals making decisions about such placements (e.g., family members, public school staff) establish goals for children. These goals may reflect skills that children should acquire, social relationships that children will develop, and the participation of each child as a member of the class (Billingsley, Gallucci, Peck, Schwartz, & Staub, 1996). For some children with disabilities, these goals may be achieved through placement in high-quality inclusive programs. That is, the ecological features of a high-quality early childhood classroom (Chapter 11) may lead to desired outcomes for children. A common assumption, however, is that a high-quality early childhood classroom is necessary but not sufficient for meeting the needs of most children with disabilities in inclusive preschool classrooms (Carta, Schwartz, Atwater, & McConnell, 1991). For most children with disabilities, individualized instruction may need to be provided in the inclusive environment (Wolery, Strain, & Bailey, 1992).

The purpose of this chapter is to describe issues related to providing individualized instruction for children with disabilities in inclusive preschool environments. This chapter begins with a definition of instruction and issues about early childhood environments. Next, the status of individualized instruction is discussed. This includes a discussion of what to teach, how to teach, when to teach, and who should teach. Barriers to providing individualized instruction in inclusive

Work on this chapter has been supported by the following grants from the U.S. Department of Education, Office of Special Education Programs: Project INTEGRATE (Grant No. H024D60012 to R.A. McWilliam), Individualizing Inclusion in Child Care (Grant No.H324M980207 to M. Wolery), and the Early Childhood Research Institute on Inclusion (Grant No. H02415960001 to S.L. Odom).

503

preschool environments are identified, and, finally, an agenda for promoting change is offered.

ISSUES RELATED TO PROVIDING INDIVIDUALIZED INSTRUCTION

Several issues related to instruction establish the context for a specific understanding of the research on instructional techniques and methodology. The definition and conceptualization of individualized instruction differs across early childhood education (ECE) and early childhood special education (ECSE) disciplines. Furthermore, the type of inclusive environment influences the ease and feasibility of individualized instruction. Teachers' beliefs and philosophies about the appropriateness of educational experiences and about inclusion affect the implementation of individualized instruction. These issues are examined in this section.

Definition and Conceptualization of Individualized Instruction

Instruction may be defined as changes in the environment or the teacher's behavior that result in a child's learning. Fletcher noted that

> Instruction is individualized to the extent that it adjusts to differences in learners. Instructional systems combine organized collections of subject-matter content with procedures and rules for presenting the content to bring about learning outcomes. . . . [T]hese procedures and rules adjust the pace, content, sequence, and/or style of instruction to the needs of individual learners. (1992, p. 613)

The definition of individualized instruction is elaborated on later in this chapter. Following this definition, differences in the conceptualizations of instruction and individualization for ECE and ECSE will become apparent, even though they are becoming closer.

In ECE, developmentally appropriate practice (Bredekamp & Copple, 1997) serves as the basis for instructional practices. Following a constructivist philosophy, a primary assumption in ECE is that children learn through their interactions with the physical and social environments in a classroom that has been tailored to their level of development (Maxim, 1997). Through these interactions, children construct an understanding of the world. Adults sometimes mediate this understanding in a way that advances children's learning and development. In this theoretical approach, instruction is enacted through the preparation of a developmentally and individually appropriate curriculum (Bredekamp, 1987). Outcomes are often defined in terms of developmental progress of groups of children in a class.

From an ECSE perspective, individualized instruction is directed toward children's learning of specific skills (Bowe, 1995). Such individualized instruction requires methods for identifying 1) the general content for children, 2) the content for individual children, and 3) the methods for teaching the identified content (Wolery & Sainato, 1996). A defining quality of this instruction is its focus on the individual child and outcomes related to that child (McLean & Odom, 1996). Although ECSE strategies have been characterized as substantially adult oriented (i.e., the teacher didactically delivers instruction to children), a range of instructional approaches, varying in the extent to which the adult leads instruction activities, exists (Wolery & Wilbers, 1994). It is important to emphasize that individualized instruction from an ECSE perspective does not necessarily mean one adult working with one child on a single learning objective. In fact, such an arrangement might occur rarely in most inclusive classrooms.

Inclusion at the preschool level requires the melding of ECE and ECSE approaches. Since the early 1990s, the two disciplines have somewhat coalesced. The most recent edition (at the time of this writing) of the National Association for the Education of Young Children's (NAEYC) developmentally appropriate practice document noted that "children construct their own understanding of concepts, and they benefit from instruction by more competent peers and adults" (Bredekamp & Copple, 1997, p. 23). At the same time, naturalistic instructional techniques, which look more similar to ECE methods than to traditional direct-instruction techniques, are frequently used by ECSE professionals to address individual goals for children (Rule, Losardo, Dinnebeil, Kaiser, & Rowland, 1998). The compatibility of ECSE and ECE instructional strategies may serve as a barrier to or facilitator of learning opportunities for young children with disabilities in inclusive classrooms.

Forms of Preschool Inclusion and Provisions of Individualized Instruction

Although individuals use the term *inclusion* to define certain services for children, inclusive preschool classrooms actually take many different forms (see Chapter 1). In a study conducted on a range of inclusive preschool programs, Odom, Horn, et al. (1999) found that programs varied in the way they provided individualized services to children. In *itinerant/direct services models*, children were enrolled in an early childhood classroom where an early childhood education teacher planned activities and instruction for all children. An itinerant special education teacher or related services personnel visited the class periodically. This person usually provided individual (i.e., one-on-one) instruction or therapy to the child in a part of the classroom that was separate from other class activities. (See the section "Models of Service Delivery" for a comparison of this *one-on-one* model

[McWilliam, 1995] and other service delivery models.) In these environments, teaching took on a rather didactic approach. *Itinerant/consultative models* differed in that the itinerant teacher's or specialist's role was to consult with the early childhood education teacher leading the class about ways in which instruction on individualized education program (IEP) objectives could be embedded in the classroom activities. In such classrooms, when instruction occurred it followed a more naturalistic (Rule et al., 1998) or integrated-therapy (McWilliam, 1996) approach. In classes using the *team teaching model*, both an early childhood education and special education teacher shared the role of lead teacher. Although the role for both teachers was to plan the curriculum activities, the special education teacher would provide instruction in small groups as well as in ongoing routines occurring throughout the day. Inclusive classrooms employing an *early childhood model* (many Head Start programs follow this model) were staffed by early childhood education teachers and assistants. Little interaction with special education staff occurred. In these classes, large-group, teacher-led instruction and child-initiated activities were prominent. In an *early childhood special education inclusive program*, also called *reverse inclusion*, the class was composed primarily of children with disabilities with a few typically developing children enrolled as peer models. This class model followed more of a special education approach with more teacher-led, small-group activities. In the final model, the *integrated-activities model*, typically developing children were enrolled in early childhood education classes and children with disabilities were enrolled in special education classes. The classes merged for a portion of the day (30 minutes to an hour), and the forms of instruction ranged from child-initiated activities to teacher-led large groups. In the classrooms studied, the forms of inclusion appeared to influence the types of instruction that teachers employed directly.

Philosophies and Beliefs

Outlooks on inclusion and teaching have provided a significant backdrop to instructional practices. The Division for Early Childhood (DEC) of the Council for Exceptional Children (CEC) stated its position on inclusion as follows:

> Inclusion, as a value, supports the right of all children, regardless of their diverse abilities, to participate actively in natural settings within their communities. A natural setting is one in which the child would spend time had he or she not had a disability. Such settings include but are not limited to home and family, play groups, child care, nursery schools, Head Start programs, kindergartens, and neighborhood school classrooms. (1993, p. 1)

This value is but one of a number of values influencing practitioners and family members. Although it might be considered desirable to have children with disabilities in child care and educational environments alongside children without disabilities, such environments might compromise the intensity of services or individualization of instruction, which are other significant values in early intervention. In making decisions about placements for children, inclusion must be considered as well as other powerful values (e.g., high-quality programs, specialized services, and family-centered practices; Bailey, McWilliam, Buysse, & Wesley, 1998).

Beliefs about inclusion have proceeded from favoring segregation (see Stainback, Stainback, & Bunch, 1989), through the normalization concept (see Bailey & McWilliam, 1990; Wolfensberger, 1972), to the principle of the "least restrictive environment," which appeared in the Education for All Handicapped Children Act of 1975 (PL 94-142). Distinctions among mainstreaming, integration, and inclusion reflect the development of the inclusion philosophy (see Erwin, 1996).

In the United States, the *inclusion philosophy* has evolved alongside legal mandates (see Chapter 4). The culmination of this development has been in the natural environments provision in the 1997 amendments of the Individuals with Disabilities Education Act (PL 105-17). This act states that "'early intervention services' means developmental services that. . .to the maximum extent appropriate, are provided in natural environments, including the home, and community settings in which children without disabilities participate" (Part C, § 632 [Definitions], pp. 81–82). Beliefs about educating young children can therefore be seen in legislative changes.

At the same time that thoughts about inclusion have been emerging, philosophies about appropriate teaching have also changed. Education of young children with disabilities was founded on behavioral principles (see Strain et al., 1992). A reasoned philosophical compromise has been reached, with behaviorists paying attention to the importance of instruction within normal routines and developmentalists paying attention to learning theory (Wolery, Strain, et al., 1992).

Philosophies about instruction highlight differences between the ECE and ECSE professions. Further differences have been found among three of the other major disciplines involved in early intervention: occupational therapy, physical therapy, and speech-language pathology (McWilliam & Bailey, 1994). The field is challenged, therefore, to provide instruction within the context of values that differ 1) in their support of inclusion, 2) in their view of the teacher's role, and 3) among disciplines.

CURRENT STATUS

Providing individualized instruction to young children with developmental delays and disabilities requires teams to face many questions. Three central ones are as follows: What skills or abilities should be taught? How can those skills be taught? What factors influence the implementation of environmental arrangements and strategies for teaching those skills?

What Skills or Abilities Should Be Taught?

The quick answer to the question of what skills or abilities should be taught is, "It depends on the individual child." This statement, although partially true, requires more explanation of the "it depends" phrase. It depends on the child's current behaviors and abilities, it depends on the desired outcomes, and it depends on factors other than children's behaviors and abilities that influence what and how they are taught.

Identifying children's current abilities requires careful assessment of children, and the procedures are described in numerous sources (e.g., Bagnato, Neisworth, & Munson, 1997; McLean, Bailey, & Wolery, 1996). Specifying types of outcomes for young children with disabilities is more complex. The outcomes promoted here are a function of the field's beliefs and values (particularly those of the child's team) and the accumulation of knowledge and experience about what seems possible to teach and, thus, what should be taught.

Early intervention, including applications in inclusive classrooms, is influenced substantially by the similar-sequence hypothesis. This hypothesis states that children with mental retardation and other disabilities acquire skills in sequences similar to those of children without disabilities, but the acquisition rate tends to be slower (Bennett-Gates & Zigler, 1998). Substantial evidence for this hypothesis can be found in the literature (e.g., Weisz & Zigler, 1979). A corollary of the hypothesis is that the more severe the disability the slower the rate of development. A qualification of the hypothesis is that children with severe sensory impairments (visual or auditory) and children with severe physical impairments may have specific deviations from the usual developmental course, particularly for those skills involving the affected body system.

The major implication of the similar-sequence hypothesis for early intervention is that the next step or skill in the developmental sequence should be taught. As a result, numerous developmental scales, criterion-referenced tests, curriculum-referenced measures, and checklists were constructed using developmental progressions as a framework (Cohen & Gross, 1979a, 1979b). The logic supporting this approach is that children without disabilities acquire skills in order of difficulty, learning the easier skills first, which sets the foundation for more complex skills. This logic applies to all children. The guidelines for developmentally appropriate practice (Bredekamp, 1987; Bredekamp & Copple, 1997) are based on the assumption that relatively invariant sequences of developmental accomplishments, producing the need for different types of practices for children of varying ages, exist.

Development is often divided into several domains to make the task of assessing and teaching the next skills in the developmental progression manageable. Common domains are language and communication skills, physical (motor) skills, cognitive abilities, adaptive and self-care skills, and social skills. As a result, many intervention teams specify goals in each of these domains. The validity of such an approach depends on the developmental theory used to generate the developmental sequences. As noted elsewhere (e.g., Bailey & Wolery, 1984), the sequences of items on many developmental scales originate from a maturational view of development and are not arranged in logical or instructional order. Furthermore, those sequences were not originally designed as curricular objectives but as markers to discriminate between children of different abilities. Nonetheless, given a nonmaturational view of development (e.g., some dialectic theory), relevant orders of developmental sequences can be specified (Dunst, 1981), and some have been translated into instructionally useful sequences (e.g., Bricker, 1993; Johnson-Martin, Attermeier, & Hacker, 1990; Linder, 1993).

Despite the popularity of development as a source of goals, other sources of outcomes have been proposed. Bailey and Wolery (1992) suggested that in addition to promoting development, the field should focus on outcomes such as promoting children's engagement and mastery of their environments, their social competence, and their ability to generalize or apply skills as well as on providing and preparing them for normalized life experiences while also preventing the emergence of future difficulties. Billingsley et al. (1996) suggested three types of outcomes for inclusive educational programs involving older children with significant disabilities: 1) promoting group membership, 2) promoting social relationships, and 3) promoting functional skill competence. Billingsley et al. (1996) provided descriptions of potential goals for each of these outcomes. Analysis of these additional outcome areas can result in many important goals for the child. The following are some examples:

- Increasing the amount and complexity of children's engagement with materials (McWilliam & Bailey, 1992)

- Increasing the frequency with which children share toys with peers, enter others' play, and initiate and respond to peers (e.g., Kohler & Strain, 1999; Odom, McConnell, et al., 1999)

- Increasing children's abilities to master social situations, such as carrying on conversations (Filla, Wolery, & Anthony, 1999)

- Increasing children's abilities to learn from the environment by teaching them to ask questions for labels of objects and events (Koegel, 1995)

- Increasing children's imitative abilities to take advantage of models in their environments (Venn et al., 1993)

- Increasing families' use of community resources and activities that provide normalized experiences for their children (Trivette, Dunst, & Deal, 1997)

Similarly, using functional communication training may reduce or prevent the occurrence of problematic behaviors that could lead to behavior disabilities (Koegel, Stiebel, & Koegel, 1998). Helping children participate in shared activities may promote group membership. Thus, a range of goals exists in addition to teaching the next skills in developmental sequences.

Another set of goals may emerge around the concept of children's quality of life (Schalock, 1996). Quality of life can be measured and analyzed at different levels, but, in general, the goals would focus on teaching skills that increase the child's acceptance by others, increase the likelihood of others' interacting with the child, increase the degree to which the child controls daily events, decrease the likelihood of painful or aversive events, and increase the ease of caring for the child (e.g., helping the child learn to console him- or herself). Additional goals may focus on children's patterns of interacting with the social and physical environment. These emerge from the general statements adults use to describe children. Examples of such patterns or styles of interacting are being flexible, showing initiative, being creative, being persistent, making choices, showing empathy, being curious, and respecting peers. Definition of such behavior patterns requires consideration of their contexts, but these interactional patterns or styles are rich sources of potential goals for individual children.

As noted previously, the quick answer to the question of what to teach ("It depends on the individual child") is only partially true because what is taught depends on the child's environments as well as the child's abilities. Some goals may be specific for the child simply because of where the child lives and spends time. Two children could have identical skills, but their teams would establish defensibly different goals for them because the children need different skills in their different environments to be independent, accepted, and valued within those ecologies (Thurman, 1997). For example, meals in one class may be served individually and in another they might be served family style (i.e., taking food from larger bowls or plates and passing them to the next child). The skills needed to participate and be independent in the two styles of meals are different. Likewise, at home, the activities and expectations may be different among children of similar abilities. For example, one family may need the child to learn to share and play with his or her siblings, whereas another family may need the child to learn to occupy his or her time with less direct attention and interaction from adults. In short, two children with similar abilities may have very different goals because their environments differ.

Finally, children's future environments may determine what is taught. Young children who are moving to other environments (e.g., other classrooms or other programs) may need to be taught the skills necessary to function in those environments (Rosenkoetter, Hains, & Fowler, 1994). Atwater, Orth-Lopes, Elliott, Carta, and Schwartz (1994) identified four characteristics of skills that facilitate children's transition to new programs. First, the skills should be useful across environments such as homes and classrooms (e.g., managing one's own materials). Second, the skills should allow the child to learn other more advanced skills (e.g., learning to follow instructions given to a group allows the child to function as part of a class and thereby learn from the activities provided for the class). Third, the skills should move the child toward greater independence (e.g., learning to complete tasks without adult assistance). Fourth, the skills should involve active engagement (e.g., learning to observe other children playing and then joining that play as an integral member of the group).

In summary, what is taught is an important decision that teams make in planning children's individualized programs in inclusive environments. Teams can identify what to teach by establishing goals to 1) promote children's developmental progress, 2) facilitate children's engagement in and mastery of their environments, 3) assist children in becoming more socially competent, 4) help children become learners who secure information from the environment and apply skills to new situations, 5) teach skills that prevent the emergence of future problems or additional disabilities, 6) support children in becoming members of groups, 7) enhance children's quality of life, 8) encourage children to use desirable patterns of interacting with their environments, and 9) ensure independence and participation in current and future environments. Although goals in these areas are not unique to inclusive classrooms, the precise goal statements that would be developed are influenced by the expectations and supports available in these environments.

How Can Identified Goals Be Taught?

The literature suggests that children with disabilities in inclusive classrooms do not have a developmental advantage over children in segregated classes but that they do have more advanced play and behavior skills (Buysse & Bailey, 1993; Lamorey & Bricker, 1993). Another finding across intervention studies in inclusive classrooms is that the baseline levels of the desired skills (e.g., communicative behaviors, social behaviors) do not change much until intervention is implemented to teach those skills (Strain, 1999). This suggests that being in an inclusive classroom is not sufficient to promote learning of some important goals; rather, instruction is needed to ensure acquisition and use of desired goals. The field of early childhood special education fortunately has a strong tradition of evaluating interventions in inclusive classrooms. From this work, many strategies have been identified and evaluated (Peck, Odom, & Bricker, 1993; Wolery & Sainato, 1996). Although the intervention procedures can be classified in different ways, two categories are discussed here: environmental arrangements and specialized procedures.

Environmental Arrangements Some child goals are to increase engagement, promote more play or different types of play, facilitate peer contacts and interactions, build group membership, support appropriate behavior, and encourage communication. Often, manipulating specific aspects of the classroom environment may result in such goals being achieved or will present opportunities

for them to be learned, practiced, or applied. Environmental arrangements involve changes in the 1) amount of space, 2) arrangement of the space, 3) sequence and duration of activities, 4) amount of materials, 5) type of materials (including preferred materials), 6) rules for gaining access to materials, and 7) number and type of peers available. A complete discussion of environmental arrangements is not possible here, but other sources exist (McWilliam & Bailey, 1992; Odom & McLean, 1996; Sainato & Carta, 1992). The following five comments about environmental arrangements, however, are important to discuss here:

1. The environmental arrangements often should be used together. For example, having toys that children prefer, a defined space for using them, a sufficient quantity of toys (including duplicates of the same toys), and peers who readily play may result in engagement and reduce conflicts between children during play.

2. Manipulating these environmental aspects does not ensure that children will learn. For example, having children in a defined play area with adequate amounts of materials does not necessarily result in children's talking with one another (Goldstein & Kaczmarek, 1992) or interacting socially with one another (Kohler & Strain, 1999). As a result, regular monitoring of the effects of environmental arrangements is necessary, and, when learning does not occur, additional intervention is required.

3. Environmental arrangements often should be supplemented by adult teaching behavior. In one example, having a restricted play space, defined number of selected peers, and choices of materials did not result in child–child conversations,

but the addition of adult prompting, which was systematically faded, produced increases in child–child conversations (Filla et al., 1999).

4. Combining intentional adult interventions in the context of environmental arrangements can result in learning multiple goals. For example, toys that children prefer should be readily available if the goal is to increase toy play. However, placing those toys on a visible shelf, thus requiring the child to ask for them, gives the adult an opportunity to promote more elaborate language (Kaiser, Yoder, & Keetz, 1992). As a result, two desirable goals are accomplished: increasing the child's play and promoting more elaborate language.

5. Adaptations of environmental arrangements and materials are often needed in inclusive classrooms. For example, using a nonslip place mat and plate guard can help keep a plate stable and help a child with severe visual impairments scoop with a spoon during meals (Demchak & Downing, 1996), using a visual schedule may help a child with autism negotiate in-class transitions more successfully (Mesibov, Schopler, & Hearsey, 1994), and using a Velcro wristband may help a child with cerebral palsy manipulate water toys and participate with his or her peers at the water table (Demchak & Downing, 1996).

Environmental arrangements, therefore, need to be considered carefully. Using elements together, manipulating environmental aspects, supplementing them with adult teaching behavior, using them as contexts for intentional adult interventions, and adapting them are five points to keep in mind.

Specialized Procedures Many goals are addressed most effectively by having adults and in some cases other children interact with the child who has disabilities in specific ways. These include using 1) responsive interaction patterns, 2) naturalistic or milieu teaching strategies, 3) procedures based on reinforcement principles, 4) prompting and fading procedures, and 5) special arrangements of peer behavior. *Responsive adult interaction patterns* are recommended when the goal of intervention is to teach children cause-and-effect relationships, initiate interactions with the environment, and sustain and elaborate children's play. Responsive adult interaction patterns include being aware of the child's behavior, engaging in game playing and waiting for the child to take turns, imitating the child, responding to the child's behavior as though it were purposeful, responding contingently to the child's behavior with animated and exaggerated expressions, providing models of more elaborate behavior, taking short rather than long turns, avoiding demands for specific behavior, and following the child's lead about the pace of interactions (Dunst et al., 1987; Field, 1982; MacDonald & Gillette, 1988; Mahoney & Powell, 1986).

Naturalistic or milieu teaching strategies are particularly useful for promoting language and communication goals. These involve incidental teaching (e.g., responding to a child's initiation, asking for more elaborate behavior, providing models if necessary, responding to the intent of the child's communication) as well as the mand-model procedure and naturalistic time delay (Kaiser et al., 1992). Several *reinforcement-based procedures* exist, including differential reinforcement, response shaping, behavioral momentum or high-probability procedure (Davis & Brady, 1993; Davis, Reichle, Southard, & Johnston, 1998), and correspondence training (Wolery & Sainato, 1996). These procedures are often useful for increasing the complexity, frequency, and duration of children's behavior; promoting more engagement and play; and encouraging appropriate behavior. Similarly, a number of *prompting and fading procedures* are available for teaching a range of behaviors including the acquisition of language, cognitive, motor, social, and self-care and adaptive skills (Wolery, Ault, & Doyle, 1992). Among others, these procedures include time delay, increasing assistance, and graduated guidance. *Peer-mediated strategies* (providing specific training to peers) have been used to increase children's social interactions and their communicative behavior with peers (Goldstein & Kaczmarek, 1992; Kohler & Strain, 1999). These strategies include social initiation training (Odom, McConnell, & Chandler, 1994), conversational training (Goldstein, English, Shafer, & Kaczmarek, 1997), and use of peer models (Werts, Caldwell, & Wolery, 1996). In addition, a number of useful specialized procedures are group friendship activities (McEvoy, Odom, & McConnell, 1992), videotaped self-modeling (Hepting & Goldstein, 1996), scripted and structured play routines (DeKlyen & Odom, 1989), use of role playing and verbal rehearsal (Holcombe, Wolery, & Katzenmeyer, 1995), systematic use of child choice (Kern et al., 1998), and teaching children to use adaptive equipment (Schepis, Reid, Behrmann, & Sutton, 1998).

Much of the research documenting the effectiveness of these procedures was conducted in inclusive classrooms. In almost all of the cases, effectiveness was dependent on the teachers' using the procedures regularly, consistently, and accurately. When inconsistent or inaccurate implementation occurs, the procedures may not be effective or may be less efficient (e.g., Holcombe, Wolery, & Snyder, 1994). Furthermore, as is recommended for inclusive classrooms, examples exist in which these procedures were used in ongoing activities of classrooms as opposed to separate, special activit-

ies (Bricker, 1998; Wolery & Wilbers, 1994).

In summary, many environmental arrangements and specialized procedures for teaching young children with disabilities exist. Those procedures are useful in inclusive classrooms as well as other contexts, but they require teacher skill and consistent use. Thus, the goals that reflect many of the outcomes identified in the previous section can be taught with the arrangements and procedures identified in this section.

What Factors Influence Implementation in Inclusive Environments?

Having specific goals and interventions (environmental arrangements and specialized procedures) does not ensure that individualized intervention will occur or that children will learn. Several factors influence whether intervention is implemented. Some of these involve specific staff supports such as having sufficient planning time, training that is relevant to the child and classroom context, regular contact with competent specialists and others who are knowledgeable about providing intervention, sufficient time to meet with those specialists, a realistic number of children in the class, teaching assistants, and leadership on the team (Scruggs & Mastropieri, 1996; Wolery et al., 1994). Without such supports, individualized intervention is unlikely in many inclusive classrooms, and even with them, individualization is complex. The following general statements can guide implementation of individualized interventions in inclusive classrooms.

Interventions should be implemented in a purposeful and comprehensive manner. This guideline implies interventions are identified for each goal, a plan exists for implementing the interventions, and someone is responsible for ensuring that the plan occurs. In addition, this guideline indicates that each event, activity, and routine should address multiple goals, and each goal should be addressed in multiple events, activities, and routines (Wolery, 1994). For example, arrival time in an inclusive classroom may be an opportunity for addressing goals such as making choices (e.g., about toys with which to play), caring for one's possessions (e.g., putting a coat in the cubby), greeting peers, and playing with toys independently. Likewise, each goal should be addressed at other times; for example, making choices can occur at center time and snack, caring for one's possessions can occur during cleanup routines, greeting peers can occur when children depart for the day, and playing with toys independently can occur during center time and outdoor play.

A balance is needed between promoting participation and independence (Wolery, 1994). One purpose of having young children with disabilities in inclusive classrooms is to allow them to participate in normalized activities with their peers. A fundamental purpose of early intervention is to assist children in learning the skills needed to be independent in a range of activities. Often, participation results in learning to be independent, and independence increases participation opportunities. In some cases, however, children's disabilities or lack of skills may preclude independent participation. Adaptation should then be made to promote participation (Baumgart et al., 1982), and, when appropriate, instruction should be given to encourage independence.

Instruction should be embedded into and distributed within and across ongoing activities and routines. Time must always be identified for providing instruction. One alternative is to have special instructional or therapeutic sessions, and another is to embed instruction and therapy into ongoing activities and routines. Although both are often effective, embedding instruction into ongoing activities is rec-ommended for inclusive classrooms. This recommendation is made because of the difficulties of staffing separate sessions, the potential for the lack of skill general-ization or application to occur, and the potential for such sessions to minimize contacts with and thus learning from peers. As a result, studies have compared whether providing instruction through special sessions or distributing it within ongoing activities results in better learn-ing. The general conclusion is that both are effective (Chiara, Schuster, Bell, & Wolery, 1995; Wolery, Doyle, Gast, Ault, & Simpson, 1993). Thus, at least three methods have been studied for embed-ding instruction into ongoing activities: fitting teaching into multiple activities (Chiara et al., 1995), embedding single opportunities into each of several transi-tions (Wolery, Anthony, & Heckathorn, 1998), and embedding multiple but dis-tributed opportunities into the same activity (Venn et al., 1993). When plan-ning such instruction, use of the activity-by-goal matrix is often useful (Bricker & Cripe, 1998; McWilliam, 1992).

Contextually relevant and integrated learning opportunities should be used. By embedding instruction into ongoing activities, teachers can take advantage of those "teachable moments" when chil-dren need the goal behavior to meet some intention they have (Drasgow, Halle, Ostrosky, & Harbers, 1996; Kaiser et al., 1992), and instruction can be pro-vided when children are attending to spe-cific and relevant stimuli (Warren & Gazdag, 1990). This allows the instruc-tion to be relevant to the context in which the child is engaged, which is thought to take advantage of children's existing motivation. *Integrated learning opportunities* are situations in which goal behaviors from multiple domains can be addressed in the same activity. For exam-ple, during storytime reading, multiple language and communication goals (e.g., pointing to pictures, answering questions, building vocabulary) can be addressed along with group membership goals (e.g., participating in an activity together, taking turns) and cognitive goals (e.g., noting relationships, making discriminations, counting).

Generalization and application of skills require specific programming. A recurring finding is that learners, including young children with disabilities in inclusive classrooms, acquire a skill in one situation but do not apply or use that skill in other situations (i.e., fail to generalize). The ultimate test of the effectiveness of interventions is whether children use and apply the skills they have learned. Warren and Horn (1996) recommended that to promote generalization, behaviors should be taught so that they occur frequently and are useful to the child, all adults who interact and care for the child should be promoting the same skills with similar procedures, the effects of interventions should be evaluated from a developmental perspective (i.e., expecting different amounts of time to be required to achieve generalization), and stringent measures of generalization should be used, continuing intervention until robust generalization effects are achieved. Brown and Odom identified three major approaches for facilitating the generalization of social skills: 1) employing natural reinforcers by using social contingencies and teaching children to recruit reinforcers; 2) training diversely by using multiple examples, training loosely, and using contingencies that are difficult for children to discriminate; and 3) employing "functional mediators" (1994, p. 109), such as using stimuli from the natural environment and teaching self-management strategies.

Children's progress and intervention implementation should be monitored regularly and adjustments made as needed. Implementation of individualized interventions in inclusive classrooms is challenging because children's development are com-

plex, the effects of disabilities on children's development are varied, and the environments in which intervention occurs are dynamic. Thus, teams are unlikely to devise plans that are maximally effective and implemented without error. As a result, teams must monitor whether their interventions are having the desired effects and must monitor whether their interventions are implemented as planned. When neither occurs, adjustments must be made.

In summary, to implement individualized interventions, teams should plan purposefully, identify multiple activities for each goal, identify multiple goals for each activity, encourage both participation and independence, embed instructional opportunities into ongoing activities and distribute their instruction across and within those activities, provide instruction at contextually relevant moments, teach goals from multiple domains simultaneously, use a range of strategies for promoting generalization, and monitor regularly both the implementation of the instruction and its effects. If teams comply with these guidelines, children are likely to experience substantial individualization of instruction and learn rapidly. Following these guidelines, however, is likely only if teams have time to plan and meet, have appropriate adult-to-child ratios, and have adequate and relevant staff development programs.

Integrated Instruction and Therapy

Numerous service providers are often involved with children with disabilities and their families. Instruction might come from a general education teacher, a special education teacher, an occupational therapist, a physical therapist, or a speech-language pathologist. Although these are the most common disciplines involved in instruction of young children, a host of others (e.g., low-vision specialists, deaf educators, orientation and mobility specialists, psychologists) could also be involved. The responsibility for instruction is almost by definition a function of educators, whether general or special. Therapists also, however, are involved in teaching children to perform certain skills as well as in *ensuring that children learn* these skills. The focus of this section is that, with changes in legislation and concepts of recommended practice, early interventionists must increasingly provide instruction indirectly, through regular caregivers.

Regular caregivers include family members, classroom teachers, and child care providers. These "generalists" are the people who spend the most time with young children. An important shift in early intervention is occurring because of the recognition that all of the effective instruction occurs *between* (as opposed to during) specialists' visits. There is no evidence that once-a-week instruction or therapy, which is a fairly common intensity of service (Kochanek & Buka, 1998), has an impact on children's development or skills. If generalists can learn from specialists during that hour per week, however, then they can provide the instruction (or "therapy") frequently during the week. Research is clear that dispersed trials are more effective with young children than are massed trials (Chiara et al., 1995).

Specialists, therefore, have a double-edged instruction sword: They must instruct adults to instruct children. To complicate matters even further, both types of instruction must often be veiled behind encouragement and support. So that children will learn to initiate and learn through discovery, many successful teaching methods must occur in response to child cues. Similarly, the consultation literature is clear that collaborative rather than expert models are more successful in effecting change (Achilles, Yates, & Freese, 1991). The following section describes different models used in early intervention, especially in inclusive environments.

Consultation Roles in Instruction

When specialists help to ensure that a child is instructed, they have choices about the approach to take with generalists (regular caregivers). Some specialists are not comfortable foregoing their role in direct instruction (McWilliam & Bailey, 1994; McWilliam, Young, & Harville, 1996), but a continuum of service delivery exists (McWilliam, 1995) to describe different ways of providing consultation. These approaches are considered next and are followed by a discussion of the importance of communication in the context of consultation.

Expert Model   Consultation involves identifying problems and developing solutions. In the expert model, consultants analyze the needs and form the solutions. They then inform the consultees, who in early intervention are usually the parents or child care providers, and expect them to follow through on the recommendations. This is the traditional method in which educational and therapeutic services have been provided. It reflects the paternalistic attitude of the educational and medical models of early intervention toward caregivers. In the medical allied health professions, this approach is especially ingrained. The problems with the expert model are that consultees do not own the needs or the solutions (i.e., the expert consultant determines what should be done), consultees might resent the expert's advice, and consultants might act with insufficient information.

Collaborative Model   The alternative to the expert model is the collaborative model in which the consultants and consultees jointly identify problems and develop solutions. The consultee thereby owns the recommendations. This is similar to a family-centered approach to working with families—one that deemphasizes concepts such as *compliance* and *follow through* and emphasizes concepts such as *partnerships* and *collaboration*. The benefits, therefore, are that the consultees own the needs and solutions, appreciate the expert's advice, and act with sufficient information.

Models of Service Delivery   Classroom teachers and family members provide direct instruction, day by day and routine by routine. What, then, is the role of the specialist who perhaps sees the child once or twice a week?

Six models of service delivery have been identified for consultants (McWilliam, 1995, 1996), defined here as specialists who are not the children's primary caregivers but consultants to these caregivers. The six models, shown in Table 22.1, range from the most segregated to the most integrated.

The Importance of Communication   Regardless of the service delivery model, the amount and quantity of communication between specialists and generalists is important. In a study of integrated versus segregated services, four times as much communication occurred when consultants worked in the classroom compared to when they used pullout services (McWilliam, 1996). In a study employing qualitative analysis of interviews with service providers and teachers, the relevance of the communication for classroom teachers was found to be very important (McWilliam & Spencer, 1993).

Effective consultation in the context of instruction involves a specialist's ensuring intervention occurs during regular routines. If specialists and teachers do not talk to each other or do so ineffectively, this is not likely to happen. Effective consultation, in the authors' experiences, requires specialists to communicate with teachers about 1) children's needs, 2) each other's preference for what in-class therapy or instruction will consist of, 3) what solutions or interventions should be tried, 4) how well the

interventions are working (both in terms of implementation and outcomes), and 5) other less task-oriented subjects. Some consultees prefer to get to know the consultant first before listening to him or her, whereas other consultees prefer to have a task-oriented relationship before beginning a personal relationship. For specialized instruction and therapy to be implemented in the classroom, consultation must be collaborative, integrated, functional, and interactive.

Teaching Contexts and Styles

Research on teaching has provided new information that should be useful for preschool inclusion. Both the context for instruction and the teacher's style are important.

Four "Teaching" Contexts   The teacher's role in instruction ranges from setting up the classroom to paying close attention to an individual child's specific responses. The discovery that teaching occurs in different contexts came from a study of teaching *styles* in early childhood classrooms (McWilliam, de Kruif, & Zulli, 1999). Ninety-three 20-minute indoor classroom sessions, using 11 teachers and 63 children, were videotaped. Fourteen of the children had disabilities including developmental delay, cerebral palsy, Apert syndrome, autism, Prader-Willi syndrome, and Williams syndrome. Extensive field notes, describing events on the videotapes, were qualitatively analyzed. One finding was that teaching was composed of four contexts, which were termed environmental, planning, approach, and interaction.

Environmental Context: The Ecology   The environmental context is the general context of the early childhood classroom, inside which the other three contexts operate. Table 22.2 shows the features of this context that influence the classroom environment. Specific to inclusion issues, the following environmental-context influences will be important. First, state

Table 22.1.   Models of service delivery

Individual pull-out	The specialist takes the child from the classroom and works with him or her one-to-one, usually in an instruction or therapy room.
Small-group pull-out	The specialist takes two or more children from the classroom and works with them, usually in an instruction or therapy room.
One-to-one in class	The specialist goes into the classroom and takes the child aside to work on goals that might not be relevant to the ongoing activities.
Group activity	With the consent of the teacher, the specialist teaches the whole class or a group in the classroom.
Individualized within routines	The specialist joins the child in ongoing classroom routines and teaches the child in that context.
Pure consultation	The specialist identifies needs with the teacher and, together, they develop solutions. Hands-on work is used only for demonstration and assessment, as needed.

guidelines for serving children with disabilities in natural environments (in the case of infants and toddlers) or in the least restrictive environment (in the case of preschoolers and older children) force professionals to figure out how to teach children in those environments. Similarly, the Americans with Disabilities Act (ADA) of 1990 (PL 101-336) is another environmental-context influence on instruction in the sense that this legislation makes it possible for children to attend community child care programs, thereby making it necessary to teach children in those environments. Second, the philosophy of the program (e.g., child care center, Head Start program, preschool) with respect to children with disabilities will have an impact on how these children are taught (McWilliam, McMillen, Sloper, & McMillen, 1997). Third, if a program offers many different types of services, then the way a child is taught might be different—and not necessarily better—than if it were to offer fewer services. Fourth, the extent to which staff are trained to teach children with disabilities affects instruction. Fifth, the smaller the number of children per adult, the easier it is for teachers to individualize instruction. These five instances are but examples of the environmental context; clearly, there are others (see Chapter 11).

Planning Context: Activities   The planning context involves the decisions teachers make every day about what activities to carry out (see Table 22.2). Whereas the environmental context consists primarily of legislative, philosophical, and administrative influences, the planning context consists primarily of teachers' plans for classroom activities.

Approach Context   The approach context involves the teacher's approach to the child, which begins the subsequent interactions. The initial interaction in a series of "turns" can follow children's existing behavior or can redirect it. Introducing a topic that has nothing to do with the child's current engagement would be a form of redirect. Table 2 shows other aspects of this context of interaction. Whereas the planning context involves the arranging of activities, the approach context involves the beginning of a teacher's interactions with a child. It is important to remember that if a child initiates the interaction, the teacher does not use the approach-context teaching in that interaction. He or she moves directly to interaction-context teaching.

Interaction Context   The interaction context involves the specific teacher behaviors during interactions with the child. These interactions can include redirectives, cessations, elaboratives,

Table 22.2.   Teaching contexts

Environmental context: influences on classroom environment	Planning context: children's experiences and activities	Approach context: beginning interactions	Interaction context: specific interaction behaviors
State guidelines	Material selection	Observation of children	Expanding, recasting, and rephrasing child behaviors
Accreditation standards	Use of thematic units	Interaction goals	
Center philosophy	Room arrangement	Seizing teachable moments	Elaborating
Child:teacher ratios	Type of child participation required by activity		Modeling
Types of children served		Maintaining child engagement in activities	Praising
Services offered	Accommodations for children with disabilities		Eliciting child behaviors
Amount of accountability		Expanding on activities	Issuing specific redirectives and cessations
Available resources	Number of available activities	Following child cues	
Staff composition	Amount of child choice between activities	Responding to child initiations	Questioning: responsive, general, wh- questions
Classroom size		Selection of children for interaction	
Teachers' levels of education			

introductions, acknowledgments, and praises. Although these teacher behaviors have technical meanings and are operationally defined in research studies (e.g., McWilliam, Scarborough, & Kim, 1998), the meanings are what they seem. In this context of teaching, teachers are—consciously or not—using different tactics at *every* "turn" (i.e., every time they interact with the child). This differs from the approach context, which is limited to the first turn—the approach.

Teaching, therefore, includes all of the conditions for which adults are responsible and that result in the child's learning. In each context, the quality can vary. To use but one component of environmental-context "teaching" as an example, the philosophy prevalent in a program might or might not promote individualization. In the planning context, some activities can be more interesting than others. In the approach context, some approaches can follow children's cues. Finally, in the interaction context, elaboratives are more likely to produce engagement than are either redirects or mere acknowledgments and praises. In the last two contexts, the extent of

responsiveness and directiveness can differentiate among teachers.

Four Styles of Teaching   In a study using the Teaching Styles Rating Scale (McWilliam, Scarborough, Bagby, & Sweeney, 1996), a cluster analysis of data on 63 child care teachers revealed four classifications of teachers (de Kruif, McWilliam, Ridley, & Wakely, in press). One group was labeled *elaborative* because they had high scores on elaborating behaviors and infrequently used redirectives. This group was similar to teachers identified as responsive-directive in a qualitative analysis of almost 100 videotaped sessions of 11 teachers (McWilliam et al., 1999). A second group was labeled *directive* because these teachers did not engage in many interaction behaviors other than redirecting and stopping the children from what they were doing. They were most similar to teachers who were identified as nonresponsive-directive in the qualitative analysis. A third group was labeled *nonelaborative* because these teachers were rated as frequently introducing topics to the children, giving them information, acknowledging their behaviors, and praising them. Furthermore, they displayed higher than average affect. They were most similar to responsive-directive teachers in the qualitative analysis. The final cluster consisted of teachers who had *average* ratings on all interaction behaviors and affect. No parallel group emerged in the qualitative analysis of 11 teachers. It might, therefore, be possible to classify teachers into four groups (including an "average" group), based on their responsiveness, directiveness, and affect. Such a classification system could be helpful for administrators in their supervision, practitioners in assessing themselves, and researchers in identifying groups of the independent variable *teaching style.*

Some research in early intervention has focused on the relationships between adult behaviors and child engagement (Lussier, Crimmins, & Alberti, 1994; Mahoney & Neville-Smith, 1996; Mc-William, 1991). For example, redirective teachers have been found to have a smaller mean percentage of children engaged in activities (82%) than average (89%), elaborative (92%), or nonelaborative (92%) teachers (de Kruif et al., in press). This study discovered a potential confound, however, in that redirective teachers tended to work in poorer quality child care and in centers with lower licensing levels. Redirective teachers were similar to nonresponsive-directive teachers, as discussed previously.

AGENDA FOR CHANGE

To promote change, barriers have to be overcome. Barriers identified include staff training, lack of materials, lack of or poor use of time, lack of specialists with whom to collaborate or lack of collaboration, and philosophical or attitudinal differences between early childhood educators and early intervention specialists (Lieber et al., 1997). The following suggestions emanate from the barriers as

well as the previous discussions about the current status and the issues confronting the early intervention field. Some of these implications are primarily for administrators, others for personnel preparation faculty, others for researchers, others for practitioners, and others for family members. Because many of these implications cut across these roles and occupations and might vary from situation to situation, they are not presented as a differentiated list.

Define individualized instruction. Every child with an individualized family service plan (IFSP) or an IEP should be able to receive individualized instruction. This is known as *special instruction* in Part C and as *special education* in Section 619 of IDEA. When a common definition of instruction, particularly in inclusive environments, is adopted, researchers will better be able to coordinate this across studies. It will be easier for them to define individualized instruction as an independent variable to ask such questions as, "How much variance in my outcome is accounted for by individualized instruction?" Perhaps more important, early intervention and school systems will better be able to agree on this intervention. This will also help families determine whether they are receiving instruction. A beginning definition of instruction might be *an adult's systematic attention to a specified need that increases the likelihood of the child's acquiring, generalizing, or maintaining behavior or knowledge that will help meet the specified need.* Each of the elements in this definition itself can be defined, as shown in Table 22.3, to provide even more specificity.

Recognize that intervention can be accomplished through environmental arrangement and specialized procedures. Although the previous definition of instruction emphasizes interaction between adults and children, adults can also systematically attend to specified needs by manip-

Table 22.3.   Elements of a proposed definition of individualized instruction

Element	Definition
Adult	A person in a teaching role, such as a teacher, assistant, therapist, or parent
Systematic attention	The adult follows certain procedures, as opposed to relying on spontaneous or chance interactions. These procedures can be naturalistic, such as those used in milieu teaching.
Specified need	A goal defined on an IEP or a child-level outcome defined on an IFSP, as opposed to a goal in the general curriculum—to be individualized, it either must be on the child's individualized plan or must be informally agreed on as a need for that particular child.
Increases the likelihood	Individualized instruction does not need to result in behavior change at the time of instruction. Some learning is not evident until later.
Acquisition	"Learning the basic requirements of a behavior or task. . .roughly a synonym for *initial learning*" (emphasis in original, Wolery, Bailey, & Sugai, 1988, p. 219)
Generalization	"When a behavior learned in one situation (i.e., training) is observed in another (i.e., nontraining)" (Wolery et al., 1988, p. 313)
Maintenance	"Response maintenance is the phase of learning in which acquired and fluent skills persist over time after training or teaching has ceased" (Wolery et al., 1988, p. 297).
Behavior	Observable and measurable action by the child
Knowledge	Mental concept, inferred by the child's behavior
Help meet	Functional instruction is designed to address needs.

ulating specific aspects of the classroom or home environment.

Define inclusion. Although common definitions that emphasize placement abound, they tend to assume one model. It might be helpful to researchers, administrators, practitioners, and families to specify whether itinerant/direct-service, itinerant/consultative, team teaching, early childhood, or integrated-activities models are being discussed (Odom, Horn, et al., 1999).

Clarify values when planning for agencies and for individual children. Because values can clash, it might be helpful for administrators to identify how they feel about the quality of the program, specialized services, and family-centered intervention. Having identified their beliefs in these matters, they could rank them to ease the process of making difficult decisions. For example, an early intervention program might need to decide whether to open another classroom so that more typically developing children can be enrolled or contract for more therapy time. Whichever value is ranked higher

could influence the decision. Similarly, when planning a child's IFSP or IEP, the family might want everything. Gently helping the family rank their priorities could help the team arrive at important decisions about goals, placement, and services.

Broaden outcomes of instruction. Beyond the traditional developmental domains, instruction should be aimed at engagement, social competence, skill generalization or application, preparation for normalized life experiences, prevention of future difficulties, and quality of life (Bailey & Wolery, 1992; Schalock, 1996). These outcomes can be identified on IFSPs and IEPs and can be the dependent variables in research on inclusion.

Instruct skills in logical order. Logic might be decided by the family's priorities, demands of the current and subsequent environments, the topography of the behavior (i.e., the elements of the skill), the elements of the concept, and the use of instructional materials in addition to normal developmental progression.

Ensure appropriate intensity. The requisite intensity for children to learn in inclusive environments needs to be addressed. Eight "name-brand" instructional programs for children with autism, for example, have been described as requiring 27–40 hours a week (McGee, 1999). In contrast, most public school preschools provide much less intensity. With all disabilities, the issue of intensity is important. Children receive instruction through the general curriculum and then, if they have child-level goals on an IFSP or IEP, they might be eligible for specific instruction (i.e., individualization) that the other children do not receive. Researchers need to figure out how to calculate the amount of instruction children receive from these two sources. This is especially difficult because the general curriculum can involve incidental learning from peers and from the adults teaching other children. Professionals also need to figure out how to make these calculations, because the IFSP and IEP require some indication of intensity of special services.

Intensity has been defined as having three dimensions: "the level of intervention occurring within a specified time interval (density), intensity defined as occurring across a longer period of time (duration), and possibly intensity defined as containing more early intervention components (comprehensiveness) may well be essential for long-term effectiveness" (Guralnick, 1998, p. 334). Most current measures of intensity focus only on the first dimension (i.e., density) and are indexed by hours per week; occasionally, researchers also report the duration of the intervention (i.e., second dimension). Thus, statements are made about hours per week and number of weeks of intervention. Few researchers report anything about the comprehensiveness of the intervention. The density measure—

hours per week (or other period)—is highly suspect because it does not focus on what occurs during those hours. Two children with the same number of hours of intervention (e.g., 20 hours) who are engaged in relevant learning opportunities at different levels (e.g., 20% for one child and 85% for the other) are likely to have different learning outcomes. Thus, improvements in how intensity is measured and reported clearly are needed.

Ensure quality of instruction. Judging instruction should not occur only by looking at whether children have learned skills but also by implementation and congruence with developmental, family, and ecological priorities. Children's learning is affected by their own characteristics (e.g., the disability) and the relevance of the skill being taught (i.e., its developmental appropriateness); therefore, the quality of teaching cannot be determined just on the basis of learning. If teaching matches the child's current abilities, is aimed at skills important to the family, and is functional for the child's everyday routines, it can be considered to have some quality. Teachers and therapists need to know the definitions of quality of instruction and the techniques for implementing those practices.

Data-based decision making. Teachers and therapists probably base much of their teaching on sequences in a curriculum and on their general impressions (i.e., their "gut instincts"). Although developmental sequencing has its place, and teachers, especially those with experience, often have a good understanding of how to teach children, these hopeful bases for making decisions are not enough. Professionals can learn some basic data collection and graphing skills, and administrators and parents can insist on them. These skills (data collection and graphing) are useful, however, only if they are used to make decisions—decisions such as whether our teaching should change, whether the child has mastered the skill, whether the child is making progress, and so forth.

Broaden instruction and inclusion issues to recognize the roles of medical allied health professionals. Too often, instruction and inclusion are considered issues for teachers. As this chapter has done, future attention to inclusion should include the parts that occupational therapists, speech-language pathologists, and physical therapists (among others) play. Although therapists attend to functioning beyond the skills that a child has to learn (e.g., range of motion is such a function), they often do teach skills either directly to the child or for implementation by someone else (e.g., a family member or a teacher). In many ways, they should be considered no different from early childhood special educators, who also function largely as consultants to regular caregivers, sometimes provide direct intervention (e.g., instruction), and provide much information and support related to disabilities. Because of the importance of instruction in habilitation, personnel preparation in the medical allied health professions should include instructional strategies. Therapists can then be more effective when teaching independent feeding, grasping objects, walking, making requests, and so forth.

Involve peers in instruction. A primary advantage of inclusive preschool classrooms (over segregated classes) is the presence of typically developing peers. Systematically planning ways for a peer to provide learning experiences that address the individual needs of children with disabilities should be an essential instructional component of inclusive preschool programs.

Elaborate the understanding about what really works in consultation (adult learning issues). Research on consultation suggests that a collaborative model is more effective than an expert model (e.g., Achilles et al., 1991). One review of the literature

concludes that the successful school consultant should be knowledgeable, competent, and congenial (Tingstrom, Little, & Stewart, 1990). Although this is not a surprising list of attributes, the importance of congeniality might be underrepresented in training programs and administrative feedback.

Recognize the four levels at which instruction occurs. Teachers and therapists should think of instruction or therapy as something that happens when they establish the environmental context, plan activities, approach children, and engage in specific interactions with them.

Prepare teachers to use interactive behaviors and styles systematically. Teaching is a science as well as an art, and preservice and in-service faculty need to train teachers in specific interactional behaviors as well as affective behaviors. Teachers, for their part, should learn the language of instruction so that they can engage in learned discourse about this most vital aspect of inclusion. If they know the jargon, they can employ the behaviors. If they cannot describe what they do, they cannot inform family members and other professionals about their interventions.

CONCLUSION

In conclusion, the previously mentioned 14 action steps provide an agenda for the next phase of instruction in inclusive settings. The quality and, to some extent, the quantity of individualized teaching bears considerably on the success of inclusion. This chapter has reviewed the importance of teachers' undertaking changes in their teaching to accommodate individual children with individual goals in individual classrooms. The significance of change is found in the definition of instruction provided earlier in the chapter: "changes in the environment or the teacher's behavior that result in a child's learning." In addition to teacher behaviors, the environments where instruction occurs and the philosophies of professionals and families have an impact on the implementation and possibly the success of inclusion. The background for the recommended steps is found in the current status of curriculum definition, teaching methods, models of service delivery, consultation roles, teaching contexts, and styles. Much has been done but much still needs to be done.

REFERENCES

Achilles, J., Yates, R.R., & Freese, J.M. (1991). Perspectives from the field: Collaborative consultation in the speech and language program of the Dallas Independent School District. *Language, Speech, and Hearing Services in Schools, 22,* 154–155.

Americans with Disabilities Act of 1990, PL 101-336, 42 U.S.C. §§ 12101 *et seq.*

Atwater, J.B., Orth-Lopes, L., Elliott, M., Carta, J.J., & Schwartz, I.S. (1994). Completing the circle: Planning and implementing transitions to other programs. In M. Wolery & J.S. Wilbers (Eds.), *Including children with special needs in early childhood programs* (pp. 167–188). Washington, DC: National Association for the Education of Young Children.

Bagnato, S.J., Neisworth, J.T., & Munson, S.M. (1997). *Linking assessment and early intervention: An authentic curriculum-based approach.* Baltimore: Paul H. Brookes Publishing Co.

Bailey, D.B., & McWilliam, R.A. (1990). Normalizing early intervention. *Topics in Early Childhood Special Education, 10*(2), 33–47.

Bailey, D.B., Jr., McWilliam, R.A., Buysse, V., & Wesley, P.W. (1998). Inclusion in the context of competing values in early childhood education. *Early Childhood Research Quarterly, 13,* 27–47.

Bailey, D.B., & Wolery, M. (1984). *Teaching infants and preschoolers with handicaps.* Westerville, OH: Glencoe/McGraw-Hill.

Bailey, D.B., & Wolery, M. (1992). *Teaching infants and preschoolers with disabilities* (2nd ed.). New York: Macmillan Publishing USA.

Baumgart, D., Brown, L., Pumpian, I., Nisbet, J., Ford, A., Sweet, M., Messina, R., & Schroeder, J. (1982). Principle of partial participation and individualized adaptations in educational programs for severely handicapped students. *Journal of The Association for the Severely Handicapped, 7*(2), 17–22.

Bennett-Gates, D., & Zigler, E. (1998). Resolving the developmental-difference debate: An evaluation of the triarchic and systems theory models.

In J.A. Burack, R.M. Hodapp, & E. Zigler (Eds.), *Handbook of mental retardation and development* (pp. 115–131). New York: Cambridge University Press.

Billingsley, F.F., Gallucci, C., Peck, C.A., Schwartz, I.S., & Staub, D. (1996). "But those kids can't even do math": An alternative conceptualization of outcomes for inclusive education. *Special Education Leadership Review, 3*(1), 43–55.

Bowe, F.G. (1995). *Birth to five: Early childhood special education.* Albany, NY: Delmar Publishers.

Bredekamp, S. (1987). *Developmentally appropriate practice in early childhood programs serving children from birth through age 8.* Washington, DC: National Association for the Education of Young Children.

Bredekamp, S., & Copple, C. (Eds.). (1997). *Developmentally appropriate practice in early childhood programs, revised edition.* Washington, DC: National Association for the Education of Young Children.

Bricker, D. (1993). *AEPS measurement from birth to three years* (Vol. 1). Baltimore: Paul H. Brookes Publishing Co.

Bricker, D. (1998). *An activity-based approach to early intervention* (2nd ed.). Baltimore: Paul H. Brookes Publishing Co.

Bricker, D., & Cripe, J.J.W. (1992). *An activity-based approach to early intervention.* Baltimore: Paul H. Brookes Publishing Co.

Brown, W.H., & Odom, S.L. (1994). Strategies and tactics for promoting generalization and maintenance of young children's social behavior. *Research in Developmental Disabilities, 15,* 99–118.

Buysse, V., & Bailey, D.B. (1993). Behavioral and developmental outcomes in young children with disabilities in integrated and segregated settings: A review of comparative studies. *Journal of Special Education, 26,* 434–461.

Carta, J.J., Schwartz, I.S., Atwater, J.B., & McConnell, S.R. (1991). Developmentally appropriate practice: Appraising its usefulness for young children with disabilities. *Topics in Early Childhood Special Education, 11*(1), 1–20.

Chiara, L., Schuster, J.W., Bell, J., & Wolery, M. (1995). Small-group massed-trial and individually distributed-trial instruction with preschoolers. *Journal of Early Intervention, 19,* 203–217.

Cohen, M., & Gross, P. (1979a). *The developmental resource: Behavioral sequences for assessment and program planning* (Vol. 1). New York: Grune & Stratton.

Cohen, M., & Gross, P. (1979b). *The developmental resource: Behavioral sequences for assessment and program planning* (Vol. 2). New York: Grune & Stratton.

Davis, C.A., & Brady, M.P. (1993). Expanding the utility of behavioral momentum with young children: Where we've been, where we need to go. *Journal of Early Intervention, 17,* 211–223.

Davis, C.A., Reichle, J., Southard, K., & Johnston, S. (1998). Teaching children with severe disabilities to utilize nonobligatory conversational opportunities: An application of high-probability requests. *Journal of The Association for Persons with Severe Handicaps, 23,* 57–68.

DeKlyen, M., & Odom, S.L. (1989). Activity structure and social interactions with peers in developmentally integrated play groups. *Journal of Early Intervention, 13,* 342–352.

de Kruif, R.E.L., McWilliam, R.A., Ridley, S.M., & Wakely, M.B. (in press). Classification of teachers' interaction behaviors in early childhood classrooms. *Early Childhood Research Quarterly.*

Demchak, M.A., & Downing, J.E. (1996). The preschool child. In J.E. Downing (Ed.), *Including students with severe and multiple disabilities in typical classrooms: Practical strategies for teachers* (pp. 63–82). Baltimore: Paul H. Brookes Publishing Co.

Division for Early Childhood (DEC) of the Council for Exceptional Children. (1993). *DEC recommended practices: Indicators of quality in programs for infants and young children with special needs and their families.* Reston, VA: Author.

Drasgow, E., Halle, J.W., Ostrosky, M.M., & Harbers, H.M. (1996). Using behavioral indication and functional communication training to establish an initial sign repertoire with a young child with severe disabilities. *Topics in Early Childhood Special Education, 16,* 500–521.

Dunst, C.J. (1981). *Infant learning: A cognitive-linguistic intervention strategy.* Hingham, MA: Teaching Resources Corp.

Dunst, C.J., Lesko, J.J., Holbert, K.A., Wilson, L.L., Sharpe, K.L., & Liles, R.F. (1987). A systematic approach to infant intervention. *Topics in Early Childhood Special Education, 7*(2), 19–37.

Education for All Handicapped Children Act of 1975, PL 94-142, 20 U.S.C. §§ 1400 *et seq.*

Erwin, E.J. (1996). *Putting children first: Visions for a brighter future for young children and their families.* Baltimore: Paul H. Brookes Publishing Co.

Field, T. (1982). Interactive coaching for high-risk infants and their parents. In H.A. Moss, R. Hess, & C. Swift (Eds.), *Early intervention programs for infants* (pp. 5–24). Binghamton, NY: The Haworth Press.

Filla, A., Wolery, M., & Anthony, L. (1999). Promoting children's conversations during play with adult prompts. *Journal of Early Intervention, 22,* 93–108.

Fletcher, F.D. (1992). Individualized systems of instruction. In M. Alkin (Ed.), *Encyclopedia of educational research* (6th ed., Vol. 2, pp. 613–620). New York: Macmillan.

Goldstein, H., English, K., Shafer, K., & Kaczmarek, L. (1997). Interaction among preschoolers with and without disabilities: Effects of across-the-day peer intervention. *Journal of Speech Language & Hearing Research, 40,* 33–48.

Goldstein, H., & Kaczmarek, L. (1992). Promoting communicative interaction among children in integrated intervention settings. In S.F. Warren & J. Reichle (Series Eds.) & S.F. Warren & J. Reichle (Vol. Eds.), *Communication and language intervention series: Vol. 1. Causes and effects in communication and language intervention* (pp. 81–111). Baltimore: Paul H. Brookes Publishing Co.

Guralnick, M.J. (1998). Effectiveness of early intervention for vulnerable children: A developmental perspective. *American Journal on Mental Retardation, 102,* 319–345.

Hepting, N.H., & Goldstein, H. (1996). Requesting by preschoolers with developmental disabilities: Videotaped self-modeling and learning of new linguistic structures. *Topics in Early Childhood Special Education, 16,* 407–427.

Holcombe, A., Wolery, M., & Katzenmeyer, J. (1995). Teaching preschoolers to avoid abduction by strangers: Evaluation of maintenance strategies. *Journal of Child and Family Studies, 4,* 177–191.

Holcombe, A., Wolery, M., & Snyder, E. (1994). Effects of two levels of procedural fidelity with constant time delay on children's learning. *Journal of Behavioral Education, 4,* 49–73.

Individuals with Disabilities Education Act Amendments of 1997, PL 105-17, 20 U.S.C. §§ 1400 *et seq.*

Johnson-Martin, N.M., Attermeier, S.M., & Hacker, B.J. (1990). *The Carolina Curriculum for Preschoolers with Special Needs.* Baltimore: Paul H. Brookes Publishing Co.

Kaiser, A.P., Yoder, P.J., & Keetz, A. (1992). Evaluating milieu therapy. In S.F. Warren & J. Reichle (Series Eds.) & S.F. Warren & J. Reichle (Vol. Eds.), *Communication and language intervention series: Vol. 1. Causes and effects in communication and language intervention* (pp. 9–47). Baltimore: Paul H. Brookes Publishing Co.

Kern, L., Vorndran, C.M., Hilt, A., Ringdahl, J.E., Adelman, B.E., & Dunlap, G. (1998). Choice as an intervention to improve behavior: A review of the literature. *Journal of Behavioral Education, 8,* 151–169.

Kochanek, T.T., & Buka, S.L. (1998). Influential factors in the utilization of early intervention services. *Journal of Early Intervention, 21,* 323–338.

Koegel, L.K. (1995). Communication and language intervention. In R.L. Koegel & L.K. Koegel

(Eds.), *Teaching children with autism: Strategies for initiating positive interactions and improving learning opportunities* (pp. 17–32). Baltimore: Paul H. Brookes Publishing Co.

Koegel, L.K., Stiebel, D., & Koegel, R.L. (1998). Reducing aggression in children with autism toward infant or toddler siblings. *Journal of The Association for Persons with Severe Handicaps, 23,* 111–118.

Kohler, F.W., & Strain, P.S. (1999). Maximizing peer-mediated resources in integrated preschool classrooms. *Topics in Early Childhood Special Education, 19,* 319–345.

Lamorey, S., & Bricker, D.D. (1993). Integrated programs: Effects on young children and their parents. In C.A. Peck, S.L. Odom, & D.D. Bricker (Eds.), *Integrating young children with disabilities into community programs: Ecological perspectives on research and implementation* (pp. 249–270). Baltimore: Paul H. Brookes Publishing Co.

Lieber, J., Beckman, P.J., Hanson, M.J., Janko, S., Marquart, J.M., Horn, E., & Odom, S.L. (1997). The impact of changing roles on relationships between professionals in inclusive programs. *Early Education and Development, 8,* 67–82.

Linder, T.W. (1993). *Transdisciplinary play-based assessment: A functional approach to working with young children.* Baltimore: Paul H. Brookes Publishing Co.

Lussier, B.J., Crimmins, D.B., & Alberti, D. (1994). Effect of three adult interaction styles on infant engagement. *Journal of Early Intervention, 18,* 12–24.

MacDonald, J.D., & Gillette, Y. (1988). Communicating partners: A conversational model for building parent–child relationships with handicapped children. In K. Marfo (Ed.), *Parent–child interaction and developmental disabilities: Theory, research, and intervention* (pp. 220–241). Westport, CT: Praeger Publishers.

Mahoney, G., & Neville-Smith, A. (1996). The effects of directive communications on children's interactive engagement: Implications for language intervention. *Topics in Early Childhood Special Education, 16,* 236–250.

Mahoney, G., & Powell, A. (1986). *The transactional intervention program: Teacher's guide.* Rock Hill, SC: Center for Excellence in Early Childhood Education.

Maxim, G.W. (1997). *The very young: Guiding children from infancy through the early years* (5th ed.). Westerville, OH: Glencoe/McGraw-Hill.

McEvoy, M.A., Odom, S.L., & McConnell, S.R. (1992). Peer social competence interventions for young children with disabilities. In S.L. Odom, S.R. McConnell, & M.A. McEvoy (Eds.), *So-cial competence of young children with disabilities: Issues and strategies for intervention* (pp. 113–133). Baltimore: Paul H. Brookes Publishing Co.

McGee, G. (1999, July 16). *Intensity of treatment: Is more always better in the treatment of autism?* Paper presented at the Office of Special Education Programs Research Project Directors' Conference, Washington, DC.

McLean, M.E., & Odom, S.L. (1996). Establishing recommended practices in early intervention/early childhood special education. In S.L. Odom & M.E. McLean (Eds.), *Early intervention/early childhood special education: Recommended practices* (pp. 1–22). Austin, TX: PRO-ED.

McLean, M., Bailey, D.B., & Wolery, M. (Eds.). (1996). *Assessing infants and preschoolers with special needs* (2nd ed.). Westerville, OH: Glencoe/McGraw-Hill.

McWilliam, R.A. (1991). Targeting teaching at children's use of time: Perspectives on preschooler's engagement. *TEACHING Exceptional Children, 23*(4), 42–43.

McWilliam, R.A. (1992). *Family-centered intervention planning: A routines-based approach.* San Antonio, TX: Communication Skill Builders.

McWilliam, R.A. (1995). Integration of therapy and consultative special education: A continuum in early intervention. *Infants and Young Children, 7*(4), 29–38.

McWilliam, R.A. (Ed.). (1996). *Rethinking pull-out services in early intervention: A professional resource.* Baltimore: Paul H. Brookes Publishing Co.

McWilliam, R.A., & Bailey, D.B. (1992). Promoting engagement and mastery. In D.B. Bailey & M. Wolery (Eds.), *Teaching infants and preschoolers with disabilities* (2nd ed., pp. 229–255). New York: Macmillan Publishing USA.

McWilliam, R.A., & Bailey, D.B. (1994). Predictors of service delivery models in center-based early intervention. *Exceptional Children, 61,* 56–71.

McWilliam, R.A., de Kruif, R.E.L., & Zulli, R.A. (1999). *The observed construction of teaching: Four contexts.* Unpublished manuscript, University of North Carolina, Frank Porter Graham Child Development Center.

McWilliam, R.A., McMillen, B., Sloper, K., & McMillen, J.S. (1997). Early education and child care program philosophy about families. In S. Riefel (Series Ed.) & C.J. Dunst & M. Wolery (Volume Eds.), *Advances in early education and day care: Vol. 9. Family policy and practice in early child care* (pp. 61–104). Stamford, CT: JAI Press.

McWilliam, R.A., Scarborough, A.A., Bagby, J.H., & Sweeney, A.L. (1996). *Teaching Styles Rating Scale*. Chapel Hill: The University of North Carolina Press, Frank Porter Graham Child Development Center.

McWilliam, R.A., Scarborough, A.A., & Kim, H. (1998). *Adult interactions and child engagement*. Manuscript under review. Chapel Hill: University of North Carolina, Frank Porter Graham Child Development Center.

McWilliam, R.A., & Spencer, A.G. (1993). *Integrated versus pull-out speech-language services in early intervention: A mixed-method study*. Manuscript submitted for publication.

McWilliam, R.A., Young, H.J., & Harville, K. (1996). Therapy services in early intervention: Current status, barriers, and recommendations. *Topics in Early Childhood Special Education, 16,* 348–374.

Mesibov, G.B., Schopler, E., & Hearsey, K.A. (1994). Structured teaching. In E. Schopler & G.B. Mesibov (Eds.), *Behavioral issues in autism* (pp. 195–207). New York: Kluwer Academic/Plenum Publishers.

Odom, S.L., Horn, E.M., Marquart, J.M., Hanson, M.J., Wolfberg, P., Beckman, P.J., Lieber, J., Li, S., Schwartz, I., Janko, S., & Sandall, S. (1999). On the forms of inclusion: Organizational context and individualized service models. *Journal of Early Intervention, 22,* 185–199.

Odom, S.L., McConnell, S.R., & Chandler, L.K. (1994). Acceptability and feasibility of classroom-based social interaction interventions for young children with disabilities. *Exceptional Children, 60,* 226–236.

Odom, S.L., McConnell, S.R., McEvoy, M.A., Peterson, C., Ostrosky, M., Chandler, L.K., Spicuzza, R.J., Skellenger, A., Creighton, M., & Favazza, P.C. (1999). Relative effects of interventions supporting the social competence of young children with disabilities. *Topics in Early Childhood Special Education, 19,* 75–91.

Odom, S.L., & McLean, M.E. (Eds.). (1996). *Early intervention/early childhood special education: Recommended practices*. Austin, TX: PRO-ED.

Peck, C.A., Odom, S.L., & Bricker, D.D. (Eds.). (1993). *Integrating young children with disabilities into community programs: Ecological perspectives on research and implementation*. Baltimore: Paul H. Brookes Publishing Co.

Rosenkoetter, S.E., Hains, A.H., & Fowler, S.A. (1994). *Bridging early services for children with special needs and their families: A practical guide for transition planning*. Baltimore: Paul H. Brookes Publishing Co.

Rule, S., Losardo, A., Dinnebeil, L., Kaiser, A., & Rowland, C. (1998). Translating research on nat-

uralistic instruction into practice. *Journal of Early Intervention, 21,* 283–293.

Sainato, D.M., & Carta, J.J. (1992). Classroom influences on the development and social competence in young children with disabilities. In S.L. Odom, S.R. McConnell, & M.A. McEvoy (Eds.), *Social competence of young children with disabilities: Issues and strategies for intervention* (pp. 93–109). Baltimore: Paul H. Brookes Publishing Co.

Schalock, R.L. (Ed.). (1996). *Quality of life: Conceptualization and measurement* (Vol. 1). Washington, DC: American Association on Mental Retardation.

Schepis, M.M., Reid, D.H., Behrmann, M.M., & Sutton, K.A. (1998). Increasing communicative interactions of young children with autism using a voice output communication aid and naturalistic teaching. *Journal of Applied Behavior Analysis, 31,* 561–578.

Scruggs, T.E., & Mastropieri, M.A. (1996). Teacher perceptions of mainstreaming/inclusion: 1958–1995: A research synthesis. *Exceptional Children, 63,* 59–74.

Stainback, W., Stainback, S., & Bunch, G. (1989). Introduction and historical background. In S. Stainback, W. Stainback, & M. Forest (Eds.), *Educating all students in the mainstream of regular education* (pp. 3–14). Baltimore: Paul H. Brookes Publishing Co.

Strain, P.S. (1999). Sometimes there is more to a baseline than meets the eye. *Journal of Early Intervention, 22,* 109–110.

Strain, P.S., McConnell, S.R., Carta, J.J., Fowler, S.A., Neisworth, J.T., & Wolery, M. (1992). Behaviorism in early intervention. *Topics in Early Childhood Special Education, 12*(1), 121–142.

Thurman, S.K. (1997). Systems, ecologies, and the context of early intervention. In S.K. Thurman, J.R. Cornwell, & S.R. Gottwald (Eds.), *Contexts of early intervention: Systems and settings* (pp. 3–17). Baltimore: Paul H. Brookes Publishing Co.

Tingstrom, D.H., Little, S.G., & Stewart, K.J. (1990). School consultation from a social psychological perspective: A review. *Psychology in the Schools, 27,* 41–50.

Trivette, C.M., Dunst, C.J., & Deal, A.G. (1997). Resource-based approach to early intervention. In S.K. Thurman, J.R. Cornwell, & S.R. Gottwald (Eds.), *Contexts of early intervention: Systems and settings* (pp. 73–92). Baltimore: Paul H. Brookes Publishing Co.

Venn, M.L., Wolery, M., Werts, M.G., Morris, A., DeCesare, L.D., & Cuffs, M.S. (1993). Embedding instruction in art activities to teach preschoolers with disabilities to imitate their peers. *Early Childhood Research Quarterly, 8,* 277–294.

Warren, S.F., & Gazdag, G.A. (1990). Facilitating early language development with milieu intervention procedures. *Journal of Early Intervention, 14,* 62–68.

Warren, S.F., & Horn, E.M. (1996). Generalization issues in providing integrated services. In R.A. McWilliam (Ed.), *Rethinking pull-out services in early intervention: A professional resource* (pp. 121–143). Baltimore: Paul Brookes Publishing Co.

Weisz, J.R., & Zigler, E. (1979). Cognitive development in retarded and nonretarded persons: Piagetian tests of the similar sequence hypothesis. *Psychological Bulletin, 86,* 831–851.

Werts, M.G., Caldwell, N.K., & Wolery, M. (1996). Peer modeling of response chains: Observational learning by students with disabilities. *Journal of Applied Behavior Analysis, 29,* 53–66.

Wolery, M. (1994). Implementing instruction for young children with special needs in early childhood classrooms. In M. Wolery & J. Wilbers (Eds.), *Including children with special needs in early childhood programs* (pp. 151–166). Washington, DC: National Association for the Education of Young Children.

Wolery, M., Anthony, L., & Heckathorn, J. (1998). Transition-based teaching: Effects on transitions, teachers' behavior, and children's learning. *Journal of Early Intervention, 21,* 117–131.

Wolery, M., Ault, M.J., & Doyle, P.M. (1992). *Teaching students with moderate and severe disabilities: Use of response prompting strategies.* White Plains, NY: Longman.

Wolery, M., Bailey, D.B., & Sugai, G.M. (1988). *Effective teaching: Principles and procedures of applied behavior analysis with exceptional students.* Needham Heights, MA: Allyn & Bacon.

Wolery, M., Doyle, P.M., Gast, D.L., Ault, M.J., & Simpson, S.L. (1993). Comparison of progresive time delay and transition-based teaching with preschoolers who have developmental delays. *Journal of Early Intervention, 17,* 160–176.

Wolery, M., Huffman, K., Holcombe, A., Martin, C.G., Brookfield, J., Schroeder, C., & Venn, M.L. (1994). Preschool mainstreaming: Perceptions of barriers and benefits by faculty in general early childhood education. *Teacher Education and Special Education, 17,* 1–9.

Wolery, M., & Sainato, D.M. (1996). General curriculum and intervention strategies. In S.L. Odom & M.E. McLean (Eds.), *Early intervention/early childhood special education: Recommended practices* (pp. 125–158). Austin, TX: PRO-ED.

Wolery, M., Strain, P.S., & Bailey, D.B. (1992). Applying the framework of developmentally appropriate practice to children with special needs. In S. Bredekamp & T. Rosegrant (Eds.), *Reaching potentials: Curriculum and assessment for 3 to 8 year olds* (pp. 92–113). Washington, DC: National Association for the Education of Young Children.

Wolery, M., & Wilbers, J.S. (1994). *Including children with special needs in early childhood programs.* Washington, DC: National Association for the Education of Young Children.

Wolfensberger, W. (1972). *The principle of normalization in human services.* Toronto, Canada: National Institute on Mental Retardation.

V

Conclusions

23

MICHAEL J. GURALNICK

An Agenda for Change
in Early Childhood Inclusion

Early childhood inclusion represents a concept and practice with the potential to alter radically the way society perceives individuals with disabilities and their families and the way individuals with disabilities and their families perceive themselves. For these families, the level of involvement in all aspects of the larger community has special meaning in the early years, as these initial experiences establish a pattern and set of expectations with respect to community participation. As noted in the chapters in this book, since the mid-1970s, there have been remarkable advances with respect to early childhood inclusion. Yet, as also revealed in this book, despite our best efforts to address factors that influence the goals of inclusion, much remains to be accomplished. In particular, significant concerns are apparent with regard to the four central goals of early childhood inclusion: 1) achieving universal access to inclusive programs, 2) agreeing on and establishing feasible programs, 3) having confidence that children's developmental and social outcomes are not compromised by participating in inclusive programs, and 4) socially integrating children with one another in meaningful

ways. Moreover, the field has yet to resolve many long-standing issues stemming from differences in values, philosophies, and practices. The figure in Chapter 1 of this volume depicting the key factors that influence the four inclusion goals is reproduced here (see Figure 23.1). The reader should consult Chapter 1 for additional details.

Perhaps of greatest concern is the absence of a national-in-scope agenda designed to address the four inclusion goals, to resolve critical issues, and to achieve an agreed-on set of principles and practices governing early childhood inclusion. Despite isolated and often impressive statewide or local community efforts, the absence of direction and leadership in this field is most obvious and may be contributing to the slow pace and the fragmented process of change that characterize the field of early childhood inclusion. What has failed to emerge are systematic goals, plans, monitoring systems, or a forum to articulate issues and to at least attempt to achieve a consensus. Similarly, there is no corresponding systematic research agenda or any movement to consider early childhood inclusion in relation to the larger community.

The purpose of this chapter is to present an outline of such a national-in-scope agenda for change in the field of early childhood inclusion and to propose a mechanism for national leadership. To do so, I have drawn extensively on the opinions and advice of the expert contributors as presented in the preceding chapters and also relied on in-depth discussions of the issues with numerous colleagues throughout the years. Nevertheless, the proposed agenda remains my responsibility, and any flaws should be attributed to me alone.

Of course, meaningful change can only occur at the state and local levels. Consequently, even with a national agenda and national leadership, extensive involvement and communication with state and local groups is essential to develop and carry out any agenda for change. A thoughtful national agenda for change and its corresponding mechanisms for change must address overarching issues, but they must be directly relevant to every state and local community. Moreover, any national-in-scope agenda must not only recognize the important

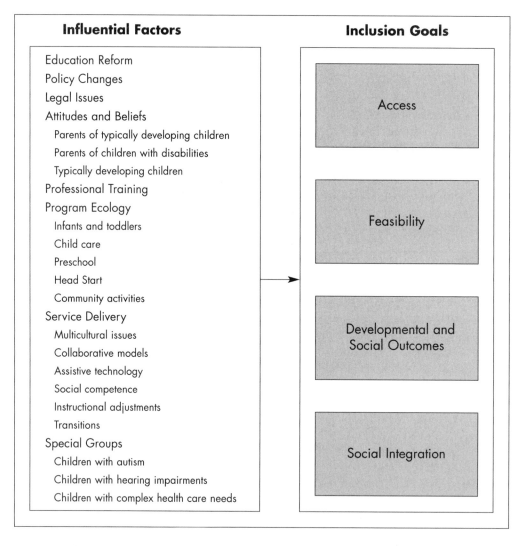

Figure 23.1.   The relationship between influential factors and the goals of inclusion.

challenge to develop solutions to promote change that have predictable and common elements across communities but must also allow reasonable flexibility for local implementation.

A NATIONAL LEADERSHIP FORUM ON EARLY CHILDHOOD INCLUSION

To provide the necessary national leadership, I propose that the U.S. Department of Education establish a national panel called the National Leadership Forum on Early Childhood Inclusion (NLF-ECI) charged with the responsibility of both developing and implementing a national agenda for change in early childhood inclusion. The four inclusion goals noted previously and elaborated on in Chapter 1 can serve as an initial framework for this group, but other goals may emerge over time. This panel should be established for a minimum period of 10 years and consist of national experts in early childhood inclusion, state and local leaders (representing Parts B and C of the Individuals with Disabilities Education Act [IDEA]), representatives of key parent groups, members of both the early childhood and early intervention communities, government officials from other federal agencies related to health and to family and child services (e.g., Head Start, child care), and representatives of professional organizations who provide related services. Sufficient resources should be made available by the Department of Education to hold forums to address specific agenda items, to develop position papers, to establish relevant databases, and to produce and distribute informational documents. The Department of Education and related agencies should also commit resources to solicit grant proposals to address high priority areas in early childhood inclusion as identified by the NLF-ECI.

In the following sections of this chapter, I suggest possible national-in-scope agenda items that are designed to provide an initial framework for the NLF-ECI. These agenda items have been organized in the areas of systems change, program development, and research. Only a brief justification for each specific item is described, as the many chapters in this volume provide the necessary background information. Where appropriate, implementation strategies are recommended, such as establishing statewide task forces or a central dissemination resource. It should be noted that no attempt has been made to be exhaustive but rather to identify possible directions that will ultimately enhance our ability to achieve the four key goals of early childhood inclusion discussed previously.

Systems Change

The nature and interrelationships among the factors influencing inclusion goals will require an agenda that addresses many systems change issues. The major influential factors that have been discussed throughout this volume (see Figure 23.1)—education reform, policy changes, legal issues, attitudes and beliefs, professional training, program ecology, service delivery approaches, and adjustments for special groups of children—all reflect the long-standing and complex forces that must somehow be considered from a comprehensive systems perspective. As such, systems change mechanisms must be in place at all levels (national, state, and local) for this to occur. Ten agenda items are identified in this section on systems change representing both mechanisms and specific goals. Emphasis is placed on state and local involvement, information gathering, and developing and disseminating information and strategies with the potential for general use.

Agenda item #1: *Establish a task force on early childhood inclusion in each state.*

Rationale: A successful national effort will require state and local support and involvement. Chairs of each state task force should be in close contact with the NLF-ECI, and the task force's goals and composition should be similar to that of the NLF-ECI. Each task force would provide input to the NLF-ECI and be the focal point for NLF-ECI developed guidelines, position papers, research summaries relevant to state and local issues, recommendations for legislation or regulations, and related issues. Each task force would be responsible for adapting, communicating, and utilizing that information at state and local levels.

Agenda item #2: *Create a national reporting system on inclusive practices at the early childhood level.*

Rationale: The absence of reliable information with respect to having access to inclusive programs is a clear impediment to change. State task forces should take responsibility for gathering relevant data, including the type of placements (especially various forms of inclusion) as well as child and family characteristics, and report annually to the NLF-ECI. The NLF-ECI should develop a streamlined reporting system with appropriate definitions to permit valid cross-state analyses.

Agenda item #3: *Establish a national dissemination unit that regularly summarizes current knowledge and practice relevant to early childhood inclusion.*

Rationale: Extensive research has been conducted with respect to feasibility, developmental and social outcomes, and social integration that should be summarized in a concise manner. Summaries of administrative or court decisions that are relevant should be included as well. Both parents and professionals should find this information valuable in making placement and program decisions. The national dissemination unit, responsible

to the NLF-ECI, would also be charged with providing state task forces with updates on new findings, reports of solutions to policy and practice problems from various sources, and any other relevant information. This unit should function as a resource to both the NLF-ECI and state task forces.

Agenda item #4: *Develop recommendations and guidelines for determining circumstances in which it is most appropriate for children to be placed in various types of inclusive placements as well as specialized placements.*

Rationale: Despite the presumption that children with disabilities should be full participants in programs for typically developing children, children with seemingly similar characteristics and needs are placed in a diverse array of programs ranging from specialized to fully inclusive, with no obvious rationale for those placements. Some universal framework needs to be established by the NLF-ECI to help guide decisions that are consistent from community to community and state to state. Guidelines can be developed that retain the integrity of the principle of individualization. Part of the framework would include not only the relationship between placement types and child characteristics and needs but also early childhood program conditions (i.e., feasibility; see the "Program Development" section) that must exist to ensure the appropriateness and effectiveness of that placement. In addition, by establishing these conditions a priori, any discrepancies or inadequacies could serve as catalysts for change.

Agenda item #5: *Develop policy guidelines on the meaning and application of natural environments for infants and toddlers with disabilities.*

Rationale: Identifying natural environments for infants and toddlers has become a divisive issue and is indeed a challenging problem. Focusing on natural environments for the family emphasizes typical family routines in which services can be integrated but threatens long-standing models of specialized, child-oriented service centers. Defining what constitutes a natural environment, determining how services and supports can be integrated effectively into a family's normal activities in the community, giving due consideration to parent preferences, and figuring out how to utilize existing professional expertise even in specialized contexts will require the NLF-ECI to develop policy guidelines that consider all of these issues. Of importance, these policy guidelines for natural environments create a rare opportunity to promote community acceptance of infants and toddlers with disabilities.

Agenda item #6: *Develop a set of strategies to help resolve potential parent–professional disagreements with respect to placement decisions.*

Rationale: Even with a more extensive knowledge base, recommendations and guidelines that may emerge from agenda item #4 will nevertheless be subject to differing interpretations. These interpretations are influenced by numerous factors, but one's individual values, preferences, and priorities are certainly among the key factors. In many instances, parents and professionals may well have widely differing values and priorities that must be articulated for a reasonable resolution to occur. Differing perceptions of the quality of programs, the adequacy of specialized and related services, or concerns about social isolation and peer rejection are likely to arise. By identifying these issues and developing strategies to consider alternatives with all relevant information available, decisions based on false and sometimes unreasonable expectations can be minimized. Moreover, these strategies would provide a context for

information exchange and, I hope, minimize administrative hearings or legal actions.

Agenda item #7: *Contribute to efforts to expand the number and improve the quality of early child care and early childhood education programs with special reference to children with disabilities.*

Rationale: The NLF-ECI can add its name and expertise to the continuing battle to improve early child care quality in the United States and to increase the availability of early childhood programs. By supporting those larger efforts, particularly by enhancing state-sponsored early childhood education and improving standards for child care, and providing information with respect to how to include children with disabilities, the quality of child care can be improved for all children.

Agenda item #8: *Explore new approaches for professional training to support inclusive practices.*

Rationale: The NLF-ECI must address a number of interrelated professional training concerns. First, strategies must be developed to improve the knowledge and skills of general early childhood educators and child care staff with respect to children with disabilities. Close collaborations with accrediting agencies and professional associations, such as the National Association for the Education of Young Children, are essential. Second, strategies at state levels must be developed to increase the availability of well-trained early childhood special educators who can assume various roles, particularly as consultants in inclusive environments. Consideration should be given to developing new professional training approaches that include a consultant specialist who would serve as the key resource for disability issues in local programs. Third, specialists from different disciplines will need more professional training coursework and practicum experiences devoted to consultant and collaborative models, as these approaches are more compatible with inclusive practices.

Agenda item #9: *Develop a set of recommended policies and procedures for consideration by states that address administrative barriers to inclusive services.*

Rationale: In view of the diverse array of public and private early childhood programs available for typically developing children in local communities, equally diverse approaches are needed to include children with disabilities. The federal and state requirements designed to ensure appropriate services for children with disabilities, however, are often not compatible with programs for typically developing children (e.g., issues of staff certification, program standards, evaluation requirements, transportation issues, restrictions placed on funding options). As most of these problems are common across states, the NLF-ECI, with state task force input, should develop a set of explicit policies and procedures to address these issues.

Agenda item #10: *Promote national efforts for education reform to further integrate the general and special education domains.*

Rationale: The historical separation between general and special education at all levels has emphasized differences in approaches to child development and educational practice rather than commonalties and minimized creative efforts to expand curricula and programs to accommodate children with diverse skills and abilities. This systems issue is critical, as it constitutes the infrastructure that generates attitudes and beliefs about the value of inclusion and the importance of developing inclusive practices. The NLF-ECI must join with higher education and state education groups to promote a reform agenda at all levels that meaningfully integrates the domains of special and general education.

Program Development

In addition to the extensive and complex agenda for systems change, there exist a number of agenda items that support these efforts but fall primarily in the domain of program development. As is seen next, many of the agenda items for program development have systems implications but are perhaps best considered as potential resources for systemwide applications. For the most part, these program development agenda items constitute model building or efforts to clarify or define issues that can serve to limit inclusive practices. The NLF-ECI can serve as the catalyst to address the following program development agenda items by promoting these topics as worthy of federal or state support and by gathering and disseminating relevant information for state task forces.

Agenda item #11: *Develop community-based child care models using the cluster concept that can appropriately and effectively support infants and toddlers with disabilities.*

Rationale: Quality child care remains a major problem in the United States, and no short-term solutions are apparent. Ideally, virtually all child care should eventually be able to accommodate children with disabilities, but this is highly unrealistic at the beginning of the 21st century. Alternatively, community models should be developed that would be designed as child care programs most appropriate for children with disabilities. These inclusive child care programs would have appropriate staff and resources adequate for all children participating. The procedures required to establish these models and to conduct a process evaluation together constitute an important agenda item.

A variety of inclusive models creating a mix of child care, family supports, and specialized services for children with disabilities could be developed. A community could then decide how many programs are needed for each geographic area. In part, this would depend on the size of the child care program and the number of children with disabilities in the community. Care must be taken to ensure that clusters of children with disabilities remain small. Moreover, work to enhance the quality of other child care programs in the community should continue.

Agenda item #12: *Develop models and guidelines for placement of children with disabilities in dual programs designed to accomplish different goals.*

Rationale: Because of parental choice and the unique needs of children, some form of dual placements may be required to provide inclusive opportunities. That is, children may participate in half-day specialized programs (or even a reverse inclusion model) and then shift to some form of a more inclusive program (usually a child care center) for the remainder of the day. For the inclusive program to be effective, coordination must occur with the more specialized program and strategies designed to ensure positive experiences for the child. Peer relationships are especially vulnerable for children with disabilities, and a well-coordinated plan is critical. The development of models for dual programs and the creation of guidelines to maximize coordination and the advantages of both programs are needed. Similarly, carefully thought-out guidelines addressing when this dual model is appropriate should be developed, as it can produce many complications for children and families.

Agenda item #13: *Develop models and guidelines for placement of preschool-age children in public and private programs.*

Rationale: The limited number of preschool programs for typically developing children operated by local education agencies restricts access, as parents often choose to place their child in available specialized programs. Local education agencies with state support must regularly pursue creative options to ensure that everyone has access to inclusive programs. Child care models outlined in agenda item #11 could be expanded for preschool-age children, cluster models could be further developed, and more extensive contractual relationships could be established with private nursery or preschool programs. Guidelines are needed to ensure placement in a quality program with resources sufficient to meet the individualized needs of children with disabilities (see agenda item #14).

Agenda item #14: *General agreement must be established with respect to the feasibility of inclusive programs.*

Rationale: The feasibility construct represents issues related to the ability of an inclusive program to maintain its integrity and to accommodate and meet children's individualized needs. At minimum, feasibility provides an index of the quality of the program from the perspective of children with disabilities. What are needed are relatively straightforward checklists (process measures) to ensure that this inclusive placement is indeed capable of effectively meeting the needs of all children in the program. From a more general perspective, domains on such checklists would likely include assessments by staff and others that their program is functioning in a manner anticipated, that all children are engaged in the curriculum as expected, and that the program's educational philosophy has not been altered to any significant degree. From the perspective of children with disabilities, these checklists would address progress toward individualized family service plan (IFSP) or individualized education program (IEP) goals, the availability of specialized services, and the extent to which stigmatization is minimized (see Chapter 1). Broader issues of overall program quality remain, but feasibility at least is intended to ensure that a program's integrity is maintained when children with disabilities are included, yet the program is able to serve as an appropriate and effective environment for these children. If inclusive programs are not feasible, the information gathered through this process could serve as a tool to encourage program modifications. In turn, this may enhance the overall quality of the program. The NLF-ECI can be helpful in coordinating the design of such checklists.

Agenda item #15: *Priority must be given at an individual program level for specialists in the disability field to engage in a dialogue with staff in the general early childhood community.*

Rationale: Discussion and debate primarily at the academic level have produced a rapprochement in many areas between the disability and general early childhood communities, yet at the day-to-day level, time constraints have not allowed a systematic dialogue to develop on a child-by-child basis to address issues of concern. Differing perspectives and assumptions about development and learning are likely to emerge at the more concrete level. Similar types of issues exist for members of various disciplines attempting to adapt service delivery models to inclusive programs. Without this dialogue, many solvable problems are not articulated and constitute a threat to feasibility and harmony. The challenge at the program development level is to ensure that this is a priority and that adequate time is available for this dialogue to occur.

Research

The agenda items in this section address problems that can benefit from the direct

and systematic efforts of researchers in the field. The number of research questions that can be legitimately asked is quite extensive, and no attempt in this section has been made to be exhaustive. Rather, the agenda items represent research relevant to program development and to systems change agenda items. Of note, the following research agenda items reflect an awareness of the practical limitations of conducting research in inclusive programs, particularly the ability of researchers to control important variables. Nevertheless, large-scale evaluation research in conjunction with smaller-scale focused studies can be carried out in a manner that does not compromise the quality of the science. Different questions will suggest correspondingly different research strategies varying from single-subject studies, the use of playgroup methodologies, small-scale randomized prospective controlled designs, and numerous others. It will be the cumulative impact and convergence of data from these various sources that will contribute to the degree of confidence in the findings and their value to the systems change and program development agendas.

Agenda item #16: *Establish a national evaluation network under the auspices of the NLF-ECI to gather developmental and social outcome data.*

Rationale: Sufficient evidence is available to suggest that inclusive programs produce at least similar developmental and social outcomes for children with disabilities in comparison with children enrolled in specialized programs and that there are no adverse effects for any group of children. Additional research employing randomized prospective controlled designs is not practical on a general basis for a variety of reasons. Nevertheless, gathering outcome data from programs differing in feasibility, related ecological characteristics, and other dimensions—and reporting that information to a national clearinghouse—would permit researchers to address important questions. Evaluation could address a wide range of programmatic or ecological factors (e.g., child characteristics, program type, educational or instructional model) that could influence outcomes. Aspects of feasibility could also be evaluated with respect to both child and family outcomes. The NLF-ECI should establish a set of common outcome measures, develop protocols to gather information on programmatic and ecological features, evaluate a program's documentation of feasibility, and provide technical assistance (e.g., on-line reporting, training in outcome measures if needed, spot-check reliability). With researchers aggregating data on a large national sample of children with and without disabilities, important information can be obtained that can also be of considerable value to program development and to systems change agenda items.

Agenda item #17: *Examine the issue of children with disabilities being stigmatized through participation in inclusive programs.*

Rationale: Participation in programs with children who have widely diverse skills and abilities invites social comparisons among children and sets the occasion for the formation of subgroups based in part on children's developmental characteristics. Outright rejection by peers is not a frequent occurrence, but exclusion of children with disabilities by typically developing children is far more common, especially during unstructured activities, and can continue to occur despite the best efforts to minimize these patterns. In addition, teachers can contribute to children's feelings of being different through their own ways of relating, instructing, and organizing their programs. Researchers have only limited

understanding of the possible stigmatizing effects of social interaction and instructional experiences, particularly their impact on the self-perceptions of children with disabilities. Accordingly, researchers should be encouraged to develop creative ways to evaluate possible stigma and to develop techniques to understand the factors that contribute to stigma should it exist. Once this has been accomplished, a more systematic program of research can be put into place to develop strategies to minimize these difficulties and provide guidelines that can be used by individual inclusive programs.

Agenda item #18: *Intensify research efforts to develop strategies that promote the peer-related social competence of children with disabilities.*

Rationale: Exclusion of children with disabilities from the social activities of typically developing children remains a common occurrence in inclusive programs despite extensive efforts. Friendships seem to be particularly affected. One major contributing factor is unusual peer competence problems characteristic of children with disabilities. Research should be encouraged to develop new means of enhancing the peer competence of children with disabilities with special emphasis on unstructured situations in which exclusion occurs most frequently.

Agenda item #19: *Develop reasonable expectations for and new approaches to maximize social integration in inclusive programs.*

Rationale: As indicated previously, social separation between children with and without disabilities is a common occurrence in inclusive programs. Researchers—working closely with parents, teachers, and others—should develop a framework to establish appropriate expectations for social integration, a framework that should be strongly influenced by developmental considerations. Among the issues to be addressed are the types of relationships that can be reasonably expected between children with and without disabilities and how the relationships are affected by the type and severity of children's disabilities. Paralleling this effort, new approaches need to be developed and systematically evaluated that are designed to maximize social integration, including friendship development within the framework of a child's current level of peer-related social competence.

Agenda item #20: *Evaluate and enhance the relationship between inclusion in early childhood programs and inclusion in community and neighborhood activities.*

Rationale: The social dynamics created by participation in inclusive programs may carry over to participation, or at least efforts to participate, in inclusive activities in one's community or neighborhood. In particular, relationships formed in inclusive programs may extend beyond the early childhood program, and parents may develop increased confidence in encouraging their child to be active in typical community activities. Researchers should attempt to evaluate this potentially important indirect result of inclusive programs and understand the mechanisms (e.g., parent activity) through which this may occur. Similarly, researchers should be encouraged to develop and evaluate explicit strategies and supports that community programs can use to encourage the participation of young children with disabilities in community activities.

Agenda item #21: *Conduct research with respect to the feasibility and effectiveness of different models of delivery of specialized services in inclusive programs.*

Rationale: There exists a range of service delivery models that can be implemented in inclusive programs. Models that attempt to integrate specialized services into routine activities seem to be particularly compatible with inclusive programs

conceptually, but only a few comparative studies of different approaches have been carried out. Researchers should be encouraged to evaluate the feasibility of various models (e.g., influence on program integrity) as well as carefully evaluate the impact of those services for specific child outcomes (effectiveness).

Agenda item #22: *Conduct research to determine the feasibility and outcomes of providing highly intensive or unique services to children with disabilities in inclusive programs.*

Rationale: One of the most difficult problems facing inclusive programs is their ability to effectively accommodate children with especially challenging behaviors or developmental characteristics (e.g., children with autism, sensory impairments, or complex health care needs). Often, services need to be provided with considerable intensity or uniqueness, increasing the risk of stigma, exacerbating social separation, and threatening the integrity of an inclusive program's model. These problems still remain despite extremely creative efforts to address these issues. Consequently, researchers should be encouraged to evaluate different existing models (e.g., cluster) when highly intensive or unique services are needed to ensure feasibility and maximize social and developmental outcomes. The role of dual models also should be given special consideration in this context. Alternative models, their timing, and their relationship to the child's larger early intervention program should also be explored.

CONCLUSION

In this chapter, I have attempted to outline major agenda items for future work on early childhood inclusion in the areas of systems change, program development, and research. Many of these agenda items are not new, but activities in the domain of early childhood inclusion since the mid-1970s have allowed a more thoughtful organization and refinement of the issues and directed questions quite specifically to the goals of inclusion that have been identified. Fortunately, the numerous fine suggestions presented in this volume by the many contributors offer an excellent beginning for a national effort focused on change. In addition, the general framework presented here highlights the interrelationships that exist among the areas of systems change, program development, and research and will, I hope, encourage even further collaborations among policy makers, parents, early childhood staff, providers of specialized services, researchers, and others who care about inclusive practices.

To pursue an agenda for change, I have proposed the establishment of a national-in-scope program coordinated by the NLF-ECI. Without vigorous and persistent leadership, the fragmented efforts that exist at the beginning of the 21st century will remain, and there will be no press for systematic change. This state of affairs is simply not acceptable in view of the far-reaching implications of inclusion in the lives of children and their families.

Finally, it is important to note that many vital yet overarching issues that can substantially affect inclusion have not been included in the agenda items. Issues related to enhancing respect for diversity in general, for example, are a matter of concern that should and, I hope, do extend well beyond more parochial interests in inclusion. It may well be that the agenda for change in the field of early childhood inclusion will serve as a catalyst for change for this and more general issues affecting young children and their families.

Author Index

Page numbers followed by *t* indicate tables; those followed by *f* indicate figures.

Subject Index

Page numbers followed by *t* indicate tables; those followed by *f* indicate figures.